**JOHN R. GUTIÉRREZ**
The Pennsylvania State University

**HARRY L. ROSSER**
Boston College

**MARTA ROSSO-O'LAUGHLIN**
Tufts University

**CHRIS McINTYRE**
Wittenberg University

**JILL WELCH**
Ohio State University

HH

**Heinle & Heinle Publishers**
An International Thomson Publishing Company • Boston, MA 02116 U.S.A.

I(T)P

Visit us on the internet http://www.thomson.com/heinle.html

**TEACHER'S EDITION**

The publication of *¡YA VERÁS! Primer nivel* Teacher's Edition was directed by the members of the Heinle & Heinle School Publishing Team:

**Editorial Director:** Beth Kramer
**Market Development Director:** Pamela Warren
**Production Editor:** Mary McKeon
**Developmental Editor:** Regina McCarthy
**Publisher/Team Leader:** Stanley J. Galek
**Director of Production/Team Leader:** Elizabeth Holthaus

Also participating in the publication of this text were:

**Manufacturing Coordinator:** Barbara Stephan
**Project Manager:** Kristin Swanson
**Interior Design:** Susan Gerould/Perspectives
**Composition:** Perspectives and Pre-Press Company
**Cover Art:** Mark Schroder
**Cover Design:** Corey McPherson Nash
**Photo/Video Specialist:** Jonathan Stark



Manufactured in the United States of America.

ISBN 0-8384-6196-4 Teacher's Edition

10 9 8 7 6 5 4 3

# To the Teacher

"The greatest strength is that this is a student-oriented textbook. The students are required to participate, especially in pair work. The next greatest strength is the book's ability to recycle previously taught material. Very little content is not reviewed and there are always plenty of exercises for the teacher to use to reteach material if necessary. Lastly, I feel that the balance the book strikes between all five skills is wonderful–it makes for easy teaching as far as our curriculum goes."

–Bartley Kirst, Ironwood High School, Glendale, AZ

"The contexts in *¡YA VERÁS!* help motivate students to learn Spanish because students put more effort into learning something which they can readily use. Students want to have the ability to 'say something in Spanish' at the end of the very first day of classes. If they see that they can understand something and say something in Spanish, then they will put forth more effort to learn."

–Diane Henderson, S.P. Waltrip High School, Houston, TX

"Students acquire the language through a natural progression, and the recycling of the material reminds students that there is a focus and inter-relatedness of linguistic functions and patterns. *¡YA VERÁS!* is user friendly! It is very easy for me to plan as well as present new material."

–Kristin Warner, Piper High School, Sunrise, FL

# Contents

# Why was the ¡YA VERÁS! program written?

As the preceding testimonials indicate, the *¡YA VERÁS!* program has had a major, positive impact on teachers and students. In large measure, our success is due to the fact that we have created a user-friendly program based on concerns expressed by you, the teachers. Before writing the first edition, we asked you to identify the most common problems you experience in the classroom and with the materials you have been using over the years. We then addressed each problem very specifically and provided solutions that have gone a long way in facilitating and enhancing your classroom experience.

**Problem:** Besides teaching my classes, I have many other assigned responsibilities. I don't have a great deal of time for preparation and I certainly don't have the time to reorganize the book, rewrite sections of it, or create a lot of new exercises. I also don't have time to create my own tests.

**Our solution:** We have organized our books in such a way that no time needs to be spent on reorganization or rewriting. Preparation time is reduced to a minimum because new and recycled materials have been carefully integrated, the four skills and culture complement each other, and there is a step-by-step progression from practice to meaningful communication.

**Problem:** My classes are very large and heterogeneous. Some students take a long time to learn something, others progress very quickly.

**Our solution:** We provide many opportunities for students to interact in small groups. This reduces anxiety in the more reticent students and allows slower students to learn from those who learn more quickly. Regular recycling provides numerous "passes" of the same material so that slower students have the time to assimilate it.

**Problem:** I should be able to express my own personality and teaching style. I should not be constrained by the textbook or by a particular method.

**Our solution:** We did not espouse one particular method in *¡YA VERÁS!* In an integrative approach such as ours, you are given a variety of options for working with the material. This allows you and your students to express your own preferences and teaching/learning styles.

**Problem:** Sometimes I feel that my teaching effectiveness is reduced by stress and fatigue. By the end of the day I feel completely drained because all of my students are totally dependent on me for all of their learning.

**Our solution:** In *¡YA VERÁS!*, we use small-group work to place more responsibility on students. Small groups give you regular "breathers" in each class period. Our student-centered approach does not, of course, remove you from the learning process. But it does teach students that they also need to look to each other and to the materials as resources for their learning.

**Problem:** No matter how hard I try, I have never been able to finish my textbook in one year. This is frustrating for me and for my students, and it causes real problems when we order textbooks because we have to order extra copies of one level to carry over to the next year. Not only is it an extra expense, but students become demoralized when they are using the same textbook two years in a row.

**Our solution:** The systematic recycling and review built into all levels of the *¡YA VERÁS!* program allows teachers to keep moving through the books because even if students have not yet "mastered" a particular vocabulary set or grammar point, they will get several more chances to practice. Additionally, each book was planned following a typical school calendar with time factored in for missed classes due to assemblies, snow days, sick days, and more. The *Capítulos preliminares* of Books 2 and 3 give an in-depth review of material from the previous level with a special emphasis on content from the last third of the previous book. If you do not complete a level in one year, you can rely on these review chapters without having to go back to the previous text. Many teachers using the first edition of *¡YA VERÁS!* have told us that with familiarity, they are now finishing a book in one year!

**Problem:** I'm held responsible for students' learning. I'm judged on how well my students communicate in Spanish and how well they perform on standardized tests. I'd also like to have the satisfaction of knowing that I've helped my students use the language effectively.

**Our solution:** In our integrative, communicative approach, students become very comfortable communicating in Spanish. The scope and sequence of grammar, vocabulary, and communicative functions over the three-year program provide students with ample time and opportunity to assimilate the material. Students are successful not only in the classroom, but on standardized tests as well. As the statements from students indicate, learning Spanish with *¡YA VERÁS!* is an enjoyable experience for them. Enjoyment is the greatest motivating factor that leads to the positive results you are looking for.

We believe that effective teaching and learning take place when textbooks accurately reflect teacher and student concerns. In our efforts to make *¡YA VERÁS!* very user friendly, we have succeeded, we believe, in creating a program that belongs to you and your students and that personalizes the Spanish language to the individual needs and interests of each learner.

## Principles of the ¡YA VERÁS! Program

The *¡YA VERÁS!* program is an integrated learning system based on a number of principles and assumptions:

- It is possible for students to use the language creatively from the outset and, therefore, free expression can and should be encouraged.
- Student-student and student-teacher interaction should be based on tasks that simulate real-world situations.
- Trial and error are a necessary part of the language-acquisition process.
- Contexts should be selected according to the frequency with which they occur in real life so that students can readily relate to them.
- Everyday spoken Spanish does not include every vocabulary item and every grammar structure available in the Spanish language. Materials should therefore include the elements most frequently used by native speakers in daily life.
- Grammar should not be presented for its own sake but as a means of transmitting a spoken or written message as accurately as possible. Grammar is the means for effective communication.
- In a proficiency-oriented, integrative approach, the four skills and culture reinforce one another in an ever-widening spiral.
- Assimilation requires sufficient time and practice.
- Teaching techniques should be student-centered.

- The goal of teaching is to make students independent users of Spanish.
- The principles of the ACTFL Proficiency Guidelines can serve as the underpinnings of a proficiency-oriented curriculum in which students learn to function as accurately as possible in situations they are most likely to encounter either in a Spanish-speaking country or with Spanish speakers in the United States.

## Use of English in ¡YA VERÁS!

Although we believe and advocate that English be used sparingly in class, we are using it in the program materials for very definite, pedagogically sound purposes. We also recognize that you, the teacher, and not the students, should decide when English is going to be used. Depending on the language-acquisition stage of your students, or the nature of a particular exercise, it will be up to you to decide whether activities can be done in Spanish (even if they are in English in the textbook). However, it would be unfortunate to inhibit students from demonstrating their aural and reading comprehension skills, as well as critical thinking abilities, because of unrealistic expectations of their speaking or writing skills. We have used the following research-supported guidelines in *¡YA VERÁS!*:

- English is used when developing comprehension skills. Since the receptive skills (listening and reading) develop more quickly than the productive skills (speaking and writing), it is important to allow students to demonstrate these skills with the least amount of frustration. For example, they may not have the speaking skills with which to demonstrate their comprehension of a reading text. Furthermore, it is unlikely that they will have the speaking skills with which to participate in discussions in Spanish, particularly early in the year.
- Throughout the textbook, the grammatical explanations are in English because it is essential that students clearly understand how the grammar structures will help them to do certain things with the language they are learning. Reading and listening comprehension exercises are largely in English in Level 1 of *¡YA VERÁS!*, although there is a gradual shifting to productive responses as the units progress. In Level 1 direction lines are in English, for the most part, until the last third of the book, when the more basic, repetitive direction lines are given in Spanish. Misunderstandings due to students' limited abilities in Spanish would be counterproductive and could lead to failure to do the homework, or even the classwork, properly. In Levels 2 and 3 of *¡YA VERÁS!* all simple direction lines are provided in Spanish. In addition, they reflect a gradual increase in the frequency of productive responses in Spanish in the listening and reading exercises.
- Using English judiciously in class tends to reduce the frustration that students often feel when learning a foreign language. Because they understand much more than they can

express, they need to have the satisfaction of working occasionally at a more abstract level rather than always being confined to the simplest concrete expression level.

- When working with cultural topics, a Spanish-only approach tends to lead to generalizations and stereotyping simply because students are unable to express more complex ideas. With limited proficiency in Spanish, they tend to reduce and simplify ideas to the point where culture becomes distorted. Using English in these instances allows you to have students discuss the risks of stereotyping and the more sophisticated cultural issues that arise through readings and cultural notes.

## The Oral Proficiency Interview and ¡YA VERÁS!

The Oral Proficiency Interview is a face-to face test that assesses an individual's speaking ability in a foreign or second language. The interview can last from 5 to about 30 minutes, depending on the interviewee's level of language use. The resulting speech sample is rated on a scale from Novice (no functional ability in the language; limited use of words and phrases) through Intermediate, Advanced, and Superior levels to Native (able to speak like an educated native speaker), with Low, Mid and High ratings that distinguish among performances within levels. Some states are starting to require the administration of the Oral Proficiency Interview (also known as the OPI test) at the end of the third year of instruction, with the expectation that students should score in the low- to mid-Intermediate range. A less staff-intensive alternative test, called the Simulated Oral Proficiency Interview or SOPI is also used. The SOPI does not require a live interview, but rather provides a list of questions to which the student responds on tape.

The emphasis on real-life, task-based use of language in the OPI has several ramifications for students. If they have been learning Spanish from a more traditional, grammar-based program, the OPI could offer some difficulty. *¡YA VERÁS!* , on the other hand, has several regular features that specifically prepare students for the OPI, such as the *¡Adelante!* section (every *etapa* culminates in an open-ended situation) and the *Ya llegamos* feature at the end of every unit (provides several realistic, broad-based situations that encompass all the material covered in the unit). Most importantly, the testing program that accompanies *¡YA VERÁS!* is proficiency based, so that students are always judged by what they can do, not by their mastery of discrete aspects of the language. After learning with *¡YA VERÁS!* for three years, students will have received all the support they need to achieve an appropriate score on the OPI.

## IMPLICATIONS FOR THE CLASSROOM

- **What students "can do" is the primary focus of instruction oriented toward the development of functional proficiency.** This is not to say that the grammar, pronunciation, syntax and cultural aspects of language study are not important, but rather that they should be viewed as tools used to accomplish various functional tasks. In *¡YA VERÁS!* students are made aware of the task at hand and the functions that are needed to carry it out. Tasks are placed in a context that is culturally realistic, as well as meaningful and interesting for the students.
- **For students to become proficient speakers of another language, they need time to engage in communicative oral activities.** The more time students spend in small-group activities, the more oral practice each of them will have. *¡YA VERÁS!* has been built around a progression of carefully planned and well-timed small-group activities, ranging from controlled to meaningful to open ended.
- **The curriculum in a proficiency-oriented program is spiral, not linear.** The scope and sequence in *¡YA VERÁS!* is based on the premise that for students to be able to use what they are learning, the curriculum cannot treat each topic or structure during only one segment of the course, but must return again and again to the same functions, the same contexts, and the same structures, each time reinforcing what has gone before while introducing some new elements.
- **The development of oral proficiency cannot be isolated from the other language skills.** The development of language proficiency can be enhanced by activities that integrate the skills, in which work in one skill can serve as stimulus material to activities in another skill. *¡YA VERÁS!* develops all four language skills as well as culture, and in keeping with its real-life focus, provides realistic, multi-faceted activities in which students implement a cross-section of skills within a given context.

# Components at a Glance

## STUDENT MATERIALS

- Student Textbook
- Student Workbook/Laboratory Manual
- *Atajo* Writing Assistant for Spanish

## TEACHER MATERIALS

- Teacher's Edition
- Testing Program
- Critical Thinking and Unit Review Blackline Masters
- Tapescript
- *Etapas preliminares* (for Level 1)

## CLASSROOM MATERIALS

- Audiocassette Program
- Pronunciation Tape (for Levels 1 and 2)
- Teacher Tape or CD
- *¡YA VERÁS!* Video Programs (VHS cassettes or videodiscs) (for Levels 1 and 2)
- Video Guide/Activity Masters (for Levels 1 and 2)
- *Mosaico cultural* Video Program (VHS cassettes or videodiscs) (for Level 3)
- *Mosaico cultural* Video Guide (for level 3)
- Color Transparencies
- *¡YA VERÁS!* Software Program
- *Nuevas dimensiones* Interactive Multimedia Program
- *Mundos hispanos* Interactive Multimedia Program

# Features of Each Component

## STUDENT TEXTBOOK

- Colorful, high-interest content
- Drawings, realia, and photos to enhance activities and infuse cultural content
- Content relating to a wide variety of subjects
- Easy-to-follow format
- Abundant practice of grammar, vocabulary, and functions in a variety of situations
- Systematic progression from mechanical practice to communicative, open-ended activities
- Full integration of the four skills and culture
- Material presented in small, manageable segments
- Cumulative *Ya llegamos* section at the end of each unit
- Critical thinking and learning strategies called out in student text margins
- Interdisciplinary lessons included in each unit
- Systematic development of reading strategies

## STUDENT WORKBOOK / LABORATORY MANUAL

*(Reading, writing, and listening activities)*

- Wide variety of exercises relating to each presentation in the Student Text
- Complete chapter *Vocabulario* reprinted at beginning of the workbook chapter so that students do not need textbook to do homework
- Recycling and reinforcement of vocabulary and structures
- Emphasis on reading and writing
- Systematic progression from mechanical practice to communicative, open-ended activities
- Systematic writing program (Level 3)

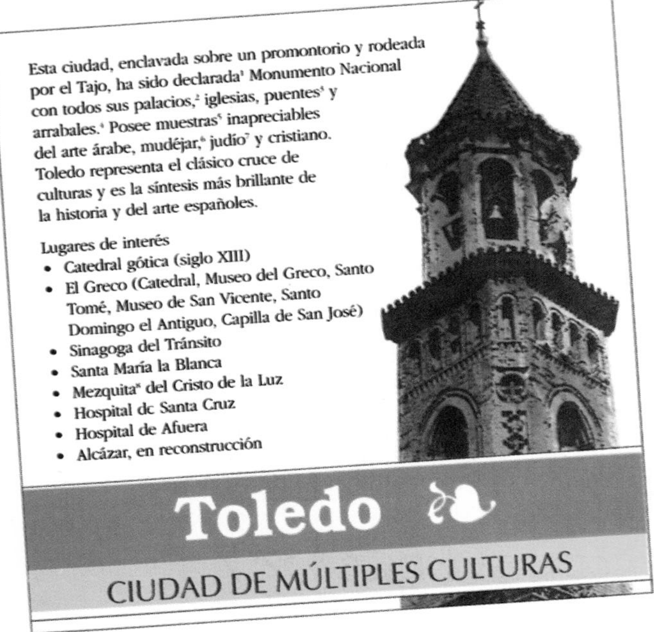

Esta ciudad, enclavada sobre un promontorio y rodeada por el Tajo, ha sido declarada[1] Monumento Nacional con todos sus palacios,[2] iglesias, puentes[3] y arrabales.[4] Posee muestras[5] inapreciables del arte árabe, mudéjar,[6] judío[7] y cristiano. Toledo representa el clásico cruce de culturas y es la síntesis más brillante de la historia y del arte españoles.

Lugares de interés

- Catedral gótica (siglo XIII)
- El Greco (Catedral, Museo del Greco, Santo Tomé, Museo de San Vicente, Santo Domingo el Antiguo, Capilla de San José)
- Sinagoga del Tránsito
- Santa María la Blanca
- Mezquita[8] del Cristo de la Luz
- Hospital de Santa Cruz
- Hospital de Afuera
- Alcázar, en reconstrucción

Toledo

CIUDAD DE MÚLTIPLES CULTURAS

- Authentic texts and documents for reading comprehension development
- Emphasis on listening comprehension
- Support activities for the Audiocassette Program

## TEACHER'S EDITION

- Introductory section that includes a program description, text organization, classroom techniques, and pedagogical principles
- Wrap-around margins for annotations (suggestions for each page). This new, expanded version of the margin notes is designed to lend increased flexibility in the selection of classroom activities, to focus teacher attention on cooperative learning activities, and to provide suggestions for the development of critical thinking skills. The annotations include:

  —Teaching suggestions for each segment of each chapter
  —Language and cultural notes for useful background information
  —Classroom management hints and strategies
  —Suggestions for grammar presentations
  —Expansion activities
  —Teaching suggestions for more- and less-prepared students
  —Reteaching ideas
  —Teaching suggestions for native speakers
  —An additional cumulative activity for each chapter
  —Homework assignments
  —Video and Teacher Tape indicators
  —Answers to selected exercises
  —Cues for use of transparencies
  —Cues for use of *Atajo*

**Note:** The pacing schedule for *¡YA VERÁS!* was based on the core of material in the textbook. If you choose to try out some of the variations and additional activities suggested in the enlarged margins, you will want to keep pacing in mind. There are many inviting options from which to choose. Attempting to do *everything*, however, could keep you from completing the book in one year.

## TESTING PROGRAM

- Quizzes and tests covering all four skills
- Quizzes for each *etapa*
- Tests for all chapters and units
- Cumulative exams for end of year
- Tests for the *Capítulos preliminares* for Levels 2 and 3 that can also be used as diagnostic tests
- Testing Manual with ideas for correction and grading
- Oral expression tests/activities accompanied by correction and grading strategies
- Portfolio assessment strategies

## CRITICAL THINKING AND UNIT REVIEW BLACKLINE MASTERS

- Critical thinking activities from the student text with fill-in grids reproduced in blackline master format
- Additional set of exercises which reviews the vocabulary and structures presented in each unit

## TAPESCRIPT

- Scripts for Audiocassette Program and Teacher Tape

## AUDIOCASSETTE PROGRAM

- Set of 12 cassettes for use in classroom or language lab
- Controlled exercises to reinforce the grammar, vocabulary, and functions presented in the textbook
- Extensive practice in listening comprehension through dictations, simulated conversations, interviews, and a variety of exchanges in many different contexts
- Pronunciation exercises correlated to the pronunciation sections in the *¡YA VERÁS!* Level 1 and Level 2 texts

## PRONUNCIATION TAPE
*(for Levels 1 and 2)*

- Pronunciation, explanations, and exercises from the Student Text recorded by native speakers and reproduced in one easy-to-use location

## TEACHER TAPE

- Supplementary single audiocassette for extra listening practice
- Monologues and dialogues from the textbook
- Nonscripted situational conversations to begin and end each chapter

## VIDEO PROGRAMS
*(Videotapes and Videodiscs for Levels 1 and 2)*

- Book-specific videos that contain segments for each chapter
- Authentic, real-life situations and conversations

## VIDEO ACTIVITY MASTERS
*(for Levels 1 and 2)*

- Black line masters that contain comprehension exercises and conversation activities based on each segment of the videos:

  —Exercises for understanding the gist
  —Exercises that require students to pay close attention to details of language, culture, and information
  —Expansion and role-playing activities
  —Video Script

## TRANSPARENCIES

- Full-color transparencies for each unit of each Student Text
- Maps of Spain and Latin America

## SOFTWARE PROGRAMS
*(for Levels 1 and 2)*

- Available in IBM and Mac platforms
- Segments that correspond to the chapters in the Student Texts
- Reinforcement of grammatical structures and vocabulary
- Independent student practice

*Mundos hispanos* is a complete, interactive multimedia program on CD-ROM that combines video, photographs, and exciting graphics in order to develop listening, speaking, reading, and writing skills and bring the culture of the Spanish-speaking world to life. Available for IBM and Mac platforms.

*Atajo Writing Assistant for Spanish* is a software program that facilitates the process of writing in Spanish. Students have access to a wide variety of on-line tools, including:

- a bilingual dictionary of some 8,000 entries, complete with examples of usage
- a verb conjugator that can call up over 500,000 conjugated verb forms
- an on-line reference grammar
- an index to functional phrases
- sets of thematically related vocabulary items

  *Ya llegamos* writing activities at the end of each unit of *¡YA VERÁS!* are correlated to *Atajo. Atajo* is available for IBM (DOS and Windows) and Mac.

*Nuevas dimensiones* is an interactive multimedia program that combines software and video in order to develop listening and writing skills and bring Spanish and Latin American culture to life. Students interact with the program as they listen, practice, test their comprehension, and complete writing exercises. Hardware requirements: IBM PS2 compatible; color VGA monitor; M-Motion Board; Mouse; Windows 3.1 with multimedia support for Toolbook; headphone or speaker. The program is also available for Mac platforms.

# Text Organization at a Glance

## PROGRAM ORGANIZATION

Each level includes some variations.

**Level 1:** 6 units
**Level 2:** 3 preliminary review chapters + 5 units
**Level 3:** 1 preliminary review chapter + 4 units

### UNIT ORGANIZATION

**Unit**
- **Chapter**
  - ***etapa***
  - ***etapa***
  - ***etapa***
  - ***Lectura cultural***
- **Chapter**
  - ***etapa***
  - ***etapa***
  - ***Lectura cultural***
- **Chapter**
  - ***etapa***
  - ***etapa***
  - ***Lectura cultural***
- ***Aquí leemos***
  - Reading
- ***Ya llegamos***
  - Practice
- ***Conexión***
  - Interdisciplinary lesson

The following observations are helpful in understanding the organization of the program:

- The number of units per book is reduced progressively as the material becomes more complex.
- The preliminary review chapters in Levels 2 and 3 highlight the major grammatical structures and vocabulary presented in Levels 1 and 2 respectively.
- The *Etapas preliminares* in Level 1 contain five preliminary lessons, one or more of which may be used as an introduction to Level 1.
- All three books integrate the four skills and culture.
- Each book also highlights one or more skills while continuing the development of the remaining skills:

  **Level 1:** Speaking and listening
  **Level 2:** Reading
  **Level 3:** Writing

## FEATURES OF THE UNIT ORGANIZATION

- Each unit consists of three chapters.
- The unit opens with photographs that illustrate the unit theme.
- The unit opener includes:
  a. the title
  b. the unit objectives
  c. chapter and *etapa* titles
  d. photographs of a young person from Spain or a Spanish-speaking country (Level 1) with questions
- This is followed by three chapters, each divided into *etapas.*
- The end of the unit includes:
  a. the *Aquí leemos* (reading section and review of the unit)
  b. the *Ya llegamos* (cumulative unit activities)
  c. *Conexión* interdisciplinary lesson

## FEATURES OF THE CHAPTER ORGANIZATION

- Each chapter presents a subtheme of the unit theme
- Each chapter opens with a photo.
- Each chapter is divided into *etapas.*
- Each chapter ends with the *Vocabulario,* which includes the expressions and vocabulary presented in the chapter, and a *Lectura cultural,* a cultural reading and practice.

## FEATURES OF THE ETAPA ORGANIZATION

- Each *etapa* presents one aspect of the chapter theme which, in turn, supports the unit theme.
- The *etapa* serves as the basic lesson plan for two or more class periods.
- Each *etapa* is self-contained, with an opening and a closing.
- Each *etapa* includes the presentation of new material, a review of the previous *etapa,* and a final review of the *etapa* being studied.

# How to Use ¡YA VERÁS!, Primer nivel

## HOW TO BEGIN THE YEAR

In the *¡YA VERÁS!* program, we provide the flexibility of beginning the school year in two ways.

### First Days without the Textbook

Because many of you like to use the first days of class as an introduction to the study of Spanish, as a way to have students get acquainted, and as a warm-up to what it is like to study a foreign language, we have designed a series of five *Etapas preliminares.* The lessons can be found in the Teacher's Edition. Cooperative learning is emphasized. **The *Etapas preliminares* are completely optional, to be used at your discretion.**

You may choose to do any, or all of these lessons before beginning Unit 1 of the text. Depending on the length of the school year and your own preferences, you may decide to devote only one class period to the *Etapas preliminares*, prefer to work through two or three suggested lessons, or want to spend as long as six days on these lessons before giving students their textbooks. The lessons not done at this time can be introduced at any time during the year or they can be given to substitute teachers to facilitate their task.

The five lessons described below can be done in whatever order you prefer.

#### *Etapa* A: Names

In this exercise, students learn the basic principles of pronunciation through a number of Spanish *nombres.* They also practice some basic greeting and leave-taking expressions. If you wish, this exercise can be used to provide each student with a Spanish name.

#### *Etapa* B: Basic Vocabulary

Students are exposed to some general ideas about learning the Spanish language. They are also made aware of some basic similarities and differences between Spanish and English. A set of exercises has them work both with word meanings and with the basic sounds of Spanish.

#### *Etapa* C: Cultural Information Quiz

In this option, students are shown that they already know some things about Spain and the Spanish-speaking world. They are also introduced to some basic facts that they may not already know. This is a good opportunity for you to begin the job of making students aware of the notion of cultural stereotypes.

#### *Etapa* D: Spanish-speaking Countries

This option familiarizes students with some geographical features of the Spanish-speaking world, particularly through the use of maps. Students are also introduced to the basic sounds of Spanish through the pronunciation of geographical proper nouns.

#### *Etapa* E: Total Physical Response

This option uses Asher's Total Physical Response approach to familiarize students with the code of language and to begin to develop their listening comprehension skills. By the end of this section, students will be able to carry out a variety of basic commands. In addition, they will be able to understand the numbers from 1 to 30, tell time, and identify some classroom objects. Finally, a short TPR lesson on understanding words for parts of the body can be introduced.

### First Days of Class with the Textbook

In classes where books are distributed on the first day of class, you may wish to enter directly into the first level, reserving the *Etapas preliminares* for other points during the year or simply omitting them.

To introduce the Spanish language and Spanish cultural symbols, have students look at the two introductory pages for Unit 1. These two pages provide sufficient material to stimulate discussion about a variety of topics:

- Symbols commonly associated with the Spanish-speaking world (what symbols do students think represent the United States?)
- Photographs of famous sites (what famous sites would they select in the United States?)
- Signs introducing sounds and cultural concepts
- Importance of Spanish and other foreign languages to various careers

Following this introduction, you can then move directly to Unit 1, Chapter 1.

## HOW TO BEGIN A UNIT

The goal of the unit opener is to provide students with the cultural context and the main theme of the unit. You may use any of the following three methods to introduce the unit.

### Teacher Tape

- Play the segment that corresponds to the unit.
- Have students do a basic comprehension activity (in Spanish or English, depending on the time of year).
- Have a short discussion about the context by comparing it to a similar situation in the United States.

## Video

- Have students view the entire video segment that corresponds to the first chapter.
- Do some comprehension activities from the Video Activity Masters.

## Unit Opener Pages

- Have students analyze the photographs and engage in a discussion about them based on the *¿Qué ves?* questions.
- Have students look at the second page while you review the unit objectives.

Once you've established the unit context, you can then proceed to the "Planning Strategy" found at the beginning of each unit in the Student Workbook. The purpose of the "Planning Strategy" is to have students match English words and expressions to the context in which they have just been introduced. As they then proceed through the unit, students will learn the equivalents of many of these expressions in Spanish.

If done on the first day of class, students brainstorm answers without prior preparation. If done on a subsequent day, this section should be assigned as homework for sharing in class.

# HOW TO BEGIN A CHAPTER

Each chapter opener page contains a photograph that features the main character of the chapter interacting with someone in the specific chapter context. A short conversational exchange is included.

- Have students engage in a short discussion analyzing the cultural content of the photograph. (See annotations in Teacher's Edition for suggestions.)

# HOW TO DO AN ETAPA

The most important aspect of *¡YA VERÁS!* is the self-contained *etapas,* which serve as the basic lesson plans for class. Each *etapa* has a clear beginning and end and includes the presentation of new material, a review of the previous *etapa,* and a final review of the *etapa* being studied.

Each *etapa* contains the vocabulary, functions, and grammar necessary for the subtheme of the *etapa*. These, in turn, contribute to the functions and contexts of the chapter, which, in turn, illustrate the larger context of the unit.

Articulation within units and between units has thus been assured through the interplay and integration of functions, contexts, and accuracy features. (See pp. 43–47 for Function/Context/Accuracy charts for each level.) As the teacher, you may therefore choose to proceed through the units in a linear fashion, without having to reorganize the material or worry about such questions as variety, the recycling of material, or pacing. You also have the flexibility, however, to reserve some parts of the *etapa* for a later date, and you may, of course, move the review activities according to your own preferences and time constraints.

Each *etapa* in Level 1 follows this pattern.

> ***Preparación***
> Vocabulary Introduction
> *¡Aquí te toca a ti!*
> ***Comentarios culturales*** (placement may vary)
> ***Pronunciación*** (in one *etapa* per chapter)
> *Práctica*
> ***Repaso*** (in all *etapas* except the first one in each unit)
> ***Estructura***
> *Aquí practicamos*
> ***Nota gramatical*** or ***Palabras útiles*** (when needed)
> ***Aquí escuchamos***
> ***¡Adelante!***

The following sections define each segment of the *etapa* and suggest generic classroom techniques that may be used. Additional suggestions can be found in the annotations of the Teacher's Edition.

## Preparación

**Definition:** This initial series of questions helps students to focus on the topic of each *etapa,* as well as serving to activate prior knowledge.

*Classroom Techniques:*

- Have students read and answer the questions in advance or in the beginning of class.
- If you have native speakers in your class, elicit more ample responses from them.
- Lead the class in a short discussion of the issues raised.

## Vocabulary Introduction

**Definition:** This first section of the *etapa* introduces the vocabulary that is central to the theme of the *etapa*. The vocabulary is presented in a variety of ways: drawings with captions, narrations, dialogues.

*Classroom Techniques:*

**1. Drawings with captions**

- Point to real objects in class or to the drawings on the transparency (first without the captions).
- Pronounce the words and have students repeat them.
- Point randomly at the drawings on the transparency and have students provide the words.
- Use the caption overlay and have students repeat the words again while they look at the spelling.

- If the objects make it possible, intersperse some personalized questions during the presentation or add a series of questions at the end: *bicicleta—¿Tienes bicicleta? ¿Montas en bicicleta con frecuencia?* Tailor the questions according to the grammar that students have already studied. You may also use the objects to say something about yourself: *A mí me gusta montar en bicicleta. ¿Y a ti?*

**2. Short narration**

- Students have books closed.
- Read through the narration, one segment at a time.
- Illustrate each segment with gestures, visuals, or real objects from class.
- Read the narration again at a normal rate of speech.
- Ask some general comprehension questions.
- Have students open the book and follow the text as you read it again.
- Have students read through the narration silently.

**3. Dialogue**

- Students have books closed.
- Present main ideas in dialogue form while illustrating the new vocabulary through gestures, visuals, or objects from class.
- Act out the dialogue taking all the parts, or having one of the better students act it out with you. Alternative: Play the dialogue from the Teacher Tape.
- Ask students some general comprehension questions.
- Have students open their books and repeat the dialogue after you, one sentence or sentence segment at a time.
- Ask students to role-play the dialogue.

## ¡Aquí te toca a ti!

**Definition:** This set of exercises allows students to practice the vocabulary learned in the Vocabulary Introduction. In most cases, the exercises progress from controlled, to meaningful, to open-ended.

### Classroom Techniques:

**1. Controlled, mechanical exercises done with the whole class**

- Books are closed.
- Have students repeat the model after you. In cases where there is no model, use the first item.
- Continue the exercise, calling on students randomly.

**2. Controlled, mechanical exercises done in pairs**

- Books are open.
- Have students repeat the model after you.
- Do the first item with the whole class.
- Then have students complete the exercise in pairs.
- When everyone is done, you may wish to spot-check items with the whole class.

**3. Open-ended exercises**

- Books are open.
- Begin by modeling the activity with a student.
- If necessary, remind students of key vocabulary and grammatical structures.
- Divide students into pairs or small groups as indicated by the activity.
- At the end of the activity, have several groups perform in front of the class.

## Comentarios culturales

**Definition:** The *Comentarios culturales* contain cultural information that expands the theme of the *etapa*. In Level 1, they are written in English to facilitate short discussions about culture.

### Classroom Techniques:

- Have students read the cultural note at home or in class.
- Ask them basic questions about the content.
- Have them draw similarities and differences between the Spanish-speaking world and the United States.

## *Pronunciación* and Práctica

**Definition:** In these sections (one per chapter), students learn the most common Spanish graphemes (letters or letter combinations) along with their phonemes (the sounds that the letters represent). The presentations always move from symbol to sound so that students are given the tools to pronounce the sounds in new words as they proceed through the program.

### *Classroom Techniques:*

- Systematic correction should occur throughout the presentation and practice.
- Write several words on the board from the list provided.
- Underline the grapheme in question.
- Have students pronounce the words after you.
- Have students read the examples from the book (books open).
- Then have students do the *Práctica* exercise with books open.
- Finally, have them close the books and repeat the *Práctica* items after you.

## Repaso

**Definition:** Found in all *etapas* except in the first of the initial chapter of a unit, these exercises provide consistent review of the structures, vocabulary, and functions of the previous *etapa*. They may be done as warm-ups at the start of a class period or as breaks in the middle of sessions.

### *Classroom Techniques:*

**1. Semi-controlled exercises done with the whole class**

- Books may be open or closed depending on the level of difficulty.
- Make the directions clear to students (preferably in Spanish).
- Have students repeat the model.
- Proceed through the exercise, calling on students randomly.
- If students encounter difficulties with a particular item, the item may be used for a rapid transformation drill. For example, students are having trouble with *Ana quiere bailar*. Use this as the base sentence to make substitutions. You say *comer*. Students say *Ana quiere comer*. You say *estudiar*. Students say *Ana quiere estudiar*. After this brief break, resume the exercise items.

**2. Semi-controlled exercises done in pairs**

- Books are open.
- Make the directions clear.
- Have students repeat the model.
- Do the first item with the whole class.
- Have students divide into pairs and complete the exercise.
- After they are done, verify by spot-checking several items.

**3. Open-ended activities**

- Books are open.
- Make the directions clear.
- With a student, model the activity.
- Divide students into pairs or small groups according to the indications in the activity.
- When students are done, have several groups perform for the class.

**Definition:** Each *etapa* contains the presentation of a new grammatical structure. In *¡YA VERÁS!,* grammar is treated communicatively—that is, grammar is tied logically to the context of the *etapa*, chapter, and unit and to the tasks that students are expected to carry out linguistically. An *Estructura* section offers one of the following three types of presentations.

1. the introduction of a new verb
2. the introduction of a more complex grammatical structure
3. the introduction of a set of lexical items that has grammatical implications (e.g., days of the week, seasons, time)

### *Classroom Techniques:*

In general, all structures can be presented either inductively or deductively, although it is recommended that, whenever possible, an inductive approach be used. In either case, students should have their books closed so that they pay close attention to your examples and explanations. It is generally preferable that you make grammatical presentations in simplified, telegraphic-style Spanish, punctuated by examples. The following demonstrates the presentation of the **preterite.**

**1. The inductive approach (from example to rule)**

- Put some drawings on the board or use a transparency that show a person going through a series of actions (e.g., some of the things a person does on a typical day).
- Have students say what the person does typically, using the present tense.
- Then put the previous day's date on the board to signal *ayer*.
- Redo each action, using the **preterite.**
- Go through the actions again and have students repeat each item.

- Use yourself and the first person singular to transform each item.
- Then have students individually use the first person to go through the actions again.
- Finally, end your presentation (in Spanish, if possible) with a short, concise explanation about the formation.
- Return to the drawings and have students redo the sequence of actions using different pronouns.

**2. The deductive approach (from rule to example)**

- This approach is most appropriate for grammar points that do not merit prolonged class time, are particularly simple, have an exact equivalent in English, or do not lend themselves readily to an inductive presentation. Examples of this type of grammatical structure are demonstrative adjectives *(este, esta, ese, esa)*, the interrogative adjective *cuánto* and its various forms, and so forth. Rather than devoting valuable class time to lengthy presentations, such grammatical topics are best dealt with as efficiently as possible to leave more time for practice. Whenever possible, presentations should be made in Spanish. Use a quick translation of the key element, if necessary.
- Put several examples on the board or on a transparency.
- Explain the rule in simple terms using the examples.
- Provide an additional series of examples by eliciting the grammatical structure through personalized questions and answers.

## Aquí practicamos

**Definition:** A series of exercises follows each *Estructura* section. The exercises usually move from controlled or mechanical drills to bridging exercises to open-ended, communicative activities. The grammatical structures are practiced in a variety of contexts.

**1. Controlled or mechanical drills**

- provide structure and meaning
- usually require some type of transformation or substitution

**2. Bridging or meaningful exercises**

- provide structure and students provide meaning
- are generally contextualized

**3. Open-ended or communicative exercises**

- require students to provide structure and meaning
- are highly contextualized and usually personalized

### *Classroom Techniques:*

**1. Controlled or mechanical drills**

- Correction should be systematic.
- You may do with the whole class or in pairs.
- Make the directions clear.
- Use the first item as a model.
- Continue with the whole class or have students complete in pairs.
- If done in pairs, follow-up with a spot check.

**2. Bridging or meaningful exercises**

- Do preferably in pairs or in small groups.
- Make the directions clear.
- Have students repeat the model.
- Divide the students into groups and have them complete the exercise.
- Spot-check some items with the whole class.

**3. Open-ended or communicative exercises**

- Do in pairs or small groups.
- Make the directions clear.
- Model the situation with a student.
- Divide the class into groups.
- When the activity is completed, have several groups role-play the situation for the class or report back the group results.

**Important Note:** Since small groups tend to progress through exercises at different rates, you can assign all three exercises or the last two as a chain. Make sure that students understand directions and instruct them to proceed to the next exercise when they are done with one. It is not necessary to wait until every pair has finished the entire chain. When the majority of pairs has reached the end of the chain, verify by doing some items with the whole class. This technique gives students the flexibility to progress at their own pace.

## Nota gramatical / Palabras útiles and Aquí practicamos

**Definition:** These follow-up sections to the *Estructura* present additional refinements to the main grammar point in the chapter or special uses of certain vocabulary items. If needed, the *Nota gramatical* (or *Palabras útiles* if the point is lexical) often comes directly after the mechanical exercise of the *Estructura* section and is followed by the meaningful and communicative exercises.

### Classroom Techniques:

Use either an inductive or a deductive approach (see *Estructura* explanation), followed by the *Aquí practicamos* exercises.

## Aquí escuchamos

**Definition:** In this section students will hear Spanish speakers carry out the function(s) that are being presented and practiced in the *etapa*. They are presented in dialogue or monologue form and also include the vocabulary introduced receptively at the beginning of each *etapa*. Students will be exposed to a wide variety of voices and accents. In order to provide a truly listening-oriented exercise, the script does not appear in the student edition of the textbook. These sections begin with pre-listening activities, designed to activate the students' background knowledge. They are followed by comprehension exercises that are meant to be completed during or after listening to the recording. Both the pre-listening and the comprehension exercises are included in the student textbook.

**Definition:** These end-of-*etapa* exercises are designed to review the vocabulary, functions, and structures of the *etapa*. They will always consist of at least two exercises: an *Ejercicio oral* and an *Ejercicio escrito*. The *¡Adelante!* review may be done at the end of a class period or as a warm-up at the beginning of a class.

### Classroom Techniques:

1. ***Ejercicio oral***

- Books are open.
- Make the directions clear.
- Model the role play with a student.
- Divide students into pairs or groups.
- As a follow-up, you may wish to ask some students to perform the role play for the class.

2. ***Ejercicio escrito***

- Books are open.
- Make the directions clear.
- Have students brainstorm vocabulary they will need to carry out the exercise.
- Have students look at and comment on each others' work.

## HOW TO END A CHAPTER

Each chapter culminates with a high interest, culturally oriented reading, called a *Lectura cultural.*

## Lectura cultural

**Definition:** This reading section appears after each chapter. It is a short passage which provides information of cultural significance in the Spanish-speaking world. These sections are presented in two parts: *Antes de leer,* which contains pre-reading activities and is designed to activate the students' background knowledge, and *Guía para la lectura,* consisting of activities designed to help the student practice various reading strategies.

## Conexión con...

**Definition:** Additional optional lessons that provide exposure to Spanish through an interdisciplinary or content-based approach. Some content areas included are mathematics, sociology, psychology, geography, and library science. Each lesson focuses on a piece of subject-area information in Spanish and includes warm-up and comprehension activities. Additional expansion activities are also available in the Teacher's Edition.

## HOW TO END A UNIT

At the end of each unit is a cumulative review of the entire unit that consists of two components.

**Definition:** This is a section-opening reading usually taken from authentic documents (newspapers, magazines, brochures, advertisements), including literature. It is usually preceded by a reading strategy that helps students focus their reading. The *Aquí leemos* is always an expansion or illustration of the unit theme and is followed by activities that serve as a verification of students' understanding of the text.

### Classroom Techniques:

- Have students read the text silently either for homework or in class.
- Impress upon them that they should not be reading word for word but should rather concentrate on the main ideas.
- Move directly to the activities.

(*Actividades orales y escritas*)

**Definition:** These cumulative, communicative activities are the culminating point of the unit. They combine the vocabulary, functions, structures, and cultural information presented in the unit. Everything in the unit leads up to this performance point, in which students can demonstrate their independence in using the Spanish language. The activities are done in pairs or in small groups. Instructions are given in English to avoid giving away the key structures and vocabulary, and to encourage students to use a variety of ways to express themselves. Using English in the direction lines also approximates the "real" situations in which students might find themselves. For example, if they were to enter a Spanish store, their reason for being there would exist in their minds in English.

The most important thing to remember is that the *Ya llegamos* activities demonstrate what language learning is all about. They show the tasks that students can accomplish with the language they know and in which contexts and with what degree of accuracy they can function. To sacrifice these activities to time constraints or to treat them as optional would be to subvert both the goals of the *¡YA VERÁS!* program and the goals of proficiency-oriented language instruction and learning. It is therefore imperative that the process be carried out fully and that students have the opportunity to demonstrate their accomplishments.

### *Classroom Techniques:*

- Select the activities you wish your students to do and reserve the rest for another time or simply skip them.
- Make the directions clear.
- Model with one or more students, if necessary.
- If needed, have students brainstorm key vocabulary ahead of time.
- Divide the students into groups.
- When the activity is ended, have a few groups role play the situation for the class.
- If you wish, you may give these groups a grade. The rest of the students can get grades at other times when they perform in front of the class.

Once you've completed the end-of-the-unit section, you can complete the unit in one of two ways (or both)

**1. Video**

You can (re)play the video segments that correspond to the unit. At this point, students should understand much of what is being said and should grasp more cultural information than they did during the first viewing. This is generally a source of real satisfaction for them and demonstrates to them how much they have learned during the unit.

**2. Teacher Tape**

You can (re)play the conversations that correspond to the unit. Again, students' understanding should be considerably enhanced because of the work done in the unit. It should be remembered, however, that audiotaped material is always more difficult to understand than video because it does not provide additional visual support.

## The Role of Culture in ¡YA VERÁS!, Primer nivel / Segundo nivel

It is important to note the various ways in which culture is integrated throughout the Level 1 and 2 texts. The role of culture in Level 3 will be discussed separately.

A variety of techniques is used to immerse students in the Hispanic cultures as they learn Spanish. Rather than isolating cultural phenomena from the language that students are learning, the culture is tightly integrated into every aspect of the textbooks.

1. Culture is ever present in that it is inseparable from language. As students learn to express themselves in various situations, the language they use and the behaviors that accompany this language are culturally authentic. This means that language in *¡YA VERÁS!* has not been doctored or modified for the sake of grammatical rules. For example, sentence fragments are acceptable because they are natural in speech. Communicative functions are taught from the outset.
2. The vocabulary in *¡YA VERÁS!* reflects the interests of young people in the Spanish-speaking world, as well as the interests of your students.
3. *¿Qué crees?* These short multiple-choice items placed in the margins at regular intervals throughout the units of Level 1 focus on interesting facts that are related to the *etapa* topics.
4. *Comentarios culturales* further student understanding of a particular topic.
5. The visual components of the program— the photos, art, realia, and video— contain a wealth of cultural material, both factual and behavioral. Their use should be fully integrated into classroom time to the greatest extent possible. Depending on facilities, the video may also be made available to students in a library or laboratory setting.
6. Reading units focus on important cultural topics and provide students with factual information about modern life and historical events.
7. Readings in the *Aquí leemos* section and throughout the Workbook expose students to a variety of texts for a multitude of purposes. Readings include ads, poems, magazine and newspaper articles, brochures, various types of guidebooks, recipes, classified ads, and literary sketches.

# Spanish for Native Speakers

In the best of all possible worlds, schools would have two Spanish language tracks—one for monolingual speakers of English and another for native speakers of Spanish. Each group would be taught with materials specifically created for them. However, we do not live in a perfect world and many schools typically enroll native speakers alongside non-native speakers in Spanish language classes. What can you do if you find yourself in this situation? *¡YA VERÁS!* is a program that has been created to teach Spanish as a foreign language to non-native speakers of the language. We have, however, included suggestions for addressing the special needs of the Hispanic students who may be enrolled in your classes.

## Who are Native Speakers?

Let us first begin by discussing the topic of what we mean by native speaker. By this we mean the broad spectrum of Hispanic students who have grown up in this country or immigrated here. If most of their education occurred in the United States, they have probably learned to speak and understand Spanish at home, but have never been taught to read or write it. Oftentimes, when they find themselves in a foreign-language classroom, native speakers feel unchallenged and/or resist the grammatical approach used to teach them a language whose grammatical structures they have already internalized. Many Hispanic students demonstrate a better command of both the listening and speaking skills in Spanish than their non-native classmates; yet too many teachers do not capitalize on the existing language proficiency of these students.

## What do Native Speakers Bring to the Classroom?

The first order of business should be to capitalize on the linguistic skills these students already bring to the classroom. Assuming a student already speaks and comprehends Spanish, he or she must be taught to read and write the language. Students raised in a Spanish-speaking home bring a great deal of oral ability to the classroom; however, few bring the knowledge of how that ability is expressed in a written mode. Contrary to popular belief, Spanish is not written just the way it sounds—it is not as phonetic as people think. While it may be more phonetic than English or French, it is certainly far from what linguists would term a phonetic language. For example, the sound of /k/ can be written with a number of symbols: qu (*que, queso*); c before a, o, u (*casa, cosa, cuna*); and even with the letter k (*kilo, kimono*). As Spanish-speaking students take their first steps toward becoming literate in Spanish, they must devote some attention to spelling. The following are some of the more problematic sound/symbol correlations they need to master.

Special attention should be paid to words with:

| | | | |
|---|---|---|---|
| b | v | z + a | z + o |
| z + u | c + e | c + i | s + any vowel |
| h | x | ll | y |
| g + e | g + i | j | |

Another area that can be addressed to improve literacy involves reading instruction. We have incorporated a number of reading activities in the *¡YA VERÁS!* program that reflect some of the latest research in this area. Hispanic students in foreign language classes generally already read English, for they have most likely been educated and learned to read in American schools. (Students who are not yet literate in English should be in ESL classes rather than foreign language classes.) However, as reading researchers have shown, the transfer of reading skills from one language to another is far from automatic. Students need support when learning to read an additional language. Special attention should be paid to having students go through all of the exercises and activities that accompany the readings in this program.

## What about "Standard" Spanish?

As we have said earlier, many Hispanic students already speak Spanish; however, it may not be the variety of language that is taught in the typical classroom. In sociolinguistic terms, people in this group are termed diglossic. This means that while one language is used for all formal or what are termed "high" functions, the other is used in all informal or "low" functions. In the case of the United States, English is generally considered appropriate for formal exchanges (political rallies, business meetings, announcements, sermons, lectures, classrooms, etc.), and Spanish is used in informal situations within the home and among other members of the speech community. Because most of these students' education has taken place in English, they have seldom had the opportunity to hear Spanish as it is used for the high or formal functions of the language. Thus (except for radio and television, where available) they have had no models for this register of the language and have not developed this aspect of Spanish. Most students can expand their range of functions in Spanish. The Spanish that they speak is not wrong. The only mistake they may make is to use the their particular variety of Spanish in an inappropriate social situation. Part of these speakers' classroom learning, then, must involve getting acquainted with formal and academic Spanish.

Many, including members of the Spanish teaching profession, often refer to what these students speak as "dialect." Popular belief holds that dialects are substandard, even defective. In fact, any variety of a language is technically a dialect, even the educated standard. Again, drawing from the field of sociolinguistics, everyone speaks a dialect. The tremendous concern over "correct" speech is explicable only when the social functions of dialects are considered, even though it can be shown that no dialect is inherently better or worse than another. It is necessary for students to be able to command educated varieties of speech if they wish to be able to hold certain kinds of jobs. However, any attempt to teach a standard dialect to a nonstandard speaker must take into account the social reasons that explain why people speak the way they do.

With regard to listening, most students will be able to understand spoken Spanish. Even those students who might be third- or fourth-generation in this country (and who may have weak speaking skills) will probably comprehend the language. What they need to work on most is to gain exposure to the variety of ways that Spanish is spoken. Remember, there are a number of ways to speak Spanish correctly. We all know that a Spaniard does not sound like a Chilean, nor a Bolivian like a Mexican, nor a Puerto Rican like an Argentine, etc. The listening activities, including the video, that accompany the *¡YA VERÁS!* program have been created with this in mind; i.e., students will hear the language as it is spoken in many parts of the Spanish-speaking world.

Finally, it is important to remember that Spanish-speaking students are not beginning from ground zero. It is up to you, the teacher, to meet them where they are and take them as far as you can. Always endeavor to be sensitive to how they express themselves, for while it may be inappropriate to use certain vocabulary words and expressions in the classroom, it may be completely appropriate to do so within their speech community. Rather than "fixing" how they speak and write Spanish, it is up to you to capitalize on the linguistic strengths they bring to your classroom and help them increase their range of linguistic functions.

## SPECIFIC SUGGESTIONS:

### ¿Qué ves?

Have students answer as much as possible in Spanish. Share some of this information with the rest of the class.

### *Etapa* opener

Ask students for variations of new vocabulary. This is a good place to begin showing them that while what they say is quite correct in their particular speech community, in order to communicate with Spanish speakers from other parts of the world it is important for them to add this new vocabulary to their linguistic repertoire.

### Estructura

Don't emphasize grammatical terminology. Students should use this section to familiarize themselves with the forms (not the names of the forms) of the Spanish language that may not be part of their linguistic repertoire. After all, it is not necessary to know the names of the 206 bones in the human body in order to walk, run, dance, etc. Have them skip some of the exercises that are very basic practice, which might be much too easy for them.

### Aquí escuchamos

Again, ask students for variations. Emphasize that what they say in their speech community is correct, but in order to communicate with other Spanish speakers outside their speech community it is important that they learn other ways of expressing the same thing.

### ¡Adelante!

#### Ejercicio oral

You must be sensitive and accept how the students carry out this speaking activity. Don't label their use of vocabulary or certain expressions as wrong. Remember, don't penalize students for something that is sociolinguistically correct within their speech community. This is a good place to point out to the students where their Spanish differs from formal Spanish and to help them work on those elements of the language that are part of a more formal Spanish. Once this is done, have them expand and go beyond the basic instructions for this exercise.

#### Ejercicio escrito

Always have students complete this section. Have them focus on what and how the book is teaching them to write. Strongly encourage the inclusion of vocabulary from the book to enhance the vocabulary that they already know. Again, stress the idea that in order to communicate with other Spanish speakers outside their speech community it is important that they learn other ways of expressing the same thing. You may want students to edit each other's work so that they might help their fellow students with any spelling errors that might occur.

### Comentarios culturales

Ask students how their specific cultural practices may be similar to or different from those expressed in this section. This is a good place to show them that while they might be a minority in this country, they are part of the vast majority of people who are living in the Western Hemisphere.

### Vocabulario

Have students pay particular attention to how words are spelled. Make a concerted effort to point out to them the words that contain the more difficult sound/symbol correlations. You might have them keep a special notebook in which they write the vocabulary words. One category could be labeled: *Así lo dice el libro ...* .

Another category could be used to allow them to write out those words that are already part of their linguistic repertoire and could be labeled: *Así lo digo yo ...* .

### Lectura cultural

Always have students go through each of the exercises in this section. Once they have completed the activities, they might be asked to summarize the reading in Spanish in order to give them additional writing practice. They might also be required to keep a notebook with a special list of new vocabulary they might find in the reading selections.

# Sample Lesson Plan for High School

## HELPFUL HINTS FOR TEACHING WITH *¡YA VERÁS!* AT THE HIGH SCHOOL LEVEL

### Primera unidad, Capítulo 1: Segunda etapa ¡Un refresco, por favor!

**Objectives:** The learner will be able to recognize and begin to have a command of various hot and cold drinks on a menu and order these drinks in a café; role play a café scene with waiter or waitress and customer.

**Materials:** A table with a tablecloth set up with most of the drinks prepared: use colored water in bottles, coffee cups, tea bags, plastic fruits and authentic soda cans; Textbook, pages 10–12; Transparencies 10, 10a, 11, 11a; Teacher Tape.

1. Model pronunciation of each drink and have students repeat vocabulary. Stop after a few words and review: *¿Qué es esto? —> un café, una limonada,* etc. Continue until the vocabulary has been introduced.
2. Return the drinks to the table and call students up to take certain drinks from the table: *Juan, ¡toma la granadina!; Ana, ¡toma el jugo de naranja!* When all of the drinks are gone, call them back by saying: *Yo quisiera una granadina, por favor,* etc. The person who has the drink gives it back to the teacher. Teacher may add *gracias* and *de nada* to the exchange.
3. Text, Ex. A, page 10: Go over the model for the exercise. Ask first student the question. He or she responds and asks the next person the question, who responds with the next answer. Keep the activity going around the room like a snake or chain with the last person asking the teacher the question.

   If you run out of questions, recycle and start at number one again.
4. Books closed. Show transparencies 10 and 11 and see how many drinks the students remember. (You may use the table setting in the room.)
5. Introduce the dialogue on page 9 with the Teacher Tape. Model pronunciation and have students repeat the new expressions.
6. Discuss some of the expressions and give meanings.

7. Ex. B, page 11: Review model with students, then divide them into groups of two and have them act out the exercise in their groups. (Role play for approximately five minutes.)
8. Call on one or two groups to present to class without notes. Students may use drinks that are already set up.
9. **Assignment:** Workbook, pages 6–7, Ex. D, E, F. Study Text, Ex. C, page 11, for skit the next day.

### *Day Two*

**Objectives:** The learner will recognize the four indefinite articles; use café vocabulary in role-playing activities; write the vocabulary.

**Materials:** Workbook, pages 6–7; colored water representing drinks; Textbook, pages 11–13; Transparencies 10, 10a, 11, 11a.

1. As teacher calls roll, have students respond with: *Yo quisiera un(a)* (and the name of a drink). See how many drinks the students remember from the previous day. Have students write the names of the drinks on the board.
2. Correct workbook orally (together).
3. Review vocabulary by asking *¿Qué es esto? ¿Qué desea tomar?* Hold up a drink and have the students respond together.
4. Introduce Exercise C. Form new groups of three. Explain the model to the students. Have students practice together until they can present without notes.
5. Have students present skits from Exercise C. Correct errors as a group.
6. Introduce concept of the indefinite article. See if students can tell you what the two singular forms are and why they are masculine and feminine. Respond by writing on the board and filling in blanks that students may leave in the explanation.
7. Show Transparencies 10 and 11 again and have students fill in the correct indefinite article on their papers. Check orally.
8. Textbook, page 12. Divide into pairs and have students work on Exercises F and G (5 minutes). Check orally together.
9. **Assignment:** Read page 13 and study vocabulary.

### *Day Three*

**Objectives:** The learner will use drink vocabulary, café expressions, indefinite articles in role-playing activities.

**Materials:** Textbook, pages 13–14; café props

1. Put a scrambled café conversation on the board and have the students write the conversation so that it makes sense. Correct together.
2. Review drink names and indefinite articles.
3. Discuss reading on page 13.

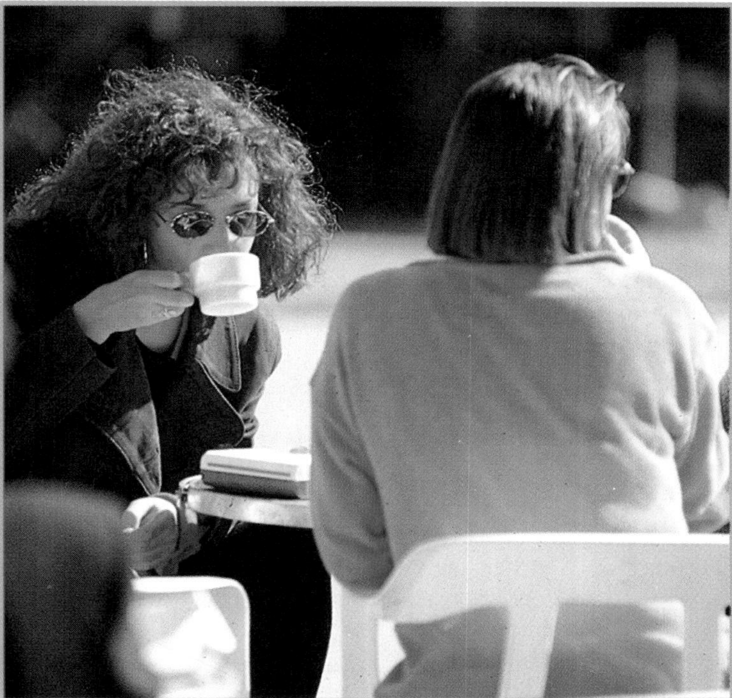

4. Divide students into groups of four and have them prepare *¡Adelante!* page 14, Ex. H. (Set up café scene in front of class.) Allow students 15–20 minutes to practice. Have them go up in front of class to present for a grade.
5. If there is time, give oral practice quiz on drink names and indefinite articles. Correct together.
6. **Assignment:** Study for *Etapa* 2 quiz the next day.

### *Day Four*

**Objectives:** The learner will take a formative quiz to check for mastery of *Segunda etapa* material; view video for visual and cultural knowledge of cafés and listen for drinks ordered.

**Materials:** Quiz for Unit I, Chapter 1, *Etapa* 2, pages 3–5; Video; Transparencies 9–11a

1. Review in pairs drink vocabulary, café phrases, and *un/una*.
2. Quiz, *Segunda etapa* from testing booklet.
3. Video — View without sound the program on ordering drinks in a café and ask students to make observations as to what they might be saying in Spanish. Discuss.
4. Now watch video with sound and have students identify the drinks that they ordered. Check student responses to see how accurate they were.
5. Close by introducing new vocabulary from Transparencies 12 and 12a. Preview what students will learn next.

# Pedagogical Considerations

A proficiency-oriented, integrative approach to teaching raises certain pedagogical issues that need to be addressed. In particular, these are questions dealing with the development of skills (listening, speaking, reading, writing, critical thinking) and culture as well as questions about classroom management (large, heterogeneous classes; cooperative learning; Total Physical Response; correction strategies; teacher behaviors).

## DEVELOPING LANGUAGE AND CRITICAL THINKING SKILLS

### Developing the Listening Skill

Through the Teacher Tape, the Video Program, the Laboratory Tapes, and appropriate teacher speech, *¡YA VERÁS!* seeks to develop the listening skill in a systematic way. The focus is on listening comprehension as it would occur in real life, using speech samples that are both scripted and unscripted and free of artificial grammatical and lexical manipulation. As you use these materials, several considerations should be kept in mind.

1. Students will not understand every word that they hear and this is not necessary. They should be encouraged to listen for gist. In real life, we do not necessarily hear every word that is said to us (noise interference, etc.) and students should become accustomed to this.
2. Students need to be able to demonstrate that they have understood something. At the beginning of the program this means that they will probably use English to indicate their comprehension. As they progress, an increased number of activities can be done in Spanish, although this will always depend on the complexity of the comprehension check.
3. Listening comprehension develops more quickly than speaking. It is therefore important to integrate listening activities fully into the learning process since it can serve as a confidence builder.
4. Since listening in real life is done for a variety of purposes, some comprehension activities are limited to understanding the main point while others require the comprehension of specific details.
5. General comprehension should usually be ascertained first, before an analysis of details is undertaken. The activities in the text and Listening Activity Masters follow this general to specific pattern.
6. Listening comprehension activities vary from simple multiple-choice and true/false items to more extensive summary-type exercises. In the *Aquí escuchamos* section, carefully designed pre-listening activities draw out students' background knowledge, which serves as a framework for comprehension. This helps students to acquire and organize new concepts. Follow-up activities check for accurate listening and the understanding of meaning in context.
7. You, the teacher, are one of the best sources for listening materials. Even your inductive presentations of grammatical structures contribute to the development of listening comprehension, providing, of course, that you speak at your normal rate of speech whenever possible.

### Developing the Speaking Skill

If speaking is to become truly functional (i.e., students can accomplish real tasks with the language), a number of conditions must be met in the classroom. It is essential that learners be surrounded with interesting, age-appropriate materials if they are to acquire a new language in its cultural context. The *¡YA VERÁS!* program provides such material, including a range of oral practice from controlled to meaningful to open ended that is necessary for the development of the speaking skill. When seeking to develop oral proficiency, the following pedagogical principles should be kept in mind.

1. Students should be corrected systematically when they're engaged in highly controlled exercises.
2. Correction should be delayed until after communicative, interactive activities have been completed. Real communication should not be interrupted with grammatical corrections.
3. The sequence of exercises in *¡YA VERÁS!* should be carried through completely whenever possible.
4. Students should be asked to speak in complete sentences when mechanical exercises require it, but sentence fragments are acceptable in communicative situations.

5. Small-group activities must be a regular part of classroom strategies. Students should work in pairs or small groups at least once and, if possible, more frequently during each class period.

6. Recognition must be given in grading for the message (content) as well as for grammatical accuracy. Students should feel that they get credit not just for how they say something but also for what they say.

When assessing spoken language, a procedure such as an oral proficiency interview or a modified version that elicits a speech sample through a somewhat standardized format, is generally quite helpful. An approach that takes into account ranges of performance at different levels allows for determining whether a student's proficiency meets or does not meet expectations. A sample of this kind of criterion-referenced scoring, which means that a speech sample should be held accountable to the criteria itself and not to other samples, is provided below. The overall evaluation should identify the sustained level of performance with regard to:

Syntactic control
Vocabulary usage and fluency
Pronunciation

9 VERY GOOD TO EXCELLENT
**Very good to excellent command of the language. Very few errors of syntax. Wide range of vocabulary, including idiomatic usage. High level of fluency.**

7–8 CLEARLY DEMONSTRATES COMPETENCE
**Good command of the language. Few errors of syntax. Above-average range of vocabulary. Good idiomatic usage and little awkwardness of expression. Good fluency and intonation.**

5–6 SUGGESTS COMPETENCE
**Comprehensible expression. Some serious errors of syntax and some successful self-correction. Some fluency, but hesitant. Moderate range of vocabulary and idiomatic usage.**

3–4 SUGGESTS INCOMPETENCE
**Poor command of the language marked by frequent serious errors of syntax. Limited fluency. Poor pronunciation. Narrow range of vocabulary and of idiomatic usage. Frequent anglicisms and structure which force interpretation of meaning by the listener. Occasional redeeming features.**

1–2 CLEARLY DEMONSTRATES INCOMPETENCE
**Unacceptable from almost every point of view. Glaring weakness in syntax and pronunciation. Few vocabulary resources. Little or no sense of idiomatic usage.**

0 IRRELEVANT SPEECH SAMPLE
**Narrative irrelevant to task or assignment.**

## Developing the Reading Skill

Of all the language skills, reading is perhaps the most durable and should be developed systematically. The *¡YA VERÁS!* program provides many opportunities for students to demonstrate their reading comprehension skills. As in listening, a number of factors have been taken into consideration in the development of the program.

1. Reading should be done in class as well as for homework.
2. Reading should be tested along with all the other skills.
3. In *Developing Reading Skills* (Cambridge: Cambridge University Press, 1981, p. 4) François Grellet points out that in real life our purposes for reading vary constantly. There also specific types of reading: (1) skimming, or quickly running one's eyes over a text to get the gist of it; (2) scanning, or quickly going through a text to find a particular bit of information; (3) extensive reading, or reading longer texts, usually for pleasure; and (4) intensive reading, or reading shorter texts to extract specific information. These different types of reading are not mutually exclusive. One often skims through a passage to see what it is about before deciding whether it is worth scanning a particular paragraph for the information one is seeking. The exercises that accompany the readings in this book have been created with this in mind, i.e., students are guided in their reading through specific reading strategies. Furthermore, reading sections include a diverse variety of text types, from menus to ads to magazine/newspaper articles to literary selections.
4. Since reading comprehension skills develop more quickly than speaking and writing skills, early comprehension checks should be done in English rather than Spanish. As students progress, these checks can be done in Spanish depending on the level of difficulty of the text and the exercise.

The reading selections are intended to further the development of students' reading skills. To this end, students work with cognates, words of the same family, and key words essential to the understanding of the texts.

In order to develop reading skills, students should be reading first for comprehension, second for detail, and finally for grammatical and/or vocabulary analysis (if you find such an analysis desirable). Vocabulary and unknown structures should be treated receptively without the expectation that students will be able to reproduce them in speaking. It is likely, of course, that they will retain some of the vocabulary for production, but this is not the aim of these lessons. As students work through the reading selections, they will become more and more comfortable with the idea of reading for meaning and for information. Since students will be timed as they read, they should also get used to reading without understanding every single word, thus increasing their reading rate. It might be helpful to point out to them that they should not be trying to decipher every word, but should look at the meaning of a whole sentence or paragraph.

### Use of English

Because comprehension of information is the primary aim of the reading selections and because students' reading ability develops more quickly than their speaking ability, English is necessary at this stage if any meaningful discussion is to take place. This limited and clearly defined use of English will relieve students of the frustration they often feel when their ideas are at a higher level than their ability to verbalize them.

## Developing the Writing Skill

Real-life writing involves many different tasks that are carried out for a variety of purposes. In *¡YA VERÁS!*, the writing skill is developed along similar lines as speaking. That is, students are required to move through a sequence of exercises, from mechanical to meaningful to communicative, at every stage of their language development. Additional writing practice is included in the *Ejercicio escrito* that appears in the *¡Adelante!* section at the end of each *etapa*.

In accordance with a proficiency orientation, the final stage of this sequence (communicative activities) is the goal of all writing tasks. Students are asked to make lists, write sentence-level notes, postcards, messages, and, finally, produce writing at the paragraph level. Since none of this writing will be error free, it is important for you to recognize and give credit to the successful communication of the message before addressing the question of accuracy. This usually means that you assign a number of points for content and message, or you may decide simply to give two grades for each major writing assignment.

In Level 3 of *¡YA VERÁS!*, we have introduced a systematic writing program (along the lines of a freshman English composition course), that moves students through the basic levels of writing: from word to sentence to multiple sentences to paragraphs to multiple paragraphs. The writing done in Level 3 therefore serves as a capstone before students move to the types of writing required of them in Spanish 4 and 5 classes.

Encouraging risk-taking is an essential factor in developing the writing skill. Traditionally, students who wrote error-free compositions that showed very little innovation and imagination have been rewarded more than students who tried to express meaningful and personalized messages. The result has usually been that students used only grammatical structures and vocabulary of which they were absolutely certain, resulting in rather boring and artificial compositions. The traditional students had few red marks on the paper. The innovative students were faced with red-pen punishment. We suggest that this trend be reversed by assigning points both for message and accuracy so that both types of students are rewarded for the efforts they have made. We would also suggest that correction techniques be modified to become less punitive. For example, comment first on what students do well before making suggestions and corrections. We further encourage you to consider underlining what is correct and to throw away the red pen! Furthermore, students can be given the opportunity to edit what they have written so that they receive two grades for their work—one grade for the first effort, another grade for their final writing sample.

## Portfolios

A portfolio is any collection of student work. Most often, it is a folder containing some of the better work a student has produced. Instructionally, a portfolio allows students to examine the work they have produced, to select special pieces of work, and to reflect on what they have learned and how they learned it. In other words, a portfolio is a collection of work that exhibits a student's efforts, progress, and achievement in a given area, in this case, writing.

The purpose of a portfolio is to record student growth over time, allowing students to think about what they have learned and how they have learned it. Throughout the process, students gain a sense of pride and confidence in their abilities. The portfolio also provides a record of student achievement for teachers, parents, and other audiences. In this way, the portfolio becomes a window through which student learning and performance can be viewed.

The *Ejercicio escrito* that is found at the end of each *etapa* can serve as the piece of writing that could be included in the students' portfolios.

## Developing Cultural Awareness

The *¡YA VERÁS!* program integrates culture at all stages of language learning. Culture is not just dealt with in terms of facts, but includes cultural analysis and appropriate behavior in terms of language use. Authenticity of expression is an essential aspect of the program so that students develop a sense of social/contextual appropriateness. In the process, it is hoped that they become more accepting and non-judgmental of other cultures, that they become less ethnocentric about their own culture, and that they realize that the Spanish language represents peoples of various cultures.

Several factors come into play in the development of cultural awareness.

1. You should avoid judgmental or stereotypical statements.
2. You should challenge judgmental or stereotypical statements.
3. Students must understand that facts are important but that they are not the only definition of culture. Culture is embedded in the language. The language is a reflection of cultural attitudes.
4. Understanding another culture depends largely on one's ability to observe and analyze. As students look at the photographs in the textbooks or view the videotapes, they should be taught to become keen observers of behavior patterns.
5. Cultural awareness should not be developed solely through the observation of differences but also through the noting of similarities between one's own culture and the target culture. For example, students should note that Spanish-speaking youth tend to dress much the same way as American youth. Similarities and differences are pointed out in the cultural observation notes in the Teacher's Edition.

6. Students should be made aware that the words they use in commenting about other cultures may tend to be judgmental and should be avoided. Words such as "weird," "bizarre," "stupid," "nerdy," (or whatever words happen to be in vogue at a particular time) indicate that the speaker assumes that his or her own culture is somehow superior to the target culture. Perhaps this lesson will carry over into students' dealings with their peers and with adults!

## Developing the Critical Thinking Skills

The foreign language class is an ideal place for developing critical thinking skills. As students acquire skills in a new language and information about a variety of cultures, they can also develop their ability to observe, analyze, synthesize, evaluate, and integrate new information in a variety of ways. In the *¡YA VERÁS!* program, activities which encourage students to practice analyzing, synthesizing, and evaluating information are labeled in the student margin. Additional critical thinking activities and strategies are suggested in the margin notes of the Teacher's Edition.

A number of general principles apply to the development of critical thinking skills.

1. Critical thinking involves a number of conditions and subskills, including the following.
   - — flexibility of mind (the ability to change one's mind)
   - — open-mindedness (sensitivity to multiple points of view)
   - — the ability to evaluate various points of view without bias
   - — the ability to observe and listen actively
   - — the ability to analyze (to break down issues into their component parts)
   - — the ability to synthesize (to combine separate elements to form a new unified, coherent whole)
   - — the ability to evaluate (to determine worth, to judge)
   - — the ability to integrate new information into what is known
   - — the ability to apply knowledge to a new issue
   - — the ability to make associations
2. The general categories of analyzing, synthesizing, and evaluating can be identified more explicitly. The following are examples and definitions of subheadings used in these groups.

   *Analysis*
   - — **Analyzing** (examining an object or an idea, studying it from every angle to see what it is, how it works, how many similarities and differences it has from other objects or ideas, and how its parts relate or fit together)
   - — **Categorizing** (organizing information into groups with similar qualities or attributes)
   - — **Comparing and contrasting** (Looking for similarities and/or differences between ideas, people, places, objects, and/or situations)
   - — **Making associations** (using an idea, person, event, or object to trigger the memory of another; seeing relationships between two or more things)
   - — **Sequencing** (arranging details in order according to specified criteria)

   *Synthesis*
   - — **Synthesizing** (pulling together pieces of information and ideas to create a new whole)
   - — **Drawing inferences** (guessing logical explanations or reasons for choices, actions, events, or situations)
   - — **Hypothesizing** (making an assertion as a basis for reasoning or argument)
   - — **Predicting** (expecting behavior, actions, or events based on prior experience and/or available facts)
   - — **Seeing cause-and-effect relationships** (anticipating a logical result from an action or event)
   - — **Creating** (producing an original product of human invention or imagination, originating, bringing about, dreaming up)

   *Evaluation*
   - —**Evaluating** (determining worth, judging)
   - —**Determining preferences** (making personal value judgments)
   - —**Prioritizing** (establishing precedence in order of importance or urgency, determining relative value)
3. Critical thinking skills can be taught and should be inherent in foreign language teaching and learning. Teaching students to think critically is an ongoing process that is enhanced by directing student attention to the examination and understanding of their own thinking.

## Developing Learning Strategies

In addition to listings of critical thinking skills, many of the activities in *¡YA VERÁS!* are labeled as to the specific learning strategies being emphasized in the activity. The learning strategies noted in the student margin can be considered to be in four different categories: **receptive strategies, productive strategies, organizational strategies,** and **multi-tasking strategies.**

The following lists provide sample entries in the four categories.

**Receptive**
- Active listening
- Reading
- Drawing meaning

**Productive**
- Describing
- Giving directions
- Listing

**Organizational**
- Brainstorming
- Interviewing
- Creating a chart

**Multi-tasking**
- Explaining
- Negotiating
- Summarizing from context

# Cooperative Learning and Classroom Management

## LARGE AND HETEROGENEOUS CLASSES

Two of the major problems in today's classrooms are the high number of students and, by definition, the varying levels of abilities represented. The *¡YA VERÁS!* program addresses these issues in a variety of ways.

1. Regular paired and small-group work maximizes student participation time and has the effect of turning a large class into many small classes.
2. In some parts of the program (e.g., *Aquí llegamos*), activities can be individualized in that different groups can be asked to work on different activities. If several weaker students are grouped together, for example, they can be given a less complex task to accomplish.
3. The *¡YA VERÁS!* program is highly motivating and thus gives the slower student a sense of accomplishment. Although some students will always learn more quickly than others, the program has a kind of leveling effect in that all students can be successful at different times.
4. Regular recycling and review of material helps weaker students "catch up" and gives stronger students the opportunity to reinforce what they know.
5. In the *¡YA VERÁS!* program, we do not expect students to learn all of the vocabulary about each topic. We assume that, for example, in lists of foods, students will focus on expressing their own likes and dislikes. In this instance, what one student likes is not necessarily the preference of another student. The same is true about vocabulary for family. Since every family has a slightly different configuration, students should first learn to speak about what applies to them, leaving the rest to be dealt with receptively. All of our materials, including the testing program, give students the flexibility to express their own situations and preferences.

## PRINCIPLES OF COOPERATIVE LEARNING

The major principles of cooperative learning techniques are inherent to the *¡YA VERÁS!* program. These principles help to define the roles of teachers and students in class and to acknowledge and utilize a variety of student learning styles. They are based on the idea that students can learn effectively from one another if their work is carefully detailed and assigned with specific information about the goal, the process, the timing, and the reporting of the results of their task. The foreign language classroom is an excellent setting for putting cooperative learning strategies into practice.

The following principles are central to cooperative learning.

- Teaching must be student centered.
- Paired and small-group work is essential to engage students in frequent communication that is meaningful, based on real-world experiences, relatively free of anxiety, and challenging to various learner styles and abilities.
- Cooperative learning encourages multiple ways of expression.
- It promotes multiple points of view through the use of heterogeneous teams.
- It reduces dependence on the teacher and fosters linguistic independence and individual accountability.
- It promotes positive interdependence and creates a positive social atmosphere in which students learn to accept the contributions that others can make to their learning.
- It fosters the willingness to be helpful to others through shared responsibility.
- It promotes individual expression of likes, dislikes, and preferences rather than "cloned" behavior.
- It gives students a chance to raise language issues that are of interest to them and that might not surface in a teacher-centered classroom.
- It allows students to manipulate language in ways that are most suitable to them.
- It gives teachers the opportunity to relax and be the observers of student behavior, thus enhancing sensitivity to student needs and interests.

It is important to recognize that in order for an activity to be considered true cooperative learning, it must call for an outcome, such as a group product or decision, resulting from initial individual input and then a final negotiated consensus developed by all members of the team.

## PAIR WORK AND SMALL-GROUP WORK IN THE ANNOTATIONS

This Teacher's Edition also contains annotations suggesting particular pair and group "structured" activities that can be used at logical places in a chapter. Each "structure" has a particular name, such as Jigsaw, Pairs Check, or Corners and is based on structures developed by researchers such as Johnson and Johnson, Slavin, and Kagan. Once you have learned to use these "structures" successfully, you can use them at other times in the course that seem appropriate to you.

Some structures are more useful for certain learning objectives than for others. For instance, Corners is particularly useful for warm-up activities because it gets students moving and communicating while setting the context for the chapter. Student Teachers (also known as Telephone) is good for pronunciation work because it forces students to listen carefully. Team Decisions (also called Numbered Heads Together) and Pairs Check are useful when your goal is mastery. Jigsaw works extremely well for reading comprehension, and Round Robin and Roundtable are useful for vocabulary practice.

Notice that in many group activities, you are asked to have students number off. This ensures that you call on students randomly to perform certain tasks or to give an individual response to a question already practiced with the group. In this way each student's individual accountability is guaranteed. Notice also that we often suggest doing warm-up activities in English. These activities appear at the beginning of the chapter in which the necessary contexts and skills to do the activity in Spanish will be taught. Students ought to be able to do a similar exercise in Spanish at the end of the chapter.

We suggest that before attempting a new and unfamiliar structure, you should (1) read through all of the directions, (2) be sure you can provide the materials, and (3) practice carrying out the activity (including saying the directions). When you become more familiar with the activities and structures, you will discover that they are not only simple and predictable, but that the results are very rewarding.

## HOW TO DETERMINE GROUP SIZE

- In *¡YA VERÁS!*, group size is usually determined by the nature of the communicative activity. A symbol in the Teacher's Edition indicates the number of students per group.
- In cases where group size may be variable, it is important to make sure that every student has the opportunity to make a valuable contribution to the activity and that no one be allowed to sit on the sidelines while others do the work. Unless each student has a clearly defined role to play, it is not advisable to have groups larger than four students. Three or four students per group is probably the optimal size unless an activity specifies paired work.
- The advantage of groups of three or four (particularly at higher levels in discussion activities) is that more than two points of view tend to eliminate the trap of "right" and "wrong." This is crucial when dealing with cultural topics.

## HOW TO DETERMINE THE COMPOSITION OF THE GROUP

- Throughout the school year it is important to vary group composition so that students can regularly interact with different classmates.
- Various group combinations can be made: 1) stronger with weaker students; 2) groups of stronger students only, weaker students only; 3) random selection of students without concern for weaknesses and strengths. All of these combinations have merit and have their advantages and disadvantages.

## HOW TO PUT STUDENTS INTO GROUPS

- If students are selected according to strengths and weaknesses, it is best to do this ahead of time during your lesson planning. Group selection wastes valuable class time which should be spent doing the activities themselves.
- Forming groups randomly can be accomplished in a variety of ways.

1. As students enter the classroom, have them take a number out of a bowl or box. All students with the same number form a group. This can also be done with colors. Note that this may become chaotic as students try to find each other in order to do the assigned activity.
2. Give students group assignments. Have them stay in the same groups for a couple of weeks. At the end of that period, change group assignments.
3. Have students count off in Spanish before the activity begins. Either groups are formed from like numbers or in numerical order (e.g., 1–3, 1–4).
4. Have students choose their own groups. Caution: This can lead to the exclusion of some students and the formation of cliques if used too often.
5. Ask students to form groups with the people sitting closest to them.
6. If students are given the option to work on different activities, they can group themselves according to the activity that interests them the most.

## GUIDELINES TO SMALL-GROUP INTERACTION

As has already been noted, small-group interaction is essential for maximizing practice time and giving students a sense of linguistic independence and accomplishment. To avoid confusion in the classroom and make the best use of time, some basic guidelines should be followed.

Students should become used to pair and small-group work from the outset. They also need to learn the rules for this type of work very quickly. You, as the teacher, need to realize that you are not relinquishing control over the class: you make the rules, you give the direction lines, you expect accountability for the work done. For students, however, you are providing the illusion of freedom. This illusion very quickly becomes a reality because students find they can use language to communicate without the constant presence of a teacher.

The following are some guidelines for small-group classroom management.

1. The task that students are to accomplish has to be clearly defined and be relatively short. Students should not have to wonder what they are supposed to do once they have divided into groups.
2. A time limit should be placed on the activity and students should not be allowed to prolong it. Time to stop occurs when the groups finish the activity.
3. It should be made clear that students have to speak Spanish in their groups. They should be taught how to ask for information from other students: *¿Cómo se dice* star *en español?* Only if communication breaks down completely should students raise their hand to get your attention. With proper preparation, this should occur very seldom.
4. The ideal group sizes are two, three, or four students. With larger groups, some students tend to dominate while others will not participate at all or only minimally.
5. Unless the activity task is obvious, it should be modeled in front of the entire class before students work on their own. This model clarifies the task and provides linguistic suggestions.
6. It is usually advisable to have a couple of groups report back to the whole class, playing out the situation or giving the information they have gathered. Since students don't know which groups will be called upon to perform, this should be an added incentive to stay on task. You may wish to use the reporting back as a way to assign grades for different students on different days. Alternative: Create a couple of new groups to perform the activity in front of the class.

## CORRECTION STRATEGIES

Students should learn very quickly that the goal of correction is not to punish them but to help them communicate more accurately. It should be a confidence builder. This suggests that we should point out the things that were done well before we make comments on what needs to be corrected.

Error correction can occur at two different times during the class.

1. When students are engaged in a controlled, mechanical, or semi-mechanical exercise, correction should be systematic. Students need the immediate feedback so that they can work on their linguistic accuracy.
2. When students are in a communicative situation, i.e., in small groups or in meaningful interaction with you, error correction should be delayed until the communication can be completed. For example, students should not be interrupted for errors when they are working in pairs or small groups or when they are performing an activity for the class. Only when they have finished the task at hand should some of the errors be pointed out, with perhaps additional controlled practice by the whole class to correct the error. At this point, it is not necessary to identify the student who made the original error.

After the reporting-back stage, discuss with students some of the alternate language structures or vocabulary they could have used in the given situation. This short discussion raises cultural questions, grammar considerations, and communicative strategies that integrate and expand what students have done in their groups.

## TEACHER BEHAVIORS

Because a proficiency orientation has as its essential premise real-life linguistic behaviors, our interaction with students should mirror the interaction we have with strangers and friends in real life. In order to simulate such behaviors in a learning environment, we will probably have to modify some of our ways of dealing with students. These behaviors can be divided into four basic categories:

### Speech and General Behavior

1. Our rate of speech should be our own. We should not slow down into artificial speech rates because we underestimate our students' ability to understand. Speech should be slowed down only when we have ascertained that there is, in fact, a comprehension problem, not because we anticipate such a problem.
2. We should limit or eliminate "teacher talk." Teacher talk *(muy bien, de acuerdo, bien)* is typically evaluative of grammatical accuracy. It rarely responds to the message. In communicative situations, i.e., when students say something personalized, the most positive feedback we can give them is to respond to the message naturally as we would in real life. This shows them that they were understood. *(¿Es verdad? ¡No me digas! ¿En serio? ¡Qué interesante!)* Then ask follow-up questions to keep the conversational ball rolling for a few seconds. The added advantage of natural speech is that students gradually learn the many expressions you use and will eventually incorporate them into their own language.
3. We should not automatically repeat everything we say *(¿Qué hiciste ayer? ¿Qué hiciste ayer?)*. Repetition underestimates students' ability to understand the first time. More importantly, it hinders the development of listening comprehension skills as students learn not to listen the first time we say something. Repetition should be used if students have truly not understood the first time, in which case the statement should probably be rephrased. If they did not hear what was said, students should be taught to say *Perdón, no comprendí.*

4. We should not finish students' sentences when they hesitate or grope for words. It is preferable to teach them to use some hesitation markers, such as, *este...* so that they can give themselves time to think. We should help out only if it becomes clear that communication has stalled completely.

5. We should not systematically repeat everything students say (Student: *El fin de semana pasado fui a una fiesta*. Teacher: *El fin de semana pasado fui a una fiesta*.) Because such repetition is often used as a correction strategy, it can become a behavior pattern even when no correction is needed. Again, repetition should be used as it would be in real life *(Ah, qué bien. ¿Fuiste a una fiesta? ¿Y qué tal la fiesta?)*.

6. We should not interrupt real communication with grammatical correction. It is important for students to be able to complete their thoughts and to feel that the message is valued. Correction can occur after conversational exchange has ended.

7. The blackboard should be used sparingly. In order to foster the development of listening comprehension skills, students should not always see everything in writing. The blackboard is a teaching tool, not a substitute for communication.

## Body Language

1. When addressing individual students, we should move as close to them as possible. Although this may be strategically more difficult in large classes, aisles can be created to reduce the space between the teacher and individual students.

2. We should keep eye contact with the student with whom we are interacting. As teachers, we are sometimes preoccupied with the next question we are going to ask the next student. Almost imperceptibly this can lead us to abandon eye contact with a student before the communication has been completed.

3. We should move around the entire classroom, not just stay at the front. Besides moving closer to students, this movement helps to maintain the energy level of the class.

4. We should avoid looking down on students physically. Since they are seated and we are standing, there is a tendency to hover over them. If we place some empty seats in different parts of the room, we can sit down for a couple of seconds and address students in that part of the room. We can also assume a half-stance by bending our knees and adjusting to students' eye level. Research has shown that eye-level interaction is less threatening and has a positive impact on student performance.

## Silence

1. It takes the mind approximately three seconds to process information (e.g., a question). Given this fact, we should give students enough time to think of a response, allowing for enough silence so that the response can be formulated. Interfering too quickly by repeating, for example, the question in different ways in rapid-fire succession inhibits thinking and is likely to be very frustrating for students.

2. We need to be sensitive to silences that are constructive and those that become uncomfortable. Only when the discomfort stage sets in should we help the student out by reformulating the question.

## General Attitude

1. We should always have a positive attitude toward students. This does not mean that we should underestimate them or teach them to rely on us in an unrealistic way. It does mean, however, that we have to have a fundamental belief that all students are able to learn Spanish, although some will learn more quickly and better than others.

2. Rather than being actors and actresses in class, we should be ourselves. We should be willing to share information about ourselves and not ask students questions we are not willing to answer ourselves. For instance, when dealing with leisure time, students are regularly put into the position of talking about their activities in detail. We should be prepared to do the same. This has the added effect of serving as a good linguistic model for students to imitate.

3. We must, at all times, be willing to give students the responsibility for their own language learning. We are essentially the facilitators for this process: in the final analysis, what matters is how well students learned what we taught. An example of this is the student who has been taught the imperfect in class but does not use it when he or she is examined in an oral test. Achievement in class in tests and classroom performance will only translate into proficiency if students have regularly been given the responsibility and the opportunity to accomplish linguistic tasks on their own.

# Yearly Syllabus for ¡YA VERÁS!, Primer nivel

The following is a suggested yearly syllabus based on 180 class days. The goal of our program is for you to be able to complete the material in Level 1 in one year (high school) or two years (middle school). We have not, however, included specific time requirements for the completion of each *etapa* because we believe that you need to retain as much flexibility as possible in designing your own yearly plan. Some *etapas* will take longer than others, depending on the general ability of the students and the complexity of the material. For example, *Estructura* sections that are essentially vocabulary based require less time than those that involve primarily grammatical structures.

**Text content:** *Etapa(s) preliminar(es),* 6 units
**Total number of class days:** 180

- 20–24 days reserved for administrative details, review, testing, and class cancellations due to extracurricular activities
- 2–6 days for the *Etapas preliminares* (optional)
- 25–30 days for each of the 6 units

The number of days for each category can be modified according to your particular school calendar and your own preferences. For example, you may prefer to allow fewer or more days for the *Etapas preliminares,* testing, and other activities.

If you use the suggested maximum number of class days for the units, you will need to adjust the number of class days for the other components accordingly.

# ¡YA VERÁS! and Longer Class Periods (Block Scheduling/ Concentrated Curriculum)

The *etapa* structure of *¡YA VERÁS!* is uniquely well-suited to the challenges and promises of longer class periods. The *etapa* is in fact a lesson plan for a 90- to 100-minute class, during which vocabulary and structures are introduced, practiced, and reinforced by student performance. The closely integrated components provide for the variety of instructional approaches that longer class periods demand, while assuring that students' attention remains focused on developing language accuracy in specific functions and contexts. Moreover, the longer instructional periods allow students to receive immediate feedback from performance and other types of evaluations, a motivating experience which keeps them learning more efficiently and effectively.

The following suggested pacing for *¡YA VERÁS!* 1 includes time for presentation, practice, performance, evaluation, and enrichment.

6 units with 3 chapters per unit
One unit presented every 15 instructional days
One chapter presented every 5 instructional days
First chapter of each unit (3 *etapas*): 1–1/2 instructional days per *etapa,* 1/2 day leeway
Second and third chapters (2 *etapas* each): 2 instructional days per *etapa*
*Ya llegamos:* 2 instructional days

The following suggested pacing for *¡YA VERÁS!* 2 includes time for presentation, practice, performance, evaluation, and enrichment.

*Capítulos preliminares*: 7–8 instructional days
5 units with 3 chapters per unit
One unit presented every 16 instructional days
One chapter presented every 5–6 instructional days
One *etapa* presented every 2 instructional days
*Ya llegamos:* 2 instructional days

The following suggested pacing for *¡YA VERÁS!* 3 includes time for presentation, practice, performance, evaluation, and enrichment.

*Capítulos preliminares:* 7–8 instructional days
4 units with three chapters per unit
One unit presented every 18 instructional days
One chapter presented every 6 instructional days
One *etapa* presented every 3 instructional days
*Ya llegamos:* 2 instructional days

# Etapas preliminares (Optional)

These **etapas** are offered as options for starting the book on the first day or two of class. They are *optional.* If you prefer, you may proceed directly to **Capítulo 1**. All material treated here— except TPR— will be covered elsewhere in *¡YA VERÁS!* Several of these **etapas** may be useful on days when a substitute is covering your class.

## ETAPA A: Names

**Objectives:** To provide each student with a Spanish name, to learn to greet and take leave of fellow students

**Time:** One class period

**Material required:** Name tags, list of names

### Suggested Classroom Procedures

1. Hand out name tags to the students. Whenever possible, give students the Spanish equivalents of their own names; otherwise, allow them to choose. See the list of names at right.
2. Introduce yourself (**Me llamo Sr..., Sra..., Srta...,**); greet each student (**Hola.../ Hola,...**); have other students repeat each name.
3. Have students introduce themselves to the class: **¡Hola! Me llamo... .**
4. Have each student introduce two others (name only): **Juan, Mónica.** The two students respond by shaking hands and saying: **Hola, Juan. Hola, Mónica.**
5. Have students greet each other, shake hands, and ask about each other: **Hola,.../ Hola,.../ ¿Qué tal?/ Bien, gracias.**

   **Variation:** Have the second student add: **¿Y tú?,** then the first one responds: **Bien, gracias.**

   **Suggestion:** Steps 4 and 5 can be modeled in front of the whole class, then you might allow students to circulate in the classroom, making introductions (step 4) and greeting each other (step 5). If there is time, you can then combine greetings and introductions.
6. At the end of the class, have one-half of the students form a "receiving line" on the way out the door. The other students go down the line, saying good-bye: **Hasta mañana,...** (or if you prefer, **Adiós,...**). The students in line respond.

## *Spanish Names (Male)*

Agustín
Alberto
Alejandro
Alfonso
Andrés
Ángel
Antonio
Arturo
Atilio
Bartolomé
Benito
Carlos
Cristóbal
Daniel
Eduardo
Emilio
Enrique
Ernesto
Esteban
Federico
Felipe
Félix
Fernando
Francisco
Gabriel
Gerardo
Germán
Gregorio
Guillermo
Hilario
Horacio
Ignacio
Isidoro
Jacinto
Jaime
Javier
Jerónimo
Jesús
Joaquín
Jorge
José
Juan
Julián
Julio
Leandro
Leonardo
Leopoldo
Lorenzo
Luis
Manuel
Marcos
Mariano
Mario
Martín
Mateo
Mauricio
Máximo
Miguel
Modesto
Narciso
Néstor
Nicolás
Octavio
Pablo
Pedro
Ramón
Raúl
Ricardo
Roberto
Salvador
Santiago
Sebastián
Silvio
Tamiro
Timoteo
Tomás
Valentín
Vicente

## *Spanish Names (Female)*

Ada
Adela
Adriana
Alejandra
Alicia
Ana
Ángeles
Antonia
Asunción
Beatriz
Carmen
Catalina
Clara
Claudia
Conchita
Consuelo
Cristina
Dalia
Delia
Dina
Dolores
Dora
Elena
Elisa
Elsa
Elvira
Engracia
Esperanza
Éster
Eugenia
Eulalia
Floriana
Gabriela
Gema
Gertrudis
Gloria
Graciela
Guadalupe
Inés
Inmaculada
Isabel
Jorgelina
Juana
Julia
Laura
Lía
Lidia
Liliana
Lourdes
Lucía
Luisa
Magdalena
Manuela
Marcela
Margarita
María
Marisa
Marta
Mercedes
Mónica
Montserrat
Nidia
Nieves
Nilse
Noemí
Nuria
Ofelia
Olga
Patricia
Paula
Pilar
Raquel
Rosa
Rosalía
Soledad
Susana
Teresa
Victoria

## ETAPA B: Basic Vocabulary

**Objectives:** To familiarize students with some simple, basic vocabulary and expressions (colors, days of the week, seasons and weather)

**Time:** One half to one class period

**Material required:** Transparencies (colors, days of the week, weather)

*Los colores*

| | |
|---|---|
| **rojo** | **negro** |
| **azul** | **blanco** |
| **verde** | **café** |

*Los días de la semana*

**¿Qué día es hoy?**

**Hoy es...**

| | | | |
|---|---|---|---|
| **lunes** | **martes** | **miércoles** | **jueves** |
| **viernes** | **sábado** | **domingo** | |

*Las estaciones del año*

**el otoño** **el invierno** **la primavera** **el verano**

*El tiempo*

**¿Qué tiempo hace hoy?**

**Hace sol. (No hace sol.)**
**Hace frío.**
**Hace calor.**
**Hace fresco.**
**Hace viento.**
**Hace buen tiempo.**
**Hace mal tiempo.**
**Llueve.**
**Nieva.**

## ETAPA C: Cultural Information Quiz

**Objective:** To give students the opportunity to show what they already know about Spain and Latin America; to introduce them to some basic facts about the Spanish-speaking world; to familiarize students with the notion of cultural stereotypes

**Time:** One class period

**Materials required:** Students need pencils and paper.

### Suggested Classroom Procedures

1. Tell students to take out a pencil and paper so that they can answer the questions you are about to ask about Spain and the Spanish-speaking world. Stress the fact that this is not a test and that they should guess at the answers.
2. When students have written out their responses, discuss the answers with them, adding some of the information provided.

### Questions

1. **What is the capital of Spain: Barcelona, Seville, Madrid, or Caracas?**

   **Answer:** Madrid

   **Discussion:** Explain that Madrid is the city where greater cultural change has occurred in the last 20 years than any other European capital. After years of conservatism, even stagnation, Madrid now enjoys the fame of being Europe's hot spot. The city of **"La movida"** has witnessed a rebirth of cinema, nightlife, fashion, tourism, industry, and "joie de vivre." Despite its regionalism, Spain remains a highly centralized country and Madrid holds the honor of being not only the main city, but the *central* city of Spain. (Point out the location of Madrid on a map of Spain.)

2. **Name two other capitals in Latin America.**

   **Answer/Discussion:** As students name some cities, you can give them the Spanish pronunciation to begin familiarizing them with Spanish sounds. Some of the capitals are **Buenos Aires** (Argentina), **Santiago de Chile** (Chile), **Montevideo** (Uruguay), **Asunción del Paraguay** (Paraguay), **La Paz / Sucre** (Bolivia) (**La Paz: sede de gobierno; Sucre: constitucional**), **Lima** (Perú), **Caracas** (Venezuela), **Bogotá** (Colombia), **Quito** (Ecuador), **La Habana** (Cuba), **Managua** (Nicaragua), **San Juan** (Puerto Rico), **San Salvador** (El Salvador), **Santo Domingo** (República Dominicana), **Panamá** (República de Panamá), **México D.F.** (México), **Tegucigalpa** (Honduras), **Guatemala** (Guatemala), **San José** (Costa Rica).

3. **Name two countries that border Spain.**

   **Answer:** Portugal and France

   **Discussion:** Ask them where the countries are located. Point out their location on the map.

4. **What regions in North America are Spanish-speaking or have Spanish heritage?**

   **Answer/Discussion:** Remember that Mexico is part of North America. Spanish is also spoken in those parts of the United States which originally belonged to Spain or Mexico, i.e., California and New Mexico (officially bilingual) and Arizona, Texas, and Florida. Because of better economic and political conditions in the United States, there are also Latin American people living in every major city of the U.S. For example: there are more Mexicans living in Los Angeles than in any city of Mexico except the capital. New York has a large Puerto Rican population, and Miami in turn received a large influx of refugees from Castro's Cuba.

5. **Approximately how many native Spanish-speakers live in the U.S.A?**

   a. more than 20,000,000
   b. between 10 and 15 million
   c. fewer than 1,000,000

   **Answer:** a

6. **Which continent does not have a Spanish-speaking country?**

   a. Africa b. North America c. Asia

   **Answer:** c. Asia

7. **Name two famous Spanish or Latin American personalities.**

   **Answer/Discussion:** Juan Carlos, king of Spain, opera singer Plácido Domingo, painters (Picasso, Miró, Dalí, etc.), writers (García Lorca, García Márquez, Pablo Neruda, etc.), musicians (Julio

Iglesias, Jon Secada, Gloria Estefan, etc.), athletes (Mary Jo Fernández, José Canseco, Nancy López), actors (Rubén Blades — also a musician; Edward James Olmos, Emilio Estevez, Julie Carmen)

8. **Name two commercial products that you associate with Spain or Latin America.**

   **Spain:** olive oil, olives, wine, sherry

   **Latin America:** coffee, sugar, rubber, fruits, textiles

9. **Which Spanish-speaking country lies right on the equator: Peru, Mexico, Ecuador, Spain?**

   **Answer:** Ecuador. Point out to students the concept of cognates and that many words will be recognizable to them because they look similar in Spanish and English.

10. **Write down three words that come to mind when you think about the Hispanic people.**

    **Discussion:** This is perhaps the most important question of this cultural quiz. It is designed to raise some of the stereotypes of Hispanics that students have in mind and to give you the opportunity to talk about the dangers of cultural stereotyping. When students have made their contributions, you might ask them how they think Americans are stereotyped and whether they feel these generalizations are valid. As the discussion progresses, it should become quickly apparent that one cannot generalize about a whole culture. Point out to students that within Spain and Latin America, as within the United States, there are many regional differences, including language. The most important message that should come out of this discussion is that stereotypes can lead to prejudices and that we need to be open to cultural differences and avoid value judgments. Different cultures are not better or worse by comparison to one's own culture; they are simply different and should be seen as interesting and worth learning about. Awareness of other cultures is one of the major goals of language study.

## ETAPA D: Spanish-Speaking Countries

**Objectives:** To familiarize students with some aspects of Spain and the Spanish-speaking world, including geographical location; to introduce students to Spanish sounds through the pronunciation of geographical proper nouns

**Time:** One class period

**Materials required:** Maps of Spain and Central and South America (available on transparencies or in the front of the textbook, list of Spanish-speaking countries below)

### Suggested Classroom Procedures

1. This entire lesson is conducted in English, but as you point out countries, have students repeat them in Spanish for pronunciation practice.
2. Begin with the maps of the Americas and Spain. Point out the following:
   a. There are approximately 250 million Spanish speakers in the world.
   b. Spoken Spanish varies from country to country, and from region to region (just as the English spoken in the north of the United States varies from that spoken in the south, the east, and the west). The differences are noticeable in pronunciation and vocabulary.
   c. The Spanish colonial heritage is multifaceted. However, what Spain gave the world was a major language. Few other languages are as widely spoken as Spanish. From New Mexico to Tierra del Fuego (the southern tip of Argentina), Spanish is understood. It is also understood in the Philippines, parts of Africa, and many islands in the Pacific and the Atlantic.
   d. The reason for the widespread use of Spanish is that Spain was a major colonial power in the past, establishing its colonies in America, the Pacific, and Africa.
3. Using the maps, point out the following Spanish-speaking countries.

   **Central America:** El Salvador, Honduras, Nicaragua, Panamá, Costa Rica, Guatemala

   **North America:** México

   **The Caribbean:** Cuba, Puerto Rico, La República Dominicana

   **South America:** Venezuela, Colombia, Ecuador, Perú, Bolivia, Paraguay, Chile, Argentina, Uruguay

   **Europe:** España

   **Africa:** Guinea Ecuatorial

4. Show the maps of Spain and the Americas. Point out the vastness and geographical diversity of the Spanish-speaking world, including its major cities and geographical features: mountain ranges, major rivers, jungle, oceans, seas, etc.
5. To personalize this lesson a bit more, ask students what Spanish-speaking place they have visited (if any) and which one(s) interest them the most. Finally, you can have them write on a piece of paper the region or country they would like to learn more about (their personal preference) and you can use this information during the year, bringing in materials or having students do some library research as homework or as an extra credit project.

## ETAPA E: TPR (Total Physical Response)

**Objectives**: To familiarize students with the code of the language; to develop students' listening skills; to have students understand and carry out a variety of commands; to have them understand and be able to identify numbers from 1 to 30, time, and basic objects.

**Time:** Two or more class periods (time to be determined by instructor)

**Material required:** Flashcards with one number (1–30) written on each card, a clock (cardboard or real) on which the hands can be easily manipulated

### Asher's Total Physical Response Approach (TPR) to Teaching

The Total Physical Response Approach to teaching was developed by James J. Asher.* This approach is based on several theories that indicate how individuals can learn a foreign language quickly and still have long-term retention. The theories are based on studies of first-language acquisition, and TPR is a condensed simulation of how children learn.

### Assumptions

1. It is easier to learn a foreign language in a stress-free environment.
2. Learning a foreign language should be enjoyable.
3. In children, listening precedes speaking: i.e., they spend thousands of hours listening to the language before they are able to utter coherent words.
4. Children associate words with actions; i.e., the movement of their entire bodies.
5. Language and actions are often transmitted to children through commands.
6. Children speak when they are ready to speak. They are not forced to do so.

Many classroom studies with children and adults have demonstrated that TPR is an effective way to teach a foreign language, particularly during the early stages of language acquisition. Although this *Etapa preliminar* limits the use of TPR to the first few hours of the course, it should be stressed that it can be used periodically throughout the school year. Consult Asher's book for a more extensive treatment of the approach and for model lessons.

* James L. Asher, *Learning Another Language through Actions: The Complete Teacher's Guidebook.* (Los Gatos, Calif.: Sky Oaks Productions, Inc., 1982).

### Suggested Classroom Procedures

1. For each of the class periods you devote to TPR, you will have a series of commands that you will teach students. These commands are not controlled grammatically.
2. Each series of commands (usually three new ones at a time) is first modeled by you so that students can associate the language with an action.
3. Put five chairs in front of the room. You sit in the middle chair and you ask four students to join you, two on each side of you. Once you have given them the introduction (see below), you begin with the first commands.
4. Modeling the command:
   a. Give the command once and model it, motioning the four students to imitate you.
   b. Say the command again and motion the whole class to act it out.
   c. Say the command again; the whole class acts it out, but you delay your response (this is to ensure that they are listening, not just imitating).
   d. Say the command again, and the class acts it out without you.
   e. Say the command again, and have individuals (or pairs) act it out.
5. After the initial **¡Levántate!** and **¡Siéntate!**, new commands can be embedded three at a time. Remember that you are training students to follow your commands exactly. Therefore, if you want them to go to the board, for example, you cannot simply say **¡Ve a la pizarra!** First you have to say **¡Levántate!** You must also remember to tell students to go back to their seats (**¡Vuelve a tu asiento!**) and to sit down (**¡Siéntate!**).
6. Students can learn to understand approximately twelve to thirty-six commands per class period. You must therefore have enough materials on hand to

cover the time in the event that your students learn the commands very quickly.

7. You can start you first TPR lesson in one of two ways:

   a. Explain to students what you're going to do. Tell them that they will be taught a series of commands that they will carry out. They will not have to say anything in Spanish for the first few class periods. You may wish to give them some of the principles mentioned above so that they have a better understanding of what will happen. (Note: in some schools it has been very helpful to explain this approach to parents and administrators so that they will realize why you are using it. You may even invite them to observe the class.)
   b. Simply tell students, "When you leave this class today, you will understand perfectly everything I'm about to say." Then utter the commands you plan to teach during the first period (see below). You should be speaking at your normal rate of speech. The usual reaction of students to this string of words is total disbelief about their ability to learn them. By the end of the period, however, they will realize what they have accomplished and they will leave the class with a great sense of achievement.

## TPR Lesson for Two Class Periods

Following are content suggestions for the first two class periods. Since many of you already use TPR, you will wish to substitute the commands that have worked best for you. Remember: ***STUDENTS DO NOT SPEAK DURING THESE LESSONS. THEY SIMPLY LISTEN TO THE COMMANDS AND ACT THEM OUT.***

### *Class 1*

**First command sequence:**

a. **¡Levántate! ¡Siéntate!**

b. **¡Levántate! ¡Ve a la pizarra! ¡Toma una tiza! ¡Deja la tiza! ¡Vuelve a tu lugar! ¡Siéntate!**

c. **¡Levántate! ¡Ve a la pizarra! ¡Toma una tiza! ¡Escribe tu nombre! ¡Deja la tiza! ¡Vuelve a tu lugar y siéntate!**

d. **¡Levántate! ¡Ve a la pizarra! ¡Toma una tiza! ¡Dibuja una casa! ¡Deja la tiza! ¡Vuelve a tu lugar y siéntate!**

e. **¡Levántate! ¡Ve a la pizarra! ¡Toma el borrador! ¡Borra la casa! ¡Deja el borrador! ¡Vuelve a tu lugar y siéntate!**

f. Now that students have learned the verb **dibujar,** you can have them draw any of the following: **un gato, un árbol, una bicicleta, un niño, una niña, el sol, un pájaro, una flor.** You can have them draw parts of the house: **una puerta, unas ventanas, una chimenea, un techo, un jardín.**

**Second command sequence:**

a. **¡Levántate! ¡Salta una vez! ¡Salta dos veces! ¡Siéntate!**

b. **¡Levántate! ¡Camina! ¡Detente! ¡Ve para atrás! ¡Siéntate!**

c. **¡Levántate! ¡Camina! ¡Detente! ¡Salta dos veces! ¡Camina! ¡Detente! ¡Vuelve a tu lugar y siéntate!**

d. **¡Levántate! ¡Toma un paso (dos, tres pasos, etc.). ¡Camina! ¡Detente! ¡Vuelve a tu lugar y siéntate!**

Students now understand approximately sixteen commands and an even larger number of concrete vocabulary words. If you cannot cover all of the material in one class period because of administrative duties, you can begin the second class with a review of the first sequence and then introduce the second sequence of commands.

### *Class 2*

You may wish to review the material from the previous day by giving students a copy of all the commands they have already learned (see Exhibit 1). They read silently as you say the commands and act them out. Then have students act them out without looking at the paper. The commands should be mixed up so that they do not form a predictable pattern.

**¡Levántate! ¡Ve a la pizarra! ¡Salta una vez! ¡Toma una tiza! ¡Deja la tiza! ¡Toma dos pasos! ¡Salta dos veces! ¡Camina! ¡Vuelve a tu lugar y siéntate!**

**¡Levántate! ¡Ve a la pizarra! ¡Toma una tiza! ¡Dibuja un gato! ¡Escribe el nombre del gato! ¡Deja la tiza! ¡Salta dos veces! ¡Vuelve a tu lugar y siéntate!**

**¡Levántate! ¡Camina! ¡Detente! ¡Ve a la pizarra! ¡Toma el borrador! ¡Borra el nombre del gato! ¡Deja el borrador! ¡Vuelve a tu lugar y siéntate!**

You can create more command combinations from what has already been learned.

**Third command sequence:**

a. **¡Levántate! ¡Ve a la pizarra! ¡Toma una tiza! ¡Escribe el número...**(numbers 1–30)! Different students should be at the board, writing the various numbers. (Teach the numbers in increments of 5.) **¡Deja la tiza! ¡Vuelve a tu lugar y siéntate!**

b. Put flashcards with numbers on them on one table. Have students pick out the correct numbers through the command: (**¡Muéstranos el número 7!**) Or distribute the flashcards to the class, and as you give the command (**¡Muéstranos el número... !**), the student with the appropriate number shows it to the class.

c. If time permits, you can have students write a number on the board and another number underneath it, then add them up. **Escribe el número 15. Debajo del número 15, escribe el número 10. Haz la suma. Bien, el resultado es 25.**

**Fourth command sequence:**
In this sequence, students apply the numbers they have learned to telling time. You can use the command **¡Dame la hora! (Son las cinco.)** Students move the hands of the clock to the right time. Instead of using a command, you could say **¿Qué hora es? (Es la una y cinco.)** Remember that all of this needs to be modeled first and students understand only the numbers up to thirty. You therefore need to model **Tres menos cinco. Una y media**, etc.

Another way to deal with time is to have students simply write the time on the board. This avoids the use of the real clock, and you can have more students at the board writing at the same time.

At the end of this period, you need to combine the new commands with the ones learned earlier.

### Subsequent Class Periods

If you can devote additional class periods to commands (students are still not speaking), you can integrate a variety of lexical topics that appear in Levels 1 and 2 of *¡YA VERÁS!* This allows students to have a receptive knowledge of a great deal of vocabulary and language structures and should facilitate subsequent presentation of that material.

The following are some of the lexical fields that you might incorporate into the initial silent period.

1. *Stores and food:* Place store signs around the room with actual objects or visuals that students can pick up.

   **Ve a la verdulería y compra lechuga.**

   **Compra el chocolate que cuesta tres dólares.**

2. *Parts of the body:* Use commands such as:

   **Toca el brazo de Ana.**

   **Dale la mano a Éster.**

   **Lávate la cabeza.**

   **Cepíllate los dientes.**

   **Cepíllate el cabello.**

   **Señala el pie.**

   This can be easily followed by **Simón dice...**(Simon says...) involving the whole class.

3. *Geographical names:* Use a large map or a transparency to have students go from city to city or country to country. As they do so, they hear the prepositions that accompany geographical nouns.

   **Ve de Madrid a Barcelona.** (Students trace their way from one city to the other).

   **Señala dónde se encuentra Caracas.**

   **Señala una ciudad que se encuentra sobre un río.**

   **Señala una ciudad al sur (norte, etc.) de México.**

   **Señala una ciudad que esté cerca de Bolivia.**

   **Señala una ciudad que esté cerca de la frontera entre México y los EE.UU.**

   **Señala una ciudad que se encuentra en los Andes.**

***Role reversal:*** When you decide that enough time has been spent on the silent period, you should give students the opportunity to try out the commands on you. Since they are speaking for the first time, their pronunciation is not going to be as good as you might wish. Tolerate this situation during their first attempts and question them only when you do not understand the command they want you to perform. Once everyone has had the chance to order you and other classmates around, you can slowly begin the refinement of pronunciation.

**Tip:** Do not ask students to carry out commands that you would not be willing to act out yourself. If you do, they are likely to take their revenge during the role reversal time!

## Exhibit 1

**¡Levántate!**
**¡Ve a la pizarra!**
**¡Toma la tiza!**
**¡Escribe tu nombre!**
**¡Dibuja una casa!**
**¡Dibuja la puerta!**
**¡Dibuja las ventanas!**
**¡Dibuja la chimenea!**
**¡Dibuja un gato!**
**¡Dibuja un árbol!**
**¡Dibuja el sol!**
**¡Dibuja una flor!**
**¡Dibuja un pájaro!**
**¡Deja la tiza!**
**¡Toma el borrador!**
**¡Borra la casa!**
**¡Borra tu nombre!**
**¡Vuelve a tu lugar!**
**¡Siéntate!**
**¡Salta una vez (dos veces)!**
**¡Camina!**
**¡Para!**
**¡Camina para atrás!**
**¡Toma un paso (dos pasos)!**
**¡Date vuelta!**

## Exhibit 2

Escribe los números.

| | | |
|---|---|---|
| **uno** | **once** | **veintiuno** |
| **dos** | **doce** | **veintidós** |
| **tres** | **trece** | **veintitrés** |
| **cuatro** | **catorce** | **veinticuatro** |
| **cinco** | **quince** | **veinticinco** |
| **seis** | **dieciséis** | **veintiséis** |
| **siete** | **diecisiete** | **veintisiete** |
| **ocho** | **dieciocho** | **veintiocho** |
| **nueve** | **diecinueve** | **veintinueve** |
| **diez** | **veinte** | **treinta** |

**¡Muéstrame el número 3!**
**¡Muéstranos el número 17!**
**¡Dame la hora!**
**Son las tres menos veinte.**
**¿Qué hora es?**
**Son las ocho menos quince.**
**Son las diez y media.**
**Es la una y cinco.**
**Son las cinco y veinte.**

# THE ¡YA VERÁS! PROGRAM

| Unit | Functions | Contexts | Accuracy |
|---|---|---|---|
| 1 | Meeting and greeting people<br>Ordering something to eat or drink<br>Discussing likes and dislikes<br>Finding out about other people | **Café, bar de tapas,** restaurant<br>Meeting and conversing with new people | **Gustar** + infinitive<br>Indefinite articles<br>Present tense **-ar** verbs<br>Subject pronouns<br>Conjugated verb + infinitive<br>Present tense **ser** |
| 2 | Identifying personal possessions<br>Discussing preferences<br>Talking about your family<br>Finding out about other people<br>Describing people and places | School, home | Definite articles<br>**Hay** + noun<br>Possessive adjectives (1st, 2nd person)<br>**Gustar** + noun<br>**Ser** + **de** for possession<br>**Ser** + adjective<br>Present tense **-er, -ir** verbs<br>Present tense **tener; Tener que** + inf. |
| 3 | Identifying and locating places / buildings in a city / town<br>Expressing desires and preferences<br>Talking about your age<br>Giving and asking for directions<br>Giving orders<br>Suggesting activities<br>Asking for and giving the time<br>Discussing feelings | Downtown, festival, various other settings (museum, park, cinema, shopping) | Present tense (continued)<br>Contractions **al, del**<br>Expressions of frequency (**rara vez,** etc.)<br>Commands with **Ud., Uds.**<br>Irregular commands<br>Telling time<br>**Estar** + adjective<br>Possessive adjectives (3rd person)<br>Prepositions, adverbs of place |
| 4 | Talking about the future<br>Identifying what to do in town<br>Giving directions for using the subway<br>Buying tickets<br>Taking a taxi<br>Making plans for a trip | Downtown, subway station, travel agency | **Ir + a** for immediate future<br>**Tener ganas de**<br>Present tense **hacer, poder, esperar**<br>Adverbs **hoy, mañana,** etc.<br>Future with **pensar**<br>Numbers 100–1,000,000 |
| 5 | Discussing leisure time activities<br>Talking about events / activities in the past, present, future<br>Talking about sports | Leisure time activities | Preterite **-ar, -er, -ir** verbs<br>Preterite **hacer, ir, andar, estar, tener**<br>Adverbs, prepositions, etc. to indicate the past (**ayer,** etc.)<br>**Hace, hace que**<br>Preterite **-gar, -car** verbs<br>Present progressive |
| 6 | Expressing likes and dislikes<br>Making purchases<br>Indicating quantities<br>Asking for prices<br>Making comparisons<br>Pointing out places, objects, people<br>Giving orders | Shopping mall, various stores (music, cards, sports, clothing, shoes)<br>Grocery store, open-air market | **Gustar** (3rd person)<br>Familiar commands<br>Negative familiar commands<br>Demonstrative adjectives<br>**Cuál, cuáles**<br>Demonstrative pronouns<br>**Tan... como** to express equality |

PRIMER NIVEL

| Unit | Functions | Contexts | Accuracy |
|---|---|---|---|
| | **Capítulos preliminares A, B,** and **C** are a review of all major functions, structures, and vocabulary covered in ***¡Ya verás! Primer nivel.*** | | |
| 1 | Describing the weather<br>Understanding weather reports<br>Describing objects<br>Describing people | Using the weather to talk about a vacation site<br>Meteorological maps<br>Watching / reading / listening to weather reports | Months / seasons of the year / date<br>Present tense of stem-changing verbs<br>Present tense of **saber, conocer**<br>Agreement and position of adjectives<br>Plural forms of adjectives<br>**Saber** vs. **conocer**<br>Personal **a**<br>**Ser para** + pronouns<br>Shortened adjectives **(buen, mal, gran)** |
| 2 | Renting and paying for a hotel room<br>Understanding classified ads / lodging brochures<br>Describing a house or apartment<br>Telling time using the 24-hour clock | **La Guía Michelín** (tourist guide)<br>Hotels, apartments, houses<br>Flight schedules, newspaper ads | Ordinal numbers<br>Preterite **dormir**<br>Present and preterite **salir, llegar, decir, poner**<br>Time expressions / Parts of an hour<br>The 24-hour clock<br>Expressions with **decir** |
| 3 | Talking about one's daily routine<br>Organizing weekend activities<br>Discussing vacation plans | School, home<br>Magazines with entertainment listings<br>Various other settings (vacation sites) | Present tense of reflexive verbs<br>**Ud., Uds., tú** commands of reflexive verbs<br>Direct object pronouns<br>Position of direct object pronouns<br>Immediate future of reflexive verbs<br>Reflexive vs. nonreflexive verbs<br>Use of pronouns with the imperative |
| 4 | Taking about health / physical condition<br>Referring to habitual actions in the past<br>Using reflexive verbs in the past<br>Indicating what you can and cannot do | Pharmacy, school<br>Sports, pastimes | The imperfect and its uses<br>Imperfect **ser, ver, ir**<br>Preterite of reflexive verbs<br>Present and preterite **dar, pedir**<br>Present tense **doler**<br>Indirect object pronouns<br>Definite articles with parts of the body<br>Expressions **desde cuándo, desde (que), cuánto tiempo hace, hace (que)** |
| 5 | Discussing leisure time activities<br>Talking about sports<br>Narrating and describing in the past | Home, school, public places, sporting events | Preterite of some irregular verbs<br>Uses of **ponerse**<br>Imperfect and preterite: past actions, descriptions, interrupted actions, changes of meaning and translation |

SEGUNDO NIVEL

| Unit | Functions | Contexts | Accuracy |
|---|---|---|---|
| | The **Capítulo preliminar** is a comprehensive review of the materials presented in ***¡Ya verás! Segundo nivel.*** | | |
| 1 | Purchasing clothing / shoes<br>Asking for information<br>Commenting on clothing / food<br>Making restaurant plans<br>Understanding a menu / recipe<br>Ordering / paying for food | Department store, clothing store, shoe store<br>Restaurant, grocery store / supermarket, open-air market | Posición de los pronombres de complemento indirecto y directo<br>**Gustar** y otros verbos<br>Usos de **se**<br>**Estar** + adjetivos para estados y condiciones<br>**Ser** y **estar** + adjetivo |
| 2 | Organizing a trip<br>Using the telephone<br>Talking about means of transportation<br>Making travel arrangements<br>Understanding a road map | Airport, train station, bus terminal, on the road | El tiempo futuro y sus usos<br>Usos especiales del tiempo futuro<br>Preposiciones para localizar<br>Otras preposiciones útiles: **antes de, después de**<br>Pronombres preposicionales<br>Los tiempos perfectos: presente y pasado |
| 3 | Offering opinions<br>Some abstract topics<br>Dealing with symbolism<br>Expressing emotions<br>Expressing wishes, preferences | Travel in various Spanish-speaking countries | El subjuntivo para expresar la imposición indirecta de la voluntad<br>El subjuntivo para expresar la emoción<br>Expresiones impersonales para expresar la emoción |
| 4 | Understanding a variety of texts about the Spanish-speaking world<br>Expressing doubt, uncertainty, improbability<br>Talking about conditions contrary to fact<br>Supporting an opinion | Cultural issues of the Hispanic world in the press, media, literature | El subjuntivo para expresar la duda, la incertidumbre, la irrealidad<br>El subjuntivo con antecedentes indefinidos<br>El subjuntivo con **creer**<br>El condicional y sus usos<br>Cláusulas con **si** + subjuntivo<br>Cláusulas con **si** + indicativo<br>El subjunctivo y la secuencia de tiempos |

TERCER NIVEL

JOHN R. GUTIÉRREZ
The Pennsylvania State University

HARRY L. ROSSER
Boston College

MARTA ROSSO-O'LAUGHLIN
Tufts University

HH
Heinle & Heinle Publishers
An International Thomson Publishing Company • Boston, MA 02116 U.S.A.
ITP

Visit us on the internet http://www.thomson.com/heinle.html

The publication of *¡Ya verás! Primer nivel* 2/e was directed by the members of the Heinle & Heinle School Publishing Team:

Editorial Director: Beth Kramer
Market Development Director: Pamela Warren
Production Editor: Mary McKeon
Developmental Editor: Regina McCarthy
Publisher/Team Leader: Stanley J. Galek
Director of Production/Team Leader: Elizabeth Holthaus

Also participating in the publication of this text were:

Manufacturing Coordinator: Barbara Stephan
Project Manager: Kristin Swanson
Interior Design: Susan Gerould/Perspectives
Composition: NovoMac Enterprises
Cover Art: Mark Schroder
Cover: Corey McPherson Nash
Photo/Video Specialist: Jonathan Stark

Gutiérrez, John R.
Ya veras! primer nivel / John R. Gutiérrez, Harry L. Rosser, Marta Rosso-O'Laughlin. — 2nd ed.
p. cm.
ISBN 0-8384-6176-X
1. Spanish language—Textbooks for foreign speakers—English.
I. Rosser, Harry L. II. Rosso-O'Laughlin, Marta. III. Title.
[PC4129.E5G88 1997]
468.2'421—dc20 95-40095
CIP
AC



Manufactured in the United States of America.

ISBN 0-8384-6176-X Student

# To the Student

We are living in a world where the most advanced nations realize that they can no longer be ignorant of the languages and cultures of other peoples on this very small planet. Learning a new language is the first step to increasing your awareness of our world. It will open up cultures other than your own: different ways of living, thinking, and seeing. In fact, there is an old Spanish proverb that underscores the importance of knowing another language. It states: **El que sabe dos lenguas vale por dos**—the person who speaks two languages is worth two people.

You are about to begin an exciting and valuable experience. Today the Spanish language is spoken all over the world by more than 300 million people. Many of you will one day have the opportunity to visit a Spanish-speaking country. Your experience will be all the richer if you can enter into the cultures of those countries and interact with their people. However, even if you don't get to spend time in one of those countries, Spanish is very much alive right here in this country, for it is spoken every day by millions of Americans!

Have you ever been exposed to a Spanish speaker or to some element of Hispanic culture? We feel sure that you have. Perhaps you have sampled some Mexican food, turned on the television to find a Spanish news broadcast on the *Univisión* cable station, or seen *MTV Internacional.* Perhaps you have listened to Gloria Estefan or Rubén Blades or maybe seen a movie with Spanish subtitles. The possibilities are endless.

Once you begin to use the Spanish language in class, you will discover that you can interact with Spanish speakers or your classmates right away. It might help to persuade you of this to know that of over 80,000 words found in the Spanish language, the average speaker of Spanish uses only about 800 on a daily basis. Therefore, the most important task ahead of you is NOT to accumulate a large quantity of knowledge ABOUT Spanish grammar and vocabulary but rather to USE what you do know as effectively and creatively as you can.

Communication in a foreign language means understanding what others say and transmitting your messages in ways that avoid misunderstandings. As you learn to do this, you will make the kinds of errors that are necessary in language learning. DO NOT BE AFRAID TO MAKE MISTAKES! Instead, try to see errors as positive steps toward effective communication. They don't hold you back; they advance you in your efforts. Learning a language is hard work, but it can also be an enriching experience. We hope your experience with *¡Ya verás!* is both rewarding and enjoyable!

# Acknowledgments

Creating a secondary program is a long and complicated process which involves the dedication and hard work of a number of people. First of all, we would like to express our heartfelt thanks to our Editorial Director, Beth Kramer, whose expertise and support were crucial for guiding the project through its realization. We are also grateful to our Developmental Editor, Regina McCarthy, who worked closely with us to facilitate our work each step of the way. Our Production Editor, Mary McKeon, managed the many facets of the process with skill, timeliness, and good humor. Vivian Novo-MacDonald flawlessly handled her typesetting responsibilities. Kristin Swanson was a particularly effective Project Manager and we greatly appreciate her keen eye, poignant comments, and excellent suggestions at every phase of the process. We would like to thank many other people who played a role in the production of the program: Susan Gerould, Mary Lemire, María Silvina Persino, Camilla Ayers, Sharon Inglis, and Esther Marshall.

Our thanks also go to others at Heinle and Heinle who helped make this project possible: Charles Heinle and Stan Galek, for their special interest and support; Vincent DiBlasi and Erek Smith for their marketing and technical knowledge; and Jeannette Bragger and Donald Rice, authors of *On y va!* We also wish to express our appreciation to the people responsible for revising the fine set of supporting materials available with the *¡Ya verás!* program: Greg Harris, Workbook; Chris McIntyre and Jill Welch, Teacher Edition; Joe Wieczorek, Laboratory Tape Program; Kristen Warner, Testing Program; Susan Malik, Activity Guide for Middle School Teachers; Sharon Brown, Software; and Frank Domínguez, Ana Martínez-Lage and Jeff Morgenstein for creating the excellent *Mundos hispanos* multimedia program.

Finally, a very special word of acknowledgment goes to the authors' children:

— To Mía (age 12) and Stevan (age 9) who are always on their daddy's mind and whose cultural heritage is ever present throughout *¡Ya verás!*

— To Susan, Elizabeth, and Rebecca Rosser, whose enthusiasm and increasing interest in Spanish inspired their father to take part in this endeavor.

***John R. Gutiérrez and Harry L. Rosser***

The publisher and authors wish to thank the following writers for the contributions to *¡YA VERÁS!* second edition.

***Critical Thinking Skills, Learning Strategies***

**Jane Harper**
Tarrant County Junior College

**Madeleine Lively**
Tarrant County Junior College

**Mary K. Williams**
Tarrant County Junior College

***Reading Strategies,*** **Aquí leemos**

**Laura Martin**
Cleveland State University

***Interdisciplinary Lessons***

**Jessie Carduner**
University of Pittsburgh

**Charles Grove**
University of Pittsburgh

**Paul D. Toth**
University of Pittsburgh

The publisher and authors wish to thank the following teachers who pilot-tested the *¡Ya verás!* program. They used the materials with their classes and made invaluable suggestions as our work progressed. Their feedback benefits all who use this final product. We are grateful to each one of them for their dedication and commitment to teaching with the program in a prepublication format.

**Nola Baysore**
Muncy JHS
Muncy, PA

**Barbara Connell**
Cape Elizabeth Middle School
Cape Elizabeth, ME

**Frank Droney**
**Susan Digiandomenico**
Wellesley Middle School
Wellesley, MA

**Michael Dock**
Shikellamy HS
Sunbury, PA

**Jane Flood Clare**
Somers HS
Lincolndale, NY

**Nancy McMahon**
Somers Middle School
Lincolndale, NY

**Rebecca Gurnish**
Ellet HS
Akron, OH

**Peter Haggerty**
Wellesley HS
Wellesley, MA

**José M. Díaz**
Hunter College HS
New York, NY

**Claude Hawkins**
**Flora Mazzucco**
**Jerie Milici**
**Elena Fienga**
**Bohdan Kodiak**
Greenwich HS
Greenwich, CT

**Wally Lishkoff**
**Tomás Travieso**
Carver Middle School
Miami, FL

**Manuel M. Manderine**
Canton McKinley HS
Canton, OH

**Grace Angel Marion**
South JHS
Lawrence, KS

**Jean Barrett**
St. Ignatius HS
Cleveland, OH

**Gary Osman**
McFarland HS
McFarland, WI

**Deborah Decker**
Honeoye Falls-Lima HS
Honeoye Falls, NY

**Carrie Piepho**
Arden JHS
Sacramento, CA

**Rhonda Barley**
Marshall JHS
Marshall, VA

**Germana Shirmer**
W. Springfield HS
Springfield, VA

**John Boehner**
Gibson City HS
Gibson City, IL

**Margaret J. Hutchison**
John H. Linton JHS
Penn Hills, PA

**Edward G. Stafford**
St. Andrew's-Sewanee School
St. Andrew's, TN

**Irene Prendergast**
Wayzata East JHS
Plymouth, MN

**Tony DeLuca**
Cranston West HS
Cranston, RI

**Joe Wild-Crea**
Wayzata Senior High School
Plymouth, MN

**Katy Armagost**
Manhattan HS
Manhattan, KS

**William Lanza**
Osbourn Park HS
Manassas, VA

**Linda Kelley**
Hopkinton HS
Contoocook, NH

**John LeCuyer**
Belleville HS West
Belleville, IL

**Sue Bell**
South Boston HS
Boston, MA

**Wayne Murri**
Mountain Crest HS
Hyrum, UT

**Barbara Flynn**
Summerfield Waldorf School
Santa Rosa, CA

The publisher and authors wish to thank the following people who reviewed the manuscript for the second edition of the *¡Ya verás!* program. Their comments were invaluable to the development of this edition.

**Georgio Arias, Juan De León, Luís Martínez** (McAllen ISD, McAllen, TX); **Katy Armagost** (Mt. Vernon High School, Mt. Vernon, WA); **Yolanda Bejar, Graciela Delgado, Bárbara V. Méndez, Mary Alice Mora** (El Paso ISD, El Paso, TX); **Linda Bigler** (Thomas Jefferson High School, Alexandria, VA); **John Boehner** (Gibson City High School, Gibson City, IL); **Kathleen Carroll** (Edinburgh ISD, Edinburgh, TX); **Louanne Grimes** (Richardson ISD, Richardson, TX); **Greg Harris** (Clay High School, South Bend, IN); **Diane Henderson** (Houston ISD, Houston, TX); **Maydell Jenks** (Katy ISD, Katy, TX); **Bartley Kirst** (Ironwood High School, Glendale, AZ); **Mala Levine** (St. Margaret's Episcopal School, San Juan Capistrano, CA); **Manuel Manderine** (Canton McKinley Sr. High School, Canton, OH); **Laura Martin** (Cleveland State University, Cleveland, OH); **Luís Millán** (Edina High School, Minneapolis, MN); **David Moffett, Karen Petmeckey, Pat Rossett, Nereida Zimic** (Austin ISD, Austin, TX); **Jeff Morgenstein** (Hudson High School, Hudson, FL); **Rosana Pérez, Jody Spoor** (Northside ISD, San Antonio, TX); **Susan Polansky** (Carnegie Mellon University, Pittsburgh, PA); **Alva Salinas** (San Antonio ISD, San Antonio, TX); **Patsy Shafchuk** (Hudson High School, Hudson, FL); **Terry A. Shafer** (Worthington Kilbourne High School, West Worthington, OH); **Courtenay Suárez** (Montwood High School, Socorro ISD, El Paso, TX); **Alvino Téllez, Jr.** (Edgewood ISD, San Antonio, TX); **Kristen Warner** (Piper High School, Sunrise, FL); **Nancy Wrobel** (Champlin Park High School, Champlin, MN)

## Middle School Reviewers:

**Larry Ling** (Hunter College High School, New York, NY); **Susan Malik** (West Springfield High School, Springfield, VA); **Yvette Parks** (Norwood Junior High School, Norwood, MA)

# CONTENTS

CINEMA 4
TODAY • HOY

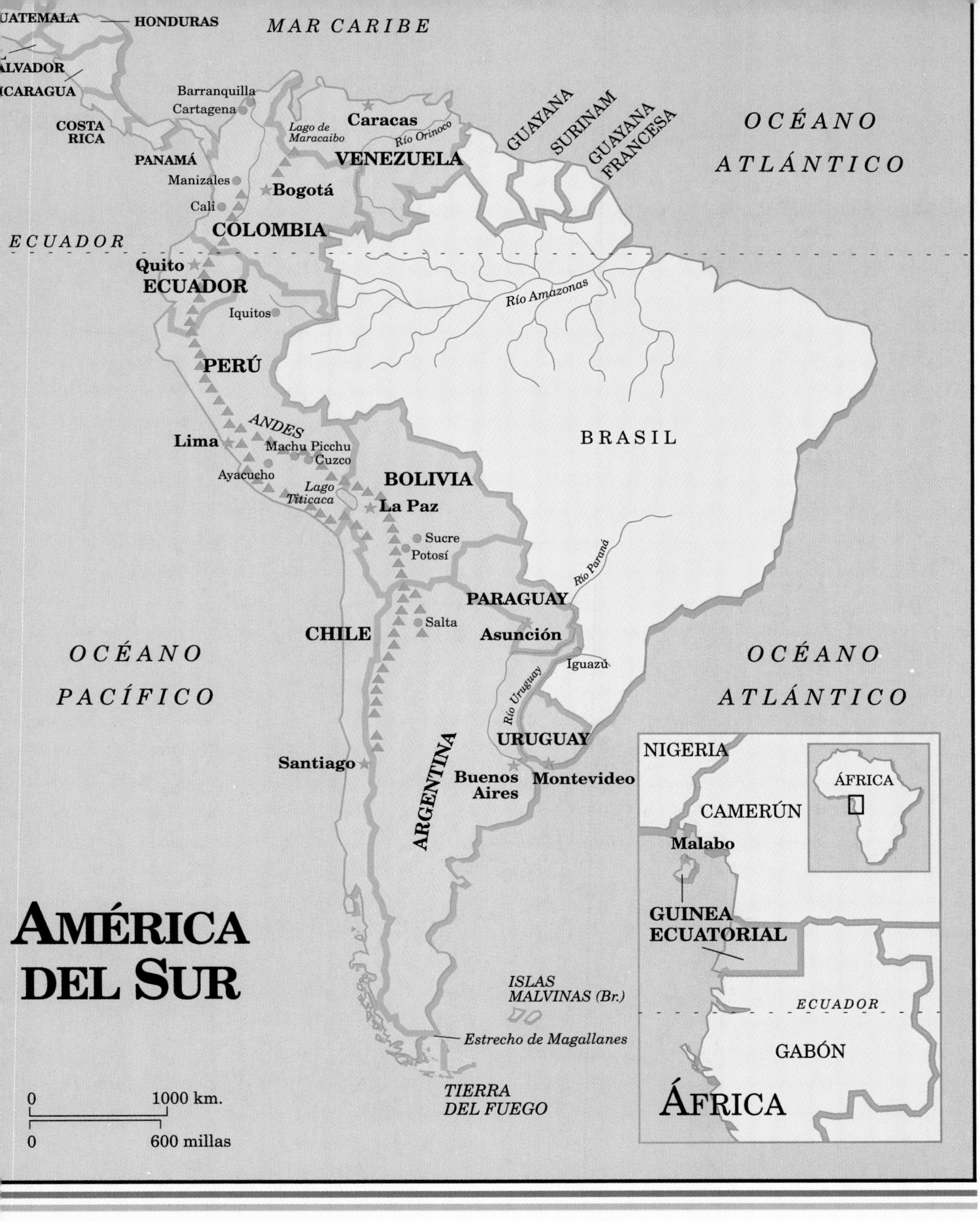
AMÉRICA DEL SUR
MAR CARIBE
OCÉANO ATLÁNTICO
OCÉANO PACÍFICO
ECUADOR
HONDURAS
COSTA RICA
PANAMÁ
Barranquilla
Cartagena
Lago de Maracaibo
Caracas
Río Orinoco
VENEZUELA
GUAYANA
SURINAM
GUAYANA FRANCESA
Manizales
Bogotá
Cali
COLOMBIA
Quito
ECUADOR
Iquitos
Río Amazonas
PERÚ
ANDES
Lima
Machu Picchu
Cuzco
Ayacucho
Lago Titicaca
BOLIVIA
La Paz
Sucre
Potosí
BRASIL
Río Paraná
PARAGUAY
Salta
Asunción
CHILE
Iguazú
Río Uruguay
URUGUAY
Santiago
Buenos Aires
Montevideo
ARGENTINA
ISLAS MALVINAS (Br.)
Estrecho de Magallanes
TIERRA DEL FUEGO
0 1000 km.
0 600 millas
NIGERIA
ÁFRICA
CAMERÚN
Malabo
GUINEA ECUATORIAL
ECUADOR
GABÓN
ÁFRICA

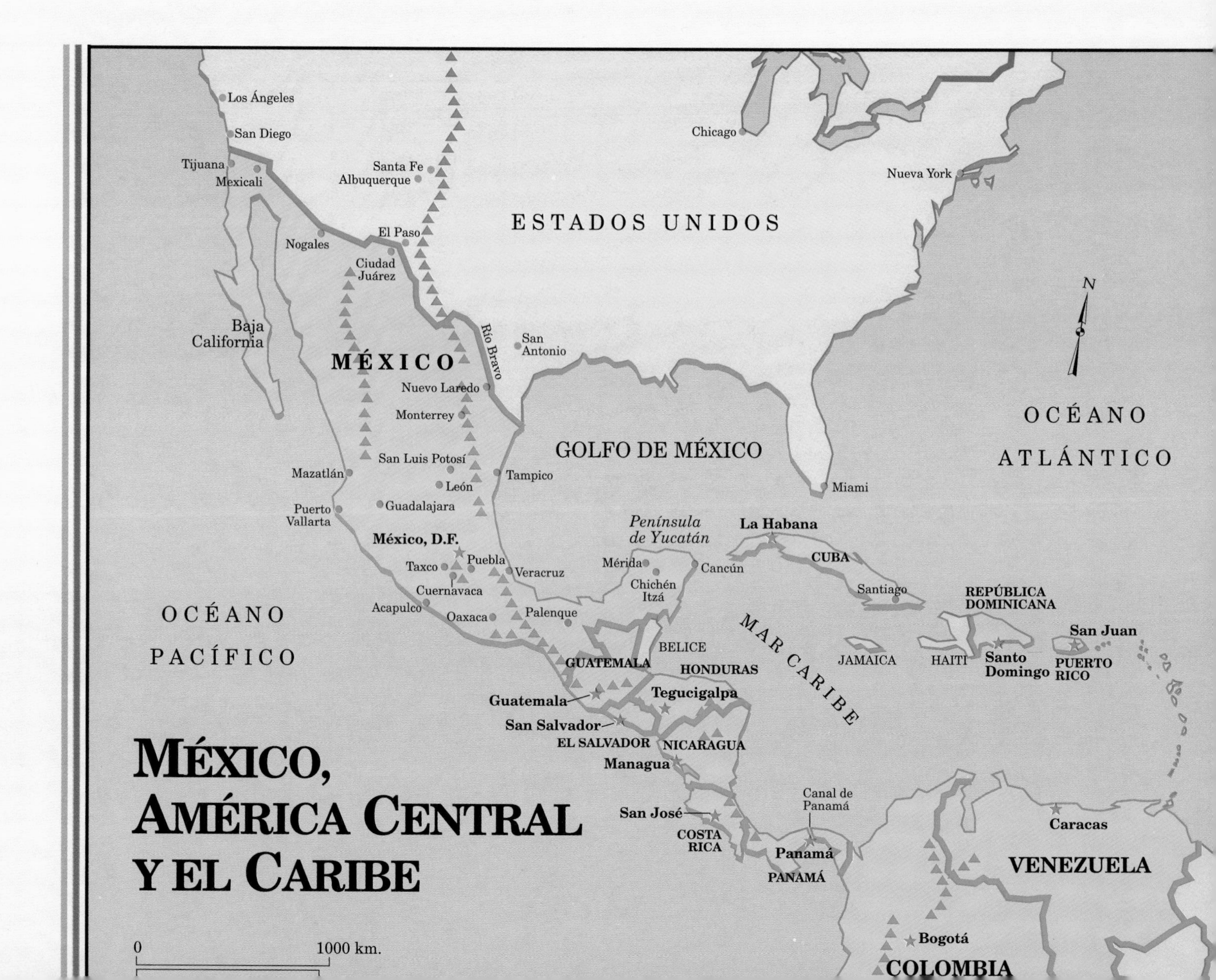

MÉXICO, AMÉRICA CENTRAL Y EL CARIBE
ESTADOS UNIDOS
MÉXICO
GOLFO DE MÉXICO
OCÉANO ATLÁNTICO
OCÉANO PACÍFICO
MAR CARIBE
N
Los Ángeles
San Diego
Tijuana
Mexicali
Santa Fe
Albuquerque
El Paso
Nogales
Ciudad Juárez
Baja California
Río Bravo
San Antonio
Chicago
Nueva York
Miami
Nuevo Laredo
Monterrey
San Luis Potosí
Mazatlán
Tampico
León
Guadalajara
Puerto Vallarta
México, D.F.
Taxco
Puebla
Veracruz
Cuernavaca
Acapulco
Oaxaca
Palenque
Península de Yucatán
Mérida
Chichén Itzá
Cancún
La Habana
CUBA
Santiago
JAMAICA
HAITÍ
REPÚBLICA DOMINICANA
Santo Domingo
San Juan
PUERTO RICO
BELICE
GUATEMALA
Guatemala
HONDURAS
Tegucigalpa
San Salvador
EL SALVADOR
NICARAGUA
Managua
San José
COSTA RICA
Canal de Panamá
Panamá
PANAMÁ
Caracas
VENEZUELA
Bogotá
COLOMBIA
0
1000 km.

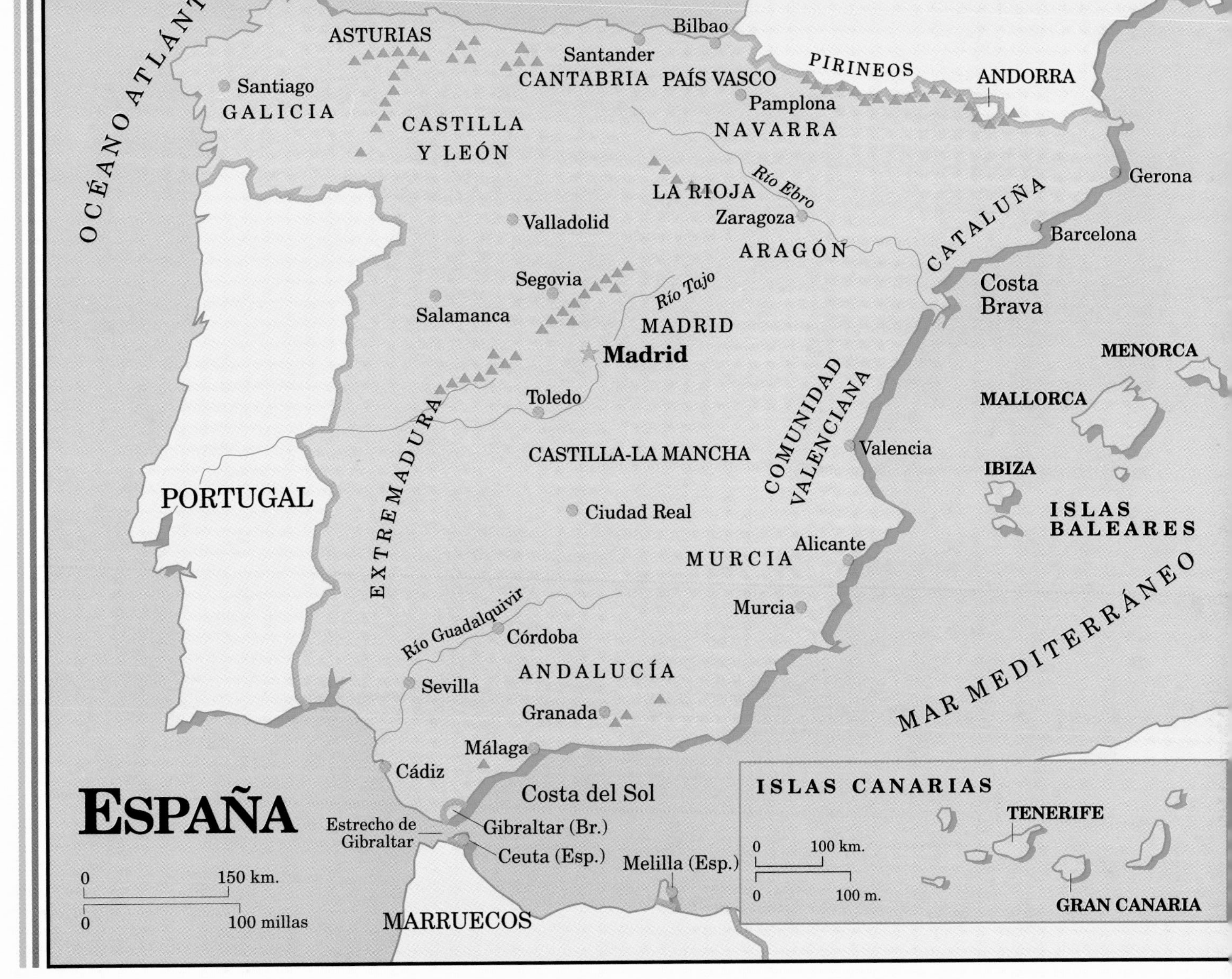

OCÉANO ATLÁNT
ASTURIAS
Santiago
GALICIA
CASTILLA
Y LEÓN
Santander
CANTABRIA
Bilbao
PAÍS VASCO
Pamplona
NAVARRA
PIRINEOS
ANDORRA
Río Ebro
LA RIOJA
Zaragoza
ARAGÓN
CATALUÑA
Gerona
Barcelona
Costa
Brava
Valladolid
Segovia
Salamanca
Río Tajo
MADRID
Madrid
Toledo
EXTREMADURA
CASTILLA-LA MANCHA
COMUNIDAD
VALENCIANA
Valencia
PORTUGAL
Ciudad Real
MURCIA
Alicante
Murcia
MENORCA
MALLORCA
IBIZA
ISLAS
BALEARES
MAR MEDITERRÁNEO
Río Guadalquivir
Córdoba
ANDALUCÍA
Sevilla
Granada
Málaga
Cádiz
Costa del Sol
ESPAÑA
Estrecho de
Gibraltar
Gibraltar (Br.)
Ceuta (Esp.)
Melilla (Esp.)
0 150 km.
0 100 millas
MARRUECOS
ISLAS CANARIAS
TENERIFE
0 100 km.
0 100 m.
GRAN CANARIA

## Cultural Context

Each unit of Level 1 of ***¡Ya verás!*** features a young person from a Spanish-speaking country; once they have been introduced, these people reappear from time to time in exercises and activities. Unit 1 features Miguel Palacios, a young man from Spain. Since Unit 1 centers on the basic task of getting food and drink, Miguel and the other characters are seen in a variety of places where young people go for refreshments or to eat. Chapter 1 deals with the café; Chapter 2 with a **tapas** bar; and Chapter 3 with Mexican restaurants. In addition to learning how to order food and beverages, students work with expressions used in greetings and introductions.

*Spanish speakers:* Have Spanish speakers mention, in Spanish, what they see. Ask them about beverages they drink that might be different from those in the photos.

### ¿Qué ves?

- Where are the people in these photographs?
- What are they doing?
- What kinds of beverages are they having?
- Where do you like to go for something to eat or drink?

### OBJECTIVES

IN THIS UNIT YOU WILL LEARN:

- To meet and greet people;
- To discuss and express your likes and dislikes about common activities;
- To get something to eat and drink;
- To read a café menu;
- To express how well or how often you do something;
- To identify and understand meal-time customs in the Hispanic world.

## Capítulo uno: Vamos al café

**Primera etapa:** ¡Hola! ¿Qué tal?
**Segunda etapa:** ¡Un refresco, por favor!
**Tercera etapa:** ¡Vamos a comer algo!

## Capítulo dos: ¡Vamos a un bar de tapas!

**Primera etapa:** Las tapas españolas
**Segunda etapa:** ¡Buenos días!... ¡Hasta luego!

## Capítulo tres: ¿Te gusta la comida mexicana?

**Primera etapa:** ¡Vamos a un restaurante!
**Segunda etapa:** ¡Qué comida más rica!

UNIDAD

# Vamos a tomar algo

*Vamos a tomar algo:* Let's get something (to eat or drink)

1

## Planning Strategy

The Planning Strategy is a brief advance organizer/warm-up to the unit. It is found on the first Workbook page of each unit.

You can assign the Planning Strategy (Workbook, p. 1) as homework or you can do it in class. If you do it in class, begin by verifying that everyone knows what a café is; then proceed to search for American "equivalents," such as fast-food restaurants. To help students become aware of the use of "formulaic" expressions in English, have them role play some of the items. Have two or three sets of students play the scene, then ask the class to identify the different formulaic expressions used in each situation.

## Cultural Observation

Have students study the photos of Miguel Palacios and his friends. Ask them to compare the way they dress with what they see in the photos.

# Chapter Objectives

Functions: Ordering food and drink; greeting, introducing, leavetaking with friends; expressing likes and dislikes; asking and answering yes/no questions
Context: Café; meeting new friends
Accuracy: **Gustar (me gusta/te gusta);** indefinite articles; present tense of regular **-ar** verbs (first and second persons)

## Chapter Warm-up: Think, Pair, Share

### *Critical Thinking Strategy: Comparing and contrasting*

- Tell the students that you are going to show them a videotape of Spanish speakers greeting and saying good-bye in a variety of social situations. Instruct the students to notice similarities and differences between Spanish greetings and American greetings (with friends, teachers, business partners, etc.)
- Show the tape. Then have students get into pairs to compare their observations. Time them so that each student has equal time to talk.
- Have each pair get together with another pair to share observations. Each pair gets equal time.
- Tell the students that they will be asked to model the greetings. Show the videotape again if necessary.
- Have each team of two pairs model one American and one Spanish greeting for the class, including culturally appropriate body language.

CAPÍTULO 1

# VAMOS AL CAFÉ

*Vamos al café:* Le
the café

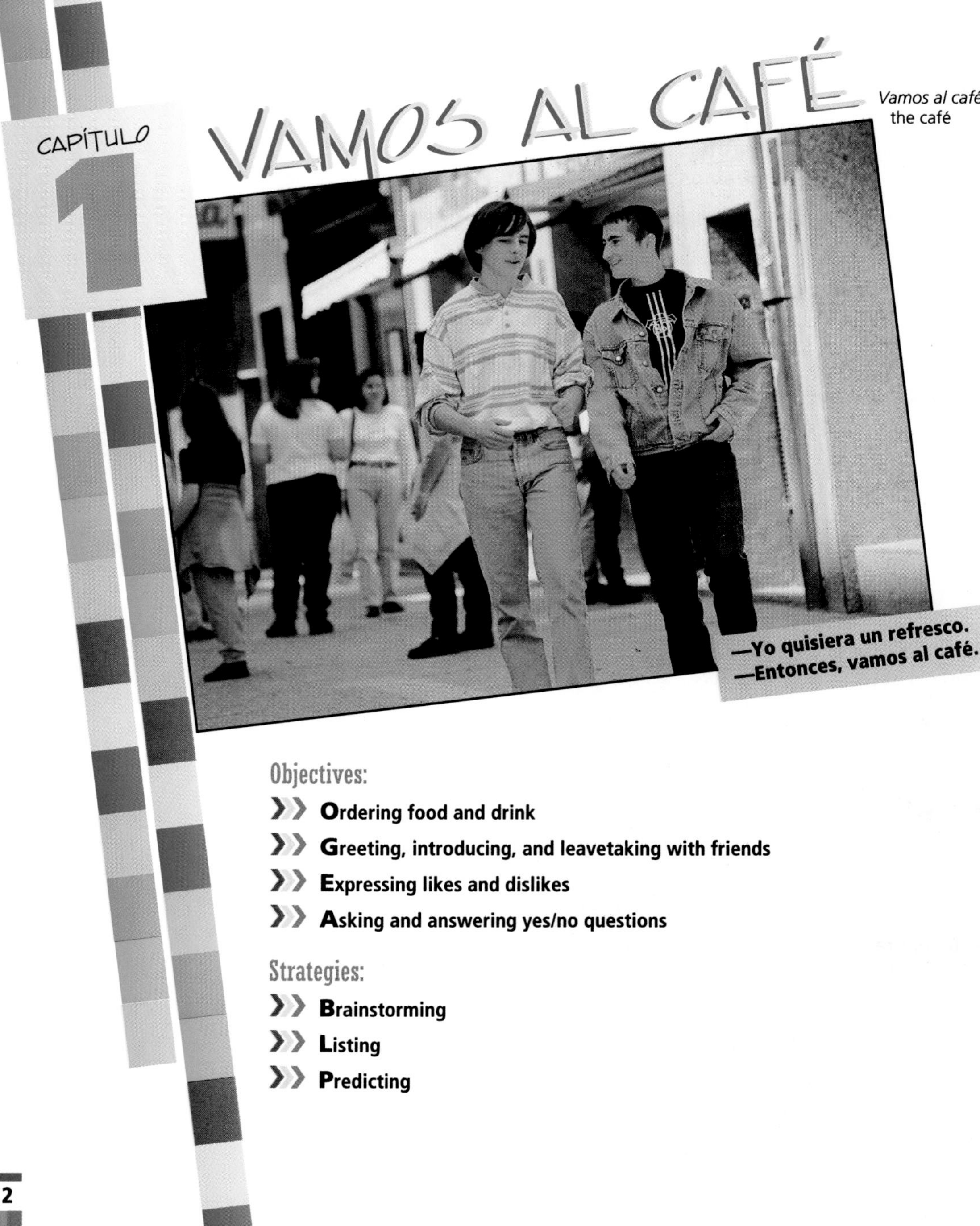

—Yo quisiera un refresco.
—Entonces, vamos al café.

Objectives:

- **Ordering food and drink**
- **Greeting, introducing, and leavetaking with friends**
- **Expressing likes and dislikes**
- **Asking and answering yes/no questions**

Strategies:

- **Brainstorming**
- **Listing**
- **Predicting**

2

## Video/CD-ROM

**Chapter 1 Video Program**
**Chapter 1 CD-ROM Program**

**These can be used at the end of the chapter as expansion activities.**

# PRIMERA ETAPA

## Preparación

- **What do you think these people are saying to each other when they meet on the street or in a public place?**
- **What gestures are the people making?**
- **When you introduce a friend to someone, what do you usually do?**
- **What are some expressions that you use in English when you meet people?**
- **What do you say when you are about to leave?**

**Learning Strategies:**

*Previewing, brainstorming, identifying culturally relevant cues*

## ¡Hola! ¿Qué tal?

—¡Hola, Anita! ¿Qué tal?
—Muy bien, Laura. ¿Y tú?
—**Bien,** gracias.
Anita, **te presento a** Juan. Juan, Anita.
—¡Hola!
—**Mucho gusto.**

—**Buenos días,** Teresa.
—Buenos días, Alba. **¿Cómo estás?**
—**Muy bien, gracias.**
**¿Y tú?**
—**Más o menos.**

*¡Hola! ¿Qué tal?:* Hello! How are you? / *Buenos días:* Good morning / *¿Cómo estás?:* How are you? / *Muy bien, gracias.:* Very well, thank you. / *¿Y tú?:* And you? / *Más o menos.:* So-so. / *Bien:* Well / *te presento a:* let me introduce you to / *Mucho gusto.:* Nice to meet you.



## Presentation: ¡Hola! ¿Qué tal?

Use the recordings on the Teacher Tape to present these dialogues. After the students have listened to the mini-dialogues on tape, read them aloud for the class, having students repeat first as a whole class, then in groups, and then individually. Then have students read the roles and play out each one with their partners. Make sure they practice several introductions and leavetakings, using the alternate expressions found on p. 4.

Point out the body language (handshakes, kissing on cheek) in the photos. Have volunteers act out the dialogues using the body language shown.

To present without the Teacher Tape, if your class has done **Etapa A** of the **Etapas preliminares,** begin by reviewing what students learned there. Have different sets of students act out mini-situations (greeting a friend, introducing two friends) in front of the class. If you have not done the **Etapas preliminares,** begin by acting out each mini-dialogue. Have students repeat, first as a whole class, then in groups, and then individually. Then have students read the roles and play out each mini-situation with their partners.

***Spanish speakers:*** Ask Spanish speakers for variations of the **saludos, respuestas,** and **despedidas** that are used here. Though they may know how to pronounce these variations, many may never have seen how they are written. Help them with the spelling of these variations by writing them on the board or overhead. Don't forget to remind them of the written accent on such words as **café, qué, cómo, tú, pasó, adiós,** etc.

***Support material, ¡Hola! ¿Qué tal?:*** Teacher Tape/CD #1 Track #1, transparency #8

## Etapa Support Materials

Workbook: **pp. 2–5**
Transparency: **#8**
Teacher Tape
Quiz: **Testing Program, p. 1**

Support material, **¡Hola! ¿Qué tal?:**
**Teacher Tape, transparency #8**

## Critical Thinking

*Critical Thinking Strategy: Comparing and contrasting*

Get students to talk about how they greet each other and make introductions; ask them what they say and do (gestures). In what situations do they shake hands? Kiss? How do they say good-bye when leaving a party or group of friends? Ask them to compare their own gestures with those in the photos on p. 3.

***Suggestion, Saludos/ Respuestas:*** Point out that some of these responses are interchangeable.

## Vocabulary Expansion

**¿Qué pasa?, Hasta pronto, Hasta mañana, Hasta la vista, Igualmente** (as a response to **Mucho gusto**). Please note that **¿Qué pasó?** is a variation of **¿Qué pasa?** that is used in some Mexican and Mexican-American communities.

## Vocabulary Activities

The **¡Aquí te toca a ti!** activities of each **etapa** always practice **etapa** vocabulary. Suggestions for groupings and for using the activities are given in this teacher margin. Most activities may be written as well as done orally.

**Ex. A:**  pair work

***Suggestions, Ex. A:*** Students may do this exercise with a partner, or you may vary the activity by having the class do it as a chain. The first student asks the student on his or her right a question; then the student who answers asks a question of the person on his or her right, and so on. Have them include students' names: **¡Hola, María!**, etc.

**Ex. B:**  groups of three

role play

***More-prepared students, Ex. B:*** The more-prepared students or the Spanish-speaking students in the class can do one or two model dialogues before having the class break into groups. Remind students to practice the body language described on p. 5 when acting out this exercise.



*Respuestas:* Answers / *Despedidas:* Farewells

| | *Saludos* | *Respuestas* | *Despedidas* | |
|---|---|---|---|---|
| Good-bye. | Buenos días. | Buenos días. | **Adiós.** | Adiós. |
| Good afternoon. / See you later. / Bye. / Good evening. / See you. | **Buenas tardes.** | Buenas tardes. | **Hasta luego.** | **Chao.** |
| | **Buenas noches.** | Buenas noches. | **Nos vemos.** | |
| | ¡Hola! | ¡Hola! | | |
| | ¿Qué tal? | Bien, gracias. ¿Y tú? | | |
| | ¿Cómo estás? | Muy bien, gracias. ¿Y tú? | | |
| How is it going? | **¿Cómo te va?** | Más o menos. ¿Y tú? | | |
| What's going on? / O.K. | **¿Qué pasó?** | **Regular.** | | |
| What's new? / Pretty good. | **¿Qué hay?** | **Bastante bien.** | | |

¡Hola!

Hasta luego.

¿Qué tal?

¿Cómo estás?

## ¡Aquí te toca a ti!

**A. *Saludos*** Answer these greetings appropriately.

1. ¡Hola!
2. Buenos días.
3. ¿Cómo estás?
4. ¿Qué tal?
5. Buenas tardes.
6. ¿Cómo te va?
7. Buenas noches.
8. ¿Qué pasó?
9. ¿Qué hay?

**B. *¡Hola! ¿Qué tal?*** You are with a new student and you meet a friend in the hallway. You and your friend greet each other, you introduce the new student, and then say good-bye to each other. Divide into groups of three to act out the situation. Follow the model.

*Modelo:*

**Tú:** *¡Hola! ¿Qué tal?*
**Amigo(a):** *Bien, gracias, ¿y tú?*
**Tú:** *Bien, gracias. Te presento a Marilú.*
**Amigo(a):** *¡Hola!*
**Marilú:** *Mucho gusto.*
**Tú:** *Hasta luego.*
**Amigo(a):** *Nos vemos.*
**Marilú:** *Adiós.*



### Exercise Progression

Ex. A is a controlled exercise designed to practice the new conversational patterns. Ex. B offers additional practice in a more open-ended situation.

## COMENTARIOS CULTURALES

### Saludos y despedidas

In Hispanic culture, the body language that accompanies greetings and good-byes is different from American customs. In both situations, it is customary for men to shake hands formally or even exchange an abrazo by embracing and patting each other on the back. Among women, the custom is to kiss each other on both cheeks in Spain and on only one cheek in Latin America. When a young man and woman who know each other meet, they generally kiss on both cheeks. Older people will usually shake hands unless they know each other well.

In addition, when Spanish-speakers of any age greet each other or engage in conversation, they generally stand closer to each other than do speakers of English. Often, when greeting each other or saying good-bye, two men may exchange an abrazo, a brief embrace with a pat or two on the back.

*Learning Strategy:*

*Reading for cultural information*

## Pronunciación: The Spanish alphabet

A good place to start your study of Spanish pronunciation is with the alphabet. Listed below are the letters of the Spanish alphabet along with their names.

| | | | | | |
|---|---|---|---|---|---|
| **a** | a | **j** | jota | **r** | ere |
| **b** | be | **k** | ka | **rr** | erre |
| **c** | ce | **l** | ele | **s** | ese |
| **ch** | che[1] | **ll** | elle[1] | **t** | te |
| **d** | de | **m** | eme | **u** | u |
| **e** | e | **n** | ene | **v** | ve |
| **f** | efe | **ñ** | eñe | **w** | doble ve |
| **g** | ge | **o** | o | **x** | equis |
| **h** | hache | **p** | pe | **y** | i griega |
| **i** | i | **q** | cu | **z** | zeta |

[1] As of 1994, the **ch** and the **ll** do not have their own separate headings in dictionaries but are listed under **c** and **l** respectively. This was viewed as a way to simplify dictionaries and make the language more internationally computer-compatible.



Point out that it is also customary for people to inquire about the family whenever they greet each other. Teach students: **¿Qué tal la familia? Bien, gracias. ¿Y tu familia?**

***Spanish speakers:*** Ask Spanish speakers if they are familiar with the customs that are mentioned in this commentary. Ask for variations.

### Presentation: Pronunciation

Pronounce the letters and have students repeat. Point out that the letters **k** and **w** are used only in words borrowed from other languages. Mention the letters found only in the Spanish alphabet: **ñ** and **rr.** (In 1994, the letters **ch** and **ll** were eliminated from the alphabet and will no longer appear as a separate entry in the dictionary.)

Additional activities appear in the Laboratory Tape Program.

***Support material, Pronunciación:*** Pronunciation Tape

## Cultural Expansion

Hispanics tend to be very demonstrative about showing affection to relatives or close friends. When greeting a close friend or relative, they often kiss him or her on one or both cheeks (depending on the country). Handshakes are used when making a new acquaintance or when two male friends greet each other. When entering or leaving a party or group of people, it is customary to shake hands or kiss on the cheek and to exchange an appropriate greeting or leavetaking expression with any friends present. An **abrazo,** or quick hug, is also common in the above situations, including between males.

***Spanish speakers, Ex. C:*** Point out those words that have spelling combinations that are problematic for Spanish speakers. For a more detailed explanation of these problematic spelling combinations, refer to p. 20 of "To the Teacher" in the Teacher's Edition. For example, the **qu** and **ll** in **mantequilla,** the **c** in **aceitunas,** the **ll** in **bocadillo,** the **j** in **naranja,** the **j** in **jamón,** and the **ll** in **tortilla.**

## Presentation: Expressing likes and dislikes

Introduce **me gusta/te gusta** as vocabulary items without explaining their construction. If you have Spanish-speaking students in your class, ask them simple questions such as **¿Te gusta escuchar música rock?**, and have them answer in complete sentences: **Sí, me gusta escuchar... .** If there are no Spanish-speaking students, make simple statements about yourself. Have students repeat them, first as a whole class, then in groups, and then individually. Suggestions: **Me gusta hablar español. Me gusta escuchar música rock. Me gusta bailar.** (Use gestures, body language, and pantomiming where possible.) Then ask questions that are likely to elicit affirmative answers from your students. For example: **Me gusta escuchar música rock. ¿Te gusta escuchar música rock?**, etc.

**Ex. D:**  pair work

 writing

## Práctica

*C.* Spell the following words using the Spanish alphabet.

1. pan
2. refresco
3. mantequilla
4. leche
5. aceitunas
6. bocadillo
7. naranja
8. limón
9. mermelada
10. calamares
11. sándwich
12. desayuno
13. jamón
14. pastel
15. tortilla

Now spell your first and last names.

## ESTRUCTURA

### *Expressing likes and dislikes: gustar + activities*

In order to express in Spanish what activities you like or do not like to do, the following structure can be used:

*Gustar + infinitive**

| | |
|---|---|
| **Me gusta** bailar. | *I like* to dance. |
| **¿Te gusta** cantar? | *Do you like* to sing? |
| **No me gusta** cantar. **Me gusta** escuchar música. | *I don't like* to sing. *I like* to listen to music. |
| **¿Te gusta** hablar español? | *Do you like* to speak Spanish? |
| Sí, pero **no me gusta** estudiar y practicar. | Yes, but *I don't like* to study and practice. |

* An *infinitive* is a verb that is not conjugated (does not show a different ending for each person). For example, in English *to introduce* is an infinitive, and *she introduces* contains a conjugated verb.

## Aquí practicamos

*D.* ***¿Qué*** (What) ***te gusta?*** Answer the following questions, according to the model.

¿Te gusta estudiar?
*Sí, me gusta estudiar.* o:
*No, no me gusta estudiar.*



***Suggestions, Ex. D:*** Have students do Ex. D first as a **pregúntale** exercise **(María, pregúntale a Juan el número uno)**. Then have them do the exercise again with their partners for more practice. The answers to this exercise will vary, but will all follow one of two formats: **Sí, me gusta... ,** or **No, no me gusta... .**

1. ¿Te gusta bailar?
2. ¿Te gusta hablar español en clase?
3. ¿Te gusta cantar óperas?
4. ¿Te gusta escuchar música rock? ¿clásica?
5. ¿Te gusta estudiar matemáticas? ¿historia?
6. ¿Te gusta cantar?

## Palabras útiles

### Expressing likes and dislikes

Here are some words that can be used to express whether you like something very much or just a little.

| | | | |
|---|---|---|---|
| **mucho** | a lot | **poco** | a little |
| **muchísimo** | very much | **muy poco** | very little |

Me gusta **mucho** bailar.
Me gusta **muy poco** escuchar música clásica.

These words are called *adverbs* and they come after the verb **gustar.**

**E. ¿Muchísimo o muy poco?** Say how much or how little you like these activities. Follow the model.

Modelo: cantar
*Me gusta mucho cantar.* o: *Me gusta muy poco cantar.*

1. bailar
2. hablar en clase
3. hablar español
4. escuchar música rock
5. escuchar música clásica
6. estudiar
7. cantar

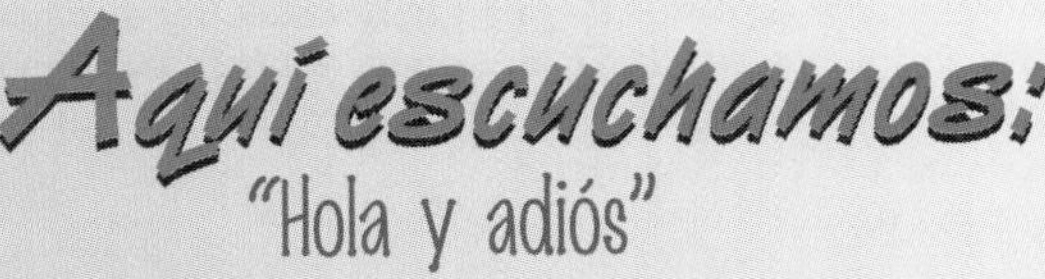

## Aquí escuchamos:

### "Hola y adiós"

#### Antes de escuchar

Think of some of the common expressions, questions, and responses typically used in Spanish when you meet people on the street.

Critical Thinking Strategy:
*Previewing*



**Ex. E:**  pair work

 writing

***Suggestions, Ex. E:*** Have students work in pairs asking the question **¿Te gusta... ?** and using the cues provided. You may also want to use this as a writing exercise. Set a time limit for students to finish writing the statements, then have them edit their partners' papers for mistakes.

***More-prepared students, Ex. E:*** More-prepared students can write and perform longer dialogues in which they introduce friends and talk about their likes and dislikes.

***Less-prepared students, Ex. E:*** Less-prepared students can review infinitives—**bailar, cantar, hablar, estudiar,** etc.

### Aquí escuchamos

This listening activity appears in every **etapa** of ***¡Ya verás!*** Guide students to listen for the overall gist of what is happening. Set the stage and help students to understand the scenario in which each dialogue is presented. For your reference, scripts for all **Aquí escuchamos** dialogues can be found in the Tapescript.

***Spanish speakers:*** Remember, most Spanish speakers will understand spoken Spanish. These students should, however, be directed to focus on "listening in context" to any new vocabulary.

***Support material, Aquí escuchamos:***
Teacher Tape/CD #1 Track #2 and Tapescript

### Presentation: Palabras útiles

Introduce these adverbs by making statements with which students are likely to agree. Have students repeat as a whole class, then in groups, and then individually. Emphasize the adverbs with the tone of your voice (and use hand gestures for **poco**). For example: **Me gusta mucho escuchar música. Me gusta poco estudiar.,** etc. Then ask simple questions such as **¿Te gusta mucho escuchar música?,** etc.

***Answers, Después de escuchar:*** First C: 1. Carlos, María Elena 2. Bastante bien, gracias. 3. Yes, no introductions are needed. They know each other's name. 4. Hasta luego. Second C: 1. Morning 2. Puerto Rico 3. José Manuel

## Review of the etapa

The **¡Adelante!** section of each **etapa** serves as the culmination of the **etapa,** providing learner-centered, task-based activities in realistic applications. These functionally driven activities allow the teacher to check for student control of the **etapa** material and serve as preparatory activities for the end of the unit.

**Ex. F:**  groups of three

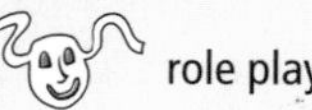 role play

***Suggestions, Ex. F:*** First do one or two model dialogues as a class. Then have students work in groups of three and write out their own dialogues. After they have finished writing the dialogues, tell them to practice them orally three times, playing a different role and using different greetings each time. (Be sure to set a time limit.) Then have volunteers present their dialogues to the class.

***Spanish speakers, Ex. F:*** Most Spanish speakers already have a command of the language in informal contexts. In this situation, students can focus on vocabulary that may be new for them. Remember to be sensitive and accept how the students do it the first time. Remember, rather than "correcting" how they speak, your objective is to expand the range of contexts in which these students can use Spanish.

**Now listen twice to the two brief exchanges between friends meeting on the street.**

*Critical Thinking Strategy:*
*Previewing*

## Después de escuchar

**First conversation**

1. **What are the names of the two people in the conversation?**
2. **What does the boy respond when asked how he is?**
3. **Do they already know each other? How do you know?**
4. **What expression do they both use when they say good-bye?**

**Second conversation**

1. **What general time of day is it when the people meet?**
2. **What country is one of the speakers from?**
3. **Who makes a reference at the end to someone's family?**

*Learning Strategies:*
*Requesting information, organizing ideas, listing*

### EJERCICIO ORAL

**F. *¡Mucho gusto!*** You and a friend are sitting in a café when another friend arrives. (1) Greet the arriving friend and (2) introduce him or her to the friend you are with. (3) Discuss which refreshments you want to order. (4) One of the two friends who have just met should ask the other a question about his or her likes or dislikes **(¿Te gusta escuchar música rock?)** and (5) the other should respond **(Sí, me gusta escuchar música rock. Me gusta cantar también.)**. Finally, (6) after finishing your drink you get up and say good-bye to your two friends.

*Learning Strategy:*
*Listing*

### EJERCICIO ESCRITO

**G. *Una postal*** (A postcard) Write a postcard to a friend. Make sure it includes a greeting, a list of three things you like to do, a question about your friend's activities, and a farewell.



**Ex. G:**  writing

***Spanish speakers, Ex. G:*** Always have Spanish speakers fully carry out this activity. Remember, while many of them already speak and understand spoken Spanish, they may not know how to write well. This is a good place to start building basic literacy skills in Spanish. Have students engage in peer-editing as well.

## SEGUNDA ETAPA

### Preparación

- **W**hat are the different beverages you can order at a restaurant or a café?
- **T**hink about what you drink at different times during the day. What do you normally drink at breakfast time? At lunch? In the evening?
- **W**hen you are really thirsty, what do you most like to drink?

*Learning Strategies:*

*Previewing, brainstorming*

## ¡Un refresco, por favor!

*¡Un refresco, por favor!:* A soft drink, please!

—Pst, **camarero.**
—Sí, señorita, **¿qué desea tomar?**
—Una limonada, por favor.
—Y usted, señorita, ¿qué desea?
—**Yo quisiera** un licuado de banana, por favor.

—**Aquí tienen ustedes.** Una limonada y un licuado de banana.
—**Muchas gracias,** señor.
—**De nada.**

*camarero:* waiter / *¿qué desea tomar?:* what do you want to drink? / *Yo quisiera:* I woud like / *Aquí tienen ustedes.:* Here you are. / *Muchas gracias:* Thank you very much / De nada.: You're welcome.



## Presentation: ¡Un refresco, por favor!

First explain the scene, then act it out playing the customers and the waiter. Have students listen to the Teacher Tape and repeat both parts. Or, read each line and have students repeat, first as a whole class, then in groups, and then in pairs. Treat **quisiera** as a vocabulary item.

Introduce the vocabulary with the transparency or while students look at the pictures in the book. Have them repeat the items while looking at the pictures.

Next, play the role of the waiter and have students get your attention to order hot or cold drinks, either using the transparency or the pictures in the book. Ask **¿Qué desea tomar?** randomly to elicit the names of different beverages. After practicing the names of beverages, ask for volunteers to act out the mini-dialogue with their books closed.

*Spanish speakers:* Ask Spanish speakers for variations of the **bebidas** that are introduced here. They may know how to pronounce the names of these drinks, but may never have seen them written. Help them with the spelling of these variations by writing them on the board or overhead.

It may be helpful to focus on the words with difficult spelling combinations, such as the **ll** in **botella,** the **j** of **jugo,** the **c** of **licuado,** and the **v** of **vaso.**

## Vocabulary Expansion

**Mesero/mesera** = waiter/ waitress. In most of the Spanish-speaking world, **café** or **cafecito** is a demi-tasse of strong black coffee. **Café con leche** is half strong black coffee and half hot milk; **chocolate** is hot milk with cocoa. In Spain and Mexico, **plátano** is used for banana, and in Puerto Rico and other parts of the Caribbean, **guineo** is the preferred word.

## Etapa Support Materials

Workbook: **pp. 6–7**
Transparencies: **#9, #10, #10a, #11, #11a**
Teacher Tape
Quiz: **Testing Program, p. 3**

Support material, **¡Un refresco, por favor!:** **Teacher Tape ; transparencies #9, #10, #10a, #11, #11a**

*Support material, ¡Un refresco, por favor!:* Teacher Tape/CD #1 Track #3 , transparencies #9, #10, #10a, #11, #11a

## Vocabulary Expansion, cont.

**Granadina** is grenadine, a non-alcoholic red syrup made from pomegranates, often mixed with mineral water and served with a wedge of lemon or lime; **licuado** (also known as **batido**) is a drink made by combining either milk or water with fresh fruit and sugar in a blender; **refresco** is any soft drink.

**Ex. A:**  pair work

 role play

*Suggestions, Ex. A:* Have students work with their partners, alternating the roles of waiter and client. Or do the exercise with the whole class by having one student play the role of waiter and asking a student seated across the aisle what he/she wishes. Continue until all students have played both roles.

*More-prepared students, Ex. A:* More-prepared students can practice longer dialogues in which they meet at the café, introduce friends, and then order refreshments.

*Less-prepared students, Ex. A:* Less-prepared students could benefit from a further review of vocabulary. Use the transparency of hot and cold drinks with the overlay, and have the students close their books while you point to choices.

Hot drinks

un café con leche

un té con leche

un té

un té con limón

un chocolate

un café

Cold drinks

UNAS BEBIDAS FRÍAS

un jugo de naranja

una granadina con agua mineral

una limonada

un refresco

una botella de agua mineral
un vaso de agua con limón

un licuado de banana

## ¡Aquí te toca a ti!

***A. En el café*** You are in a café and want to order the following drinks. Follow the model.

un café con leche
—*¿Qué desea, señorita (señor)?*
—*Un café con leche, por favor.*

1. un refresco
2. un té con limón
3. una granadina con agua mineral
4. un chocolate
5. una botella de agua mineral
6. un licuado de banana
7. una limonada
8. un café
9. un té con leche
10. un jugo de naranja
11. un vaso de agua con limón
12. un té



## Exercise Progression

Ex. A is a controlled exercise designed to familiarize students with beverage vocabulary and the basic waiter–client exchange. Exs. B and C offer practice in more open-ended situations. If you have not used transparencies to present the material, the following suggestions will be helpful as you work with these exercises in class.

*B.* **Camarero(a), por favor.** You need to get the waiter's (waitress's) attention and order the drink of your choice. Follow the model.

**Modelo:** *—Pst, camarero(a).*
*—Sí, señor (señorita), ¿qué desea tomar?*
*—Un licuado de banana, por favor.*

*C.* **Aquí tienen.** Play the role of the waiter (waitress) or one of two students at a café. The students each order a drink, but the waiter (waitress) forgets who ordered what. Work in groups of three. Follow the model.

**Modelo:**
**Camarero(a):** *¿Qué desean tomar?*
**Estudiante 1:** *Una granadina con soda, por favor.*
**Camarero(a):** *¿Y Ud., señor (señorita)?*
**Estudiante 2:** *Quisiera un refresco, por favor.*

**Camarero(a):** *Aquí tienen. Un refresco para Ud....*
**Estudiante 1:** *No, señor(a), una granadina.*
**Camarero(a):** *¡Ah, perdón* (sorry)*! Una granadina para Ud., y un refresco para Ud.*
**Estudiante 2:** *Sí, gracias.*
**Camarero(a):** *De nada.*

## Pronunciación: *The vowel a*

The sound of the vowel **a** in Spanish is pronounced like the *a* of the English word *father* except that the sound is shorter in Spanish. Listen as your teacher models the difference between the Spanish **a** and the English *a* of *father.*

## Práctica

*D.* Listen and repeat as your teacher models the following words.

1. hola
2. va
3. pan
4. patatas
5. tapas
6. canta
7. habla
8. hasta
9. calamares
10. cacahuetes

## Repaso

*E.* **Hola, te presento a...** The Spanish Club has organized a meeting for its new members to get to know each other. Select a partner and introduce each other to three new people.



### Presentation: Pronunciation

Point out that the Spanish **a** sounds more tense or clipped than the English *a.* Demonstrate this by mispronouncing a few words in Spanish, drawing out the **a** sound (such as **ahh-ni-mahhl**). Then pronounce them correctly in Spanish, shortening the sound of the **a.**

Read the words in the **Práctica** and have students repeat first as a whole class, then in groups, and then in pairs or individually.

*Spanish speakers, Ex. D:* Have the Spanish speakers focus on the **h** of **hola, habla, hasta,** and **cacahuetes** and the **v** of **va.**

Additional activities appear in the Laboratory Tape Program.

*Support material, Pronunciación:* Pronunciation Tape

### Recycling Activity

The **Repaso** activity in the second (and third) **etapa(s)** of each chapter recycle material from the previous **etapa.**

**Ex. E:** pair work

*Suggestion, Ex. E:* This activity can be done with groups as large as you wish. Pairs of students may circulate around the whole class or you may divide students into groups of six or more.

**Ex. B:** 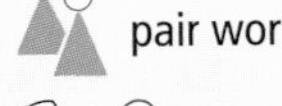 pair work

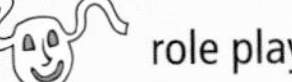 role play

*Suggestion, Ex. B:* You play the waiter/waitress or have more-prepared students do so. Have each student in the class get your attention and order a drink. No order may be repeated until all drinks have been mentioned. If your students have already learned the numbers in the **Etapas preliminares,** ask them to keep track of the orders and do a summary at the end: **tres limonadas, dos licuados de banana, cinco refrescos,** etc.

**Ex. C:**  groups of three

 role play

*Variation, Ex. C:* Have students work in groups of three and write out a different dialogue following the model. Then have groups volunteer to act out the dialogues for the class. They may use the photos on p. 10 for reference.

*Follow-up, Ex. C:* During these early stages of instruction when conversation is limited, or later in the year for a diversion, students can play a blackboard version of "Pictionary" to practice concrete nouns or a game of charades to practice verbs.

## Presentation: Indefinite articles

Pointing to students, say **un hombre, una mujer** or **un estudiante, una estudiante**, stressing the indefinite article (with your voice) each time. Then continue by saying some of the drinks learned, stressing the article each time. For example: **Deseo una granadina, no un refresco.** After students understand the use of **un** with masculine nouns and **una** with feminine nouns, point out the plural forms **unos** and **unas.** Have students repeat singular and plural forms of the drinks they have learned.

**Exs. F and G:**  pair work

*Suggestions, Exs. F and G:* Have students close their books and do the exercises using the transparency of drinks without the overlay. Students could also do them as a writing exercise. Set a time limit and then have students edit their partners' answers for mistakes in articles or spelling.

*Answers, Ex. F:* 1. un 2. unas 3. un 4. un 5. unos 6. un

*Answers, Ex. G:* 1. Yo quisiera un chocolate. ¿Y tú? 2. un té 3. un vaso de agua mineral 4. una granadina con agua mineral 5. un licuado de banana 6. un té con leche



# ESTRUCTURA

### *The indefinite articles un, unos, una, unas*

The singular (one person or thing) indefinite articles in Spanish are:

| *Masculino* | *Femenino* |
|---|---|
| **un** refresco<br>**unos** refrescos | **una** limonada<br>**unas** limonadas |

1. The English equivalent of **un, una** is *a* or *an*; **unos** and **unas** mean *some.*
2. Every noun in Spanish has a grammatical gender; that is, it is either masculine or feminine. The gender of a noun has nothing to do with what the word means.
3. If a noun is masculine, it often ends with the vowel **-o, un jugo.** If a noun is feminine, it often ends with the vowel **-a, una granadina.** But other words, like **té** or **café,** do not fall into these categories. For this reason, it is best to learn the noun with its corresponding article.
4. If a noun is plural it ends with an **-s,** whether it is masculine or feminine. Note that **uno** is always shortened to **un** when it comes before a noun.

## Aquí practicamos

**F.** ***¿Un o unos? ¿Una o unas?*** Add the correct indefinite article to these nouns. Follow the model.

**Modelo:** botella de agua mineral
*una botella de agua mineral*

1. jugo de naranja
2. botellas de agua mineral
3. té
4. vaso de agua
5. refrescos
6. café con leche

**G.** ***Yo quisiera... ¿Y tú?*** You and your friend are deciding what to have. Express what you want and then ask your friend. Follow the model.

**Modelo:** café con leche
*Yo quisiera un café con leche. ¿Y tú?*

1. chocolate
2. té
3. vaso de agua mineral
4. granadina con agua mineral
5. licuado de banana
6. té con leche



*Follow-up, Exs. F and G:* With books closed, read the drinks without the articles. Have one student repeat the item with the correct indefinite article and then have the next student give the item in its plural form with its corresponding article.

### Exercise Progression

Exs. F and G are both controlled drills designed to coordinate the use of the indefinite articles. They offer students multiple opportunities to use a structure correctly, keeping its form in their minds.

# COMENTARIOS CULTURALES

## Los cafés

In the Spanish-speaking world, young and old people enjoy meeting at a **café** for a drink and a snack at different times during the day. In every neighborhood of a town or city one can find cafés, each with its own particular clientele and atmosphere. In a café near a school or university, for example, it is possible to see groups of students sitting at tables discussing their studies and politics or just laughing and chatting with friends. Older people may prefer sitting in a quieter café where they can listen to music while they read the newspaper, play cards, or simply relax watching the passersby. In the summertime, tables are usually set outside for the enjoyment of the customers.

Learning Strategy:

*Reading for cultural information*

## Aquí escuchamos: "En un café"

Ana and her friends are having something to drink at a café. Listen to their conversation and do the following exercises.

### Antes de escuchar

Based on the information you have learned in this chapter, answer the following questions.

1. What are some beverages you expect Ana and her friends will order?
2. What do you say to order something in Spanish?

START

Learning Strategy:

*Previewing*

### Después de escuchar

Look at the following list and tell what Ana and her friends ordered.

| | | | |
|---|---|---|---|
| limonada | licuado | café | agua mineral |
| té | leche | refresco | |

Learning Strategy:

*Listening for details*



***Spanish speakers:*** Ask Spanish speakers if they are familiar with the types of places that are mentioned in this commentary. If they don't exist in the students' immediate community, perhaps they may have been to one on a trip to Mexico, Puerto Rico, the Dominican Republic, El Salvador, Nicaragua, Colombia, or another Spanish-speaking country.

## Cultural Expansion

Introduce the concept of the **tertulia** in the Spanish-speaking world (particularly Spain): a group of friends who meet usually at the same time and place every day or every week to discuss politics, sports, or current events, or just to chat about everyday happenings. **Tertulias** generally take place at cafés or bars, where young people have soft drinks or coffee and where adults usually drink coffee, soft drinks, wine, or beer.

### Aquí escuchamos

***Spanish speakers:*** Remember, most Spanish speakers, even those that are third or fourth generation, will understand spoken Spanish. The exercises that accompany this section should pose relatively little problem for Spanish speakers. They should, however, be directed to focus on "listening in context" to any vocabulary that may be new for them.

***Answers, Después de escuchar:*** una limonada, un café, una botella de agua mineral

***Support material, Aquí escuchamos:*** Teacher Tape/CD #1 Track #4 and Tapescript

**Ex. H:** 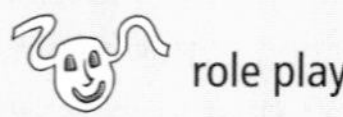 groups of four or more

role play

*Suggestion, Ex. H:* You may wish to have any Spanish-speaking/more-prepared students in the class model this before students work with their classmates. Then divide the class into groups of four. Have students do the conversation several times, allowing each group member to play a different part. Insist that students vary the drinks they order, or even change their orders: **"Una limonada—no, un chocolate, por favor."**

*Spanish speakers, Ex. H:* Remember that most Spanish speakers already have a command of a variety of Spanish that is used in informal, very familiar contexts. This situation is a fairly informal one, but have the students focus on using vocabulary that may be new for them. Emphasize that it may be necessary to use such vocabulary when talking to speakers who are from other parts of the Spanish-speaking world. Again, remember to be sensitive and accept how the students say it the first time. What they have said may be totally appropriate in their speech community. This is a good place to have them focus on the differences between how they may say something in their speech community and how the book is teaching them to express this. Remember, rather than "correcting" how they speak, your main objective is to expand the range of real-world contexts in which these students can use Spanish.

# ¡Adelante!

## EJERCICIO ORAL

**H. *¿Qué desean tomar?*** You and two friends are in a café. Decide what each person will order, call the waiter (waitress), and place your order. Work in groups of four and follow the model.

**Modelo:** —*¿Qué desean tomar?*
—*Yo quisiera una limonada.*
—*Un café para mí* (for me).

—*Pst, camarero(a).*
—*Sí, señorita (señor), ¿qué desean?*
—*Una limonada, un café y un té con limón, por favor.*
—*Muy bien, señorita (señor).*

## EJERCICIO ESCRITO

**Cooperative Learning**

**Learning Strategy:**
*Listing*

**Critical Thinking Strategies:**
*Prioritizing, comparing and contrasting*

**I. *A mí me gusta...*** Working with a classmate, each of you (1) list six different beverages in the order in which you prefer them personally. Then (2) exchange lists and compare your preferences. Finally, (3) determine three beverages that both of you like (adding to your original lists, if necessary).

**Ex. I:**  pair work

*Spanish speakers, Ex. I:* Always have Spanish speakers fully carry out this activity. Remember, while many of them already speak and understand spoken Spanish, they may not know how to write the language. This is a good place to start building basic literacy skills in Spanish. Have them pay special attention to the spelling of the vocabulary that has been introduced in this **etapa,** especially those words that may have problematic spelling combinations. This is also a good place to have them engage in peer-editing. Have them look at the written work of a partner and focus on the spelling.

## TERCERA ETAPA

### Preparación

- ›› **What are some of the things you can order for breakfast in a restaurant?**
- ›› **What is your favorite breakfast food?**
- ›› **What do you generally like to eat for lunch?**
- ›› **What do you have for a snack now and then?**

*Learning Strategies:*

*Brainstorming, previewing*

# ¡Vamos a comer algo!

un pastel de fresas

un sándwich de jamón y queso

un bocadillo

una rebanada de pan

un pan dulce

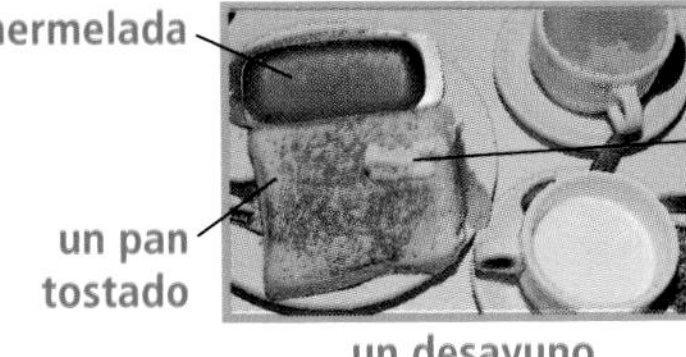

un desayuno

un croissant (Spain)

### DOS AMIGAS EN UN CAFÉ

*Dos amigas:* Two friends

**Ana:** Quisiera tomar un café. ¿Y tú?
**Clara:** Yo quisiera **comer algo.** (to eat something)
**Ana:** En **este** café **tienen** bocadillos, sándwiches y pasteles. (this / they have)
**Clara:** **Pues, voy a comer** un pastel, mm… con un café con leche. (Then, I'm going to eat)
**Ana:** Y **para mí** un sándwich de jamón y queso. (for me)

**un bocadillo:** sandwich made with a French roll; may have different fillings, such as cheese, ham, sausage, an omelette, etc.; most common in Spain

**un pan dulce:** any kind of sweet roll, cinnamon roll, danish, etc.; usually eaten with hot chocolate; this expression is commonly used in Mexico



## Etapa Support Materials

Workbook: **pp. 8–12**
Transparencies: **#12, #12a**
Listening Activity masters: **p. 3**
Tapescript: **p. 1**
Teacher Tape

Quiz: **Testing Program, p. 6**
Chapter Test: **Testing Program, p. 9**
Support material, ¡Vamos a comer algo!:
**Teacher Tape** **; transparencies #12, #12a**

## Presentation: ¡Vamos a comer algo!

With books closed, show students the transparency without the overlay. Have them repeat the items and order breakfast. Then repeat the process for lunch, adding the overlay if necessary. With books still closed, have students listen to the Teacher Tape. Then read each line of the dialogue again, having them repeat first as a whole class, then in groups, and then in pairs or individually.

Or, without the Teacher Tape, with books open, have students repeat the names of foods for breakfast and for lunch. Have several students order breakfast; then have several others order lunch. Finally act out the café scene, asking students to repeat as a whole class, then in groups, and then individually.

***Spanish speakers:*** Ask Spanish speakers for variations of the foods that are listed here. Though they may know how to pronounce these variations, many may never have seen how they are written. Help them with the spelling of these variations by writing them on the board or overhead. Point out those problematic spelling combinations like the **j** in **jamón; qu** in **queso; ll** in **bocadillo; y** in **desayuno;** the **qu** and **ll** in **mantequilla;** the **b** in **rebanada.** Don't forget to remind them of the written accent on such words as **sándwich** and **jamón.**

***Support material, ¡Vamos a comer algo!:*** Teacher Tape/CD #1 Track #5, transparencies #12, #12a

## Cultural Expansion

Point out that a typical breakfast consists of a cup of **café con leche** and a piece of bread or toast with butter and/or jam. Discuss the difference between an American sandwich and a **bocadillo** (**torta** in Mexico). Bread for this kind of sandwich is baked fresh two or three times a day in all parts of the Hispanic world.

**Ex. A:**  pair work

 role play

*Suggestions, Ex. A:* Have students work with their partners, telling them to vary their answers using **yo quisiera** or **yo voy a comer.** Or do the exercise as a whole class using the **pregúntale** format: **María, pregúntale a Juan el número uno,** etc.

*Variation, Ex. A:* After looking at the model, students close their books and make choices from the transparency.

**Ex. B:**  pair work

role play

 groups of four or more

*Suggestions, Ex. B:* Have students work in pairs, ordering several different breakfasts and lunches and alternating in the roles of the waiter and the customer. You could also have students work in groups of three or four, ordering several different meals and taking turns playing the waiter. Then have your Spanish-speaking students (or other volunteers) present their dialogues to the class.

*Suggestion, Ex. B:* More- and less-prepared students can present a longer dialogue together, with the number of lines varying accordingly among the students. Have them pretend to meet after class at a local restaurant, greet each other, introduce new students, talk about what they like, and order snacks and drinks. This would serve as preparaton for Ex. D.



# ¡Aquí te toca a ti!

**A. *¿Vas*** (Are you going) ***a comer algo?*** You and a friend are in a snack bar. Using the items suggested, decide what snack you will have.

un sándwich de queso / un sándwich de jamón
—*¿Vas a comer algo tú?*
— *Yo quisiera un sándwich de queso.*
— *Yo voy a comer un sándwich de jamón.*

1. un bocadillo de jamón / un bocadillo de queso
2. un pastel de fresas / un pastel de banana
3. un croissant / un pan dulce
4. un sándwich de queso / un sándwich de jamón y queso
5. un pan tostado / una rebanada de pan
6. un licuado de banana / un pan con mantequilla
7. un pan con mermelada / un pan dulce
8. un sándwich de jamón / un sándwich de queso

**B. *El desayuno*** You are having breakfast in a café in Condado, Puerto Rico. What would you like to order? Work with a partner and follow the model.

**Camarero(a):** *¿Qué desea, señor (señorita)?*
**Tú:** *Un café y un pan tostado, por favor.*

## Pronunciación: The vowel e

The sound of the vowel **e** in Spanish is pronounced like the *e* of the English word *bet* except that the sound is shorter in Spanish. Listen as your teacher models the difference between the Spanish **e** and the English *e* of *bet.*

## Práctica

**C.** Listen and repeat as your teacher models the following words.

| | |
|---|---|
| 1. que | 6. tres |
| 2. leche | 7. nene |
| 3. Pepe | 8. té |
| 4. este | 9. es |
| 5. café | 10. ese |



### Exercise Progression

Ex. A is a controlled exercise designed to practice the new vocabulary and the expressions **yo quisiera** and **yo voy a comer.** Ex. B provides an open-ended situation for conversational practice.

### Presentation: Pronunciation

Point out that just like the Spanish **a,** the Spanish **e** sounds more tense or clipped than the English *e.* Read the words in the **Práctica,** having students repeat first as a whole class, then in groups, and then individually.

Additional activities appear in the Laboratory Tape Program.

*Support material, Pronunciación:* Pronunciation Tape

## Repaso

**D. *Después de clase*** (After class) You are meeting a friend in a nearby café. She or he arrives with a person that you have never met before. (1) Greet your friend. (2) She or he introduces you to the new person, and the three of you sit down for a drink. (3) The waiter (waitress) comes and takes your orders. While you wait, (4) you ask the new person what things she or he likes to do. Work in groups of four, assigning each person the role of the first person, the friend, the new person, or the waiter (waitress).

**Learning Strategies:**

*Interviewing, participating in culturally appropriate social interactions*

## ESTRUCTURA

### The present tense of regular -ar verbs — first and second persons

| | |
|---|---|
| **Yo tomo** un refresco. | *I am drinking* a soft drink. |
| **Tú deseas** un bocadillo. | *You want* a sandwich. |
| **Ud. habla** con los amigos. | *You are talking* with your friends. |
| **Nosotros cantamos** en el café. | *We sing* in the café. |
| **Vosotros bailáis** bien. | *You dance* well. |
| **Uds. escuchan** música. | *You are listening* to music. |

### Subject pronouns

| Spanish | English |
|---|---|
| **yo** | *I* |
| **tú** | *you* (used when you are on a first-name basis) |
| **usted (Ud.)** | *you* (more formal, used with people you do not know very well, your superiors, and older people in general; it can be abbreviated to **Ud.**) |
| **nosotros(as)** | *we* (**nosotros** has a feminine form, **nosotras,** that is used when referring to a group of all women) |
| **vosotros(as)** | *you* (used with more than one person with whom you are on a first-name basis; like **nosotros,** it has a feminine form, **vosotras. Vosotros[as]** is used only in Spain.) |
| **ustedes (Uds.)** | *you* (used with more than one person; it can be abbreviated to **Uds.**) |

1. Verbs consist of two parts: a *stem,* which carries the meaning, and an *ending,* which indicates the subject or person the verb refers to.



Using gestures, establish the difference between the different pronouns: **yo, tú, nosotros,** and **ustedes.** Then, using gestures and verbs used earlier in the infinitive with **gustar,** form simple sentences and have students repeat them. Say a few sentences in the **yo** form, continue with a few in the **tú** form, and then with the **ustedes** and **nosotros** forms. Use cognates and pantomime as much as possible. Suggestions: **Yo canto en las fiestas. Yo bailo en las fiestas también. Tú escuchas música moderna. Tú estudias español.**

Explain the difference between **tú** and **usted** and give the plural forms of each one. Point out the abbreviations **Ud.** and **Uds.**

Should you choose not to use **vosotros,** point out to students that its forms are included in the charts and that they should be aware of its existence. Explain that its use is widespread in Spain, but that the **ustedes** form is more common worldwide and will be used in class.

*Spanish speakers:* Most students will know the present indicative tense, they just don't know what it is called. It is not necessary to focus on the specific names of the various grammatical components mentioned in the **Estructura** sections. With rare execeptions, few native speakers of *any* language know the grammatical names of the components of their language.

**Ex. D:**  groups of four or more

 role play

*Suggestion, Ex. D:* Explain the activity and allow groups five minutes to prepare. Then have two or three groups present their versions. This activity serves as a preparation for Ex. A in the **Ya llegamos** section at the end of Unit 1.

*More-prepared students, Ex. D:* Encourage students who presented a longer dialogue in Ex. B to resolve a problem this time in their dialogue.

### Presentation: Present tense of regular -ar verbs

Only first- and second-person forms are presented here in order to allow students to practice talking to each other before referring to other people. This way they can concentrate on the interplay between **tú/Ud.,** and **yo/Uds./nosotros.** The third-person form is presented in Chapter 2.

## Presentation: Regular -ar verbs, cont.

Make simple statements and then ask students related questions that are likely to elicit affirmative answers. For example: **Yo escucho la radio. ¿Tú escuchas la radio?** etc. Then, using gestures, continue with the plural forms. **Nosotros hablamos español. ¿Uds. hablan español?** Use the verbs from this page and as many cognates and gestures as possible. Once enough students have responded correctly, write the verb endings on the board and continue asking questions.

You may want to try a **pregúntale** exercise here. To make it easier for students, point to the correct form on the chalkboard when they are asking or responding to the questions. Example: **María, pregúntale a Juan si estudia español.** Ask your Spanish-speaking/more-prepared students first.

*Suggestions, Ex. E:* Do this exercise with the whole class (choral response) or have the students work in pairs. You may also want to have students write out the responses for practice. Then have them edit their partner's work for mistakes in spelling or verb endings.

2. In English, verb endings seldom change (with the exception of the third-person singular in the present tense—*I read,* but *she reads*). In Spanish, verb endings are very important, since each verb ending must agree in *person* (first, second, or third) and *number* (singular or plural) with its subject.
3. There are three types of Spanish verbs. One type ends in **-ar**.
4. To conjugate a regular **-ar** verb, drop the **-ar** and add the appropriate endings for each person: for example, look at the following conjugation of **tomar**.

| *Subject* | *Stem* | *Ending* | *Conjugated verb form* |
|---|---|---|---|
| yo | tom- | **-o** | tom**o** |
| tú | | **-as** | tom**as** |
| Ud. | | **-a** | tom**a** |
| nosotros(as) | | **-amos** | tom**amos** |
| vosotros(as) | | **-áis** | tom**áis** |
| Uds. | | **-an** | tom**an** |

Other verbs you already know that follow this form are: **bailar, cantar, desear, escuchar, estudiar, hablar, practicar,** and **tomar.** Two new **-ar** verbs are:

**trabajar** *(to work)* **viajar** *(to travel)*

The present tense is used in Spanish as the equivalent of *I dance, I am dancing,* and *I do dance* in English.

## Aquí practicamos

*E.* Replace the subjects in italics and make the necessary changes.

*Modelo:* *Yo* bailo mucho. (tú / usted / nosotros / vosotros)
*Tú bailas mucho.*
*Usted baila mucho.*
*Nosotros bailamos mucho.*
*Vosotros bailáis mucho.*

1. *Tú* cantas en el café. (usted / yo / nosotros / ustedes / vosotros)
2. *Nosotros* practicamos en la clase. (tú / usted / yo / ustedes / vosotras)
3. *Usted* habla español. (ustedes / yo / nosotras / tú / vosotras)
4. *Yo* viajo a México. (tú / usted / nosotros / ustedes / vosotros)
5. *Ustedes* estudian mucho. (yo / tú / usted / nosotras / vosotros)
6. *Nosotras* escuchamos música. (tú / yo / usted / ustedes / vosotras)



## Exercise Progression

Ex. E is a substitution drill designed to coordinate the subject-ending relationship in the student's mind. Ex. F is a personalized exercise that allows students to express themselves in an open-ended form.

**Ex. F:** pair work writing

*Suggestions, Ex. F:* Have students ask their partners questions with the cues provided. Encourage them to add different adverbs to vary their answers. This would also be a good writing exercise. Set a time limit and then have students check their partners' work for mistakes.

*Answers, Ex. F:* 1. Yo (no) canto muy bien. 2. ...hablo mucho. 3. ...practico el piano. 4. ...trabajo mucho. 5. ...escucho música rock. 6. ...hablo en clase. 7. ...estudio poco. 8. ...viajo a España.

### F. *¡Muy bien!* Say whether you do or do not do the following activities.

bailar bien
*Yo no bailo bien.* o:
*Yo bailo bien.*

1. cantar muy bien
2. hablar mucho
3. practicar el piano
4. trabajar mucho
5. escuchar música rock
6. hablar en clase
7. estudiar poco
8. viajar a España

## Palabras útiles

### Expressing frequency

The following words and phrases are used in Spanish to express how well or how often you do something.

| | | | |
|---|---|---|---|
| **bien** | well | **todos los días** | every day |
| **muy bien** | very well | **siempre** | always |
| **mal** | poorly | **a veces** | sometimes |

### G. *Hablo español todos los días.* Say how well or how often you engage in the following activities. Follow the model.

estudiar
*Yo estudio todos los días.*

1. hablar español
2. bailar
3. cantar en clase
4. estudiar
5. escuchar música popular
6. trabajar

### H. *Preguntas personales* (Personal questions) Answer the questions.

¿Cantas bien?
*No, canto mal.* o:
*Sí, canto bien.*

1. ¿Bailas mucho?
2. ¿Hablas español muy bien?
3. ¿Trabajas después de *(after)* clase?
4. ¿Estudias mucho o poco?
5. ¿Viajas todos los días a Nueva York?
6. ¿Escuchas música popular? ¿rock? ¿clásica?
7. ¿Cantas todos los días?
8. ¿Practicas el tenis?



*Spanish speakers:* Point out the **b** in **bien** and the **v** in **veces;** some speakers may use a variation of this expression, i.e., use **en veces** for **a veces.** The former may be totally appropriate in their speech community, the latter is simply another way to say the same thing.

**Ex. G:** pair work

writing

*Suggestion, Ex. G:* Do as a writing exercise by having six students write out the answer to one of the cues on the board, while the rest of the class does it at their seats. Have the class read the sentences on the board and point out any errors. Be sure to reinforce good points so that students do not feel embarrassed if they have made any mistakes.

*Answers, Ex. G:* 1. Yo hablo español... 2. Yo bailo... 3. Yo canto en clase... 4. Yo estudio... 5. Yo escucho música popular... 6. Yo trabajo...

**Ex. H:** pair work

writing

*Variation, Ex. H:* Divide the class into two teams and send a student from each team to the board. Read a question from the exercise and tell them if they should answer *yes* or *no.* The students at the board will write their answer as quickly and accurately as possible. The faster, more accurate team gets a point. If the answers are incorrect, students may hand off to another member of their team. Students at the board should be of similar ability.

## Exercise Progression

Exs. G and H are personalized exercises designed to give students practice in using the adverbs and phrases in the **Palabras útiles** section. Ex. I is also personalized, but gives students more open-ended practice of the same expressions. Ex. J reviews the **etapa** by allowing students to create their own conversation. Exercise K is a writing exercise designed to review vocabulary.

*Reteaching:* Students may benefit at this point from a short dictation exercise. If you dictate the six sample sentences on page 17, students can then correct their work themselves.

### Presentation: Palabras útiles

Review adverbs from the previous **etapa** by asking simple questions: **¿Estudias mucho o poco? ¿Viajan Uds. mucho o poco?** etc. Then create sentences with the new adverbs; have students repeat first as a whole class, then in groups, and then individually. **Yo hablo español bien. Yo hablo ruso mal.**

**Ex. I:** pair work

*More-prepared students, Ex. I:* Sit in front of the class and have more-prepared students "interview" you about your typical week for the school newspaper, asking you **Ud.** questions based on the various activities they have been practicing. This allows them to be creative at the same time that it reinforces the **Ud./yo** format.

*Less-prepared students, Ex. I:* Less-prepared students can sit with the interviewer, taking notes for a bilingual newspaper.

## Cultural Expansion

In Spanish-speaking countries, the typical breakfast (**desayuno**) consists of **café con leche** and **pan,** with butter and/or jam and sometimes cheese. A mid-morning snack or brunch (called the **almuerzo** in Mexico) is eaten between 10:30 and 12:00. People usually eat regional snacks or have **licuados** at this time. The main meal of the day is generally eaten between 1:30 and 3:30, and it is called the **comida** (Spain and Mexico) or **almuerzo** (South America and the Caribbean). There is usually a late afternoon snack between 5:00 and 6:00 called the **merienda** (called **once** in Chile), which usually consists of coffee or tea and pastry or regional sweets. Supper (**cena**) is normally a light meal of leftovers or regional foods, and perhaps a dessert such as fruit, cheese, **flan,** or **arroz con leche.**

**Critical Thinking Strategy:** *Comparing and contrasting*

**Learning Strategy:** *Reading for cultural information*

**I. Mi amigo(a) y yo** Talk with a classmate about what you each do in a typical week, and compare these activities with what your parents do. Using **-ar** verbs that you know, think of at least three pairs of examples in all. Follow the model.

**Modelos:**
*—Mi amigo y yo estudiamos mucho.*
*—Y nuestros padres trabajan mucho.*

*—Yo escucho música rock.*
*—Y mi madre escucha música clásica.*

## COMENTARIOS CULTURALES

### Las comidas

**In Spanish-speaking countries, there are usually cafés near schools and universities where students meet before or after class. It is very common to have a snack in the morning at about 11:00 and at about 6:00 or 7:00, because lunch and dinner are frequently served late. Lunch is around 2:00 in the afternoon, and dinner may be as late as 10:00 in the evening.**

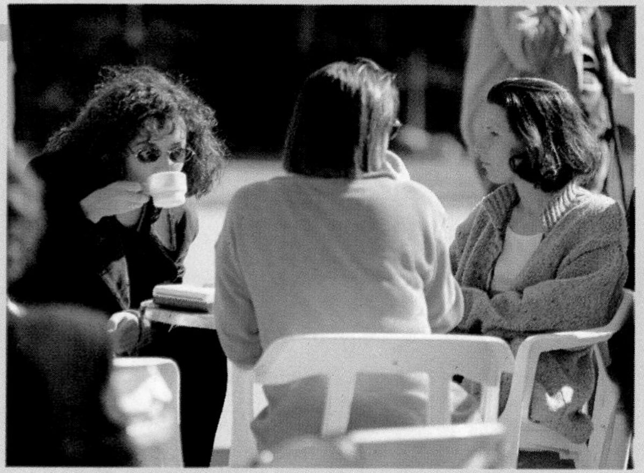

**Learning Strategy:** *Listening for details*

**Critical Thinking Strategy:** *Predicting*

## Aquí escuchamos:

### "¡A comer!"

**Luis and his friends are having a bite to eat at a café. Listen to their conversation and do the following exercises.**



*Spanish speakers:* Ask students what their eating habits are in this country. Perhaps some of them may still maintain some of the customs of the country where their family orginiated.

*Support material, **Aquí escuchamos:*** Teacher Tape/CD #1 Track #6  and Tapescript

## Antes de escuchar

**Based on what you have learned about food in this chapter, answer the following questions.**

1. **What are some of the things you expect Luis and his friends will order?**
2. **What question does the waiter or waitress usually ask when first taking your order?**

## Después de escuchar

**Take a moment to copy the following words on a separate sheet of paper. Indicate with a check mark what Luis and his friends ordered.**

| | | |
|---|---|---|
| croissant | pan tostado | pastel |
| pan dulce | sándwich | agua mineral |
| bocadillo | jugo | café |

EJERCICIO ORAL

**J. *La merienda*** (The snack) You go to a café at about 11:00 in the morning for a snack and run into a classmate whom you recognize, but whom you don't know very well. (1) Greet each other; then (2) order something to eat. While waiting for your food, (3) ask each other questions in order to get acquainted. Suggestions: Find out if the other person likes to (**¿te gusta... ?**) travel, dance, and sing, how well and how frequently (**bien, mal, mucho, todos los días, a veces, poco**), if he or she works, how often, and if he or she likes to work or not, etc.

EJERCICIO ESCRITO

**K. *¿Qué vamos a comer?*** Work with another classmate and plan a lunch for your friends and family. Make a list of everything that you are going to have to eat and drink.

*Learning Strategies:*

*Interviewing, listening for and providing information*

*Critical Thinking Strategy:*

*Comparing and contrasting*

*Learning Strategies:*

*Brainstorming, making plans*



### Aquí escuchamos

***Spanish speakers:*** Remember, most Spanish speakers, even those that are third or fourth generation, will understand spoken Spanish. The exercises that accompany this section should pose relatively little problem for Spanish speakers. They should, however, be directed to focus on "listening in context" to any vocabulary that may be new for them.

***Answers, Después de escuchar:*** sándwich, pan dulce, café, pastel

**Ex. J:**  pair work

 role play

***Suggestion, Ex. J:*** You play the waiter and first do one or two dialogues as a class. Then have students work with their partners. You may want them to write out their scripts and then practice them several times, varying their answers each time. Then have your Spanish-speaking students or other volunteers present their dialogues to the class.

***Less-prepared students, Ex. J:*** Less-prepared students could play the part of the waiter, perhaps writing their questions on a pad of paper, until they are comfortable with more extensive dialogue.

***Spanish speakers, Ex. J:*** Remember that most Spanish speakers already have a command of a variety of Spanish that is used in informal, very familiar contexts. This situation is a fairly informal one, but have the students focus on using vocabulary that may be new for them. Emphasize that it may be necessary to use such vocabulary when talking to speakers who are from other parts of the Spanish-speaking world. Again, remember to be sensitive and accept how the students say it the first time. What they have said may be totally appropriate in their speech community. This is a good place to have them focus on the differences between how they may say something in their speech community and how the book is teaching them to express this. Remember, rather than "correcting" how they speak, your main objective is to expand the range of real-world contexts in which these students can use Spanish.

**Ex. K:** writing

***Spanish speakers, Ex. K:*** Always have Spanish speakers fully carry out this activity. Remember, while many of them already speak and understand spoken Spanish, they may not know how to write the language. This is a good place to start building basic literacy skills in Spanish. Have them pay special attention to the spelling of the vocabulary that has been introduced in this **etapa,** especially those words that may have problematic spelling combinations. This is also a good place to have them engage in peer-editing. Have them look at the written work of a partner and focus on the spelling.

# Vocabulario

The **Vocabulario** includes high-frequency vocabulary that students have used in the chapter's exercises and activities. These words and expressions are found again in the comprehensive Glossary at the back of the book, along with other vocabulary found in the readings and realia. English translations are not included in the **Vocabulario.** This allows students to distinguish the words they know from those they do not remember.

*Spanish speakers:*
Point out the words with problematic spelling combinations that were highlighted on p. 20 of "To the Teacher" in the Teacher's Edition. Students could be encouraged to keep a special spelling notebook with various categories such as: **Palabras con ll, Palabras con v, Palabras con b,** etc. Another category might be headed with **Así lo digo yo** in order for students to work on the spelling of those words and expressions that they already know and that might be variations to what has been presented in the book.

The **Vocabulario** consists of all new words and expressions presented in the chapter. When reviewing or studying for a test, you can go through the list to see if you know the meaning of each item. In the glossary at the end of the book, you can check the words you do not remember.

## *Para charlar*

### *Para saludar*

Buenos días.
Buenas tardes.
Buenas noches.
¿Cómo estás?
¿Cómo te va?
¿Qué hay?
¿Qué pasó?
¿Qué tal?
¡Hola!

### *Para despedirse*

Adiós.
Chao.
Hasta luego.
Nos vemos.

### *Para contestar*

Buenos días.
Buenas tardes.
Buenas noches.
Bien, gracias. ¿Y tú?
Más o menos.
Muy bien, gracias.
Regular.
Bastante bien.
¡Hola!

### *Para expresar gustos*

(No) Me gusta...
(No) Te gusta...

### *Para presentar*

Te presento a...

### *Para contestar*

Mucho gusto.
¡Hola!

### *Para hablar en un restaurante*

¿Qué desea tomar?
¿Qué desean tomar?
Yo quisiera...
¿Y Ud.?
Voy a comer...
Aquí tienen.
Para mí...
¡Un refresco, por favor!
Vamos al café.
Vamos a tomar algo.

## Temas y contextos

### Bebidas

una botella de agua mineral
un café
un café con leche
un chocolate
una granadina (con agua mineral)
un jugo de naranja
un licuado de banana
una limonada
un refresco
un té
un té con leche
un té con limón
un vaso de agua (con limón)

### Comidas

un bocadillo
un croissant
un desayuno
mantequilla
mermelada
un pan dulce
un pan tostado
un pastel de fresas
una rebanada de pan
un sándwich de jamón y queso

## Vocabulario general

### Adverbios

a veces
bien
después
mal
muchísimo
mucho
muy
poco
siempre
todos los días

### Pronombres

yo
tú
usted (Ud.)
nosotros(as)
vosotros(as)
ustedes (Uds.)

### Sustantivos

un(a) camarero(a)
una merienda
música
un señor
una señora
una señorita

### Verbos

bailar
cantar
comer
desear
escuchar
estudiar
hablar
practicar
tomar
trabajar
viajar

### *Otras palabras* (words) *y expresiones*

algo
este
Gracias.
Muchas gracias.
pues

# Chapter Culminating Activities

You may want to play **el juego de las categorías** as a wrap-up exercise for practicing the vocabulary. You name a category (**saludos, respuestas, bebidas, comidas, adverbios, verbos,** etc.); with books closed, students write as many items as they can remember for each category. Give points for the most answers. Alternate version: students write words beginning with a certain letter. (For this chapter, **b, d, e, c,** and **t** are particularly good.)

Give a spelling dictation at this time to reinforce the sounds of the Spanish alphabet.

Have students make a list of the masculine nouns and another of the feminine nouns, including the articles.

***Support material, Capítulo 1:*** Improvised Conversation, Teacher Tape/CD #1 Track #7 and Tapescript; Lab Manual listening activities, Laboratory Program, Tapescript, and Teacher's Edition of the Workbook/Lab Manual

# Lectura cultural

Explain to students that it is common for us to take for granted the foods and products we see and use every day and to think of everything around us as typically "American." Point out the number of English's linguistic borrowings from the Spanish language, as well as food items from the Americas as described in this short reading. See how many students can name common food items that have their origins in other areas of the world.

*Spanish speakers:* Have the students go through each of the exercises in this section. Spanish-speaking students in foreign language classes already read English, for they have been educated in U.S. schools. However, as reading researchers have shown, the transfer of reading skills from one language to another is far from automatic. People must learn to read in each language. Special attention should be paid to having these students go through all of the exercises and activities that accompany the readings in this program. Once they have completed the activities, they might be asked to summarize the reading in Spanish in order to give them additional writing practice. They might also be required to keep a notebook with a special list of new vocabulary they might find in the reading selections.

## DE AMÉRICA A EUROPA: EL MAÍZ, EL TOMATE, LA PAPA

### Antes de leer

1. Look at the title of this brief reading and make a guess about its content.
2. Look at the pictures to help you confirm your guess.
3. What are the vegetables pictured?

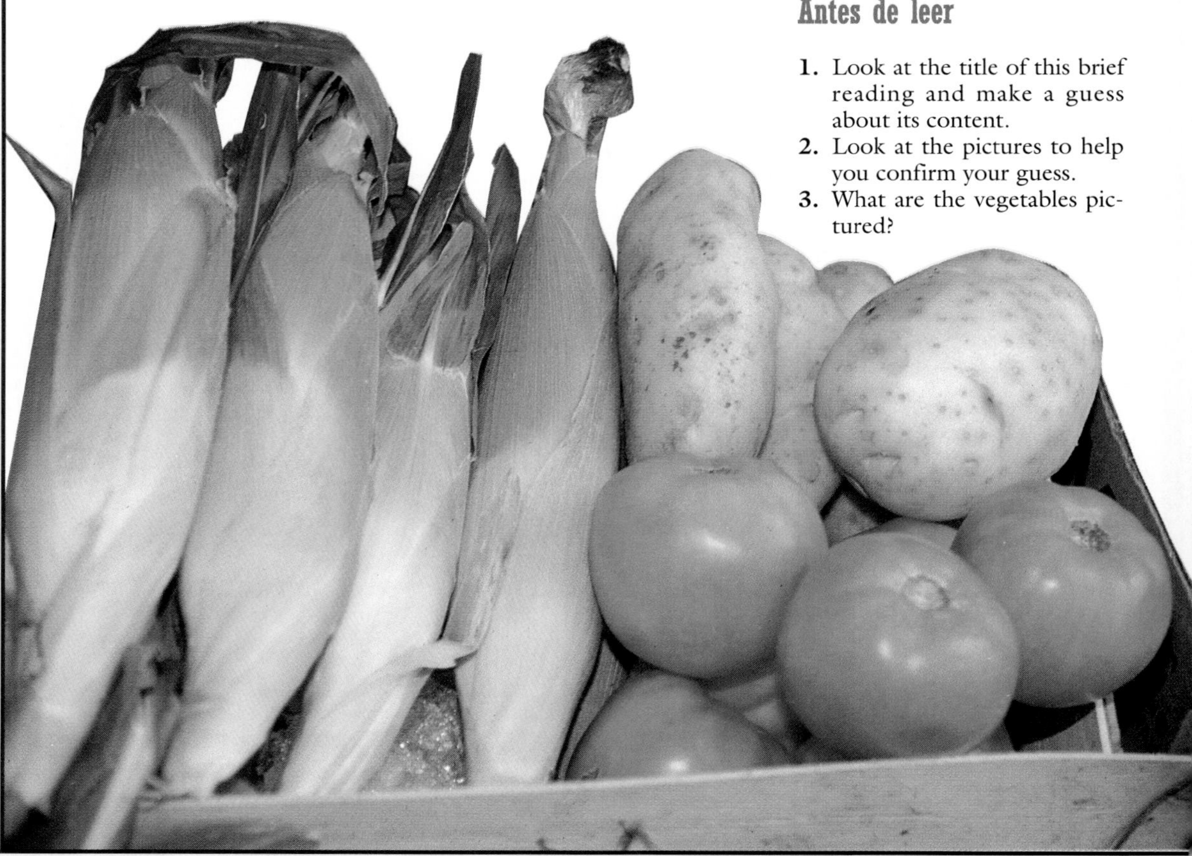

## Guía para la lectura

**A.** Now read the first paragraph quickly, skipping over any words you don't know, and answer the following questions.

1. What are the main food items featured?
2. How do you say them in Spanish?

**B.** Now read the second paragraph and list three countries that are mentioned.

**C.** Now write down on a piece of paper each vegetable and the country it came from.

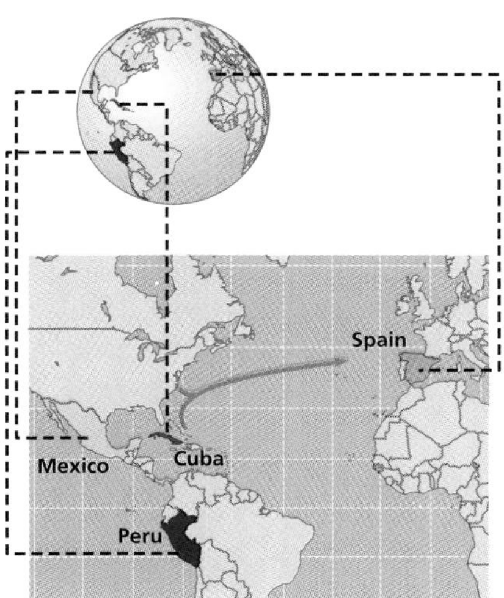


**Learning Strategies:**

*Skimming for gist, scanning for specific details*

### De América a Europa: El maíz, el tomate, la papa

Las comidas de muchas de las naciones de Europa tienen ingredientes de origen americano. En Francia, Italia, Inglaterra y España, por ejemplo, preparan platos especiales con productos típicos de las Américas. Muchas personas comen el maíz, el tomate y la papa todos los días.

En 1492 los españoles exploran el interior de Cuba. Hablan con los nativos que usan el maíz. Después, cuando los españoles llegan a México en 1519, comen el tomate con los aztecas. Otra de las plantas importantes de América es la papa, que tiene su origen en Perú.

## Chapter Objectives

**Functions:** Ordering something to eat; greeting, introducing, and leavetaking
**Context:** **Tapas** bars; meeting people
**Accuracy:** Present tense of regular **-ar** verbs (third person); asking and answering yes/no and tag questions; conjugated verb with infinitive

## Cultural Observation

Have students study the photo on this page. What type of establishment is this? Which foods do they recognize? Are they familiar with any of the foods pictured on p. 27?

*Spanish speakers:* Have Spanish speakers mention, in Spanish, what they see. Ask them what they see in the photos that might be similar to or different from their community.

CAPÍTULO 2

# ¡VAMOS A UN BAR DE TAPAS!

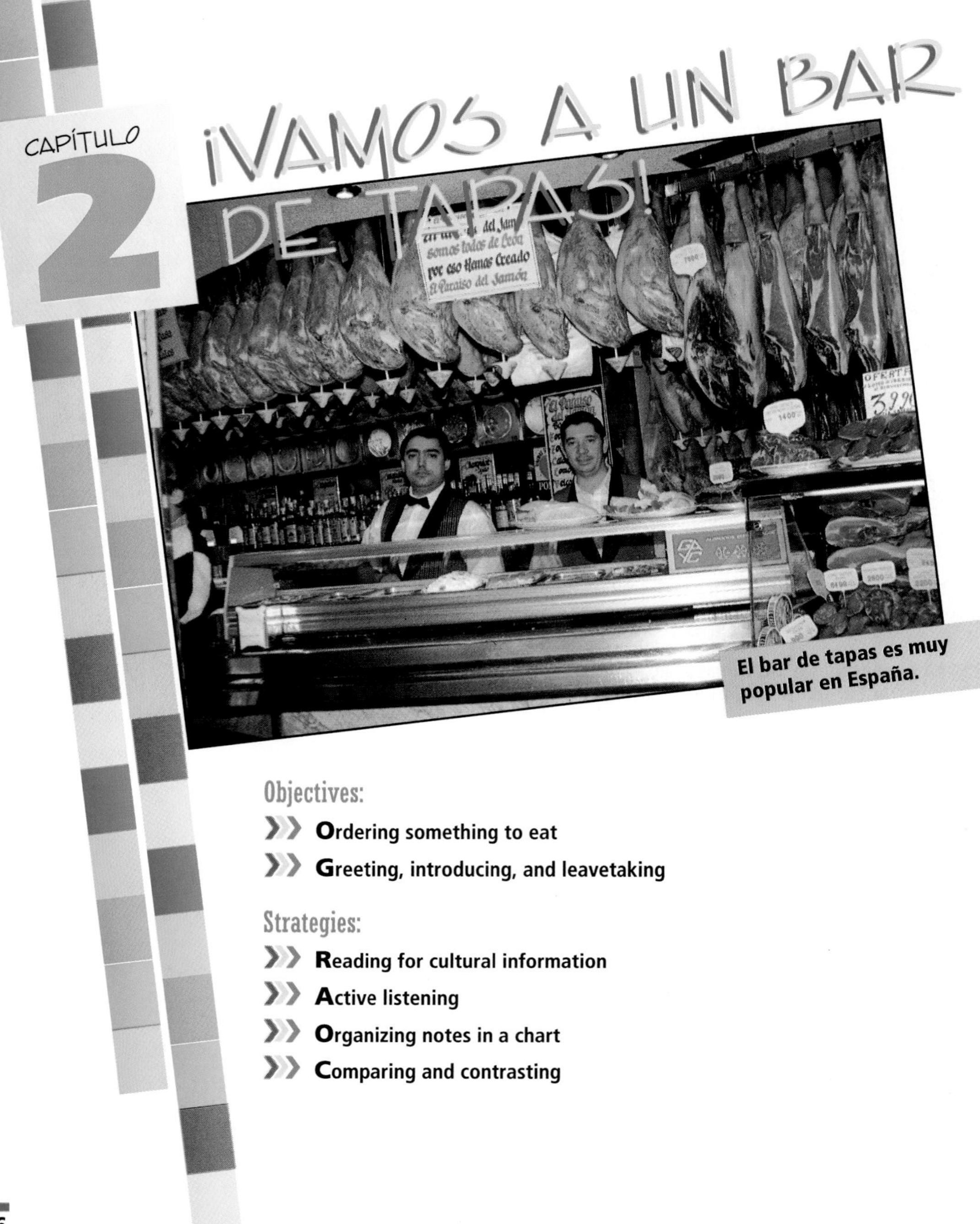

El bar de tapas es muy popular en España.

**Objectives:**

- **O**rdering something to eat
- **G**reeting, introducing, and leavetaking

**Strategies:**

- **R**eading for cultural information
- **A**ctive listening
- **O**rganizing notes in a chart
- **C**omparing and contrasting

26

## Video/CD-ROM

**Chapter 2 Video Program**
**Chapter 2 CD-ROM Program**

**These can be used at the end of the chapter as expansion activities.**

# PRIMERA ETAPA

## Preparación

» **As you noticed in Capítulo uno, people eat different kinds of food when it is time for a snack. Here are some typical snacks from Spain.**

» **Try to identify the different tapas in the picture. Do you recognize any of them?**

» **Have you ever had a tapa? Would you like to try this kind of snack? Why or why not?**

*Learning Strategies:*

*Previewing, supporting opinions*

*Critical Thinking Strategy:*

*Making judgments based on available information*

## Las tapas españolas

*Las tapas españolas:* Spanish snacks

pan con chorizo

calamares

aceitunas

queso

cacahuetes

patatas bravas

tortilla (de patatas)

**patatas bravas:** cooked potatoes diced and served in a spicy sauce

**tortilla (de patatas):** an omelette made with eggs, potatoes, and onions; served in small bite-sized pieces



Begin with a brief planning strategy, asking students what they eat after school if they are hungry. Then introduce the **tapas** with the transparency or point them out in the text. Ask simple questions that students will recognize: **¿Te gustan los cacahuetes? ¿Te gusta el queso?** Then explain what the other foods are.

Point out that the **tortilla** in the picture is called a **tortilla española** to distinguish it from the **tortilla** known in Mexico and Central America as a thin cornmeal pancake. **Chorizo** is a very spicy sausage similar in taste to pepperoni, but softer in texture. **Calamares** are served in many ways (marinated, in sauces, deep-fried, etc.) and are very popular.

*Spanish speakers:* Ask Spanish speakers if they are familiar with the foods that are listed here. Ask them what sorts of foods they and their families snack on. Point out to them that **chorizo** is spelled with a **z** and that **tortilla** is spelled with a **ll.**

This is also a good time to mention the basic differences between **tortilla** in Spain and **tortilla** in Mexico where they can be made of flour (**harina**) or corn (**maíz**). The corn **tortillas** can also be made of various types of corn: blue, yellow, white.

*Support material, Las tapas españolas:* Transparencies #13, #13a

### Vocabulary Expansion

**Cacahuetes** (or **cacahuates**) is used for peanuts in Spain, Mexico, and Central America; **maní** is used in South America and the Caribbean. **Patata** is potato in Spain; **papa** is used in the Americas.

## Etapa Support Materials

Workbook: pp. 13–19
Critical Thinking Master: p. 1
Transparencies: #13, #13a
Quiz: Testing Program, p. 14

Support material, Las tapas españolas: Transparencies #13, #13a

### Presentation: Las tapas españolas

As you saw in Chapter 1, there are different kinds of food people eat when it is time for a snack. In the picture you will see some typical snacks from Spain. Try to identify the different **tapas** in the picture. Do you recognize any of them? Have you ever had a **tapa**? Would you like to try this kind of snack? Why or why not? Do we have anything similar to a **tapas** bar in the United States?

**Ex. A:** pair work

role play

**Ex. B:**  pair work

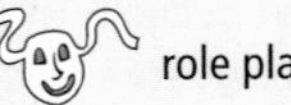
role play

*Answers, Ex. B:* All answers will follow the same format: **No, pasa... , por favor.**

*Variation, Ex. B:* Have students ask their partners questions with the foods using **o.** Example: **¿Deseas la tortilla o las patatas? ¿Deseas los cacahuetes o las aceitunas?** They answer with their preference. You may want to do a few of these with the whole class first.

**Ex. C:**  groups of four or more

role play

*Suggestion, Ex. C:* Tell students to use foods that others in their group haven't already chosen. Suggest that they also order drinks. Then have volunteer groups present their dialogues to the class.

*Less-prepared students, Ex. C:* Less-prepared students might benefit from a quick review of Chapter 1 vocabulary from transparencies, for example. They could then design a menu to be used during the dialogues in this exercise.

*More-prepared students, Ex. C:* More-prepared students could select a number of **tapas** and brainstorm their possible ingredients, and then find actual recipes to share with the class.



# ¡Aquí te toca a ti!

**A. *¡Camarero(a), más* (more) *aceitunas, por favor!*** You are in a **bar de tapas** with your friends, and you want to order more **tapas**. Ask the waiter or waitress to bring you some.

aceitunas
*Camarero(a), más aceitunas, por favor.*

1. cacahuetes
2. tortilla
3. patatas bravas
4. aceitunas
5. pan con chorizo
6. queso
7. calamares

**B. *Pasa* (Pass) *las patatas, por favor.*** The **tapas** that you want to eat are too far away from you. Ask your friend to pass them to you. Work in pairs and follow the model.

Modelo:
**Amigo(a):** ¿Deseas la tortilla? (las patatas)
**Tú:** *No, pasa las patatas, por favor.*

1. ¿Deseas los cacahuetes? (las aceitunas)
2. ¿Deseas el queso? (el chorizo)
3. ¿Deseas la tortilla de patatas? (el pan)
4. ¿Deseas los calamares? (la tortilla)
5. ¿Deseas las aceitunas? (el queso)
6. ¿Deseas el chorizo? (las patatas bravas)
7. ¿Deseas el pan? (los calamares)

**C. *¡Qué hambre!* (I'm starving!)** You are very hungry and want something more to eat than **tapas.** What do you order? Work in groups of four. One person is the waiter or waitress and the others are customers. Take turns ordering something to eat. Use some of the vocabulary that you already know from **Capítulo uno.** Follow the model.

**Camarero(a):** *¿Qué desean comer?*
**Tú:** *Yo quisiera un sándwich de jamón y queso.*

## Pronunciación: The vowel *i*

The sound of the vowel **i** in Spanish is pronounced like the *ee* of the English word *beet,* except it is shorter in Spanish. Listen as your teacher models the sound for you.



## Exercise Progression

Exs. A and B offer controlled practice of the new vocabulary. Ex. C provides a more open-ended situation in which to practice ordering these new food items.

### Presentation: Pronunciation

Point out that the Spanish **i** is like the Spanish **a** and the Spanish **e**, in that the sound is more tense and clipped than the English vowels. Point this out by contrasting the difference between the *i* sound of the English word *see* and the sound in the Spanish word **sí**. Other examples: *dee*/**di**; *me*/**mi**; *tea*/**ti**; *knee*/**ni.**

*Spanish speakers, Ex. D:* Point out the **h** in **hija,** the **z** in **tiza,** the **ll** in **silla,** and **allí** as well as the accent mark on **sí** and **allí.**

Additional activities appear in the Laboratory Program.

*Support material, Pronunciación:* Pronunciation Tape

# Práctica

*D.* Listen and repeat as your teacher models the following words for you.

| | | | |
|---|---|---|---|
| 1. sí | 4. allí | 7. hija | 10. tiza |
| 2. mi | 5. y | 8. mochila | 11. Lili |
| 3. silla | 6. mira | 9. ti | 12. libro |

## COMENTARIOS CULTURALES

### Las tapas

In Spain, one of the most popular meeting places for friends is the **bar de tapas.** Spaniards commonly stop in these places after work or before dinner for a snack and something to drink. These snacks are called **tapas** and include such things as peanuts, olives, cheese, and bite-sized pieces of **tortilla.** Sometimes these **tapas** are provided at no charge with each beverage order. More substantial food, such as **bocadillos** and different kinds of fried fish, can also be ordered. **La Chuleta** is one of the better-known **tapas** bars in Madrid.

*Learning Strategy:*

*Reading for cultural information*

# Repaso

*E.* ***Mis actividades*** (My activities) Say whether or not you do the following activities. If you do them, say how often or how well.

cantar
*Yo no canto muy bien.*

| | | |
|---|---|---|
| 1. trabajar | 4. cantar | 7. hablar español |
| 2. escuchar música | 5. hablar inglés | 8. estudiar matemáticas |
| 3. viajar | 6. bailar | |

*F.* ***Una conversación en un café*** You and two other students meet in a café for a snack. One of you should make introductions. Then place your order. While waiting for the waiter or waitress to bring your food and beverages, ask each other questions about the things you like to do. On a signal from your teacher, end your conversation and say good-bye.

**¿Qué crees?**

**In Spain, a typical breakfast would be:**

**a) bacon and eggs**
**b) coffee and toast**
**c) pancakes with hot syrup**

**respuesta**

**Ex. E:** pair work

***Suggestions, Ex. E:*** Do as a **pregúntale** exercise, asking questions with the cues but adding adverbs. Example: **María, pregúntale a Juan si viaja mucho o poco.** Or have students ask their partners similar questions, using the cues and adding adverbs.

***Follow-up, Ex. E:*** You may want to practice **Uds./nosotros** questions before beginning the third person of **-ar** verbs. Ask **Uds.** questions using the cues or other vocabulary that students will recognize.

**Ex F:**  groups of three

 role play

***Suggestion, Ex. F:*** You or any Spanish-speaking/more-prepared students in class should model for students before they work with their classmates. Then divide students into groups of three. Have them do the conversation a few times to allow each group member to play a different part. You could circulate around the room and play the part of the waiter, or possibly the manager, asking how the meal is, how everyone is doing, etc.

## Cultural Expansion

ecause mealtimes are so late in Spain, **tapas** are an impor- nt part of the Spanish diet, normally eaten between the two ain meals of the day: lunch and dinner. Traditional **tapas** bars e called **tascas** and they are favorite places for friends to ather. Some **tascas** serve only one or two different **tapas,** ut others offer a variety of dishes that are usually placed at e bar in earthenware dishes.

Explain to students that Spanish cuisine is very different om Mexican cuisine. It is Mediterranean and uses many ingre- ents found in Greek or Italian cooking, especially olive oil.

Ask students if they have ever heard of **paella** or **gazpacho,** two common regional dishes known worldwide.

***Spanish speakers:*** Ask students about snacks that are typical in their respective communities. Sometimes Spanish speakers refer to these foods as **algo para picar** (something to nibble on). Some common snacks may be **quesadillas, nachos, tostadas,** and **salsa** among students of Mexican ancestry; fried plantains called **tostones** among Cubans and Puerto Ricans; thin corn cakes filled with cheese, meat, or other fillings called **pupusas** among Salvadorans.

## Presentation: Regular -ar verbs, third person

Begin by doing a quick oral drill on third-person subject pronouns. Repeat the gestures you used previously to explain **yo, tú, ustedes,** and **nosotros.** Then establish references for **él, ella, ellos,** and **ellas.** Substitute pronouns for proper names, pointing to different members of the class: **Alicia–ella, José–él, María y Ana–ellas, Juan y Jorge–ellos,** etc. Point out that a large group of females with only one male would still be substituted with the pronoun **ellos.**

Then ask simple **tú** questions, such as **¿Cantas tú bien? ¿Estudias tú mucho?,** etc. Summarize using third-person forms. **María canta bien. Ella canta bien.,** etc. Continue with **ustedes** questions. **¿Uds. viajan mucho o poco? ¿Uds. hablan español bien?** Point to two or three students as you direct these questions and then have one answer as a spokesperson for the others. **Viajamos poco. No hablamos español bien.,** etc. Then summarize. **Alicia y Jorge viajan poco. Ellos viajan poco.,** etc.



# ESTRUCTURA

## *The present tense of regular -ar verbs — third person*

1. ¿Miguel? **Él viaja** mucho.

2. ¿Anita? **Ella habla** español muy bien.

3. ¿Jaime y Tomás? **Ellos cantan** bien.

4. ¿Paquita y Laura? **Ellas no estudian** mucho.

b

5. ¿Juan y Clara? **Ellos bailan.**

## Subject pronouns

| Spanish | English |
|---|---|
| **él** | *he* |
| **ella** | *she* |
| **ellos** | *they* (two or more males or a group of males and females) |
| **ellas** | *they* (two or more females) |

1. To form the present tense of an **-ar** verb in the third person, add the appropriate ending to the stem. Remember, the stem is found by dropping the ending **(-ar)** from the infinitive **(estudiar — estudi-).**

2. You will notice that the endings for **él, ella, ellos,** and **ellas** are the same as those used for the formal second persons, **usted** and **ustedes.**

| Subject | Ending | Conjugated verb form | |
|---|---|---|---|
| | | **trabajar**<br>**trabaj-** | **escuchar**<br>**escuch-** |
| él | **-a** | trabaj**a** | escuch**a** |
| ella | **-a** | trabaj**a** | escuch**a** |
| ellos | **-an** | trabaj**an** | escuch**an** |
| ellas | **-an** | trabaj**an** | escuch**an** |

Some additional **-ar** verbs and expressions are:

**ganar (dinero)** (*to earn [money]*)
**mirar** (*to look at, to watch*)
**tocar** (*to touch, to play an instrument*)

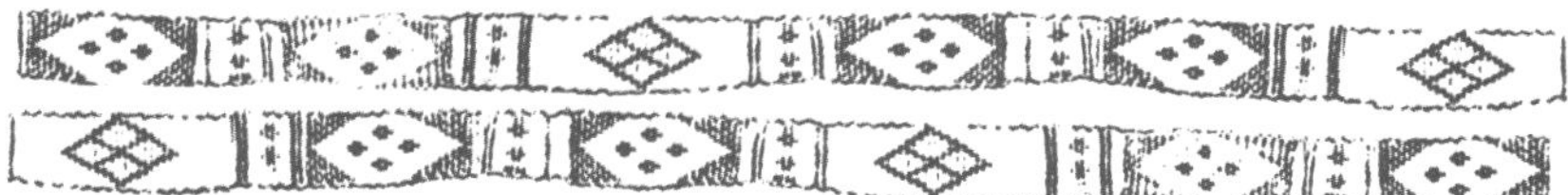



## Presentation: Regular -ar verbs, cont.

Write the pronouns and verb forms on the board. Then make up sentences and have students repeat first as a whole class, then in groups, and then individually. Example: **Uds. estudian mucho. Los profesores trabajan mucho,** etc. Continue by having students change sentences from the singular to the plural. Suggestions: **Ella baila muy bien. Él mira la televisión mucho. Ud. escucha música clásica.**

Point out that **Ud.** and **Uds.** use third-person forms. The origin of **Ud.** is **Vd.,** an abbreviation for **Vuestra Merced,** a term that was used in addressing royalty or the aristocracy. It is now used formally to show respect.

After students have practiced third-person endings sufficiently, review the first and second person again by asking simple questions. Then have them change simple statements from the singular to the plural. Remind them that the plural of the **tú** form is the **Uds.** form, unless you have chosen to use the **vosotros** form.

***Suggestion, Ex. G:*** These column exercises are meant to provide controlled practice. A possible way to present these would be through the creation of a "word web." On a separate piece of paper, students would draw a web, and then connect elements from the columns in ways that form grammatically correct sentences. (They would have to write in the correct form of the verb in the middle column.) See the diagram below for a sample word web format. Word web formats will vary from exercise to exercise.

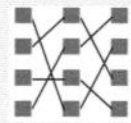

***Suggestion, Ex. G:*** You can personalize this activity by having students use people they know as the subjects for these sentences. Provide a list of examples on the board: **Mis padres, mi hermano(a), mis amigos(as), mi familia y yo, mis amigos y yo.**

***Follow-up, Ex. G:*** Students who learn better by listening could benefit from a guessing game. The teacher can describe a member of the class—**Esta persona canta en el coro y practica la música todos los días**—and students can guess who is being described. More-prepared students can do some of the descriptions themselves.

**Ex. H:**  pair work

 writing

# Aquí practicamos

**G. *Las actividades*** Describe the activities of the people in the left-hand column by forming sentences with phrases from the other two columns.

| A | B | C |
|---|---|---|
| ellos | cantar | en un café |
| yo | hablar | una limonada |
| Juan y Alicia | trabajar | en clase |
| vosotras | escuchar | inglés |
| Carlos | mirar | dinero |
| Patricia y yo | bailar | música clásica |
| ustedes | tomar | todos los días |
| tú | viajar | en casa |
| ellos | desear | patatas bravas |
| el señor Suárez | estudiar | a Madrid |
| el (la) profesor(a) | practicar | la televisión |
| mis hermanos | necesitar | |

**H. *Mis amigos colombianos*** (My Colombian friends) Your Colombian friends have some questions for you and your classmates. Answer their questions using subject pronouns and the expressions in parentheses. Follow the model.

¿John habla español mucho? (poco)
*No, él habla español poco.*

1. ¿Jack baila muy poco? (muchísimo)
2. ¿Nancy y Kay estudian poco? (mucho)
3. ¿Helen trabaja todos los días? (a veces)
4. ¿Julie y Tom viajan mucho? (poco)
5. ¿Ed y Andy escuchan música clásica todos los días? (a veces)
6. ¿Lisa gana mucho? (muy poco)

### *Asking and answering yes/no questions*

| | |
|---|---|
| **¿Tú estudias** mucho? | *Do you study* a lot? |
| **Sí, yo estudio** mucho. | *Yes, I study* a lot. |



***Suggestions, Ex. H:*** You may want to do this first as a **pregúntale** exercise to make sure that students substitute the subject pronouns correctly. Then have students ask their partners the questions for extra practice. Point out that one of the purposes of this exercise is to practice the subject pronouns.

***Answers, Ex. H:*** 1. No, él baila muchísimo. 2. ...ellas estudian... 3. ...ella trabaja... 4. ...ellos viajan... 5. ...ellos escuchan... 6. ...ella gana...

## Exercise Progression

Ex. G provides creative practice in forming complete sentences and making meaningful statements about people. Ex. H offers controlled practice with the third-person verb endings and the subject pronouns.

***Reteaching:*** Following practice with Ex. H, students could review **gustar** by repeating the exercise, and adding information: **No, Jack baila muchísimo. Le gusta mucho bailar.** Be sure to tell students how to use **le** and **les** in their statements.

**Sr. y Sra. García:** Buenos días, Lucas.
**Lucas:** ¡Oh! Buenos días, señor García. Buenos días, señora. **¿Cómo están ustedes?** — How are you?
**Sra. García:** Muy bien, gracias. ¿Y tú?
**Lucas:** **Estoy** muy bien, gracias. **Quisiera presentarles a mi amigo** Jaime Torres. El señor y la señora García. — I am / I would like to introduce you to my friend
**Sr. y Sra. García:** Mucho gusto, Jaime.
**Jaime:** **Encantado,** señora. Mucho gusto, señor. — Delighted
**Sr. García:** ¿**Van a** tomar un café? — Are you going to
**Lucas:** No, **acabamos de** tomar unos refrescos. — we've just finished
**Sr. García:** ¡Ah! Pues, hasta luego. **Saludos a tus padres.** — Greetings to your parents.
**Lucas:** Gracias.
**Lucas y Jaime:** Adiós, señor, señora.
**Sr. y Sra. García:** Adiós.

| *Saludos* | *Presentación* |
|---|---|
| Buenos días. | Quisiera presentarles(le) a... |
| ¿Cómo están ustedes? | Encantado(a). |
| ¿Cómo está usted? | |
| (Estoy) Bien, gracias. ¿Y Ud.? | |

*Presentación:* Introduction

## COMENTARIOS CULTURALES

### *Saludos informales y formales*

When greeting people and making introductions, there are expressions that denote different degrees of formality or informality: **¡Hola!, ¿Qué tal?, ¿Cómo estás?, ¿Cómo te va?, Te presento a...** are used informally with people you know well and with peers. **¿Cómo está usted?, ¿Cómo están ustedes?, Quisiera presentarles(le) a...** are more formal and are used with older people or people you do not know very well. It is not uncommon for older people or superiors to speak informally to a younger person who addresses them as **usted,** as you saw in the conversation between Lucas, Jaime, and señor and señora García.

*Learning Strategy:*

*Reading for cultural information*

37

When practicing greetings and introductions, you will probably wish to have students use **tú** when talking among themselves, and **Ud.** when speaking to you. For more practice with the formal expressions, designate several students to play "older people." It would help (and be more fun) to give each "older person" a prop (hat, briefcase) that signals his/her new identity.

Explain that when someone has been introduced to you and says either **Encantado/Encantada** or **Mucho gusto**, an appropriate response would be **Igualmente.** Other expressions: **Tanto gusto. El gusto es mío. ¿Cómo le va?** (formal version of **¿Cómo te va?**)

*Spanish speakers:* Ask students for variations of the **Saludos informales y formales** presented in the **Comentarios culturales.** Help them with the spelling of these variations by writing them on the board or overhead. Point out that their **saludos** and **despedidas** are some of the many, many ways that Spanish speakers have to say hello and good-bye to each other.

## Vocabulary Expansion

Take this opportunity to stress the importance of recognizing and respecting levels of language. With the help of students, make the following lists on the board: expressions (and gestures) that go along with **tú,** with **Ud.,** and with both **tú** and **Ud.** Some expressions will include the words **tú** or **Ud.** (**¿Cómo está Ud.? ¿Cómo estás?,** etc.) and others will not (**¿Qué tal? ¿Cómo te va?**).

**Ex. A:** pair work

*Follow-up, Ex. A:* Review other phrases from Chapter 1, addressing the students randomly. Encourage them to vary their responses as much as possible.

**Ex B:**  groups of three

*Suggestions, Ex. B:*
Divide the class into groups of three, telling them to practice the exercise several times, varying their roles and answers each time. You may want to expand the exercise by choosing several students to play the role of "older persons" (as suggested on p. T37). Students will thus have the opportunity to switch levels of language as they work their way around the class.

### Presentation: Pronunciation

Continue to emphasize the tense clipped nature of the Spanish vowels. Point this out by contrasting the difference of the sound in the English word *no* and that of the Spanish word **no.** Other examples: *low*/**lo**; *tow*/**to**; *sew*/**so**; *poe*/**po**; *bow*/**bo.**

*Spanish speakers, Ex. C:*
Point out to the students the **j** of **ojo** and **jugo;** the **z** of **chorizo;** the **v** of **vaso.**

Additional activities appear in the Laboratory Tape Program.



## ¡Aquí te toca a ti!

*A.* ***¿Qué respondes?*** (What do you answer?) Complete the conversation with an appropriate expression, and don't forget to address the person in parentheses by name. Follow the model.

*Modelo:* Buenos días, Alberto. (Sr. Pérez)
*Buenos días, señor Pérez.*

1. ¿Cómo estás, Adela? (Sr. Carrillo)
2. ¡Hola, Lourdes! (Sra. Ramírez)
3. Quisiera presentarle a mi amigo Pepe. (Sra. Ruiz)
4. ¿Cómo están ustedes, señores? (Margarita)
5. Mucho gusto, Raquel. (Sra. Castillo)

*B.* ***Buenos días, señor (señora, señorita).*** Greet and shake hands with your teacher, introduce a classmate to him or her, and then say good-bye.

## Pronunciación: *The vowel o*

The sound of the vowel **o** in Spanish is pronounced like the *o* in the English word *open,* except it is much shorter in Spanish. Listen as your teacher models the difference between the English *o* and the Spanish **o.**

### Práctica

*C.* Listen and repeat as your teacher models the following words.

| | | | |
|---|---|---|---|
| 1. ojo | 4. chorizo | 7. jugo | 10. vaso |
| 2. con | 5. año | 8. política | 11. nosotros |
| 3. algo | 6. como | 9. por | 12. disco |

## Repaso

*D.* ***Escuchen bien.*** (Listen carefully.) Play the roles of the following students and enact their conversation according to the model. Anita asks Marcos a question. After Marcos answers, Claudia asks Ada what he said. If Ada has been listening, she should be able to answer with no problem.

 hablar inglés
**Anita:** *Marcos, ¿tú hablas inglés?*



### Exercise Progression

Ex. A is a controlled exercise designed to practice using the expressions. Ex. B offers some limited open-ended communicative practice.

**Marcos:** *No, yo no hablo inglés.*
**Claudia:** *Ada, ¿habla inglés Marcos?*
**Ada:** *No, él no habla inglés.*

1. tocar la guitarra
2. tomar café con leche todos los días
3. viajar a Bolivia
4. bailar muy bien
5. mirar mucho la TV
6. estudiar francés *(French)*
7. cantar muy mal
8. trabajar muchísimo

**E. Mi amigo(a)** In pairs, (1) ask questions of your partner in order to gather information about him or her. Then (2) create a profile of the two of you on a grid like the one below. Put an *X* under each activity that each of you does well or often. (3) Prepare to report on your similarities and differences. Copy the grid on a separate sheet of paper.

| | hablar | estudiar | cantar | bailar | viajar | trabajar | tocar |
|---|---|---|---|---|---|---|---|
| yo | | | | | | | |
| mi amigo(a) | | | | | | | |

**Modelo:** —*Carmencita, cantas bien, ¿verdad?*
—*Sí, canto bien.*

*Mi amiga Carmencita canta bien. Yo no canto bien, pero bailo muy bien.*

*Cooperative Learning*

*Learning Strategy:*
*Active listening*

*Critical Thinking Strategy:*
*Comparing and contrasting*

## ESTRUCTURA

### The conjugated verb followed by an infinitive

**Ellas necesitan estudiar** mucho. — *They need to study* a lot.
**¿Deseas trabajar?** — *Do you want to work?*
**¿Quisieras bailar?** — *Would you like to dance?*

1. When there are two verbs in the same sentence or in the same part of a sentence, the first verb is conjugated (that is, made to agree with the subject), but the second verb remains in the infinitive form. This construction occurs frequently with some verbs and expressions you already know: **desear** and **yo quisiera,** for example. It also occurs with these new verbs and expressions:

**acabar de** *(to have just done something)*
**necesitar** *(to need)*
**tú quisieras** *(you would like)*

39

### Presentation: The conjugated verb followed by an infinitive

*Reminder:* The word **quisieras** is introduced here as a vocabulary item. There is no need to explain tense or mood at this point. You can introduce this structure by asking simple questions with verbs learned in Chapter 1. **¿Te gusta bailar? ¿Quisieras bailar? ¿Deseas bailar?** Continue with statements and have students repeat. Examples: **Me gusta hablar español. Uds. desean hablar español bien. Yo quisiera hablar francés también.,** etc. Then write a few sentences on the board to show the two verbs. Point out the conjugated verbs and the infinitive forms. Explain that only the first verb is conjugated.

Practice a few sentences with **acabar de.** Explain that it is an idiomatic expression and that they should not try to translate it. Examples: **Nosotros acabamos de practicar los verbos. El profesor García acaba de viajar a España.,** etc.

*Spanish speakers:* The grammatical terminology doesn't need to be emphasized for Spanish-speaking students. The important concept to remember is that you conjugate the first verb and leave the second one in the form that ends in **-r**.

**Ex. D:**  groups of four or more

*Answers, Ex. D:* Some answers may vary. Examples: 1. Anita: Marcos, ¿tú tocas la guitarra?; Marcos: No, yo no toco la guitarra.; Claudia: Ada, ¿toca la guitarra Marcos?; Ada: No, él no toca la guitarra. 2. Anita: Marcos, ¿tú tomas café con leche todos los días?; Marcos: No, yo no tomo café con leche todos los días.; Claudia: Ada, ¿toma Marcos café con leche todos los días?; Ada: No, él no toma café con leche todos los días. Follow this pattern for numbers 3–8.

**Ex. E:** pair work

*Suggestion, Ex. E:* Have the pairs regroup by four or six to report the similarities and differences recorded on their grids.

**Ex. F:** pair work

***Suggestion, Ex. F:*** Have students work with their partners. Encourage them to be creative in their answers and to try to practice vocabulary that they have learned thus far. Remind them that the purpose of this exercise is to practice **quisiera** and that they should use it in all of their questions and answers.

**Ex. G:**  pair work

 groups of four or more

***Suggestion, Ex. G:*** Ask two or three pairs to do the first several items on the grid before having students work on their own. Answers will vary but will all contain the **yo** form of the verbs. Partners' responses will all contain a **también** in affirmative statements and a **tampoco** in negative statements, according to the model. Have the pairs regroup by four or six to report the similarities and differences recorded on their grids. Give students time to refine and present as skits to the class.



**2.** The words **tampoco** *(neither)* and **también** *(also)* are often used to confirm what someone has just said:

| | |
|---|---|
| **—Deseo bailar.** | **—No deseo estudiar.** |
| **—Deseo bailar también.** | **—No deseo estudiar tampoco.** |

## Aquí practicamos

**Learning Strategy:**

*Interviewing*

**F. *¿Quisieras tú...?*** At a party, you try to impress a boy or a girl whom you like by asking in Spanish if he or she would like to do certain things. Use the suggested expressions to form your questions. He or she can answer either affirmatively or negatively.

comer algo *(something)*
—*¿Quisieras comer algo?*
—*Sí, quisiera comer unas patatas bravas.* o:
—*No, quisiera bailar.*

1. bailar
2. cantar
3. escuchar música española *(Spanish)*
4. tomar algo
5. hablar español
6. comer unas tapas

**Cooperative Learning**

**Learning Strategies:**

*Active listening, organizing notes in a chart*

**Critical Thinking Strategy:**

*Comparing and contrasting*

**G. *¿Deseas o necesitas?*** Copy the following grid on a separate sheet of paper. Then indicate whether you want or need to do the following activities. Mark your decisions by placing an *X* in each appropriate space for each *yes* response. Then check with your classmate to see if he or she wants or needs to do the same things. If your classmate gives the same positive response as you, he or she will add **también** to the answer. If your classmate gives the same negative response as you, he or she will add **tampoco.** Look at the models for examples. Be prepared to report (1) one activity you both want to do, (2) one you both need to do, (3) one that neither one of you wants to do, and (4) one that neither of you needs to do.

**Gathering information:** estudiar
—*Necesito estudiar.*
—*Yo necesito estudiar también.* o:
—*No deseo estudiar.*

—*No necesito estudiar.*
—*Yo sí necesito estudiar.* o:
—*Yo no deseo estudiar tampoco.*

## Exercise Progression

This structure builds primarily on what students already know (i.e., the conjugation of regular **-ar** verbs and the expression **quisiera**), so Exs. F–H provide meaningful and controlled practice using the infinitives.

| | Yo necesito... | Yo deseo... | Mi amigo(a) necesita... | Mi amigo(a) desea... |
|---|---|---|---|---|
| viajar a Sud *(South)* América | | | | |
| hablar español | | | | |
| tomar un refresco | | | | |
| trabajar mucho | | | | |
| tocar el piano | | | | |
| mirar la TV | | | | |
| estudiar mucho | | | | |
| ganar mucho dinero | | | | |

**Modelo:** **Reporting:** *Mi amiga Ana y yo deseamos viajar a Sud América. Los (Las) dos* (The two of us) *no deseamos trabajar mucho.*

**H. Consejos** (Pieces of advice) Your mother tells you what you need to do but you have already done everything she mentions. Follow the model.

**Modelo:** estudiar matemáticas
—*Necesitas estudiar matemáticas.*
—*Pero* (But) *acabo de estudiar matemáticas.*

1. estudiar inglés
2. trabajar mucho
3. comer bien
4. hablar en español
5. ganar dinero
6. practicar el piano

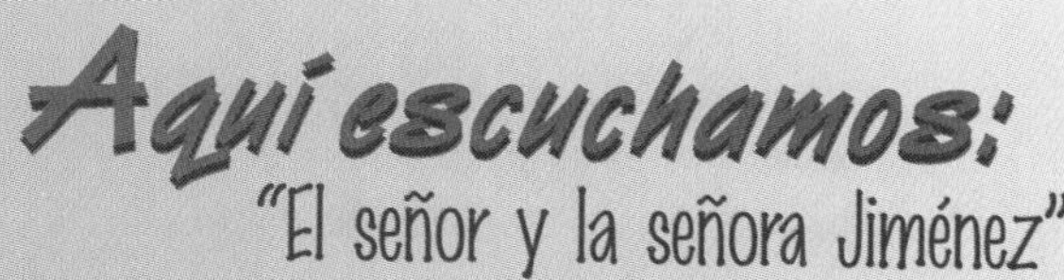

## Aquí escuchamos: "El señor y la señora Jiménez"

**Alicia and her friend Reynaldo meet some friends of her parents as they are walking through the park. Listen to the conversation and then do the exercises that follow.**

*Learning Strategy:*

*Listening for cultural information*



**Ex. H:** pair work

***Suggestion, Ex. H:*** Have students do the exercise with their partners or do as a whole class exercise by having one student give the mother's statement and another give the student's reply. Example: **Juan, ¿qué dice mamá? María, ¿qué dice el estudiante?**

***Answers, Ex. H:*** 1. Necesitas estudiar inglés. Pero acabo de estudiar inglés. 2. Necesitas trabajar mucho. Pero acabo de trabajar mucho. Numbers 3–6 follow this pattern.

### Aquí escuchamos

***Spanish speakers:*** Remember, most Spanish speakers, even those that are third or fourth generation, will understand spoken Spanish. The exercises that accompany this section should pose relatively little problem for Spanish speakers. They should, however, be directed to focus on "listening in context" to any vocabulary that may be new for them.

***Answers, Después de escuchar:*** 1. Alicia. She is speaking to someone older. 2. Sr. and Sra. Jiménez; because Alicia is younger. 3. They decide to go to a café. 4. Quisiera presentarles, mucho gusto, gracias, muy amables

***Support material, Aquí escuchamos:*** Teacher Tape/CD #1 Track #10 and Tapescript

**Ex. I:**  groups of three

 role play

*Suggestion, Ex I:* Let your Spanish-speaking students model the conversation or help three volunteers present it before having students do the exercise in groups of three. This activity serves as preparation for Ex. A in the **Ya llegamos** section at the end of this unit.

**Ex. J:** writing

*Spanish speakers, Ex. J:* Always have Spanish speakers fully carry out this activity. Remember, while many already speak and understand spoken Spanish, they may not know how to write the language. This is a good place to start building basic literacy skills in Spanish. Have students pay special attention to the spelling of the vocabulary that has been introduced in this **etapa,** especially those words that may have problematic spelling combinations. This is also a good place to have Spanish-speaking students engage in peer-editing. Have them look at the written work of a partner and focus on the spelling.

## Antes de escuchar

**Review some of the set phrases you know in Spanish for greetings, introductions, and farewells, found on page 37. Now listen to the conversation, paying particular attention to the use of usted and ustedes.**

START

## Después de escuchar

1. Who uses the more formal **usted** form in the conversation? Why is this so?
2. Who uses the more informal **tú** form? Why?
3. What do the two couples decide to do?
4. What are some of the set courtesy phrases that you hear more than once in the conversation?

## ¡Adelante!

EJERCICIO ORAL

***I. Buenos días, señor (señora).*** While walking with a friend, you run into a Spanish colleague of your parents, Sr. or Sra. Ruiz. Introduce your friend to him or her. Sr. or Sra. Ruiz will ask the two of you about what you like to do.

EJERCICIO ESCRITO

***J. Preferencias*** Write six different things that you prefer doing as opposed to other activities. Follow the model.

Modelo: *No deseo mirar la televisión, pero deseo escuchar música.*

# ocabulario

## Para charlar

| *Para saludar* | *Para contestar* |
|---|---|
| ¿Cómo está Ud.? | (Estoy) Bien, gracias. ¿Y Ud.? |
| ¿Cómo están Uds.? | Muy bien, gracias. |
| Buenos días. | |
| Saludos a tus padres. | |

| *Para presentar* | *Para contestar* |
|---|---|
| Quisiera presentarle(les) a… | Encantado(a). |

## Temas y contextos

### *Tapas españolas*

unas aceitunas
unos cacahuetes
unos calamares
chorizo
pan
unas patatas bravas
queso
una tortilla (de patatas)

## Vocabulario general

| *Pronombres* | *Verbos* | *Otras palabras y expresiones* | |
|---|---|---|---|
| él | acabar de | dinero | tampoco |
| ella | ganar | mi amigo(a) | van a… |
| ellas | mirar | el (la) señor(a) | ¿verdad? / ¿no? |
| ellos | necesitar | la señorita | |
| | tocar | también | |

# hapter ulminating ctivities

ou may want to play **el juego de las categorías** as a rap-up exercise for practicing the vocabulary. Good cate- ories for this chapter might be **tapas u otras comidas spañolas,** and **expresiones para saludar, contestar presentar.**

Have students make two lists: one for all the masculine nouns and another for the feminine nouns.

Ask students what they remember about Spanish **tapas** and other foods discussed in this chapter. Then ask them what they remember about meal times discussed in the last chapter. Have them compare Spanish eating habits to theirs.

*Vocabulario, Spanish speakers:* Point out the words that have problematic spelling combinations that were highlighted on p. 20 of "To the Teacher" in the Teacher's Edition. Students could be encouraged to keep a special spelling notebook with various categories such as: **Palabras con ll, Palabras con v, Palabras con b,** etc. Another category might be headed with **Así lo digo yo** in order for students to work on the spelling of those words and expressions that they already know and that might be variations to what has been presented in the book.

## Vocabulario: Round Robin

### *Critical Thinking Strategy: Categorizing*

 groups of three

- Have students sit in teams of three with books closed, to review the vocabulary.
- Tell them that you will announce a category and that they should take turns (moving from left to right) saying a word or expression that fits the category.
- Announce the category, such as **tapas españolas**. Tell students to name everything they think of when they hear that word. Stress that the point of the exercise is to review the vocabulary, but that they may include words they associate with **tapas españolas**, provided that they are in Spanish.
- Keep the exercises moving by limiting the time for each category. Remind students that each person has to take a turn, but that teammates may help each other by suggesting words when needed.
- When finished, announce the first category, and go around the room with one person from each team saying a word for that category. Continue with the other categories.

*Support material, Capítulo 2:* Improvised Conversation, Teacher Tape/CD #1 Track #11 and Tapescript; Lab Manual listening activities, Laboratory Program, Tapescript, and Teacher's Edition of the Workbook/Lab Manual

# Lectura cultural

Have students talk in small groups about different kinds of restaurants and foods served, and then compare answers with the whole class. Can they think of any restaurants that provide snacks before the main meal? (Chips and **salsa** at Mexican restaurants, warm bread and butter at Italian restaurants, etc.) Do Americans ever go to restaurants just to talk and snack?

*Spanish speakers:* Have the students go through each of the exercises in this section. Spanish-speaking students in foreign language classes already read English, for they have been educated in U.S. schools. However, as reading researchers have shown, the transfer of reading skills from one language to another is far from automatic. People must learn to read in each language. Special attention should be paid to having these students go through all of the exercises and activities that accompany the readings in this program. Once they have completed the activities, they might be asked to summarize the reading in Spanish in order to give them additional writing practice. They might also be required to keep a notebook with a special list of new vocabulary they might find in the reading selections. Point out the **h** of **huevos** and the **c** and **ll** of **cebolla.**

## IR DE TAPAS

*Learning Strategy:*
*Reading for details*

### Antes de leer

1. Look at the photos and the title that go with this reading passage.
2. What do you think the reading is about?
3. Can you identify some of the items in the photos?

### Guía para la lectura

**A.** After reading the first paragraph, decide which statement below best describes a **tapa.**

- **a.** a place where people meet to eat and chat
- **b.** a small helping of food served with bread

**B.** Now read the second paragraph and decide which of the following ingredients are used in a **tortilla española.**

- **a.** **queso**
- **b.** **patatas**
- **c.** **chorizo**
- **d.** **cebolla**
- **e.** **jamón**
- **f.** **huevos**

Spain

## Ir de tapas

"Ir de tapas" es una costumbre popular de España. Los españoles tienen la tradición de comer "tapas", o pequeñas porciones de comida, generalmente con pan. Muchas personas comen en bares de tapas todos los días. Es una manera tradicional de comer y hablar con los amigos y la familia.

Las tapas siempre son productos de las diferentes regiones de España. Las tapas típicas combinan varios quesos o tienen jamón o chorizo. La tapa más famosa de todas es la tortilla española. La tortilla española es fácil de preparar: patatas, cebolla, huevos y un excelente aceite de oliva.

El famoso restaurante "Casa Botín" en Madrid, España

# Chapter Objectives

**Functions:** Ordering something to eat; finding out about people
**Context:** Mexican restaurants
**Accuracy:** Present tense of **ser;** adjectives of nationality; nouns of profession

# Cultural Observation

Have students study the photo on this page. Ask them if they have ever bought any fast food from a street vendor, such as a hot dog at a hot dog stand or food from a booth at a county fair. Have they ever eaten fast food at a Mexican restaurant? Do they recognize the food in the photo?

*Spanish speakers:* Have Spanish speakers mention, in Spanish, what they see. Ask them what they see in the photos that might be similar or different in their community. Point out the **h** in **hambre** in the caption.

# Cooperative Learning

## Chapter Warm-up: TPR Cluster Activity

### *Critical Thinking Strategies: Categorizing, analyzing, prioritizing*

- Have the four corners represent popular types of restaurants that are found in your area, for example: pizza, Mexican, hamburger, barbecue, cafeteria, etc.
- Ask the students to indicate their preferences by going to the corresponding corner. With the other members of the group selecting the same type of restaurant, have them list (in English) the reasons for their choice in the form of single-phrase attributes, or characteristics, such as price, formality, service, speed, quality of food, who goes there, atmosphere, and convenience.
- Write the types of restaurants on the board and under each one list the reasons from each group. (You may choose to write these in Spanish now.)
- Select the four most frequently named reasons and designate each corner of the classroom to represent a different one of these four.
- Have students recluster by selecting their one most important reason for selecting a restaurant. An extension might be to have them recluster several times to observe changes in priorities by naming each time a certain occasion for the restaurant outing, such as a family outing, lunch with a parent, lunch with a best friend, their birthday, their parents' anniversary.

CAPÍTULO 3

# ¿TE GUSTA LA COMIDA MEXICANA?

*la comida mexicana* Mexican food

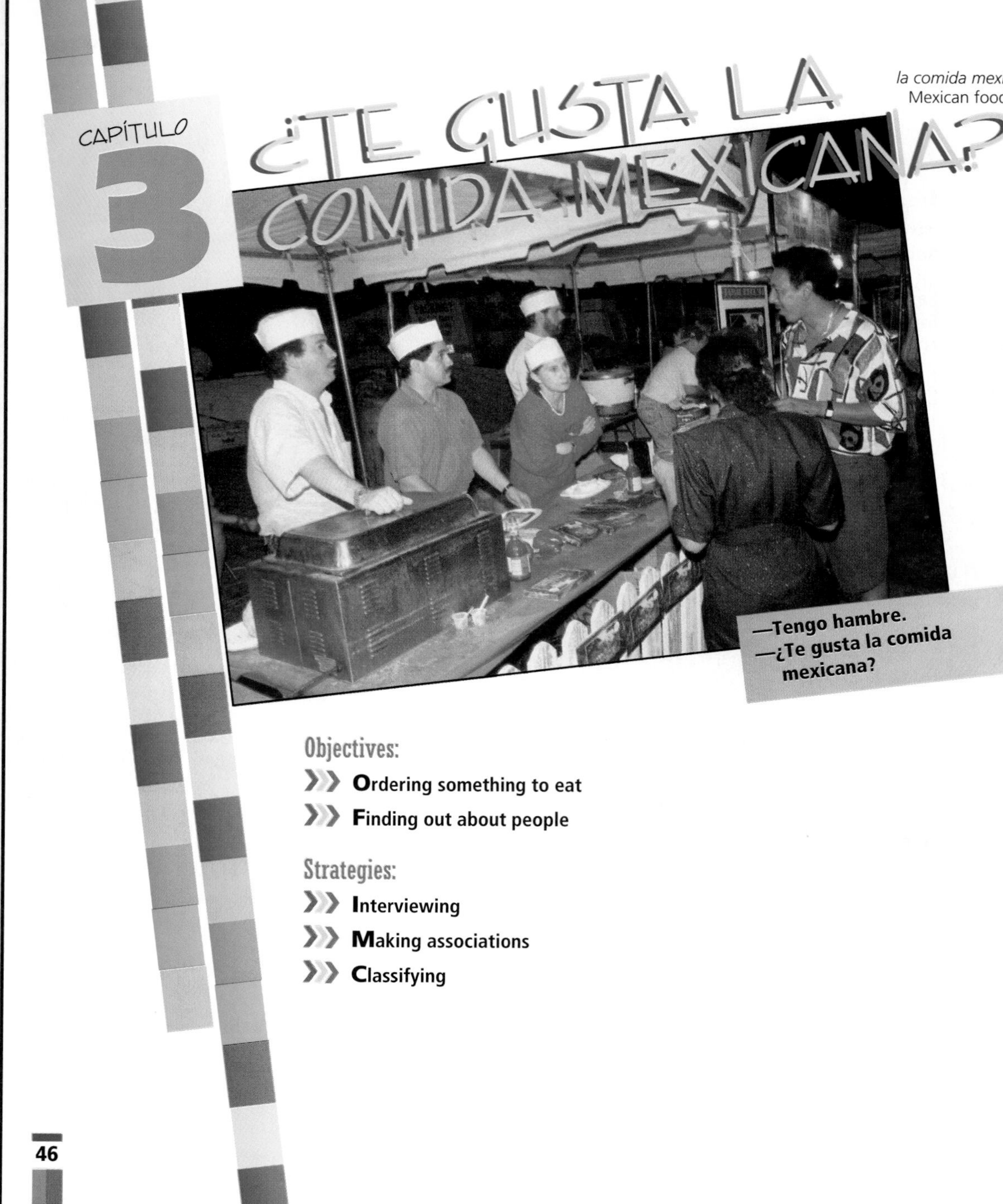

—Tengo hambre.
—¿Te gusta la comida mexicana?

**Objectives:**

- **Ordering something to eat**
- **Finding out about people**

**Strategies:**

- **Interviewing**
- **Making associations**
- **Classifying**

46

## Video/CD-ROM

**Chapter 3 Video Program**
**Chapter 3 CD-ROM Program**

**These can be used at the end of the chapter as expansion activities.**

## PRIMERA ETAPA

### Preparación

**>> Before you start working on this etapa, consider what you already know about Mexican food. Given the popularity of Mexican food in the United States, it is likely that you are already familiar with some of the dishes you are going to learn about in this etapa. Make a list of all the Mexican dishes you know.**

**>> Now think of several features that you feel best describe or characterize this kind of food, for example, colors, spices, vegetables, meats, the kinds of dishes and utensils used for serving and eating them, etc.**

Learning Strategies:

*Brainstorming, previewing*

## ¡Vamos a un restaurante!

Rafael y Pablo **están** en un restaurante en México.

**Camarero:** Buenos días, señores. **¿Qué van a pedir?**
**Rafael:** Yo quisiera comer un **taco de pollo** con **frijoles**.
**Pablo:** Para mí, una **enchilada de carne** con **arroz**.
**Camarero:** ¿Y para tomar?
**Rafael:** Un vaso de agua con limón.
**Camarero:** ¿Y para Ud., señor?
**Pablo:** Una limonada, **bien** fría, por favor.
**Camarero:** Muy bien.

*están:* are / *¿Qué van a pedir?:* What will you have? / *taco de pollo:* chicken taco / *frijoles:* beans / *enchilada de carne*: meat enchilada / *arroz:* rice / *bien:* very

47

As a lead-in to this chapter, play the recording of the short dialogue on the Teacher Tape or read it for the students, acting out the scene. Afterwards ask what happened and what was ordered.

Point out that in spoken Spanish, **bien** may be used to mean *very:* **bien fría** = *very cold*, **bien caliente** = *very hot.*

*Spanish speakers:* Ask Spanish speakers if they are familiar with the foods that are listed here. Ask them for variations. Help them with the spelling of the variations they provide. Point out to them that **pollo** is spelled with a **ll** and **arroz** with a **z** and **frijoles** with a **j.** This is a good time to talk about the basic differences between Mexican and Tex-Mex food.

### Vocabulary Expansion

**guacamole; tostadas** (crisp flat tortillas with toppings such as beans, lettuce and onions, cheese, and shredded chicken with salsa); **huevos rancheros** (eggs served on a corn tortilla and topped with a spicy tomato sauce); **pollo con mole** (chicken served in a sauce made up of over 20 ingredients, including chocolate and chile); **quesadilla** (a tortilla with cheese inside folded over and fried, served with hot sauce); **burrito** (flour tortilla with beans and cheese)

*Support material, ¡Vamos a un restaurante!:* Teacher Tape/CD #1 Track #12, transparency #15

## Etapa Support Materials

Workbook: **pp. 25–28**
Critical Thinking Masters: **p. 4**
Transparencies: **#15, #16, #17, #18**
Teacher Tape 
Quiz: **Testing Program, p. 23**

Support material, **¡Vamos a un restaurante!:**
**Teacher Tape, transparency #15**

### Presentation: ¡Vamos a un restaurante!

Given the popularity of Mexican food in the U.S., it is likely that students are already familiar with some of the dishes they are going to learn about in this **etapa.** Ask students to make a list of all the Mexican dishes they know. Have them think of several features of this kind of food, for example: colors, spices, vegetables, meats, the kinds of dishes and utensils used for serving and eating them.

*Support material, Ex. A:* Transparency #16. Use the transparency of Mexican food to introduce the food items mentioned in the dialogue.

**Ex. A:** pair work

 role play

*Suggestions, Ex. A:* You play the waiter. Have students get your attention and order something. No orders may be repeated until all items have been chosen. Or have students work with their partners asking each other questions until they have practiced all of the food items shown.

## Cultural Expansion

Take this opportunity to discuss more about Mexican food. What are some of the names of Mexican restaurants with which students are familiar? Explain that much of the food served at these different chain restaurants are really American inventions. The typical ground beef **taco** at the fast-food restaurants would surprise most Mexicans, for whom a **taco** is anything you roll up inside a soft corn tortilla (except ground beef). Traditional Mexican **tacos** are usually served with chopped onion and cilantro and with a choice of sauces. **Flautas** are rolled and fried and are usually served with sour cream, crumbled fresh white cheese, shredded lettuce, and hot sauce.

Suggest having a Mexican fiesta with your students. Have them bring in foods and discuss which of the foods would be authentically Mexican.



**enchilada:** soft corn **tortilla** filled with cheese, meat, or chicken, and served with hot sauce
**frijoles:** pinto or black beans cooked until tender; served mashed, most often as a side dish
**taco:** a corn **tortilla** filled with meat, chicken, or other fillings, and topped with lettuce, tomato, grated cheese, and sauce
**tortilla:** made of corn meal and shaped like a pancake; in Mexico, the **tortilla** is served with all meals and takes the place of bread

## ¡Aquí te toca a ti!

**A.** ***¿Qué va a pedir?*** You are in a Mexican restaurant. Look at the pictures below and decide what you are going to order.

enchilada de queso
—*¿Qué va a pedir?*
—*Yo quisiera comer una enchilada de queso.*
—*Muy bien.*

1. enchilada de carne

2. enchilada de queso

3. tacos de pollo

4. tacos de carne

5. arroz con frijoles

6. frijoles

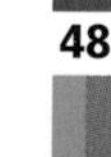


## Exercise Progression

Ex. A is designed to introduce the new vocabulary in an open-ended format. Ex. B invites students to focus on what they have learned about food from Spain and Mexico. Ex. C practices some of the foods learned in Chapter 1 along with the new food items.

# ¡Aquí te toca a ti!

**A. ¿Qué tal es?** Complete the sentences according to your preferences in food. If the noun is masculine, use the ending **-o** for the adjective; if it is feminine, use the ending **-a**.

*El flan es* delicios*o*.

1. ____________ riquísimo(a).
2. ____________ rico(a).
3. ____________ malo(a) *(bad)*.
4. ____________ horrible.
5. ____________ bueno(a).
6. ____________ picante.

**B. ¿Cómo (How) son?** What is your opinion of the following foods?

un taco con salsa
*Un taco con salsa es muy picante. No me gusta.*

1. una hamburguesa *(hamburger)*
2. un pastel de fresas
3. una enchilada de queso
4. un croissant
5. un flan
6. un bocadillo de jamón

## Repaso

**C. ¿De dónde son estas comidas?** Ask a classmate where these foods come from. Follow the model.

Modelo: la salsa de chile
*—¿De dónde es la salsa de chile?*
*—Es de México.*

1. las medialunas
2. la tortilla de patatas
3. el croissant
4. las hamburguesas
5. las patatas bravas

## ESTRUCTURA

### Adjectives of nationality

| | |
|---|---|
| Ricardo es **peruano.** | Ricardo is *Peruvian.* |
| Alfredo y Paco también son **peruanos.** | Alfredo and Paco also are *Peruvians.* |
| Mirta es **peruana.** | Mirta is *Peruvian.* |
| Ada y Alejandra también son **peruanas.** | Ada and Alejandra also are *Peruvians.* |



**Ex. B:** pair work

*Suggestions, Ex. B:* Do with the whole class as a **pregúntale** exercise (**María, pregúntale a Juan si le gusta...**) or have students work with partners, asking questions with **¿Te gusta... ?** Make sure that they follow the model. You may want to do a couple as a whole class before they work in pairs.

**Ex. C:** pair work

*Suggestions, Ex. C:* Have students work in pairs or do as a whole class activity using the **pregúntale** format. Point out that if the food item is plural, they must use **¿De dónde son... ?** in the question and **Son de...** in the answer. Continue the exercise by asking about foods from earlier chapters.

*Answers, Ex. C:*
1. Argentina 2. España 3. Francia (España) 4. Estados Unidos 5. España

## Cultural Expansion

Have students study the photo on p. 56. Explain that the food stand is at a street market (called **tianguis** in Mexico). At these markets people buy and sell everything from household goods to clothing to food, and they are set up every week on the same day and in the same place.

## Exercise Progression

Since students have had considerable practice ordering foods, the two exercises provided are open-ended, to afford students the opportunity to practice the new adjectives presented while giving their opinion about different Mexican foods.

**Ex. A:** writing

*Variation, Ex. A:* Students could use a chart to describe how they feel about each of these foods (by placing an "X" under the appropriate descriptor).

Creat a chart with 7 columns and 9 rows. Starting at row 1, column 2, each column will contain a heading: **picante, riquísimo(a), rico(a), bueno(a), malo(a), horrible.** Starting at row 2, column 1 will contain row headings: **una hamburguesa, un pastel de fresas, una enchilada de queso, un licuado de banana, un croissant, un flan, un bocadillo de jamón, un taco de pollo.**

## Presentation: Adjectives of nationality

Ask yes/no questions with adjectives of nationality as you show pictures of famous foreign people. Or make statements about famous people (both male and female) that students are likely to know, and have students repeat. Stress the endings in these statements to emphasize the differences in masculine and feminine forms.

Then introduce the adjectives of nationality that appear in point two. Write them on the board in two groups, masculine and feminine. Point out the differences in spelling between forms, such as adding an **-a** and dropping the accent.

The term **americano** is often synonymous with citizens of the United States, but it is sometimes offensive to people outside the U.S., since all inhabitants of North, Central, or South America are **americanos**. Thus, **norteamericano** is the preferred word to refer to people from the United States.

*Spanish speakers:* Have students work on the spelling of those words with any problematic combinations. For example, the **rr, c,** and **s** in **costarricense; v** in **boliviano; cu** in **ecuatoriano; h** in **hondureño; güe** in **nicaragüense; y** in **paraguayo** and **uruguayo; rr** and **qu** in **puertorriqueño; z** in **venezolano.**



In Spanish, adjectives agree in gender *(masculine or feminine)* and number *(singular or plural)* with the person or thing to which they refer.

1. Adjectives that end in **-o** are *masculine.* Change the **-o** to **-a** to obtain the *feminine* form.

| | |
|---|---|
| Él es **argentino.** | Ella es **argentina.** |
| Él es **chino.** | Ella es **china.** |
| Él es **italiano.** | Ella es **italiana.** |
| Él es **ruso** *(Russian).* | Ella es **rusa.** |

2. Adjectives that end in a consonant **(-l, -n, -s)** form the *feminine* by adding an **-a.**

| | |
|---|---|
| Él es **español** *(Spanish).* | Ella es **española.** |
| Él es **inglés** *(English).* | Ella es **inglesa.** |
| Él es **francés** *(French).* | Ella es **francesa.** |
| Él es **japonés** *(Japanese).* | Ella es **japonesa.** |
| Él es **alemán** *(German).* | Ella es **alemana.** |

3. Some adjectives have identical *masculine* and *feminine* forms.

| | |
|---|---|
| Él es **estadounidense.** | Ella es **estadounidense.** |
| Él es **canadiense.** | Ella es **canadiense.** |

4. To form the plural of the adjectives that end in a vowel, simply add **-s** to the masculine or feminine singular forms. If the singular form ends in a consonant, add **-es** for masculine adjectives and **-as** for feminine adjectives.

| | |
|---|---|
| Ellos son **mexicanos.** | Ellas son **mexicanas.** |
| Ellos son **españoles.** | Ellas son **españolas.** |
| Ellos son **canadienses.** | Ellas son **canadienses.** |
| Ellos son **alemanes.** | Ellas son **alemanas.** |

| *País* | *Adjetivo* | *País* | *Adjetivo* |
|---|---|---|---|
| Argentina | argentino(a) | Honduras | hondureño(a) |
| Bolivia | boliviano(a) | México | mexicano(a) |
| Colombia | colombiano(a) | Nicaragua | nicaragüense |
| Costa Rica | costarricense | Panamá | panameño(a) |
| Cuba | cubano(a) | Paraguay | paraguayo(a) |
| Chile | chileno(a) | Perú | peruano(a) |
| Ecuador | ecuatoriano(a) | Puerto Rico | puertorriqueño(a) |
| El Salvador | salvadoreño(a) | La República Dominicana | dominicano(a) |
| España | español(a) | Uruguay | uruguayo(a) |
| Guatemala | guatemalteco(a) | Venezuela | venezolano(a) |



## Vocabulary Expansion

The use of the article with certain countries is becoming optional. Some countries such as **(la) Argentina, (el) Canadá, (la) China, (el) Ecuador, (los) Estados Unidos, (el) Japón, (el) Paraguay, (el) Perú,** and **(el) Uruguay** may or may not take an article. Point out that, in Spanish, adjectives of nationality are not capitalized. Other adjectives of nationality: **camboyano, coreano, filipino, haitiano, laosiano, samoano** (all with four forms like **cubano** and **peruano**); **tailandés** (with four forms like **inglés** or **francés**); **israelí, iraquí, iraní** (all with only two forms like **iraní, iraníes**); **vietnamita** (with only two forms: **vietnamita** for masculine or feminine singular and **vietnamitas** for the plural).

Students do not need to learn all of these additional adjectives of nationality for production. They should be encouraged to choose those that are most related to their personal family situations.

## Aquí practicamos

**D. ¿Y David?** Answer the questions according to the model. In the first four items, the first person is female and the second is male.

Alicia es venezolana. ¿Y Alberto?
*Él es venezolano también.*

1. Gladis es colombiana. ¿Y Fernando?
2. Éster es cubana. ¿Y José?
3. Adelita es peruana. ¿Y Pepito?
4. Marilú es española. ¿Y Paco?

Now the first person is male and the second person is female.

Pancho es boliviano. ¿Y Marta?
*Ella es boliviana también.*

5. Luis es costarricense. ¿Y Clara?
6. Pedro es argentino. ¿Y Luisa?
7. Miguel es panameño. ¿Y Teresa?
8. Tomás es puertorriqueño. ¿Y Elena?

### Más adjetivos de nacionalidad

| País | Adjetivo | País | Adjetivo |
|---|---|---|---|
| Alemania | alemán (alemana) | Inglaterra | inglés (inglesa) |
| Canadá | canadiense | Italia | italiano(a) |
| China | chino(a) | Japón | japonés (japonesa) |
| Estados Unidos | estadounidense | Rusia | ruso(a) |
| Francia | francés (francesa) | | |

**E. Las nacionalidades** You are with a group of young people from all over the world. Find out their nationalities by making the assumptions indicated and then correcting your mistakes. Follow the model.

Margarita — argentina / Nueva York
*—¿Margarita es argentina?*
*—No, ella es de Nueva York.*
*—Ah, ella es estadounidense entonces* (then).
*—Claro, es estadounidense.*

1. Lin-Tao (m.) — japonés / Beijin
2. Sofía — mexicana / Roma
3. Jean-Pierre — francés / Québec
4. Jill — canadiense / Londres
5. Hilda y Lorena — colombianas / Berlín
6. Olga y Nicolás — venezolanos / Moscú



## Exercise Progression

Exs. D and E are controlled exercises providing practice in making the adjectives of nationality agree. You may wish to personalize this structure by doing the follow-up suggested for Ex. D.

x. D:  pair work

 writing

*Suggestions, Ex. D:* Have students work in pairs following the model carefully. Make sure that they substitute the names with subject pronouns when responding. You could also do this exercise with the whole class by having one student read each item and having another respond. Example: **Juan, lee el número uno. María, contesta.**

*Answers, Ex. D:* 1. Él es colombiano también. 2. ...cubano... 3. ...peruano... 4. ...español... 5. Ella es costarricense también. 6. ...argentina... 7. ...panameña... 8. ...puertorriqueña...

*Follow-up, Ex. D:* Teach students the expressions **Mi familia es italiana/francesa/alemana,** etc., and **Yo soy de origen italiano/francés/alemán,** etc. Then have them tell you and each other about their family backgrounds and origins.

**Ex. E:** groups of four or more

*Answers, Ex. E:* 1. ¿Lin-Tao es japonés? No, él es de Beijín. Ah, él es chino entonces. Claro, es chino. 2. ¿Sofía es mexicana? No, ...es de Roma. ...es italiana... . 3. ¿Jean-Pierre es francés? No, ...es de Québec. ...es canadiense... . 4. ¿Jill es canadiense? No, ...es de Londres. ...es inglesa... . 5. ¿Hilda y Lorena son colombianas? No, ...son de Berlín. ...son alemanas... . 6. ¿Olga y Nicolás son venezolanos? No, ...son de Moscú. ...son rusos... .

*Follow-up, Ex. E:* Test students' knowledge of Latin American and Spanish capitals by saying, **Soy de Tegucigalpa** and having them guess, **¿Es usted de Honduras? (Sí, soy hondureña.)** The class could form teams and earn extra credit points.

## Cultural Expansion

Ask students what they know about Puerto Ricans. Remind them that Puerto Ricans are citizens of the United States and are able to enter and leave the country without passports or visas. Mention that Puerto Rico is a commonwealth of the U.S. and uses the same currency. However, Puerto Ricans can't vote in U.S. elections unless they establish their residency on the mainland.

## Presentation: Nouns of profession

Make statements with the cognates, stressing (with voice inflection) the difference between the masculine and feminine forms. Bring in pictures of people in different identifiable occupations and have students repeat sentences about them. Have students repeat the names of occupations listed in the first item on p. 60. Make statements using the masculine form and have students change them to the feminine. Continue this procedure with items two, three, and four.

## Vocabulary Expansion

**actor, actriz, asistente social** (**trabajador/trabajadora social** in some countries), **carpintero/capintera, científico/científica, consejero/consejera, electricista, empleado/empleada, fotógrafo/fotógrafa, gerente, jefe, programador/programadora, sicólogo/sicóloga, vendedor/vendedora**

Write the list of occupations from the Vocabulary Expansion on the board and ask students about their parents' occupations: **Mi mamá es enfermera. ¿Tú mamá es enfermera también?** or **¿Qué es tu mamá/papá?**

*Follow-up, Nouns of profession:* Have students look at the photographs on p. 60 and ask them: What do you think are the professions of these two people? Why do you think that? Have them list logical possibilities and supporting reasons.



# Nota gramatical

### Nouns of profession

Most nouns that refer to work or occupation follow the same patterns as adjectives of nationality.

1. If the masculine ends in **-o,** the feminine form changes **-o** to **-a.**

| | |
|---|---|
| Él es **abogado** *(lawyer).* | Ella es **abogada.** |
| Él es **secretario** *(secretary).* | Ella es **secretaria.** |
| Él es **ingeniero** *(engineer).* | Ella es **ingeniera.** |
| Él es **enfermero** *(nurse).* | Ella es **enfermera.** |
| Él es **médico** *(doctor).* | Ella es **médica.** |

2. Nouns that end in the consonant **-r** form the feminine by adding **-a** to the end of the word.

| | |
|---|---|
| Él es **contador** *(accountant).* | Ella es **contadora.** |

3. Nouns that end in the vowel **-e,** as well as those that end in **-ista,** have the same masculine and feminine forms.

| | |
|---|---|
| Él es **estudiante.** | Ella es **estudiante.** |
| Él es **periodista** *(journalist).* | Ella es **periodista.** |

4. Nouns of profession form their plural in the same way as the adjectives of nationality. Add **-s** to the masculine or feminine singular form if the noun ends in a vowel. If the singular form ends in a consonant, add **-es** or **-as.**

| | |
|---|---|
| Ellos son **abogados.** | Ellas son **abogadas.** |
| Ellos son **estudiantes.** | Ellas son **estudiantes.** |
| Ellos son **profesores.** | Ellas son **profesoras.** |



## Critical Thinking

### *Critical Thinking Strategy: Making inferences and drawing conclusions*

Write a chart on the board and ask the students where they would most likely find these people at work.

Create the chart with 5 columns and 9 rows. Starting at row 1, column 2, each column has a heading: **escuela, oficina, hospital, fábrica** *(factory).* Starting at row 2, column 1 has row headings: **professor(a), contador(a), enfermero(a), gerente, programador(a), consejero(a), abogado(a), ingeniero(a).**

## Aquí practicamos

**F. ¿El señor Martínez? Él es...** You and a friend are attending a function with your parents. You point out to your friend various acquaintances of your parents and state their professions.

Sr. Martínez / abogado
*¿El señor Martínez? Él es abogado.*
Sr. y Sra. Martínez / ingeniero
*¿El señor y la señora Martínez? Ellos son ingenieros.*

1. Sr. y Sra. Herrera / médico
2. Sr. Pérez / profesor
3. Sr. y Sra. López / abogado
4. Sra. Quintana / secretario
5. Sra. Dávila / ingeniero
6. Sr. y Sra. Valdés / profesor
7. Patricio / estudiante de universidad
8. Sra. González / contador
9. Roberta / estudiante de colegio
10. Sr. y Sra. Chávez / periodista

**G. Yo quisiera ser abogado(a).** From the following list, choose several careers or jobs that you would like and several that you would not like. Which of these careers or jobs would you most like to have? Why? Which of these careers or jobs would you not want to have? Why?

*Yo quisiera ser médico(a), pero yo no quisiera ser abogado(a).*

periodista
dentista
profesor(a)
secretario(a)
hombre (mujer) de negocios *(businessman, businesswoman)*
abogado(a)
camarero(a)
médico(a)
ingeniero(a)
enfermero(a)
contador(a)

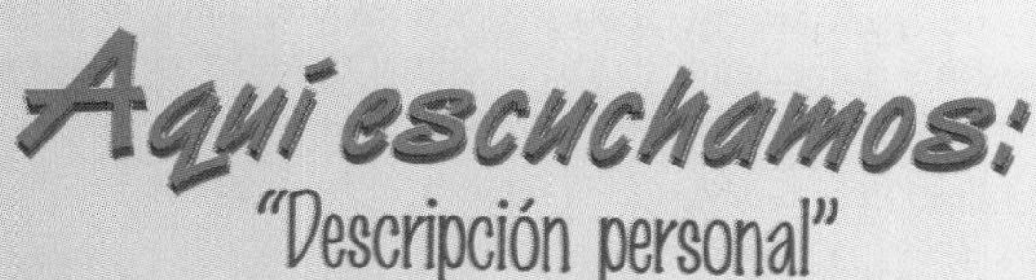


### "Descripción personal"

**María Victoria Rodríguez is a Mexican-American. Listen to what she says about herself before doing the exercises that follow.**

### Antes de escuchar

**Before you listen to the personal description, think about the sort of information that you would expect to hear. To help you prepare for what you are about to hear, first read the true/false statements in the *Después de escuchar* section to give you a better idea of the content.**

**¿Qué crees?**

**Approximately how many people of Spanish-speaking origin are in the United States?**
**a) fewer than 10 million**
**b) 15 million**
**c) more than 20 million**

**respuesta**

*Critical Thinking Strategy:*
*Evaluating*

*Learning Strategy:*
*Listening for details*



## Critical Thinking

*Critical Thinking Strategy: Analyzing*

*Learning Strategies: Polling, tallying, making observations from a survey*

This activity serves as preparation for the **Ya llegamos** section at the end of Unit 1.

- Have students get into groups of six or eight and answer the question, **¿Qué quisieras ser?** The group recorder keeps a tally of the professions mentioned.
- Then have another student from each group report which professions were selected by their group and by whom: **Billy quisiera ser abogado; Ana y Bryan quisieran ser médicos.**
- Record on the board each profession and put a mark beside it each time it is selected.
- Ask the whole class such questions as **¿Qué profesiones son las más populares? ¿Cuáles requieren más educación? ¿...más talento musical? ¿Para qué profesiones es necesario viajar? ¿...estudiar matemáticas? ¿...hablar español? ¿En cuáles se gana más dinero?**

### Aquí escuchamos

***Spanish speakers:*** Most Spanish speakers will understand spoken Spanish. These students should be directed to focus on "listening in context" to any new vocabulary.

***Support material, Aquí escuchamos:*** Teacher Tape/CD #1 Track #15 and Tapescript

## Exercise Progression

Ex. F offers controlled practice for making agreement with nouns of profession. Ex. G allows students to use this vocabulary in a personalized context. Both exercises reinforce the use of the noun of profession without an article. If students are able to follow the model automatically, there should be no need for further explanation.

Ex. F: pair work

***Suggestion, Ex. F:*** Have students work in pairs, following the model. Point out the use of the definite article **el/la** before the titles **Sr./Sra.** Mention that when saying *Mr. and Mrs.* in Spanish (**el Sr. y la Sra.**), Spanish speakers generally use an abbreviated version: **los Sres. García**.

***Answers, Ex. F:*** 1. ¿El Sr. y la Sra. Herrera? Ellos son médicos. 2. ...Él es profesor. 3. ...Ellos son abogados. 4. ...Ella es secretaria. 5. ...Ella es ingeniera. 6. ...Ellos son profesores. 7. ...Él es estudiante. 8. ...Ella es contadora. 9. ...Ella es estudiante. 10. ...Ellos son periodistas.

*Answers, **Después de escuchar:*** 1. False, she is from San Antonio, Texas. 2. True 3. True 4. True 5. False, she wants to study to be a lawyer and hopes to become a politician. 6. True

**Ex. H:**  pair work

*Less-prepared students, Ex. H:* Less-prepared students can first review by listing various countries, nationalities and brief descriptions of some foods from that country.

*More-prepared students, Ex. H:* More-prepared students can go a bit further, pretending to introduce their friends to each other (the teacher can play the role of the international friend), and having a brief conversation about the food fair.

*Spanish speakers, Ex. H:* Remember that most Spanish speakers already have a command of a variety of Spanish that is used in informal, very familiar contexts. This situation is an informal one, but have the students focus on using vocabulary that may be new for them. Emphasize that it may be necessary to use such vocabulary when talking to speakers who are from other parts of the Spanish-speaking world. Remember to be sensitive and accept how the students say it the first time. What they have said may be totally appropriate in their speech community. This is a good place to have them focus on the differences between how they say something in their speech community and how the book is teaching them to express this. Remember, rather than "correcting" how they speak, your main objective is to expand the range of contexts in which these students can use Spanish.

**Ex. I:**  writing

c

## Después de escuchar

**Listen to María Victoria's description once more before indicating whether the statements below are true or false. If something is false, provide the correct information in English.**

1. María Victoria is from New Mexico.
2. María Victoria's parents are originally from Mexico.
3. Playing the guitar is one of María Victoria's favorite activities.
4. Studying is an important part of María Victoria's routine.
5. Someday María Victoria would like to be an actress.
6. María Victoria is concerned about the needs of other people.

*Critical Thinking Strategy:*

*Making associations*

EJERCICIO ORAL

**H. *En la feria de la comida*** You and your friend are walking through an international food fair. (1) You each name three foods that you wish to sample, describing each one. Choose foods from at least two different booths, representing two different countries. (2) Each of you then points out someone from another country whom you have met at the fair, telling the person's name, nationality, profession, and two things that the person likes to do that make him or her interesting to you.

*Allí está Juan. Él es cubano. Él es fotógrafo. Juan canta y baila bien.*

EJERCICIO ESCRITO

**I. *Mini-descripción*** Write a brief personal description (four to six sentences) in Spanish about an adult you interviewed. Include basic information about the person, such as his or her interests, activities, and profession. Be prepared to report back to the class about what you learned about this person.



*Spanish speakers, Ex. I:* Always have Spanish speakers fully carry out this activity. Remember, while many already speak and understand spoken Spanish, they may not know how to write the language. This is a good place to start building basic literacy skills in Spanish. Have students pay special attention to the spelling of the vocabulary that has been introduced in this **etapa,** especially those words that may have problematic spelling combinations. This is a good place to have Spanish speaking students engage in peer-editing. Have them look at the written work of a partner and focus on the spelling.

*Follow-up, Ex. I:* Have students illustrate or collect photo to accompany their descriptions, and then have students compile them for a "Getting to Know You" section of a classroom newsletter. This is also a good hands-on activity for students who learn better by manipulating and responding to materia

## Para charlar

### Para comentar sobre la comida

¡Qué bueno(a)!
¡Qué comida más rica!
¡Qué picante!
¡Es riquísimo(a)!
¡Es delicioso(a)!

## Temas y contextos

### Las nacionalidades

alemán (alemana)
argentino(a)
boliviano(a)
canadiense
chileno(a)
chino(a)
colombiano(a)
costarricense
cubano(a)
dominicano(a)
ecuatoriano(a)
español(a)
estadounidense
francés (francesa)
guatemalteco(a)
hondureño(a)
inglés (inglesa)
italiano(a)
japonés (japonesa)
mexicano(a)
nicaragüense
norteamericano(a)
panameño(a)
paraguayo(a)
peruano(a)
puertorriqueño(a)
ruso(a)
salvadoreño(a)
uruguayo(a)
venezolano(a)

### Las profesiones

un(a) abogado(a)
un(a) contador(a)
un(a) dentista
un(a) enfermero(a)
un(a) estudiante
un hombre (una mujer) de negocios
un(a) ingeniero(a)
un(a) médico(a)
un(a) periodista
un(a) profesor(a)
un(a) secretario(a)

***Suggestion, Vocabulario:*** Students may use the **Vocabulario** as a checklist for vocabulary recognition. A Spanish–English Glossary is provided at the end of the book if students need to consult it for definitions. Review the adjectives by mentioning different foods and having students describe them.

***Spanish speakers:*** Point out the words that have problematic spelling combinations that were highlighted on p. 20 of "To the Teacher" in the Teacher's Edition. Students could be encouraged to keep a special spelling notebook with various categories such as: **Palabras con ll, Palabras con v, Palabras con b,** etc. Another category might be headed with **Así lo digo yo** in order for students to work on the spelling of those words and expressions that they already know and that might be variations to what has been presented in the book.

***Support material, Capítulo 3:*** Improvised Conversation, Teacher Tape/CD #1 Track #16 and Tapescript; Lab Manual listening activities, Laboratory Program, Tapescript, and Teacher's Edition of the Workbook/Lab Manual

# Chapter Culminating Activities

 groups of four or more

Collect or, if feasible, have students bring in a set of photos (from magazines and newspapers) of people of various nationalities and occupations. This collection can serve as the basis for several communicative-type activities. (1) Show each photo to the class; students try to guess the nationality and occupation. You (or the student who found the photo) confirms the correct answer.

(2) Divide the class into groups of four or five students. Each student shows a photo; the group tries to guess the nationality and occupation. (3) Proceed as with the second activity, but have students exchange photos after the first round. Then, create new groups in which students present the "new" photos to a different set of classmates.

You may want to play a game as a wrap-up exercise for practicing the **Vocabulario.** With books closed, name a country and have students write down the corresponding adjective of nationality. Give points for each correct answer. You could divide the class into teams. Each team member must answer when it is his/her turn and if this person cannot give the correct answer, then the other team has the opportunity to do so. You could also have students write the corresponding adjective on the board.

# Cultural Observation

See if students remember the origin of different foods discussed in the last three chapters. Name a food and see if they can give the country in Spanish.

*La comida mexicana*

arroz
carne
chile
una enchilada
flan
unos frijoles
una hamburguesa
pollo
salsa
un taco
una tortilla

*Los países*

Alemania
Argentina
Bolivia
Canadá
Chile
China
Colombia
Costa Rica
Cuba
Ecuador
El Salvador
España
Estados Unidos
Francia
Guatemala
Honduras
Inglaterra
Italia
Japón
México
Nicaragua
Panamá
Paraguay
Perú
Puerto Rico
La República Dominicana
Rusia
Uruguay
Venezuela

## *Vocabulario general*

*Verbos*

ser

*Otras palabras y expresiones*

Allí está…
Aquí hay otro(a)…
¿De dónde es (eres)?
ésta
¡Mira!
¿Qué es?
¿Qué van a pedir?
¿quién?
ser de

## Vocabulario: Team Charades

 groups of four or more

- Have the vocabulary words indicating nationality and occupation written out on individual cards. Put all the cards into a **sombrero** or other type of hat.
- Divide the class into teams of four. Place the teams in different parts of the room, so that teammates can communicate with each other without other teams overhearing.
- Ask one member from each team to pull a card from the ha It will be each team's responsibility to plan a charade representing the occupation or nationality they have drawn, and to present the charade to the other teams so they can try to guess their word. In planning the charade, each teammate must contribute one idea for an action that illustrates the vocabulary word.
- It is important with this exercise to leave sufficient time aft the charades for a discussion of stereotypes. Encourage the students to discuss their reactions to the images put forwa to represent the nationalities and the occupations. Don't forget the representations of genders.

# Lectura CULTURAL

## MAGIA Y COLOR EN LOS ÁNGELES

### Antes de leer

1. Look at the picture that accompanies the text.
2. What does the picture let you know about the content of the reading?
3. Now look at the title, "Magia y color en Los Ángeles." To what location (city/area) will the content of the article be related?

### Guía para la lectura

A. Notice that **combina** and **técnica** are similar to the English words *combine* and *technique*. Words that look alike in different languages are called *cognates*. Now read the first paragraph and find as many cognates as you can. How many did you spot? Compare your list with another classmate's list.

B. Some of the cognates look more alike than others, for example, **combina, popular,** and **americano.** Can you guess these cognates that are not so similar to their English counterparts?
- **celebrados**
- **delicadeza**
- **sirven**

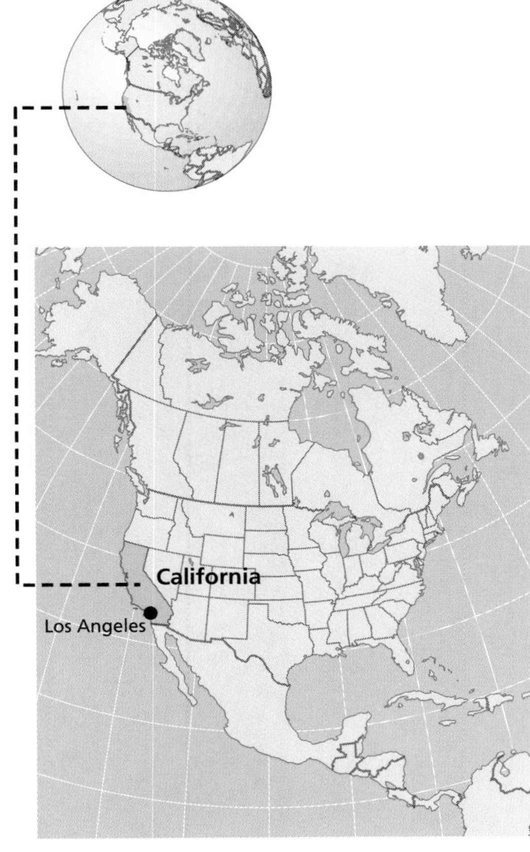


65

## ectura cultural

ve students talk about what comes to mind upon hearing word *chef*. What differentiates *chef* from *cook*? What areas the world are known for their fine cuisine? Do your students ssify Mexican food as elegant and expensive or as fast, ap food?

*panish speakers:* Have the students go through each the exercises in this section. Spanish-speaking students in eign language classes already read English, for they have been educated in U.S. schools. However, as reading researchers have shown, the transfer of reading skills from one language to another is far from automatic. People must learn to read in each language. Special attention should be paid to having these students go through all of the exercises and activities that accompany the readings in this program. Once they have completed the activities, they might be asked to summarize the reading in Spanish in order to give them additional writing practice. They might also be required to keep a notebook with a special list of new vocabulary they might find in the reading selections.

*Answers, Guía para la lectura:* **D.** 1. Sedlar was born in Santa Fe 2. Tacos, tamales, enchiladas, chiles rellenos

C. Now read the second paragraph and look for more cognates.

D. Answer the folowing questions

1. Why is Santa Fe mentioned?
2. What Mexican dishes are listed in the text?

*Learning Strategy:*

*Skimming for gist*

## Magia y color en Los Ángeles

John Sedlar, dueño de "St. Estèphe" en Los Ángeles y uno de los chefs más celebrados del país, combina la técnica de la "nouvelle cuisine" francesa con la cocina popular del suroeste americano. Sedlar nació en Santa Fe y uno de sus recuerdos más vivos es la comida de su abuela, Eloísa Rivera, cuyas recetas para empanaditas y bizcochitos se sirven hoy día en el elegante comedor "St. Estèphe".

Tacos, tamales, enchiladas y chiles rellenos se transforman en platos de una delicadeza extraordinaria. Para que sus platos también agraden a la vista, Sedlar se inspira en los colores y texturas del suroeste. "El suroeste", explica, "es un espíritu intenso que uno siente en la luz viva de Nuevo México, sus desiertos quemados por el sol, sus paisajes rústicos y su comida vital y robusta."

John Sedlar

# Aquí leemos

## Estrategia para la lectura

It is not necessary to know every word in order to read and understand many kinds of writing in Spanish. A lot of information is carried by the layout or format of the passage. By thinking in advance about the information you expect to find in a passage and by looking for familiar words, you can often read as much as you need to.

*Reading Strategies:*

*Be aware of the context of the reading.*
*Examine format and layout for clues to content.*
*Decide what you expect the content to be.*
*Look for words you know or can guess.*

## Antes de leer

Before looking at the reading in this section, answer these questions about restaurant menus:

- **What categories are usually included on restaurant menus?**
- **What information is essential on a menu?**
- **What headings do you expect to see on a menu?**

Use your experience with menus as well as layout and familiar-looking words to help you understand the menu from a Mexican restaurant on page 68. Try to guess words you do not know.

## Actividades

*A.* You are at the restaurant with a friend who does not speak much Spanish. She tells you what she would like to eat or drink, and you tell her (in English, of course!) what she should order and how much it will cost. For example, if she says, "I've always wanted to try Mexican sausage. Do they have it here?," you could suggest she try the **sándwich de chorizo,** which costs 22 **pesos**.

1. I'm not very hungry. All I want is a cup of coffee.
2. I don't eat meat. Maybe I could get something with cheese.
3. I'm really thirsty. I'd like something cold to drink.
4. I'm in the mood for something sweet.
5. I'm hungry! I feel like having chicken.



## Objectives

[T]his section contains a reading (**Aquí leemos**) and a set of [o]ral and written communicative activities (**Ya llegamos**) that [r]epresent the culminating performance point of the unit.

## Support Materials

Workbook: **pp. 34–36**
Unit Review Blackline Masters: **Unit 1 Review**
Transparency: **#20**
Listening Activity masters: **p. 21**
Tapescript: **p. 28**
Unit exam: **Testing Program, p. 33**
Atajo, writing assistant software

### Prereading

Discuss a Spanish menu. What strategies might you use to figure out unfamiliar words? Do you play it safe and order a **sándwich** and a **café**? Do you take a wild guess? Emphasize that it is unusual for a non-native speaker of Spanish to recognize every item on a menu. Encourage them to make intelligent guesses based on: (1) cognates (**fruta**, **sándwich**, etc.); (2) context (the general categories, such as **Entradas**); (3) word association (**agua mineral**). Have the students recall the many Mexican food words we now use so commonly in the U.S.

**Ex. A:** pair work

### Ex. A: Numbered Heads Together

- Form teams of three. Have team members choose a family identity (**padre, hijo,** etc.).
- Give the teams a situation from Ex. A, such as "I'm not very hungry." Each "family" is to confer to decide what to order. Family members must make sure everyone understands the answer.
- Call out a word for a family member: **madre, padre,** etc. Students who chose that identity can indicate that they know the answer by raising their hands. When the teacher calls on a student and gets an incomplete response, he/she might ask another student with the same identity to add to the response.

*Answers, Ex. A:* 1. coffee ($10) 2. cheese **enchiladas** with **guacamole** ($30) or cheese sandwich ($15) 3. soft drink ($15) or mineral water ($15) 4. any **postre** 5. chicken **tacos** ($27), chicken **tostada** ($22) or chicken in **mole** sauce ($35)

*Spanish speakers:* Special attention should be paid to having these students go through all of the exercises and activities that accompany this reading. Once they have completed the activities, they might be asked to create a menu of their own in order to give them additional writing practice. They might be asked to keep a notebook with a special list of new vocabulary they might find in the reading selections.



## Restaurante "La Estancia"

| Entradas | |
|---|---|
| Enchiladas de queso con guacamole | $30 |
| Enchiladas de carne | $35 |
| Tacos con frijoles | $25 |
| Tacos de pollo con salsa picante | $27 |
| Pollo en mole | $35 |
| Huevos rancheros | $20 |
| Tostada de pollo | $22 |
| **Sándwiches** | |
| Sándwich de queso | $15 |
| Sándwich de jamón | $20 |
| Sándwich de chorizo | $22 |
| **Postres** | |
| Flan | $15 |
| Fruta | $10 |
| Pastel de fresas | $20 |
| Helados | $15 |
| **Bebidas** | |
| Té | $10 |
| Café | $10 |
| Refrescos varios | $15 |
| Agua mineral | $15 |

Todos los platos se acompañan con arroz y frijoles.

*B.* What do you tell the waiter she wants? Match these orders to your friend's wishes in Activity A. One answer is left over. Which of the orders could it apply to?

___ a. **Sólo quiere un agua mineral, bien fría.**
___ b. **No come carne. Va a probar los tacos con frijoles.**
___ c. **Para ella, las enchiladas de queso con guacamole.**
___ d. **Quiere los tacos de pollo con salsa picante.**
___ e. **Va a tomar un café, no más.**
___ f. **El pastel de fresas, por favor.**

*C.* You are traveling in Mexico with your family. They are not very familiar with Mexican food. Using the photographs on p. 48, describe these dishes in English.

1. **arroz con frijoles**
2. **tacos de pollo**
3. **enchilada de queso**
4. **enchilada de carne**

*D.* List all the words you know (or can guess from the readings) that you could use to describe in Spanish the dishes in Activity C.

## ostreading

eading comprehension questions are in English because at is point students understand more than they can communiate. Receptive skills develop before productive skills in the arning process.

*nswers, Ex. B:* a. 3 b. left over, could use for #2
2 d. 5 e. 1 f. 4

**Ex. C:**  pair work

*Answers, Ex. C:* Encourage full descriptive answers, e.g., "a soft **tortilla** wrapped around meat in a sauce, sprinkled with cheese, lettuce, tomato, and onions" instead of "meat **enchilada**."

# Objectives

As the title suggests, **Ya llegamos** is the culminating section of the unit, providing open-ended situational activities to practice unit material. These activities provide an opportunity to pull together and apply the vocabulary, functions, and structures studied in the unit, as well as allow teachers to check the students' control of these elements in realistic applications. Plan to spend approximately one class period doing the activities that you and your class prefer.

**Ex. A:** 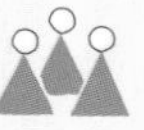 groups of three

**Ex. B:** groups of four or more

*Spanish speakers, Exs. A and B:* Remember that most Spanish speakers already have a command of a variety of Spanish that is used in informal, very familiar contexts. These situations are informal, but have the students focus on using that vocabulary that may be new for them. Emphasize that it may be necessary to use such vocabulary when talking to speakers who are from other parts of the Spanish-speaking world. Remember to be sensitive and accept how the students say things the first time. What they have said may be totally appropriate in their speech community. This is a good place to have them focus on the differences between how they say something in their speech community and how the book is teaching them to express this. Remember, rather than denigrating how they speak, your main objective is to expand the range of contexts in which these students can use Spanish.



# Ya llegamos

## Actividades orales

**Learning Strategies:**

*Interviewing, listening for and providing information, selecting information, participating in culturally appropriate social interactions*

**Critical Thinking Strategies:**

*Sequencing, evaluating information to share, comparing and contrasting*

**A. *En el café*** **Scene 1, Take 1:** You and a friend meet at a café after school. You (1) greet each other and (2) order something to eat and/or drink (perhaps from an imaginary waiter). Then another friend arrives. (3) Introduce him or her to your first friend. To help the two people who have just met get to know each other better, (4) mention two interesting facts that you know about each person to the other friend. Consider their likes and dislikes and what they do particularly well.

**Scene 1, Take 2:** Now replay the scene, expanding on your conversation. This time, after doing the first part, the new friends should go on to (1) comment on an interest or activity they have in common or would like to develop. They should then (2) ask each other questions about their nationalities or family origin, (3) inquire about what languages they speak or would like to speak, and then (4) add one other interesting detail about themselves or their family. Don't forget to have the third person (5) order something as well.

**Learning Strategies:**

*Negotiating, persuading, supporting opinion, participating in culturally appropriate social interactions*

**Critical Thinking Strategies:**

*Evaluating, prioritizing, decision-making*

**B. *¿Dónde desean comer?*** While downtown on a Saturday afternoon, you and a friend run into two or three other classmates. You decide that you are hungry. Each member of the group (1) suggests a type of place to go for something to eat (café, **bar de tapas,** restaurant). (2) Support your suggestion by mentioning the appealing features of your choice. (Be convincing; you want your suggestion to win out!) (3) As each suggestion is offered, say what you do or do not like about that place and its menu. (4) Reach an agreement with your group members, and when you have decided, (5) go to that place together and order your food. (If you can't all agree, split into smaller groups, say good-bye, and go off to the place of your choice for ordering.)



*Support material, Unidad 1:* Lab Manual Ya llegamos listening activities, Laboratory Program, Tapescript, and Teacher's Edition of the Workbook/Lab Manual

**Ex. C, D, and E:** writing

*Spanish speakers, Exs. C, D, and E:* Have Spanish speakers fully carry out writing activities. Remember, while many already speak and understand spoken Spanish, they may not know how to write the language. This is a good place to start building basic literacy skills in Spanish. Have students pa

## Actividades escritas

*C. Para comer* Write down what you are going to serve two or three friends at a small lunch at your house on Saturday to honor the new exchange student from Spain who is visiting your school. Be sure to include beverages and dessert.

*D. Preferencias* Write down six different activities that you like to do and include how well or how often you do them.

*E. ¿Quién soy yo?* Assume the identity of an international celebrity—actor or actress **(actor o actriz),** political figure **(político[a]),** or author **(autor[a]).** Write a brief description of yourself, your nationality, where you are from, and what you like to do, eat, etc. Be prepared to read this description to your classmates who will try to guess your identity. (Limit yourself as much as possible to words and structures you have studied in this first unit.)

Miguel Palacios
Soy español. Estudio mucho y trabajo a veces en la cafetería. Deseo viajar a México y a los Estados Unidos.

*Topic vocabulary:* Bread; breakfast; cheeses; cooking; drinks; fish and seafood; fruits; languages; legumes and vegetables; meals; meat; nationality; pastry; personality; professions; spices, seasonings, condiments; trades; etc.

*Grammar:* Verb summary; verbs: present; interrogative; **ser;** adjectives: descriptive; etc.

**Ex. E:** role play

## Critical Thinking

### *Critical Thinking Strategy: Comparing and contrasting*

Ask students to compare and contrast Spain with Mexico or another Spanish-speaking country on the basis of what they learned in the first unit or on previous knowledge. How have the countries influenced each other? Then have them compare Latin American countries to the United States. What is different? How are some things the same? Do they see any signs of American influence in Spanish-speaking countries? Are there any signs of Latin American influence in the United States? (If possible, get them to discuss both positive and negative points of view when answering the questions.)

ecial attention to the spelling of the vocabulary that has en introduced in this **etapa,** especially those words that ay have problematic spelling combinations. This is a good ace to have Spanish speaking students engage in peer-edit-g. Have them look at the written work of a partner and focus the spelling.

### Writing Activities

*Writing suggestion:* Remind students to refer for help writing to the **Para charlar** and **Temas y contextos** sec-ns of the chapter **Vocabulario,** as well as to the **Estruc-ra** and **Nota gramatical** sections in the **etapa.** If you have access to **Atajo** software, students will find similar help there, both in the dictionary and in the indexes labeled *Functional Vocabulary, Topic Vocabulary,* and *Grammar.* For instance, in Unit 1 students might refer to the following **Atajo** categories:

### *Atajo, Writing Assistant Software*

*Functional vocabulary:* Asking for information; describing people; greeting and saying good-bye; introducing; etc.

# Objectives

The interdisciplinary lessons that have been included at the end of each unit provide a unique opportunity for teachers and students to study the Spanish language through the medium of another subject area, (i.e., math, science, or social studies) as recommended in the most recent draft of the National Standards for Foreign Language Education. These lessons are completely optional, and none of this material has been included in the testing program.

Each lesson centers around a short reading and includes warm-up and follow-up activities with ample support to walk students through the lesson. In some cases, additional extension activities are provided in the teacher edition margins.

*Alternate warm-up activity:*

You may want to ask students to work in small groups of 3–5 students to complete the following activity. Copy the information below onto the board or an overhead transparency. One student in each group will act as the "asker," posing the question **¿Dónde te gusta merendar?** to the other students in the group. Another student will act as "scribe," recording the responses of each group member. After the group has finished, members should be prepared to provide a "group report" to the entire class.

# Conexión

## La merienda y la nutrición

- What do you think the reading is about based on the title?
- Can you predict what the author will say about the topic?
- What words might be important ones to know when reading about this topic?

### AL EMPEZAR

Reading Spanish is not as difficult as you might think because of the large number of cognates (words that look similar and share similar meaning) in English and Spanish. In addition, your teacher will help you organize ideas about the reading before you get started. First, look at the title of the following reading.

### LA MERIENDA Y LA NUTRICIÓN

Es importante pensar en la nutrición antes de seleccionar un **alimento**. Las mejores meriendas tienen menos calorías y son muy bajas en **grasa**. La leche **descremada**, por ejemplo, contiene todos los minerales, vitaminas y proteínas de la leche entera, pero con menos grasa, colesterol y calorías. Es una buena idea variar la dieta. Los alimentos que contienen más **fibra** son muy buenos para la salud, por ejemplo—**las palomitas de maíz** (sin mantequilla), las frutas y los vegetales.

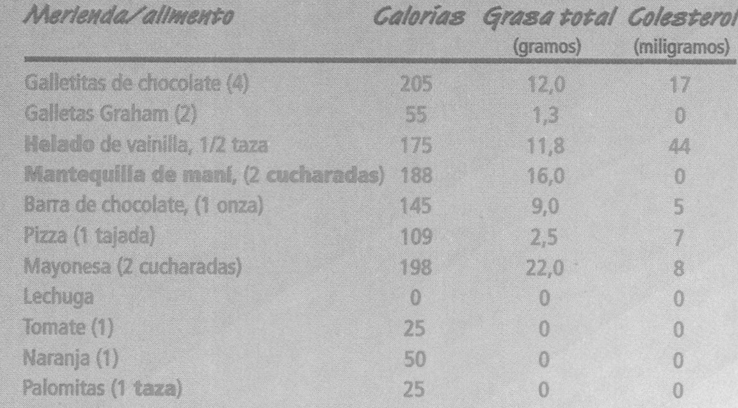

| *Merienda/alimento* | *Calorías* | *Grasa total* (gramos) | *Colesterol* (miligramos) |
|---|---|---|---|
| Galletitas de chocolate (4) | 205 | 12,0 | 17 |
| Galletas Graham (2) | 55 | 1,3 | 0 |
| **Helado** de vainilla, 1/2 taza | 175 | 11,8 | 44 |
| **Mantequilla de maní**, (2 **cucharadas**) | 188 | 16,0 | 0 |
| Barra de chocolate, (1 onza) | 145 | 9,0 | 5 |
| Pizza (1 tajada) | 109 | 2,5 | 7 |
| Mayonesa (2 cucharadas) | 198 | 22,0 | 8 |
| Lechuga | 0 | 0 | 0 |
| Tomate (1) | 25 | 0 | 0 |
| Naranja (1) | 50 | 0 | 0 |
| Palomitas (1 **taza**) | 25 | 0 | 0 |

*merienda* snacking / *alimento* food / *grasa* fat / *descremada* skim / *fibra* dietary fiber / *las palomitas de maíz* popcorn / *helado* ice cream / *mantequilla de maní* peanut butter/ *cucharadas* tablespoons / *taza* cup

72

**¿Dónde te gusta merendar?**

*En casa*

En la cocina ______

Enfrente de la televisión ______

En el sofá ______

En mi cama ______

¿ ? ______

*En la escuela*

En la clase de español ______

En la cafetería ______

En el patio de la escuela ______

En el autobús ______

En los pasillos ______

**¿Cuándo te gusta merendar?**

Por la mañana ______

Por la tarde ______

Por la noche ______

Todo el día ______

Antes de dormir ______

Después de hacer ejercicios ______

¿ ? ______

# PRIMERA ETAPA

## Preparación

» As you get ready to begin this **etapa,** think about the items you take to school. Make a list of at least five items that you usually take to school.

» In this **etapa** you will also learn to say that something belongs to someone else. If you have borrowed a calculator from a friend, how would you say, in English, whose calculator it is?

*Learning Strategies:*

*Previewing, listing*

## ¿Qué llevas a la escuela?

*¿Qué llevas a la escuela?:* What do you take to school?

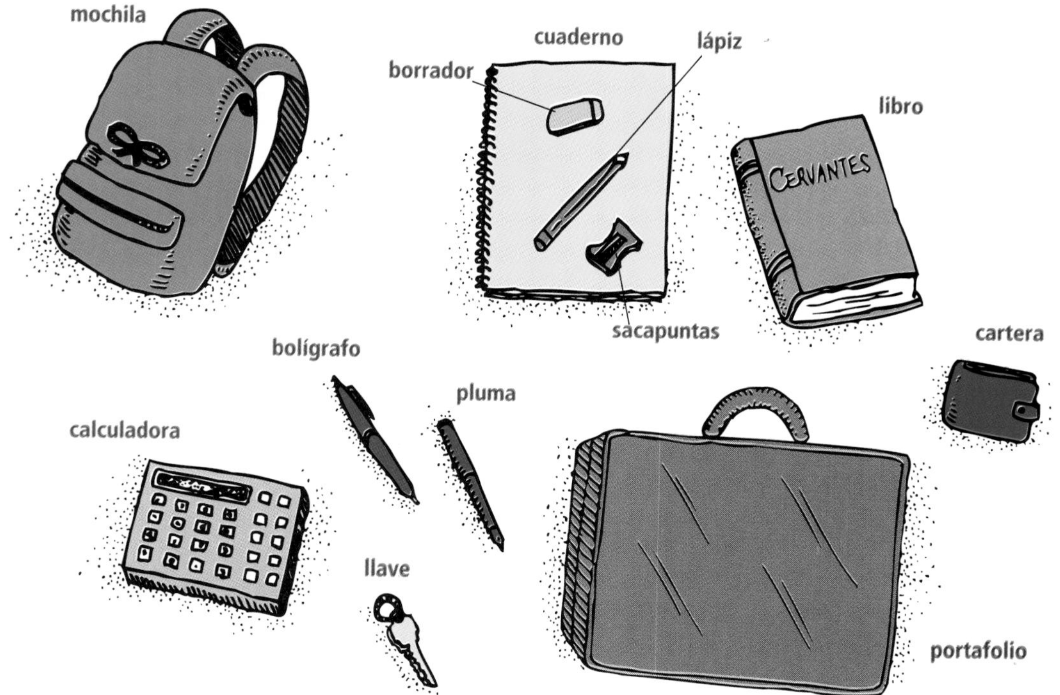

### Presentation: ¿Qué llevas a la escuela?

Use actual objects for the most effective presentation of this vocabulary: **Es una mochila. ¿Qué es? Es una mochila. ¿Qué es?** (pointing to a pen) **¿Es una mochila también? No, es un bolígrafo.** Point to other objects, using this pattern. As you progress, go back to other groups to review and reinforce.

### Vocabulary Expansion

**papel, una hoja de papel, tijeras**

Point out that **billetera** is also used for *wallet*. **Un bolígrafo** is a ball-point pen. **Una pluma** is a fountain pen. **Borrador** is the generic term for eraser. Another common word for the eraser on a pen or pencil is **goma.**

***Support material, ¿Qué llevas a la escuela?:*** Transparencies #21, #21a

## Etapa Support Materials

Workbook: pp. 38–42
Critical Thinking Master: pp. 5–6
Transparencies: #21, #21a, #22

Quiz: Testing Program, p. 39

Support material, ¿Qué llevas a la escuela?: Transparencies #21, #21a

# ¡Aquí te toca a ti!

**A. *¿Qué es?*** Identify the objects in the numbered drawings.

**Modelo:** *Es un lápiz.*

1. 
2. 
3. 
4. 
5. 
6. 
7. 
8. 

**B. *No es...*** Correct the initial assumption on the basis of the numbered drawings in the previous exercise.

**Modelo:** ¿Es un libro?
*No es un libro. Es un lápiz.*

1. ¿Es un bolígrafo?
2. ¿Es una cartera?
3. ¿Es un cuaderno?
4. ¿Es un lápiz?
5. ¿Es un sacapuntas?
6. ¿Es un borrador?
7. ¿Es un portafolio?
8. ¿Es una llave?

**C. *¿Qué llevas tú a la escuela?*** Indicate what each person takes to school. Follow the model.

**Modelo:** Juan
*Juan lleva un libro a la escuela.*

1. Julia
2. Jaime
3. tú
4. nosotros



*Support material, Exs. A and B:* Transparency #22.

**Ex. A:** pair work

*Answers, Ex. A:* 1. Es un libro. 2. Es una mochila. 3. Es una calculadora. 4. Es un bolígrafo. 5. Es un cuaderno. 6. Es una cartera. 7. Es un borrador/una goma. 8. Es un sacapuntas. (Point out that this word is masculine even though it has a feminine plural ending.)

**Ex. B:** pair work

*Suggestions, Ex. B:* Have students work in pairs or do as a whole class activity by using the **pregúntale** format.

*Answers, Ex. B:* 1. No es un bolígrafo. Es un libro. 2. ...Es una mochila. 3. ...Es una calculadora. 4. ...Es un bolígrafo. 5. ...Es un cuaderno. 6. ...Es una cartera. 7. ...Es un borrador/una goma. 8. ...Es un sacapuntas.

**Ex. C:** pair work

writing

*Suggestions, Ex. C:* Have students write out sentences and edit their partners' mistakes. You could also have six students write the answers on the board and then have the whole class point out any errors. Be sure to reinforce good points so that students don't feel embarrassed or intimidated in front of the class.

*Answers, Ex. C:* 1. Julia lleva una mochila a la escuela. 2. Jaime lleva un cuaderno... 3. Tú llevas unos bolígrafos... 4. Nosotros llevamos unos cuadernos... 5. Yo llevo un bolígrafo... 6. Él lleva una cartera... 7. Ella lleva una bolsa... 8. Ud. lleva una calculadora...

*Follow-up, Ex. C:* Showing students drawings, transparencies, or actual objects, ask **¿Llevas un/una... a la escuela?** A willing student could also volunteer his or her backpack for a guessing game. **¿Qué tiene X en la mochila?** Students could guess school items within.

## Exercise Progression

Exs. A and B, which can be done either with the transparency or with the book, are designed to help students associate the word with the object and also to practice **es un/una** and **no es un/una.** Ex. C continues to practice word/object association while also practicing forms of the verb **llevar.**

5. yo
6. él
7. ella
8. Ud.

## Pronunciación: The consonant p

The sound of the consonant **p** is similar to the sound of *p* in English, but is pronounced without the puff of air that accompanies the English sound. Put your hand in front of your mouth and note the puff of air that is produced when you pronounce the English word *pan* and the absence of this puff of air when you say *speak.* The Spanish **p** is more like the *p* in the English word *speak.*

## Práctica

*D.* Listen and repeat as your teacher models the following words.

1. papa
2. política
3. pájaro
4. pintura
5. problema
6. póster
7. pronto
8. pluma
9. lápiz
10. sacapuntas

## ESTRUCTURA

### The definite article

| | |
|---|---|
| **el** libro, **el** bolígrafo, **el** portafolio | *the* book, *the* pen, *the* briefcase |
| **la** mochila, **la** calculadora, **la** pluma | *the* knapsack, *the* calculator, *the* pen |
| **los** libros, **los** bolígrafos, **los** portafolios | *the* books, *the* pens, *the* briefcases |
| **las** mochilas, **las** calculadoras, **las** plumas | *the* knapsacks, *the* calculators, *the* pens |

In Spanish, the definite article has two singular forms and two plural forms. The English equivalent of these four forms is simply *the.*

**el** **los** **la** **las**



### Presentation: Pronunciation

Demonstrate that the puff of air that accompanies the sound of *p* in English can be shown by holding a piece of paper in front of your mouth as you pronounce English words that begin with *p.*

Additional activities appear in the Laboratory Tape Program.

### Presentation: The definite article

Introduce definite articles by contrasting them with indefinite articles. Read several sentences where you stress the articles, and then have students repeat them. **Julia lleva un libro a la escuela. Allí está el libro de Julia.** Other objects: **calculadora, llaves, bolígrafos, cuaderno.**

You may want to point out that the definite article is omitted in direct address: **Buenos días, señor García; Hasta mañana, doctora Hernández.**

*Support material, Pronunciación:*
Pronunciation Tape

## Exercise Progression

Exs. E and F offer controlled practice with the definite articles.

**Ex. E:** writing

*Suggestion, Ex. E:* Have students do this exercise with their books closed. Read the words with the indefinite articles and have students repeat them, substituting the corresponding definite articles.

1. One of the two main uses of the definite article is to designate a noun in a general or collective sense:

   **El café** es una bebida popular aquí. *Coffee* is a popular drink here.
   **La leche** tiene vitamina D. *Milk* has vitamin D.

Notice how Spanish uses the article when talking about these nouns in a general sense while English does not.

2. The other main use of the definite article is to designate a noun in a specific sense. **Necesito los libros** means I need the specific books that have already been mentioned. **La mochila de Juan** refers to the particular knapsack that belongs to Juan.

3. The definite article is also used in Spanish with such titles as **Sr., Sra., Srta., Dr., Dra.,** etc.

   **El señor Herrera** come en un café. *Mr. Herrera* eats in a café.
   **La señora Martínez** lleva un libro a la escuela. *Mrs. Martínez* takes a book to school.

You will note that English does not use the article with these titles.

## Aquí practicamos

*E.* Replace the indefinite article with the appropriate definite article **(el, la, los, las).**

**Modelo:** un cuaderno — *el cuaderno*
unos libros — *los libros*

1. un café
2. una estudiante
3. un sándwich
4. una mochila
5. unas bebidas
6. unos médicos
7. un bolígrafo
8. una cartera
9. unos refrescos
10. un jugo
11. una profesora
12. unos estudiantes
13. una llave
14. una calculadora
15. un borrador
16. un sacapuntas

**Me llamo Jorge.**
**En mi cuarto hay...**

## ¡Aquí te toca a ti!

**A. *¿Dónde hay...?*** (Where is/are there . . . ?) Based on the pictures, answer the following questions about Marta's and Jorge's rooms.

**Modelos:** ¿un televisor?
*En el cuarto de Jorge hay un televisor.*

¿una cama?
*En el cuarto de Marta hay una cama y en el cuarto de Jorge hay una cama también.*

1. ¿una computadora?
2. ¿una grabadora?
3. ¿un radio despertador?
4. ¿una cama?
5. ¿un estéreo?
6. ¿unos pósters?
7. ¿una máquina de escribir?
8. ¿una cámara?
9. ¿unas cintas?
10. ¿unos discos compactos?
11. ¿unas plantas?
12. ¿unos estantes?
13. ¿una silla?
14. ¿una alfombra?

**Learning Strategies:** Collecting information, reporting

**B. *¿Y tú?*** Indicate what you have and do not have in your room at home.

**Modelo:** *En mi cuarto, hay una cama y una cómoda, pero no hay un escritorio. También hay pósters en la pared* (on the wall).



**Ex. B:** writing

*Learning Strategy: Writing a report from information organized in a chart*

***Suggestion, Ex. B:*** Expand into a writing exercise, being sure to set a time limit if done in class. Have students write a paragraph comparing their room with those of their partners. They should draw from information gathered in interviews with their partners and recorded on a chart. Then have them check their partners' papers for errors in spelling or agreement of articles. You might also have volunteers read their paragraphs to the class. This activity provides preparation for the **Ya llegamos** section at the end of Unit 2.

***More-prepared students, Ex. B:*** More-prepared or Spanish-speaking students could draw diagrams of their rooms on the board, pointing out where items are.

***Less-prepared students, Ex. B:*** Less-prepared students could sketch an empty bedroom with closet, windows, and door indicated. They could then cut out pictures of bedroom furnishings from a magazine and glue them in the room, labeling each item in Spanish.

## Exercise Progression

Ex. A is designed to associate the word with the drawing of the item. Ex. B is a personalized version of this activity.

***Answers, Ex. A:*** 1. En el cuarto de Marta hay una computadora. 2. Jorge—grabadora 3. Marta—radio despertador 4. Marta—cama, Jorge—cama 5. Marta—estéreo 6. Marta—pósters 7. Jorge—máquina de escribir 8. Jorge—cámara 9. Jorge—cintas 10. Marta— discos compactos 11. Marta—plantas 12. Marta—estantes 13. Marta—silla, Jorge—silla 14. Jorge—alfombra

## Presentation: Pronunciation

Have students pronounce English words that begin with *t,* telling them to take notice of the position of the tip of the tongue. Then have them move the tip of the tongue from the gum ridge to the back of the upper front teeth and practice saying *ta, te, ti, to, tu.*

Additional activities appear in the Laboratory Tape Program.

*Follow-up, Ex. D:* Review by doing a **pregúntale** exercise. **(María), pregúntale a... si lleva un/una... a la escuela.**

## Presentation: Numbers from 0 to 20

You may have presented these numbers in the **Etapa preliminar.** If that is the case, review them quickly. To present numbers for the first time, have students repeat number series in chorus: 0; 0, 1; 0, 1, 2; etc. Then have them count backwards and in twos, with books closed, introducing the notion of **pares** (even numbers) and **impares** (odd numbers). You could also have students practice saying zip codes.

*Support material, Pronunciación:* Pronunciation Tape



# Pronunciación: The consonant *t*

The sound of **t** in Spanish is produced by placing the tip of the tongue behind the back of the upper front teeth, while *t* in English is pronounced by placing the tip of the tongue on the gum ridge behind the upper front teeth. Pronounce the English word *tea* and note where the tip of your tongue is. Now pronounce the Spanish word **ti** being careful to place the tip of the tongue on the back of the upper front teeth.

## Práctica

*C.* Listen and repeat as your teacher models the following words.

1. tú
2. tomo
3. tapas
4. taza
5. tipo
6. tenis
7. tonto
8. política
9. fútbol
10. cinta

## Repaso

*D. ¿Qué llevan a la escuela?* Look at the drawings below and tell what each person takes to school.

## Palabras útiles

### Numbers from 0 to 20

| | | | | | |
|---|---|---|---|---|---|
| **cero** | 0 | **tres** | 3 | **seis** | 6 |
| **uno** | 1 | **cuatro** | 4 | **siete** | 7 |
| **dos** | 2 | **cinco** | 5 | **ocho** | 8 |

| | | | | | |
|---|---|---|---|---|---|
| **nueve** | 9 | **trece** | 13 | **diecisiete** | 17 |
| **diez** | 10 | **catorce** | 14 | **dieciocho** | 18 |
| **once** | 11 | **quince** | 15 | **diecinueve** | 19 |
| **doce** | 12 | **dieciséis** | 16 | **veinte** | 20 |

## Aquí practicamos

*E.* Follow the directions in Spanish.

1. Cuenta *(Count)* de 0 a 10. Cuenta de 11 a 20.
2. Cuenta los números pares *(even)*: 0, 2, 4, 6, 8, 10, 12, 14, 16, 18, 20.
3. Cuenta los números impares *(odd)*: 1, 3, 5, 7, 9, 11, 13, 15, 17, 19.

*F.* ***Sumando y restando*** (Adding and subtracting) Make a complete sentence out of the following problems in addition and subtraction by solving them. Follow the model.

2 + 1 =
*Dos más uno son tres.*

3 − 1 =
*Tres menos uno son dos.*

| | | | |
|---|---|---|---|
| **1.** 2 + 5 = | **5.** 4 − 1 = | **9.** 7 + 13 = | **13.** 3 + 5 = |
| **2.** 6 − 3 = | **6.** 0 + 4 = | **10.** 18 − 2 = | **14.** 1 + 2 = |
| **3.** 6 + 10 = | **7.** 5 + 4 = | **11.** 8 − 3 = | **15.** 9 − 4 = |
| **4.** 17 − 2 = | **8.** 19 − 6 = | **12.** 12 + 5 = | **16.** 19 − 8 = |

## Palabras útiles

### *Hay + noun*

**Hay** un libro en mi cuarto. — *There is* a book in my room.
**Hay** tres libros en mi cuarto. — *There are* three books in my room.

As you have already seen in this **etapa,** the Spanish word **hay** means either *there is* or *there are.* Note that **hay** does not change and combines with both *singular* and *plural* nouns. **Hay** can be combined with nouns that are preceded by an indefinite article **(un, una, unos, unas)** or any number.



**Ex. E:** pair work

**Ex. F:** pair work

*Variation, Ex. F:* You do the calculations, making errors from time to time and having students correct you.

*Follow-up, Ex. F:* Dictate some simple math problems to students with their books closed. Have students volunteer to read out loud the problems with the answers.

*More-prepared students, Ex. F:* More-prepared students would enjoy hearing and solving a much longer equation with both addition and subtraction said quite quickly.

### Presentation: Hay + noun

Place some school supplies and classroom objects on a desk or table. Then ask: **¿Qué hay sobre (en) la mesa (el escritorio)? ¿Hay unos libros? ¿Hay un bolígrafo?** Have students point out other objects around the room.

You might also want to introduce **cuántos/cuántas** as a lexical item and ask questions such as, **¿Cuántas ventanas hay aquí?, ¿Cuántos pósters hay en la pared?** etc.

Point out that **hay** is never followed by a definite article, only by indefinite articles or numbers.

### Exercise Progression

Ex. E can easily be incorporated into the presentation. Ex. F practices the numbers in easy mathematical problems.

**Ex. G:** pair work

*Suggestion, Ex. G:* Have students ask each other questions with the items given, and then respond according to the drawing. Example: **¿Hay una cama? Sí, hay una cama.**

*Answers, Ex. G:* Hay: (1) unos pósters (2) una silla (4) una computadora (6) un estéreo (7) unos libros (8) unos lápices (9) unos bolígrafos (10) un escritorio (11) unas plantas (13) un radio despertador. No hay: (3) unas cintas (5) un televisor (12) una máquina de escribir (13) unos cuadernos.

*Follow-up, Ex. G:* Since the **Palabras útiles** note is lexical in nature, there is only one controlled meaningful exercise. If you wish further practice, you could follow up by having students review the transparencies (without overlays) or by showing a photo of a different room.

**Ex. H:** pair work

*Answers, **Después de escuchar:*** plantas, escritorio, cama, silla, grabadora, cintas, póster

*Support material, **Aquí escuchamos:*** Teacher Tape/CD #1 Track #18 and Tapescript

Learning Strategy:
*Collecting information*

**G. *El cuarto de Marta*** Indicate whether each item is or is not found in the room pictured on page 84.

**Modelos:**

| una cama | una grabadora |
|---|---|
| *Hay una cama.* | *No hay una grabadora.* |

1. unos pósters
2. una silla
3. unas cintas
4. una computadora
5. un televisor
6. un estéreo
7. unos libros
8. unos lápices
9. unos bolígrafos
10. un escritorio
11. unas plantas
12. una máquina de escribir
13. unos cuadernos

**H. *Hay...*** Working with another student, take turns pointing out items in the room on page 85. Each of you should also point out one item that does not appear in the room. Stop when each of you has discussed five items.

**Modelo:** *Hay una cama allí* (there).

Critical Thinking Strategy:
*Predicting*

Learning Strategy:
*Listening for details*

## Aquí escuchamos:
### "¿Qué hay en tu cuarto?"

### Antes de escuchar

**Think about what you have in your room at home. Before you listen to Carmen's short monologue, think about the items you think she might have in her room. Before your instructor plays the tape, take a moment and copy onto a separate sheet of paper the list of words that follows:**

START

| | | | |
|---|---|---|---|
| estantes | escritorio | silla | discos compactos |
| plantas | computadora | grabadora | póster |
| estéreo | cama | cintas | |

### Después de escuchar

**Listen to the tape again and this time check off on your list the items that Carmen has in her room.**

**Carmen's room**

EJERCICIO ORAL

*I.* ***¿Qué hay?*** Find out from several of your classmates what they have and do not have in their rooms at home. Then tell them what you have and do not have in your own room.

 —*¿Qué hay en tu cuarto?*
—*En mi cuarto hay dos plantas, una cama...*

*Learning Strategy:* Reporting

EJERCICIO ESCRITO

*J.* ***Cosas importantes*** Your school has just received a foreign exchange student. The couple with no children who live across the street from the school has agreed to host the student. They have asked for help in furnishing their guest's room appropriately for a teen. With a partner, decide on the six most important items to include.

*Cooperative Learning*
*Learning Strategy:* Negotiating
*Critical Thinking Strategy:* Prioritizing



## Critical Thinking

*Critical Thinking Strategy: Drawing inferences*

Have students study the photo on this page. On the basis of what they observe there, what can they deduce about this person? Then ask them to compare this room with their own or that of a friend or sibling. What, if anything, looks particularly "Hispanic"?

**Ex. I:** groups of four or more

## Cooperative Learning

*Learning Strategy: Polling*

*Critical Thinking Strategies: Interpreting information in a chart, drawing inferences*

Take a class survey on the board by having groups report how many students in their group have each item discussed in their room. Write the name of an item on the board as it is mentioned by the "reporter." **(Hay plantas en los cuartos de tres alumnos, y hay escritorios en los cuartos de dos.)** Enter the appropriate number of "tick" marks after each item as they are mentioned.

Do a follow-up discussion to determine the highest and lowest frequency items while practicing the **hay** and **gustar** structures. **(¿De qué cosa hay más en nuestros cuartos? Hay más escritorios; hay diez y nueve escritorios. ¿De qué cosa hay menos en nuestros cuartos? Hay menos plantas; sólo hay cinco plantas.)** Then encourage the students to draw inferences on the "sample group" (their class) by asking such questions as: **¿Por qué hay muchos escritorios? Porque somos alumnos. ¿Por qué hay muchos discos compactos? Porque nos gusta la música.**

This activity provides preparation for the **Ya llegamos** section at the end of Unit 2.

**Ex. J:** 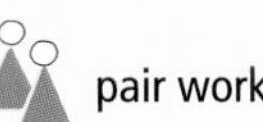 writing

pair work

## Cooperative Learning

*Learning Strategies: Surveying*

*Critical Thinking Strategies: Interpreting information in a chart, drawing inferences*

Do a follow-up class summation survey on the board to determine the top priorities for the entire group. (Refer to suggestions for Ex. I for format of doing a survey and drawing inferences from it.)

Ask such summative questions as: **¿Qué cosa es más importante? (la prioridad número uno, número dos, etc.) ¿Por qué?**

## Presentation: En nuestra casa

Using the transparency of houses and possessions, begin each vocabulary group by talking about yourself: **Yo vivo en una casa, ¿y tú? ¿Quién vive en un apartamento? En nuestra casa hay un estéreo y un televisor a colores. ¿Qué hay en tu casa?**

If you do not use the transparencies, describe two people (drawing items on the board when necessary): **Marta vive en una casa. En su casa hay un televisor a colores y... ,** etc.

## Vocabulary Expansion

**sillón** (armchair, easy chair), **sofá, condominio**

The technical word for *VCR* is **videocasete** or **videocasetera.** In Spain, the word **vídeo** is used for both the VCR and the tape that it plays.

***Support material, En nuestra casa:***
Transparencies #25, #25a



# TERCERA ETAPA

### Preparación

- **As you get ready to begin this etapa, think about where you and your friends and relatives live (house, apartment, condominium, etc.); what you have where you live; and how you get around town.**
- **Make a list with house, apartment, condominium and/or townhouse on it; then list one to three acquaintances under each heading who lives in that type of residence.**
- **By each name, list three different items of interest that you and those friends or relatives have at their home.**
- **Then name the different modes of transportation that each of you uses to get to school, go shopping, and to go to a friend's house.**

*Learning Strategies:*

*Contextualizing, previewing, listing*

## En nuestra casa

*En nuestra casa:* In our house

I live in . . .

**Vivo en...**

una casa

un apartamento



## Etapa Support Materials

Workbook: **pp. 47–51**
Transparencies: **#25, #25a**
Listening Activity masters: **p. 23**
Tapescript: **p. 31**
Quiz: **Testing Program, p. 44**

Chapter Test: **Testing Program, p. 46**

Support material, **En nuestra casa:**
**Transparencies #25, #25a**

**Allí** hay… — There

un estéreo

un vídeo

un televisor a colores

**Para ir al centro, voy en…** — To go downtown, I go in…

coche

(bici) bicicleta

(moto) motocicleta

autobús

## ¡Aquí te toca a ti!

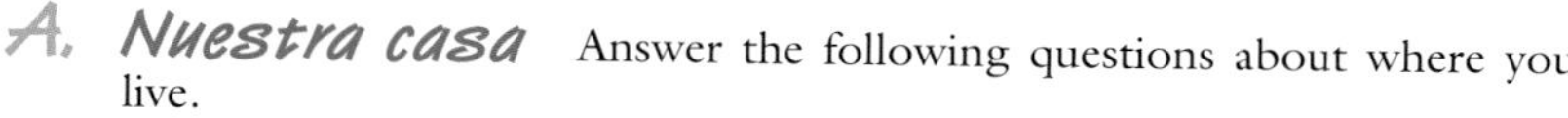

**A. *Nuestra casa*** Answer the following questions about where you live.

1. ¿Vives tú *(Do you live)* en una casa o en un apartamento?
   Vivo…
2. ¿Hay un estéreo en tu casa? ¿un televisor? ¿una computadora? ¿un vídeo?
3. ¿Cómo vas *(How do you go)* al centro? ¿En coche? ¿En moto? ¿En bicicleta? ¿En autobús?
   Yo voy…



### Vocabulary Expansion

**camioneta** (*van*), **autobús, camión** (*truck, bus* in Mexico)

**Ex. A:** pair work

***Suggestion, Ex. A:*** Have students ask their partners the questions and then call on certain students to report back to the class.

### Cultural Observation

Use the drawings as the basis for a discussion of typical means of transportation. Begin by having students talk about how they move about; then give them some information about Spanish-speaking countries.

### Exercise Progression

Ex. A is a personalized exercise designed to practice using the vocabulary. Ex. B offers additional controlled practice with the vocabulary items.

### *Possible answers, Ex. B:*

1. Vivo en una casa. Allí hay unas plantas, un televisor (a colores) y un sillón (un gato, una ventana), pero no hay un estéreo (una videocasetera). Para ir al centro, voy en coche. 2. ...un apartamento (un condominio). ...un televisor (a colores), una videocasetera, un estéreo, ...no hay una computadora. ...motocicleta. 3. ...una casa. ...una computadora y una grabadora, no hay un televisor a colores. ...bicicleta.

## Ex. B: Strip Stories

### *Learning Strategy: Peer tutoring*

- Divide students into teams of two pairs.
- Have each pair work together to prepare a completion of each strip story.
- Have pairs present variations of their strip stories to their team partners. (They may consult each other to confirm understanding.)



**Learning Strategies:**

*Reporting based on visual information, listing*

**B. *María, Antonio y Cristina*** On the basis of the drawings, complete each person's description of where he or she lives.

1. Me llamo María González. Vivo en... Allí hay..., pero no hay... Para ir al centro, voy en...

2. Me llamo Antonio Martínez. Yo vivo en... Allí hay... y... Para ir al centro, voy en...

3. Me llamo Cristina Sánchez. Yo vivo en... Allí hay..., pero no hay... Para ir al centro, voy en...

## Pronunciación: The sound of /k/

In Spanish the sound of **/k/** can be spelled with a **c** before the vowels **a, o, u,** as in **caso, cosa, culpa,** or before the consonants **l** and **r** as in **clase** and **cruz.** It can also be spelled with **qu** as in **Quito** and **queso;** in this combination, the **u** is always silent. A few Spanish words that have been borrowed from other languages are spelled with the letter **k,** for example, **koala, kimono,** and **kilómetro.** In all of these cases the sound of **/k/** in Spanish is identical to the sound of /k/ in English.

### Práctica

*C.* Listen and repeat as your teacher models the following words.

1. casa
2. cómoda
3. cama
4. computadora
5. calculadora
6. que
7. quien
8. queso
9. pequeño
10. kilómetro

## Repaso

*D.* Ask the following questions of a classmate, who will answer them.

1. En tu cuarto, ¿hay libros? ¿plantas? ¿pósters en la pared?
2. ¿Hay un estéreo en tu casa? ¿unos discos compactos? ¿unos discos compactos de jazz? ¿de rock? ¿de música clásica?
3. ¿Hay un radio despertador en tu cuarto? ¿un estéreo? ¿unas cintas?
4. En tu casa, ¿hay una máquina de escribir? ¿una computadora? ¿una cámara?

### Presentation: Pronunciation

Introduce the concept of linguistic borrowings. Explain that it is common for languages to borrow words from other languages. Give examples of words that English has borrowed from Spanish, such as *patio, rodeo, plaza, mosquito,* and *chocolate.* Then point out that any word spelled with a **k** in Spanish has been borrowed from another language.

*Suggestion, Ex. C:* Stress the fact that the **qu** in Spanish is always pronounced like the *k* in English, and never like the *qu* in the English word *queen.*

Additional activities appear in the Laboratory Tape Program.

**Ex. D:**  pair work

*Suggestion, Ex. D:* Have students ask their partners the questions and then have volunteers report back to the class.

## Presentation: Possessive adjectives, first and second persons

Possessive adjectives are presented in two parts in order to establish the notion of double agreement (agreement with the modified noun as well as with the possessor) before the confusing his/her problem is introduced. Third-person possessive adjectives are presented in Chapter 9. You may wish to review gender and number before beginning the presentation of the possessive adjectives.

Collect some items from the students and place them on your desk or table. Ask: **¿Es tu libro? ¿Son tus lápices?,** etc. Have students respond using negative or affirmative statements: **Sí, es mi libro**, or **No, no es mi libro.** Then practice the plural forms. Walk around the room, stopping occasionally to take objects from students. Ask one of the neighbors: **¿Son sus cuadernos?,** etc. Instruct them when to respond with the **nuestro** form. (It may be helpful to write this pattern on the board.)

**Vuestro** and its other forms have not been introduced. You may present them here if you wish.

Point out that the possessive adjective **tu** is written without the accent mark, unlike the subject pronoun **tú.**

**Ex. E:** writing



# ESTRUCTURA

### Possessive adjectives—first and second persons

| | |
|---|---|
| —¿Tú necesitas **tu** libro?<br>—Sí, yo necesito **mi** libro. | Do you need *your* book?<br>Yes, I need *my* book. |
| —¿Dónde está **su** cuarto?<br>—Allí está **nuestro** cuarto. | Where is *your* room?<br>There is *our* room. |
| —¿Dónde están **mis** llaves?<br>—Allí están **tus** llaves. | Where are *my* keys?<br>There are *your* keys. |

Like articles, possessive adjectives in Spanish agree in gender and number with the noun they modify. Consequently, Spanish has two forms for *my* and *your* and four forms for *our.* The following chart summarizes the first- and second-person possessive adjectives.

| Subject | Masc. singular | Fem. singular | Masc. plural | Fem. plural | English |
|---|---|---|---|---|---|
| yo | **mi** | **mi** | **mis** | **mis** | *my* |
| tú | **tu** | **tu** | **tus** | **tus** | *your* |
| usted | **su** | **su** | **sus** | **sus** | *your* |
| nosotros | **nuestro** | **nuestra** | **nuestros** | **nuestras** | *our* |
| ustedes | **su** | **su** | **sus** | **sus** | *your* |

## Aquí practicamos

**E.** Replace the nouns in italics and make the necessary changes.

1. Es mi *libro.* (lápiz / apartamento / bolígrafo)
2. Es mi *casa.* (calculadora / cámara / máquina de escribir)
3. Son mis *discos compactos.* (llaves / amigos / plantas)
4. ¿Dónde está tu *casa*? (apartamento / cuaderno / cámara)
5. ¿Dónde están tus *discos compactos*? (cintas / pósters / plantas)
6. Nosotros necesitamos nuestros *libros.* (cuadernos / calculadoras / computadora)
7. ¿Es su *coche*? (cuarto / mochila / calculadora)
8. ¿Son sus *libros*? (cintas / amigos / llaves)
9. Es nuestra *escuela.* (disco compacto / llave / televisor)
10. Llevamos nuestros *libros* a clase. (calculadoras / cuadernos / mochilas)



## Exercise Progression

Ex. E. is a mechanical drill designed to practice using possessive adjectives with nouns. Exs. F and G provide more controlled practice with this structure.

**F. ¡Qué confusión!** All of a sudden everyone seems confused about what belongs to whom. First, a stranger tries to take your school possessions, but you politely set him or her straight. Remember to use **es** with a singular noun and **son** with a plural noun.

—Ah, mi lápiz.
—*Perdón* (Excuse me). *No es su lápiz. Es mi lápiz.*

1. Ah, mi cuaderno.
2. Ah, mi mochila.
3. Ah, mi calculadora.
4. Ah, mi borrador.

—Ah, mis libros.
—*Perdón. No son sus libros. Son mis libros.*

5. Ah, mis cintas.
6. Ah, mis llaves.
7. Ah, mis cuadernos.
8. Ah, mis discos compactos.

Now your neighbors get confused about what belongs to them and what belongs to your family.

—¿Es nuestro coche?
—*No, no es su coche. Es nuestro coche.*

9. ¿Es nuestro televisor a colores?
10. ¿Es nuestro radio despertador?
11. ¿Es nuestra cámara?
12. ¿Es nuestra computadora?

—¿Son nuestras plantas?
—*No, no son sus plantas. Son nuestras plantas.*

13. ¿Son nuestros discos compactos?
14. ¿Son nuestras bicicletas?
15. ¿Son nuestras llaves?
16. ¿Son nuestras cintas?

Finally, your friend thinks your possessions belong to him or her.

—Dame *(Give me)* mi llave.
—*Perdón. No es tu llave. Es mi llave.*

17. Dame mi cuaderno.
18. Dame mi cinta.
19. Dame mi borrador.
20. Dame mi mochila.

Modelo:
—Dame mis libros.
—*Perdón. No son tus libros. Son mis libros.*

21. Dame mis pósters.
22. Dame mis discos compactos.
23. Dame mis llaves.
24. Dame mis cuadernos.

**¿Qué crees?**

**Spanish television often features *telenovelas,* both here in the United States and in other parts of the Spanish-speaking world. *Telenovelas* are:**

**a) TV plays**
**b) novels read on TV**
**c) soap operas**
**d) game shows**

**respuesta**



***Answers, Ex. F:*** 1. Perdón. No es su cuaderno. Es mi cuaderno. 2. ...No es su mochila. Es mi mochila. 3. ...No es su calculadora. Es mi calculadora. 4. ...No es su borrador. Es mi borrador. 5. ...No son sus cintas. Son mis cintas. 6. ...No son sus llaves. Son mis llaves. 7. ...No son sus cuadernos. Son mis cuadernos. 8. ...No son sus discos compactos. Son mis discos compactos 9. No, no es su televisor a colores. Es nuestro televisor a colores. 10. No, no es su radio despertador. Es nuestro radio despertador. 11. No, no es su cámara. Es nuestra cámara. 12. No, no es su computadora. Es nuestra computadora. 13. No, no son sus discos compactos. Son nuestros discos compactos. 14. No, no son sus bicicletas. Son nuestras bicicletas. 15. No, no son sus llaves. Son nuestras llaves. 16. No, no son sus cintas. Son nuestras cintas. 17. Perdón, no es tu cuaderno. Es mi cuaderno. 18. ...No es tu cinta. Es mi cinta. 19. ...No es tu borrador. Es mi borrador. 20. ...No es tu mochila. Es mi mochila. 21. ...No son tus pósters. Son mis pósters. 22. ...No son tus discos compactos. Son mis discos compactos. 23. ...No son tus llaves. Son mis llaves. 24. ...No son tus cuadernos. Son mis cuadernos.

**Ex. G:** pair work

***Variation, Ex. G:***
After denying ownership of an item, the student states that the questioner owns it. **No, no es mi libro, es tu libro.**

***Answers, Ex. G:*** 1. ¿Es tu calculadora? No, no es mi calculadora. 2. tus lápices/mis lápices 3. tus bolígrafos/mis bolígrafos 4. tu mochila/mi mochila 5. tu computadora/mi computadora 6. tu portafolio/mi portafolio 7. tu borrador/mi borrador 8. tu bicicleta/mi bicicleta 9. tu moto/mi moto 10. tu coche/mi coche 11. tus discos compactos/mis discos compactos 12. tus llaves/mis llaves 13. tu cuaderno/mi cuaderno 14. tus libros/mis libros 15. tu cartera/mi cartera

***More-prepared students, Ex. G:*** Have the more-prepared students redo the exercise with their partners, this time using the **su/nuestro** format: **¿Es su cámara? No, no es nuestra cámara.**

***Less-prepared students, Ex. G:*** Have less-prepared students write several of the items first, and then do the exercise orally.

**G. *No, no. No es mi libro.*** Now you're confused! When you point out the following items and ask a classmate if they belong to him or her, your classmate responds negatively.

**Modelos:** —*¿Es tu cámara?*
—*No, no es mi cámara.*

—*¿Son tus plantas?*
—*No, no son mis plantas.*

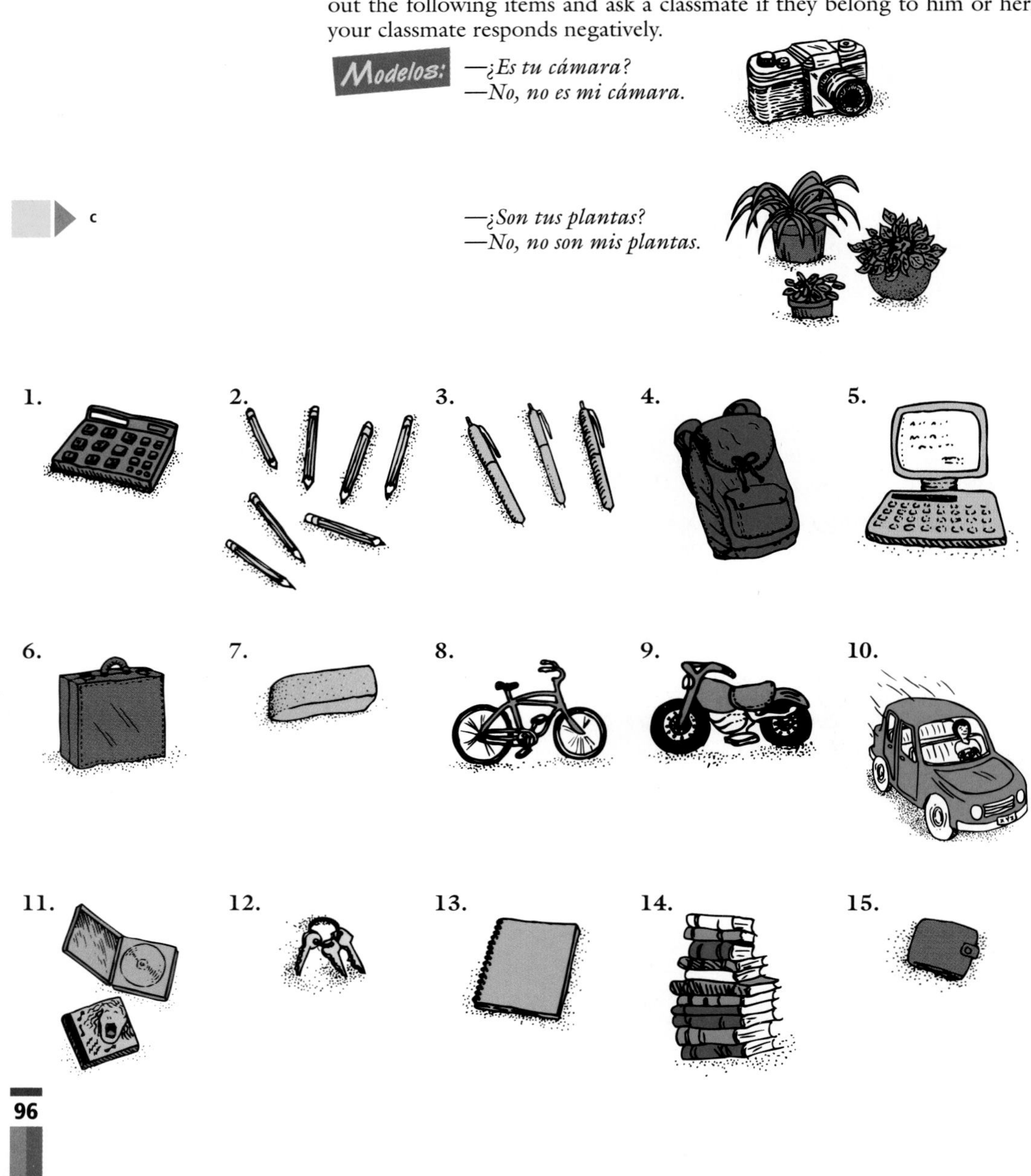

# Aquí escuchamos:

## "¿Dónde vives?"

### Antes de escuchar

Think about (1) where you live, (2) what items you have there, and (3) how you get around town. Before you listen to Carmen's short monologue, think about (4) where you think she lives, (5) what she has there, and (6) how she gets around town. Before your instructor plays the tape, take a moment and look at the list that follows.

| | | | |
|---|---|---|---|
| casa | vídeo | televisor | motocicleta |
| apartamento | pósters | plantas | bicicleta |
| estéreo | libros | coche | |

START

### Después de escuchar

Listen to the tape again and this time write down on a separate sheet of paper what Carmen has to say about where she lives, what she has there, and how she gets around.

**Critical Thinking Strategy:**

*Predicting*

**Learning Strategy:**

*Listening for details*

# ¡Adelante!

EJERCICIO ORAL

**H. Mi casa y tu casa** Share information with your partner about your home and belongings. (1) Ask what he or she has: **¿Qué hay en tu casa?** and (2) describe your own home, **En mi casa hay... .** While listening to your partner's description, (3) point out something he or she has that you also have at home: **Hay un coche americano y un coche japonés en mi casa también.** (4) Also listen for something that is at your partner's home but not at yours and comment on it: **No hay moto en mi casa, pero hay tres bicicletas.** Finally, prepare a report together in

**Cooperative Learning**

**Learning Strategies:**

*Providing and gathering information, organizing, and reporting*

**Critical Thinking Strategies:**

*Comparing and contrasting, synthesizing*



**Answers, Después de escuchar:** 1. Vive en un apartamento. 2. Hay un estéreo, un televisor, unas plantas y muchos libros. 3. Va al centro en bicicleta.

**Ex. H:** pair work

*Ex. H:* This activity provides preparation for the **Ya llegamos** section at the end of Unit 2.

*Variation, Ex. H:* Have students ask their partners questions about the photograph on page 98. They could also compare their room to the one in the photo, saying what they have that the photo does not.

**Support material, Aquí escuchamos:**
Teacher Tape/CD #1 Track #19 and Tapescript

**Ex. I:** writing

*Variation, Ex. I:* For extra practice, have students draw on the information in their strip stories to produce a written group story, including the similarities and differences among individual members of their group. Help students with additional vocabulary and phrases they may need.

*Suggestion, Ex. I:* You may want to have the students do the individual part of this writing activity at home. They could also prepare an illustration of their own strip story. The group could prepare an illustration of their strip story for use in a full group presentation. This activity provides preparation for the **Ya llegamos** section at the end of Unit 2.

*More-prepared students, Ex. I:* More-prepared students could create two very different fictitious characters who become good friends, despite differences in homes, possessions, modes of transportation, talents, and likes and dislikes.

which you identify (1) a few items that are in both of your homes: **En nuestras casas hay...,** (2) other items that are either only in your home: **En *mi* casa hay..., pero no hay... en *su* casa,** and those that are only in his/hers: **En *su* casa hay..., pero no hay... en *mi* casa.**

## EJERCICIO ESCRITO

*Critical Thinking Strategy:*

*Making associations between possessions and activities*

**I. *Mi vida...*** Prepare your own personal picture strip story describing your own home, what you have in it, and how you travel when you go out, based on the models in Activity B on page 92. In your writing, include things you have in your home or room and mention what you like to do with those things. You may wish to start out with: **En mi casa (or cuarto) hay...** (Example: **En mi cuarto hay un estéreo y muchos discos compactos. Mis discos compactos son de música rock. Me gusta escuchar música cuando estudio. Hay un teléfono también en mi cuarto. Me gusta mucho hablar con mis amigos. También me gusta visitar en casa de mis amigos. A veces voy a casa de mis amigos en bicicleta.**) Don't forget to include in your description things you do not have at home **(En mi casa no hay...).**

**En mi cuarto hay muñecas por todas partes.**

## Vocabulario

### Para charlar

#### Para expresar posesión

¿De quién es...?
¿De quién son...?
Es de...
Son de...

mi(s)
tu(s)
su(s)
nuestro(s)
nuestra(s)

### Temas y contextos

#### En la escuela

un(a) alumno(a)
un bolígrafo
una bolsa
un borrador
una calculadora
un cuaderno
un lápiz
un libro
una mochila
una pluma
un portafolio
un sacapuntas

#### En mi cuarto

una alfombra
una cama
una cámara
una cartera
una cinta
una cómoda
una computadora
un disco compacto
un escritorio
un estante
un estéreo
una grabadora
una llave
una máquina de escribir
una planta
un póster
un radio despertador
una silla
un televisor (a colores)
un vídeo

#### Los medios de transporte

un autobús
una bicicleta
un coche
una motocicleta

#### Las viviendas

un apartamento
una casa
un cuarto

### Vocabulario general

#### Definite articles

el
la
los
las

#### Verbos

llevar

#### Otras palabras y expresiones

allí
¿Cuántos hay?
¿Dónde hay?
Me llamo...
Para ir al centro, voy en...
¿Qué llevas tú a la escuela?
Vivo en...

***Suggestion, Vocabulario:*** Students may use the **Vocabulario** as a checklist for vocabulary recognition. A Spanish–English Glossary is provided at the end of the book.

## Chapter Culminating Activities

You might want to play **el juego de las categorías** as a wrap-up exercise. You name a category, for example, **la escuela, el cuarto,** or **los medios de transporte.** With books closed, students write as many items as they can remember for each category. Give points for each correct answer or for the most unique items. Alternate version: open categories, but students must write a word or words beginning with a certain letter (for this chapter, **a, c, e,** and **m** are particularly good).

Another game: Have a student start out with **En mi mochila hay un/una...**, and other students add new items repeating the previous ones. Variation: **En mi cuarto/casa hay...**

Have students make two lists: one for all the masculine nouns and another for the feminine nouns.

***Support material, Capítulo 4:*** Improvised Monologue, Teacher Tape/CD #1 Track #20 and Tapescript; Lab Manual listening activities, Laboratory Program, Tapescript, and Teacher's Edition of the Workbook/Lab Manual

# Lectura cultural

Have students discuss the various uses of the bicycle, and why it is such a popular mode of transportation in so many places around the world, including New York City. Then have students talk about the attraction to cycling as a sport.

## ¡VIVA LA BICICLETA!

*Critical Thinking Strategy:*

*Predicting*

### Antes de leer

1. Among the things that you own, do you have a bicycle? If so, what kind?
2. Look at the pictures that accompany this reading. What do you think the reading may tell you about bicycles?
3. Look at the title. What does it suggest to you? HINT: Notice the exclamation marks.

*Learning Strategy:*

*Scanning for specific details*

### Guía para la lectura

A. Read the first paragraph and identify three cognates.

B. Which one of the following ideas does the writer emphasize in this paragraph?

1. There are many bicycle lanes in Spanish cities.
2. Lots of Spanish young people like to ride their bikes in the city parks.
3. Bicycling is a preferred activity among young people in Spain.

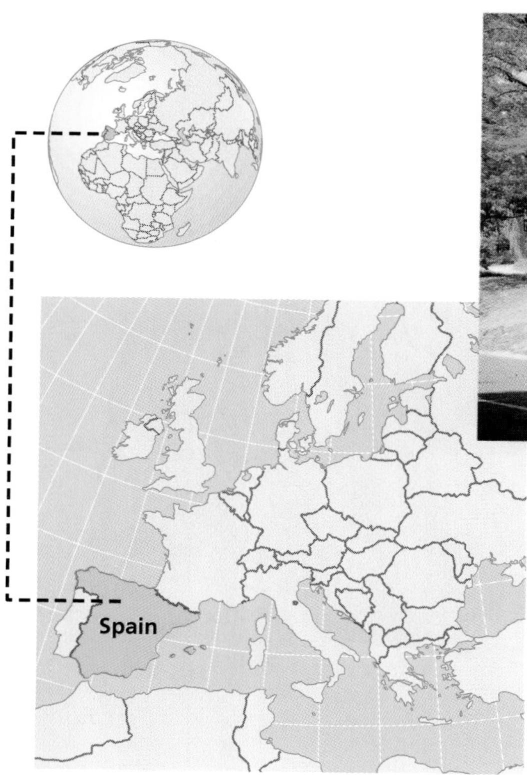

C. Now read the second paragraph. Can you guess the English equivalents for some of the following reasons (in Spanish) for the mountain bike's popularity?

| Spanish | English |
| --- | --- |
| 1. No contamina el aire. | |
| 2. Es un buen ejercicio. | |
| 3. No gasta petróleo. | |

## ¡Viva la bicicleta!

El ciclismo es un deporte que cada día es más popular en España. Más y más estudiantes van a la escuela en bicicleta a pesar de que no hay carriles-bici en las ciudades. Cada fin de semana, los chicos españoles cambian los libros y los bolígrafos por las bicicletas.

La "mountain bike" también es muy popular entre los jóvenes. Los jóvenes que montan sus bicicletas en el campo piensan que es menos aburrido y peligroso que pedalear en la ciudad. También prefieren la "mountain bike" por razones ecológicas. No contamina el aire. No hace ruido. No gasta petróleo. Es buen ejercicio y ayuda a estar en forma. ¡Viva la bicicleta!

# Chapter Objectives

**Functions:** Talking about preferences; getting information about other people
**Context:** Various settings
**Accuracy:** **Gustar** (**me gustan/ te gustan**); review of **ser** + **de** for possession; **-er** and **-ir** verbs

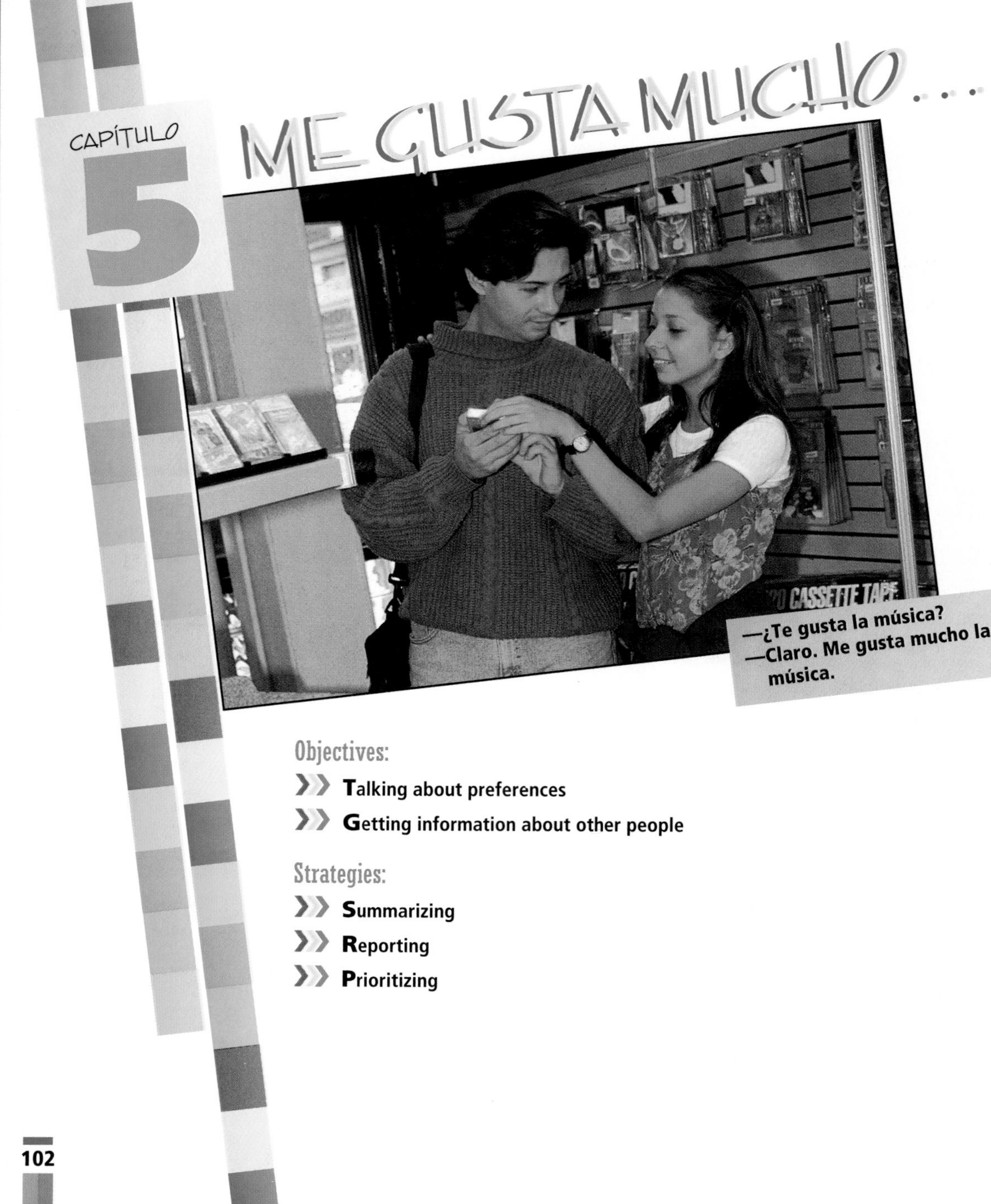


—¿Te gusta la música?
—Claro. Me gusta mucho la música.

### Objectives:

- Talking about preferences
- Getting information about other people

### Strategies:

- Summarizing
- Reporting
- Prioritizing

102

## Video/CD-ROM

Chapter 5 Video Program
Chapter 5 CD-ROM Program

These can be used at the end of the chapter as expansion activities.

# PRIMERA ETAPA

## Preparación

›› **As you get ready to begin this etapa, think about your likes and dislikes. On a sheet of paper, make headings for two lists: (1) *I like . . .* and (2) *I don't like . . . .***

›› **Write each of the following interests under the appropriate heading to express your personal tastes: music, animals, sports, nature, art, certain classes (science, history, foreign language, math).**

*Learning Strategies:*

*Previewing, listing*

# Mis gustos

*Mis gustos:* My tastes

Buenos días. Me llamo José. Ésta es Ana. Es mi **novia,** pero nuestros gustos son muy diferentes.

girlfriend

**José:** No me gusta la música.
**Ana:** Me gusta la música.

**José:** Me gustan los animales.
**Ana:** No me gustan los animales.



## Presentation: Mis gustos

You may introduce the new vocabulary by using transparencies and the Teacher Tape (with students' books closed), or you may read it for the class. Prepare students for the listening comprehension by telling them that they are about to hear a conversation between a male student (José) and his girlfriend (Ana). They like each other a lot, but they have very different interests. After playing the tape (or reading) once or twice, ask questions such as, **¿A quién le gusta la música, a Ana o a José?** Tell students to answer with just the name. Or you could read different statements, such as, **Me gustan los animales,** and have students say who made the statement, Ana or José. If students are unable to answer, verify comprehension, then read the dialogue, having students repeat first as a whole class, then in groups, and then individually. Then ask again those questions with which they had difficulty.

*Support material, Mis gustos:* Teacher Tape/CD #1 Track #21, transparencies #26, #27

## Etapa Support Materials

Workbook: **pp. 52–57**
Critical Thinking Master: **pp. 7–8**
Transparencies: **#26, #27**

Teacher Tape
Quiz: **Testing Program, p. 49**

Support material, **Mis gustos:**
**Teacher Tape, transparencies #26, #27**

## Presentation: Mis gustos, cont.

Point out that in most cases the adjective of nationality is also the word used for the languages.

## Vocabulary Expansion

**física, matemáticas (álgebra, trigonometría, cálculo, geometría), arte surrealista, arte moderno, pintura (cuadro), museo**

Write the words from the vocabulary expansion on the board and then ask students simple questions with the new vocabulary, using either **gustar** or other **-ar** verbs that they have learned. **¿Qué ciencia estudias? ¿Te gusta el arte surrealista? ¿Visitas los museos mucho o poco?**

## Cultural Expansion

You may want to take this opportunity to discuss one of the twentieth century's greatest surrealist painters, Salvador Dalí, from Spain. Try to bring in some pictures of his paintings. You may also want to mention or discuss other great painters of this century, such as Pablo Picasso or Rufino Tamayo (Mexico).

sports / nature

**José:** Me gustan los **deportes.**
**Ana:** No me gustan los deportes.

**José:** Me gusta la **naturaleza.**
**Ana:** No me gusta la naturaleza.

languages

**José:** No me gusta el arte.
**Ana:** Me gusta el arte.

**José:** Me gustan las **lenguas.**
**Ana:** No me gustan las lenguas.

sciences
chemistry

**José:** No me gustan las **ciencias...** no me gusta la **química.**
**Ana:** Me gustan las ciencias... me gusta la química.

**José:** No me gusta la biología.
**Ana:** Me gusta la biología.

# ¡Aquí te toca a ti!

**A. ¡(No) Me gusta!** Indicate how you feel about each activity pictured below.

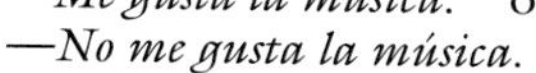

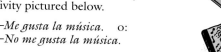

**Modelo:** *—Me gusta la música.* o:
*—No me gusta la música.*

1. 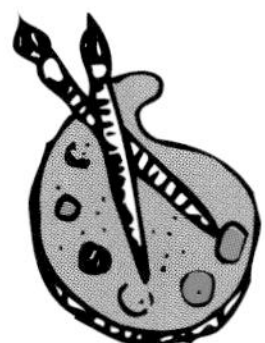
2. 
3. 
4. 
5. 

6. 

**B. ¿Y tú?** Ask a classmate whether he or she likes the activities pictured in the previous exercise.

**Modelo:** *—¿Te gusta la música?*
*—No, no me gusta la música.*

## ESTRUCTURA

### The verb *gustar*

| | |
|---|---|
| **Me gusta** el disco compacto. | *I like* the compact disc. |
| **Te gusta** la cinta. | *You like* the tape. |
| **Me gustan** las cintas. | *I like* the tapes. |
| **Te gustan** los discos compactos. | *You like* the compact discs. |
| **Me gusta** estudiar. | *I like* to study. |
| **Te gusta** trabajar. | *You like* to work. |

***Answers, Ex. A:*** 1. (No) Me gusta el arte. 2. (No) Me gusta la química. 3. (No) Me gusta la naturaleza. 4. (No) Me gustan los animales. 5. (No) Me gustan las lenguas. 6. (No) Me gustan los deportes.

***Variation, Ex. A:*** Have students work in pairs, telling them to give a response to their partners' statements by adding either **también** or **tampoco.** Example: **Me gusta la música también. No me gusta la música tampoco.**

**Ex. B:** pair work

## Presentation: Gustar

Students have already heard and used the plural of **gustar (me gustan/te gustan)** in the vocabulary activities on the previous pages. Reinforce this structure by making simple statements, using voice inflection to stress the singular and plural endings of **gustar.** Have students repeat first as a whole class and then individually. **Me gustan las ciencias. Me gusta mucho la biología.,** etc. Then ask simple questions (stressing the endings with voice inflection) and have students answer. You may want to ask plural questions to your Spanish-speaking students first.

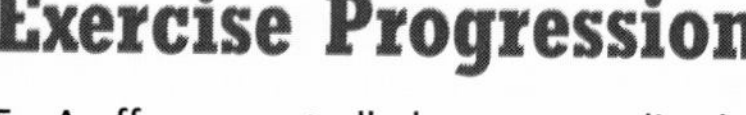

## Exercise Progression

Ex. A offers a controlled yet personalized practice of the vocabulary. Ex. B provides more practice using a communicative approach.

**Ex. A:** pair work  writing

***Suggestions, Ex. A:*** Have students work orally in pairs or have them write out the sentences and then edit their partners' work. You could also have students write the answers on the board and then have the class point out any errors.

Ex. C: writing

*Suggestion, Ex. C:* These column exercises are meant to provide controlled practice. A possible way to present these would be through the creation of a "word web." On a separate piece of paper, students would draw a web, and then connect elements from the columns in ways that form grammatically correct sentences. (They would have to write in the correct form of the verb in the middle column.) See the diagram below for a sample word web format. Word web formats will vary from exercise to exercise.

*Suggestion, Ex. C:* Have students work in pairs and then report their number one mutual interest and top mutual dislike. You might take a tally on the chalkboard (with tick marks) to determine the most and least popular tastes of the whole class. Label each column, **Nos gusta(n) más** and **Nos gusta(n) menos.** Follow-up discussion can include questions like **¿A quién(es) le(s) gusta más... ? ¿Qué nos gusta menos?** with responses practicing the different structural forms of the **gustar** expression. This activity provides preparation for the **Ya llegamos** section at the end of Unit 2.

*Learning Strategies: Polling, Reading a graph*

*More-prepared students, Ex. C:* More-prepared students can interview each other as if they were looking for a compatible roommate for a study abroad program or for college. Have them list their likes and dislikes and then find others with similar interests.



The Spanish verb for *to like* is **gustar.** You have already learned one way to use **gustar,** so you know it is different from other verbs in that it does not use the subject pronouns you learned in Chapter 1. Instead, to say *I like* and *you like,* you use the pronouns **me** and **te.** Only two forms of **gustar** are used. These are the singular form **gusta** and the plural form **gustan.** Use **gusta** if what is liked is a singular noun and **gustan** if what is liked is a plural noun.

Remember that you learned in Unit 1 to use the singular form **gusta** with infinitive verbs to express activities you like and dislike. Infinitive verbs are always treated as a singular item with **gustar.**

## Aquí practicamos

**C.** Create a sentence by combining an element from Column A, one from Column B, and one from Column C.

**Modelo:** *Me gustan los licuados.*

| A | B | C |
|---|---|---|
| me | gusta | el sándwich |
| te | gustan | los licuados |
| | | los refrescos |
| | | el póster |
| | | el disco compacto |
| | | los deportes |
| | | la música clásica |
| | | las ciencias |
| | | las lenguas |
| | | los animales |

**D. *¡Me gustan muchísimo los deportes!*** An exchange student from Peru will be living with your family for the next six months. You are getting to know each other and he or she is asking you about your likes and dislikes. Be as specific as possible in your answers.

**Modelo:** ¿Te gustan los deportes?
*¡Sí, me gustan muchísimo los deportes!* o:
*No, no me gustan los deportes.*

1. ¿Te gusta estudiar?
2. ¿Te gusta bailar?
3. ¿Te gusta la química?
4. ¿Te gustan las lenguas?
5. ¿Te gustan los animales?
6. ¿Te gusta la música?



*Less-prepared students, Ex. C:* Less-prepared students can find magazine ads and photos to create a personal poster on which they write their likes and dislikes and illustrate them in a creative way.

## Exercise Progression

Ex. C is designed to practice composing sentences using the singular and plural endings of gustar. Ex. D provides a more personalized communicative activity. Ex. E offers more controlled practice.

**E. *Me gustan los deportes, pero no me gusta la política.*** You and your friends are talking about what you like and dislike. In each case, say that the person indicated likes the first activity or item but dislikes the second.

**Modelo:** me / deportes / política
—*Me gustan los deportes, pero no me gusta la política.*

1. me / naturaleza / animales
2. te / música / arte
3. me / lenguas / literatura
4. me / lenguas / ciencias
5. te / política / matemáticas
6. te / música / deportes

# Pronunciación: The consonant *d*

In Spanish, when **d** is the first letter of a word or comes after **l** or **n,** it is produced by placing the tip of the tongue behind the back of the upper front teeth. In English, *d* is pronounced by placing the tip of the tongue on the gum ridge behind the upper front teeth. Pronounce the English word *dee* and note where the tip of your tongue is. Now pronounce the Spanish word **di** being careful to place the tip of the tongue on the back of the upper front teeth.

## Práctica

**F.** Listen and repeat as your teacher models the following words.

1. disco
2. de
3. domingo
4. dos
5. diez
6. grande
7. aprender
8. Donaldo
9. Aldo
10. donde

# Repaso

**G. *¿Cuántos hay?*** Tell how many objects are in each of the drawings below.

 *Hay dos lápices.*

1. 

2. 

3. 

4.



**Ex. D:** pair work

role play

***Answers, Ex. D:*** Endings will vary according to students' preferences. 1–3 and 6: **Sí, me gusta... / No, no me gusta...** 4 and 5: **Sí, me gustan... / No, no me gustan...**

***Follow-up, Ex. D:*** Ask more questions in the **pregúntale** format, using other vocabulary that students already know. For example: **María, pregúntale a Juan si le gustan los discos compactos de rock.** This format lets them know whether to use **te gusta** or **te gustan** when asking the questions.

**Ex. E:** pair work

writing

***Suggestions, Ex. E:*** Have students write out sentences using the cues, and then have them check the verb endings and articles on their partner's papers. Or have them do the activity in pairs, then personalize it by having them tell about other things that they like and dislike.

***Answers, Ex. E:*** 1. Me gusta la naturaleza, pero no me gustan los animales. 2. Te gusta..., pero no te gusta... 3. Me gustan..., pero no me gusta... 4. Me gustan..., pero no me gustan... 5. Te gusta..., pero no te gustan... 6. Te gusta..., pero no te gustan...

### Presentation: Pronunciation

Have students pronounce English words that begin with *d* and tell them to notice the position of the tip of the tongue. Then have them move the tip of the tongue from the gum ridge to the back of the upper front teeth and practice saying **da, de, di, do, du.**

Additional activities appear in the Laboratory Tape Program.

***Suggestions, Ex. G:*** Dictate the numbers to students with their books closed. Then have them read the numbers back to you in Spanish from their papers. Students could then do simple addition problems orally. Others can comment on the results.

***Answers, Ex. G:*** 1. tres bolígrafos 2. cinco plantas 3. una calculadora 4. cuatro sillas

***Support material, Pronunciación:*** Pronunciation Tape

***Answers, Ex. G, cont.:***
5. tres cintas 6. siete lápices 7. once libros 8. ocho discos compactos

**Ex. H:**  writing

 groups of four or more

Exercise H provides preparation for the **Ya llegamos** section at the end of Unit 2.

## Presentation: Ser + de

This review allows students to perfect what they learned and practiced in Chapter 4. Remind them that to express possession in Spanish they must change the word order of possessives in English. Instead of "John's keys" they must think "the keys of John."

**Ex. I:**  pair work

 writing

***Suggestions, Ex. I:*** Have students do the exercise orally with their partners or have them write out the statements and check their partners' work for mistakes.

***Answers, Ex. I:*** 1. La calculadora es de Anita. 2. La computadora es de Elena. 3. La cámara es de Juan. 4. Los bolígrafos son de ella. 5. La bicicleta es de Tomás. 6. Los lápices son de Julián. 7. Las cintas son de él. 8. La mochila es de Carmen. 9. La radio es de Alicia y Susana. 10. Las llaves son de ellos.



5. 
6. 
7. 
8. 

*Learning Strategies:*

*Polling, organizing information in a chart*

*Critical Thinking Strategy:*

*Comparing and contrasting*

**H. Nosotros llevamos...** Make a list of five things you take to school every day. Compare your list with those of several other people in class. When you find that an item on your list is also on someone else's list, put a check mark beside it to show how many other people take it to school. Keep a careful record of the information so that you can count the marks and report which items are most and least popular.

## Nota gramatical

### Ser + de for possession

| | |
|---|---|
| El libro **es de Juan.** | The book *is John's.* |
| La calculadora **es de María.** | The calculator *is Mary's.* |
| Los lápices **son de él.** | The pencils *are his.* |
| Las mochilas **son de ellos.** | The knapsacks *are theirs.* |

In Chapter 4 you learned to talk about possession using **de** plus a noun or the possessive adjectives **(mi, tu, su, nuestro).** You can use the verb **ser** with **de** and a noun or a pronoun to show possession. Remember that Spanish uses the preposition **de** and not the apostrophe to show possession, as in English.

**I. El libro es de...** Look at the drawings and indicate to whom the items belong, according to the models.

*El cuaderno es de José.*

José

*Los libros son de Bárbara.*

Bárbara



***Follow-up, Ex. I:*** Hold up specific students' belongings and ask to whom they belong. For example, ask (holding up a schoolbag): **¿Es la mochila de Jane?** Students answer: **No, no es la mochila de Jane. Es la mochila de Carmen.,** etc.

## Exercise Progression

Ex. I is a controlled exercise designed to practice possessives with **de** and to review everyday school vocabulary. Ex. J offers more controlled practice with possessive statements, and reinforces questions with **¿De quién?**

1. Anita

2. Elena

3. Juan

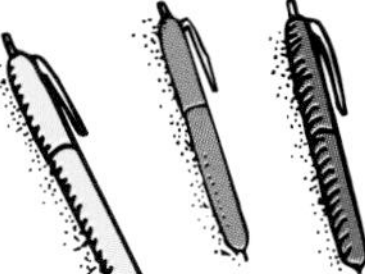
4. ella

5. Tomás

6. Julián

7. él

8. Carmen

9. Alicia y Susana

10. ellos

**J. *¿De quién es?*** Indicate to whom each of the following items belongs, using **ser + de.**

*¿De quién es la mochila?*
*La mochila es de María.*

María

*¿De quién son los cuadernos?*
*Los cuadernos son de José.*

José

1. Juan

2. ella

3. Catarina

4. Alicia

5. Miguel

6. él

7. Anita

8. Lorenzo

**Ex. J:**  pair work

 writing

***Suggestion, Ex. J:*** Do a singular and a plural example for the class first, before having them work in pairs. Stress **¿De quién es... ?** for singular questions and **¿De quién son... ?** for plural.

***Answers, Ex. J:*** 1. ¿De quién es la computadora? La computadora es de Juan. 2. ...son los discos compactos? Los discos compactos son de ella. 3. ...es el bolígrafo? El bolígrafo es de Catarina. 4. ...es la llave? La llave es de Alicia. 5. ...son los lápices? Los lápices son de Miguel. 6. ...son los libros? Los libros son de él. 7. ...son las plantas? Las plantas son de Anita. 8. ...son las cintas? Las cintas son de Lorenzo.

## Aquí escuchamos

This activity provides preparation for the **Ya llegamos** section at the end of Unit 2.

***Answers, Después de escuchar:*** She likes: **animales, biología, matemáticas** she doesn't like: **arte, literatura**

***Support material, Aquí escuchamos:*** Teacher Tape/CD #1 Track #22 and Tapescript

# Aquí escuchamos:
## "Mis gustos"

*Learning Strategy:*

*Previewing*

### Antes de escuchar

Think about your likes and dislikes. Before listening to Carmen's short monologue, think about (1) how she will say that she likes something, (2) how she will say that she doesn't like something, and (3) how the words **también, tampoco, y,** and **pero** relate ideas to each other.

START

*Learning Strategy:*

*Listening for details and main ideas*

### Después de escuchar

Before your teacher plays the tape, take a moment to copy the following chart onto a separate sheet of paper. While you listen, check the appropriate column to show which courses Carmen likes and which she doesn't like. Do not check the courses that she does not mention.

| | She likes | She doesn't like |
|---|---|---|
| animales | | |
| arte | | |
| biología | | |
| lenguas | | |
| literatura | | |
| matemáticas | | |
| música | | |
| química | | |

Based on this monologue, which subject area is most likely Carmen's favorite: liberal arts, science, or technology?

EJERCICIO ORAL

**K. *Los gustos de la clase*** Prepare a profile of a classmate's likes and dislikes. Begin by making a list like the one that follows. Then interview your partner, writing the appropriate number by each item. Use the following scale to record your partner's responses.

**no** = 0 **mucho** = 3
**poco** = 1 **muchísimo** = 4
**bastante** *(okay, pretty well)* = 2

**Modelo:** —*¿Te gusta mucho la biología?*
—*No, me gusta la biología muy poco.* (_1_ *la biología*) o:
—*No, pero me gusta la biología bastante.* (_2_ *la biología*)

| | | |
|---|---|---|
| ___ la biología | ___ la música clásica | ___ los animales |
| ___ la química | ___ el jazz | ___ los deportes |
| ___ las ciencias | ___ el arte moderno | ___ la comida italiana |
| ___ la historia | ___ el arte clásico | ___ la comida vietnamita |
| ___ la literatura | ___ los pósters | ___ bailar |
| ___ las lenguas | ___ la política | ___ viajar |
| ___ la música rock | ___ la naturaleza | ___ cantar |

*Learning Strategies:*

*Polling, recording information on a chart*

*Critical Thinking Strategy:*

*Prioritizing*

EJERCICIO ESCRITO

**L. *Entrevista*** Using the list in the previous exercise, along with other Spanish vocabulary you have learned, write a brief description of your likes and dislikes. Mention (1) at least three things you like a lot and (2) at least two that you don't like very much. Among them, (3) mention something that you do well **(muy bien),** (4) something that you do every day, and (5) something else that you do occasionally (a total of at least five items). Don't forget to use **también, tampoco, y,** and **pero** to connect your ideas. Compare your paragraph with that of a classmate. What are the similarities? What are the differences?

*Learning Strategy:*

*Linking ideas in a paragraph*

*Critical Thinking Strategy:*

*Comparing and contrasting*



## Cooperative Learning

*Learning Strategies: Polling, reading a graph*

*Critical Thinking Strategy: Categorizing*

Develop a sample profile of the class from their interview responses:

- Select one category of items from the list for your sample (school courses or pastimes, for example).
- On the board, label your activity **Nuestros gustos** and then write the category title. Have students help you select all the items from the list that fit in that category.
- Then have students, working in pairs, tally their numbers for the items on the board.
- Write those sums on the board and add them together to get a cumulative "profile" for the class.
- To cap the activity, have the class determine how they have collectively ranked the items in that category. If you have done this activity in another section of the same course, the classes might be interested in comparing their profiles. This activity provides preparation for the **Ya llegamos** section at the end of Unit 2.

**Ex. K:** pair work

***Suggestions, Ex. K:*** Encourage your students to ask and answer their questions in complete sentences in Spanish. Tell them to say **"¿Cómo?"** or **"Repite, por favor"** if they don't understand a classmate's response.

**Ex. L:** writing

*Ex. L:* This activity provides preparation for the **Ya llegamos** section at the end of Unit 2.

## Presentation: ¿Qué te gusta más?

Most new vocabulary words are not glossed because they are cognates.

Point out the appropriate pictures on the transparencies as you read the statements about the people. Then have several students answer the questions. **¿Qué te gustan más—las películas de horror o las películas de aventura?,** etc. If you do not use the transparencies, read the dialogue, having students repeat. Then ask them questions based on the pictures.

## Vocabulary Expansion

**pez de colores** *(goldfish)*, **hámster** (pl. **hámsters**), **loro** *(parrot)*, **perico/periquito** *(parakeet)*, **natación, ciclismo, atletismo, lucha libre** *(wrestling)*, **boxeo, los juegos olímpicos/las olimpiadas**

Write the words from the Vocabulary Expansion on the board and continue discussing students' preferences: **¿Qué deportes practicas?/¿Qué deportes te gusta practicar? ¿Qué deportes miras en la televisión?,** etc.

*Support material, ¿Qué te gusta más?:* Teacher Tape/CD #1 Track #23, transparency #28



# SEGUNDA ETAPA

*Learning Strategy:*

*Previewing*

*Critical Thinking Strategies:*

*Comparing and contrasting, determining preferences*

### Preparación

**In this etapa you will continue to learn to talk about your likes and dislikes. Before you begin, think more specifically about the things you like and dislike. For example:**

- **Various sports**
- **Kinds of movies**
- **Types of art**
- **Types of animals**
- **Kinds of music**
- **Your school subjects**

## ¿Qué te gusta más?

*¿Qué te gusta más?:* What do you like better?

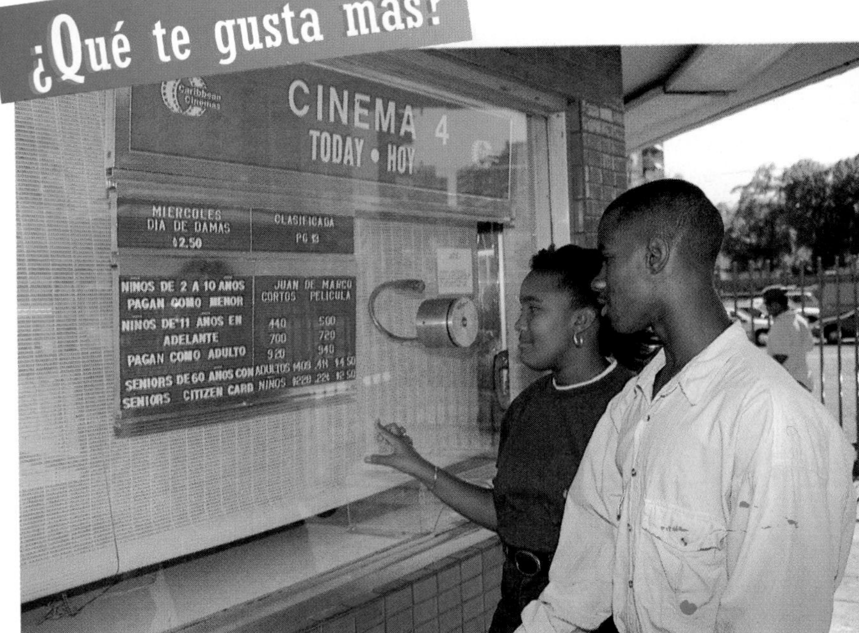


—Me gustan las películas.
—¿Qué te gustan más —las películas cómicas, las películas de horror, las películas de aventura o las películas de ciencia ficción?
—Me gustan más las películas de horror.



## Etapa Support Materials

Workbook: **pp. 58–63**
Critical Thinking Master: **p. 9**
Transparencies: **#28, #29**
Listening Activity masters: **p. 30**
Tapescript: **p. 41**

**Teacher Tape**
Quiz: **Testing Program, p. 51**
Chapter Test: **Testing Program, p. 53**

Support material, **¿Qué te gusta más?:**
**Teacher Tape** **, transparencies #28, #29**

# Aquí practicamos

**E.** Create original sentences using words from each column.

| A | B | C |
|---|---|---|
| Raúl | comer | en la cafetería |
| Teresa y Sara | vivir | en un apartamento |
| yo | comprender | español |
| nosotros | compartir | un cuarto |
| Uds. | | |
| tú | | |

**F.** Tell what you and your friends do and don't do during the summer. Write five sentences, one sentence about each of five of your classmates, using the words in Columns A, B, and C. Use a different verb from Column B in each sentence. Follow the model.

**Learning Strategy:**
Reporting

*John corre todos los días.* o:
*John no corre todos los días.*

| A | B | C |
|---|---|---|
| (no) | comer | en la cafetería |
| | correr | todos los días |
| | leer | muchos libros |
| | beber | muchas cartas *(letters)* |
| | recibir | en España |
| | vivir | leche cada mañana |
| | escribir | en un restaurante |

**G.** ***¿Qué hacen?*** (What are they doing?) Look at the drawings below and on the following page and indicate what these people are doing.

1. Miguel

2. Rogelio y Lilia

3. Adela y Nívea



**Ex. E:** writing

**Ex. F:** writing

**Ex. G:**  pair work

writing

*Answers, Ex. G:* 1. Miguel escribe una carta. 2. Rogelio y Lilia comparten (beben) un licuado. 3. Adela y Nívea corren.

*Variation, Ex. G:* Have students ask their partners simple questions based on the pictures. For example: **¿Qué escribe Miguel?** Have them answer with a subject pronoun: **Él escribe una carta.** Or pretend that your drawing is unclear, and make a false statement about it. Have students correct you. **("Miguel lee el menú." "No, Miguel escribe una carta.")**

## Exercise Progression

Ex. E is a mechanical drill designed to coordinate the verb endings with the subjects. Ex. F provides controlled personalized practice, and Ex. G provides more controlled practice with the verbs and the new vocabulary in response to drawings. Ex. H offers a more personalized communicative activity.

*Answers, **Después de escuchar:*** Carmen likes: **películas de horror;** doesn't like: **películas de aventura.** José likes: **fútbol americano, básquetbol;** doesn't like: **películas.**

*Answers, Ex. G, cont.:*
4. Leo recibe una carta. 5. Nosotros leemos revistas. 6. Antonio come una hamburguesa.

*Support material, **Aquí escuchamos:***
Teacher Tape/CD #1 Track #24 and Tapescript

**4.** Leo

**5.** nosotros

**6.** Antonio

# Aquí escuchamos:

## "¿Qué te gusta más?"

*Critical Thinking Strategy:*
*Predicting*

### Antes de escuchar

**Think about your likes and dislikes again. Before you listen to Carmen and José's short conversation, think about how they will say that they like something, and how they will say that they don't like something.**

*Learning Strategy:*
*Listening for details*

### Después de escuchar

**Now listen to the tape again and write down on a separate sheet of paper what Carmen and José say they like and don't like.**

| | José | Carmen |
|---|---|---|
| animales | | |
| películas | | |
| de horror | | |
| de aventura | | |
| de ciencia ficción | | |

| | José | Carmen |
|---|---|---|
| deportes | | |
| tenis | | |
| fútbol americano | | |
| béisbol | | |
| básquetbol | | |
| música | | |

EJERCICIO ORAL

**H. *Yo me llamo...*** Imagine this is your first day in an international school where the common language is Spanish. Go up to another student and (1) introduce yourself. (2) Tell where you are from. (3) Ask his (her) name and (4) where he (she) is from. Then try to get better acquainted by sharing information about yourselves. (5) Indicate at least three things that you like and (6) one thing that you do not like.

**Learning Strategies:**

*Organizing, providing information*

EJERCICIO ESCRITO

**I. *Mi familia y yo*** Write a short paragraph in which you describe where you and your family live and what you have in your home. Mention (1) where you are from if you do not live in your birthplace, (2) whether you live in a house or apartment, (3) at least three items in your home, and (4) the mode of transportation that each family member uses to go to the office or school.

**Learning Strategies:**

*Summarizing, reporting, providing information*

*—Mi familia y yo somos de Nueva York, pero vivimos en Pennsylvania. Vivimos en una casa. En nuestra casa hay un estéreo, un televisor y una grabadora. No hay una computadora. Yo voy al centro en bicicleta, pero mis padres van al centro en coche.*



**Ex. H:** pair work

role play

*More-prepared students, Ex. H:* More-prepared students can extend the conversation, asking and answering questions: **¿Qué necesito en esta escuela? ¿Una mochila? ¿Cuántos cuadernos?**

**Ex. I:** writing

***Suggestions, Vocabulario:*** Students may use the **Vocabulario** as a checklist for vocabulary recognition. A Spanish–English Glossary is provided at the end of the book.

# Chapter Culminating Activities

Have students make two lists: one for all the masculine nouns and another for the feminine nouns.

You may want to play **el juego de las categorías** as a wrap-up exercise. Use any of the categories on this page and accept words from the vocabulary expansions. Have students write down answers and give a point for each correct response, or divide the class into teams and do the game orally.

Name famous Hispanic sports figures, singers, or painters. See if students can remember who they are. This can also be done as a game orally or in writing.

***Support material, Capítulo 5:*** Improvised Monologue, Teacher Tape/CD #1 Track #25 and Tapescript; Lab Manual listening activities, Laboratory Program, Tapescript, and Teacher's Edition of the Workbook/Lab Manual

## Temas y contextos

*Los animales*

un gato
un pájaro
un perro

*El arte*

la escultura
la pintura

*Las ciencias*

la biología
la química

*Los deportes*

el básquetbol
el béisbol
el fútbol
el fútbol americano
el tenis
el vólibol

*La música*

el jazz
la música clásica
la música rock

*Las películas*

cómicas
de aventura
de ciencia ficción
de horror

## Vocabulario general

*Verbos*

aprender
beber
compartir
comprender
correr
escribir
leer
recibir
vender
vivir

*Otras palabras y expresiones*

¡Claro!
Me gusta más...
las lenguas
la naturaleza
una novia
un novio
la política
¿Qué te gusta más?

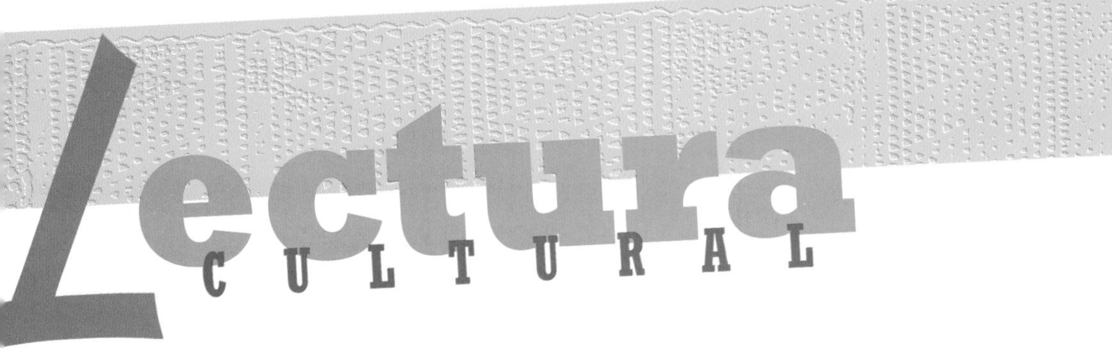

# Las tortugas de las islas Galápagos

## Antes de leer

1. Look at the picture and title of this reading. Can you find the Spanish word for this reptile?
2. Have you ever seen a turtle this size?
3. What do you know about turtles?

*Critical Thinking Strategy:*

*Predicting*

## Lectura Cultural

Have students share what they know about turtles—from school, from books, from menus, from personal experience. How many ever had turtles as pets? How much do they know about the present endangerment of turtles?

*Answers, Guía para la lectura:* **A.** Turtles have not changed for millions of years. There are almost 300 species of turtles. Many are in danger of extinction. **B.** Turtles are killed both for the meat and the shell. **C.** Ecuador



**Learning Strategy:**
*Paraphrasing*

## Guía para la lectura

**A.** Read the first paragraph and list three things that it says about turtles.

**B.** In the second paragraph, what two reasons are given for why turtles are in danger of extinction.

**C.** In the third paragraph, according to the reading, what country is working hard to protect turtles and how?

### Las tortugas de las Islas Galápagos

La tortuga, un animal inofensivo y simpático, no ha cambiado desde hace millones de años. Hoy en día existen casi 300 especies de tortugas, distribuidas por todas partes del mundo, menos en las regiones muy frías. Pero muchas de estas tortugas están en peligro de extinción.

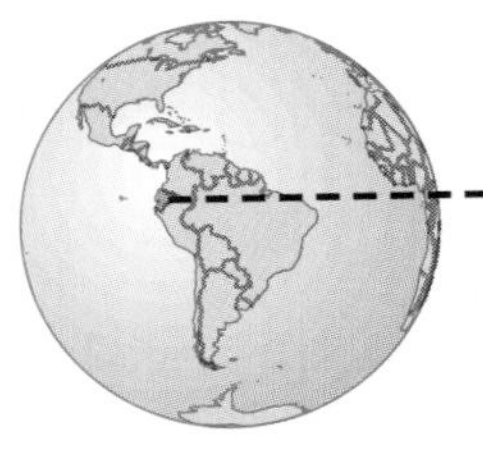

Las tortugas son perseguidas por muchas razones. En algunas regiones es por su carne, en otras por su caparazón que se usa para hacer peines, gafas y otros objetos. A pesar de ser protegidas, hay cada vez menos tortugas en el mundo.

En las Islas Galápagos, que son parte del Ecuador, hay un proyecto para proteger a estos animales en una reserva especial. El dinero que pagan los turistas para visitar las Islas se usa para mantener el santuario para las magníficas tortugas.

CAPÍTULO 6

# ¡ÉSTA ES MI FAMILIA!

Ésta es mi familia: mi madre, mi hermano y mi hermana con su marido.

### Objectives:

- **T**alking about one's family
- **G**etting information about other people

### Strategies:

- **I**nterviewing
- **R**eading a chart
- **S**eeing cause-and-effect relationships



## Video/CD-ROM

**Chapter 6 Video Program**
**Chapter 6 CD-ROM Program**

**These can be used at the end of the chapter as expansion activities.**

## Chapter Objectives

Functions: Talking about one's family; getting information about other people
Context: Home
Accuracy: Present tense of the verb **tener** (including **tener que** + infinitive); questions with **dónde, cuántos/cuántas, quién, qué, por qué; ser** + descriptive adjectives

## Cultural Observation

Have students study the photo on this page. Ask them to compare Carmen Candelaria's family to their own. Is this a typical "nuclear family"? What do they observe about the decor of the house? About the way the family members are dressed? Do they notice anything that is different? Anything similar?

*Teacher's Note:* Throughout this chapter students will be studying the subject of family. If any student is hesitant to share his or her family's attributes, or if they don't know a lot about their family, assure them that it's ok, and that they can still do the exercises using an imaginary family tree (or using any family they know of as a model, if they wish). Most families in the U.S. today are non-traditional, so let students know that their trees will probably differ from those shown in the book.

## Presentation: Yo vivo con...

With books closed, play the Teacher Tape while students look at the transparency. After listening to the tape of Ernesto's monologue, you may want to replay it, stopping from time to time to ask students personal questions. Do not insist that they answer in complete sentences; comprehension should be the goal at this time. If you do not use the transparency and Teacher Tape, have students look at the picture in the book while you read the monologue. Then read it again, stopping occasionally to ask questions.

## Vocabulary Expansion

**bisabuelo/bisabuela** *(great-grandfather/grandmother)*, **tío abuelo/tía abuela** *(great uncle/aunt)*

***Support material, Yo vivo con...:*** Teacher Tape/CD #1 Track #26, transparency #30



# PRIMERA ETAPA

### Preparación

*Learning Strategy: Previewing*

**As you get ready to begin this etapa, think about the various members of your immediate family.**

- **Do you have a traditional family?**
- **Do you have stepparents?**
- **Do you have brothers and sisters?**
- **Do you have stepbrothers or stepsisters?**

## Yo vivo con...

Buenos días. Me llamo Ernesto Torres. Ernesto es mi **nombre** y Torres es mi **apellido**. Hay siete personas en mi familia. **Tengo** un **padre**, una **madre**, un **hermano** y una **hermana**. **Mi padre se llama** Alberto, y mi madre se llama Catalina. Mi hermano se llama Patricio, y mi hermana se llama Marta. Vivimos en una casa en **la ciudad de México** con mi **abuelo** y mi **abuela.**

first name
last name / I have / father / mother / brother / sister / My father's name is
Mexico City / grandfather / grandmother



## Etapa Support Materials

**Workbook:** pp. 64–70
**Transparency:** #30
**Teacher Tape** 

**Quiz:** Testing Program, p. 57
**Support material, Yo vivo con...:** Teacher Tape , transparency #30

# ¡Aquí te toca a ti!

**A. *Tú y tu familia*** First complete the following sentences with information about you and your family.

1. Me llamo...
2. Mi nombre es...
3. Mi apellido es...
4. Hay... personas en mi familia.
5. Mi padre se llama...
6. Mi madre se llama...
7. Tengo... hermanos. (o: No tengo hermanos.)
8. Ellos se llaman...
9. Tengo... hermanas. (o: No tengo hermanas.)
10. Ellas se llaman...
11. Vivo con mis abuelos. (o: No vivo con mis abuelos.)

Vocabulary Expansion

| | |
|---|---|
| padrastro | *stepfather* |
| madrastra | *stepmother* |
| hermanastro | *stepbrother* |
| hermanastra | *stepsister* |

**B. *La familia de un(a) compañero(a)*** (a classmate) Now ask one of your classmates the following questions about himself or herself and his or her family.

1. ¿Cómo te llamas? *(What's your name?)*
2. ¿Cuál *(What)* es tu nombre?
3. ¿Cuál es tu apellido?
4. ¿Cuántas *(How many)* personas hay en tu familia? (Hay...)
5. ¿Cómo se llama tu padre?
6. ¿Cómo se llama tu madre?
7. ¿Cuántos hermanos tienes?
8. ¿Cómo se llaman?
9. ¿Cuántas hermanas tienes?
10. ¿Cómo se llaman?
11. ¿Cuántos abuelos tienes?

*Learning Strategy:*

*Interviewing*

## COMENTARIOS CULTURALES

### Los apellidos

**Perhaps you have noticed that Hispanics often use more than one last name. This is because many use their mother's maiden name along with their father's last name. For example, Mario González Cruz would use the last name of his father first (González), followed by his mother's (Cruz). Mario might also use the initial instead of the complete second name (Mario González C.). When addressing someone, you use the first of the two last names (Mario González). What would be your complete name if we had this tradition here in the United States?**

*Learning Strategy:*

*Reading for cultural information*



*Answers, Ex. B:* Endings will vary. 1. Me llamo... 2. Mi nombre es... 3. Mi apellido es... 4. Hay... personas en mi familia. 5. Mi padre se llama... 6. Mi madre se llama... 7. Tengo... hermanos. / Tengo un hermano. / No tengo hermanos. 8. Se llaman... y... / Se llama... 9. Tengo... hermanas. / Tengo una hermana. / No tengo hermanas. 10. Se llaman... y... / Se llama... 11. Tengo dos abuelos. / Tengo un abuelo. / No tengo abuelos.

*Suggestion, Comentario cultural:* You may want to discuss names a little more, since students may find them confusing. Write **José Pérez Morales** and **Beatriz García Sánchez** on the board. Explain to students that the first last name is called the **apellido paterno.** (Circle both of the **apellidos paternos** on the board.) The second last name is called the **apellido materno** and is the mother's maiden name. Ask students what would be the full name of **José** and **Beatriz's** first-born son, **José,** if this couple were to marry. If they can't answer, point to the circled name of the father (**Pérez**) and write it on the board, adding **José** before it. Then point to the circled name of the mother (**García**) and write it down after **Pérez.** Thus, **José Pérez García** would be their son's name.

## Exercise Progression

Exs. A and B provide communicative practice with the vocabulary and expressions associated with the family. Ex. A stresses the vocabulary in statement form. Ex. B works with the same vocabulary in a question/answer format.

**. A:**  writing

*Suggestion, Ex. A:* Have students write out the statements in paragraph form like the reading. Then have volunteers read their paragraphs to the class.

**Ex. B:** pair work

*Suggestion, Ex. B:* You may want to do this first as a **pregúntale** exercise. Have students answer in complete sentences and point out mistakes if necessary. (Students tend to say **Me llamo es...** and may be confused about how to form some of the other answers in this exercise.) You could also have students ask you the questions so they could hear your model.

## Presentation: Pronunciation

Have students pronounce English words beginning with *b*, such as *Bob, Bill,* and *Betty.* Explain that this is also the sound for the Spanish consonant **v.** Then read the words in the **Práctica,** stressing the sound of the **v** pronounced as a *b* in numbers 4, 5, and 7.

Additional activities appear in the Laboratory Tape Program.

**Ex. D:** pair work

*Suggestions, Ex. D:* Have students make statements to their partners or tell them to write out the answers and have them edit their partners work. You could also have six students write the answers on the board while the rest write at their seats. Then have the whole class point out any errors.

*Possible answers, Ex. D:*
1. Alicia y Carlos comen en un restaurante. 2. Ana lee un libro. 3. Alberto escribe una carta. 4. Marirrosa y Juan corren. 5. El Sr. García vende libros. 6. Sofía bebe leche.

*Support material, Pronunciación:*
Pronunciation Tape



# Pronunciación: The sound of /b/

In Spanish the sound of /**b**/ can be spelled with the letter **b** or **v** and is pronounced like the *b* in *Bill* when it is the first letter of a word or after *n* or *m.*

## Práctica

C. Listen and repeat as your teacher models the following words.

1. bueno
2. bien
3. bocadillo
4. vaso
5. vamos
6. hombre
7. un vídeo
8. un beso
9. también
10. hambre

## Repaso

D. ***¿Qué hacen?*** Describe what the people in the drawings are doing.

1. Alicia y Carlos

2. Ana

3. Alberto

4. Marirrosa y Juan

5. el Sr. García

6. Sofía

**E. *¿Qué te gusta más?*** From the choices below, ask a classmate what he or she likes more.

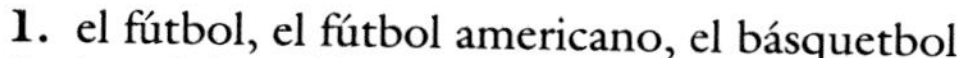

1. el fútbol, el fútbol americano, el básquetbol
2. la música, el baile *(dance)*, las películas
3. la música rock, el jazz, la música clásica
4. las hamburguesas, los sándwiches de jamón, las hamburguesas con queso
5. las películas de horror, las películas de aventura, las películas cómicas
6. la historia, las lenguas, las ciencias

**¿Qué crees?**

**When a woman marries she usually adds *de* plus her husband's last name to her own name. If María Pérez Clemente married José Román Caño, what would her name be?**

**a) María Clemente de Caño**
**b) María Pérez de Román**
**c) María Clemente de Román**
**d) María Pérez de Caño**

**respuesta** 

# ESTRUCTURA

## *The verb tener*

| | |
|---|---|
| **Yo tengo** dos hermanas. | *I have* two sisters. |
| **¿Tienes tú** un hermano? | *Do you have* a brother? |
| **Nosotros tenemos** dos gatos. | *We have* two cats. |
| **Ellos no tienen** un perro. | *They don't have* a dog. |
| **Él tiene** un abuelo en Miami. | *He has* a grandfather in Miami. |

In Spanish the verb **tener** can be used to talk about possessions.

The verb **tener** *(to have)* is irregular. Here are its conjugated forms.

| *tener* | | | |
|---|---|---|---|
| yo | **tengo** | nosotros(as) | **tenemos** |
| tú | **tienes** | vosotros(as) | **tenéis** |
| él / ella / Ud. | **tiene** | ellos / ellas / Uds. | **tienen** |

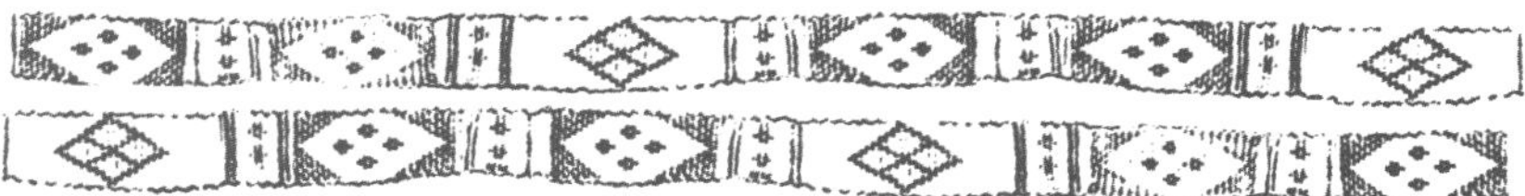



**Ex. E:** pair work

***Suggestions, Ex. E:*** Do as a **pregúntale** exercise with books closed to develop listening skills or have students work in pairs.

### Presentation: The verb tener

Students have seen and used some forms of **tener** in the vocabulary activities, so it should be easy to present the verb inductively. Start out by making a statement about yourself, then ask a **tú** question based on your statement and summarize using the third-person singular form. Example: **Yo tengo dos hermanos. ¿Cuántos hermanos tienes tú? Ella (Él) tiene un hermano.,** etc. Continue by making statements using the **nosotros** and the **Uds.** forms. **Nosotros tenemos muchos libros. Uds. tienen muchos libros también.,** etc. Then make other **nosotros** statements and ask **Uds.** questions based on those statements. Point to two or three students as you direct these questions and have one answer as a spokesperson for the others. **Nosotros tenemos muchos amigos. ¿Tienen Uds. muchos amigos?,** etc. Then summarize their answers using the third-person plural form. **Ellas (Ellos) tienen muchos amigos.**

*Suggestions, Ex. G:* Have students do this exercise orally in pairs or have them write out sentences and edit their partners' work.

*Answers, Ex. G:* Answers will vary, but should reflect Ana and Esteban's possesions accurately: Ana tiene una cámara, tres libros, un radio, un cuaderno, un lápiz y una mochila. Esteban tiene un portafolio, dos lápices, una cartera, una calculadora y un sacapuntas.

*Variation, Ex. G:* Tell students they have 30 seconds to look at the drawings for Ex. G and then they must close their books. When you say, **"Preparados, listos, ¡ya!"** they will have to write down as many items as they can remember in front of each person. Have volunteers read their answers; the one with the most items correct wins.

## Aquí practicamos

*F.* Tell what your friends have and don't have, using words from Columns A, B, C, and D.

| A | B | C | D |
|---|---|---|---|
| José<br>yo<br>nosotros<br>Juan y Catarina<br>tú<br>Uds. | (no) | tener | dos hermanos<br>una hermana<br>un gato<br>dos perros<br>un pájaro |

 b

*Critical Thinking Strategy:*
*Comparing and contrasting*

*G.* ***¿Qué tienen Ana y Esteban?*** Look at the drawings below and tell what Ana and Esteban have and don't have. Follow the model.

**Modelo:** *Ana tiene una cámara, pero Esteban no tiene una cámara.* o: *Ellos tienen unos lápices.*

## Exercise Progression

Ex. F is designed to practice the agreement of verb endings with the subjects while students create their own sentences. Ex. G offers controlled practice with the verb **tener** and the new vocabulary.

## Palabras útiles

### *Tener + que + infinitive*

| | |
|---|---|
| **Yo tengo que** comer. | *I have to* eat. |
| **Tú tienes que** estudiar. | *You have to* study. |
| **Él tiene que** escribir la lección. | *He has to* write the lesson. |

In Spanish, when you want to say that you have to do something, you do so by using the verb **tener** followed by **que** followed by the *infinitive* form of the verb that expresses what must be done.

*H.* Replace the words in italics and make the necessary changes.

1. Yo tengo que *comer.* (trabajar / estudiar / correr)
2. *Ellos* no tienen que estudiar. (Juan / Bárbara y Alicia / tú / vosotros)
3. ¿Tienes *tú* que trabajar hoy? (Julio y Santiago / Elena / Uds.)

*I.* Tell what you and your friends have to do, using words from Columns A, B, C, and D.

| A | B | C | D |
|---|---|---|---|
| yo | tener que | trabajar después *(after)* de la escuela | hoy |
| nosotras | | estudiar para un examen | mañana |
| Jaime | | hablar con un(a) amigo(a) | el viernes |
| tú | | comprar un disco compacto | esta noche |
| Uds. | | hacer un mandado para su padre (madre) | |

## "Mi familia"

### Antes de escuchar

**Carmen is going to provide some basic information about her family. What information about her family do you expect her to include in her short monologue?**

*Learning Strategy:*

*Previewing*

129

### Exercise Progression

Ex. H is a mechanical drill designed to practice the use of **tener que** before an infinitive. Ex. I provides more controlled practice of the expression.

### Presentation: Tener + que + infinitive

Make statements telling students what you have to do today. For example: **Tengo que comer. Tengo que leer. Tengo que escribir una carta.,** etc. Then write, **¿Qué tienen que hacer?** on the board and circle the **que.** Explain that you must use the conjugated form of **tener** plus the **que** before an infinitive. Then start asking the question **¿Qué tienes que hacer?** randomly, telling students to make up activities using vocabulary that they know.

*Answers, Ex. H:* 1. Yo tengo que trabajar. ( ...que estudiar; ...que correr) 2. Juan no tiene que estudiar. (Bárbara y Alicia no tienen que...; Tú no tienes que...; Vosotros no tenéis que...) 3. ¿Tienen Julio y Santiago que trabajar hoy? (¿Tiene Elena que... ?; ¿Tienen Uds. que... ?)

*Suggestion, Ex. I:* Have five students write the answers on the board while the rest write at their seats. Then have the whole class point out any errors.

*Follow-up, Ex. I:* Get dramatic for a moment and act out some situations while saying, for example, **"Tengo hambre," "Tengo sed,"** or *"I live far away from school but I don't have a car."* Students will listen and then tell you what you have to do: **"Ud. tiene que comer... beber... comprar un coche",** etc. Ask students to make up similar situations to tell the class.

*Support material, Aquí escuchamos:* Teacher Tape/CD #1 Track #27 and Tapescript

**Answers, *Después de escuchar:*** familia: pequeña; padre: ingeniero; madre: periodista; un hermano; perros



**Before your instructor plays the tape, take a moment to copy the list that follows on a separate sheet of paper.**

## Después de escuchar

**Now listen to the tape again and circle the choices that match what Carmen says about her family.**

| familia | padre | madre | un hermano |
|---|---|---|---|
| grande | contador | enfermera | dos hermanos |
| pequeña | ingeniero | periodista | animales |
| | mecánico | profesora | gatos |
| | | | perros |

Esta semana tengo que estudiar para un examen, ir al cine y jugar al fútbol con mis amigos. Y tú, ¿qué tienes que hacer?

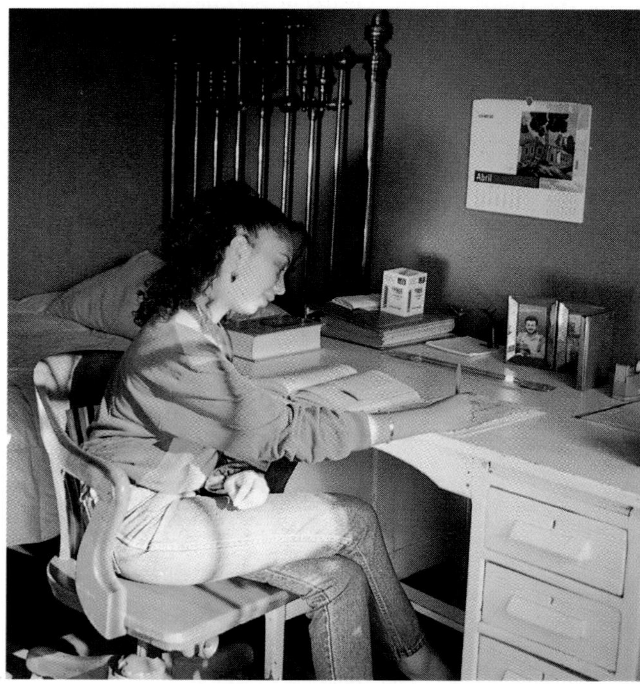

# ESTRUCTURA

## *Information questions with: dónde, cuántos, cuántas, quién, qué, por qué*

You have already learned how to ask questions that take *yes* or *no* for an answer. Frequently, however, you ask a question because you seek specific information. In Chapter 4 you will recall you learned to ask to whom something belongs, using **¿De quién es?** and **¿De quién son?** The following words are the most commonly used in Spanish when seeking information.

1. To find out *where* something is or someone is located, use **¿dónde?**

| | |
|---|---|
| **¿Dónde** vive tu hermano? | *Where* does your brother live? |
| Él vive en Pittsburgh. | He lives in Pittsburgh. |
| **¿Dónde** está mi libro? | *Where* is my book? |
| Tu libro está en la mesa. | Your book is on the table. |

2. To ask *how many* there are, you use **¿cuántos?** if what you are asking about is masculine.

| | |
|---|---|
| **¿Cuántos** hermanos tienes? | *How many* brothers do you have? |
| Tengo dos. | I have two. |
| **¿Cuántos** perros tienes? | *How many* dogs do you have? |
| Tengo uno. | I have one. |

To ask *how many* there are, you use **¿cuántas?** if what you are asking about is feminine.

| | |
|---|---|
| **¿Cuántas** hermanas tiene él? | *How many* sisters does he have? |
| Él tiene seis. | He has six. |
| **¿Cuántas** cintas tienes? | *How many* tapes do you have? |
| Tengo diez. | I have ten. |
| Tengo una. | I have one. |

3. To find out *who* does something, use **¿quién?**

| | |
|---|---|
| **¿Quién** come en la cafetería? | *Who* eats in the cafeteria? |
| Bárbara come en la cafetería. | Bárbara eats in the cafeteria. |
| **¿Quién** estudia en la biblioteca? | *Who* studies in the library? |
| Roberto estudia en la biblioteca. | Roberto studies in the library. |

Remember, the words that you use to ask an information question always take a written accent.

4. To find out *what* someone wants or is seeking, use **¿qué?**

| | |
|---|---|
| **¿Qué** buscan ellos? | *What* are they looking for? |
| Ellos buscan la casa de Marta. | They are looking for Martha's house. |
| **¿Qué** compran ellos? | *What* are they buying? |
| Ellos compran una mochila. | They are buying a knapsack. |



*(continued from page bottom)*

Write the interrogative words on the board, pointing out the accents and where they are placed (on the stressed vowel). Remind students to use the upside-down question mark when writing questions.

You may want to mention that Spanish has two forms for *who* and add the plural form on the board (**quiénes**). Then give some examples: **¿Quiénes estudian en la biblioteca?** Explain that Spanish speakers use the plural form when they expect a plural answer.

You may want to introduce **cuál** at this time for recognition only. Tell students that **cuál** is used in some information questions such as **¿Cuál es tu apellido?** or **¿Cuál es tu número de teléfono?** and that it means *what.*

Make statements and see if students can form questions that would have elicited your statement as an answer. Sample statement: **María estudia en la biblioteca.** Question: **¿Dónde estudia María?** Start out with third-person questions and then work up to the first person. If students find this difficult, have them write down the statements before changing them. Or have a few students go to the board and dictate a sentence to each of them. Then have the whole class suggest how they could be changed to questions.

### resentation: Information questions ith interrogative words

ake statements about your family and then ask students out theirs, using information questions. The first time you use particular form, follow it up with some possible answers. For ample: **Mi mamá trabaja en un hospital. ¿Tu mamá trabaja, Juan? ¿Sí? ¿Dónde trabaja tu mamá? ¿En un hospital también? ¿En... ?** (Choose some local businesses.) **Ah, ella trabaja en... . Y tu mamá, José, ¿dónde trabaja?** Then have one student ask questions of another using the **pregúntale** format: **María, pregúntale a Juan dónde trabaja su mamá.** Continue in a similar fashion with the other question words.

## Exercise Progression

Ex. E is a mechanical exercise designed to familiarize students with the basic information questions. Ex. F has students use questions as a means of following up on a statement they have just heard.

**5.** To ask *why,* use **¿por qué?** The answer to a question that includes **¿por qué?** may sometimes include **porque** *(because).*

| | |
|---|---|
| **¿Por qué** estudias? | *Why* are you studying? |
| **Porque** tengo un examen mañana. | *Because* I have a test tomorrow. |
| **¿Por qué** comes pizza? | *Why* do you eat pizza? |
| **Porque** me gusta. | *Because* I like it. |

**Me llamo Lourdes. Ahora estoy en los Estados Unidos pero vivo en Bogotá, Colombia. Tengo dos hermanos y una hermana. Mis hermanos trabajan en Cartagena y mi hermana es estudiante de escuela secundaria. ¿Cuántos hermanos tienes tú? ¿Qué hacen?**

## Aquí practicamos

**E.** Create original questions using words from each column.

| A | B | C |
|---|---|---|
| dónde | trabajar | Josefina |
| qué | tener | tu padre |
| por qué | buscar | tú |
| quién | estudiar | Juan y Pablo |
| cuándo | comer | ellas |
| | vivir | Uds. |
| | correr | |

**F.** ***Más detalles*** (More details) Conversation depends on the listener paying attention to the speaker's comments and reacting to them. You are talking with some of the Hispanic exchange students in your school. After a student makes a statement, ask a logical follow-up question.

**Learning Strategy:**
*Formulating questions*

Esteban Candelaria:
—No vivo en Valencia.
—*¿Dónde vives?*

**Esteban Candelaria**

1. Tengo hermanos, pero no tengo hermanas.
2. Mis hermanos no viven con nosotros.
3. Ellos no estudian ciencias.

**Bárbara Martínez**

4. Mi padre y mi madre trabajan.
5. Mi hermana estudia muchas horas todos los días.
6. Mi hermano tiene muchos discos compactos.

**Carlos López**

7. No tengo una clase de química.
8. Como en la cafetería.
9. No vivo aquí.



**Ex. F:** pair work

*Possible answers, Ex. F:*
1. ¿Cuántos hermanos tienes? 2. ¿Dónde viven tus hermanos? 3. ¿Qué estudian? 4. ¿Dónde trabajan tus padres? 5. ¿Cuántas horas estudia tu hermana? 6. ¿Cuántos discos compactos tiene? 7. ¿Qué estudias? 8. ¿Qué comes? 9. ¿Dónde vives?

*Follow-up, Ex. F:* Make statements about members of your family. Have students ask you follow-up questions. You might want to write **su/sus** on the board and point out that the **Ud.** form of the possessive is **su.**

Ex. G: pair work

*Suggestions, Ex. G:* Since this is the first time that students will be doing an exercise of this type, you may want to work through the items with the whole class before students work with partners. Pair students up with partners other than those with whom they worked in Ex. B.

*Possible answers, Ex. G:*
1. ¿Dónde viven tus abuelos?
2. ¿Cuántos hermanos tienes? ¿Cuántas hermanas tienes?
3. ¿Cuántos animales (perros, gatos, pájaros) tienes en tu casa?
4. ¿Qué estudias?

*Follow-up, Ex. G:* Put interrogatives on slips of paper in a hat. Have students draw a question word out of the hat, form a question with it, and call on someone to answer. The student who answers correctly can draw the next word out of the hat.



**G. ¿Dónde vives?** Ask a classmate questions in order to get the following information. Do not translate word for word. Instead, find a Spanish expression that will get the information for you. Your classmate will answer your questions. Follow the model.

**Modelos:** where he or she lives
*—¿Dónde vives?*
*—Vivo en Los Ángeles.*

where his or her father and mother work
*—¿Dónde trabajan tu padre y tu madre?*
*—Mi padre trabaja en First National Bank of Los Ángeles, y mi madre trabaja en City Hospital.*

1. where his or her grandparents live
2. how many brothers and sisters he or she has
3. how many pets (dogs, cats, birds) he or she has
4. what he or she is studying

## ESTRUCTURA

### Ser + adjective

**Ser** plus an adjective can be used to describe someone or something.

| | |
|---|---|
| Él es **alto.** | He is *tall.* |
| Ella es **alta.** | She is *tall.* |
| Juan y José son **altos.** | Juan and José are *tall.* |
| María y Carmen son **altas.** | María and Carmen are *tall.* |

1. Adjectives that end in **-o** in the masculine singular have four different forms—masculine singular, masculine plural, feminine singular, and feminine plural—and must agree in number and gender with the nouns they modify, as you saw with the adjective **alto.** Here are some adjectives used to describe people and things:

| | |
|---|---|
| **aburrido** *(boring)* | **bajo** *(short)* |
| **alto** *(tall)* | **bonito** *(pretty)* |
| **antipático** *(disagreeable)* | **bueno** *(good)* |

**delgado** *(thin)*
**divertido** *(fun, amusing)*
**feo** *(plain, ugly)*
**gordo** *(fat)*
**guapo** *(handsome)*
**malo** *(bad)*
**moreno** *(dark haired, brunet)*
**pelirrojo** *(red haired)*
**pequeño** *(small)*
**rubio** *(blond)*
**serio** *(serious)*
**simpático** *(nice)*
**tonto** *(stupid, foolish)*

pelirroja moreno rubia

2. Adjectives that end in **-e** have only two forms, one singular and one plural, and must agree in number with the nouns they modify.

Some common adjectives that have only a singular and a plural form are:

**inteligente** **interesante** **grande**

Él es **inteligente.** He is *intelligent.*
Ella es **inteligente.** She is *intelligent.*
Juan y José son **inteligentes.** Juan and José are *intelligent.*
María y Bárbara son **inteligentes.** María and Bárbara are *intelligent.*

El libro es muy interesante.



## Presentation: Ser + adjective

Students have used **ser** with adjectives of nationality and adjectives that describe food, so they know how to make adjectives agree. To reinforce adjective agreement, show pictures of famous people and describe them using the descriptive adjectives presented in this section (and other cognates if you choose to do so). Or describe yourself and different students in the class using all forms of the adjectives, so that students associate the adjective endings with the gender and number of the people being described. For example: **Teresa y Ana son rubias. También son bonitas y simpáticas. Karen es pelirroja.**, etc.

## Vocabulary Expansion

Cognates that describe people's personal traits: (ending in **-e**) **elegante, eficiente, independiente, paciente, responsable, valiente;** (ending in **-a**—these have only one singular and one plural form) **egoísta, realista, idealista, optimista, pesimista, materialista;** (ending in **-o**) **extrovertido, introvertido, impulsivo, sincero, tímido, generoso, romántico;** (ending in **-l**—these have only one singular and one plural form) **cruel, emocional, sentimental.**

After writing these cognates on the board, say different adjectives and have students give their opposites, telling them to look at the lists on pp. 138 and 139 or on the board to find the answer.

## Presentation: ¿Cómo es... ? / ¿Cómo son... ?

To introduce **¿Cómo es... ?** or **¿Cómo son... ?,** make statements about your family, and then ask students about theirs. Follow up your questions with some possible answers. For example: **Mi mamá es paciente y generosa. ¿Cómo es tu mamá? ¿Es generosa también? Mis amigos son simpáticos. ¿Cómo son tus amigos? ¿Son simpáticos también?,** etc.

*Ex. H:* These column exercises are meant to provide controlled practice. A possible way to present these would be through the creation of a "word web." On a separate piece of paper, students would draw a web, and then connect elements from the columns in ways that form grammatically correct sentences. (They would have to write in the correct form of the verb in the middle column.) See the diagram below for a sample word web format. Word web formats will vary from exercise to exercise.

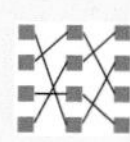

**Ex. I:** pair work

*Less-prepared students, Ex. I:* Give less-prepared students more practice with adjectives by having them name famous people or characters and having them say an adjective that readily describes that person: (**Michael Jordan—alto; la Madre Teresa—generosa; Bugs Bunny—divertido,** etc.).

*More-prepared students, Ex. I:* Have more-prepared students describe in some detail a famous person or character and others will guess who it is.

### ¿Cómo es...?/¿Cómo son...?

In Spanish, to ask what someone or something is like, you use **¿Cómo es...?** or **¿Cómo son...?**

| | |
|---|---|
| **¿Cómo es** Juan?<br>Juan es inteligente. | *What is* Juan *like?*<br>Juan is intelligent. |
| **¿Cómo es** el libro?<br>El libro es aburrido. | *What is* the book *like?*<br>The book is boring. |
| **¿Cómo son** María y Bárbara?<br>María y Bárbara son simpáticas. | *What are* María and Bárbara *like?*<br>María and Bárbara are nice. |

**H. ¿Cómo son?** Describe the following people, using words from Columns A, B, and C.

Modelo: *Él es alto.* o: *Él no es alto.*

| A | B | C |
|---|---|---|
| él | (no) ser | alto |
| tú | | inteligente |
| Elizabeth | | bajo |
| Linda y Paula | | rubio |
| Javier y Roberto | | moreno |
| nosotros | | pelirrojo |
| | | aburrido |
| | | tonto |
| | | antipático |
| | | bueno |

Critical Thinking Strategy: Contrasting

**I. No, no es..., es...** Someone asks you about a quality of one of your friends and you respond with the opposite. Follow the model.

Modelo: alto / María
—*¿Es María alta?*
—*No, no es alta, es baja.*

1. gordo / Juan
2. rubio / Anita
3. inteligente / David
4. divertido / Marina
5. simpático / Antonio
6. feo / Miguel y Luis
7. bajo / Éster y Marisa
8. simpático / ellos
9. aburrido / ellas
10. bueno / los hijos



### Exercise Progression

Ex. H is a sentence-formation activity designed to focus on the agreement of adjectives with the nouns they modify. Ex. I offers controlled practice with the adjectives in a question/answer format.

*Answers, Ex. I:* 1. ¿Es Juan gordo? No, no es gordo, es delgado. 2. ¿Es Anita rubia? No, ..., es morena. 3. ¿Es Dav inteligente? No, ..., es tonto. 4. ¿Es Mariana divertida? No, . es aburrida. 5. ¿Es Antonio simpático? No, ..., es antipático. 6. ¿Son feos Miguel y Luis? No, ..., son guapos. 7. ¿Son baja Éster y Marisa? No, ..., son altas. 8. ¿Son simpáticos ellos? No, ..., son antipáticos. 9. ¿Son aburridas ellas? No, ..., son divertidas. 10. ¿Son buenos los hijos? No, ..., son malos.

# Aquí escuchamos: "La familia de Isabel"

## Antes de escuchar

Isabel, a friend of Carmen's, is going to provide some basic information about her family. Given what you have learned in this **etapa,** what information about her family do you expect her to include in her short monologue?

Before your instructor plays the tape, take a moment and copy the list that follows onto a separate sheet of paper.

- familia
  - grande
  - pequeña
- padre
  - contador
  - ingeniero
  - mecánico
- madre
  - enfermera
  - periodista
  - profesora
- un hermano
- dos hermanos
- animales
  - gatos
  - perros
  - pájaros

## Después de escuchar

Now listen to the tape again and circle the items that match what Isabel says about her family.

*Learning Strategy:* *Predicting*

*Learning Strategy:* *Listening for details*



*Answers,* ***Después de escuchar:*** familia: grande; padre: contador; madre: profesora; dos hermanos; perros; pájaros

*Support material,* ***Aquí escuchamos:*** Teacher Tape/CD #1 Track #29 and Tapescript

**Ex. J:** pair work

*Support material, Ex. J:* Transparency #32

**Ex. K:** writing

*Suggestion, Ex. K:* Have students write out the descriptions and then have them edit their partners' papers.

*Spanish speakers, Ex. K:* Spanish-speaking students can interview a Spanish-speaking relative and write about him/her. Perhaps he/she could record the interview and play it for the class.

*Less-prepared students, Ex. K:* Less-prepared students can list relatives and then list positive and negative traits for each, before moving to complete sentences.

*More-prepared students, Ex. K:* More-prepared students can write three different descriptions of themselves—one from their own point of view (**Yo soy...**), another as if their mother (father, brother, teacher) were doing the describing (**Mi hijo [hermano, estudiante] Andrew es...**), and the last one as if their best friend (or pet dog) were writing (**Mi mejor amigo Andrew es...**). Encourage students to think about how everyone sees them from a different perspective.

EJERCICIO ORAL

**J. *Una fiesta*** Describe as many people as you can in the picture below.

EJERCICIO ESCRITO

*Learning Strategies:*

*Reporting, providing details*

**K. *Tu familia*** Choose three members of your family (mother, father, brother, sister, grandfather, grandmother, uncle, aunt, or cousin) and write a description of each that includes at least three adjectives.

## Para charlar

### Para preguntar

¿Cuántas?
¿Cuántos?
¿Dónde?
¿Por qué?
¿Qué?
¿Quién?
¿Cómo es? / ¿Cómo son?

## Temas y contextos

### La familia

una abuela
un abuelo
una esposa
un esposo
una hermana
un hermano
una hija
un hijo
una madre
un padre
una prima
un primo
una tía
un tío

## Vocabulario general

### Adjetivos

aburrido(a)
alto(a)
antipático(a)
bajo(a)
bonito(a)
bueno(a)
delgado(a)
divertido(a)
feo(a)
gordo(a)
guapo(a)
inteligente
interesante
malo(a)
moreno(a)
pelirrojo(a)
pequeño(a)
rubio(a)
serio(a)
simpático(a)
tonto(a)

### Sustantivos

un apellido
una ciudad
un nombre
unas personas

### Verbos

tener
tener que

### Otras expresiones

cada domingo
Está casado(a) con...
Se llama(n)...

# Cooperative Learning

## Vocabulario: Round Table

- Divide the class into several teams with equal numbers of students.
- Hand one person in each team a piece of paper.
- Announce a category, such as **la familia.**
- The first person writes down a word that fits the category, then passes the sheet of paper to the next student who writes down another word, and so on. They should work quickly.
- Change categories to cover the vocabulary to be reviewed.
- When finished, check each team's sheet. The team with the most words written correctly wins.

*Suggestion, Vocabulario:* Students may use the **Vocabulario** as a checklist for vocabulary recognition. A Spanish–English Glossary is provided at the end of the book.

# Chapter Culminating Activities

You may want to play **¿Quién es?** to practice the vocabulary. Have students describe celebrities using simple terms, without giving the name. The class tries to guess the famous person on the basis of the description.

You might prefer a game of opposites to practice the adjectives. Read a list of adjectives, including the cognates from the vocabulary expansion, and have students write down the opposites. You could also do this orally by dividing the class into teams.

This chapter also lends itself to a listening comprehension exercise. Talk to the class about your family and have the students take notes. Then ask them questions about what you have said.

*Support material, Capítulo 6:* Improvised Conversation, Teacher Tape/CD #1 Track #30 and Tapescript; Lab Manual listening activities, Laboratory Program, Tapescript, and Teacher's Edition of the Workbook/Lab Manual

# Lectura cultural

Crown Prince Felipe graduated from Georgetown University's School of Foreign Service with a master's of science in foreign services (May, 1995). At his own graduation ceremony, Felipe's parents both received honorary doctoral degrees.

Have students talk about the relative advantages and disadvantages of growing up in a famous and/or powerful family. What would they like most and least about growing up in the White House, for example, or as the child of a famous rock star?



# Lectura cultural

## LA FAMILIA REAL DE ESPAÑA

In this chapter you have been talking about your family and family members. Look at the family tree below. What kind of family do you think this is? Who is the father? Who is the mother? Who are the children?

### Antes de leer

1. Look at the pictures of this family tree and the title of the reading. Where is this family from?
2. What are the names of the parents?
3. What are the children's names?

## Guía para la lectura

**A.** Which child is talked about in the first paragraph?

**B.** What words in this paragraph suggest to you that this is a very important family in Spain?

**C.** Read the second paragraph to find out what his friends say about Felipe.

**D.** What is Felipe's favorite sport? Look at the photo to help you determine what **vela** means.

*Learning Strategies:*

*Reading for details, drawing meaning from context*

### La familia real de España

Los hijos del rey y la reina son como los otros jóvenes. Por ejemplo, la princesa Elena de España es gran aficionada a la música moderna. Sus cantantes preferidos son la cubana Gloria Estefan y el inglés Sting. Recientemente, después de un concierto, Elena habló con Gloria Estefan. Gloria dice que Elena es como los otros jóvenes.

El príncipe Felipe también es como los otros jóvenes, pero sus amigos dicen que estudia mucho. En su tiempo libre es un gran deportista. El deporte que más prefiere es la vela. Él participó en las Olimpiadas de Barcelona en 1992 en el equipo de vela de España.

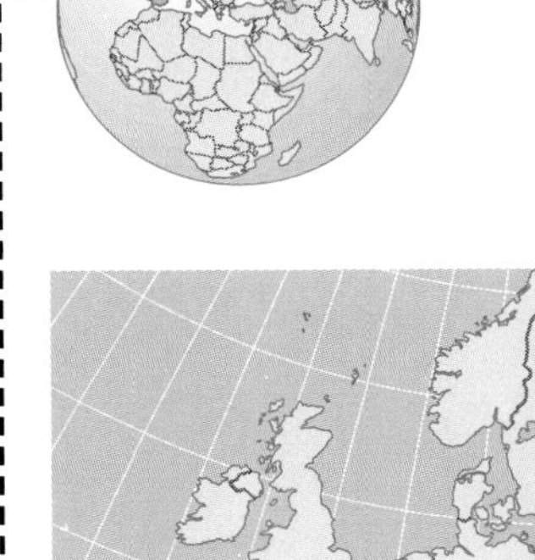

Spain

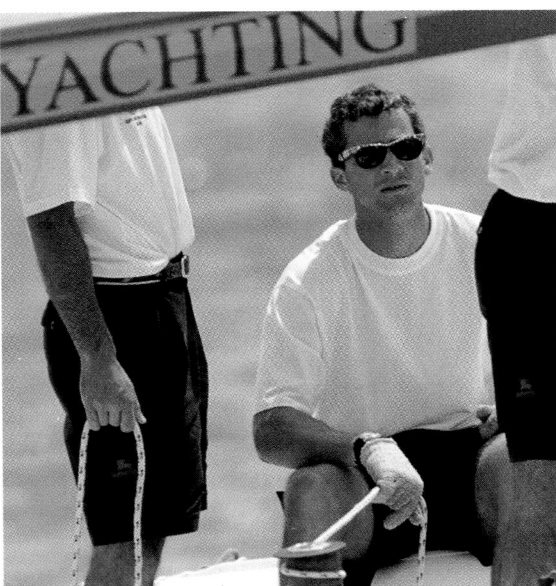


El príncipe Felipe de España



*Answers, Guía para la lectura:* **A.** Princess Elena **B.** rey, reina, princesa **C.** He studies a lot. **D.** Sailing

## Prereading

Ask students how they determine a person's identity. Have them look at the photos on pp. 147 and 148 and try to guess the identity of each person. Check students' predictions and guesses about the identities of the writers.

**Reading Strategies:**

*Use cognates and pay attention to the context of a reading passage.*

*Try to predict content on the basis of topic and layout: What information do you expect to find? What words or types of words do you expect to find? What does the writer seem to want you to learn?*

## Estrategia para la lectura

Your ability to read in Spanish develops more rapidly than the skills of speaking, listening, or writing. There are several reasons. First, you already know how to read and can apply that knowledge to reading in Spanish. Next, reading passages are usually part of a known background or context, that you can make predictions about. Finally, many words in Spanish look like English words with similar meanings. These words are called *cognates*, and you can use them to get a general idea of what a reading is about.

## Antes de leer

This reading is a series of autobiographical statements with photographs. Before looking at them, answer these questions.

- **When people talk about themselves, what information do they usually mention?**
- **What kinds of words do you use to describe yourself? Words for your relatives? Names of occupations? Personal adjectives? Body-part words? Lists of your possessions? Animals? Sports? Others?**
- **What kinds of verb forms would you expect in an autobiographical statement?**

Now look at the photographs and try to guess the identity of each person.

## Support Materials

Workbook: **pp. 77–79**
Unit Review Blackline Masters: **Unit 2 Review**
Listening Activity masters: **p. 41**
Tapescript: **p. 61**
Unit Exam: **Testing Program, p. 65**
**Atajo,** writing assistant software

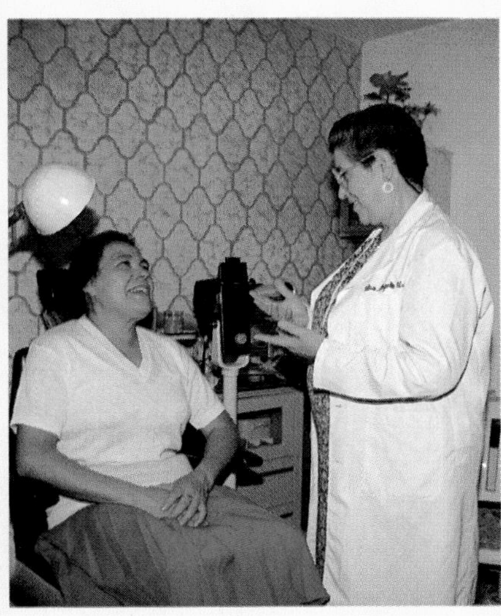

Yo soy médica y madre de familia. Trabajo en el Hospital Santa Ana en Guadalajara. Mi esposo es profesor. Él está mucho en casa con los niños. Tenemos un hijo y tres hijas. **Durante** el **fin de semana pasamos tiempo** con nuestros hijos. **A veces vamos de campamento** o a un **partido** de fútbol. A veces vamos a las montañas. Me gusta el arte, y a veces mi esposo y yo vamos a los museos de arte. Llevamos a nuestros hijos con nosotros porque mi hijo **quiere** ser arquitecto, y una de mis hijas quiere estudiar pintura en la universidad.

During
weekend / we spend time
Sometimes we go
camping / game
wants

Yo soy estudiante en la Escuela Secundaria de Santa Fe, Nuevo México. Estudio lenguas modernas —el francés y el español— porque me gusta mucho la literatura y también porque **quiero** viajar a Europa y a América Latina **algún día.** Mis padres están divorciados. Vivo con mi madre. Ella trabaja en un banco. Mi padre es ingeniero; vive en Albuquerque. Tengo un hermano **menor** que se llama Alejandro. No tengo hermanas. No tenemos mucho dinero.

I want
some day
younger

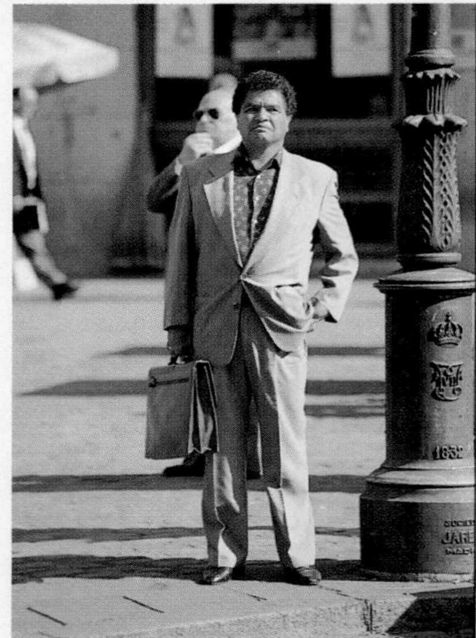

Yo soy presidente de una compañía grande. Tengo una casa grande, tres televisores a color y dos coches en el garaje. Mi esposa y yo viajamos mucho. Tenemos un condominio en Puerto Rico y un apartamento en Madrid. Mis hijos no viven en casa y **asisten** a una escuela privada. Contribuimos mucho dinero a diferentes instituciones **benéficas** cada año. Tenemos una **vida** muy **cómoda.**

attend
charitable
life / comfortable

Yo estoy **jubilado.** Mi esposa **murió** en 1985. Vivo con mi hijo en Quito, Ecuador. Él es dentista y está casado. Su esposa se llama Cecilia. Ellos tienen dos hijos. Yo no trabajo. Me gusta la naturaleza y me gusta mucho **caminar** en el parque. **Por la noche,** como con la familia y **después de** comer miro la televisión. Mi vida es muy tranquila y agradable.

retired / died
to walk / At night
after

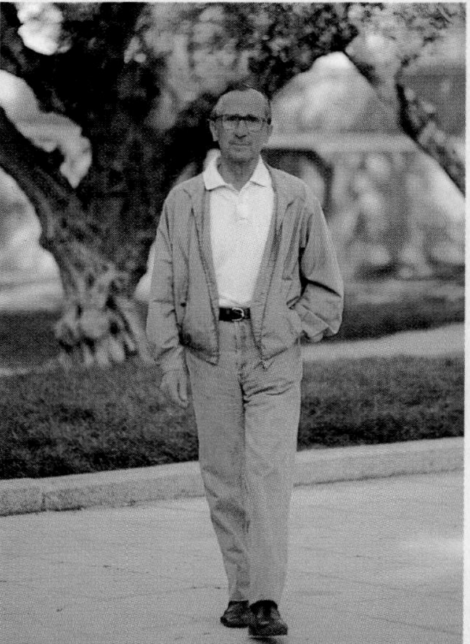

Ex. A: writing

*Suggestion, Ex. A:* Do the activity with the whole class. Afterwards, have students read the passages in order to do Ex. B.

*Answers, Ex. B:* 1. F, F, T, T 2. F, F, T, F 3. F, T, T, F 4. T, F, F, T

*Suggestion, Ex. C:* This recycling activity can be done for writing practice or can be used as a group exercise in class with students working in pairs and presenting the statements and questions to the class for responses.

## Actividades

**A.** Go back over the readings and make a list of all the cognates you can find.

**B.** Reread each passage to decide whether each of the following statements is true or false for the person indicated. Support your decisions with relevant information from the paragraphs.

**1.** la médica
- **a.** Tengo cuatro hijas.
- **b.** Mi esposo trabaja todos los días en una oficina.
- **c.** Me gusta la naturaleza.
- **d.** Paso mucho tiempo con mis hijos.

**2.** la estudiante
- **a.** Vivo con mi padre y mi madre en Santa Fe, Nuevo México.
- **b.** Hablo alemán y español.
- **c.** Tengo una familia pequeña.
- **d.** Soy rica.

**3.** el presidente de la compañía
- **a.** No me gustan mucho las cosas materiales.
- **b.** Tengo un apartamento en Madrid.
- **c.** Contribuyo mucho dinero a las causas benéficas.
- **d.** Paso mucho tiempo con mis hijos.

**4.** el hombre jubilado
- **a.** Vivo con la familia de mi hijo en Quito.
- **b.** A veces camino en el parque con mi esposa.
- **c.** Por la noche, siempre como solo.
- **d.** Por la noche, me gusta mirar la televisión.

**C.** Outline your own autobiographical statement in Spanish, using the paragraphs you just read as models. Exchange statements with a partner who will compose questions similar to those in Activity B. Pass your statement and the questions to a third student, who will select the right statements to describe you.

## ooperative Learning

### nside/Outside Circle

- Play popular Spanish music and set up equal numbers of chairs in two concentric circles, with the inside circle facing out and the outside circle facing in.
- Have the students sit. Stop the music when they are seated. Announce a question, which the students on the inside circle are to ask the students they are facing on the outside circle. Students on the outside circle answer, and then ask the student on the inside circle the same question.
- After both students have asked and answered the question, ask the students to stand, start the music, and have the students proceed around their circles until the music stops again.
- Repeat the exercise untill all students have asked and answered all of the questions.
- To ensure individual accountability, call on students randomly to answer questions.

*Suggestion, Exs. A, B, and F:* If you have students for whom their personal family tree will be a sensitive issue, tell them they can create an imaginary family tree (or use another family as a model, if they wish). Most families in the U.S. today are non-traditional, so be supportive of students in their expression of their individual lives. Let students know that the book portrays a number of families and affirm that families are unique and many possibilities exist.

**Ex. A:** pair work

*Suggestion, Ex. A:* Pair students who have not yet worked together on an interview-type of exercise.

**Ex. B:** groups of three

role play

*Suggestion, Ex. B:* You can circulate, playing the role of the **mesero/mesera.**

**Ex. C:** pair work

*Suggestions, Ex. C:* Students will need time to prepare this exercise. They might want to write out their dialogues and then practice reading them before presenting them to the class.

# Ya llegamos

## Actividades orales

*Learning Strategies:*

*Interviewing, listening for and providing relevant information*

**A. *Vamos a conocernos.*** **Scene 1:** Get to know another student better by exchanging personal information. Find out from your partner:

1. his or her name,
2. where he or she currently lives,
3. where he or she is from,
4. the size of his or her family,
5. his or her relationship to family members who live with the family.

Your partner will ask you for the same information about yourself and your family. You may want to bring family photographs to class for this activity.

**Scene 2:** Now continue to find out more things about your friend and his or her interests. Ask him or her to tell you:

1. three activities that he or she likes,
2. three activities that he or she does not like,
3. three of his or her possessions that are usually in his (her) room at home.

Your partner will ask you for the same information about yourself.

*Cooperative Learning*

*Learning Strategies:*

*Interviewing, listening for and providing relevant information*

*Critical Thinking Strategies:*

*Comparing and interacting*

**B. *Comemos en un café.*** You go to a café for lunch with a person whom you've just met. When you arrive, you see a friend of yours. Along with two other members of the class, play the roles of the students in this situation. During the conversation, make introductions, order lunch, and find out as much as possible about each other.

**C. *Un diálogo de contrarios*** **Scene 1:** Imagine that you and your partner have a relationship similar to that of the two people at the beginning of Chapter 5 (Review their differences on pages 103–104). The two of you are friends, despite great differences in your lives. Invent the details of your two imaginary lives, creating opposites or differences in such factors as:

1. where you are from,
2. where you live,
3. the size of your family,
4. the family members who live at your home,
5. your parents' occupations.

**Scene 2:** You and your partner are fascinated by the lack of similarity between you. So you continue to explore your differences in other factors such as:

1. what you have in your room at home,
2. what you carry to class,
3. how you get to school,
4. your interests in school subjects,
5. your interests in music,
6. your interests in sports.

Present the details of your greatly different lives to the class in the form of a dialog of opposites.

## Actividades escritas

D. ***Yo soy...*** Using the Spanish you've learned so far, write a short paragraph in which you give as much information as you can about yourself: your family, your interests, your activities, and the things you own.

E. ***Mis gustos*** You are filling out an application for a summer school in Spain. In order to match you with a compatible roommate, employees at the school want to know what your likes and dislikes are. Create a list with as much information as possible about what you like and don't like.

F. ***El árbol genealógico*** Construct your family tree as far back as your grandparents. Provide several bits of information for each living person: (1) where he or she lives, (2) what he or she does and has, and (3) what he or she likes and dislikes. If possible bring photos to class.

Me llamo Carmen Candelaria. Me gusta la música rock y los deportes. En mi cuarto tengo una raqueta de tenis, un póster de Gloria Estefán y muchos discos compactos.



**Exs. D, E, and F:**  writing

### Writing Activities

***Atajo, Writing Assistant Software*** 

*Functional vocabulary:* Describing objects; describing people; etc.

*Topic vocabulary:* Animals; automobile; family members; house; leisure; musical instruments; people; professions; sports; trades; etc.

*Grammar:* Adjectives: numbers; articles: definite; possession with **de; hay;** adjectives: possessive; verbs: **gustar**-type; verbs: present irregular; verbs: **tener** and **haber;** verb summary; verbs: present; adverbs: interrogative; pronouns: interrogative; verbs: **ser** and **estar;** etc.

*Support material, Unidad 2:* Lab Manual Ya llegamos listening activities, Laboratory Program, Tapescript, and Teacher's Edition of the Workbook/Lab Manual

## Presentation: Tipos de familias

You may want to ask some of the following questions to help guide students through the reading:

1. **¿Cuáles tipos de familias tienen dos padres?**
2. **¿Cuáles grupos no tienen dos padres?**
3. **¿Cuántos padres hay en una familia monoparental?**
4. **¿Qué tipo de famlia quisieras tener en veinte años?**

# La familia en nuestra sociedad

### AL EMPEZAR

Hay muchos tipos de familias diferentes. Algunas familias son grandes y algunas son pequeñas. Nuestra **sociedad** es interesante y diversa porque todos tenemos familias diferentes.

society

### ACTIVIDAD A

***¿Con quién vives?*** Go over the following list of people. Write down relatives you live with and how many of each you have in your family.

nephew

| | | |
|---|---|---|
| madre | tía | hermanastro |
| padre | primo | hijo |
| hermano | prima | hija |
| hermana | padrastro | **sobrino** |
| abuelo | madrastra | sobrina |
| abuela | hermanastra | otros: ____________ |
| tío | | Tengo _____ personas en mi familia. |

### TIPOS DE FAMILIAS

**La familia nuclear:** La familia nuclear es el tipo de familia más común del mundo. En esta familia, hay dos esposos que viven con sus hijos o **hijastros**. Otros **parientes** no viven con ellos.

**Las familia extendida:** Cuando otros parientes viven con dos esposos y sus hijos, es una familia extendida. En muchas familias extendidas, los abuelos, los primos o los tíos viven en la misma casa. Hay muchas familias extendidas en Latinoamérica.

**La familia monoparental:** En una familia monoparental, hay **sólo** una madre o un padre que vive con los hijos o hijastros. No hay dos padres. A veces la madre o el padre está divorciado y a veces la madre o el padre es **viudo**.

*hijastros* stepchildren / *parientes* relatives / *sólo* only / *viudo(a)* widower (widow)

## ACTIVIDAD B

Now complete the chart below using your knowledge from the reading to identify the kinds of families that the following people have.

| *persona* | *vive con* | *tipo de familia* |
|---|---|---|
| **Carmen** | su madre y padre, sus hermanos y hermanas | |
| **Luis** | sus abuelos, padres y hermanos | |
| **Elena** | su esposo y su hijo | |
| **Carlos** | su hijo | |
| **Mónica** | su hijo y sus dos hijas | |
| **Yo** | ¿? | ¿? |

El siguiente gráfico tiene información **sobre** el número de padres y madres en las familias de los Estados Unidos. about

## ACTIVIDAD C

Answer **verdad** or **falso** based on the information in the pie graph.

1. En esta gráfica, hay información sobre personas solteras.
2. La gráfica tiene información sobre las familias extendidas.
3. 12% de las personas viven con su madre, pero no con su padre.
4. 15% de las personas viven en familias monoparentales.
5. La sección azul *(blue)* representa las familias nucleares.

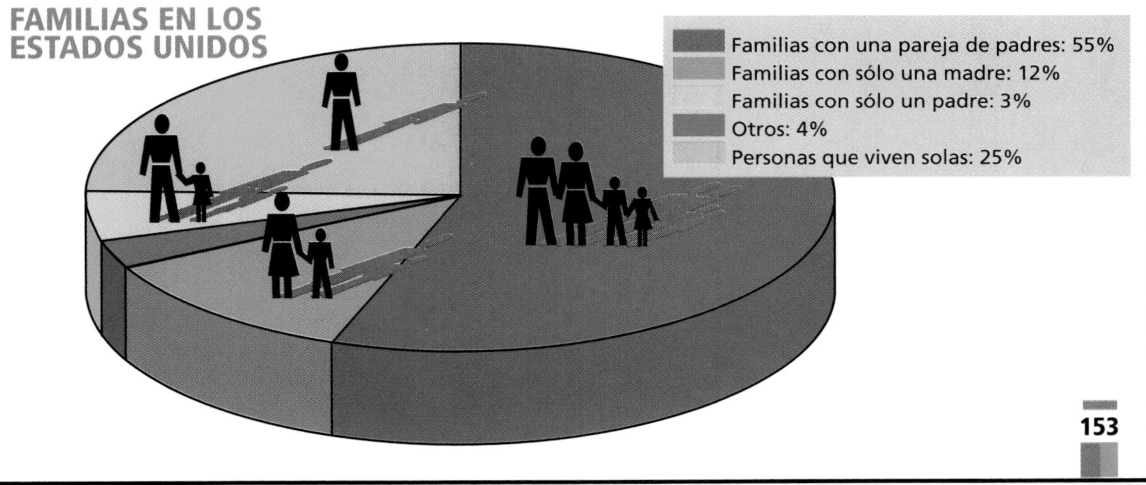




*Activity B:*

*Answers, Activity B:* Carmen—familia nuclear, Luis—familia extendida, Elena—familia nuclear, Carlos—familia monoparental, Mónica—familia monoparental

*Answers, Activity C:* 1. V 2. F 3. V 4. V 5. V

*Follow-up, Activity C:* You may want to put the following sentences on an overhead transparency or on the board and ask students to decide which kind of family each describes.

Mark **N** for **una familia nuclear, E** for **una familia extendida,** or **MP** for **una familia monoparental.**

_____ **El padre y la madre no viven en la misma casa.**
_____ **Los abuelos viven con los padres y sus hijos.**
_____ **Los padres están divorciados.**
_____ **Los esposos viven con todos sus hijos.**
_____ **Los hijos viven con su madre y su padrastro.**
_____ **Los tíos y tías viven con los padres y sus hijos.**
_____ **Los esposos viven con los padres de la esposa.**

## Cultural Context

Unit 3 features José Rivas, a young man from Spain. The basic theme of the unit is getting around towns and cities. Chapter 7 offers a generic introduction to a town or city. Chapter 8 focuses on how to give directions for getting around in a city. Chapter 9 discusses many of the celebrations in the Hispanic world.

## Cultural Observation

Ask students to study the photos on this page. Where do they think the picture was taken? Could a photo like this be taken in their town or city? What do they notice that looks particularly Hispanic? (This might be a good time to read and discuss **La ciudad típica** in the **Comentario cultural** on p. 158.)



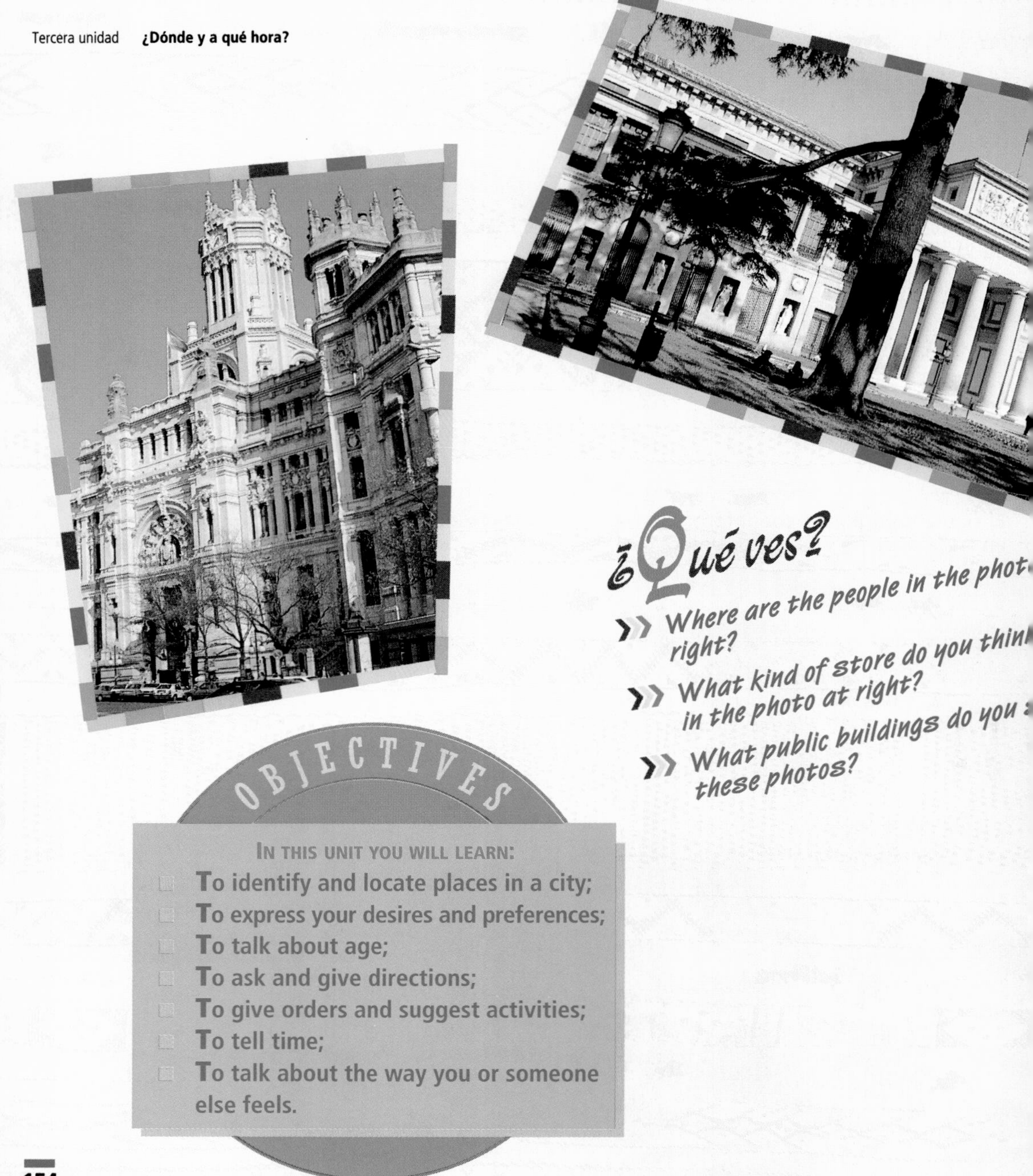

## ¿Qué ves?

- Where are the people in the phot[o]
right?
- What kind of store do you thin[k]
in the photo at right?
- What public buildings do you [s]
these photos?

## OBJECTIVES

IN THIS UNIT YOU WILL LEARN:

- To identify and locate places in a city;
- To express your desires and preferences;
- To talk about age;
- To ask and give directions;
- To give orders and suggest activities;
- To tell time;
- To talk about the way you or someone else feels.

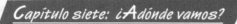

## Capítulo siete: ¿Adónde vamos?

**Primera etapa:** Los edificios públicos
**Segunda etapa:** ¿Quieres ir al cine?
**Tercera etapa:** Las tiendas

## Capítulo ocho: ¿Dónde está... ?

**Primera etapa:** ¿Está lejos de aquí?
**Segunda etapa:** ¿Cómo llego a... ?

## Capítulo nueve: ¡La fiesta del pueblo!

**Primera etapa:** ¿A qué hora son los bailes folklóricos?
**Segunda etapa:** ¿Cómo están Uds.?

# Unidad tres

*¿Dónde y a qué hora?:* Where and at what time?



## Planning Strategy

If you do not assign the Planning Strategy (Workbook, p. 81) for homework, or if students have difficulty coming up with English expressions, you might try asking several students to role play each of the situations in English: you can ask someone to find out from a stranger the location of the town library; you can have another student find out from a friend if there is a drugstore nearby; etc. After each response, point out the expressions used and then ask the class to suggest other possibilities.

## Cultural Observation

Have students study the photo of José Rivas on p. 156. Ask them to compare and contrast the way he dresses to the way people his age in the U.S. do.

# Chapter Objectives

**Functions:** Identifying places in a city; identifying public buildings
**Context:** City or town
**Accuracy:** Present tense of the verb **ir;** the prepositions **a** and **de** with the definite article **el;** the present tense of **querer** and **preferir;** numbers from 20 to 100; expressions with **tener**

### *Critical Thinking Strategies: Comparing and contrasting, hypothesizing*

Show students a map of a typical Hispanic city (you can refer them to p. 166 of the text or p. 94 of the Workbook). Ask them to compare the layout of the town or city where they live to that of the Hispanic town or city. What differences do they notice? How might they explain these differences?

CAPÍTULO 7

# ¿ADÓNDE VAMOS?

*¿Adónde va[mos?]* Where are [we] going?

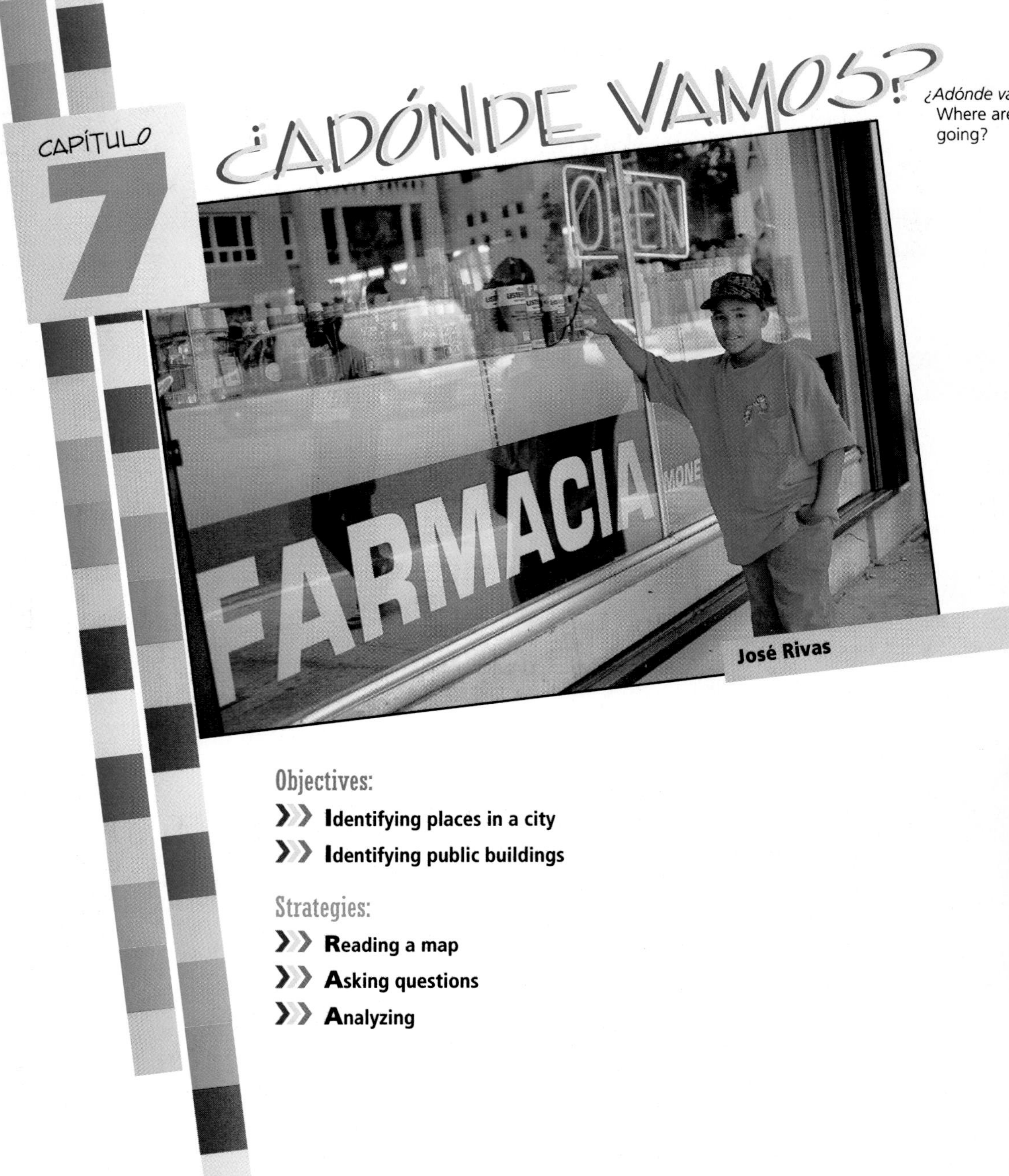


José Rivas

Objectives:

- **I**dentifying places in a city
- **I**dentifying public buildings

Strategies:

- **R**eading a map
- **A**sking questions
- **A**nalyzing

156

## Video/CD-ROM

**Chapter 7 Video Program**
**Chapter 7 CD-ROM Program**

**These can be used at the end of the chapter as expansion activities.**

# PRIMERA ETAPA

## Preparación

- What are some typical buildings that can be found in any city or town?
- What does the word **plaza** make you think of?
- Where are most of the public buildings located in your city or town?
- Which public buildings are within walking distance from where you live?

**Learning Strategy:**
*Previewing*

## Los edificios públicos

*Los edificios públicos:* Public buildings

### En nuestra ciudad hay:

| | | | |
|---|---|---|---|
| un aeropuerto | una catedral | una **biblioteca** | library |
| una estación de trenes | una **iglesia** | una **oficina de correos** | church / post office |
| una estación de autobuses | una universidad | una estación de policía | |
| una plaza | un **mercado** | un hospital | market |
| una **escuela secundaria** | un **colegio** | | secondary (high) school / school |

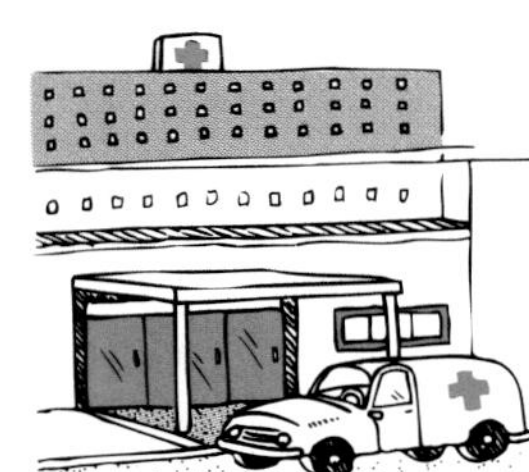

### Presentation: Los edificios públicos

With students' books closed, show the class the transparency. Introduce all the vocabulary, using the following pattern: **un hospital / ¿Qué es? / (Es un hospital.) / Sí, es un hospital.** Then continue by making mistakes and having students correct you: **Es una iglesia. (No, no es una iglesia, es un hospital.)** If the class performs well with the transparency, move directly to Ex. B.

If you do not wish to use a transparency, write the names of the places (grouped by category: transportation, schools, public buildings) on the board. Many of the words are recognizable as cognates. Have students ask you about the others: **¿Qué es una iglesia?,** etc.

*Support material,* ***Los edificios públicos:*** Transparency #33

### Etapa Support Materials

Workbook: **pp. 82–85**
Transparency: **#33**
Quiz: **Testing Program, p. 72**

Support material, **Los edificios públicos:**
**Transparency #33**

## Cultural Expansion

Most towns and cities in Spain date back to the Middle Ages, a period when the major concern in city planning was protection. Often the town grew around a **castillo** or a church, with the houses crowded together within defensive walls. (Try to bring in pictures of Ávila.) As a result, the streets were narrow and winding and did not follow any predetermined pattern. The basic street pattern of Spanish cities has changed very little since the fifteenth century. Most of the walls have come down and the towns have expanded, but you still find a plaza with its church in the center of the city or town.

*Support material, Ex. A:* Transparency #33

*Suggestion, Ex. A:* This exercise could be written or done orally in pairs.

*Answers, Ex. A:* 1. Es una estación de autobuses. 2. ...el centro 3. ...una estación de policía 4. ...un mercado 5. ...un aeropuerto 6. ...una estación de trenes 7. ...un hospital 8. ...una oficina de correos 9. ...una iglesia

*Learning Strategy:*

*Reading for cultural information*

## COMENTARIOS CULTURALES

### La ciudad típica

**Many cities in the Spanish-speaking world are built in the same pattern. There is usually a plaza in the middle of town with several important buildings facing into it: the cathedral or main church at one end; the main government building and a police station at the other; and shops, banks, hotels, and cafés on the two sides in between. Families as well as young people gather at the central plaza on weekends and summer evenings to take a walk, see their friends, and have a drink or a meal. Walking around a city and its plaza is considered one of life's pleasures by people in all sectors of Spanish-speaking societies. The streets are full of life, movement, and music.**

## ¡Aquí te toca a ti!

**A. *¿Qué es?*** Identify each building or place in the drawings that follow. Follow the model.

*Es una catedral.*

1.

2.

3.



## Exercise Progression

Exs. A, B, and C are all mechanical exercises designed to practice the new vocabulary. In addition, Ex. A practices **Es un/una**, Ex. B associates a definite article with the word, and Ex. C introduces the expression **Allí está.**

4.

5.

6.

7.

8.

9

**B. *¿Dónde está... ?*** (Where is . . . ?) You have just arrived in town and are looking at a map. Using the appropriate form of the definite article (**el, la**), ask where each building or place is located. Follow the model.

**Modelo:** oficina de correos
*¿Dónde está la oficina de correos?*

1. estación de trenes
2. aeropuerto
3. iglesia
4. estación de autobuses
5. universidad
6. plaza
7. escuela secundaria
8. biblioteca
9. catedral
10. oficina de correos
11. estación de policía
12. hospital
13. mercado
14. colegio

**C. *¡Allí está!*** (There it is!) Now that you are familiar with the map of the town, other newcomers ask you where certain buildings and places are. Using the expression **Allí está,** indicate the various locations on the map.

**Modelo:** la plaza
*—¿Dónde está la plaza?*
*—¿La plaza? Allí está.*

1. la catedral
2. la oficina de correos
3. la universidad
4. la biblioteca
5. la estación de trenes
6. la escuela secundaria
7. el aeropuerto
8. la estación de policía
9. la iglesia
10. el hospital
11. la estación de autobuses
12. el colegio



**Ex. B:** writing

***Answers, Ex. B:*** 1. ¿Dónde está la estación de trenes? 2. ...el aeropuerto? 3. ...la iglesia? 4. ...la estación de autobuses? 5. ...la universidad? 6. ...la plaza? 7. ...la escuela secundaria? 8. ...la biblioteca? 9. ...la catedral? 10. ...la oficina de correos? 11. ...la estación de policía? 12. ...el hospital? 13. ...el mercado? 14. ...el colegio?

**Ex. C:** pair work

***Suggestion, Ex. C:*** Have students work in pairs to create imaginary town maps in which they include buildings from Ex. C. Then have pairs exchange maps and do Ex. C. You could also draw a map on the board and have students role play this exercise in front of the class.

***Answers, Ex. C:*** All answers follow the model; students simply substitute the cues. All questions begin with **¿Dónde está... ?** The replies are a repetition of the words and articles given, with the addition of **Allí está.**

## Pronunciation

Additional activities appear in the Laboratory Tape Program.

**Support material, Pronunciación:**
Pronunciation Tape

## Presentation: The present tense of the verb ir

To present the verb **ir** inductively, you can combine the presentation of the verb with that of the adverbs frequently used with the idea of going (see the **Palabras útiles** on pp. 161–162). Write these new adverbs and the adverbs of frequency learned in Chapter 1 on the board (**nunca, rara vez, a veces / de vez en cuando, a menudo, todos los días / siempre**). Illustrate their meanings with verbs that students already know (**estudiar, cantar, hablar español,** etc.) Then choose a well-known city and start by telling about yourself. **Yo voy a Chicago rara vez, pero voy a Nueva York a menudo.** Then ask a student: **¿Tú vas a Chicago a menudo?** Summarize using third-person forms. **Él (Ella) nunca va a Chicago.** Continue until you have used all of the forms, stressing the conjugated forms of **ir** each time with voice inflection. (Make statements using the **nosotros** form, then ask **Uds.** questions, and summarize the answers in the third-person plural.) End the presentation by writing the forms of **ir** on the board.

Deductive method: Have students repeat the conjugation while you write the subject pronouns on the board: **yo / tú / él, ella, Ud. / nosotros(as) / vosotros(as) / ellos, ellas, Uds.** Repeat with the negative. Then add the verb forms to the pronouns on the board.

# Pronunciación: The consonant *g*

In Spanish, **g** is pronounced like the *g* in the English word *goal* when it is before the vowels **a, o,** and **u**, as in **gato, gota,** and **gusta** or before the consonants **l** and **r** as in **globo** or **grupo**. It also has this sound before **ue** and **ui** as in **guerra** and **guitarra**, in which cases the **u** is silent. The letter **g** is pronounced like this when it is the first letter of a word or follows the consonant **n**.

## Práctica

*D.* Listen and repeat as your teacher models the following words.

1. gato
2. grupo
3. gordo
4. ganas
5. gracias
6. globo
7. Gustavo
8. tengo
9. un gato
10. un globo

# ESTRUCTURA

### The present tense of the verb *ir*

¿Adónde **vamos?** — Where *are we going*?
Alicia **va** al centro. — Alicia *is going* downtown.
Ellos **no van** al colegio. — They *don't go* to school.

Vamos al mercado central.

The present-tense forms of the verb **ir** *(to go)* are:

| *ir* | | | |
|---|---|---|---|
| yo | **voy** | nosotros(as) | **vamos** |
| tú | **vas** | vosotros(as) | **vais** |
| él / ella / Ud. | **va** | ellos / ellas / Uds. | **van** |



## Exercise Progression

Ex. E is a contextualized practice with the verb **ir** and also includes new vocabulary from the chapter. Ex. F is a more mechanical exercise designed to practice the change from negative to positive.

## Aquí practicamos

*E.* Pick an activity from the first column, then choose the place associated with it from the second column. Form a sentence, following the model.

**Modelo:** Me gusta viajar. — el aeropuerto
*Me gusta viajar; por eso voy al aeropuerto.*

| | |
|---|---|
| 1. Tienes que ver al médico. | la biblioteca |
| 2. Necesitamos más libros. | el banco |
| 3. Quisieran comprar fruta. | el museo |
| 4. Me gusta caminar. | la oficina de correos |
| 5. Usted necesita dinero. | la estación de policía |
| 6. Ellos tienen que aprender. | el hospital |
| 7. Me gusta el arte moderno. | la iglesia |
| 8. Tengo que mandar una carta. | la escuela |
| 9. Quiero hablar con un policía. | el mercado |
| 10. Desean escuchar música religiosa. | el aeropuerto |
| | el parque |

*Critical Thinking Strategy:*
*Making associations*

*F.* ***En la estación de trenes*** You are at the railroad station with a group of friends who are all leaving to visit different Spanish cities. Each time you ask if someone is going to a certain city, you find out that you are wrong. Ask and answer questions following the model.

**Modelo:** Raquel / Salamanca / Cádiz
*—¿Va Raquel a Salamanca?*
*—No, Raquel no va a Salamanca. Ella va a Cádiz.*

1. Teresita / León / Burgos
2. Carlos / Valencia / Granada
3. Antonio / Málaga / Córdoba
4. Carmencita / Sevilla / Toledo
5. Miguel / Pamplona / Ávila
6. Mariquita / Barcelona / Valencia
7. Juan / Córdoba / Segovia

### *Expressions of frequency*

Here are some more phrases used in Spanish to say how often you do something.

**rara vez** rarely
**nunca** never
**a menudo** frequently, often
**de vez en cuando** from time to time



## Cultural Expansion

You might want to point out facts about a few of the cities mentioned in Ex. F and bring in pictures if you can. Suggestions: Pamplona (**Fiesta de San Fermín** [in July] and the running of the bulls, location of Hemingway's novel *The Sun Also Rises*); Granada (site of the Alhambra, a magnificent palace built by the Arabs); Valencia (Spain's third largest city, probably best known for the millions of orange trees that surround it); Barcelona (Spain's second largest city and site of the 1992 Summer Olympics, probably best known for **las Ramblas, el Museo de Picasso,** and the buildings by the architect Antonio Gaudí).

### Presentation: Expressions of frequency

If you have not introduced these adverbs along with **ir,** put on the board a continuum running from **nunca** to **siempre** (see the notes for p. 160). Use expressions such as **ir a la biblioteca, ir al centro,** etc. to practice the adverbs and expressions. Note: The use of **nunca** after the verb will be presented later. For now, students should use it only before the verb.

**Ex. E:**  pair work  writing

***Suggestion, Ex. E:*** Since it may not be immediately apparent to students, point out that the subject for the second verb (**ir**) may be logically deduced from that of the first verb.

**Ex. F:** pair work

***Answers, Ex. F:*** All answers follow the model. Students simply substitute the name of the person and places in each of their questions and answers. 1. **¿Va Teresita a León? No, Teresita no va a León. Ella va a Burgos.,** etc.

**Ex. G:**  groups of four or more

**Ex. H:**  groups of four or more

 writing

## Cooperative Learning

### Exs. G and H: Three-step Interview

- Combine Exs. G and H in one three-step interview. Divide the class into teams of four to conduct **una encuesta.**
- Each question in Exs. G and H will be answered by a different student, who will then ask each of his/her team members the same question. For example, the first student might say, **Voy a menudo a la iglesia. Tomás, ¿vas tú a la iglesia a menudo?**
- Each team should designate a "recorder" to keep track of everyone's answers.
- Tell the recorder to summarize the responses for his or her teammates for **Los resultados.** Each team member must agree on the results.
- Call on one member of each team (not the recorder) to report the team's results to the class in complete sentences.

*Support material, Aquí escuchamos:*
Teacher Tape/CD #1 Track #31 and Tapescript

**Nunca** usually precedes the verb. The other adverbs may be placed at the beginning or end of a sentence.

| | |
|---|---|
| **Nunca** vamos a la estación de policía. | We *never* go to the police station. |
| **Rara vez** voy al hospital. | I *rarely* go to the hospital. |
| Andrés va a la biblioteca **a menudo**. | Andrés goes to the library *often*. |

**G. *Una encuesta*** (A survey) Ask three other students the questions below and note their answers. They do not need to answer with complete sentences. (Remember the other expressions of frequency you have already learned: **siempre, todos los días, a veces**.) Follow the model.

Modelo:
¿Vas al aeropuerto a menudo?
—*¿Vas al aeropuerto a menudo?*
—*Muy rara vez.* o:
—*Sí, a menudo.* o:
—*No, nunca.*

1. ¿Vas a la iglesia a menudo?
2. ¿Vas a la catedral a menudo?
3. ¿Vas a la plaza a menudo?
4. ¿Vas al mercado a menudo?
5. ¿Vas a la biblioteca a menudo?
6. ¿Vas al hospital a menudo?

*Learning Strategy:*
*Reporting*

**H. *Los resultados*** (The results) Now report your findings from Activity G to other members of your class. This time use complete sentences.

Modelo:
*Josh nunca va a la biblioteca. Linda va a la biblioteca de vez en cuando y Denise va a menudo.*

## Aquí escuchamos:
### "El autobús"

**Listen to the information about the route the city bus takes on a typical day.**

*Learning Strategy:*
*Previewing*

### Antes de escuchar

**Review the names of the public buildings in a typical city or town to prepare you for what you are going to hear about where the bus stops.**

## Después de escuchar

Listen to the announcement again. This time make a list of the stops the bus makes (in the order in which they are given) as it goes around the city.

**Learning Strategies:**

*Listing, listening for details*

# ¡Adelante!

EJERCICIO ORAL

*I.* ***En la calle*** (In the street) You run into a classmate in the street. (1) Greet each other. (2) Then ask where your classmate is going, (3) what he or she is going to do there, and (4) whether he or she goes there often.

**Student 1:** *¡Hola! ¿Qué tal?*
**Student 2:** *Muy bien, ¿y tú?*
**Student 1:** *Bien, gracias. ¿Adónde vas?*
**Student 2:** *Voy a la biblioteca.*
**Student 1:** *¿Qué vas a hacer?*
**Student 2:** *Voy a estudiar.*
**Student 1:** *¿Vas a menudo a la biblioteca?*
**Student 2:** *Sí, todos los días.* o: *No, voy de vez en cuando.*

EJERCICIO ESCRITO

*J.* ***¿Cuándo?*** Write a list of sentences using each of the following expressions **(rara vez, nunca, siempre, a menudo, de vez en cuando, todos los días, a veces)** to indicate the frequency with which you go to certain public buildings in your town or city.

**Learning Strategy:**

*Listing*



*More-prepared students, Ex. I:* For more-prepared students, have them interview as many other classmates as possible with as many different destinations and expressions of frequency as possible. In order to enhance the interview, perhaps another question could be added to the end, **¿Por qué?** For example, **Voy a la biblioteca a menudo porque me gusta leer.** Remind students that they may then be called upon to perform a dialogue in front of the class.

**Ex. J:** writing

*Less-prepared students, Ex. J.* Have less-prepared students work together in pairs and write a joint list on the board.

*More-prepared students, Ex. J:* For more-prepared students, have them expand their writing by contrasting their information with that collected from other students in Ex. G. For example: **Yo nunca voy al hospital, pero Jenny va a menudo al hospital (porque ella trabaja allí).**

*Suggestions, Ex. J:* After students have chosen a destination, they circulate in class, competing to see who can meet the most friends. Or you can have them work in pairs. Give them a few minutes to work out the exercise and then ask your Spanish-speaking students or other volunteers to present a dialogue to the class.

*nswers, Después de escuchar:* aeropuerto, iversidad, centro, catedral, la oficina de correos, la escuela cundaria, hospital, mercado, estación de autobuses

**Ex. I:** 

*Less-prepared students, Ex. I:* For less-prepared students, make a list on the board of possible greetings, another of expressions of frequency, and another of different destinations so that there is extra reinforcement of these items as students improvise their dialogues and then perform them for the class or for their group.

## Presentation: ¿Quieres ir al cine?

Describe the town where your school is located. Begin by using words from the previous **etapa: En esta ciudad, hay un colegio, pero no hay una universidad... .** Move from the public buildings to the entertainment topic by using cognates: **En esta ciudad hay lugares interesantes y divertidos. ¿Te gusta bailar? ¿Vas a las discotecas? ¿Te gusta ver películas en el cine? Hay... cines en nuestra ciudad,** etc. Have students repeat the new vocabulary items after each sentence or two. Work in non-cognate expressions, mentioning also what the town does not have. After introducing the vocabulary, play the Teacher Tape to present the dialogue. Or, you may want to read it to the students, having them listen carefully, trying to understand as much as possible.

### *Support material, ¿Quieres ir al cine?:*

Teacher Tape/CD #1 Track #32 (headphones icon), transparency #34



# SEGUNDA ETAPA

**Learning Strategies:**

*Listing, brainstorming, organizing ideas, previewing*

**Critical Thinking Strategies:**

*Classifying, evaluating*

### Preparación

» **What other public buildings or public places can you think of that are meant for leisure-time activities, recreation, or entertainment?**

» **What is your favorite place for recreation in your city or town?**

» **What do you wish your town had for recreation that it currently does not have?**

## ¿Quieres ir al cine?

*¿Quieres ir al cine?:* Do you want to go to the movies?

Una conversación telefónica

—¡Hola! ¿Celia?

—Sí. ¿Quién habla?

—Habla Isabel.

—Hola, Isabel. ¿Qué tal?

—Muy bien. Delia y yo vamos al cine esta tarde. **¿Quieres venir** con nosotras? *(Do you want to come)*

—Mm..., **lo siento,** pero no es posible porque voy al **museo** con Marcos, y esta noche vamos a la discoteca. *(I'm sorry / museum)*

—Bueno, **en otra oportunidad.** *(some other time)*

—Gracias, Isabel. Hasta luego.

—De nada. Adiós.

### *Otros lugares en la ciudad:*

*lugares:* places

| | | |
|---|---|---|
| un teatro | un parque | un **estadio** |
| una **piscina** | un club | un café |

stadium / swimming pool

164

## Etapa Support Materials

Workbook: **pp. 86–90**

Transparencies: **#34, #35, #36**

Teacher Tape (headphones icon)

Quiz: **Testing Program, p. 74**

Support material, ¿Quieres ir al cine?:

**Teacher Tape** (headphones icon)**, transparency #34**

## COMENTARIOS CULTURALES

### El teléfono

There are different ways of answering the phone in Spanish, depending on the country. **Bueno** is used in Mexico, **hola** is used in several South American countries, and **diga** or **dígame** is used in Spain.

**Learning Strategy:**

*Reading for cultural information*

## ¡Aquí te toca a ti!

***A. ¿Qué lugares son?*** Identify each building or place below.

1.

2.

3.

4.

5.

6.

***B. ¿Hay un(a)... en el barrio** (neighborhood)?* Ask a passerby if the places on page 166 are in the area. The passerby will answer affirmatively and indicate the street where each can be found. Act this out in pairs.

**Learning Strategy:**

*Asking for information*

**Modelo:** restaurante / en la Calle *(street)* San Martín
—*Perdón, señor (señorita). ¿Hay un restaurante en el barrio?*
—*Sí, hay un restaurante en la Calle San Martín.*



### Exercise Progression

Exs. A and B are mechanical exercises designed to focus on the new vocabulary. In addition, Ex. B introduces a conversational strategy (asking for information) and prepares students for using the expressions **en la calle** and **en la avenida.** Ex. C is a meaningful exercise that reinforces the structure **hay un/una** and **no hay un/una.**

### Vocabulary Expansion

Other variations for answering the phone: **¡Aló! ¿Sí?**

**Ex. A:** writing

***Support material, Ex. A:*** Transparency #35.

***Suggestion, Ex. A:*** Use the transparency and ask simple questions using cognates. For example: **¿Dónde practicamos la natación? ¿Dónde podemos mirar obras de Shakespeare o de Tennessee Williams?,** etc.

***Answers, Ex. A:*** 1. Es un estadio. 2. ...un teatro 3. ...un parque 4. ...una piscina 5. ...un cine 6. ...un museo

**Ex. B:** 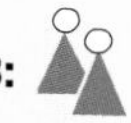 pair work

 role play

***Answers, Ex. B:*** Following the model, students substitute the cues given and add the articles to these words: 1. un parque 2. una discoteca 3. un teatro 4. un museo 5. un cine 6. una piscina 7. una oficina de correos

**Ex. C:** pair work

*Support material, Ex. C:* Transparency #36

*Less-prepared students, Ex. C:* After less-prepared students have made their lists, have them relate the information orally to each other as a double check. Write a model on the board for them to follow: **En Nerja hay un/una ____________ pero no hay un/una____________.**

*More-prepared students, Ex. C:* Have more-prepared students explain in Spanish why their additional buildings are most needed and why others aren't (the teacher may need to supply additional vocabulary). Suggest that they try to also use expressions of frecuency in their work. For example, **Nerja necesita un hospital porque a menudo hay accidentes. Nerja no necesita una librería porque las personas van a la biblioteca frecuentemente.**

## Cultural Expansion

Nerja is a beach town on the Costa del Sol, 45 km east of Málaga. It is visited by many tourists in the summer months and boasts the **Balcón de Europa,** a palm-fringed promenade built on the top of a cliff that juts out onto the Mediterranean Sea.

**Cooperative Learning**

**Learning Strategies:**

*Reading a map, listing, negotiating*

**Critical Thinking Strategy:**

*Analyzing*

1. parque / en la Calle Libertad
2. discoteca / en la Calle Tucumán
3. teatro / en la Avenida 9 de Julio
4. museo / en la Calle Cervantes
5. cine / en la Avenida Lavalle
6. piscina / en la Calle Bolívar
7. oficina de correos/ en la Calle Independencia

**C. *¿Qué hay en Nerja?*** Below are examples of public buildings that are found in many cities and towns. Using the map of Nerja, indicate what there is and what there is not in this small beach town. Create a list for each group. Then you and your partner decide on the three additional public buildings that you think the town most needs to add.

**Modelo:** *En Nerja hay un hotel, pero no hay un aeropuerto.*

estación de trenes | museo | parque | restaurante | hospital | oficina de correos | cine | estadio

café | biblioteca | iglesia | plaza | hotel | discoteca | aeropuerto

## Pronunciación: The consonant g (continued)

When the letter **g** (in the same combinations you studied in the previous **etapa**) follows a vowel or any consonant except **n**, it is pronounced like the *g* in the English word *sugar* when it is said very quickly.

### Práctica

*D.* Listen and repeat as your teacher models the following words.

1. lago
2. amigo
3. llego
4. nos gusta
5. conmigo
6. Ortega
7. regular
8. lugar
9. hasta luego
10. jugar

## Repaso

*E.* ***¿Adónde van?*** Félix and his family are visiting Córdoba, Spain, for the day. Because they all want to go to different places, they decide to split up. Using the drawings, give Félix's explanation of where each person is headed. Follow the model.

mi tío
*Mi tío va a la catedral.*

1. mis padres

2. mi prima y yo

3. mi tía



*Support material, Pronunciación:* Pronunciation Tape

### Cultural Expansion

Point out that Córdoba's history is marked by two different Golden Ages: the Romans made it the largest city on the Iberian peninsula; then, in the Middle Ages, it became one of the cultural centers of Europe under Muslim rule, well-known for its science and art. After the Reconquest, it was the custom for the Catholic Spaniards to destroy mosques and build churches on the ruins. Fortunately, in Córdoba they spared one of the world's largest and most beautiful mosques, begun in the year 785. However, they built a cathedral inside it (the Mezquita-Catedral).

**Ex. E:** writing

*Answers, Ex. E:* 1. Mis padres van al parque. 2. Mi prima y yo vamos a la estación de trenes. 3. Mi tío va a la oficina de correos.

### Pronunciation

Additional activities appear in the Laboratory Tape Program.

*Reteaching:* Very quickly, before doing the **Repaso** Ex. E, review family vocabulary orally. You may ask, **¿Cómo se dice** *brother* (etc.) **en español?** Or vary this question with, **¿Qué significa (quiere decir) primo** (etc.)? Have students give one-word answers as a group.

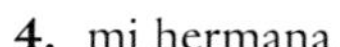

**4.** mi hermana

**5.** mi hermano

**6.** mis primas

## Nota gramatical

### *The preposition a and the definite article el*

Nosotros vamos **al** museo. — We go *to the* museum.
Mi familia va **a la** piscina. — My family goes *to the* swimming pool.

When the preposition **a** *(to)* is followed by the article **el,** they contract to form one word, **al.**

**a + el = al**

**F. *¿Adónde quisiera ir... ?*** You are talking to a friend about where your other friends want to go this weekend. Ask about each of the following people and your friend will answer using the places suggested. Follow the model.

**Modelo:** Miguel / el club
—*¿Adónde quisiera ir Miguel?*
—*Miguel quisiera ir al club.*

1. Elsa / la piscina
2. Isabel / el parque
3. Roberto / la discoteca
4. Mónica / el cine
5. Manuel / el museo
6. Pilar / el teatro
7. Luis / el estadio
8. Lidia / el café



### Presentation: The preposition a and the definite article el

Use the transparency of public buildings and amusement sights. Ask students **¿Adónde van?,** pointing to one of the buildings or sights. Begin with **a la** and then proceed to **al.** If you prefer not to use the transparency, you can present this structure by putting drawings on the board or writing names of places, grouping them by gender. (Feminine: **biblioteca, estación, catedral, piscina, discoteca, escuela,** etc.; masculine: **cine, estadio, teatro, museo,** etc.) Ask students, **¿Adónde van Uds.?,** and have them respond, **Nosotros vamos...** using places from each list. Then have students pick out three places to go. Ask: **¿Adónde vas tú? Yo voy a la escuela, luego voy a la biblioteca y al cine.** Encourage students to substitute other places they actually go, using vocabulary they know.

**Ex. F:** pair work

*Reteaching:* Before doing Ex. F, review the idea of conjugated verb + infinitive, using **quisiera** as your example on the board. As alternatives to **quisiera,** you may wish to also include verbs such as **desear, necesitar,** and **acabar de** in this exercise after listing them on the board. This also will serve as an introduction to the verbs **querer** and **preferir,** presented on p. 169.

*Answers, Ex. E, cont.:*
4. Mi hermana va a la iglesia.
5. Mi hermano va al centro.
6. Mis primas van a la piscina.

*Answers, Ex. F:* 1. ¿Adónde quisiera ir Elsa? Elsa quisiera ir a la piscina. 2. ...Isabel? ...al parque. 3. ...Roberto? ...a la discoteca. 4. ...Mónica? ...al cine. 5. ...Manuel? ...al museo. 6. ...Pilar? ...al teatro. 7. ...Luis? ...al estadio. 8. ...Lidia? ...al café.

# TERCERA ETAPA

## Preparación

- What is the difference between a department store and a mall?
- How would you describe a specialty shop?
- Make a list of five different kinds of specialty shops that you can think of.
- On your list, mark the shops where you like to go. Be prepared to discuss why you prefer them to a department store or a large discount center.

*Learning Strategies:*

*Listing, brainstorming, previewing*

*Critical Thinking Strategies:*

*Analyzing differences, evaluating*

## Las tiendas

*Las tiendas:* Stores

*En nuestra ciudad hay:*

una **librería**
una **farmacia**
un mercado
un banco
un hotel
una **florería**
una **carnicería**
una **panadería**

bookstore / butcher's
drugstore / bakery
flower shop



## Presentation: Las tiendas

The suggestions in the previous two **etapas** can be used for presenting this vocabulary. You might also try to find one or two large photos of Spanish street scenes that illustrate the shops introduced here.

## Vocabulary Expansion

**Salchichonería** (similar to a deli; they sell sausages, cold meats, and cheeses of all kinds); **pastelería, zapatería**

## Cultural Expansion

Point out that the bread sold in the **panadería** is usually baked fresh at least twice daily. It is crusty on the outside and soft on the inside and is usually sold in several sizes. Fancy pastries are sold at **pastelerías.**

## Etapa Support Materials

Workbook: pp. 91–96
Critical Thinking Master: p. 10
Transparency: #37
Listening Activity masters: p. 43
Tapescript: p. 65
Quiz: Testing Program, p. 77
Chapter Test: Testing Program, p. 79

**Ex. A:** writing

***Support material, Ex. A:***
Transparency #37

***Suggestion, Ex. A:***
You may want to use the suggestions given for Ex. A on p. 165.

***Answers, Ex. A:*** 1. Es un mercado. 2. una florería 3. un banco 4. una librería 5. una panadería 6. una carnicería



**Learning Strategy:**

*Reading for cultural information*

## COMENTARIOS CULTURALES

### Las tiendas

In many parts of the Spanish-speaking world, the small store is more common than the large supermarket. Each one of these stores sells only one type of article or food. The name of the shop is taken from the products sold; for example, **pan** *(bread)* is sold at the **panadería; flores** *(flowers)* are sold at the **florería.**

## ¡Aquí te toca a ti!

**A. *¿Qué es?*** Identify each building or place below.

1.

2.

3.

4.

5.

6.



## Exercise Progression

Ex. A is a mechanical exercise designed for practicing the vocabulary. Exs. B and C, in addition to working with the vocabulary, review information-getting strategies.

**B. Cerca de aquí** (Near here) You ask a passerby whether certain stores and places are nearby. The passerby will answer affirmatively and indicate the street where each can be found. Follow the model.

**Modelo:** banco / en la Calle Alcalá
*—Perdón, señorita (señor). ¿Hay un banco cerca de aquí?*
*—Sí, hay un banco en la Calle Alcalá.*

1. farmacia / en la Avenida Libertad
2. hotel / en la Calle Perú
3. librería / en la Calle Mayor
4. banco / en la Calle San Marco
5. panadería / en la Avenida Independencia
6. florería / en la Avenida Colón

**C. ¿Adónde vamos primero** (first)**?** Whenever you run errands with your friend, you like to know where you are headed first. However, each time you suggest a place, your friend has another idea. Follow the model.

banco / librería
*—¿Adónde vamos primero? ¿Al banco?*
*—No, primero vamos a la librería. Luego* (Then) *vamos al banco.*

1. carnicería / mercado
2. librería / florería
3. museo / banco
4. farmacia / panadería
5. hotel / oficina de correos
6. biblioteca / colegio

## Pronunciación: The sound of Spanish jota

The Spanish **jota** is similar to the sound of the *h* in the English word *hot.* This sound is spelled with **g** when it is followed by the vowels **e** or **i.** The consonant **j (jota)** is always pronounced in this way.

## Práctica

**D.** Listen and repeat as your teacher models the following words.

1. Juan
2. trabajo
3. julio
4. jueves
5. jugar
6. tarjeta
7. geografía
8. biología
9. general
10. Jorge



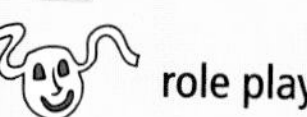

**Ex. B:** pair work

role play

*Answers, Ex. B:* Following the model, students substitute the cues provided and add definite articles to these words: 1. ...una farmacia 2. ...un hotel 3. ...una librería 4. ...un banco 5. ...una panadería 6. ...una florería

**Ex. C:** pair work

*Suggestion, Ex. C:* Write the model sentences on the board, then have students close their books. Prepare ahead small pieces of paper or cards with photocopied icons of the different places, hand one out to each student, then, using the icons, do a chain **pregúntele** exercise with the whole class.

*Answers, Ex. C:* Following the model, students supply the preposition **a** with the correct definite article along with the other cues provided. 1. ...a la carnicería / ...al mercado 2. ...a la librería / ...a la florería 3. ...al museo / ...al banco 4. ...a la farmacia / ...a la panadería 5. ...al hotel / ...a la oficina de correos 6. ...a la biblioteca / ...al colegio

### Pronunciation

Additional activities appear in the Laboratory Tape Program.

*Support material, Pronunciación:* Pronunciation Tape

Ex. E:  writing

*Less-prepared students, Ex. E:* For less-prepared students, split the task into two parts. First let them do the five items with **trabajar,** then go back and work with **ir.**

*More-prepared students, Ex. E:* For more-prepared students, after they finish the five items, have them give information about the parents of real-life friends and classmates (teacher may need to supply additional vocabulary).

*Answers, Ex. E:* Following the model, students supply the preposition with the correct definite article. 1. ...en la estación de trenes / ...al cine 2. ...en la universidad / ...al parque 3. ...en la oficina de correos / ...al museo 4. ...en el restaurante / ...al mercado 5. ...en la biblioteca / ...a la librería

## Presentation: The numbers from 20 to 100

Start out by having students count from 1 to 20. Continue by saying slowly, **veintiuno, veintidós, veintitrés,** and then point to a student to continue, **veinticuatro,** and then another and so on up to 29. Then say slowly **treinta, treinta y uno, treinta y dos, treinta y tres,** and point to a student to continue. Proceed in this manner up to 100. Then count to 100 by fives and then by tens, having the class repeat. Have volunteers count to 100 by fives and then by tens. Then write **veintiún, veintiuna** and **treinta y un, treinta y una** on the board. Explain how they are used before masculine and feminine nouns. Mention that the other numbers are invariable and do not agree with nouns. You may also want to point out the accents written on the last stressed vowel in the numbers **veintidós, veintitrés,** and **veintiséis.**





# Repaso

*E.* ***Los padres de tus amigos*** Your parents are curious about your friends. Tell them where your friends' parents work and where they often go when they're not working. Follow the model.

*Modelo:* el padre de Cristina (hospital / biblioteca)
*El padre de Cristina trabaja en el hospital. Va a la biblioteca a menudo.*

1. el padre de Roberto (estación de trenes / cine)
2. la madre de Isabel (universidad / parque)
3. el padre de Vicente (oficina de correos / museo)
4. la madre de Marilú (restaurante / mercado)
5. el padre de Josefina (biblioteca / librería)

# Estructura

## *The numbers from 20 to 100*

| | | | | | | | |
|---|---|---|---|---|---|---|---|
| 20 | veinte | 25 | veinticinco | 30 | treinta | 60 | sesenta |
| 21 | veintiuno | 26 | veintiséis | 31 | treinta y uno | 70 | setenta |
| 22 | veintidós | 27 | veintisiete | 32 | treinta y dos | 80 | ochenta |
| 23 | veintitrés | 28 | veintiocho | 40 | cuarenta | 90 | noventa |
| 24 | veinticuatro | 29 | veintinueve | 50 | cincuenta | 100 | cien |

The numbers 21–29 may be written as one word or three words. For example, 23 can be written as **veintitrés** or **veinte y tres.**

# Aquí practicamos

*F.*
1. Cuenta *(Count)* de 0 a 30, de 30 a 0.
2. Cuenta de 20 a 100 de cinco en cinco.
3. Cuenta los números pares *(even)* de 0 a 100.
4. Cuenta los números impares *(odd)* de 1 a 99.
5. Cuenta de diez en diez de 0 a 100.

*G.* ***¿Cuántos... hay en la ciudad?*** While working for the tourist bureau during the summer, you have to research the number of hotels,



## Exercise Progression

Ex. F is designed to give students varied practice in saying the numbers. Ex. G offers more practice and at the same time reviews the use of **cuántos/cuántas.** Ex. H provides more practice with the new numbers in a functional exercise.

cinemas, etc., that the city has. Interview the city's leading statistician in order to collect this information. Work in pairs. Remember to use **¿Cuántos?** or **¿Cuántas?** according to the noun that follows. Follow the model.

hoteles / 15
—*¿Cuántos hoteles hay?*
—*Hay quince hoteles.*

piscinas / 17
—*¿Cuántas piscinas hay?*
—*Hay diecisiete piscinas.*

1. librerías / 11
2. panaderías / 18
3. clubes / 13
4. mercados / 26
5. farmacias / 16
6. carnicerías / 27
7. teatros / 14
8. cines / 12
9. florerías / 20
10. cafés / 22

**H. ¡Diga!** You want to make several telephone calls from a small town where you need to talk to the operator to connect you. Tell him or her the number that you want. Follow the model.

30–89–70
*Treinta, ochenta y nueve, setenta, por favor.*

1. 25–59–78
2. 54–67–83
3. 22–51–60
4. 82–67–91
5. 43–56–90
6. 37–40–87
7. 95–46–70
8. 97–55–30

## Palabras útiles

### Expressions with *tener*

To ask someone's age in Spanish, use **tener.**

| | |
|---|---|
| **—¿Cuántos años tienes?** | *How old are you?* |
| **—Tengo catorce años.** | *I am fourteen years old.* |
| **—¿Cuántos años tiene** tu hermana? | *How old is* your sister? |
| **—Tiene cuatro.** | *She's four.* |

**¿Qué crees?**

**You are traveling in Uruguay and the schedule says that your bus leaves at 22:00 hrs. When will it go?**

**a) It's a misprint; you don't know when the bus leaves.**
**b) at 2 o'clock**
**c) at 10:00 p.m.**

**respuesta**

**Ex. H:** pair work

*Answers, Ex. H:* 1. Veinticinco, cincuenta y nueve, setenta y ocho, por favor. 2. Cincuenta y cuatro, sesenta y siete, ochenta y tres... 3. Veintidós, cincuenta y uno, sesenta... 4. Ochenta y dos, sesenta y siete, noventa y uno... 5. Cuarenta y tres, cincuenta y seis, noventa... 6. Treinta y siete, cuarenta, ochenta y siete... 7. Noventa y cinco, cuarenta y seis, setenta... 8. Noventa y siete, cincuenta y cinco, treinta...

*Follow-up, Ex. H:* Have students practice their own phone numbers by asking several of their classmates, **¿Cuál es tu número de teléfono?** For seven-digit numbers, have them say a single number first and then the rest of the numbers in pairs. For example: 7-61-09-38 (**siete, sesenta y uno, cero nueve, treinta y ocho**). As students say their phone numbers out loud, have other students write the numbers on the board as the whole class listens as double check. You may also wish to have an/other student/s write out several of the phone numbers in words.

### Presentation: Expressions with tener

Bring in some photos of people of various ages (including children and elderly people) and indicate their age by saying, **Este niño tiene ocho años.** etc. Then ask some students how old they are. To vary this, you can guess (sometimes incorrectly on purpose) different students' ages and have them correct you.

**Ex. G:** pair work role play

*Answers, Ex. G:* 1. ¿Cuántas librerías hay? / Hay once librerías. 2. ...panaderías... / ...dieciocho panaderías. 3. ¿Cuántos clubes hay? / ...trece clubes. 4. ...mercados... / ...veintiséis mercados. 5. ¿Cuántas farmacias hay? / ...dieciséis farmacias. 6. ...carnicerías... / ...veintisiete carnicerías. 7. ¿Cuántos teatros hay? / ...catorce teatros. 8. ...cines... / ...doce cines. 9. ¿Cuántas florerías hay? / ...veinte florerías. 10. ¿Cuántos cafés hay? / ...veintidós cafés.

## Presentation: Expressions with tener, cont.

To introduce the expressions **tener hambre** and **tener sed,** use gestures to indicate hunger and thirst while making statements. Then ask students follow-up questions. For example: **Quiero comer ahora porque tengo hambre. ¿Tienes hambre tú? También quiero tomar un refresco porque tengo sed. ¿Quieres tomar algo? ¿Tienes sed?,** etc. Then ask more questions, such as, **¿Qué tomas cuando tienes mucha sed? ¿Qué te gusta comer cuando tienes mucha hambre?**

### Exercise Progression

Ex. I is a mechanical drill in which students practice the expression **tener... años** in the **él/ella** form. Ex. J is a personalized and open-ended exercise in which students use the **yo** and **tú** forms of the verb **tener** in expressions of hunger and thirst. In the **Adelante** section, Ex. K allows students to combine the material they have learned in the **etapa** in an improvisational activity.

**Ex. I:** writing

*Answers, Ex. I:* 1. Carmelita tiene diecisiete años. 2. sesenta y cuatro 3. veinte 4. doce 5. ochenta y dos 6. cincuenta y cinco



Other expressions that also use **tener** are **tener hambre** *(to be hungry)* and **tener sed** *(to be thirsty).*

| | |
|---|---|
| **—Tengo hambre.** ¿Y tú? | *I'm hungry.* And you? |
| —No, **yo no tengo hambre,** pero **sí, tengo mucha sed.** | *No, I'm not hungry,* but *I am very thirsty.* |

**I. *¿Cuántos años tienes?*** In the process of getting to know your friends, you find out how old they are. Remember to use the verb **tener** and the word **años.** Follow the model.

—¿Cuántos años tiene Felipe? (13)
—*Felipe tiene trece años.*

1. ¿Cuántos años tiene Carmelita? (17)
2. Y el señor Ramos, ¿cuántos años tiene? (64)
3. ¿Cuántos años tiene Ana María? (20)
4. ¿Cuántos años tiene Roberto? (12)
5. ¿Cuántos años tiene don Alberto? (82)
6. Y doña Éster, ¿cuántos años tiene ella? (55)

**J. *¿Tienen hambre?*** You are hosting a picnic and you want to know if your guests are hungry or thirsty and what they would like to have. Walk around the class asking five people what they want. Follow the model.

—*¿Tienes hambre? ¿Tienes sed?*
—*Sí, tengo mucha hambre. No tengo sed.*
—*¿Qué quieres comer?*
—*Un taco, por favor.*

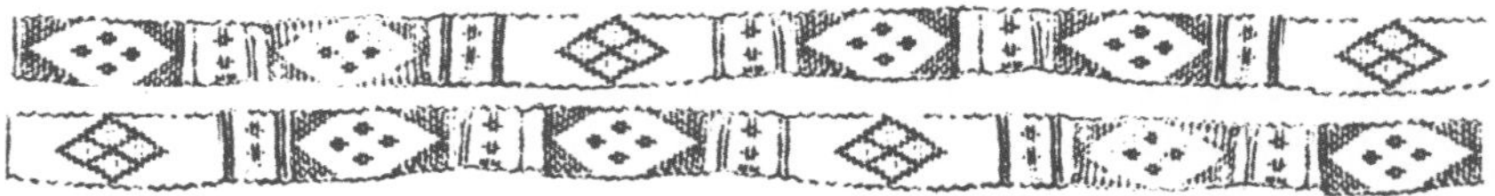

c



*Less-prepared students, Ex. I:* Very quickly, review family vocabulary. Have less-prepared students write-out a list of questions such as: **¿Cuántos años tienes tú? ¿Cuántos años tiene tu mamá/papá/hermano/hermana/primo,** etc.? Remind students to chart or take notes of other students' answers so that they can report back to the class.

*More-prepared students, Ex. I:* Have more-prepared students ask three other students about as many family members as they can. Then, either orally or in writing, have them report back on the family of one of the students they interviewed.

**Ex. J:** groups of four or more  role play

*More-prepared students, Ex. J:* Call on more-prepared students to report back in a chain all of the informatic they found out. For example, **Joe quiere comer un taco, pero Mary y John tienen sed y quieren tomar agua. Ann tiene hambre y quiere comer enchiladas.**

*Answers, Guía para la lectura:* **B.** la iglesia, las oficinas del gobierno, la oficina de correos, el banco **C.** 1. los mayas, los aztecas, los incas 2. los romanos

## Antes de leer

Learning Strategy:

*Previewing*

1. What does the word **plaza** mean to you? This Spanish word is now regularly used in the English language, but you may find that its Spanish meaning is different from what you thought.
2. Look at the photos on page 182. Where do you think these **plazas** are?
3. Look at the title and the photos to see what the reading may be about.

## Guía para la lectura

Learning Strategies:

*Reading for details, supporting choices*

A. Read the first paragraph and identify some of the cognates.

B. 1. What are some of the buildings that are built around the **plaza**?
2. What other group contributed to the idea of the **plaza**?

C. What were three ancient civilizations in the Americas?

### La plaza: El centro social del mundo hispano

En los pueblos y en las ciudades de los países del mundo hispano, siempre hay una plaza. La plaza es su centro original. Una plaza siempre tiene la forma de un cuadrado o de un rectángulo y no hay edificios en el centro. Los edificios públicos están alrededor de la plaza: la iglesia, las oficinas del gobierno, la oficina de correos y el banco. También hay espacios para algunas tiendas, un hotel y un restaurante.

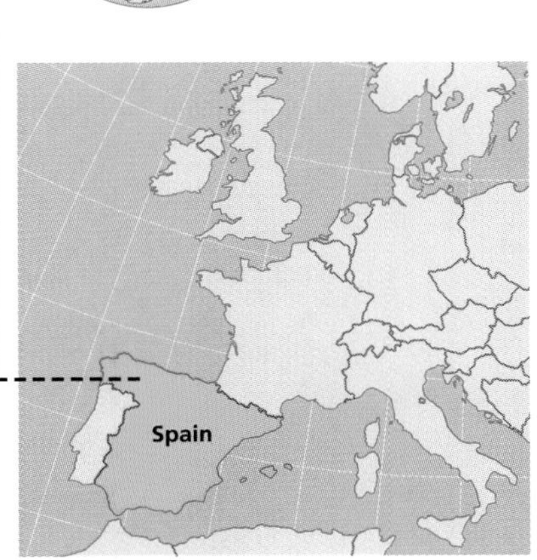


La larga tradición de la plaza data desde las grandes civilizaciones de América, como las de los mayas y los aztecas en México, o los incas en Perú. Las ciudades más antiguas de América tienen plazas ya construidas antes de la llegada de los españoles en el año 1492. También es evidente la influencia de los romanos sobre los españoles en el sistema de la construcción de plazas en España, así como más tarde en los países de América Latina y en el suroeste de los Estados Unidos.

Hoy en día la plaza todavía es un lugar importante en la vida hispana. Puede ser grande, como la Plaza Mayor de Madrid, el Zócalo en la Ciudad de México o la Plaza de Armas en Lima. También puede ser pequeña, como la plaza de muchos pueblitos. En todo caso, se reune la gente allí para hablar con los amigos, para divertirse o para ir de compras. En la plaza siempre hay color, movimiento y mucha vida.

# Chapter Objectives

Functions: Asking for directions; giving directions; getting people to do something
Context: City or town
Accuracy: The preposition **de** and the definite article; prepositions of place; present tense of **estar;** commands with **Ud.** and **Uds.**

## Cultural Observation

Ask students what museums they have visited and in what cities. What other museums in the United States have they heard about? Are they familiar with any famous museums in Spain? Have they ever heard of the **Museo del Prado?** Do they know where it is located?

## Cultural Context

You might want to point out that Madrid has over 30 museums, the newest of which is the **Centro de Arte Reina Sofía,** which houses the most famous of Picasso's paintings, the ***Guernica.*** Try to bring in a picture of the ***Guernica*** and discuss it, or have students research the painting and bring in a picture.

CAPÍTULO 8

# ¿DÓNDE ESTÁ...?

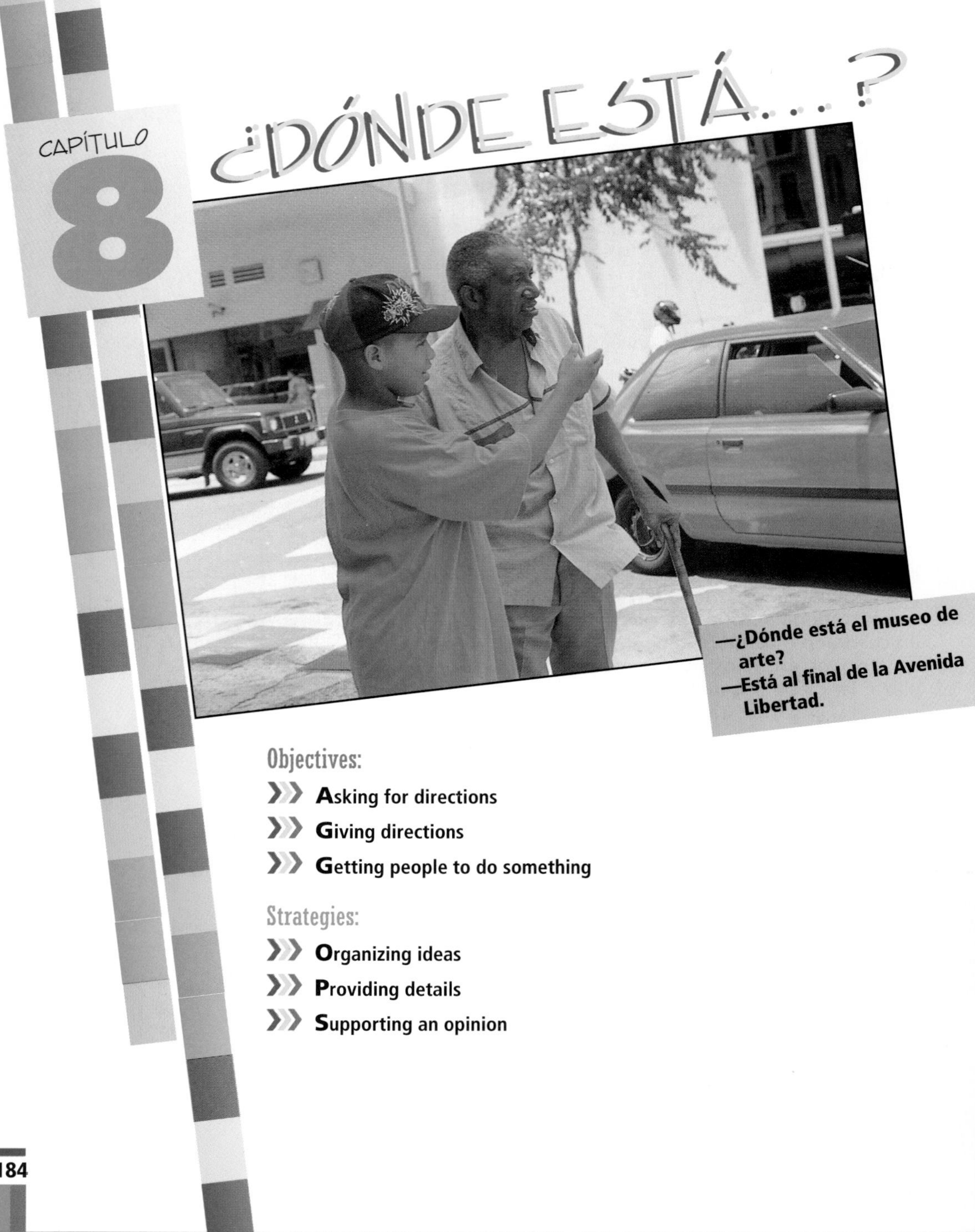

**—¿Dónde está el museo de arte?**
**—Está al final de la Avenida Libertad.**

Objectives:

- Asking for directions
- Giving directions
- Getting people to do something

Strategies:

- Organizing ideas
- Providing details
- Supporting an opinion

184

## Video/CD-ROM

**Chapter 8 Video Program**
**Chapter 8 CD-ROM Program**

**These can be used at the end of the chapter as expansion activities.**

# PRIMERA ETAPA

## Preparación

- **How do you find your way around a city when you have never been there before?**
- **When you ask for directions, what do you generally hope to find out?**
- **If someone asks you how to get to a particular place in town, what information do you give?**

**Learning Strategy:**

*Previewing*

*¿Está lejos de aquí?:* Is it far from here?

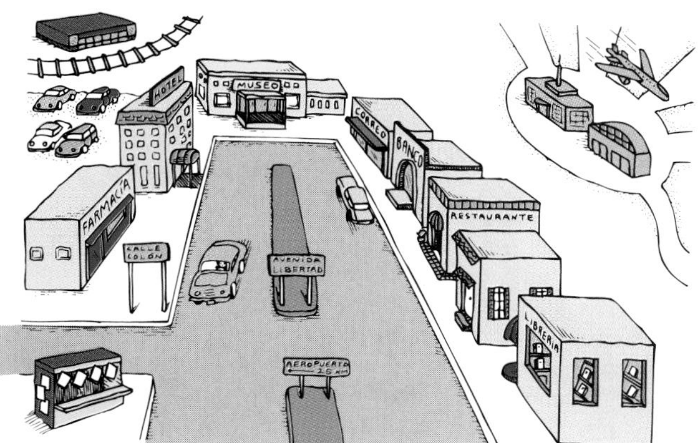


| | | |
|---|---|---|
| ¿Dónde **está** el aeropuerto? | Está lejos de la ciudad. | is (located) |
| ¿Dónde está la estación de trenes? | Está **cerca del** hotel. | near |
| ¿Dónde está la oficina de correos? | Está **frente al** hotel. | across from (facing) |
| ¿Dónde está la farmacia? | Está **al lado del** hotel. | next to |
| ¿Dónde está el museo? | Está **al final de** la Avenida Libertad. | at the end of |
| ¿Dónde está el **quiosco de periódicos**? | Está **en la esquina** de la Calle Colón y la Avenida Libertad. | newspaper kiosk / at the corner |
| ¿Dónde está el coche de Mario? | Está en una **playa de estacionamiento detrás** del hotel. | parking lot<br>behind |
| ¿Dónde está el coche de Teresa? | Está en la avenida **delante del** banco. | in front of |
| ¿Dónde está el banco? | Está **entre** el restaurante y la oficina de correos. | between |



## Presentation: ¿Está lejos de aquí?

Introduce the new vocabulary and prepositions of place by using the transparency. Have students keep their books closed as they look at the transparency and listen to you say the expressions. After each pair or group of expressions, have students repeat. If you do not use the transparency, read the expressions while students look at the picture in their books, having them repeat after each pair or group of expressions.

There is no recorded material on the teacher tape to accompany this *etapa* opener.

***Support material, ¿Está lejos de aquí?:***
Transparency #38

## Etapa Support Materials

Workbook: **pp. 97–102**
Transparency: **#38**
Teacher Tape
Quiz: **Testing Program, p. 82**

Support material, **¿Está lejos de aquí?:**
**transparency #38**

# ¡Aquí te toca a ti!

*Learning Strategy:*
*Reading a map*

**A. *Mi ciudad*** When someone asks you about the town pictured on page 185, you answer using the suggested expressions. Follow the model.

**Modelo:** —¿Dónde está la estación de trenes? (cerca del hotel)
—*Está cerca del hotel.*

1. ¿Dónde está el hotel? (al lado de la farmacia)
2. ¿Dónde está el banco? (frente a la iglesia)
3. ¿Dónde está el aeropuerto? (lejos de la ciudad)
4. ¿Dónde está la oficina de correos? (cerca del restaurante)
6. ¿Dónde está la farmacia? (en la esquina de la Calle Colón y la Avenida Libertad)
7. ¿Dónde está la estación de trenes? (al lado del museo)
8. ¿Dónde está el restaurante? (entre la florería y el banco)

*Learning Strategy:*
*Reading a map*

**B. *No, te equivocas* (you're wrong), *el banco está...*** You are asked for information about the town on page 185 and the people you talk to are not quite right. In a subtle way, you tell them they're wrong and point out the correct information. Follow the model.

**Modelo:** —El aeropuerto está cerca de la ciudad, ¿no? (lejos de)
—*No, te equivocas, está lejos de la ciudad.*

1. El restaurante está al lado de la iglesia, ¿verdad? (frente a)
2. La estación de trenes está lejos del museo, ¿no? (cerca de)
3. La florería está frente a la librería, ¿verdad? (al lado de)
4. El quiosco de periódicos está al final de la Avenida Libertad, ¿verdad? (en la esquina de la Avenida Libertad y la Calle Colón)
5. El museo está al lado del banco, ¿no? (al final de la Avenida Libertad)
6. El coche de Teresa está detrás de la iglesia, ¿verdad? (delante del banco)
7. La florería está frente a la librería y el restaurante, ¿no? (entre)

*Critical Thinking Strategy:*
*Sequencing*

**C. *En la cola* (In line)** While waiting to get into the movies, you point out some of your friends to your brother. You do so by indicating each person's place in line. Use the drawing on page 187 to give your answers. Follow the model.

Estela / detrás
*¿Estela? Ella está detrás de Alejandro.*

1. Amanda / delante
2. Pablo / detrás
3. Marcos / entre
4. Antonio / detrás
5. Alejandro / delante
6. Estela / entre



**Ex. A:** pair work

*Variation, Ex. A:* Situate your school in relationship to places around it. For example: **La escuela está en la esquina de la calle... y la avenida...** Ask students: **¿Qué hay delante de la escuela? ¿un parque? ¿una avenida?**

**Ex. B:** pair work

*Answers, Ex. B:* 1. No, te equivocas, está frente a la iglesia. 2. ...cerca del museo. 3. ...al lado de la librería. 4. ...en la esquina de la avenida Libertad y la calle Colón. 5. ...al final de la avenida Libertad. 6. ...delante del banco. 7. ...entre la librería y el restaurante.

## Cooperative Learning

### Ex. C: Information Gap Pairs

*Learning Strategies: Describing spatial relationships, listening for details, taking notes*

For this information gap activity, have each student rearrange the people in line in the drawing on p. 187. They can do this simply by copying the names onto a sheet of paper, writing them down in an order different from that in the textbook. Working in pairs, they can take turns describing the position of the people in line, while their partner takes notes, trying to duplicate the order of the other's list.

## Exercise Progression

Exs. A and B provide controlled practice with the prepositions. Ex. C visually reinforces the meanings of **delante de** and **detrás de.**

**Ex. C:** pair work

*Less-prepared students, Ex. C:* For less-prepared students, have other volunteers come to the front of the room and arrange them so that all the prepositons can be used. Have the less-prepared students explain the positionality as you point to different students in the arrangement. (**Mary está delante de Joe, Joe está al lado de Tom,** etc.). Have the volunteers change places, then have students restate new positions, etc.

*More-prepared students, Ex. C:* After this demonstration, call on more-prepared students to explain the position of students at their desks. (**Ann está al lado de Tom, Mary está entre Joe y Beth,** etc.)

## Pronunciación: The sound of /s/

The sound of Spanish **/s/** is spelled with the consonants **s** or **z**. Usually, these are pronounced in the same way as *s* in the English word *say.* Note that **z** is never pronounced as the *z* in the English words *zoo, zebra,* and *zero.*

## Práctica

*D.* Listen and repeat as your teacher models the following words.

1. siempre
2. salsa
3. sábado
4. zapato
5. plaza
6. señor
7. semana
8. López
9. arroz
10. lápiz

## Repaso

*E.* ***¿Vas a... a menudo?*** Find out how often your partner goes to the places on page 188. Keep track of his or her answers so that you can make a list of places ranging from most to least frequently visited. When you have interviewed each other, compare your lists to see which places you go to with the same frequency. Follow the model.

la panadería
—*¿Vas a la panadería a menudo?*
—*No, nunca voy a la panadería.* o:
—*Voy a la panadería todos los días.*

**Learning Strategies:**

*Asking questions, taking notes, providing personal information*

**Critical Thinking Strategies:**

*Comparing and contrasting, ranking*



### Presentation: Pronunciation

You may want to mention that in Spain, the **z** is pronounced like the *th* in the English word *think.* Stress the fact that the **z** in the Spanish spoken in Latin America is pronounced like the **s** in the name **Silvia.**

Additional activities appear in the Laboratory Tape Program.

***Support material, Pronunciación:***
Pronunciation Tape

**Ex. E:** pair work

***Reteaching:*** Before doing Ex. E, quickly review expressions of frequency by asking **"cómo se dice"** or **"qué significa"** questions. Alternatively, the teacher could ask, **¿Cuál es una palabra/expresión similar a frecuentemente? (a menudo),** etc.; or work with opposites, **¿Cuál es el contrario de nunca? (siempre),** etc.

Before doing Ex. F, quickly review numbers from 1 to 100 orally. Divide the class in half or in smaller groups. Have one group count by 10s to 100, the other by 5s, then by 3s, then by 4s. Perhaps offer a small reward to the group(s) who count the best.

*Answers, Ex. F:* 1. ¿Qué cuarto tiene Claudia? Claudia tiene el cuarto número sesenta y ocho. 2. Bill tiene... veinte. 3. Betty y Rosa tienen... quince. 4. Paul tiene... treinta y seis. 5. Martha y Ann tienen... setenta y dos. 6. Antonio tiene... ochenta y nueve. 7. Sue y Clara tienen... cuarenta y siete. 8. John y Tom tienen... once.

## Cultural Expansion

Ask students what they know about Mexico City. The center of the city, called the **zócalo,** was also the main part of the ancient Aztec city called the **Gran Tenochtitlán.** (Bring pictures if possible.) The Spaniards destroyed the Aztecs' palaces and pyramids and built the National Cathedral, a palace for the **conquistador** Hernán Cortés, and many other splendid buildings of Spanish sixteenth century architecture over the ruins. Today Cortés' palace is called the **Palacio Nacional.** It is the official seat of the presidency and houses paintings by the great Mexican muralist Diego Rivera. In the early 1980s, archeologists began to explore the area under the palace and cathedral and discovered rich Aztec treasures and ceremonial buildings.

1. la farmacia
2. el banco
3. la librería
4. la panadería
5. la florería
6. la piscina
7. la oficina de correos
8. la carnicería

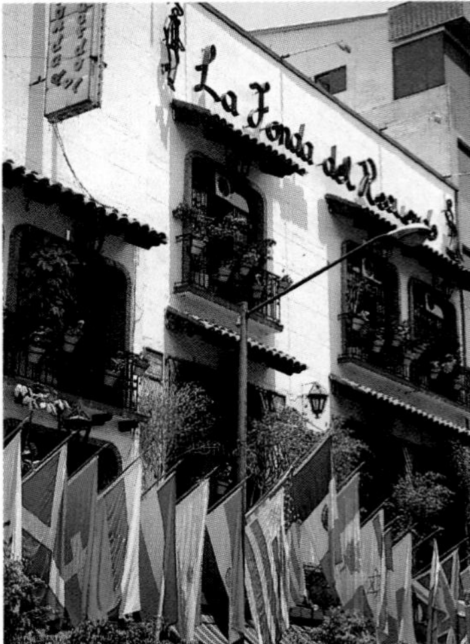


**F. *¿Qué cuarto tienes?*** Your class has just arrived at a hotel in Mexico City where you are going to spend a week. You want to find out your friends' room numbers. Follow the model.

**Modelo:** Anita / 23
*—¿Qué cuarto tiene Anita?*
*—Anita tiene el cuarto número veintitrés.*

1. Claudia / 68
2. Bill / 20
3. Betty y Rosa / 15
4. Paul / 36
5. Martha y Ann / 72
6. Antonio / 89
7. Sue y Clara / 47
8. John y Tom / 11

## Nota gramatical

### *The preposition* de *and the definite article* el

El coche de Teresa está al lado **del** hotel.
Es el portafolio **del** profesor.

When the preposition **de** is followed by the definite article **el**, the two words contract to form one word, **del.**

**de + el = del**

Many of the prepositions of place presented in this **etapa** include **de:**

| | |
|---|---|
| **lejos de** | **al final de** |
| **cerca de** | **detrás de** |
| **al lado de** | **delante de** |

Remember to follow the same rules for contraction: **lejos del centro, cerca del cine, al lado del restaurante.**



### Presentation: The preposition de and the definite article el

You can combine the presentation of contractions with **de** and contractions of prepositions of place by using the transparency for the buildings or by having them look at the drawing on p. 185. Begin by using two places that have the article **la** and are near each other. Then find two places that use the article **el** that are near each other. For each place, ask: **¿Qué está cerca de... ?** or **¿Dónde está... ?** (Point to a place that is near or next door or across the street.) Once you have established the patterns for **de la** and **del,** you can then mix genders.

**G.** Replace the words in italics and make the necessary changes.

1. El banco está *cerca* de la estación. (al lado de / detrás de / lejos de)
2. Nosotros vivimos *al lado del* restaurante. (detrás de / delante de / frente a)
3. ¿Hay una farmacia frente *a la iglesia*? (museo / estadio / cine / casa)
4. Hay un café lejos de la *panadería*. (carnicería / hotel / oficina de correos / florería)
5. —¿De quién es el coche nuevo?
   —*Es de la señorita Galdós.* (profesor / Sr. Álvarez / Sra. Ruiz / muchacho)

**H. Direcciones** Using the drawing on page 185, answer these questions that strangers ask about the city. Be as precise as possible.

**Modelo:** —Perdón. ¿Dónde está el quiosco de periódicos, por favor?
—*¿El quiosco? Está en la esquina de la Calle Colón y la Avenida Libertad, cerca de la farmacia.*

1. Perdón, ¿el restaurante, por favor?
2. Perdón. ¿Dónde está el hotel, por favor?
3. Perdón, ¿el museo, por favor?
4. Por favor, ¿la farmacia?
5. ¿Dónde está la oficina de correos, por favor?
6. ¿Hay una librería cerca de aquí?

**Learning Strategies:**

*Reading a map, describing spatial relationships*

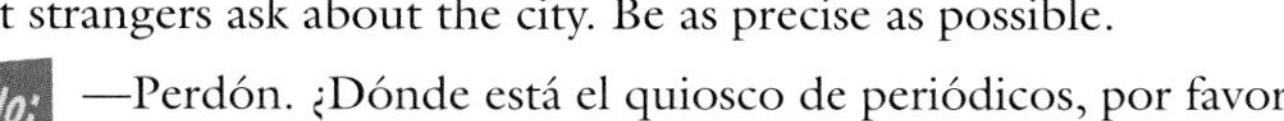


### *The present tense of the verb estar*

| | |
|---|---|
| Yo **estoy** en el Hotel Trinidad. | I *am* in the Hotel Trinidad. |
| Ana y Raúl **están** en el coche. | Ana and Raúl *are* in the car. |
| Nosotros **estamos** muy bien. | We *are* very well. |

The present tense forms of the verb **estar** *(to be)* are:

| *estar* | | | |
|---|---|---|---|
| yo | **estoy** | nosotros(as) | **estamos** |
| tú | **estás** | vosotros(as) | **estáis** |
| él / ella / Ud. | **está** | ellos / ellas / Uds. | **están** |



***Answers, Ex. G:*** 1. al lado de / detrás de / lejos de 2. detrás del / delante del / frente al 3. al museo / al estadio / al cine / a la casa 4. de la carnicería / del hotel / de la oficina de correos / de la florería 5. del profesor / del señor Álvarez / de la señora Ruiz / del muchacho

**Ex. H:** pair work

***Answers, Ex. H:*** Answers may vary slightly. 1. Está al lado del banco. 2. ...frente a la oficina de correos. 3. ...al final de la avenida Libertad. 4. ...al lado del hotel en la esquina de la calle Colón. 5. ...al lado del banco y frente al hotel. 6. ...frente al quiosco de periódicos.

## Presentation: The present tense of the verb estar

To introduce this verb inductively, follow the suggestions given for presenting other verbs on p. T169. Make statements in the **yo** form using prepositions of location: **Estoy en la escuela.,** etc. Continue by asking a **tú** question and summarize the answer in the third person. Proceed with the plural forms. Point out the written accents on the second- and third-person forms.

## Exercise Progression

Ex. G provides mechanical practice with the structure. Ex. H offers more meaningful practice using the transparency or the map.

**Ex. J:** pair work

*Answers, Ex. J:* 1. ¿Dónde está tía Ana? Está en la piscina. 2. ...están papá y mamá? Están en el banco. 3. ...está Lourdes? Está en el café de la esquina. 4. ...está Ángel? Está en el cine. 5. ...están las primas? Están en el estadio. 6. ...está mi perro? Está en tu cuarto.

You will note that only the **yo** form **(estoy)** is irregular. In Chapter 1, you learned to use **estar** to inquire and talk about health—**¿Cómo estás?** *(How are you?).* In this chapter you are learning to use **estar** to talk about where something or somebody is.

## Aquí practicamos

**I. ¿Cómo y dónde?** Taking information from each column, use a form of the verb **estar** to create a complete sentence.

Mario / Madrid
*Mario está en Madrid.*

| A | B | C |
|---|---|---|
| Graciela y Ana | | en Buenos Aires |
| el (la) profesor(a) | | en el banco |
| mi amigo(a) | | cerca de la iglesia |
| la biblioteca | estar | con José |
| tú | | mal |
| los abogados | | en la calle Alameda |
| nosotros | | cerca de la iglesia |
| la panadería | | bastante bien |
| yo | | al lado del hotel |
| Esteban | | |

**J. ¿Dónde están?** When you get home, only your brother is there. You ask him where everybody is.

la abuela / mercado
—*¿Dónde está la abuela?*
—*Está en el mercado.*

1. tía Ana / piscina
2. papá y mamá / banco
3. Lourdes / café de la esquina
4. Ángel / cine
5. las primas / estadio
6. mi perro / tu cuarto

## Exercise Progression

Ex. I is a mechanical drill designed to coordinate the forms of the verb with the subjects. Ex. J provides controlled practice in a question and answer format while reviewing vocabulary and structures from this **etapa** and the previous chapter.

¿Dónde estamos?

# Aquí escuchamos:

## "No está lejos"

### Antes de escuchar

Look at the following questions before you listen to the conversation. Also, review the prepositions of place on page 185.

1. What is the opposite of **lejos de**?
2. What verb is always used in Spanish to indicate location of people, animals, places, or things?

Now listen to two people talk about the location of a building.

**Learning Strategy:**
*Previewing*

### Después de escuchar

Write down the four places that are mentioned in the conversation. Then listen to the conversation again before deciding whether the following statements are true or false. If a statement is false, provide the correct information in English.

**Learning Strategy:**
*Listening for details*



**Answers, Después de escuchar:** la biblioteca, el banco, la oficina de correos, la biblioteca en la universidad

1. F, She wants to go to the library. 2. T 3. T 4. F, the university is far away. 5. T

**Support material, Aquí escuchamos:**
Teacher Tape/CD #1 Track #36 and Tapescript

**Ex. K:**  pair work

*Less-prepared students, Ex. K:* Have less-prepared students work in pairs to answer the questions in writing, then have them do the exercise again orally.

*More-prepared students, Ex. K:* Have more-prepared students approach the exercise as a conversation, reminding them that often after one person answers a question, he/she asks a related question in return, this could be something as simple as **¿y tú?.** In this way students can turn the exercise into a real conversation.

**Ex. L:** pair work

 role play

*Less-prepared students, Ex. L:* Have less-prepared students prepare their "script" on the board, using it as needed when they perform their dialogue in front of the class or group. Hand out cards with place names or icons to more-prepared students and have them improvise on the spot.

*Variation, Ex. L:* Have some students describe the location of a certain place without naming it. The class has to identify the place being described. You can have students use the expression **Este lugar está... .** You may wish to organize a game of "pictionary." Divide the class into teams, have one person from one team come to the board and draw the vocabulary item from a card handed to them. Have the translation on the reverse side, but charge a point if the drawer must refer to it. Give each person 45 sec. to 1 min. to draw their item while team members try to guess the word. If the first team fails to guess correctly, the other team has one chance to identify the word correctly. Then it is the other team's turn to draw and so on.



1. The woman wants to go to the bank.
2. The man indicates that the place the woman is looking for is nearby.
3. The woman finds out that the bank and the post office are on the same street.
4. The man says there is a university right in the downtown area of the city.
5. The woman discovers that there are two libraries she can visit.

## ¡Adelante!

### EJERCICIOS ORALES

*Learning Strategies:*
*Asking questions, providing information*

**K. *Intercambio*** Ask a classmate the following questions.

1. ¿Vas al aeropuerto de vez en cuando? ¿Está cerca de la ciudad? ¿cerca de tu casa?
2. ¿Vas al cine a menudo? ¿Hay un cine cerca de tu casa? ¿Qué hay al lado del cine?
3. ¿Hay una panadería cerca de tu casa? ¿Qué hay frente a la panadería?
4. ¿Qué hay entre tu casa y la escuela? ¿Casas? ¿Edificios de apartamentos? ¿Una biblioteca? ¿Tiendas?
5. ¿Qué hay delante de la escuela? ¿Detrás de la escuela?

**L. *Por favor, ¿dónde está... ?*** You are walking down the street in your town when a Spanish-speaking person stops you and asks where a certain place (movie theater, bank, train station, drugstore, etc.) is located. You indicate the street or avenue and then try to describe the area (such as what it is near, next to, across from, behind, between).

### EJERCICIO ESCRITO

*Learning Strategy:*
*Providing information*

**M. *Para ir a mi escuela*** Write out in Spanish directions to your school for some out-of-town guests from Spain. Tell them how to get from your school to the downtown area of your city or town, where you will meet them at a restaurant for lunch. Refer to specific buildings as well as streets in your description.



**Ex. M:**  writing

*Suggestion, Ex. M:* You may also wish to modify the meeting place for lunch to a well-known shopping mall, etc. since many downtowns are no longer "tourist" areas.

*Less-prepared students, Ex. M:* Brainstorm with less-prepared students a list of expressions/vocabulary they c use in their directions before letting them begin. You may als wish to let them work in pairs.

*More-prepared students, Ex. M:* You may wish to supply more-prepared students with additional vocabulary items to be presented in the next **etapa** (p. 193) in order to give more complex directions.

## SEGUNDA ETAPA

### Preparación

- What do you say when you stop somebody on the street to ask for directions?
- Can you give examples of the kinds of details about distance and direction that you need to find a place?
- Is it easy for you to understand directions? Why or why not?
- What helps you to remember directions?

**Learning Strategy:**
*Previewing*

## ¿Cómo llego a... ?

*¿Cómo llego a... ?:* How do I get to . . . ?

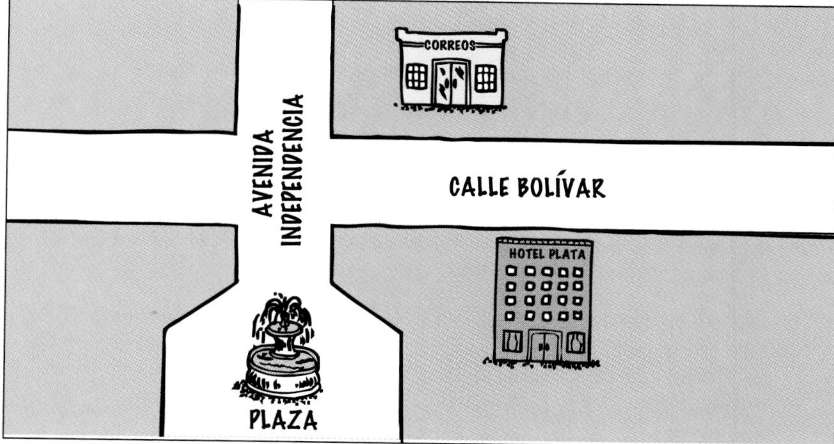


—Perdón, señor. ¿Hay una oficina de correos cerca de aquí?
—Sí, señora. En la Calle Bolívar.
—¿Cómo llego a la Calle Bolívar, por favor?
—Mm..., **cruce** la plaza y **tome** la Avenida Independencia, **siga derecho por** Independencia **hasta** llegar a la Calle Bolívar. **Doble a la derecha**. La oficina de correos está **a la izquierda**, frente al Hotel Plata.
—Muchas gracias.
—De nada.

cross / take / go straight along / until / Turn right
on the left



## Presentation: ¿Cómo llego a... ?

Begin by having students listen to the recording of the dialogue on the Teacher Tape. Ask: **¿Qué busca la señora?** Then replay the dialogue while students look at the transparency. **¿Qué cruza la señora para ir a la oficina de correos? ¿Ella sigue derecho por qué calle? ¿Adónde dobla al llegar a la calle Bolívar, a la derecha o a la izquierda? ¿Dónde está la oficina de correos?** The goal is to make clear the meanings of the new expressions. Use gestures whenever necessary and accept phrases as answers. You may wish to let different pairs of students read the dialogue after initially listening to the teacher or tape, correcting pronunciation as needed. Have the whole class repeat correctly some of the words, too.

If you do not use the transparency, follow the suggestions given above, but read the dialogue with students' books closed, and then read it again while they look at the drawing in the book.

**Support material, ¿Como llego a...?:**
Teacher Tape/CD #1 Track #37, transparency #39

## Etapa Support Materials

Workbook: **pp. 103–106**
Transparencies: **#39, #40, #41**
Listening Activity masters: **p. 52**
Tapescript: **p. 78**
Teacher Tape

Quiz: **Testing Program, p. 86**
Chapter Test: **Testing Program, p. 88**

Support material, **¿Cómo llego a... ?:**
**Teacher Tape, transparency #39**

## Cultural Expansion

Ask students if they know the names of any official languages (other than Spanish) spoken in Spain. Point out that Catalán is spoken in the region of Cataluña, and that it is similar to both French and Spanish. At the Barcelona Olympic Games, the scores and other announcements were given in Catalán, Spanish, English, and French. Then mention that Gallego is spoken in Galicia. The Basque language (Vascuence or Euskera) is not related to any other European language and is the oldest language spoken in Spain.

**Ex. B:** pair work

 role play

*Support material, Ex. B:* Transparency #40.

*Suggestion, Ex. B:* Do the first destination with the class (or have one of your more-prepared students do it), using the transparency of the city map. Then have students work in pairs. Finally, verify their work by using the transparency and having various students go over the directions they came up with while working in pairs.

*Variation, Ex. B:* With students looking at the map in their book, describe an itinerary students are to follow with their fingers on the page. When you arrive at your final destination, ask someone to indicate where you are. Once you have done this receptive activity a few times, divide the students into pairs and have them do the exercise. This is a good listening comprehension activity.

**Learning Strategy:**

*Reading for cultural information*

## COMENTARIOS CULTURALES

### El español en el mundo

**Spanish is the fourth most widely spoken language in the world after Chinese, Hindi, and English. It is spoken by more than 400 million people in Spain, the Americas, and in other areas of the world that were once Spanish possessions. Today, other than English, Spanish is by far the most widely spoken and studied language in this country.**

## ¡Aquí te toca a ti!

**A.** Give the following directions by replacing the words in italics.

1. Cruce *la calle.* (la plaza / la avenida / el parque)
2. Siga derecho hasta *la Avenida de las Américas.* (la plaza San Martín / la Calle Corrientes / la catedral)
3. Doble a la derecha *en la esquina.* (al llegar al río *[river]* / en la Calle Córdoba / al llegar a la Avenida Libertad)
4. Doble a la izquierda en *la Avenida 9 de Julio.* (la Calle Santa Fe / la Calle Florida / Calle Esmeralda)

**Learning Strategies:**

*Reading a map, organizing and giving directions*

**B.** ***Perdón, señorita. ¿Cómo llego a... ?*** With your partner, take turns playing the role of the police officer at **La Puerta del Sol** (circled in red on the map on page 195). Explain how to get to the following places. Follow the model.

la estación de metro Antón Martín
—*Perdón, señor (señorita). ¿Cómo llego a la estación de metro Antón Martín?*
—*Tome la Calle Carretas hasta llegar a la Plaza Benavente. Tome la Calle Atocha a la izquierda de la plaza. Siga derecho. La estación de metro Antón Martín está a la izquierda.*

1. La Plaza Mayor
2. la Capilla del Obispo
3. La Plaza de la Villa
4. El Teatro Real
5. La Telefónica en la Gran Vía



## Exercise Progression

Ex. A is designed to familiarize students with the expressions. Ex. B affords communicative practice with giving directions.

¿Qué crees?

**In which Latin American city were many archaeological findings discovered while building a subway system? One of the stations is decorated by an excavated pyramid.**

**a) Buenos Aires (Argentina)**
**b) Mexico City**
**c) Caracas (Venezuela)**

**respuesta** 

## *Pronunciación: The sound of /s/ (continued)*

The sound of **/s/** can also be spelled with the consonant **c** when it is before the vowels **e** and **i** as in **cena** and **cine.**

### Práctica

*C.* Listen and repeat as your teacher models the following words.

1. cena
2. centro
3. cerca
4. dulce
5. a veces
6. cine
7. cinta
8. cita
9. cien
10. gracias

## Repaso

*D. ¿Por favor... ?* Some tourists stop you in the **Zócalo** to ask where certain places are located. Using the map on page 196, locate as precisely as possible the places that they are looking for. Follow the model.

**Modelo:** la Antigua Aduana
—*¿La Antigua Aduana, por favor?*
—*La Antigua Aduana está frente al Antiguo Palacio de la Inquisición.*

**Learning Strategies:**
*Reading a map, organizing and giving directions*



**Ex. D:** pair work
role play

*Support material, Ex. D:* Transparency #41.

*Less-prepared students, Ex. D:* The reteaching note should be especially useful for less-prepared students and serves as a lead in to the exercise for all students.

*More-prepared students, Ex. D:* Encourage more-prepared students to expand their answers by explaining how to get from #1 to #2, etc., using other direction-giving vocabulary.

**resentation: Pronunciation**

nt out that in some regions of Spain, the **c** before an **i** or an s pronounced like the *th* in the English word *think*, just like Spanish **z.**

ditional activities appear in the Laboratory Tape Program.

*Support material, Pronunciación:* Pronunciation Tape

*Reteaching:* Quickly review prepositions of place before doing the **Repaso.** Use suggestions from previous reteaching sections and/or ask students to supply the words while you write them on the board.

## Presentation: Commands with **Ud.** and **Uds.**

This is the perfect opportunity to use a variation of the total physical response described in **Etapa preliminar E** on pp. 39–42. Introduce the commands inductively by doing a whole class activity. Use commands such as **levántense/siéntense**, then move on to verbs such as **mirar** (**por la ventana, a la profesora,** etc.), **hablar, bailar, cantar, correr, escribir (en la pizarra),** doing both positive and negative forms, as well as singular and plural (one student or whole class). Allow students to use gestures for verbs such as **cantar, correr,** and **comer.**



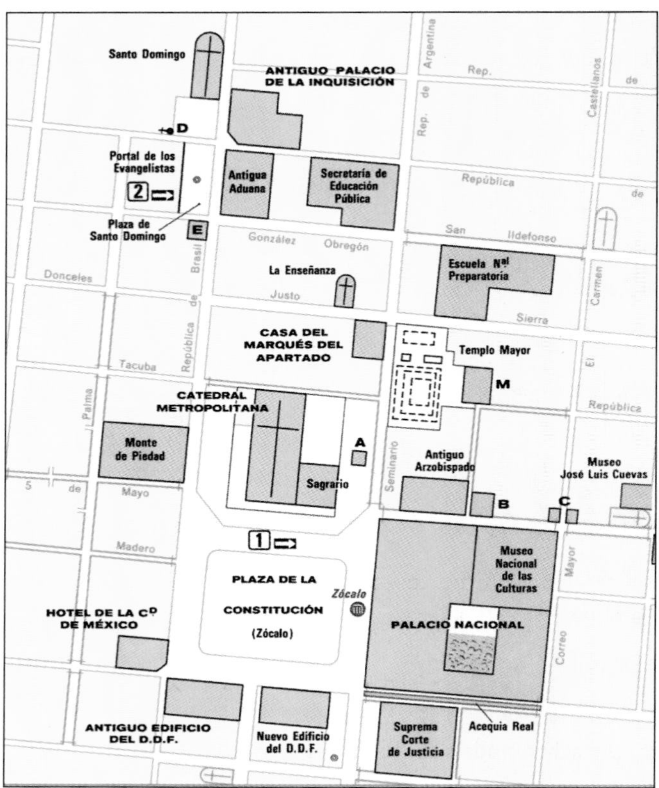


1. Casa del Marqués del Apartado
2. Monte de Piedad
3. Suprema Corte de Justicia
4. Secretaría de Educación Pública
5. Antiguo Arzobispado
6. Nuevo Edificio del D.D.F.

b

# ESTRUCTURA

## Commands with *Ud.* and *Uds.*

| | |
|---|---|
| **Tome** la Calle Atocha. | *Take* Atocha Street. |
| ¡**Escuchen** bien! | *Listen* well! |

1. Command forms of a verb are used to tell someone to do something, such as to give orders, directions, and suggestions. Spanish has two command forms: formal (**Ud.** and **Uds.**) and informal (**tú** and **vosotros**). Here you will learn how to make formal commands.

*Formal Commands*

| Verbs ending in **-ar: cantar** | Verbs ending in **-er: comer** | Verbs ending in **-ir: escribir** |
|---|---|---|
| **Cante** Ud.<br>**Canten** Uds. | **Coma** Ud.<br>**Coman** Uds. | **Escriba** Ud.<br>**Escriban** Uds. |

2. To form the **Ud.** and **Uds.** commands, drop the **o** from the **yo** form of the present tense and add **e/en** for **-ar** verbs and **a/an** for **-er** and **-ir** verbs.

| | | | |
|---|---|---|---|
| yo **hablo** → | **habl-** → | **hable** Ud. | **hablen** Uds. |
| yo **bebo** → | **beb-** → | **beba** Ud. | **beban** Uds. |
| yo **escribo** → | **escrib-** → | **escriba** Ud. | **escriban** Uds. |
| yo **tengo** → | **teng-** → | **tenga** Ud. | **tengan** Uds. |

3. The negative command is formed by placing **no** before the verb: **¡No baile!**, **¡No canten!**

## Aquí practicamos

**E.** Give the **Ud.** and **Uds.** command forms of the following verbs.

doblar a la derecha
*Doble a la derecha.*
*Doblen a la derecha.*

1. estudiar
2. no beber mucho
3. aprender español
4. tener paciencia
5. no comer mucho
6. leer todos los días

**F. *A mi profesor(a)*** Use the **Ud.** command with your teacher.

no bailar en clase
*No baile en clase.*

1. tener paciencia
2. no trabajar mucho
3. escribir las instrucciones
4. leer en la biblioteca
5. viajar mucho
6. no hablar tan despacio *(so slowly)*

**G. *¡Vamos!*** Using the suggested verbs, tell two or three of your classmates to do something. They are obliged to obey you! Use these verbs:

| | | | |
|---|---|---|---|
| mirar | cantar | escuchar | bailar |
| trabajar | usar | correr | escribir |

**Modelos:** *Luisa y Marta, ¡canten bien!*
*Antonio y Marta, ¡bailen mucho!*



**Ex. E:** pair work

***Answers, Ex. E:*** 1. Estudie/Estudien. 2. No beba/beban mucho. 3. Aprenda/Aprendan español. 4. Tenga/Tengan paciencia. 5. No coma/coman mucho. 6. Lea/Lean todos los días.

**Ex. F:** pair work

writing

***Less-prepared students, Ex. F:*** Have less-prepared students work in pairs and write out the commands, then really direct them orally at the teacher (it is nice to turn the tables occasionally!).

***More-prepared students, Ex. F:*** Have more-prepared students improvise additional commands to put the teacher on the spot. You may wish to put a list of verbs on the board for them to use.

***Answers, Ex. F:*** 1. Tenga paciencia. 2. No trabaje mucho. 3. Escriba las instrucciones. 4. Lea en la biblioteca. 5. Viaje mucho. 6. No hable tan despacio.

**Ex. G:** groups of four or more

## Exercise Progression

Ex. E offers mechanical practice with the command forms of **-ar** and **-er** verbs. Exs. F and G provide mini-contexts for the commands.

## Presentation: Irregular command forms

Point to several students and gesture for them to start to move, telling them, **Vayan a la pizarra.** Then use a command to ask each one to write a different verb that involves a spelling change for the command form. For example **Juan, escriba "llegar,"** etc.

Then ask the class to give the **yo** form of the verbs. The student who wrote the verb also writes the **yo** form. Then tell each student to erase the **o.** Ask the class to give the command ending and have the students at the board write it down. Then ask students to pronounce what is written.

Remind them that **g** before an **i** or an **e** is pronounced like the English *h* in *hot.* A **u** is needed to make it sound like **llegue.** Explain the spelling rules, pointing out that in **cruce** a spelling change is necessary because the **z** usually changes to a **c** before an **i** or an **e** in Spanish. Have the class point out how the other verbs will be spelled to form the commands correctly.

**Ex. H:** pair work

*Answers, Ex. H:* 1. Sea bueno./Sean buenos. 2. Vaya/Vayan a bailar. 3. No sea antipático./Sean antipáticos. 4. Vaya/Vayan a clase. 5. Practique/Practiquen el piano. 6. No llegue/lleguen tarde. 7. No cruce/crucen la calle. 8. Busque/Busquen las llaves.

*Support material, Aquí escuchamos:* Teacher Tape/CD #1 Track #38 and Tapescript

### Irregular command forms

1. Verbs that end in **-car**, **-gar**, or **-zar**, such as **practicar**, **llegar**, and **cruzar**, have a spelling change in the **Ud.** and **Uds.** command forms: **c → qu: practique; g → gu: llegue; and z → c: cruce.**

2. The verbs **ir** and **ser** have irregular command forms.

| ir | ser |
|---|---|
| **vaya** Ud. | **sea** Ud. |
| **vayan** Uds. | **sean** Uds. |

*H.* Give the **Ud.** and the **Uds.** command forms of these verbs. Follow the model.

ir de vacaciones
*Vaya de vacaciones.*
*Vayan de vacaciones.*

1. ser bueno
2. ir a bailar
3. no ser antipático
4. ir a clase
5. practicar el piano
6. no llegar tarde *(late)*
7. cruzar la calle
8. buscar *(look for)* las llaves

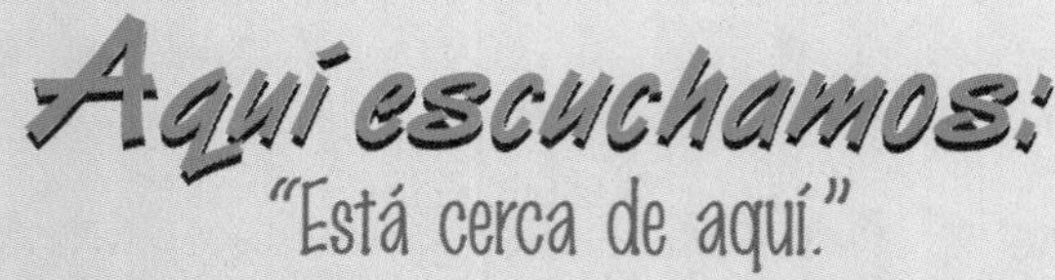

"Está cerca de aquí."

Learning Strategy: *Previewing*

### Antes de escuchar

**Read the following questions before listening to the conversation. Review the command forms on pages 196, 197 and above.**

1. How do you say *turn to the left?*
2. What is the difference between **derecho** and **derecha**?
3. What is the word in Spanish for *street blocks?*

Now listen to the conversation to find out the name of the street the man is looking for. Write the name of the street as well as any other street names you hear.

## Después de escuchar

Listen to the conversation again before summarizing in English the steps the man needs to take to get where he wants to go.

*Learning Strategies:*

*Listening for details, listing*

EJERCICIO ORAL

I. ***Vamos a la escuela*** Explain to another student how you get from where you live to your school. (1) Give specific directions, including every street name and turn. (2) Name at least three buildings that you pass on the way. Include in your explanation the verbs **ir, cruzar,** and **doblar.**

*Learning Strategies:*

*Organizing ideas, providing information*

EJERCICIO ESCRITO

J. ***Para ir a la Plaza Mayor*** You and a Peruvian pen pal have just arrived in Madrid. While having lunch at **La Puerta del Sol,** you look at a map similar to the one on page 195 and find the red circle marking where you are. Discuss the best way to get to your destinations. You are going to **La Plaza Mayor** and your friend is meeting his or her family in front of **El Teatro Real**. Together write down specific directions in Spanish from your current location to each destination.

*Cooperative Learning*

*Learning Strategies:*

*Reading a map, organizing ideas, providing information*

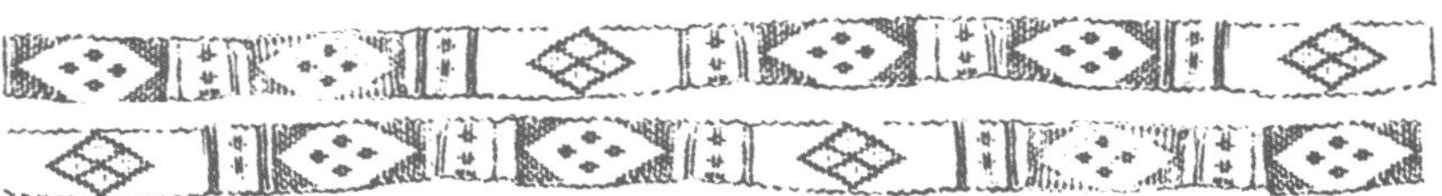



**Ex. I:** pair work

***Less-prepared students, Ex. I:*** Help less-prepared students brainstorm and organize a list of verbs, vocabulary expressions, and street names to use when giving directions. Allow them to look at these notes as they do the exercise orally.

***More-prepared students, Ex. I:*** For more-prepared students, have one partner explain how to get from home to school and have the other partner explain how to get from the school back to the first partner's house (reversing the destination) and viceversa. This requires good listening skills and vocabulary use.

***Variation, Ex. I:*** Have students use the **Ud.** command form to explain how to get to their house.

**Ex. J:** pair work

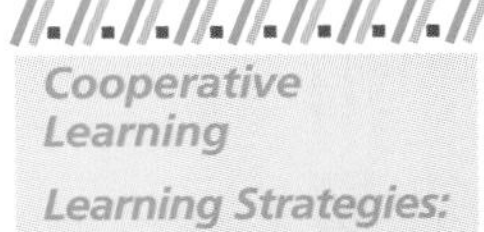

writing

***Less-prepared students, Ex. J:*** Have less-prepared students trace their route with a finger or lightly in pencil first. Then have them return to **Sol** and retrace, this time stopping to write down the street names and the directions as they go along.

***More-prepared students, Ex. J:*** Have more-prepared students design alternate routes to their destinations, including other sights to see along the way.

***Answers, Después de escuchar:*** calle Bolívar. Go straight until you reach the Plaza de la Independencia. Then turn left and go three blocks and there is calle Bolívar.

# Chapter Culminating Activities

Use a map of the town or city where your school is located. Have students give directions for getting around town. Show them how a Spanish speaker might adapt American street names; for example: Maple Street—**la calle Maple,** Washington Avenue—**la avenida Washington.**

Begin with a receptive exercise. Describe several itineraries, with students following your directions on the map. Ask them to identify your destination. Have students work in groups to prepare itineraries which they can read to the class and have them identify. Prepare in advance sets of starting and end points for less-prepared students. Have more-prepared students try to "lose" the class by taking lots of twists and turns and roundabout ways to get to their destinations.

*Support material, Capítulo 8:* Improvised Conversation, Teacher Tape/CD #1 Track #39 and Tapescript; Lab Manual listening activities, Laboratory Program, Tapescript, and Teacher's Edition of the Workbook/Lab Manual

## Para charlar

### Para dar direcciones

Cruce la calle...
Doble a la derecha.
a la izquierda.
Está al final de...
al lado de...
cerca de...
delante de...
detrás de...
en la esquina de...
entre...
frente a...
lejos de...
Tome la calle...
Siga derecho por...

### Para pedir direcciones

¿Cómo llego a... ?
¿Dónde está... ?
¿Está lejos/cerca de aquí?

## Vocabulario general

### Sustantivos

la playa de estacionamiento
un quiosco de periódicos

### Verbos

estar
llegar

### Otras palabras y expresiones

del
Sea Ud....
Sean Uds....
Vaya Ud....
Vayan Uds....

# ESTRUCTURA

## ¿Qué hora es?

Es la una.

Son las dos.

Son las dos y diez.

Son las dos y cuarto.

Son las dos y media.

Son las tres menos veinte.

Son las tres menos cuarto.

Es **medianoche**.

Es **mediodía**.

midnight / noon

1. To distinguish between a.m. and p.m., use the expressions **de la mañana** *(in the morning)*, **de la tarde** *(in the afternoon)*, or **de la noche** *(in the evening)*.
2. Notice that in Spanish **es la** is used for one o'clock and **son las** is used for all other hours.



### Presentation: ¿Qué hora es?

Use a model clock (or draw one on the board). Begin by having students repeat the hours from one to midday (contrast with midnight). Then have them repeat the time every five minutes.

Once students have learned to tell time, it is important to return to this point on a regular basis in subsequent class periods. You can begin and end each class by asking someone what time it is, or you can have several students become responsible for giving the time whenever anyone needs to know it for a few weeks (to know when a dance begins, when a football game starts, etc.).

### Vocabulary Expansion

In order to say *on the dot* or *sharp* when telling time, Spanish speakers use the expression **en punto.** Therefore, *It is two o'clock sharp* becomes **Son las dos en punto** in Spanish.

**Ex. F:** pair work

*Answers, Ex. F:* 1. Son las ocho y veinte de la mañana. 2. Es la una (en punto) de la tarde. 3. Es la una y media de la mañana. 4. Son las tres y diez de la tarde. 5. Son las once menos cinco de la mañana. 6. Son las doce menos cuarto de la noche. 7. Son las cuatro y cuarto de la tarde. 8. Son las seis menos veinticinco de la mañana. 9. Son las ocho menos cuarto de la mañana. 10. Son las diez y veinticinco de la noche.

*Follow-up, Ex. F:* Write additional times on the board.

### Presentation: Questions about time

Begin by talking to the students about their Spanish class. **Nuestra clase de español comienza a las... y continúa hasta las... . La clase dura desde las... hasta las... . Entonces, hablamos español entre las... y las... .** Then ask them to verify the information: **¿A qué hora comienza nuestra clase de español? ¿Hasta qué hora continúa? ¿Cuándo es que hablamos español? (Desde las... hasta...** or **Entre las... y las...)** Then switch topics. For example, talk about when they eat lunch or dinner, when they arrive at school or get home, etc. Have students refer to the schedule of events on p. 204 and ask them similar questions.



## Aquí practicamos

**E.** Give the time for every five minutes between 9:00 and 10:00.

**F.** ***¿Qué hora es?*** Find out the time from a classmate. Indicate whether it is morning **(de la mañana)**, afternoon **(de la tarde)**, or evening **(de la noche)**. Follow the model.

**Modelo:** 2:20 a.m.
—*¿Qué hora es?*
—*Son las dos y veinte de la mañana.*

1. 8:20 a.m.
2. 1:00 p.m.
3. 1:30 a.m.
4. 3:10 p.m.
5. 10:55 a.m.
6. 11:45 p.m.
7. 4:15 p.m.
8. 5:35 a.m.
9. 7:45 a.m.
10. 10:25 p.m.

## Palabras útiles

### Questions about time

1. To ask someone what time something happens, use **¿A qué hora... ?** The response to this question requires the preposition **a**.

| | |
|---|---|
| —**¿A qué hora** comes? | *What time* do you eat? |
| —**A las 6:15.** | *At 6:15.* |

2. To ask someone when something occurs, use **¿cuándo?** To indicate that something happens *between* two times, use either **entre las... y las...** or **desde las... hasta las... .**

| | |
|---|---|
| —**¿Cuándo** corres? | *When* do you run? |
| —**Entre las 5:00 y las 6:00.** | *Between 5:00 and 6:00.* |
| —**¿Cuándo** trabaja tu madre? | *When* does your mother work? |
| —**Desde las 9:00 hasta las 5:00.** | *From 9:00 to 5:00.* |

**G.** ***¿A qué hora... ?*** Tell your friend between what times you do the activities on the next page. Follow the model.

mirar la TV
—*¿A qué hora miras la TV?*
—*Miro la TV entre las 7:00 y las 9:00 de la noche.*



### Exercise Progression

Ex. E could be used as part of the presentation on telling time. Ex. F offers controlled practice with the time structure. Ex. G gives students practice with the related time expression, **¿A qué hora?**

1. preparar la lección (*lesson*) de español
2. usar el laboratorio de lenguas
3. comer
4. practicar el tenis
5. trabajar
6. leer

# ESTRUCTURA

## The present tense of *venir*

¿A qué hora **viene** Mónica? — What time does Mónica *come*?
Nosotros **venimos** a las 3:00. — We *come* at 3:00.

The present tense forms of the verb **venir** are:

| *venir* | | | |
|---|---|---|---|
| yo | **vengo** | nosotros(as) | **venimos** |
| tú | **vienes** | vosotros(as) | **venís** |
| él / ella / Ud. | **viene** | ellos / ellas / Uds. | **vienen** |

You will note that the verb **venir** follows the same pattern as the verb **tener** except in the **nosotros** and **vosotros** forms.

## Aquí practicamos

*H.* Create original sentences using words from each column.

| A | B | C |
|---|---|---|
| Laura | venir | a la fiesta |
| Cristina y yo | | de Acapulco |
| Uds. | | a mi casa |
| tus amigos | | del supermercado |
| la profesora | | |
| tú | | |



**Ex. G:** pair work

*Suggestion, Ex. G:* Do first as a whole class, using the **pregúntale** format to practice listening comprehension. Call on more-prepared students first to establish the pattern. Then have the students do again in pairs, teaming up a more-prepared student with a less-prepared one.

### Presentation: The present tense of venir

Begin by making statements in the **yo** form. Continue by asking questions in the **tú** form and then summarize the answers in the third-person plural. Proceed in the same way for the plural forms. (See the presentation for the **-er** and **-ir** verbs on p. T116.) Then write the conjugation on the board and proceed with the exercises.

### Exercise Progression

Ex. H is a mechanical exercise designed to coordinate the forms of the verb with the subjects. Ex. I offers controlled practice with the new verb. Ex. J provides a more open-ended communicative activity.

## Cooperative Learning

*Learning Strategies: Listing, compiling information, reading a graph*

*Critical Thinking Strategy: Comparing and contrasting*

You may want to expand and personalize Ex. G while still doing a lot of practice. Begin by brainstorming with the class, reviewing vocabulary for day-to-day activities. Then have students list activities that they normally do or participate in during the week. With each activity, have them tell what time of day they usually do these activities. When the lists are completed, the results can be examined on a "tick mark" graph on the blackboard to determine: which activities appear on the most lists, which ones come earlier or later in the day, and which ones might be limited to certain seasons.

**Ex. I:**  pair work

*Answers, Ex. I:* 1. Elena y su hermano no vienen al baile. 2. Elvira no viene... 3. Tú vienes... 4. Mis abuelos vienen... 5. David y Juliana vienen... 6. Vosotros no venís...

**Ex. J:** groups of four or more

role play

*More-prepared students, Exs. I and J:* Have more-prepared students make a list of personalized questions similar to those in the exercises to ask their classmates. The teacher may also wish to intersperse her/his own questions, too.

*Less-prepared students, Exs. I and J:* Work with less-prepared students as a group to practice answering short questions as a way of reinforcing verb forms and listening comprehension, for example, **¿Vienes tú?/¿Viene Ud.?/¿Viene María?** and so on. After this initial practice, ask longer, more meaningful questions. Then have these students make up questions for each other or the rest of the class.

*More-prepared students, Ex. J:* Have more-prepared students give potential guests directions to get to the party.

*Less-prepared students, Ex. J:* Have less-prepared students circulate with a chart (**sí/no/porque**), and check off or make notes to facilitate reporting back.

I. ***¿Quién viene al baile con nosotros?*** You and your boyfriend or girlfriend are going to the dance for **El Día de la Independencia**. You want to know who else is coming with you. Follow the model.

**Modelo:** Ana / sí
*Ana viene al baile.*

1. Elena y su hermano / no
2. Elvira / no
3. tú / sí
4. mis abuelos / sí
5. David y Juliana / sí
6. vosotros / no

J. ***¿Quieres venir a mi fiesta esta noche?*** You are giving a party tonight and you are inviting people in your class. Ask five people whether they want to come. If they cannot come, they must give you an excuse. Follow the model.

**Modelo:** *—Rob, ¿quieres venir a mi fiesta esta noche?*
*—Sí, ¡cómo no!* o:
*—No, lo siento, pero tengo que estudiar.*

## Aquí escuchamos:
### "La hora"

**You will hear people talking about time: class times, time zones, bus schedules, and plans for an evening's activity. You will hear each short conversation twice.**

*Learning Strategy:* *Listening for details*

### Antes de escuchar

**Review telling time, on pages 207 and 208. Now listen to the information in each conversation and pay special attention to the times given. Write down as many of the times as you can in preparation for the questions that follow.**

### Después de escuchar

**Answer the following questions in Spanish.**

**CONVERSACIÓN 1:**
**1.** ¿Cuándo es la clase de inglés? **2.** ¿Hasta qué hora es la clase?



*Answers, Después de escuchar:* 1. a las diez de la mañana 2. hasta las once y media 3. Es la una. 4. Son las diez de la mañana. 5. a las siete y media 6. a las nueve 7. a las dos y media de la tarde 8. a las cuatro y media

*Support material, Aquí escuchamos:* Teacher Tape/CD #1 Track #40 and Tapescript

**CONVERSACIÓN 2:**

3. **¿Qué hora es en Nueva York cuando son las 7:00 en Madrid?**
4. **¿Qué hora es en Los Ángeles cuando son las 7:00 en Madrid?**

**CONVERSACIÓN 3:**

5. **¿A qué hora van a un restaurante el muchacho y la muchacha?**
6. **¿A qué hora es la película que van a ver?**

**CONVERSACIÓN 4:**

7. **¿A qué hora va el autobús a Santa Fe?**
8. **¿A qué hora llega el autobús a Santa Fe?**

## ¡Adelante!

### EJERCICIO ORAL

**K. *En la fiesta del pueblo*** Imagine that your class is in Guatemala for the annual **Día de la Independencia**. Consulting the poster on page 204, (1) decide on three events that you would like to attend. Then, working with two classmates, (2) reach an agreement on at least one event on each person's list that you will attend together. Finally, (3) create a schedule, indicating what time each event begins and how long you will be at the **fiesta**. Be prepared to report on your choices and your schedule.

*Learning Strategies:*

*Scheduling, reporting, negotiating*

*Critical Thinking Strategies:*

*Prioritizing, comparing and contrasting*

### EJERCICIO ESCRITO

**L. *Un programa*** Work with a classmate and prepare a poster in Spanish for a celebration in your town or city for the Fourth of July, or some other holiday of your choice. Write down the events for an entire day and evening as well as the times they will take place. If you wish, you can use the program on page 204 to give you ideas.

*Learning Strategies:*

*Listing, scheduling*



**Ex. K:** groups of three

*Suggestion, Ex. K:* Follow up with a discussion of the group decisions. Elicit these from the group reporters, keeping track of the activities mentioned, how many different groups plan to attend them, and how long each group plans to spend at the **fiesta.** (Given a model, students can respond to the question, **¿Cuántas horas van a pasar en la fiesta?** by converting times expressed in such terms as **entre/desde las diez de la mañana y/hasta las ocho y media de la noche** into total hours.) Have students determine which events are most popular and the average length of time to be spent at the celebration.

**Ex. L:** pair work

writing

## Presentation: ¿Cómo están Uds.?

Discuss with students what details have to be settled when making plans: for example, where to go, when and where to meet. Then have them listen to the dialogue on the Teacher Tape and answer the following questions in Spanish or English. If you do not use the tape, you can treat this as a reading activity. After students have read the dialogue, ask them: **¿Qué quiere hacer Julia? ¿Adónde van Consuelo y Miguel? ¿Dónde se van a encontrar con Julia?,** etc. Then have students find the expressions used to (1) suggest going somewhere, (2) agree about going somewhere, and (3) arrange a place to meet. These expressions will then be practiced in the **¡Aquí te toca a ti!** exercises.

*Support material, ¿Cómo están Uds.?:*
Teacher Tape/CD #1 Track #41, Transparency #44

# SEGUNDA ETAPA

## Preparación

*Learning Strategy:* *Brainstorming*

- **What kind of special events does your town or city plan for special holidays?**
- **If you could help plan events for a public holiday celebration, what suggestions would you make?**

## ¿Cómo están Uds.?

Hay muchas actividades para ver durante la fiesta del pueblo.

| | | |
|---|---|---|
| Then | **Ana:** | **Entonces,** ¿adónde vamos ahora? ¿Hay más actividades? |
| Of course / tired / rest | **Julia:** | **Por supuesto,** pero estoy muy **cansada.** Quisiera **descansar** por una hora. |
| ready | **Miguel:** | Pues, yo estoy muy bien. Estoy **listo** para continuar la fiesta. |
| Now | **Consuelo:** | **Ahora** es el concurso de poesía. Yo quiero ver quién gana el premio. |
| | **Julia:** | Bueno, vayan Uds. |
| are we meeting | **Ana:** | Muy bien. ¿Dónde **nos encontramos**? |
| | **Miguel:** | Delante del cine Odeón en la Avenida Los Andes. |
| O.K. (We are in agreement.) | **Julia:** | **De acuerdo**. ¡Hasta luego! |



## Etapa Support Materials

Workbook: **pp. 112–115**
Transparency: **#44**
Teacher Tape
Listening Activity masters: **p. 58**
Tapescript: **p. 87**

Quiz: **Testing Program, p. 94**
Chapter Test: **Testing Program, p. 98**

Support material, ¿Cómo están Uds.?:
**Teacher Tape, transparency #44**

# ¡Aquí te toca a ti!

**A. *De acuerdo*** You and a classmate are planning to attend the **fiesta del pueblo** in Guatemala. Ask your classmate what he or she wants to do at the festival. When your classmate suggests an activity, indicate your agreement or disagreement by saying **De acuerdo, ¡Buena idea!**, or **No, prefiero...** . Agree on three of the activities listed. Follow the model.

ir a ver el desfile
—*Entonces, ¿adónde vamos?*
—*Vamos a ver el desfile.*
—*De acuerdo. ¡Buena idea!*

1. ir a la feria de las comidas regionales
2. ir a mirar los fuegos artificiales
3. ir a ver los bailes folklóricos
4. ir al banquete
5. ir al baile popular

Cooperative Learning

Learning Strategy

*Negotiating*

**B. *¿A qué hora nos encontramos? ¿Y dónde?*** You and your classmate have decided where to go. Now you need to arrange a time and place to meet. Follow the model.

10:00 / delante del cine Odeón
—*¿A qué hora nos encontramos?*
—*A las 10:00.*
—*¿Dónde?*
—*Delante del cine Odeón.*
—*De acuerdo, a las 10:00, delante del cine Odeón.*

1. 11:00 / delante de la catedral
2. 3:00 / delante del Club San Martín
3. 4:00 / en la Avenida Los Andes, esquina de la Calle Corrientes
4. 9:00 / en el Parque Nacional

**¿Qué crees?**

**One of the shows that is common in town festivals in Spain is the** Toros de Fuego ***(Bulls of fire)*. What do you think they are?**

**a) bullfights**
**b) The bulls are set on fire.**
**c) people dressed as bulls carrying fireworks on their backs**

**respuesta** 

## Pronunciación: The consonant ñ

The consonant **ñ** is pronounced like the *ni* in the English word *onions.*

## Práctica

**C.** Listen and repeat as your teacher models the following words.

1. año
2. mañana
3. señorita
4. baño
5. señor
6. español



**Ex. A:**  pair work

**Ex. B:** pair work

### Cultural Expansion

Most Latin American countries celebrate their independence from Spain. Ask students if they know any of the leaders in the 19th-century movements for independence from Spain. Mention that Simón Bolívar is known as the **Libertador** of South America. He is to South America what George Washington is to the United States. Bolívar had a dream of forming a "United States of South America" modeled after the U.S.A. However, he never achieved this, due to all of the rivalries among regions. You may also want to mention Miguel Hidalgo (who led the movement for independence in Mexico) and Bernardo O'Higgins (Chile's hero), among others.

### Pronunciation

Additional activities appear in the Laboratory Tape Program.

***Support material, Pronunciación:***
Pronunciation Tape

### Exercise Progression

Exs. A and B are designed to teach students the conversational strategies involved in making plans. Students should be encouraged to treat the models as suggestions, not as dialogues to be imitated exactly.

**Ex. D:** pair work

*Answers, Ex. D:* 1. Son las siete y veinticinco. 2. Son las doce menos ocho. 3. Son las diez y cuarto. 4. Son las tres y media. 5. Son las ocho y diez. 6. Son las dos menos cuarto. 7. Son las cinco menos veinte. 8. Son las doce y cinco. 9. Son las nueve menos veintisiete. 10. Son las nueve y dieciséis.

### Presentation: Estar + adjectives of condition

Bring in pictures from magazines that show different physical states or emotional conditions. Make statements about the pictures and ask students follow-up questions about themselves. For example: **Estos jugadores de básquetbol están cansados. ¿Estás tú cansado ahora?,** etc. Point out that **estar** is only used with adjectives that describe physical or mental states and emotional conditions (or feelings).

Remind students that adjectives ending in **-e**, like **triste,** have the same feminine and masculine form. They only change in the plural.

### Vocabulary Expansion

**desilusionado, sorprendido, preocupado, nervioso, decepcionado, celoso**



**D. *¿Qué hora es?*** Answer according to the cues, following the model.

**Modelo:** 2:30
*—¿Qué hora es?*
*—Son las dos y media.*

1. 7:25
2. 11:52
3. 10:15
4. 3:30
5. 8:10
6. 1:45
7. 4:40
8. 12:05
9. 8:33
10. 9:16

## ESTRUCTURA

### *Estar + adjectives of condition*

| | |
|---|---|
| Yo **estoy muy cansada**. | *I am very tired.* |
| Yo **estoy listo** para continuar la lección. | I *am ready* to continue with the lesson. |

1. **Estar** is used with adjectives that describe physical or emotional conditions:

| | |
|---|---|
| **aburrido** *(bored)* | **enojado** *(angry)* |
| **cansado** *(tired)* | **listo** *(ready)* |
| **contento** *(happy)* | **tarde** *(late)* |
| **enfermo** *(sick)* | **triste** *(sad)* |

c

2. These adjectives agree in gender and number with the person they describe.

| | |
|---|---|
| **Ella** está **cansada.** | **Ellas** están **cansadas.** |
| **Él** está **cansado.** | **Ellos** están **cansados.** |

*Critical Thinking Strategies:*

*Seeing cause-and-effect relationships, making associations*

**E. *¿Qué hacen?*** Complete the following sentences with an adjective from the box above to tell you how you and the following people feel in each situation. Follow the model.

**Modelo:** Voy al cine cuando...
*Voy al cine cuando estoy aburrido(a).*

1. Voy al hospital cuando...
2. Tomamos una siesta cuando...
3. Ustedes necesitan correr cuando...
4. Mis amigos comen cuando...
5. Mi hermana va de compras cuando...



**Ex. E:** writing

*Possible answers, Ex. E:* 1. Voy al hospital cuando estoy enfermo(a). 2. Tomamos una siesta cuando estamos cansados(as). 3. Ustedes necesitan correr cuando están tardes. 4. Mis amigos comen cuando están listos. 5. Mi hermana va de compras cuando está aburrida. 6. Escuchamos música cuando estamos contentos(as). 7. Llamo a mi mejor amigo(a) cuando estoy aburrido(a). 8. Raquel y Pablo no hablan cuando están enojados. 9. Tomas el examen cuando estás listo. 10. Voy al centro cuando estoy contento(a).

6. Escuchamos música cuando...
7. Llamo a mi mejor amigo(a) cuando...
8. Raquel y Pablo no hablan cuando...
9. Tomas el examen cuando...
10. Voy al centro cuando...

**F. ¿Estás bien?** Look at the pictures and describe how these people feel today.

1. Marisol

2. Graciela

3. Santiago

4. Diego y Fernando

5. Julia

6. Benjamín y Laura

**G. ¿Cómo están Uds.?** Ask five of your classmates how they are feeling today. Then report to the class. Follow the model.

Modelo: —*¿Cómo estás?*
—*Estoy muy contento(a).*



Ex. G:  groups of four or more; writing

*Less-prepared students, Ex. G:* Have less-prepared students take notes on their classmates' responses to facilitate being able to report back.

*More-prepared students, Ex. G:* Have more-prepared students ask follow-up questions, like **¿Por qué estás contento?** and have them include that information when they report back to the class.

*Follow-up, Ex. G:* Ask students questions so that they can report what they found out. For example: **¿Cómo están tus amigos?**

Ex. F:  writing

*Possible answers, Ex. F:* 1. Marisol está cansada. 2. Graciela está enferma. 3. Santiago está contento. 4. Diego y Fernando están tristes. 5. Julia está aburrida. 6. Benjamín y Laura están enojados.

*Follow-up, Ex. F:* Write the adjectives from the Vocabulary Expansion on p. T214 on the board. Practice listening comprehension by asking personal questions. For example: **¿Cómo estás cuando no tienes clases? ¿Aburrido?** Start out with simple questions and work up to more complicated ones such as, **Si tú llegas a casa a la 1:00 de la mañana, ¿cómo reacciona tu mamá?** Call on less-prepared students to perform charades of adjectives and let the more-prepared students identify them.

## Presentation: Possessive adjectives—third person

Students are now familiar with the basic notion of possessive adjectives, so the transition to the third person should be fairly easy. Begin by asking: **¿De quién es el libro?** Students respond: **El libro es de (Juan).** You say: **Sí, es su libro.** After a few more similar examples, put together objects belonging to two students and ask: **¿De quiénes son los... ?** Students respond: **Los... son de Pedro y Miguel.** You say: **Sí, son sus...,** etc. Work your way through various objects, alternating singular and plural things to underline the fact that the possessive adjectives agree with the objects, not the possessor(s). To make sure that they understand how to use these possessives, ask questions in English such as: *How do you say "their house" or "his cars" in Spanish?* If they answer incorrectly, write a few examples on the board and point out again how these adjectives agree.

**Ex. H:** writing

# Nota gramatical

### Possessive adjectives—third person

| | |
|---|---|
| —¿Es la bicicleta de Vicente? | Is it Vincent's bike? |
| —Sí, es **su** bicicleta. | Yes, it's *his* bike. |
| —¿Son ellos los amigos de tu hermana? | Are they your sister's friends? |
| —Sí, son **sus** amigos. | Yes, they are *her* friends. |

The third-person singular possessive adjective is **su**. The plural form is **sus**. These adjectives agree in number with the noun they modify. They have several equivalents in English.

**su / sus** = *his, her, its, your (formal),* and *their*

In order to clarify meaning, sometimes the phrases **de él, de ella, de Ud., de Uds., de ellos**, and **de ellas** are used in place of the possessive adjective.

| | |
|---|---|
| —¿Es **su** coche? | Is it *his* car? |
| —Sí, es el coche **de él.** | Yes, it's *his* car. |

H. Answer the questions on page 217 affirmatively, following the model.

Modelo: —¿Es el cuaderno de Pedro?
—*Sí, es su cuaderno.*

Pedro

1. Ana María

2. Antonio

3. Raquel y Susana

4. Pilar

5. Mariano y Adela

6. Marcos y Carmen

7. Raúl

8. Benito

1. ¿Es el libro de Ana María?
2. ¿Son las llaves de Antonio?
3. ¿Son las amigas de Raquel y Susana?
4. ¿Es el perro de Pilar?
5. ¿Es el gato de Mariano y Adela?
6. ¿Son las hijas de Marcos y Carmen?
7. ¿Es la hermana de Raúl?
8. ¿Es la casa de Benito?

# Aquí escuchamos:

## "¿Cómo están?"

### Antes de escuchar

Listen to five people tell how they are and why they feel this way. Write down (1) the name of each person, (2) how he or she is, and (3) the main reason each one gives for feeling this way. Do the best you can the first time around, and then listen again to fill in any information you may have missed.

Review the adjectives of condition or mood on page 214 and answer the following questions.

1. What verb is used in Spanish with the kinds of adjectives the speakers used to describe how they felt?
2. What ending does the adjective have if referring to a male? to a female?

START

*Learning Strategies:*

*Listening for details, taking notes*



**Answers, Ex. H:** 1. Sí, es su libro. 2. Sí, son sus llaves. 3. Sí, son sus amigas. 4. Sí, es su perro. 5. Sí, es su gato. 6. Sí, son sus hijas. 7. Sí, es su hermana. 8. Sí, es su casa.

**Follow-up, Ex. H:** Continue the exercise by asking questions using various objects that belong to students.

**Support material, Aquí escuchamos:**
Teacher Tape/CD #1 Track #42 and Tapescript

***Answers, Después de escuchar:*** 1. She feels sick because it is cold, she doesn't sleep well, and she doesn't eat well. 2. Ramón is happy because his father is going to buy him a car. 3. She is worried because she has two exams tomorrow and she has a lot of work to do. 4. He wants a raise and he's mad. 5. Alejandra is sad because there are no more tickets available for the concert.

**Ex. I:** pair work

***Suggestion, Ex. I:*** Pair up a less-prepared and a more-prepared student to work together on this oral exercise.

**Ex. J:** groups of four or more

 writing

## Después de escuchar

**Now answer the following questions in English, checking the notes you took to help you remember who said what.**

1. **How does Raquel feel and why does she feel this way?**
2. **Which person is happy and what is the reason?**
3. **What does Patricia say about the mood she is in?**
4. **What does Raimundo want and how is he?**
5. **What about Alejandra? How does she feel?**

### EJERCICIO ORAL

*Cooperative Learning*

*Critical Thinking Strategy:*

*Comparing and contrasting*

**I. *¿Cómo estás?*** You and your partner compare how you feel when you engage in the following activities. Follow the model.

*Modelo:* Cuando voy a un concierto...
*Cuando voy a un concierto, estoy contento(a).*

1. Cuando corro...
2. Cuando voy a clase...
3. Cuando escucho música...
4. Cuando estudio...
5. Cuando hablo con mis amigos...
6. Cuando recibo una F...

### EJERCICIO ESCRITO

*Learning Strategies:*

*Interviewing, taking notes, organizing notes in a chart*

**J. *Una encuesta* (A poll)** Take a poll of four classsmates. Then, (1) write down a sentence or two about how your classmates feel today, and (2) include the reason each person gives for feeling that way. (3) Then organize a chart based on your findings, grouping the names of your classmates interviewed by the feeling they expressed. Be prepared to report back to the class.

## Para charlar

### Para preguntar y dar la hora

¿Qué hora es?
Es la una y media.
Son las tres menos veinte.

¿A qué hora?
¿Cuándo?
A las cinco de la mañana.
A la una de la tarde.
A las nueve de la noche.
Desde… hasta…
Entre… y…
Al mediodía.
A la medianoche.

## Temas y contextos

### La Fiesta del Pueblo

un baile popular
unos bailes folklóricos
un concurso de poesía
un desfile
el Día de la Independencia
una feria
unos fuegos artificiales
la misa de Acción de Gracias
un premio

## Vocabulario general

### Adjetivos

aburrido(a)
cansado(a)
contento(a)
enfermo(a)
enojado(a)
hispano(a)
listo(a)
triste

### Verbos

anunciar
celebrar
descansar
venir

### Otras expresiones

ahora
de acuerdo
¿Dónde nos encontramos?
entonces
mejor
para
por supuesto
su/sus
todo(a)
una vez al año

# Chapter Culminating Activity

For integrating various aspects of this chapter, have students plan activities for celebrating the 4th of July or some other local or regional festival. They could also make plans for some other special day in their lives, such as their birthday.

Plan activities for a traditional celebration from the Spanish-speaking world (this will depend on when the class reaches this chapter), such as **el 5 de mayo** from Mexico, **el 6 de enero** all over the Spanish-speaking world, or **el 25 de mayo,** Argentine Independence Day. You may wish to expand or have students expand upon the celebrations mentioned in the **Lectura cultural** on page 221. Pair up a more-prepared and a less-prepared student to research different countries to find out when they have celebrations and why, or to research any of the previously mentioned ones. This information can be written up in Spanish and reported back to the class. Perhaps the class can vote on a holiday to plan appropriate activities for, or choose the one closest to the current date of the class.

***Support material, Capítulo 9:*** Improvised Conversation, Teacher Tape/CD #1 Track #43 and Tapescript; Lab Manual listening activities, Laboratory Program , Tapescript, and Teacher's Edition of the Workbook/Lab Manual

# Lectura CULTURAL

## LAS FIESTAS EN EL MUNDO HISPANO

**El Festival de la Virgen de Guadalupe en México y la Fiesta de San Fermín en Pamplona, España**

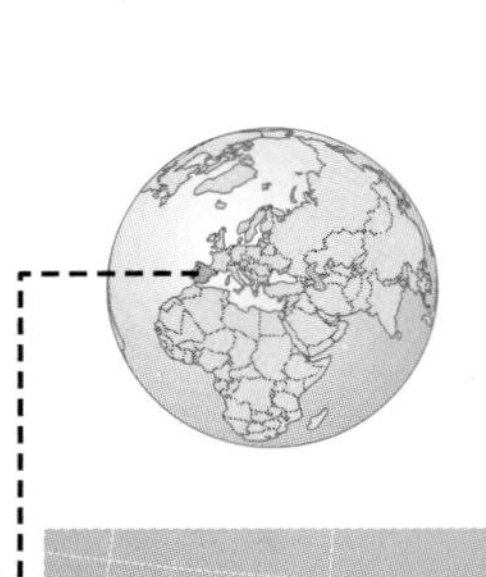

### Antes de leer

1. Look at the title and the photos. What do you think the reading is
2. What are some major holidays that are celebrated in the United Sta
3. Do any of these holidays have a religious significance? Which ones?

## Guía para la lectura

A. Read the first paragraph to determine what traditions are combined in celebrations throughout the Spanish-speaking world.

B. Look quickly at the three paragraphs that follow and identify the festival that is described in each.
Paragraph 2: Paragraph 3:
Paragraph 4:

C. Describe in your own words in English one of the celebrations mentioned.

Una celebración de los Reyes Magos en la Pequeña Habana, Miami, Florida

**Learning Strategies:**

*Reading for gist, drawing meaning from key words, reading for cultural information*

**Answers, *Guía para la lectura*:** **A.** Christian traditions are combined with traditions of native cultures. **B.** Día de los Reyes Magos, las fiestas de San Fermín, la fiesta de la Virgen de Guadalupe

### Las fiestas en el mundo hispano

En España y en Latinoamérica hay numerosas fiestas, de gran interés y color, que forman parte de la cultura de cada región. En América Latina las fiestas casi siempre combinan tradiciones cristianas de España y las tradiciones de las antiguas culturas nativas.

El 6 de enero es el Día de los Reyes Magos, que dejan sus regalos dentro de los zapatos de los niños del mundo hispano. Esta celebración tiene su origen en la visita de los Reyes Magos al niño Jesús. En algunas ciudades, personas famosas se visten de Rey Mago y caminan por las calles.

En la ciudad de Pamplona, en el norte de España, las fiestas de San Fermín tienen lugar entre el 6 y el 14 de julio. La actividad tradicional de una multitud de personas es correr por las calles delante de los toros, que van desde los corrales hasta la plaza de toros.

En México, celebran la fiesta de la Virgen de Guadalupe el 12 de diciembre. Cada año, miles y miles de personas vienen de todo México y de los otros países de Centroamérica. Algunos caminan durante semanas para hacer el viaje a la basílica de Guadalupe.

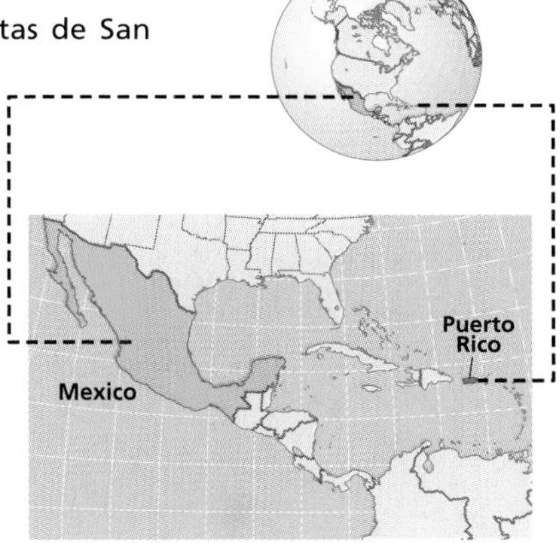

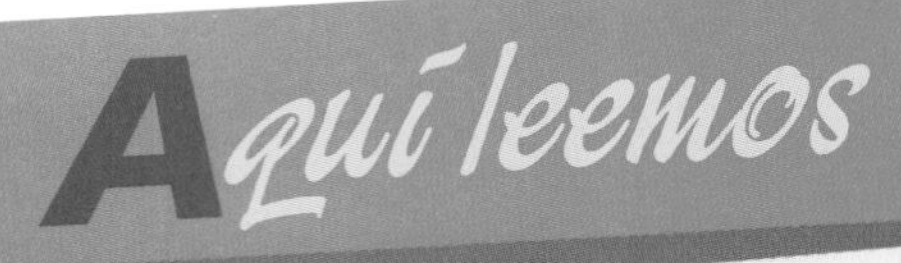


## Prereading

Use photos, reproductions of El Greco's work, or a short encyclopedia homework assignment to encourage students to learn something about Toledo before working with these readings. Emphasize how they can use this background information to help get the gist of the passages.

Glossing is purposely kept to a minimum in reading passages. By using the background information provided earlier, students should be able to guess all the important words they need. Help by reminding them they do not need to translate the reading.

## Cultural Expansion

Discuss Toledo further by bringing in some pictures and/or explaining some of the sights in the reading with more detail. The **Catedral Gótica** was started in the year 1222 and its construction lasted for more than two and a half centuries. The sacristy is in itself a museum of art, containing, among others, 16 paintings by El Greco.

**La Sinagoga del Tránsito** was built by Samuel Levi, a fourteenth-century Jewish financier. He had the temple built next to his house, and the walls were intricately and elaborately adorned by Muslim artists. **Santa María la Blanca** is also a synogoue that was converted into a church.The **Hospital de Santa Cruz** is a sixteenth-century hospital that is now a museum, and contains many of El Greco's paintings. The **Alcázar,** originally built by the Romans, has been destroyed and rebuilt many times.

*Reading Strategies:*

*Use cognates and layout to help you identify the topic.*

*Use your background knowledge to make educated guesses about content.*

*Look over the entire passage to guess where to find important information.*

## Estrategia para la lectura

You do not have to understand every word to get the gist of a reading passage as well as a good idea of the information it contains. For example, in reading a tourist brochure about the Spanish city of Toledo, any background knowledge you have about Toledo will be even more useful than vocabulary or grammar. Whenever you know what kind of information to expect, you can make educated guesses about where to find it. By concentrating on what you already know about a topic, you can have a better idea about what vocabulary might occur, making it easier to recognize cognates and to guess meanings. When you first begin to read, always take a moment to look the entire passage over quickly to see its organization and get an idea of the likely content.

## Antes de leer

- **What do you know about the Spanish city of Toledo?**
- **Imagine you have a tourist brochure about Toledo. What three types of information do you expect the brochure might tell you about the city?**

Here is some information to use for the reading on page 223.

Toledo is built on a hill surrounded by the Tajo River. It is a very old city that served as a crossroads of many cultures, including Christian, Arabic, and Jewish. The mixing of Christian and Islamic cultures produced a special blend of art and culture known as **mudéjar**. Toledo is the site of a famous castle, the Alcázar. It was also the adopted home of the Greek artist El Greco, who painted a famous view of the city. What else you can find out about Toledo?

This tourist brochure for the city of Toledo is published by the **Dirección General de Promoción y Turismo** of Spain. Imagine that your family is planning a trip to Spain and you are trying to convince them to include a visit to Toledo. Look over this brochure quickly to see how it is organized. Then read it more carefully to find out more about the tourist attractions in Toledo.



## Support Materials

Workbook: **pp. 116–119**
Unit Review Blackline Masters: **Unit 3 Review**
Transparency: **#45**
Listening Activity masters: **p. 64**
Tapescript: **p. 96**
Unit Exam: **Testing Program, p. 102**
Atajo, **writing assistant software**

Esta ciudad, enclavada sobre un promontorio y rodeada por el Tajo, ha sido declarada Monumento Nacional con todos sus palacios, iglesias, puentes y arrabales. Posee muestras inapreciables del arte árabe, mudéjar, judío y cristiano. Toledo representa el clásico cruce de culturas y es la síntesis más brillante de la historia y del arte españoles.

Lugares de interés

- Catedral gótica (siglo XIII)
- El Greco (Catedral, Museo del Greco, Santo Tomé, Museo de San Vicente, Santo Domingo el Antiguo, Capilla de San José)
- Sinagoga del Tránsito
- Santa María la Blanca
- Mezquita del Cristo de la Luz
- Hospital de Santa Cruz
- Hospital de Afuera
- Alcázar, en reconstrucción

realia 9-3 pick up realia from 1st ed. film, p. 266

**Toledo**

CIUDAD DE MÚLTIPLES CULTURAS

*arrabales:* suburbs, outskirts

## Actividades

A. Go through the reading again and mark all the cognates or words you can guess.

B. Reread the passage and list at least three facts about the city of Toledo. Was the information you expected to find included?

C. Select two tourist attractions mentioned in the brochure and explain why you think you might like to visit them.



## Cultural Expansion

Toledo has always been the religious capital of Spain. In the twelfth and thirteenth centuries it was one of the cultural centers of Europe and home to some of the best poets, historians, and philosophers in the world.

*Support material, Ex. A:* Transparency #45

**Ex. B:** writing

*Less-prepared students, Ex. B:* Have less-prepared students follow along with a finger as the teacher or other more-prepared student(s) read(s) the text. When they re-read on their own, remind them to look at/for groups of words together and to use punctuation to help them understand the material.

**Ex. C:** writing

**Exs. D and E:**  writing

*Less-prepared students, Ex. D:* Brainstorm with less-prepared students a list of features they could include in a tourist brochure about their town or city.

*More-prepared students, Ex. D:* Have more-prepared students write a draft for the tourist brochure. The teacher may need to supply some additional vocabulary.

## Cooperative Learning

### Ex. E: Team Project (Co-op, Co-op)

*Learning Strategies: Brainstorming, targeting different audiences, organizing ideas and tasks, proofreading, persuasive writing and speaking, negotiating a response*

*Critical Thinking Strategies: Analyzing, synthesizing, evaluating*

- Divide the class into teams of four. Each group will make a poster to attract Spanish-speaking tourists to their town.
- Have each team brainstorm about what aspects of their town would likely attract Spanish-speaking tourists. Advise students to consider which Spanish speakers of the world they are trying to attract. Tourists from Spain may be attracted by different items than tourists from Mexico or the Caribbean, for example.
- Instruct students to divide the tasks so that all students participate equally in making suggestions about what to put on the poster, how to write it correctly, and how to present it on the poster. They may need to proceed in round robin fashion, to ensure equal participation.
- When the poster is completed, direct each team to send a person to present the poster to another team. Each poster will be presented to four teams so that every student presents the poster once to a group.
- Tell the students that after each presentation, team members will discuss and agree on a written response to the poster and to the presentation. Tell them to write their responses on the backs of the posters and sign them.



*D.* Create a poster encouraging tourists to visit Toledo. You might include some special information about El Greco or perhaps a small map. Use expressions such as **¡Visite Toledo!, ¡Visite sus palacios!, ¡Visite sus iglesias históricas!**

*E.* Create a poster similar to the one you created for Toledo that will attract Spanish-speaking tourists to your town or area.

**Una vista de Toledo, ciudad con un papel muy importante en la historia española y con muchos lugares de interés.**

# Ya llegamos

## Actividades orales

**A. *Para ir a la Plaza Mayor...*** You and a friend have just arrived in Madrid. While having lunch at the **Puerta del Sol**, you look at the map on page 195 and discuss the best way to get to your next destination. You are going to the **Palacio Real** and your friend is meeting his or her family in the **Rastro** flea market at **La Latina**. Together write down specific directions from the **Corte Inglés** to each destination.

**B. *El festival*** You and two of your classmates are in Guatemala for the annual festival. Using the poster on page 204, plan your activities for the day. Decide on at least two activities to do together and one activity that each of you will do alone. Make plans to meet later in the day. Be sure to set a time and place where you will all meet at the end of the day!

*Learning Strategies:*

*Organizing details, sequencing, negotiating*

## Actividades escritas

**C *¿Dónde están?*** Make a list of six public buildings in your town and indicate where they are located.

**D. *¿Cuándo?*** Make a schedule of six things you do in a typical day and write the number of times you do them. Be prepared to report to the class.

**E. *Mi amigo(a)*** Interview a classmate and write down the following information: (1) name, (2) family background, (3) where he (she) lives, (4) three of his (her) interests, (5) three of his (her) possessions, (6) two things he (she) likes, (7) two things he (she) dislikes. Using this information, write a report about your friend.

*Learning Strategies:*

*Interviewing, organizing details, reporting*



## Cultural Context

You might want to take time here to review the culture presented in this unit. Discuss how and when festivals are celebrated, along with the other information you introduced to the class.

**Ex. A:**  pair work

**Ex. B:** groups of three

***Suggestion, Ex. B:*** This activity can be used to encourage listening. After students make their plans, they tell their plans to another student who was not part of their original group. This student, in turn, will answer questions about his/her partners' activities when you conduct a verification check at the end of the exercise.

**Exs. C and D:**  writing

**Ex. E:**  pair work

 writing

### Writing Activities

***Atajo, Writing Assistant Software***

***Functional vocabulary:*** Asking for information, describing people, giving directions, etc.

***Topic vocabulary:*** City, direction and distance, family members, people, personality, time expressions, time of day, etc.

***Grammar:*** **Ir; estar;** article: contractions **al** and **del;** verbs: present irregular; adjectives: numbers; verbs: **tener** and **haber;** prepositions: locatives; verbs: imperative; verbs: **ser** and **estar;** adjectives: possessive; etc.

***Support material, Unidad 3:*** Lab Manual Ya llegamos listening activities, Laboratory Program, Tapescript, and Teacher's Edition of the Workbook/Lab Manual

*Answers, Activity A:*
1. 11:00 2. 10:00 3. Chicago
4. Los Ángeles

*Answers, Activity B:*
1. Bogotá, Lima, La Habana
2. Londres 3. Answers will vary.
4. 5, 3, 8, 0

*Expansion, Activity B:*
Ask students to work with a partner to complete a chart like the one at the base of this page. One student will look at the map on page 227, and the other will look at the chart. The person with the chart must rely on the person with the map to provide the information necessary to complete the chart. Be sure students include the part of the day (morning, afternoon, night) with the hour for each city. Have them follow the model.

Student 1 (looking at the chart): **Son las diez de la mañana en Nueva York. ¿Qué hora es en Madrid?**

Student 2 (looking at the map): **Son las cuatro de la tarde en Madrid.**

# Conexión

» Have you ever taken a trip to a place located in a different time zone? Where?

» Do you have friends or family who live in a different time zone?

## Los husos horarios

### AL EMPEZAR

Nuestro planeta tiene veinticuatro husos horarios (zonas de tiempo) porque hay veinticuatro horas en el día. Mientras el planeta **da vueltas**, las horas del día pasan de un huso horario a otro. Por ejemplo, en el **dibujo** siguiente, la hora «mediodía» pasa de Nueva York a Chicago, y luego de Chicago a Denver. Cuando es mediodía en Denver, es la una en Chicago y son las dos en Nueva York.

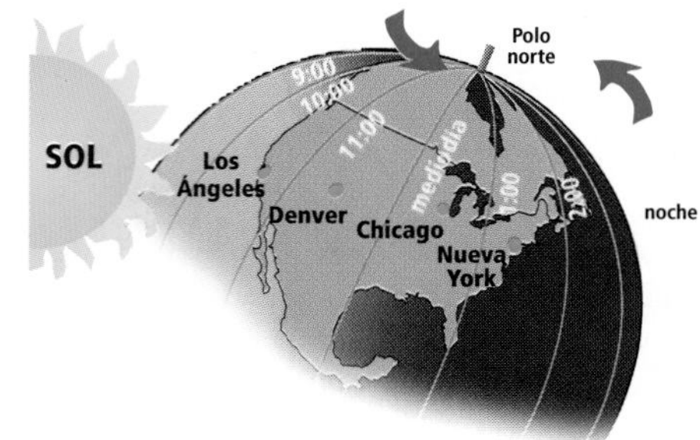


### ACTIVIDAD A

Answer the following questions based on the drawings and the reading passage.

1. Cuando es la una en Nueva York, ¿qué hora es en Denver?
2. Cuando es la una en Nueva York, ¿qué hora es en Los Ángeles?
3. Cuando es mediodía en Denver, ¿dónde es la una?
4. Cuando es mediodía en Denver, ¿dónde son las once?

El mapa en la página 227 tiene todos los husos horarios del mundo. Siempre es la misma hora en las ciudades que están en el mismo huso horario. Con este mapa, es posible contar la diferencia de horas entre dos ciudades que están muy lejos.

*da vueltas* rotates / *dibujo* drawing



| | México, D.F. | Nueva York | Buenos Aires | Londres | Madrid |
|---|---|---|---|---|---|
| **Son las . . .** | | **10:00 de la mañana** | | | |
| **Son las . . .** | | | **12:00 medianoche** | | |
| **Son las . . .** | | | | | **1:30 de la mañana** |
| **Son las . . .** | | **11:45 de la noche** | | | |

# con la geografía

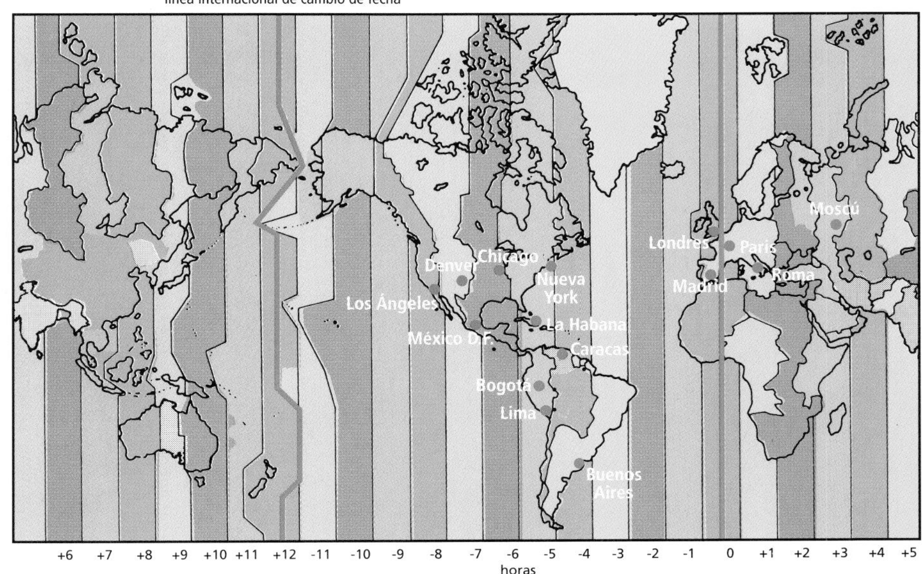


Países que tienen diferencias de media hora con los husos horarios al lado, o que no participan en el sistema de husos horarios.

## ACTIVIDAD B

1. ¿Cuáles ciudades latinoamericanas están en el mismo huso horario que Nueva York?
2. ¿Hay otras ciudades europeas que están en el mismo huso horario que Madrid? ¿Cómo se llaman?
3. ¿En que huso horario está tu ciudad?
4. ¿Cuántos husos horarios hay entre Nueva York y Madrid? ¿entre Nueva York y Los Ángeles? ¿entre Los Ángeles y Madrid? ¿entre Londres y Madrid?

## ACTIVIDAD C

Work with a partner and find out when he or she performs the following daily activities. Make a list of the activities and the time your partner does each activity.

comer el desayuno
**Estudiante 1:** *¿A qué hora comes el desayuno?*
**Estudiante 2:** *Desayuno a las siete de la mañana.*

1. estudiar
2. ir a la escuela
3. llegar a casa
4. estar cansado(a)
5. descansar en la cama
6. mirar la televisión
7. comer en la cafetería
8. pasar tiempo con amigos



**Activity C:**  pair work

 writing

### *Expansion, Activity C:*

Students can use the time zone map to find out what time it is in other parts of the world when their partner performs his or her daily activities. Tell them first to copy down the time that their partner does the activities listed in the chart below using his or her answers from Activity C. Then have the partner use the map to count the hours ahead or behind your time zone to see what time it is in other cities while he or she performs these activities.

Student 1 (looking at chart):
**Llegas a casa a las tres de la tarde. ¿Qué hora es en Moscú?**

Student 2 (looking at the map):
**Son las once de la noche.**

## Expansion Activity

Now have students use their knowledge of time zones to speculate about what people in other parts of the world do when their partner is performing his or her daily activities.

**pansion, Activity C**

| **Cuando mi compañero(a) . . .** | **. . . en Buenos Aires son las . . .** | **. . . en Madrid son las . . .** | **. . . en Moscú son las . . .** |
|---|---|---|---|
| . . . va a la escuela | | | |
| . . . come en la cafetería | | | |
| . . . llega a casa | | | |
| . . . estudia | | | |

## Cultural Context

Unit Four features Elena González, a young high school student from Madrid. The basic task of this unit is getting around a city. Chapter 10 centers on making plans for typical city activities (shopping, errands, meeting people). Chapter 11 deals with the Madrid metro system. Chapter 12 focuses on cars and taxis.

## Cultural Observation

Have students study the photos on this page and p. 229. Ask them to compare these streets with a typical street in their town or city. Some features to point out: the cobblestones, the narrowness of the street, the pedestrians walking in the street.

*Spanish speakers, ¿Qué ves?:* Have Spanish speakers mention, in Spanish, what they see. Ask them about the people in the various photos.



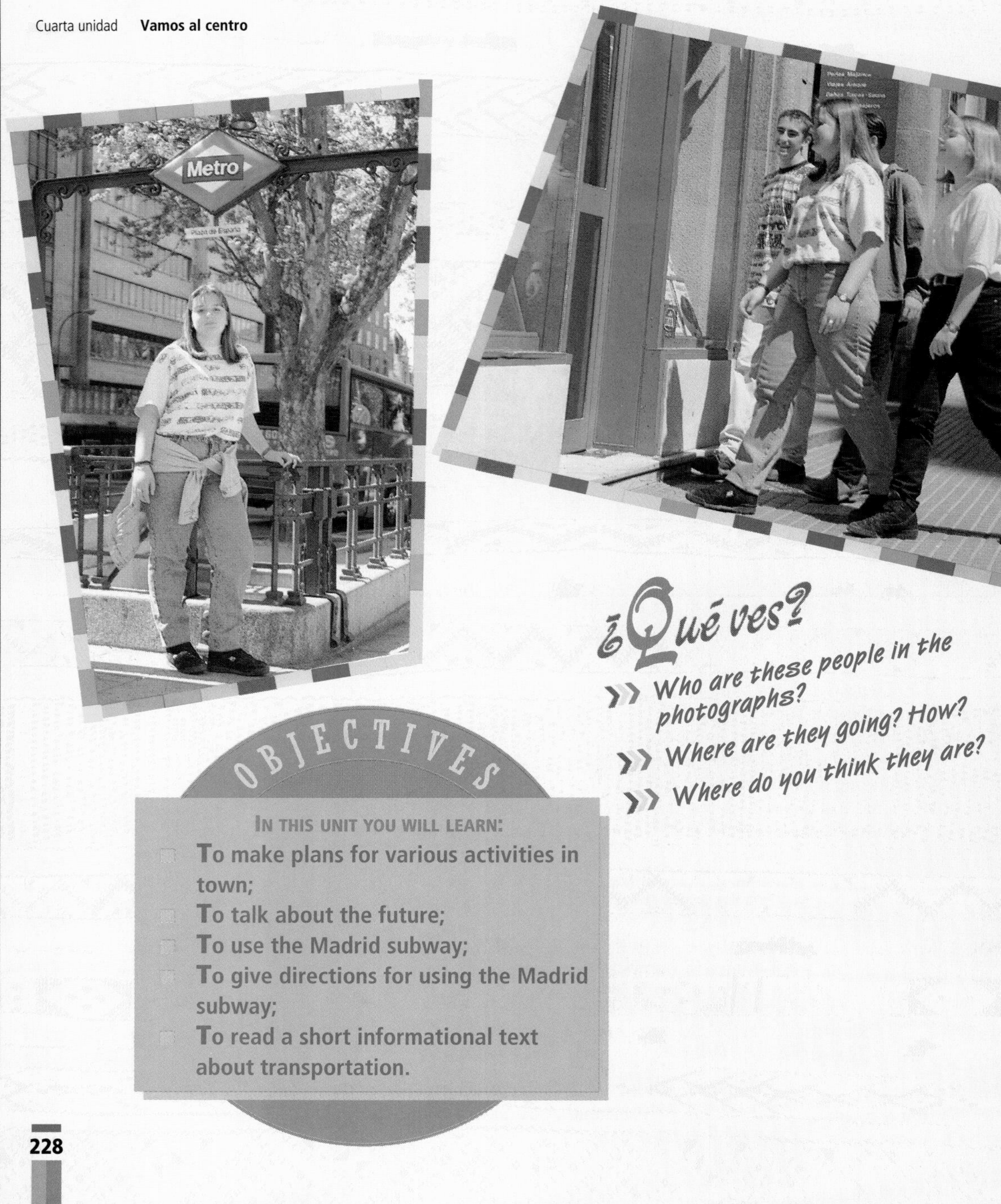


## ¿Qué ves?

- Who are these people in the photographs?
- Where are they going? How?
- Where do you think they are?

### OBJECTIVES

**In this unit you will learn:**

- To make plans for various activities in town;
- To talk about the future;
- To use the Madrid subway;
- To give directions for using the Madrid subway;
- To read a short informational text about transportation.

## Capítulo diez: ¿Quieres ir al centro?

Primera etapa: **¿Para qué?**
Segunda etapa: **¿Cuándo vamos?**
Tercera etapa: **¿Cómo prefieres ir, en coche o a pie?**

## Capítulo once: Vamos a tomar el metro

Primera etapa: **¿En qué dirección?**
Segunda etapa: **En la taquilla**

## Capítulo doce: ¿Cómo vamos?

Primera etapa: **¡Vamos a tomar un taxi!**
Segunda etapa: **En la agencia de viajes**

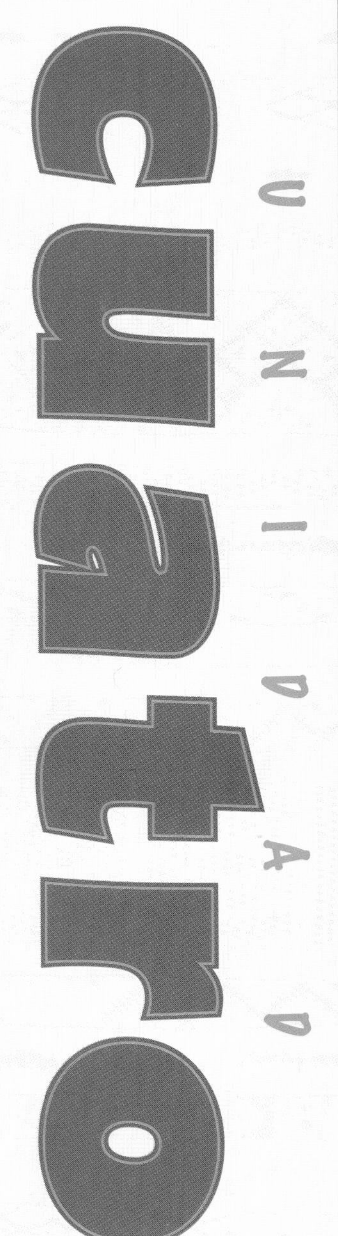




## Planning Strategy

If you do not assign the Planning Strategy for homework (Workbook, p. 121), do it in class by having students role play inviting a friend to go somewhere. Then have them invite a friend's parents to do something. Discuss modes of transportation in small towns and cities. Note what kinds of information you need for each form of transportation.

# Chapter Objectives

**Functions:** Making plans to go downtown; identifying what to do in town; talking about when and how to go downtown
**Context:** Town or city
**Accuracy:** The immediate future; **tener ganas de** + infinitive; the days of the week; the present tense of the irregular verbs **hacer** and **poder**

## Chapter Warm-up: Getting to Know You

- Tell students to walk around the room, greeting other students.
- Have them find the person they know least well. Then tell them that one student should say what he or she is going to do after school. The other student will first confirm his or her understanding by paraphrasing what the partner said, and then tell the partner what he or she is going to do.
- Ask students at random to report on what other students do after school.

*Brainstorming: Anti-stereotyping* Have students study the photo on this page. Does the picture of Elena González and her friends fit the image of what they had considered "Hispanic"? Why or why not? Ask students if they often go downtown with their friends. What do they do there?

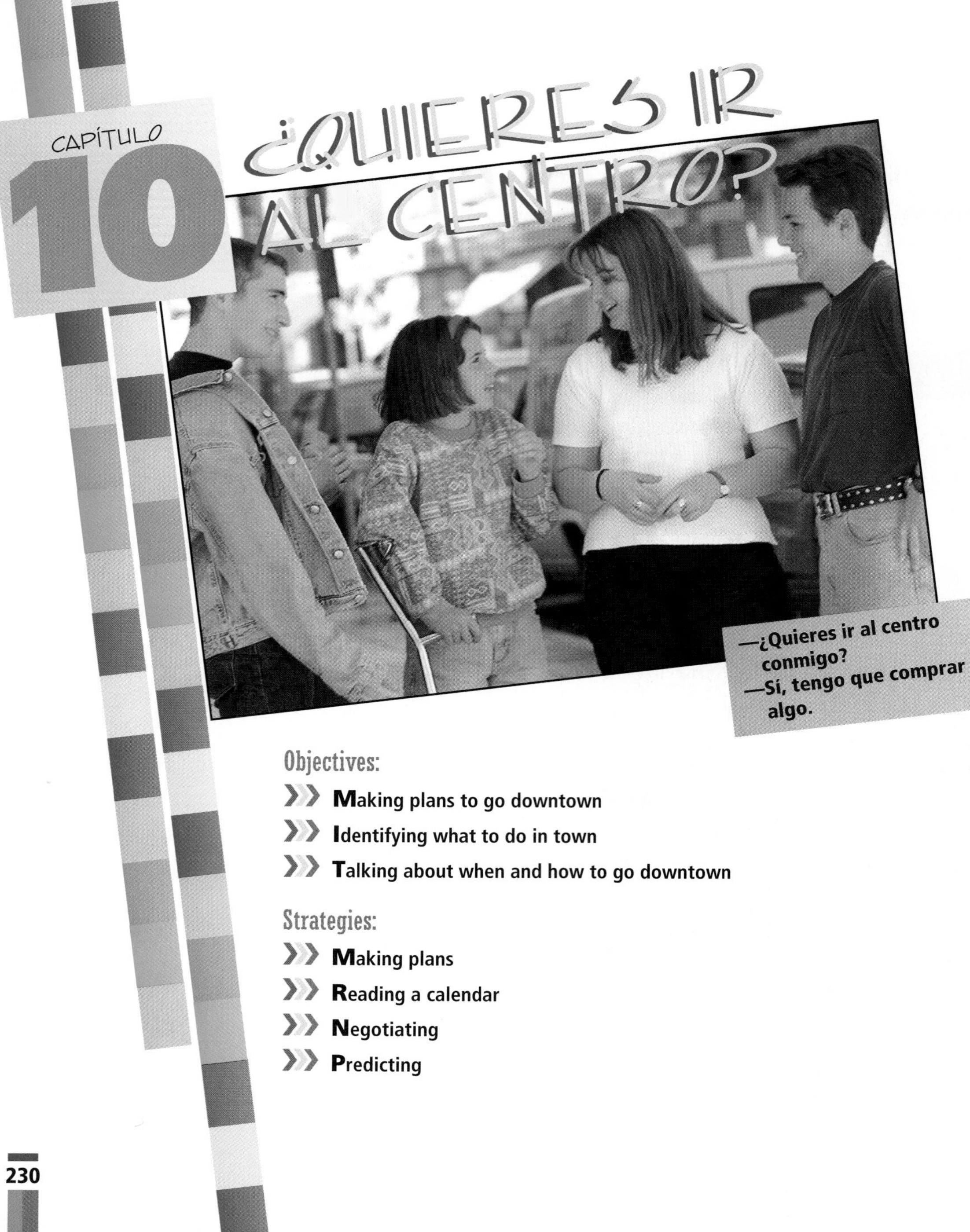
CAPÍTULO
10
¿QUIERES IR AL CENTRO?

—¿Quieres ir al centro conmigo?
—Sí, tengo que comprar algo.

**Objectives:**

- **M**aking plans to go downtown
- **I**dentifying what to do in town
- **T**alking about when and how to go downtown

**Strategies:**

- **M**aking plans
- **R**eading a calendar
- **N**egotiating
- **P**redicting

230

## Video/CD-ROM

**Chapter 10 Video Program**
**Chapter 10 CD-ROM Program**

**These can be used at the end of the chapter as expansion activities.**

# PRIMERA ETAPA

## Preparación

- What do you do when you go downtown?
- Why do you go there?
- How do you invite someone to go with you?

**Learning Strategy:**
*Previewing*

## ¿Para qué?

*¿Para qué?* For what reason?

—Voy al centro para ver a mis amigos.
—Ah, tienes una **cita** con tus amigos.

—Voy al centro para **ir de compras.**
—Ah, quieres comprar algo.

to go shopping
date

—Voy al centro para ir al cine.
—Ah, **tienes ganas de** ver una película.

—Voy al centro para **hacer un mandado** para mi madre.
—Ah, **debes** hacer un mandado.

do an errand
you feel like
you should



### Etapa Support Materials

Workbook: **pp. 122–126**
Transparencies: **#46, #47**
Teacher Tape
Quiz: **Testing Program, p. 109**

Support material, ¿Para qué?:
**Teacher Tape , transparency #46**

### Presentation: ¿Para qué?

Have students look at the drawings on the transparency while they listen to the short conversations on the Teacher Tape. After each conversation ask questions, moving from comprehension of the dialogue (**¿Adónde va para ver a sus amigos?**) to personalized variations (**¿Adónde vas tú para ver a tus amigos?**). If you do not use the transparency and the Teacher Tape, read the short conversations while students look at the pictures in the book.

This **etapa** shows that an idea can be expressed in more than one way. Students need not learn to produce all of the expressions. They should understand both forms and be able to use one of the expressions for each activity. Encourage more-prepared students to learn each expression actively and to interchange them. Have less-prepared students concentrate on one, incorporate it well, then learn the other. It is important for all students to realize that there is always more than one way to express an idea.

***Spanish speakers, ¿Para qué?:*** Ask Spanish speakers for variations to the places and reasons young people go downtown. They may know how to pronounce these variations, many may have never seen how they are written. Help them with the spelling of these variations by writing them on the board or overhead. Have them focus on the more difficult spelling combinations such as the **c** in **cita** and **cine,** the **h** and **c** in **hacer** and the **s** in **paseo.**

***Support material, ¿Para qué?:*** Teacher Tape/CD #1 Track #44 , Transparency #46

## Vocabulary Presentation

Here are some additional questions that you may use while presenting and practicing this new vocabulary: **¿Vas tú al centro a veces para ir de compras? ¿Con quién? ¿Adónde vas? ¿Qué compras? ¿Te gusta el cine? ¿Tienes ganas de ver una película esta noche? ¿Haces mandados para tu madre? ¿Vas a la oficina de correos? ¿al supermercado? ¿Te gusta dar paseos? ¿Dónde? ¿Qué vas a hacer después de la escuela hoy? ¿Tienes ganas de ir al centro para ver las cosas?** Remember: the idea during the presentation is to familiarize students with the meanings and basic structures of these expressions, not to get them to produce complete sentences.

**Ex. A:** pair work

*Support material, Ex. A:* Transparency #47

*More-prepared students, Ex. A:* Have more-prepared students alternate the format of their answers in order to express the same idea in different ways. After finishing each situation, have them ask each other or you ask them personalized questions on the same material.

*Less-prepared students, Ex. A:* Have less-prepared students practice the whole exercise using one expression, then again using another. If the exercise is done in writing, have them leave room after each number to add the alternate expression. Then have them redo the exercise for the third time, looking at their papers and reading both alternatives for each question. This could also be done at the board.



—¿Para qué vas al centro?
—Voy al centro para **dar un paseo.**

take a walk

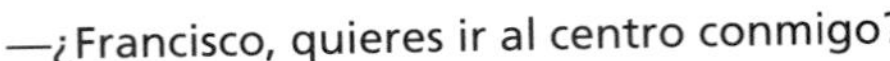

—¿Francisco, quieres ir al centro conmigo?
—¿Para qué?
—Para hacer un mandado para mi padre. Tengo que ir a la farmacia.
—Mm, bueno, quiero comprar un disco compacto. ¡Vamos!
—De acuerdo. ¡Vamos!

# ¡Aquí te toca a ti!

**Learning Strategy:**

*Reporting based on visual cues*

**A. *¿Para qué va al centro?*** Your teacher wants to know why the following students are going downtown. On the basis of the drawings on page 233, explain why. Follow the model.

**Modelo:** ¿Para qué va María al centro?
*Ella va al centro para ver a una amiga.*

*Possible answers, Ex. A:*
1. Él va al centro para ver una película. 2. Ella va al centro para ir al banco. 3. Él va al centro para comprar un disco compacto. 4. Ella va al centro para ir de compras. 5. Ellos van al centro para comer en un restaurante. 6. Ellos van al centro para estudiar en la biblioteca.

1. ¿Para qué va Vicente al centro?

2. ¿Para qué va Anita al centro?

3. ¿Para qué va José al centro?

4. ¿Para qué va Laura al centro?

5. ¿Para qué van Patricio y Julia al centro?

6. ¿Para qué van Mario y Luis al centro?

## Exercise Progression

Ex. A provides an opportunity to work with two ways to express an idea. Ex. B provides open-ended communicative practice with the new vocabulary and expressions.

**Ex. B:** pair work

*Less-prepared students, Ex. B:* Write a list of alternative expressions on the board for less-prepared students to refer to as they do this exercise. Have them use at least two different expressions over the course of the exercise.

*More-prepared students, Ex. B:* Encourage more-prepared students to alternate and vary as much as possible their responses. Afterwards, call on pairs of both groups of students to perform one of the situations for the class.

*Answers, Ex. B:* The answers to Ex. B require no grammatical changes. Students add these cues, following the model: 1. a la biblioteca 2. a la librería 3. a la panadería 4. al banco 5. a la farmacia

*Spanish speakers, Ex. C:* Have students focus on the silent **h** in these words. Perhaps they can enter them in their notebook under **"Palabras con h."** See p. 20 of "To the Teacher" in the Teacher's Edition for a more detailed discussion of special spelling issues unique to Spanish speakers.

## Pronunciation

Additional activities appear in the Laboratory Tape Program.

*Support material, Pronunciación:* Pronunciation Tape



**Learning Strategy:**

*Reporting based on visual clues*

**B. *¿Quieres ir al centro conmigo?*** You are going downtown and invite a friend to go along. When you explain the reason for going, your friend decides to accompany you. Base your reasons for going on the following drawings. Follow the model.

**Modelo:**
—*¿Quieres ir a la oficina de correos conmigo?*
—*¿Para qué?*
—*Tengo que ir a la oficina de correos.*
—*Bueno. Vamos.*

1.

2.

3.

4.

5.

## *Pronunciación: The consonant h*

In Spanish, unlike English, the letter **h** is always silent.

### Práctica

**C.** Listen and repeat as your teacher models the following words.

| | | | |
|---|---|---|---|
| **1.** hay | **4.** hoy | **7.** hablar | **9.** ahora |
| **2.** hospital | **5.** hace | **8.** hispano | **10.** hora |
| **3.** hola | **6.** hotel | | |



## Cultural Expansion

You may want to take this time to point out some of the highlights of Barcelona and its history. Try to bring in some pictures. Begin by asking students what they know about the city.

Have them locate it on the map. Point out that due to its location as a port on the Mediterranean, Barcelona has been Spain's link to many cultures. To understand the people of Barcelona, one must also be familiar with the Catalán-Spanish duality. Cataluña was an independent nation with its own language and parliamentary system long before the formati of the Spanish state. It was one of the main commercial pow of the Mediterranean during the fourteenth and fifteenth ce turies. Later, while Spain was colonizing the Americas and m ing its wealth, Cataluña became an industrialized nation. By the year 1850 it achieved status as the world's fourth manu turing power.

**En el centro de Madrid, España**

# ESTRUCTURA

## The immediate future

| | |
|---|---|
| **Voy a comer.** | *I am going to eat.* |
| **Vamos a estudiar.** | *We are going to study.* |
| ¿Qué **vas a hacer** esta tarde? | What *are you going to do* this afternoon? |
| **Voy a dar** un paseo. | *I am going to take* a walk. |

What you have learned to say in Spanish so far refers mainly to the present or to a general situation. It is now time to learn how to talk about the future. One way to express a future action, especially one that will occur in the not-too-distant future, is to use a present-tense form of **ir + a +** *infinitive.* This structure is equivalent to the English use of *going to + verb.*

| | |
|---|---|
| **Voy a bailar.** | *I'm going to dance.* |
| **Vas a hablar** español. | *You're going to speak* Spanish. |
| **¿Va a comer Juan** en el centro? | *Is John going to eat* downtown? |
| **Vamos a escuchar** la cinta. | *We're going to listen to* the tape. |
| **Uds. van a estudiar.** | *You're going to study.* |
| **Ellos van a dar** un paseo. | *They're going to take* a walk. |

To form the negative, **no** is placed before the conjugated form of **ir.**

| | |
|---|---|
| **No voy a comer** en el centro. | *I'm not going to eat* downtown. |
| **Ellos no van a estudiar.** | *They're not going to study.* |



Since the marriage of Fernando de Aragón to Isabel de Castilla in 1469, Cataluña has had to fight constant suppressions by the Spanish government. Since the end of the Franco regime in 1975, Cataluña has undergone a cultural resurgence. Point out some of the region's world-famous artists: painters Pablo Picasso, Joan Miró, and Salvador Dalí; musician Pablo Casals; and the sculptor and architect Antoni Gaudí. Try to bring in examples of their work.

### Presentation: The immediate future

Since students are already familiar with the conjugation of **ir** and its meaning, begin using the future in a conversational-type question-and- answer format. Start by asking what they are going to do tonight and then, without giving them the opportunity to answer, say what you and others are going to do. Then ask them questions, occasionally summarizing their answers and adding comments. For example: **¿Qué van a hacer Uds. esta noche? Yo voy a comer con mis hijos y voy a ver la televisión un poco. Después voy a preparar las lecciones para mañana y voy a leer un libro divertido.** etc.

After several students have answered correctly, write **ir** + **a** + infinitive on the board and explain the idiomatic nature of this expression. Then proceed with the exercises.

*Spanish speakers:* Most students will know how to conjugate the verb **ir** and how to use it to form this tense, they just don't know that it is called the immediate future tense. It is not necessary to have students focus on the specific names of the various grammatical components mentioned in the **Estructura** sections.

*Suggestion, Ex. D:* These column exercises are meant to provide controlled practice. A possible way to present these would be through the creation of a "word web." On a separate piece of paper, students would draw a web, and then connect elements from the columns in ways that form grammatically correct sentences. (They would have to write in the correct form of the verb in the middle column.) See the diagram below for a sample word web format. Word web formats will vary from exercise to exercise.

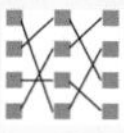

*Spanish speakers, Ex. D:* Have Spanish speakers skip some of the very easy exercises like Ex. D. You might have them come up with their own places to go that reflect the real world in their daily lives. Help them with the spelling of what they come up with.

**Ex. E:** pair work

*Answers, Ex. E:* 1. Voy a estudiar... 2. Va a ver... 3. Van a dar... 4. Van a ir... 5. Voy a comprar...

**Ex. F:** pair work

*More-prepared students, Ex. F:* Have more-prepared students ask two or three others about their plans and then report back, including their own plans, too: **John va a escribir una carta, Mary va a comprar un disco compacto y yo voy a estudiar español.**

## Aquí practicamos

**D.** Use words from each column to form sentences expressing future plans.

| A | B | C |
|---|---|---|
| yo | ir a | dar un paseo |
| Susana | | comer en un restaurante |
| Marcos | | estudiar en la biblioteca |
| nosotros | | comprar un disco compacto |
| Juan y su novia | | mirar un programa de televisión |
| Uds. | | |
| tú | | |
| vosotros | | |

**E.** ***¿Qué vas a hacer el sábado por la tarde* (Saturday afternoon)?**
You are trying to find out what your friends are going to do Saturday afternoon. Your classmates will answer the questions using the expressions in parentheses. Follow the model.

*Modelo:* Marcos, ¿qué vas a hacer el sábado por la tarde? (comer en un restaurante)
*Voy a comer en un restaurante.*

1. Carlos, ¿qué vas a hacer el sábado por la tarde? (estudiar en la biblioteca)
2. ¿Y qué va a hacer Juan? (ver a una amiga en el centro)
3. ¿Y Fernando y su amigo? (dar un paseo)
4. ¿Y Bárbara y Julián? (ir de compras)
5. Marcos, ¿qué vas a hacer? (comprar un disco compacto)

**Learning Strategy:**
*Providing information*

**F.** ***¿Qué vas a hacer este fin de semana* (this weekend)?**
Answer the following questions about your weekend plans.

1. ¿Vas a estudiar español?
2. ¿Vas a leer un libro? ¿Qué libro?
3. ¿Vas a comprar algo?
4. ¿Vas a mirar un programa de televisión? ¿Qué programa?
5. ¿Vas a bailar en una fiesta?
6. ¿Vas a hablar por teléfono con un(a) amigo(a)? ¿Con qué amigo(a)?

## Exercise Progression

Ex. D is a controlled drill designed to review the conjugation of **ir** while practicing it in this new structure. Ex. E provides controlled practice in a question/answer format. Ex. F offers a more personalized communicative exercise.

*Less-prepared students, Ex. F:* Have less-prepared students ask one other and then report back.

*Follow-up, Ex. F:* After students have done the exercise in the singular, have them redo it, using **Uds./nosotros** form. You may wish to have less-prepared students write the questions on the board. Have one student ask a group of others for their plans. Designate one student to answer for the whole group. You may also wish to have more-prepared students reuse the Suggestion for Ex. F.

# SEGUNDA ETAPA

## Preparación

- In this etapa you will be talking about various activities that you do on certain days and at specific times of the day. How do you divide a day into different parts?
- Do you know the names of the days of the week in Spanish?
- How do you ask someone what he or she is going to do on a specific day or during a specific part of a day?

*Learning Strategy:*
*Previewing*

## ¿Cuándo vamos?

HOY | MAÑANA

today / tomorrow

Esta mañana, yo voy a la escuela.

**Mañana por la mañana,** voy a dormir tarde.

*viernes:* Friday
*sábado:* Saturday

This morning / Tomorrow morning

**Esta tarde,** yo voy a estudiar.

**Mañana por la tarde,** voy a ir de compras.

This afternoon / Tomorrow afternoon



### Presentation: ¿Cuándo vamos?

Begin by writing today's date on the board. Have the class repeat: **Hoy es el... .** Then write tomorrow's date and have students say: **Mañana es el... .** Under today's date, write 9:30; have students repeat **esta mañana**. Continue with an afternoon and an evening time. Then have students look at the transparency while you read the captions, having them repeat. Finally have them listen to the Teacher Tape recording of the conversation. Then ask comprehension questions such as, **¿Adónde van? ¿Cuándo? ¿Esta mañana?** etc.

If you do not use the transparency and the Teacher Tape, have students look at the pictures in the book while you read the captions, having them repeat. Then read the dialogue and follow up with comprehension questions. Before proceeding to the exercises, ask personalized questions: **¿Vas a estudiar esta noche? ¿Vas a escribir una carta esta tarde? ¿Cuándo vas a escribir?**

***Spanish speakers, ¿Cuándo vamos?:*** Ask Spanish speakers for variations of times and the things to do that are introduced here. Help them with the spelling of these variations by writing them on the board or overhead. You may want to point out the written accent on **televisión.**

***Support material, ¿Cuándo vamos?:***
Teacher Tape/CD #1 Track #46, Transparency #48

### Etapa Support Materials

Workbook: **pp. 127–131**
Transparency: **#48**
Teacher Tape

Quiz: **Testing Program, p. 112**
Support material, ¿Cuándo vamos?:
**Teacher Tape , transparency #48**

**Ex. A:** pair work

*Ex. A: Partners*

- Direct students to form pairs and sit or stand back-to-back.
- Distribute the questions from Ex. A to one student and drawings indicating dates and times of day to the other.
- Tell the student with the questions to begin by asking **¿Cuándo van a ir al cine tus padres?** The partner answers, using an appropriate date and time of day chosen from the drawings.
- After three questions, tell students to switch roles. The second student asks a question, and the first student answers with a different time of day than the one used by the second student.
- Direct the pairs to continue until finished. Then tell them to turn toward each other to make up questions about other students in the class.
- Reconvene the class as a whole and have the pairs ask their personalized questions.

*Spanish speakers, Ex. A:* Remind students that **marzo** is spelled with a **z.**

*Answers, Ex. A:* 1. Ellos van al cine esta noche. 2. Él va al centro mañana por la tarde. 3. Ella va a estudiar esta mañana. 4. Él va a comprar el disco compacto mañana por la mañana. 5. Voy a ver a mis amigos mañana por la noche. 6. Mis hermanos van a hacer el mandado esta tarde.

Tonight / Tomorrow night

**Esta noche,** yo voy a mirar la televisión en casa.

**Mañana por la noche,** voy a ver a mis amigos en el cine.

—¿Quieres ir al centro conmigo? Tengo que ir a la oficina de correos.
—Sí, yo también. Tengo que hacer un mandado para mi padre. ¿Cuándo quieres ir? ¿Esta mañana?
—No, es imposible. **No puedo ir.** Tengo que estudiar hasta las 12:00. ¿Esta tarde? **¿Está bien?**
—Sí, está bien. Vamos al centro esta tarde.

I can't go.
Is that O.K.?

## ¡Aquí te toca a ti!

**A. *¿Cuándo vas al centro?*** Based on the drawings below and on page 243, indicate when the following activities take place. Today's date is the fifth of March.

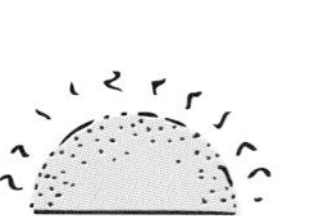
la mañana

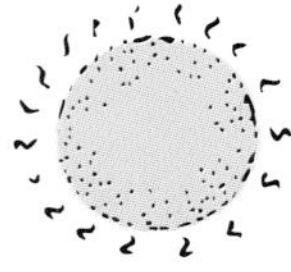
la tarde

la noche

¿Cuándo va Anita al centro?
*Ella va al centro esta noche.*

el 5 de marzo

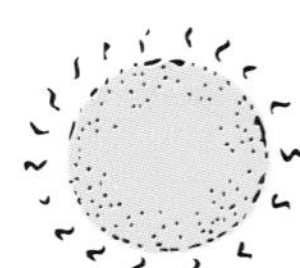

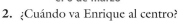

1. el 5 de marzo — ¿Cuándo van a ir al cine tus padres?
2. el 6 de marzo — ¿Cuándo va Enrique al centro?
3. el 5 de marzo — ¿Cuándo va a estudiar tu hermana?



### Exercise Progression

Ex. A provides controlled practice with the vocabulary. Ex. B on the following page introduces these expressions into typical short exchanges and presents conversational fillers and helpers, such as, **¿Está bien?; No es posible; Claro que sí; Sí, por supuesto.**

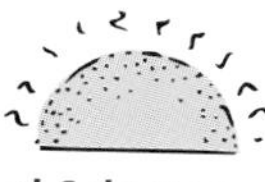

el 6 de marzo

4. ¿Cuándo va a comprar Julián el disco compacto?

el 6 de marzo

5. ¿Cuándo vas a ver a tus amigos?

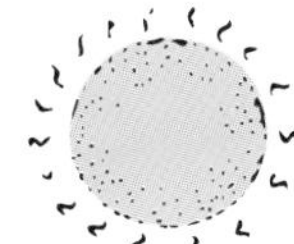

el 5 de marzo

6. ¿Cuándo van a hacer el mandado tus hermanos?

**B. ¿Cuándo quieres ir?** Using the information provided, imitate the model conversations.

Modelo: ir al cine, esta noche / sí
*—¿Quieres ir al cine conmigo?*
*—Sí. ¿Cuándo quieres ir?*
*—Esta noche. ¿Está bien?*
*—Sí, por supuesto. Vamos al cine esta noche.*

1. ir al centro, esta noche / sí
2. ir a la biblioteca, mañana por la tarde / sí
3. ir a la piscina, mañana por la tarde / sí

Modelo: ir al centro, esta tarde / no (trabajar) / mañana por la tarde / sí
*—¿Quieres ir al centro conmigo?*
*—Sí, ¿cuándo quieres ir?*
*—Esta tarde. ¿Está bien?*
*—No, es imposible. Tengo que trabajar. ¿Mañana por la tarde?*
*—Claro que sí. Vamos al centro mañana por la tarde.*

4. ir al museo, esta tarde / no (hacer un mandado) / mañana por la tarde / sí
5. dar un paseo, esta mañana / no (dormir) / esta tarde / sí
6. ir al cine, esta noche / no (estudiar) / mañana por la noche / sí

# Repaso

**C. Preguntas** Your partner will play the role of an exchange student who has just arrived at your school. He or she wants to get to know you. Answer his or her questions (below and on page 244), paying close attention to whether each question is general and therefore requires the present tense, or whether it deals with a specific future time and thus calls for **ir + a +** *infinitive*.

**Learning Strategies:**

*Indicators of time, providing information*

1. ¿Estudias mucho? ¿Vas a estudiar esta noche?
2. Usualmente, ¿qué haces por la noche? ¿Qué vas a hacer esta noche?



**Ex. B:** pair work

***Less-prepared students, Ex. B:*** Encourage less-prepared students to use one or two different expressions as they do the dialogues.

***More-prepared students, Ex. B:*** Encourage more-prepared students to experiment with variations (see Reteaching, p. 238). Afterwards, call on students from both groups to perform a sample for the class.

***Follow-up, Ex. B:*** Have each student in the class write one or two cues (**ir al cine/mañana por la tarde, hacer un mandado/esta tarde,** etc.). Then redistribute the cues and have students work out the dialogues. Write a list of conversational fillers such as **por supuesto** on the board for students to use.

**Ex. C:** role play

***More-prepared students, Ex. C:*** Have more-prepared students write up their own double sets of questions as they create a new conversation similar to the book model. They can take turns being the exchange student. You may wish to have some students perform for the class.

*Less-prepared students, Ex. C:* Emphasize the importance of the different time frames to less-prepared students by continuing to ask them double questions in a personalized format. For example: **¿Tú estudias a menudo? ¿Tú vas a estudiar esta noche?** Try to use vocabulary that students know best.

## Presentation: The days of the week

First, have students repeat the days of the week. Then write on the board today's date and the dates for the next six days. Ask: **¿Qué día es hoy? Ah, hoy es (lunes, el 9 de...). Y el 10 de..., ¿es (miércoles)? Ah, bien, es (martes).** etc. Continue by writing the days of the week on the board, beginning with **lunes**. Then write **el** before the days and make a statement with each one. Explain that when you use an article before the days of the week, it means *on.* Then make more statements (with follow-up questions) using both **el** or **los** before the days mentioned. You might also want to add **por la noche,** etc. For example: **Yo voy de compras los sábados. ¿Y tú? Yo voy a una fiesta el viernes por la noche. ¿Tú vas a una fiesta el viernes por la noche también?** etc.

Have students point out which two days are written with an accent mark. Then write **fin de semana** on the board and explain its meaning in Spanish using the days of the week. For example: **Me gusta mucho el fin de semana. Los viernes por la noche, voy a comer en un restaurante y voy al cine. Los sábados voy de compras y leo un buen libro. También trabajo en la casa. Los domingos... ¿Te gusta también el fin de semana? ¿Qué te gusta hacer?** etc.



3. ¿Vas frecuentemente al centro? ¿Qué haces en el centro? ¿Vas al centro mañana?
4. ¿Estudias español? ¿ruso? ¿chino? ¿francés? ¿Vas a estudiar otra lengua?
5. ¿Te gusta dar un paseo? ¿Vas a dar un paseo esta noche?

## ESTRUCTURA

### *The days of the week*

| | |
|---|---|
| —**¿Qué día es hoy?** | —*What day is it today?* |
| —Es **miércoles**. | —It is *Wednesday.* |
| **El jueves** yo voy al cine. | *On Thursday* I'm going to the movies. |
| **El domingo** vamos a dar un paseo. | *On Sunday* we're going to take a walk. |
| **Los domingos** vamos a la iglesia. | *On Sundays* we go to church. |
| **Los sábados** no vamos a la escuela. | *On Saturdays* we don't go to school. |

To express the idea *on a certain day* or *days*, use the definite article **el** or **los**. Note that in the first example, when you are simply telling what day it is, the article is omitted.

In Spanish the days of the week are:

| | | |
|---|---|---|
| **lunes** *(Monday)* | **jueves** *(Thursday)* | **sábado** *(Saturday)* |
| **martes** *(Tuesday)* | **viernes** *(Friday)* | **domingo** *(Sunday)* |
| **miércoles** *(Wednesday)* | | |

Spanish speakers consider the week to begin on Monday and end on Sunday. The names of the days are masculine and are not capitalized.

## Aquí practicamos

**D. *Hoy es...*** Form questions using the day indicated. Then, answer each question negatively using the following day in your response. Follow the model.

lunes
*¿Es hoy lunes?*
*No, hoy no es lunes. Hoy es martes.*

1. jueves
2. sábado
3. miércoles
4. domingo
5. viernes
6. martes



*Spanish speakers, The days of the week:* Everyone knows the days of the week, but not everyone may know how to spell them. Have Spanish speakers focus on the **j** of **jueves** and the **v** of **viernes.**

**Ex. D:**  pair work

*Answers, Ex. D:* 1. No, hoy no es jueves. Hoy es viernes. 2. ...sábado. Es domingo. 3. ...miércoles. Es jueves. 4. ...domingo. Es lunes. 5. ...viernes. Es sábado. 6. ...martes. Es miércoles.

*Follow-up, Ex. D:* It is important to have students work o recognizing the time frame of questions (present, general or specific, future). Continue asking students double questions. F example: **¿Tú vas de compras a veces con tus padres? ¿Vas a ir de compras esta noche?** etc. Suggested expressions: **ver la televisión a menudo, escuchar discos co pactos de vez en cuando,** etc.

**E. *Ellos llegan el jueves.*** Some students from Bolivia are going to visit your school. They come from different cities and will arrive on different dates. Using the following calendar, indicate on what day of the week various students will arrive. Follow the model.

Miguel va a llegar el 18.
*Ah, él llega el jueves.*

1. Enrique va a llegar el 15.
2. Mario y Jaime van a llegar el 17.
3. María y Anita van a llegar el 20.
4. Francisco va a llegar el 21.
5. Roberto va a llegar el 16.
6. Todos los otros *(All the others)* van a llegar el 19.

**Learning Strategy:**

Reading a calendar

| ENERO | | | | | | |
|---|---|---|---|---|---|---|
| L | M | M | J | V | S | D |
| 15 | 16 | 17 | 18 | 19 | 20 | 21 |

## Nota gramatical

### The verb hacer

The verb **hacer** *(to do, make)* is conjugated as follows:

| *hacer* | | | |
|---|---|---|---|
| yo | **hago** | nosotros(as) | **hacemos** |
| tú | **haces** | vosotros(as) | **hacéis** |
| él / ella / Ud. | **hace** | ellos / ellas / Uds. | **hacen** |

Note that, except for the **yo** form **(hago), hacer** is conjugated in the same way as the other regular **-er** verbs you have studied.



### Presentation: The verb hacer

Begin by asking, in English, what several students are going to do later in the week. Point out that while a form of the verb *to do* is part of the question, it is not part of the answer. The response contains a form of the verb that expresses what they will do, but not the verb *to do* itself. Then present the verb in a manner similar to other verbs that you have presented, making statements and then asking follow-up questions, etc. **Yo hago ejercicios a menudo. ¿Haces tú ejercicios a menudo también?** Continue by writing the verb on the board, and have students point out its similarities and differences from other verbs that they have studied.

***Spanish speakers, The verb hacer:*** Many students will already know this verb and how to conjugate it, but many will never have been taught to spell the forms. Have them focus on the **h** and on the **c** as they learn to spell these verb forms.

### Exercise Progression

Ex. D provides mechanical practice with the days of the week; you do not need to follow the order of the questions in the book. Ex. E offers controlled yet meaningful practice.

Ex. F:  pair work

 writing

*Answers, Ex. F:* 1. hace Anita, haces tú, hacen Uds., hacen Susana y Enrique, hago yo, hacéis vosotros 2. vas a hacer tú, van a hacer Uds., va a hacer Alberto, voy a hacer yo, van a hacer Linda y Mario, vais a hacer vosotros

*Spanish speakers, Ex. F:* Have Spanish speakers skip some of the very easy exercises like this one.

**Ex. G:** pair work

*Answers, Ex. G:* 1. ...mira la televisión. 2. ...come en un restaurante. 3. ...van al cine. 4. ...va de compras. 5. ...dan un paseo.

**Ex. H:** pair work

*Answers, Ex. H:* 1. ...va a escuchar discos compactos. 2. ...va a estudiar. 3. ...van a ir al museo. 4. ...va a ver a una amiga. 5. ...van a hacer un mandado.



When asked a question that includes **hacer** or one of its forms, you normally answer with the verb that expresses what it is you do. For example:

| | |
|---|---|
| —¿Qué **haces** los lunes? | What *do you do* on Mondays? |
| —**Voy** a la escuela. | *I go* to school. |
| —¿Qué **vas a hacer** el viernes? | What *are you going to do* on Friday? |
| —**Voy a estudiar.** | *I'm going to study.* |

**F.** Replace the words in italics, making all necessary changes.

1. ¿Qué hace *Juan* los sábados? (Anita / tú / Uds. / Susana y Enrique / yo / vosotros)
2. ¿Qué van a hacer *ellos* el domingo por la tarde? (tú / Uds. / Alberto / yo / Linda y Mario / vosotros)

**G. *¿Qué hace Juan... ?*** Someone asks you what your friends do on a certain day of the week. Respond with what is in parentheses. Follow the model.

**Modelo:** ¿Qué hace Martín los lunes por la noche? (estudiar)
*Martín estudia.*

1. ¿Qué hace Martín los martes por la noche? (mirar la televisión)
2. ¿Qué hace Lucía los viernes? (comer en un restaurante)
3. ¿Qué hacen Elisa y Jaime los sábados por la noche? (ir al cine)
4. ¿Qué hace Marina los jueves en el centro? (ir de compras)
5. ¿Qué hacen Mario y Susana los domingos? (dar un paseo)

**H. *¿Qué va a hacer Timoteo... ?*** Someone asks you what your friends are going to do on a certain day. Respond with what is in parentheses. Follow the model.

¿Qué va a hacer Timoteo esta noche? (leer)
*Timoteo va a leer esta noche.*

1. ¿Qué va a hacer José esta noche? (escuchar discos compactos)
2. ¿Qué va a hacer Ernestina el viernes? (estudiar)
3. ¿Qué van a hacer Antonio y Catarina mañana? (ir al museo)
4. ¿Qué va a hacer Pepita en el centro el martes? (ver a una amiga)
5. ¿Qué van a hacer Teodoro y Alicia el sábado? (hacer un mandado)



## Exercise Progression

Exs. F and G provide controlled practice with the verb **hacer** and with the new vocabulary from this chapter. Ex. H is a more open-ended communicative activity.

# Aquí escuchamos:

## "¿Cuándo vamos?"

### Antes de escuchar

Think about when you do certain things during the day. Before you listen to the short conversation between Elena and Francisco think about (1) how she will invite him to do something, (2) how he will agree or disagree, and (3) how they will settle on a time of day.

START

**Learning Strategy:**

*Listening for details*

### Después de escuchar

1. What does Elena have to do downtown?
2. Why does Francisco have to go downtown?
3. Why can't Francisco go in the morning?
4. When do they decide to go?
5. How does Francisco say "no way"?

## ¡Adelante!

EJERCICIO ORAL

*I.* ***¿Qué haces los fines de semana?*** When your teacher gives you the signal, circulate around the room and ask your classmates what they do on the weekends. Keep track of your findings and be ready to report back to the class. See how many classmates you can ask—you won't have much time!

EJERCICIO ESCRITO

*J.* ***Este fin de semana*** Write a note to a friend, explaining what you are going to do this weekend. Include at least five activities. Be sure to ask what your friend is going to do.

**Learning Strategies:**

*Listing, requesting and providing information, organizing ideas in a letter*



***Spanish speakers, Ex. I:*** Most Spanish speakers already have a command of a variety of Spanish that is used in informal, very familiar contexts. This situation is a fairly informal one, but have the students focus on using that vocabulary that may be new for them. Emphasize that it may be necessary to use such vocabulary when talking to speakers who are from other parts of the Spanish-speaking world. Again, remember to be sensitive and accept how the students do it the first time. What they have said may be totally appropriate in their speech community. This is a good place to have them focus on the differences between how they may say something in their speech community and how the book is teaching them to express this. Remember, rather than "correcting" how they speak, your main objective is to expand the range of real-world contexts in which these students can use Spanish.

***Suggestion, Ex. J:*** After students write their notes, have them exchange papers and edit each other's work. Try pairing-up a less-prepared student with a more-prepared one for this exercise.

***Spanish speakers, Ex. J:*** Always have Spanish speakers fully carry out this activity. Remember, while many of them already speak and understand spoken Spanish, they may not know how to write the language. This is a good place to start building the basic literacy skills in Spanish. Have them pay special attention to the spelling of the vocabulary that has been introduced in this **etapa;** especially those words that may have more difficult spelling combinations. This is a good place to have them engage in peer-editing. Have them look at the written work of a partner and focus on the spelling.

***panish speakers, Aquí escuchamos:*** Most anish speakers, even those that are third or fourth generation, ll understand spoken Spanish. The exercises that accompany s section should pose relatively little problem for Spanish eakers. They should, however, be directed to focus on "listen- in context" to any vocabulary that may be new for them.

***Answers, Aquí escuchamos:*** 1. go to the post office 2. to do an errand for his mother 3. he studies until noon 4. in the afternoon 5. "No, es imposible."

***Support material, Aquí escuchamos:*** Teacher Tape/CD #1 Track #47 and Tapescript

## Presentation: ¿Cómo prefieres ir, en coche o a pie?

Have students repeat the expressions while looking at the transparency. Then make false statements and have students correct them. For example: **¿El Sr. Valdés va en su coche? No, él va en metro,** etc. Then have students listen to the short scene on the Teacher Tape. Ask comprehension questions such as, **¿Adónde quiere ir Andrés? ¿Cómo van a ir allí?** etc. Then replay the tape and have students repeat the dialogue.

If you do not use the transparency, have students repeat the expressions as they look at the pictures in the book. Then tell them in a short monologue about a Spanish family, **los García: Los Sres. García trabajan. El Sr. García va a su oficina en metro. La Sra. García va en autobús. Sus hijos van a la escuela. Su hija va en bicicleta. Su hijo va a pie.** Act out or draw on the board the various means of transportation. Then proceed as above with the taped dialogue.

***Support material, ¿Cómo prefieres ir, en coche o a pie?:*** Teacher Tape/CD #1 Track #48, Transparency #49

# TERCERA ETAPA

### Preparación

*Learning Strategy:* *Previewing*

- **H**ow do you get around town? Car? Bus? Bike?
- **H**ow do you ask someone if he or she can do something?
- **H**ow do you politely say you can't do something?

## ¿Cómo prefieres ir, en coche o a pie?

*a pie:* on foot

### PARA IR AL CENTRO

El Sr. Valdés va en metro.

La Sra. Candelaria va en coche.

La Sra. López va en autobús.

El Sr. Cano va en taxi.



## Etapa Support Materials

Workbook: pp. 132–136
Transparency: #49
Listening Activity masters: p. 67
Tapescript: p. 99
Teacher Tape

Quiz: Testing Program, p. 114
Chapter Test: Testing Program, p. 117

Support material, **¿Cómo prefieres ir... ?:** Teacher Tape, transparency #49

Pedro va en bicicleta.

Fernando va a pie.

**Andrés:** ¿Quieres ir al Museo del Prado hoy?
**Gabriela:** Sí. Me gustan las pinturas de Velázquez. ¿Vamos a pie?
**Andrés:** No. Está muy lejos. Vamos en metro.
**Gabriela:** Bien, de acuerdo. Vamos a tomar el metro.

## ¡Aquí te toca a ti!

**A. *¿Cómo van?*** Based on the drawings below, tell how each person gets around town. Follow the model.

Jorge va...
*Jorge va en bicicleta.*

1. Francisco va...

2. La Sra. Fernández va...

3. Carlos va...

4. Marta va...

5. El Sr. González va...

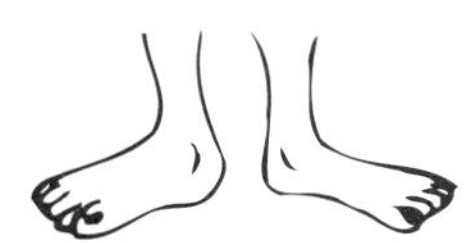

6. Santiago y su hermana van...

7. El Sr. López va...



***Spanish speakers:*** Ask Spanish speakers for variations of modes of transportation that are listed here. It is common for people in Mexico to call a bus a **camión** while in Puerto Rico, Cuba, and the Dominican Republic the word **guagua** is heard. You may also hear **carro** and **auto** for **coche.** Allow the students to use these words in the subsequent exercises since to use a word like **autobús** in Puerto Rico would sound funny there just as it would sound funny in Mexico. Although they may know how to pronounce these variations, many may have never seen how they are written. Help them with the spelling of these variations by writing them on the board or overhead.

**Ex. A:**  pair work

***Answers, Ex. A:*** 1. en autobús 2. en metro 3. a pie 4. en bicicleta 5. en coche 6. a pie 7. en taxi

### Exercise Progression

Ex. A focuses directly on vocabulary. On the following page, Ex. B uses vocabulary in a structured, communicative format; Ex. C incorporates other structures and vocabulary from the chapter in a question/answer review format.

**Ex. B:** pair work

*Suggestions, Ex. B:* When possible, we introduce functional expressions in exercises rather than in isolated lists, in order to provide for immediate practice with the expressions: e.g., **claro que sí, de acuerdo.** Encourage students to try several ways of performing the same function (here, agreeing to a suggestion). By learning to use these functional expressions in several different contexts, they will be taking an important step in becoming truly communicative in the language, even though the "quantity" of Spanish they know may still be quite limited. One way of emphasizing these expressions is to have students do the exercise first in pairs. Then correct the exercise with the whole class, eliciting alternative versions and expressions wherever appropriate. See also Follow-up and More- and Less-prepared notes for Ex. B, p. 243.

**Ex. C:** pair work

*Suggestions, Ex. C:* Have students work in pairs and then ask them follow-up questions to give them the opportunity to report back. You might also want to do it as a **pregúntale** exercise with students' books closed to practice listening comprehension. Pair-up students of equal abilities, or pair-up a more-prepared with a less-prepared student for student-to-student teaching and learning.

**B. *¿Tú quieres ir... ?*** You invite a friend to go somewhere with you. He or she responds affirmatively, saying **"claro que sí."** Your friend then suggests a way of going there, but you have a different idea. Follow the model.

**Modelo:** museo / metro / a pie
*—¿Quieres ir al museo?*
*—Claro que sí. ¿Vamos en metro?*
*—No. ¡Vamos a pie!*
*—De acuerdo. Vamos a pie.*

1. cine / a pie / autobús
2. centro / autobús / coche
3. biblioteca / taxi / metro
4. parque / coche / a pie
5. restaurante / metro / autobús
6. farmacia / metro / autobús
7. estadio / bicicleta / a pie
8. mercado / a pie / coche

## Repaso

**C. *Intercambio*** Ask the following questions of a classmate, who will answer them. Follow the model.

1. ¿Qué tienes ganas de hacer el sábado próximo *(next)*?
2. ¿Qué haces los domingos por la mañana?
3. ¿Qué haces los lunes por la mañana? ¿Por la tarde?
4. ¿Cuándo estudias? ¿Cómo vas a la escuela? ¿Cuándo vas al centro? ¿Para qué? ¿Cuándo vas al cine?

## ESTRUCTURA

### *The verb poder (to be able to)*

To express in Spanish whether you are able or not able to do something, use the irregular verb **poder.**

| *poder* | | | |
|---|---|---|---|
| yo | **puedo** | nosotros(as) | **podemos** |
| tú | **puedes** | vosotros(as) | **podéis** |
| él / ella / Ud. | **puede** | ellos / ellas / Uds. | **pueden** |



*Presentation: The verb **poder**:* Begin by making **yo** statements and then ask follow-up questions based on the statements. Proceed in a manner similar to the way in which you have presented other verbs. (See the Teacher's Notes on pp. 127 and 160.) **Yo quiero ir al cine hoy pero no puedo. Tengo que preparar las lecciones para mañana. ¿Puedes tú ir al cine hoy?** etc. After presenting all of the forms, write the conjugation on the board and have students point out its irregularities. Stress the fact that there is no stem change in the **nosotros** form.

*Spanish speakers, The verb **poder**:* Most students will know this verb, they just don't know how to spell the forms. One possible variation might occur in the **nosotros** form where some students, by analogy with the other forms, will say **"puedemos."** This is a good place to have them focus on the more widely accepted form **"podemos."**

You will note that the **o** of the stem of the verb **poder** becomes **ue** in all forms except **nosotros** and **vosotros.** Later in this book you will learn other verbs that follow this pattern.

| | |
|---|---|
| —**¿Puedes** ir al cine conmigo? | *Can you* go to the movies with me? |
| —Sí, **puedo** ir. | Yes, *I can* go. |

To say you cannot do something, place **no** before the conjugated form of **poder.**

| | |
|---|---|
| —**¿Puede** hablar Marcos francés? | *Can* Marcos speak French? |
| —No, **no puede** hablar francés, pero **puede** hablar español. | No, *he can't* speak French, but *he can* speak Spanish. |
| —**¿Puedes** ir al centro ahora? | *Can you* go downtown now? |
| —No, **no puedo** ir. | No, *I can't* go. |

Note in the above examples that the conjugated form of the verb **poder** can be followed directly by an infinitive.

## Aquí repasamos

**D.** Tell what the following people can do, using words from each column.

| A | B | C |
|---|---|---|
| Linda | poder | ir al centro |
| yo | | ir a un restaurante |
| tú | | ir al concierto |
| Gregorio y Verónica | | ir al museo |
| Uds. | | ir al cine |
| nosotros | | |

**E.** ***Hoy no puedo...*** A classmate invites you to do something. You cannot do it at the time he or she suggests, but you suggest another time when you can. Follow the model.

ir al cine, hoy / sábado por la noche
—*¿Puedes ir al cine hoy?*
—*No, hoy no puedo, pero puedo ir el sábado por la noche.*

1. ir al centro, ahora / viernes por la tarde
2. ir a un restaurante, esta noche / mañana por la noche
3. ir al museo, esta tarde / domingo por la tarde
4. ir al concierto, esta semana / la semana próxima
5. ir de compras, esta mañana / sábado por la mañana

**¿Qué crees?**

***Las meninas*** **is a famous painting by:**

**a) Diego Rivera**
**b) Diego Velásquez**
**c) Francisco de Goya**
**d) Pablo Picasso**

**respuesta**



***Suggestion, Ex. D:*** These column exercises are meant to provide controlled practice. A possible way to present these would be through the creation of a "word web." On a separate piece of paper, students would draw a web, and then connect elements from the columns in ways that form grammatically correct sentences. (They would have to write in the correct form of the verb in the middle column.) See the diagram below for an sample word web format. Word web formats will vary from exercise to exercise.

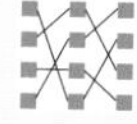

***Spanish speakers, Ex. D:*** Have Spanish speakers skip some of the very easy exercises like Ex. D. You might have them come up with their own places to go that reflect the real world and their daily lives.

**Ex. E:**  pair work

## Exercise Progression

Ex. D: is a controlled drill that focuses on the forms of the new verb. Ex. E provides controlled practice in a more communicative format.

*Ex. F:* This activity provides preparation for the **Ya llegamos** section at the end of Unit 4.

## Cultural Expansion

The **Museo del Prado** is one of Madrid's greatest attractions. It houses what is without a doubt the world's greatest collection of Spanish paintings, in addition to hundreds of foreign masterpieces. It was commissioned to be built by Charles III at the end of the eighteenth century and was supposed to serve as a museum of natural history. Its construction was interrupted by the Napoleonic wars and it wasn't finished until 1819. It was then opened up as an art museum and filled with treasures collected by Spain's Hapsburg and Bourbon kings and other patrons of the arts, as well as by monasteries and convents from all over the country. Try to bring in some pictures of paintings by El Greco, Velázquez, Goya, or some of the other artists mentioned. Suggestions: *Las Meninas* by Velázquez, *Nobleman with a Hand on His Chest* by El Greco, the *Majas* and *Executions of the Rioters* by Goya, *Holy Family with a Little Bird* by Murillo.



**F. No, no puedo.** You suggest an activity to a friend. He or she is interested, but cannot do it on the day you have proposed and gives you his or her reason why not. You then suggest a different day, which is fine with your friend. Follow the model.

dar un paseo, mañana / trabajar / sábado
*—¿Puedes dar un paseo mañana?*
*—No, no puedo. Tengo que trabajar.*
*—¿El sábado? ¿Está bien?*
*—Sí. Vamos a dar un paseo el sábado.*

1. ir al centro, esta noche / ir al cine con mis padres / mañana por la noche
2. hacer un mandado, el sábado / trabajar / domingo
3. ir al museo, esta tarde / estudiar / sábado
4. ir a tomar un café, el sábado / ir de compras con mi madre / domingo
5. ir al cine, mañana / hacer un mandado / viernes
6. ir a la biblioteca, hoy / ver a un amigo / martes

*Learning Strategy:*

*Reading for cultural information*

## COMENTARIOS CULTURALES

### El Museo del Prado

**This museum is located in Madrid and is considered one of the most important art museums in the world. It contains over 6,000 works by such Spanish artists as Goya, Velásquez, El Greco, Murillo, and Zurbarán. It also exhibits works of other artists such as Bosch, Dürer, Rafael, Tiziano, Tintoretto, and Rubens.**

 b



*Spanish speakers, Aquí escuchamos:* Most Spanish speakers, even those that are third or fourth generation, will understand spoken Spanish. The exercises that accompany this section should pose relatively little problem for Spanish speakers. They should, however, be directed to focus on "listening in context" to any vocabulary that may be new for them.

*Answers, Aquí escuchamos:* 1. Museo del Pra 2. in the afternoon 3. the next morning 4. by train 5. "S icómo no!"

# Aquí escuchamos:
## "¿Puedes ir conmigo?"

### Antes de escuchar

**Think about inviting someone to accompany you to do something. Before you listen to the short conversation between Elena and Francisco, try to predict (1) how she will invite him to do something, (2) how he will agree or disagree, and (3) how they will settle on a means of transportation.**

START

**Learning Strategy:**
*Previewing*

### Después de escuchar

1. **Where does Elena invite Francisco?**
2. **When does she want to go?**
3. **When does Francisco suggest they go?**
4. **How do they decide to go?**
5. **What phrase does Elena use to agree when Francisco suggests a new time?**

**Learning Strategy:**
*Listening for details*

EJERCICIO ORAL

**G. *¿Puedes ir conmigo?*** Ask a classmate if she or he can do something with you. When you get an affirmative response, arrange a day, a time, and a place to meet. Then agree on a means of transportation.

**Learning Strategy:**
*Negotiating*

EJERCICIO ESCRITO

**H. *El sábado…*** Write a short note to a classmate in which you (1) ask if he or she can accompany you to do something on Saturday. Mention (2) where you want to go and (3) what you plan to do when you get there, as well as (4) how you expect to get there. Be sure to (5) suggest a time of day.

**Learning Strategies:**
*Organizing ideas in an invitation, providing information*



**Ex. H:** pair work

*Ex. H:* This activity provides preparation for the **Ya llegamos** section at the end of Unit 4.

*Less-prepared students, Ex. H:* Brainstorm with less-prepared students places, ways and reasons to go there. Have them jot down some of these possibilities, or assign a "secretary" to list some of them on the board before they write.

*More-prepared students, Ex. H:* Encourage more-prepared students to be creative and add alternate plans and/or means of transportation.

*Spanish speakers, Ex. H:* Always have Spanish speakers fully carry out this activity. Remember, while many of them already speak and understand spoken Spanish, they may not know how to write the language. This is a good place to start building the basic literacy skills in Spanish that they may lack. Have them pay special attention to the spelling of the vocabulary that has been introduced in this **etapa**; especially those words that may have more difficult spelling combinations. This is a good place to have them engage in peer-editing. Have them look at the written work of a partner and focus on the spelling.

*Support material, Aquí escuchamos:* Teacher Tape/CD #1 Track #49 and Tapescript

*panish speakers, Ex. G:* Most Spanish speakers eady have a command of a variety of Spanish that is used in ormal, very familiar contexts. This situation is a fairly inforl one, but have the students focus on using vocabulary that y be new for them. Emphasize that it may be necessary to such vocabulary when talking to speakers who are from er parts of the Spanish-speaking world. Again, remember to sensitive and accept how the students do it the first time. at they have said may be totally appropriate in their speech nmunity. This is a good place to have them focus on the difences between how they may say something in their speech nmunity and how the book is teaching them to express this. Remember, rather than "correcting" how they speak, your main objective is to expand the range of real-world contexts in which these students can use Spanish.

**Ex. G:** pair work

*Reteaching, Ex. G:* First review the days of the week. Then ask students questions such as, **¿Qué día es hoy? ¿Qué días vamos a la escuela? ¿Qué días no vamos a la escuela?** This activity provides preparation for the **Ya llegamos** section at the end of Unit 4.

## Chapter Culminating Activity

pair work

Have students write to a classmate asking if they can do something together. Have all students exchange notes with each other. Instruct them to write an answer saying they can't go at the suggested day or time, but offering an alternative. Students can exchange notes one more time, this time writing to agree to the alternative. Remind all students to use communicative, filler phrases, like **claro que sí** in their responses.

*Support material, Capítulo 10:* Improvised Conversation, Teacher Tape/CD #1 Track #50 and Tapescript; Lab Manual listening activities, Laboratory Program, Tapescript, and Teacher's Edition of the Workbook/Lab Manual

# Vocabulario

## Para charlar

*Para hablar de planes*

ir + a + *infinitive*
poder + *infinitive*
tener ganas + de + *infinitive*

*Para decir para qué vas*

Voy a dar un paseo.
...hacer un mandado.
...ir de compras.
...ver a un amigo.

*Para preguntar qué día es*

¿Qué día es hoy?

*Para decir cuándo*

Vamos esta mañana.
...esta tarde.
...hoy.
...mañana.
...mañana por la mañana.
...mañana por la tarde.
...mañana por la noche.

*Para decir sí o no*

¡Claro que sí!
Sí, puedo.
Sí, tengo ganas de...
Es imposible.
No, no puedo.

*Para ir al centro*

Voy en autobús.
...a pie.
...en bicicleta.
...en coche.
...en metro.
...en taxi.

## Temas y contextos

*Los días de la semana*

el lunes
el martes
el miércoles
el jueves
el viernes
el sábado
el domingo
el fin de semana

## Vocabulario general

*Verbos*

deber
hacer
poder

*Otras palabras y expresiones*

una cita
conmigo
frecuentemente
próximo(a)
usualmente

*Spanish speakers, Vocabulario:* Point out the words that have more difficult spelling combinations that were highlighted on p. 20 of "To the Teacher" in the Teacher's Edition. Students could be encouraged to keep a special spelling notebook with various categories such as: **Palabras con "c"; Palabras con "z"; Palabras con "j"; Palabras con "x"** etc. Another category might be headed with **"Así lo digo yo"** (this could include words like **guagua** and **camión)** in order for students to work on the spelling of those words and expressions that they already know and that might be variations to what has been presented in the book.

# Lectura CULTURAL

## LOS GUSTOS DE LOS JÓVENES ESPAÑOLES

## Lectura cultural

*Spanish speakers:* Have the students go through each of the exercises in this section. Spanish-speaking students in foreign language classes probably already read English. However, as reading researchers have shown, the transfer of reading skills from one language to another is far from automatic. People must learn to read in each language. Special attention should be paid to having these students go through all of the exercises and activities that accompany the readings in this program. Once they have completed the activities, they might be asked to summarize the reading in Spanish in order to give them additional writing practice. They might also be required to keep a notebook with a special list of new vocabulary they might find in the reading selections.

***Answers, Guía para la lectura:*** **A.** 1. 2  2. 3  3. 1 **B.** ages **C.** designer clothing, Walkmans, and videogames

*Critical Thinking Strategy:*

*Predicting*

## Antes de leer

1. Look at the pictures on page 255. How old do you think the young people are?
2. What do you think the reading will be about?
3. What does the title suggest to you?

*Learning Strategies:*

*Reading for details, skimming, scanning*

## Guía para la lectura

**A.** Skim the passage to determine in which paragraph you find the following information.

| | Paragraph |
|---|---|
| 1. movies that younger people enjoy | ________ |
| 2. clothing that they prefer | ________ |
| 3. what they spend their money on | ________ |

**B.** Scan the passage for numbers. To what do the numbers refer?

**C.** Now read the passage again and find three things young people like to buy.

### Los gustos de los jóvenes españoles

Los jóvenes españoles gastan su dinero en lo que más les apasiona: la música y la ropa de marca. El walkman y los juegos de vídeo son sus juguetes favoritos.

Van bastante al cine y ven todo tipo de película. Aunque muchos jóvenes entre 13 y 16 ven películas para adultos, también son populares entre los chicos las películas de dibujos animados, como *La bella y la bestia.*

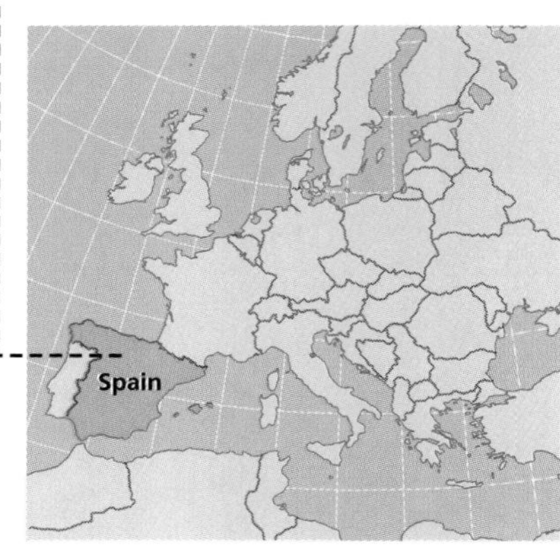


Los chicos llevan vaqueros, camisetas y, a veces, un pendiente en la oreja. Las chicas también llevan vaqueros durante la semana, pero para ir a las discotecas durante el fin de semana, prefieren las faldas cortas o los vestidos largos.

CAPÍTULO 11

# VAMOS A TOMAR EL METRO

—¿Tomamos un autobús?
—No, vamos a tomar el metro.

Objectives:

- **T**alking about taking the Madrid subway
- **B**uying subway tickets
- **M**aking and accepting invitations

Strategies:

- **R**eading a subway map
- **O**rganizing and giving directions
- **S**equencing
- **P**rioritizing



## Video/CD-ROM

Chapter 11 Video Program
Chapter 11 CD-ROM Program

These can be used at the end of the chapter as expansion activities.

## Chapter Objectives

Functions: Talking about taking the Madrid subway; buying subway tickets; making and accepting invitations
Context: Subway station
Accuracy: Adverbs used for the present and the future; talking about future plans with **pensar**

## Cultural Observation

Have students study the photo on this page. Point out that the girls are looking at a **plan del Metro** like the one on p. 259. Ask students if they have ever traveled in a subway system, either in the U.S. or in a foreign country. Mention that the subways in the Spanish-speaking world are excellent but very busy, especially during rush hours, as in the U.S.

*Spanish speakers:* Have Spanish speakers mention, in Spanish, what they see. Ask them what they see in the photo that might be similar or different to their community.

## Chapter Warm-up: Team Map-reading

 groups of three

- Put students who have not worked together into teams of three and have them number off. Give each team a map of their hometown.
- Tell students to explain in Round robin fashion (taking turns clockwise) how to get to three local landmarks from school.
- Ask Student 1 of each team to explain to the class how to get to one of the landmarks. Have Student 2 ask questions about the directions. Then have Student 3 rephrase the directions, answering the questions.

## Presentation: ¿En qué dirección?

Because of the large amount of cultural information involved in doing the metro exercises, you may wish to have students follow along in the text while they listen to the Teacher Tape. You can then ask them if there are things they do not understand. Use the transparency of the metro map to point out the basic information given in the **Comentario cultural (líneas, estaciones,** etc.) as well as to trace the girls' route.

***Spanish speakers, ¿En qué dirección?:*** Ask students for variations to the vocabulary and/or expressions introduced here. A common variation might be the use of the verb **quedar** for **estar** when asking where some building is. For example, **¿Dónde queda el Museo del Prado?** This is appropriate in all Spanish-speaking countries and if students want to use it, help them with the spelling of **queda** and **quedan** which are probably the only forms of this verb that are used in this context. Point out to them the spelling of the forms of the verb **bajar** (i.e., with a **j**).

**Ex. A:** pair work

***Support material, ¿En qué dirección?:*** Teacher Tape/CD #2 Track #1, transparency #50

# PRIMERA ETAPA

## Preparación

Learning Strategy: *Previewing*

- **Have you ever ridden a subway?**
- **What cities in the U.S. have subways? Have you heard of the "L" in Chicago; the "T" in Boston; "BART" in San Francisco; "MARTA" in Atlanta; the Metro in Washington, DC?**

## ¿En qué dirección?

Elena y su prima Clara van a tomar el metro al Museo del Prado. Están cerca de la Plaza de España, donde hay una estación de metro. Las dos jóvenes miran el plano del metro en la **entrada** de la estación.

**Elena:** Bueno. Estamos aquí, en la Plaza de España.
**Clara:** ¿Dónde está el Museo del Prado?
**Elena:** Está cerca de la Estación Atocha. Allí.
**Clara:** Entonces, ¿qué hacemos?
**Elena:** Es fácil. Tomamos la dirección de Legazpi.
**Clara:** ¿Es necesario **cambiar** de trenes?
**Elena:** Sí. Cambiamos en Sol, dirección de Portazgo.
**Clara:** Y debemos **bajar** en Atocha, ¿verdad?
**Elena:** Exacto, allí en Atocha bajamos.

*entrada:* entrance / *cambiar:* to change / *bajar:* to get off

## ¡Aquí te toca a ti!

**A. *Cambiamos en... / Bajamos en...*** Based on the cues, answer each person's questions about where to change lines and where to get off the subway, in order to get to the destination mentioned. The place to change lines is listed first and the destination is second. Follow the model.

Sol / la Plaza de España
*—¿Es necesario cambiar de trenes?*
*—Sí, tienes que cambiar en Sol.*
*—¿Dónde bajo del tren?*
*—Debes bajar en la Plaza de España.*

1. Pacífico / Manuel Becerra
2. Callao / Lavapiés
3. Bilbao / Goya
4. Ópera / Cuatro Caminos
5. Ventas / Banco de España
6. Goya / Sol

## Etapa Support Materials

Workbook: **pp. 137–142**
Transparencies: **#50, #51**
Teacher Tape
Quiz: **Testing Program, p. 122**

Support material, ¿En qué dirección?:
**Teacher Tape 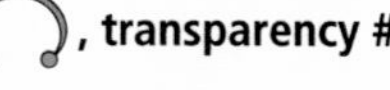, transparency #50**

## Exercise Progression

Ex. A practices the conversational formulae necessary for giving metro directions. Ex. B on the following page allows students to practice following routes on the map. Give additional starting points and destinations if students seem to be enjoying it or if they are having particular problems.

Ex. B: pair work

***Suggestions, Ex. B:*** You may want to demonstrate the model using the transparency or by holding up your book while students follow along with their fingers. Then have them work in pairs. If students read the **Comentarios culturales** first on p. 260, the exercise will be easier to understand.

***Possible answers, Ex. B:***
1. Marcos, es necesario tomar la dirección de Esperanza, tú tienes que cambiar de tren en A. Martínez, dirección de Canillejas, y debes bajar en Rubén Darío.
2. Pilar...de la Plaza de Castilla,... en Sol, ...de Legazpi, ...en Embajadores. 3. Felipe...de Moncloa, ...en Sol, ...de Portazgo, ...en Atocha. 4. Nilda...de la Ciudad Universitaria, ...en Nuevos Ministerios, ...de Fuencarral, ...en la Plaza de Castilla.

**B. *¡Vamos a tomar el metro!*** Follow the model and use the **metro** map below to explain how to use the subway. The **metro** line number (shown in parentheses after the name of each station) will help you locate the stations. Follow the model.

**Learning Strategy:**
*Reading a subway map*

Juan / la Plaza de España (3, 10) → Ventas (2)
*Juan, para ir a Ventas desde la Plaza de España, es necesario tomar la dirección Legazpi. Tienes que cambiar de tren en Callao, dirección de Canillejas, y debes bajar en Ventas.*

1. Marcos / Argüelles (4) → Rubén Darío (5)
2. Pilar / Nueva Numancia (1) → Embajadores (3)
3. Felipe / Delicias (3) → Atocha (1)
4. Nilda / Manuel Becerra (6) → Plaza de Castilla (1)

# Cultural Expansion

Ask students to look at the guide on this page and see if they can find out how long the metro is open every day (from 6:00 a.m. to 1:30 a.m.). It follows this schedule seven days of the week. All metro stations are marked by a sign like the one at the top right hand corner of this guide. Tell students that after buying a ticket, they should ask for **el plan del Metro,** which will be similar to this one.

## Pronunciation

*Spanish speakers:* Students should have no problem with the spelling of words with the **c** and **h** combination. Remind them that **ch** is no longer part of the Spanish alphabet. It was decided by the **Real Academia Española de la Lengua** in 1993 to eliminate both the **ch** and the **ll** as letters. (Words that start with **ch** and **ll** will now be put under the **c** and **l** categories.)

Additional activities appear in the Laboratory Tape Program.

**Ex. D:** pair work

*Reteaching:* Quickly review the forms of the verb **ir**, days of the week and modes of transportation before doing the **Repaso.** Use **¿Cómo se dice?/¿Qué quiere decir?** question format.

*Follow-up, Ex. D:* Review the other forms of **ir** by asking personalized questions in both the **tú** and the **Uds.** forms. For example: **¿Adónde vas mañana por la mañana? ¿El domingo por la mañana? ¿Cómo vas? ¿Adónde van tú y tus amigos/amigas los sábados por la noche?** etc.

*Support material, Pronunciación:* Pronunciation Tape

# *Pronunciación: The consonant ch*

The sound of **ch** in Spanish is like the *ch* in the English word *church.*

## Práctica

*C.* Listen and repeat as your teacher models the following words.

1. chocolate
2. Chile
3. mucho
4. muchacho
5. coche
6. ocho
7. leche
8. noche
9. ochenta
10. mochila

*Learning Strategy:*

*Reading for cultural information*

## COMENTARIOS CULTURALES

### *El metro*

The **metro** is one of the most popular means of transportation in Madrid, the capital city of Spain. The rate for each trip on the subway is fixed. Booklets of tickets are available, and buying tickets by the booklet is cheaper than buying individual tickets. To get around on the **metro** you must first find the **línea** on which you want to travel. Then look in the direction you want to go on that line and find the name of the last station. Follow the signs for that station.

## Repaso

*D.* ***Como de costumbre*** (As usual) Some members of your family follow a regular routine. On a certain day of the week, they always do the same thing. Describe where they go and how they get there, based on the drawings on page 261.

tu madre
*Los lunes mi madre va al centro. Usualmente ella va a pie.*

1. tu abuelo

2. tu primo

3. tu hermana

4. tu tío y tu tía

5. tus primas

6. tus padres

## ESTRUCTURA

### Adverbs that designate the present and the future

| | |
|---|---|
| Mi mamá trabaja **hoy.** | My mother is working *today.* |
| **Mañana** ella no va a trabajar. | *Tomorrow* she's not going to work. |
| ¿Dónde están **ahora?** | Where are they *now?* |

You have already learned several adverbs that express present or future time:

| | | |
|---|---|---|
| **hoy** | **esta noche** | **mañana por la tarde** |
| **esta mañana** | **mañana** | **mañana por la noche** |
| **esta tarde** | **mañana por la mañana** | |

Here are some additional expressions:

| | |
|---|---|
| **ahora** *(now)* | **la semana próxima** *(next week)* |
| **esta semana** *(this week)* | **el mes próximo** *(next month)* |
| **este mes** *(this month)* | **el año próximo** *(next year)* |
| **este año** *(this year)* | |



*Answers, Ex. D:*
1. Los sábados mi abuelo va al café. Usualmente él va a pie. 2. ...mi primo va al museo. ...él va en taxi. 3. Los martes mi hermana va a la escuela. ...ella va en autobús. 4. Los viernes mis tíos van al banco. ...ellos van en coche. 5. Los jueves mis primas van al cine. ...ellas toman el metro. 6. Los domingos mis padres van a la iglesia. ...ellos van a pie.

### Presentation: Adverbs that designate the present and the future

On the board write today's date, dates for this week and next, the present year, and next year. Review and introduce the adverbs by using the dates. Begin with the present and move to the future. Continue by giving a short personal monologue about your plans for next week and next year. Then have students answer questions about their plans, gradually familiarizing them with the notion of **próximo(a).** For example: **¿Qué van a hacer Uds. la semana próxima? ¿En las próximas vacaciones?**

*Suggestion, Ex. E:* These column exercises are meant to provide controlled practice. A possible way to present these would be through the creation of a "word web." On a separate piece of paper, students would draw a web, and then connect elements from the columns in ways that form grammatically correct sentences. (They would have to write in the correct form of the verb in column B.) See the diagram below for a sample word web format. Word web formats will vary from exercise to exercise.

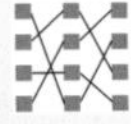

**Ex. F:** pair work

*Answers, Ex. F:* 1. El miércoles por la noche no... . Vamos al centro el miércoles por la tarde. 2. ...Voy a hacer un mandado el sábado por la mañana. 3. ...Va a comer en un restaurante la semana próxima. 4. ...Va a estudiar español el año próximo. 5. ...Vamos al cine el viernes por la noche. 6. ...Va a llevar el coche el domingo por la tarde. 7. ...Van a llegar el jueves próximo. 8. ...Voy a estudiar esta noche.

In addition, the expressions **por la mañana**, **por la tarde**, **por la noche**, and **próximo(a)** can be combined with the days of the week: **el lunes por la mañana**, **el sábado por la tarde**, **el domingo por la noche**, **el lunes próximo**, etc. Time expressions are usually placed at the very beginning or end of a sentence.

## Aquí practicamos

*E.* Create original sentences using words from each column.

| A | B | C | D |
|---|---|---|---|
| yo | ir | al cine | hoy |
| Roberto | | a Madrid | esta tarde |
| nosotros | | al museo | el viernes por la noche |
| mi hermana | | al banco | el domingo por la mañana |
| Uds. | | a la iglesia | la semana próxima |
| tú | | a la escuela | el jueves por la noche |
| | | | el año próximo |
| | | | ahora |

*F.* ***Esta noche no...*** Your mother is always asking about people's activities, but then she gets them confused. Correct her statements, using the information given. Follow the model.

Modelo: ¿Van al cine tú y Luis esta noche? (mañana por la noche)
*Esta noche no podemos ir al cine. Vamos al cine mañana por la noche.*

1. ¿Van tú y Felipe al centro el miércoles por la noche? (miércoles por la tarde)
2. ¿Vas a hacer un mandado mañana por la mañana? (el sábado por la mañana)
3. ¿Va a comer Mario en un restaurante esta semana? (la semana próxima)
4. ¿Va a estudiar español tu hermano este año? (el año próximo)
5. ¿Van al cine tú y Yolanda esta noche? (el viernes por la noche)
6. ¿Va a llevar el coche tu hermana esta tarde? (el domingo por la tarde)
7. ¿Van a llegar tus abuelos hoy? (el jueves próximo)
8. ¿Vas a estudiar ahora? (esta noche)

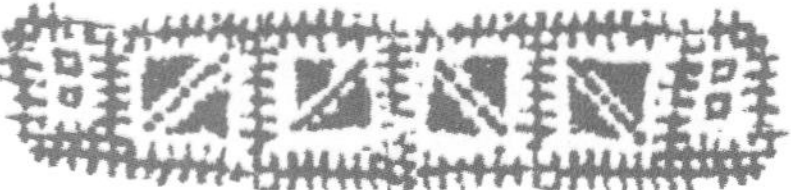



## Exercise Progression

Ex. E is a mechanical drill designed to focus on the expressions. Exs. F and G provide meaningful practice, with Ex. G on the following page requiring that they work with a Spanish calendar. You may want to remind them that the Spanish week begins with **lunes.**

**Ex. G:** pair work

**G. *El horario* (schedule) *de los González*** Answer the questions about the González family's activities during the month of February. Choose the appropriate time expressions, assuming that *today* is the morning of February 15. Follow the model.

*Learning Strategy:*
*Reading a schedule*

**FEBRERO**

| lunes | martes | miércoles | jueves | viernes | sábado | domingo |
|---|---|---|---|---|---|---|
| 1 | 2 | 3 | 4 | 5 restaurante | 6 | 7 iglesia |
| 8 | 9 | 10 | 11 | 12 restaurante | 13 | 14 iglesia |
| 15 Sr y Sra: teatro en el centro (noche) | 16 Sr: jugar al tenis | 17 Sr: trabajo (noche) | 18 Sra: museo | 19 Sra: trabajo (mañana) restaurante | 20 Sra: curso de francés (tarde) | 21 iglesia |
| 22 catedral | 23 los Martínez | 24 | 25 | 26 restaurante | 27 | 28 iglesia |

¿Cuándo va a visitar el museo la Sra. González?
*El jueves.*

1. ¿Qué noche va a trabajar el Sr. González?
2. ¿Cuándo van a visitar los González la catedral?
3. ¿Cuándo van a comer en un restaurante?
4. ¿Cuándo van a llegar los Martínez?
5. ¿Cuándo va a jugar *(play)* al tenis el Sr. González?
6. ¿Qué mañana va a trabajar la Sra. González?

¿Qué va a hacer el Sr. González el miércoles por la noche?
*Él va a trabajar.*

7. ¿Qué van a hacer los González esta noche?
8. ¿Qué van a hacer el Sr. y la Sra. González el domingo?
9. ¿Qué va a hacer la Sra. González el sábado por la tarde?
10. ¿Qué van a hacer los González el viernes próximo?



*Support material, Ex. G:* Transparency #51

*Answers, Ex. G:* 1. El miércoles. 2. El lunes próximo. 3. Este viernes y el viernes próximo. 4. El martes próximo. 5. Mañana. 6. El viernes. 7. Van al teatro. 8. Van a la iglesia. 9. Va al curso de francés. 10. Van al restaurante.

*Follow-up, Ex. G:* Have students practice giving the date of some of the González' activities as well.

*Less-prepared students, Ex. G:* Have less-prepared students write three questions in the **Ud.** form to ask you about next week, using new expressions.

*More-prepared students, Ex. G:* Have more prepared-students improvise questions to you in the **Ud.** format.

***Spanish speakers, Aquí escuchamos:*** Remember, most Spanish speakers, even those that are third or fourth generation, will understand spoken Spanish. The exercises that accompany this section should pose relatively little problem for Spanish speakers. They should, however, be directed to focus on "listening in context" to any vocabulary that may be new for them.

***Answers, Aquí escuchamos:*** 1. buy a CD 2. see a movie 3. by bus 4. Ventas 5. Ópera

***Support material, Aquí escuchamos:***
Teacher Tape/CD #2 Track #2
 and Tapescript

# Aquí escuchamos:

## "¿Tomamos el metro?"

**Critical Thinking Strategy:**
*Predicting*

### Antes de escuchar

**Elena and Francisco are making plans to go downtown. Based on what you've learned in this etapa, what information do you expect Elena and Francisco to give about why they have to go downtown and how they will get there?**

START

**Learning Strategy:**
*Listening for details*

### Después de escuchar

1. Why does Elena want to go downtown?
2. What does Francisco want to do?
3. How does Francisco suggest they go?
4. Where will they get the subway?
5. Where do they change trains?

# ¡Adelante!

## EJERCICIO ORAL

*H.* ***¿Qué dirección tomamos?*** You and your family are staying in Madrid at a hotel near the Plaza de Castilla (line 1). You need to go to the American Express office near Banco de España (line 2). You have just arrived in Madrid and don't understand the subway system yet, so you ask the desk clerk for help. When he or she explains how to get there, you repeat the instructions to make sure you have understood. (Another student will play the role of the desk clerk.) Consult the **metro** map on page 259.

> **Learning Strategies:**
> *Reading a subway map, organizing and giving directions, verifying*

## EJERCICIOS ESCRITOS

*I.* ***Muchas cosas por hacer*** A foreign exchange student from Caracas will arrive next week. You and your partners want to introduce the student to some of your favorite places and activities. You will have a week of vacation left before classes, so you can pace your schedule over several days. (1) Begin by brainstorming on places to go (favorite restaurants, museums, parks) and things to do (concerts, movies, parties, sports). (2) Narrow your list down so that you can do it all during your vacation. (3) Then make out a schedule, beginning when your guest arrives **(llega).** Decide which days and what time of day you will do each item on your list **(el sábado próximo por la tarde, martes entre mediodía y las tres).**

> **Cooperative Learning**
> **Learning Strategies:**
> *Brainstorming, negotiating, organizing ideas*
> **Critical Thinking Strategies:**
> *Prioritizing, sequencing*

*J.* ***Mi horario este mes...*** Make a calendar for the current month and indicate what you will be doing on various days of the month. Use the calendar in Activity G on page 263 as an example.

> **Learning Strategy:**
> *Recording a schedule*



**x. H:** role play

***Suggestions, Ex. H:*** Model this exercise first for less-prepared students. Then pose an alternate problem: You are at **pensión** near the Legazpi Station (3) and want to go to the ullfights near the Ventas Station (2). For a controlled version f this mini-situation, write these guidelines on the board: (1) xplain to the desk clerk that you want to take the subway. ) Ask if the American Express office near the Banco de España tation is near or far from the hotel. (3) Find out what direction take. (4) Ask if you have to change trains. (5) Summarize what you have heard. Vary this exercise by changing the location of the hotel and/or the destination. Prepare cards with several different destinations for your more-prepared students to role play.

***Spanish speakers, Ex. H:*** Most Spanish speakers already have a command of a variety of Spanish that is used in informal, very familiar contexts. Be sensitive and accept how the students say things the first time. What they have said may be totally appropriate in their speech community. Have them focus on the differences between how they say something and how the book is teaching them to express this. Remember, your main objective is to expand the range of contexts in which these students can use Spanish.

**Ex. I:**  groups of three

***Suggestion, Ex. I:*** Have students brainstorm while a "secretary" makes a chart on the board (places/things to do). Then divide the class into groups of three to prepare the schedule. Group students of similar abilities together.

***Spanish speakers, Ex. I:*** Always have Spanish speakers fully carry out this activity. While many of them already speak and understand spoken Spanish, they may not know how to write it. This is a good place to start building the basic literacy skills in Spanish that they need.

***Follow-up, Ex. I:*** Ask the different groups what they have on their itineraries. Write the places and activities on the board. Then have the class decide which three items are most important.

## Critical Thinking

*Critical Thinking Strategies: Prioritizing, Categorizing*

You may want to have a follow-up discussion about the cultural relevance of the students' choices of sites and activities to share with a foreign visitor. Have them come up with categories such as *"typically American," "unique to our city," "ways to meet people."* Help them see that "fun" activities, e.g., local theme parks, have cultural significance, especially for foreign visitors.

***Suggestion, Ex. J:*** Brainstorm with students to help them come up with a variety of activities not on the calendar on page 263.

*Learning Strategy: Brainstorming*

## Presentation: En la taquilla

You might want to begin by having students look at the tickets on p. 268 and by going over the information in the **Comentarios culturales** on p. 268. You may wish to ask your students if they are familiar with any subway systems in the U.S. that have automated ticket sales, like the metro in Washington, D.C. Then play the Teacher Tape or read the dialogue with students' books closed. Ask simple comprehension questions, such as **¿Van a comprar un billete sencillo? ¿Por qué no? ¿Cuánto cuesta un billete de diez viajes?** etc. Then read the dialogue again (students' books open) and have students repeat.

*Spanish speakers, Vocabulary:* Ask Spanish speakers for variations of the vocabulary that is presented here. A common variation for **billete** is **boleto.** Although they may know how to pronounce these variations, many may have never seen how they are written. Help them with the spelling of these variations by writing them on the board or overhead. Point out to them the spelling of **billete** with an **ll** and **sencillo** with an **ll** and **c.**

*Support material, En la taquilla:* Teacher Tape/CD #2 Track #3 🎧, transparency #52

## Previewing

### *Learning Strategies: Drawing context from visual cues, looking for details in a photo*

Have students study the photo on this page. Ask them to compare this station to one in the U.S. (if they are familiar with subway stations). What else do they notice?



# SEGUNDA ETAPA

## Preparación

*Learning Strategies:*

*Previewing, brainstorming*

- What does it cost to ride public transportation in your town or city?
- Do you pay with currency or can you use tokens?
- Can you use a pass?
- What if you don't have the exact change?

## En la taquilla

*En la taquilla:* At the ticket window

**Elena y Clara entran en la estación del metro y van a la taquilla.**

| | | |
|---|---|---|
| single ticket | **Elena:** | ¿Vas a comprar un **billete sencillo**? |
| ten-ride ticket / cheap | **Clara:** | No, voy a comprar un **billete de diez viajes**. Es más **barato.** Un billete sencillo cuesta 125 pesetas y un billete de diez viajes cuesta 625. ¿Y tú, vas a comprar un billete? |
| commuter pass / a whole month | **Elena:** | No, yo tengo una **tarjeta de abono transportes**. Con esta tarjeta puedo tomar el metro o el autobús sin límite por **un mes entero**. |
| | **Clara:** | ¡Qué bien! Por favor, señorita, un billete de diez viajes. |
| | **La empleada:** | Seiscientas veinticinco pesetas, señorita. |



## Etapa Support Materials

Workbook: **pp. 143–146**
Transparency: **#52**
Listening Activity masters: **p. 73**
Tapescript: **p. 108**
Teacher Tape 

Quiz: **Testing Program, p. 125**
Chapter Test: **Testing Program, p. 127**
Support material, **En la taquilla:**
**Teacher Tape 🎧, transparency #52**

## ¡Aquí te toca a ti!

**A. *En la taquilla*** Buy the indicated **metro** tickets. Follow the model.

1 ticket
*Un billete sencillo, por favor.*

1. 2 tickets
2. 1 book of ten tickets
3. 2 books of ten tickets
4. 1 ticket that allows you to travel for a month

**B. *¡En el metro!*** Explain to each person how to take the subway. Specify the kind of ticket to buy. Consult the **metro** map on page 259. (**Metro** line numbers are given in parentheses.) Follow the model.

**Learning Strategies:**

*Reading a subway map, organizing and giving directions*

*Tú vas (Ud. va) a la estación Atocha.*
*Compras (Ud. compra) un billete sencillo, tomas (Ud. toma) la dirección de... etc.*

1. Gina, your Italian friend, is in Madrid for a couple of days. Her hotel is near Cuatro Caminos (2). She wants to go see a church that is near Atocha (1).
2. Mr. and Mrs. Dumond, French friends of your family, are spending three weeks in Madrid. Their hotel is near the Cruz del Rayo Station (9) and they want to go to the bullfights. The Madrid Plaza de Toros *(bullring)* is near the Ventas Station (2).
3. Near the Delicias Station (3), you meet a disoriented tourist who wants to get to the American Express office near the Banco de España Station (2).

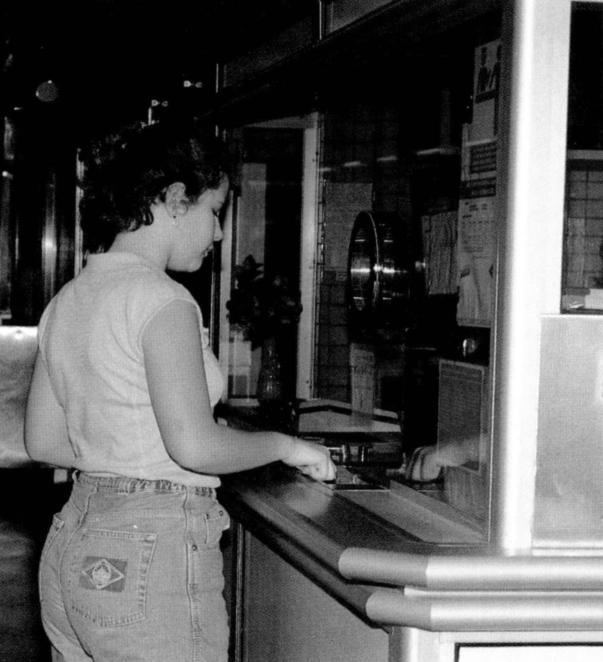

—Un billete sencillo, por favor.



**Ex. A:** pair work

***Answers, Ex. A:***
1. Dos billetes sencillos, por favor. 2. Un billete de diez viajes, por favor. 3. Dos billetes de diez viajes, por favor. 4. Una tarjeta de abono transportes, por favor.

**Ex. B:** groups of three

***Suggestion, Ex. B:*** Have students work in groups of three. Each student takes a destination and the other group members follow along. You may wish to write expressions on the board for continued reference.

***Less-prepared students, Ex. B:*** Brainstorm a list of expressions, such as **debes tomar/debes cambiar/en dirección,** with less-prepared students before they begin. You may wish to write the expressions on the board for continued reference.

***More-prepared students, Ex. B:***

Have more-prepared students role play this activity. The roles will vary, but always have two students giving contradictory or different directions to the same destination.

### Exercise Progression

Ex. A practices the new vocabulary associated with buying tickets. Ex. B also functions as a review of the metro material presented in the previous **etapa.**

## Critical Thinking

### *Critical Thinking Strategies: Evaluating, Supporting Opinion*

Ask students what might be the advantages of having a full month bus pass. You may want to point out that there are 90 bus routes in Madrid and they all provide excellent and efficient service.

**Ex. C:** 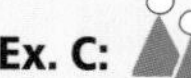 pair work

*Reteaching:* Before doing Ex. C, quickly review days of the week using **¿Cómo se dice?/¿Qué quiere decir?** format. Also review the verb **ir.**

*Variation, Ex. C:* Ask the students personalized questions based on the information from Ex. C. In order to emphasize the habitual vs. future time, ask things like, **¿Qué haces los sábados por la tarde?** vs. **¿Qué vas a hacer el sábado próximo?,** perhaps writing the two questions on the board. Once you establish a pattern, you could continue this as a **pregúntale** exercise. This can also serve as an introduction to the next **estructura,** a variation of the future.

*Learning Strategy:*

*Reading for cultural information*

## COMENTARIOS CULTURALES

### *Billetes para el transporte público*

**Metro** tickets can be bought singly **(un billete sencillo)** or in groups of ten **(un billete de diez viajes)**. Also available are three-day or five-day tourist tickets **(un metrotour de tres días** or **de cinco días)**. You can also buy a full-month commuter pass **(una tarjeta de abono transportes)**, which allows unlimited use of the buses as well as the subway for the specific month.

## Repaso

**C.** ***¿Qué haces?*** Using the adverbs of time provided on page 269, tell your classmates about your usual activities (**los sábados, los lunes por la mañana,** etc.) and then about your upcoming plans (**el sábado próximo, el lunes próximo,** etc.). Follow the model.

 los lunes / el lunes próximo
*Usualmente, los lunes voy a la escuela.*
*Pero el lunes próximo voy a visitar a mis abuelos.*

# Lectura cultural

## LOS METROS

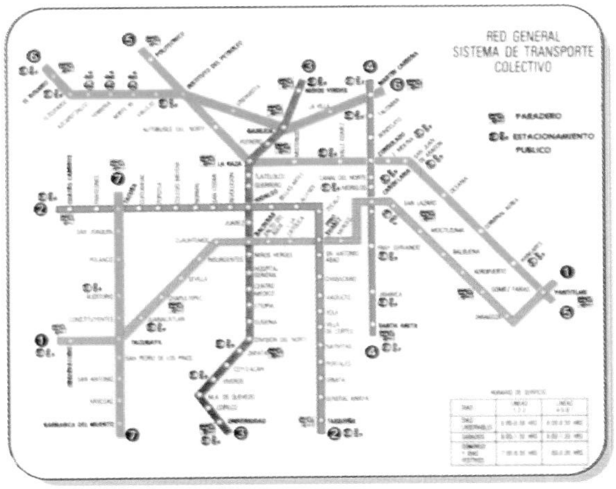

Dirección PALO VERDE
Dirección PROPATRIA
SALIDA
SAL

RED GENERAL SISTEMA DE TRANSPORTE COLECTIVO

PARADERO
ESTACIONAMIENTO PUBLICO

TAQUILLA



# Lectura cultural

*Spanish speakers:* Have the students go through each of the exercises in this section. Spanish-speaking students in foreign language classes probably already read English. However, as reading researchers have shown, the transfer of reading skills from one language to another is far from automatic. People must learn to read in each language. Special attention should be paid to having these students go through all of the exercises and activities that accompany the readings in this program. Once they have completed the activities, they might be asked to summarize the reading in Spanish in order to give them additional writing practice. They might also be required to keep a notebook with a special list of new vocabulary they might find in the reading selections. Ask students, especially those of Mexican ancestry, if they have been on the metro in Mexico City.

**Answers, Guía para la lectura:** **A.** Tokio, París, Nueva York, Buenos Aires, Madrid, la Ciudad de México; all have subway systems **B.** 9 different subway lines, 105 stations, 136 kilometers of rails, 90 kilometers per hour speed, 5 million daily passengers **C.** 1. excavations 2. workers 3. exhibitions **D.** They contain ruins and artifacts of ancient civilizations.



*Learning Strategies:*

*Brainstorming, drawing inferences, previewing*

## Antes de leer

1. What cities in the U.S. do you know of that have a subway system?
2. Have you ever ridden a subway in one of these cities? If so, when and where?
3. Look at the map and photos on page 273. In what city do you think the subway featured in this passage is located?

*Learning Strategies:*

*Scanning, drawing meaning from cognates, reading for details*

## Guía para la lectura

A. Scan the first paragraph and pick out all the cities that are mentioned. What do these cities have in common?

B. Scan the second paragraph for numbers. Did you find five? To what do the numbers refer?

C. Read the last paragraph. What do you think the following words mean?
 1. **excavaciones**
 2. **trabajadores**
 3. **exhibiciones**

D. Why are some of the stations in the Mexico City subway like museums?

### Los metros

Los metros, como saben Uds., son trenes subterráneos. Como son subterráneos, no hay tráfico y pueden llegar de un lugar a otro más rápidamente. En muchas ciudades del mundo hay metros: Tokio, París, Nueva York, Buenos Aires, Madrid y la Ciudad de México.

La Ciudad de México tiene uno de los metros más extensos del mundo. Tienen nueve líneas de diferentes colores, 105 estaciones y más de 136 kilómetros de vías. El metro corre a una velocidad máxima de 90 kilómetros por hora. Todos los días más de cinco millones de personas viajan en el metro.

Durante las excavaciones para construir el sistema subterráneo en la Ciudad de México, los trabajadores encontraron muchas ruinas de las antiguas civilizaciones: pequeños templos, figuras de barro y joyas de oro y de plata. Algunas de las estaciones son como museos que contienen una exhibición de objetos artísticos. Viajar por la Ciudad de México en el metro es una experiencia interesante.

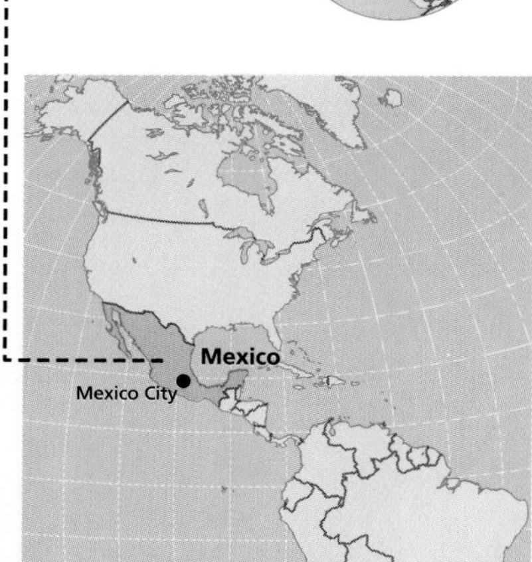

CAPÍTULO 12

# ¿CÓMO VAMOS?

—¿Cómo vamos? ¿A pie o en el coche de tu padre?
—Vamos en autobús.

Objectives:

- Taking a taxi
- Expressing wishes and desires

Strategies:

- Polling
- Supporting an opinion
- Researching and organizing information
- Reading for main ideas
- Skimming and scanning



## Chapter Objectives

**Functions:** Taking a taxi; expressing wishes and desires
**Context:** Town or city
**Accuracy:** Numbers from 100 to 1,000,000; expressions for discussing plans (**esperar** and **querer** + infinitive)

## Cultural Observation

Have students look at the photo on this page. Do they ever go places with their friends by bus? Point out that **microbuses** are smaller and more comfortable than the regular ones but are just as efficient and only cost about 10 **pesetas** more.

*Spanish speakers:* Have Spanish speakers mention, in Spanish, what they see. Ask them what they see in the photo that might be similar or different to their community.

## Video/CD-ROM

Chapter 12 Video Program
Chapter 12 CD-ROM Program

These can be used at the end of the chapter as expansion activities.

## Presentation: ¡Vamos a tomar un taxi!

Begin by doing a mini-planning strategy about taking a taxi. Have students generate the need to know the address, how long the trip will take, and how much it will cost. Then have students listen to the recording on the Teacher Tape. Ask: **¿Adónde van Linda y Julia? ¿Cuál es la dirección del Restaurante Julián Rojo? ¿Cuánto tarda en llegar? ¿Cuesta mucho el taxi?** Since this conversation is fairly difficult, you will probably want to replay it with students looking at the book. You can then ask again any questions that may have caused difficulty.

*Spanish speakers, ¡Vamos a tomar un taxi!:* Ask Spanish speakers if they are familiar with the situation that is presented here. If they bring up any variations, help them with the spelling of the variations they provide. Point out to them the spelling of **ciento, quinientas,** and **trescientas.** The word **chófer** is also pronounced **chofer.** Both pronunciations are acceptable.

## Cultural Expansion

If you have Spanish **pesetas,** show them to the students after reading the dialogue, and ask them to identify them. Find out the present exchange rate (**pesetas** to dollars) and have students figure out the price of the taxi and the tip.

*Support material, ¡Vamos a tomar un taxi!:* Teacher Tape/CD #2 Track #6



# PRIMERA ETAPA

### Preparación

*Learning Strategy:* *Previewing*

- **H**ave you ever taken a taxi?
- **W**hat information must you give to the taxi driver?
- **W**hat information can you expect him or her to give you?
- **W**hat about payment?
- **A**re you expected to give a tip?

## ¡Vamos a tomar un taxi!

Linda y Julia van a una **agencia de viajes,** pero antes van a almorzar en un restaurante que está cerca de la agencia. Piensan tomar un taxi.

travel agency

**Linda:** ¡Taxi! ¡Taxi!
**El chófer:** ¿Señoritas? ¿Adónde van?

*Ellas suben al taxi.*

**Linda:** Queremos ir al Restaurante Julián Rojo, Avenida Ventura de la Vega 5, por favor. **¿Cuánto tarda** para llegar?
**El chófer:** Diez minutos... quince **como máximo**.

How long does it take

at most



## Etapa Support Materials

Workbook: **pp. 147–152**
Teacher Tape
Quiz: **Testing Program, p. 131**

Support material, **¡Vamos a tomar un taxi!:**
**Teacher Tape**

*Ellas llegan al restaurante. Julia baja del taxi y Linda va a* ***pagar.***

**Linda:** ¿Cuánto es, señor?
**El chófer:** **Trescientas ochenta** pesetas, señorita.
**Linda:** Aquí tiene **quinientas** pesetas, señor.
**El chófer:** Aquí tiene Ud. el **cambio, ciento veinte** pesetas.

*Linda le* ***da*** *70 pesetas al chófer como* ***propina.***

**Linda:** Y **esto es para Ud.**, señor.
**El chófer:** Muchas gracias, señorita. Hasta luego.

pagar: to pay
Trescientas ochenta: Three hundred eighty
quinientas: five hundred
cambio / ciento veinte: change / one hundred twenty
da / propina: gives / tip
esto es para Ud.: this is for you

## ¡Aquí te toca a ti!

**A. *¿Adónde van... ?*** A taxi driver asks you where you and a friend are going and you tell the driver the name of the place and the address. Follow the model.

**Modelo:** Restaurante Capri / Calle Barco 27
—*¿Adónde van?*
—*Queremos ir al Restaurante Capri, Calle Barco 27.*

1. Hotel Praga / Calle Antonio López 65
2. Restaurante Trafalgar / Calle Trafalgar 35
3. Hotel Don Diego / Calle Velázquez 45
4. Café Elche / Calle Vilá-Vilá 71
5. Hotel Ramón de la Cruz / Calle Don Ramón de la Cruz 91

**B. *¿Cuánto tarda para ir?*** As you make plans with your friends, you discuss how long it will take to get to your destination. The answer will depend on the means of transportation you choose. Remember that in Spanish the preposition **en** is used in the expressions **en coche, en autobús, en metro, en taxi,** and **en bicicleta,** but **a** is used in **a pie.** Follow the model.

**Modelo:** al parque / en autobús (10 minutos) / a pie (30 o 35 minutos)
—*¿Cuánto tardas para ir al parque?*
—*Para ir al parque en autobús, tardo diez minutos.*
—*¿Y para llegar a pie?*
—*¿A pie? Tardo treinta o* (or) *treinta y cinco minutos.*

1. a la biblioteca / a pie (25 minutos) / en bicicleta (10 minutos)
2. a la catedral / en metro (20 minutos) / en autobús (25 o 30 minutos)
3. al aeropuerto / en taxi (45 minutos) / en metro (30 o 35 minutos)
4. a la estación de trenes / en coche (20 minutos) / en metro (10 minutos)
5. al centro / a pie (35 minutos) / en autobús (15 minutos)



**Ex. A:** pair work

***Follow-up, Ex. A:*** Ask students personalized questions about places in their town or city. For example: **¿Cuánto tardas para ir a tu casa de la escuela?** etc.

**Ex. B:** pair work

***Follow-up, Ex. B:*** Have pairs of students of equal abilities make up questions to ask the class, using the new expressions. Instruct them to write both singular and plural versions, such as **¿Cuánto tardas en ir a tu casa de la escuela?** and **¿Cuánto tardan Uds. en ir al centro de la casa?** Call on a variety of students to ask and answer the questions.

### Exercise Progression

Ex. A provides meaningful practice with giving destinations and addresses. Ex. B is designed to teach students the expression **¿Cuánto tardas para ir... ?**

## Pronunciation

***Spanish speakers:*** The spelling of words with **ll** can pose a problem for Spanish speakers as was discussed on p. 20 of "To the Teacher" in the Teacher's Edition. Students often want to spell words with **ll** with a **y.** They will probably know all these words, but have them focus on the spelling of the words listed here. Remind them that **ll** is no longer counted as one letter in the Spanish alphabet. It was decided by the **Real Academia Española de la Lengua** in 1993 to eliminate both the **ch** and the **ll** as letters.

Additional activities appear in the Laboratory Tape Program.

**Ex. D:**  groups of four or more

***Variation, Ex. D: Three-Step Interview***

- Direct the students to form teams of four and number off.
- Explain that Student 1 will state the task (**Pregúntales a los otros si...**), Student 2 will ask the question (**¿Piensas ir de compras?...**), Student 3 will answer the question, and Student 4 will summarize the answers.
- Tell the students to rotate roles.
- When they have finished, you may want to ask one question of every student in the class, and then ask a volunteer to try to remember and summarize the answers.

***Support material, Pronunciación:*** Pronunciation Tape

# Pronunciación: The consonant ll

You will recall when you learned the alphabet in **Capítulo 1** that the letters **ll** represent a sound in Spanish that is similar to the *y* in the English word *yes.*

## Práctica

**C.** Listen as your teacher models the following words.

1. llamar
2. calle
3. milla
4. tortilla
5. ellos
6. llegar
7. ella
8. Sevilla
9. maravilla
10. pollo

## Repaso

*Cooperative Learning*

*Learning Strategies:*

*Listing, negotiating*

*Critical Thinking Strategy:*

*Comparing and contrasting*

**D. *Pensamos hacer...*** Think of four different things that you plan to do during the coming week and write them down. Then circulate among your classmates, asking about their plans. When you find someone who also plans to do something on your list, try to arrange a day and time that you can do it together. Follow the model.

*Modelo:*

**Student 1:** *¡Hola! ¿Qué piensas hacer esta semana?*
**Student 2:** *Pienso ver una película el sábado próximo por la tarde.*
**Student 1:** *Bueno, yo quiero ir al cine también. Vamos juntos.*
**Student 2:** *Buena idea. ¿A qué hora quieres ir?*
**Student 1:** *¿A la una?*
**Student 2:** *De acuerdo.* o: *No puedo a la una porque tengo que hacer mandados con mi madre. ¿Puedes ir a las cuatro?*



***Suggestion, Ex. D:*** Brainstorm with students to help them come up with a variety of activities that can be done with classmates. Examples: **ir de compras, hacer mandados, mirar un vídeo, ir al cine, visitar el museo, preparar un examen, jugar al básquetbol, ir a la biblioteca, dar un paseo, comer al café, ir a un concierto, estudiar el español.** To elicit expressions with **pensamos,** poll the different groups to find out what they plan to do and when they plan to get together. This activity provides preparation for the **Ya llegamos** section at the end of Unit 4.

# COMENTARIOS CULTURALES

## La Puerta del Sol en Madrid

**La Puerta del Sol** is one of the most lively and popular plazas in Madrid. Several metro lines intersect there, and it is the location of **kilómetro 0**, the point from which official distances from Madrid to other cities in Spain and Portugal are measured. Below are the official distances from the capital to some major Spanish and Portuguese cities.

| | | | | | |
|---|---|---|---|---|---|
| Barcelona | 627 km | Granada | 430 km | Málaga | 548 km |
| Burgos | 239 km | Lisboa | 658 km | Pamplona | 385 km |
| Cádiz | 646 km | Segovia | 87 km | Porto | 591 km |
| Córdoba | 407 km | Valencia | 351 km | Salamanca | 205 km |

Note that distances are measured in kilometers **(km)**, the metric equivalent of about 5/8 of a mile **(milla)**.

*Learning Strategy:*

*Reading for cultural information*

# Palabras útiles

### The numbers from 100 to 1,000,000

| | | | |
|---|---|---|---|
| 100 | **cien** | 900 | **novecientos(as)** |
| 101 | **ciento uno** | 1.000 | **mil** |
| 102 | **ciento dos** | 2.000 | **dos mil** |
| 200 | **doscientos(as)** | 4.576 | **cuatro mil quinientos setenta y seis** |
| 300 | **trescientos(as)** | | |
| 400 | **cuatrocientos(as)** | 25.489 | **veinticinco mil cuatrocientos ochenta y nueve** |
| 500 | **quinientos(as)** | | |
| 600 | **seiscientos(as)** | | |
| 700 | **setecientos(as)** | 1.000.000 | **un millón** |
| 800 | **ochocientos(as)** | 2.000.000 | **dos millones** |

**¿Qué crees?**

**The distance between Madrid, Spain and Paris, France is approximately equal to the distance between:**

**a) Detroit, MI and Atlanta, GA**
**b) Boston, MA and Washington, DC**
**c) Chicago, IL and New Orleans, LA**
**d) Albuquerque, NM and Oklahoma City, OK**

**respuesta**

## Presentation: The numbers from 100 to 1,000,000

Begin by having students count from one to ten and then by tens to 100. Then count slowly from 101 to 110 and then by tens to 200, and so on up to 1,000. Continue by writing a few three-digit numbers on the board; say them out loud and have students repeat. Explain rules 1–5 on p. 280, then write some dates on the board, show how they are formed, and have the class repeat them. Write **nací** and **nació** on the board and have students write out in Spanish the year in which they were born: **Nací en mil novecientos... .** Then have them do the same for one of their parents or siblings using **mi papá (mamá, hermano, hermana,** etc.) **nació en... .**

***Spanish speakers, Numbers from 100 to 1,000,000:*** Have students focus on the spelling of these numbers, especially words like **cien** and **ciento** and the **sc** combination in **doscientos, trescientos, seiscientos**. Also mention the **qu** in **quinientos** and the **ll** in **millón.**

**Ex. E:** writing

*Follow-up, Ex. E:* Divide the class into two teams and then dictate some simple math problems. Have one student keep score at the board. Teams win a point for coming up with the correct answer first. Write the plus, minus, multiplication, and division symbols on the board and write out their Spanish equivalents to use in the math problems: **más, menos, por, dividido por.**

**Ex. F:** pair work

*Answers, Ex. F:* 1. trescientos kilómetros, seiscientos treinta y dos kilómetros 2. cuatrocientos veintitrés kilómetros, quinientos sesenta y un kilómetros 3. cuatrocientos y un kilómetros, novecientos sesenta y tres kilómetros 4. doscientos treinta y siete kilómetros, cuatrocientos kilómetros



1. The word **cien** is used before a noun: **cien discos compactos**.
2. **Ciento** is used with numbers from 101 to 199. There is no **y** following the word **ciento**: 120 = **ciento veinte**.
3. **Cientos** changes to **cientas** before a feminine noun: **doscientos hombres, doscientas mujeres**.
4. Notice that Spanish uses a period where English uses a comma: 3.400 = 3,400 (three thousand four hundred).
5. **Millón/millones** is followed by **de** when it accompanies a noun: **un millón de dólares, tres millones de habitantes**.

## Aquí practicamos

**E.** Read the following numbers out loud.

| 1. | 2. | 3. | 4. | 5. |
|---|---|---|---|---|
| 278 | 1.800 | 11.297 | 225.489 | 1.500.000 |
| 546 | 2.450 | 35.578 | 369.765 | 2.800.000 |
| 156 | 9.600 | 49.795 | 569.432 | 56.250.000 |
| 480 | 4.267 | 67.752 | 789.528 | 76.450.000 |
| 610 | 5.575 | 87.972 | 852.289 | |
| 817 | 7.902 | 98.386 | | |
| 729 | 3.721 | | | |
| | 6.134 | | | |

*Cooperative Learning*

*Learning Strategies:*

*Reporting, listening for details, taking notes*

*Critical Thinking Strategy:*

*Comparing and contrasting*

**F.** *¿Cuál es la distancia entre Madrid y... ?* Take turns with your partner asking and answering questions about the distance between Madrid and each of the following cities. Follow the model and consult the map on page 281 for the information you will need for your answers. Take notes and together create a list of the cities in the order of their distance from Madrid. Start your list with the city that is closest.

*Modelo:* Segovia / Lisboa
**Student 1:** *¿Cuál es la distancia entre Madrid y Segovia?*
**Student 2:** *Noventa y nueve kilómetros.*
**Student 1:** *¿Está más lejos que Lisboa?*
**Student 2:** *No, Lisboa está a seiscientos treinta y dos kilómetros.*

1. Valencia / Lisboa
2. Granada / Porto
3. Pamplona / Barcelona
4. Burgos / Málaga

a



## Exercise Progression

Ex. E is a mechanical exercise designed to give students more practice with numbers. Ex. F is a more meaningful exercise using a question-and-answer format.

Distancias entre las ciudades principales
Distancias entre as cidades principais
Distances entre principales villes
Distanze tra le principali città
Entfernungen zwischen den größeren Städten
Distances between major towns

cete

| | Alicante/Alacant | Almería | Andorra la Vella | Badajoz | Barcelona | Bayonne | Bilbao/Bilbo | Burgos | Cáceres | Cádiz | Coimbra | Córdoba | La Coruña/A Coruña | Granada | León | Lérida/Lleida | Lisboa | Logroño | Madrid | Málaga | Murcia | Oviedo | Pamplona/Iruñea | Perpignan | Porto | Salamanca | San Sebastián/Donostia | Santander | Segovia | Sevilla | Valencia | Valladolid | Vigo | Vitoria/Gasteiz |
|---|---|---|---|---|---|---|---|---|---|---|---|---|---|---|---|---|---|---|---|---|---|---|---|---|---|---|---|---|---|---|---|---|---|---|
| Almería | 88 | | | | | | | | | | | | | | | | | | | | | | | | | | | | | | | | | |
| Andorra la Vella | 80 | 930 | | | | | | | | | | | | | | | | | | | | | | | | | | | | | | | | |
| Badajoz | 71 | 630 | 1017 | | | | | | | | | | | | | | | | | | | | | | | | | | | | | | | |
| Barcelona | 32 | 782 | 190 | 1014 | | | | | | | | | | | | | | | | | | | | | | | | | | | | | | |
| Bayonne | 87 | 1058 | 398 | 814 | 536 | | | | | | | | | | | | | | | | | | | | | | | | | | | | | |
| Bilbao/Bilbo | 06 | 946 | 548 | 701 | 608 | 154 | | | | | | | | | | | | | | | | | | | | | | | | | | | | |
| Burgos | 49 | 788 | 601 | 542 | 598 | 276 | 164 | | | | | | | | | | | | | | | | | | | | | | | | | | | |
| Cáceres | 74 | 682 | 920 | 95 | 917 | 722 | 610 | 450 | | | | | | | | | | | | | | | | | | | | | | | | | | |
| Cádiz | 38 | 452 | 1239 | 340 | 1103 | 1127 | 1015 | 857 | 392 | | | | | | | | | | | | | | | | | | | | | | | | | |
| Coimbra | 33 | 923 | 1130 | 287 | 1127 | 815 | 701 | 541 | 340 | 633 | | | | | | | | | | | | | | | | | | | | | | | | |
| Córdoba | 17 | 327 | 1004 | 275 | 868 | 893 | 780 | 623 | 328 | 239 | 568 | | | | | | | | | | | | | | | | | | | | | | | |
| La Coruña/A Coruña | 32 | 1165 | 1133 | 706 | 1130 | 730 | 576 | 511 | 656 | 1111 | 430 | 1000 | | | | | | | | | | | | | | | | | | | | | | |
| Granada | 50 | 165 | 991 | 468 | 843 | 926 | 814 | 656 | 520 | 290 | 761 | 170 | 1033 | | | | | | | | | | | | | | | | | | | | | |
| León | 58 | 891 | 792 | 506 | 788 | 467 | 354 | 191 | 414 | 804 | 504 | 726 | 320 | 760 | | | | | | | | | | | | | | | | | | | | |
| Lérida/Lleida | 06 | 756 | 159 | 861 | 154 | 394 | 456 | 445 | 764 | 1084 | 974 | 849 | 954 | 883 | 636 | | | | | | | | | | | | | | | | | | | |
| Lisboa | 06 | 820 | 1252 | 232 | 1248 | 1012 | 898 | 738 | 324 | 530 | 201 | 507 | 621 | 658 | 701 | 1096 | | | | | | | | | | | | | | | | | | |
| Logroño | 54 | 882 | 478 | 663 | 474 | 222 | 137 | 126 | 571 | 952 | 662 | 718 | 633 | 751 | 316 | 322 | 859 | | | | | | | | | | | | | | | | | |
| Madrid | 17 | 554 | 621 | 397 | 617 | 507 | 394 | 237 | 300 | 624 | 513 | 389 | 612 | 423 | 342 | 465 | 632 | 333 | | | | | | | | | | | | | | | | |
| Málaga | 70 | 206 | 1111 | 427 | 963 | 1037 | 924 | 767 | 480 | 250 | 720 | 167 | 1143 | 123 | 870 | 992 | 618 | 861 | 532 | | | | | | | | | | | | | | | |
| Murcia | 83 | 218 | 725 | 745 | 577 | 823 | 789 | 632 | 657 | 568 | 916 | 442 | 1015 | 280 | 742 | 551 | 936 | 700 | 400 | 400 | | | | | | | | | | | | | | |
| Oviedo | 69 | 1001 | 834 | 617 | 894 | 439 | 285 | 309 | 525 | 914 | 614 | 837 | 302 | 870 | 119 | 741 | 811 | 423 | 452 | 981 | 852 | | | | | | | | | | | | | |
| Pamplona/Iruñea | 57 | 907 | 480 | 797 | 477 | 132 | 159 | 215 | 661 | 1020 | 754 | 785 | 729 | 819 | 406 | 324 | 951 | 92 | 401 | 929 | 702 | 438 | | | | | | | | | | | | |
| Perpignan | 11 | 961 | 167 | 1187 | 185 | 482 | 633 | 771 | 1090 | 1283 | 1300 | 1049 | 1203 | 1022 | 961 | 327 | 1421 | 647 | 790 | 1142 | 756 | 912 | 564 | | | | | | | | | | | |
| Porto | 81 | 1087 | 1168 | 392 | 1164 | 819 | 705 | 546 | 445 | 797 | 116 | 674 | 312 | 925 | 397 | 988 | 307 | 667 | 561 | 885 | 964 | 500 | 757 | 1337 | | | | | | | | | | |
| Salamanca | 26 | 759 | 823 | 308 | 820 | 506 | 394 | 234 | 216 | 606 | 307 | 594 | 468 | 628 | 198 | 667 | 504 | 356 | 209 | 738 | 609 | 309 | 445 | 993 | 355 | | | | | | | | | |
| San Sebastián/Donostia | 34 | 1005 | 449 | 760 | 554 | 55 | 100 | 223 | 668 | 1075 | 761 | 840 | 670 | 874 | 413 | 401 | 958 | 169 | 453 | 984 | 779 | 379 | 79 | 534 | 764 | 452 | | | | | | | | |
| Santander | 00 | 939 | 644 | 667 | 704 | 249 | 95 | 152 | 575 | 1009 | 666 | 775 | 486 | 808 | 280 | 551 | 863 | 233 | 388 | 919 | 783 | 195 | 255 | 728 | 636 | 359 | 196 | | | | | | | |
| Segovia | 16 | 648 | 713 | 393 | 709 | 469 | 356 | 199 | 301 | 718 | 468 | 484 | 567 | 517 | 255 | 557 | 623 | 318 | 99 | 628 | 499 | 406 | 408 | 882 | 515 | 164 | 415 | 350 | | | | | | |
| Sevilla | 00 | 415 | 1147 | 217 | 1011 | 1036 | 923 | 766 | 270 | 124 | 510 | 148 | 930 | 253 | 681 | 991 | 408 | 860 | 531 | 212 | 530 | 792 | 927 | 1191 | 616 | 483 | 982 | 917 | 626 | | | | | |
| Valencia | 77 | 427 | 504 | 747 | 356 | 603 | 604 | 582 | 650 | 753 | 867 | 519 | 966 | 489 | 693 | 331 | 981 | 470 | 350 | 609 | 222 | 802 | 472 | 536 | 914 | 560 | 549 | 693 | 449 | 662 | | | | |
| Valladolid | 10 | 742 | 716 | 423 | 713 | 391 | 279 | 119 | 331 | 812 | 422 | 578 | 453 | 611 | 140 | 560 | 619 | 241 | 193 | 722 | 593 | 258 | 330 | 886 | 470 | 115 | 338 | 244 | 112 | 598 | 543 | | | |
| Vigo | 24 | 1156 | 1144 | 550 | 1141 | 795 | 682 | 522 | 603 | 955 | 275 | 831 | 165 | 1025 | 354 | 965 | 466 | 644 | 603 | 1042 | 1007 | 402 | 733 | 1314 | 158 | 424 | 741 | 585 | 557 | 773 | 957 | 444 | | |
| Vitoria/Gasteiz | 60 | 899 | 563 | 655 | 560 | 157 | 67 | 117 | 563 | 969 | 654 | 735 | 637 | 768 | 308 | 407 | 851 | 89 | 348 | 879 | 743 | 346 | 95 | 636 | 659 | 347 | 104 | 156 | 310 | 878 | 564 | 232 | 635 | |
| Zaragoza | 98 | 748 | 309 | 709 | 306 | 306 | 307 | 297 | 612 | 932 | 822 | 697 | 805 | 731 | 487 | 153 | 944 | 173 | 313 | 841 | 543 | 586 | 176 | 479 | 839 | 515 | 253 | 396 | 405 | 840 | 322 | 412 | 816 | 259 |

603 km

Madrid - Vigo

# Aquí escuchamos:

## "¡Taxi, taxi!"

### Antes de escuchar

**Elena and Francisco are going to take a taxi to a museum in the city. Based on what you've learned in this etapa, what do you expect them (1) to ask the taxi driver, (2) to tell the taxi driver, and (3) to be told by the taxi driver?**

START

### Después de escuchar

1. **Where do they want to go?**
2. **What is the name of the street?**
3. **What is the street number?**
4. **How long will it take to get there?**
5. **How much did the taxi ride cost?**

*Critical Thinking Strategy:*

*Predicting*

*Learning Strategy:*

*Listening for details*



***Spanish speakers, Aquí escuchamos:*** Remember, most Spanish speakers, even those that are third or fourth generation, will understand spoken Spanish. The exercises that accompany this section should pose relatively little problem for Spanish speakers. They should, however, be directed to focus on "listening in context" to any vocabulary that may be new for them.

***Answers, Aquí escuchamos:*** 1. Museo Reina Sofía 2. Calle Santa Isabel 3. 52 4. about 15 minutes 5. 730 ptas. + 70 ptas. as tip

***Support material, Aquí escuchamos:*** Teacher Tape/CD #2 Track #7 and Tapescript

EJERCICIO ORAL

**G. *Tenemos que tomar un taxi.*** You are in Madrid with your parents, who don't speak Spanish. They want to go from their hotel (the Euro Building) to the Plaza Mayor. They don't like the subway; so they ask you to go with them in a taxi. (1) Hail the taxi and (2) tell the driver where you want to go. Then (3) ask if it's nearby and (4) how long the trip will take. On arriving at your destination, (5) ask how much to pay for the ride and (6) give the driver a tip. (A classmate will play the role of the taxi driver.)

EJERCICIO ESCRITO

**Learning Strategies:**

*Researching and organizing information, providing specific details in a letter*

**H. *¿Cuál es la distancia entre Washington, DC, y... ?*** In Washington, DC, we also have a point from which distances are measured. It is on the Ellipse, between the White House and the Washington Monument. A friend from Spain writes to you and is curious about distances between Washington, DC, and some other major cities, including where you live. Choose two cities in addition to your own and find out what the distances are. Write a short letter, giving your friend the information.



**Ex. G:**  role play

pair work

***Suggestion, Ex. G:*** Create activity cards by writing the destination on one side of the card **(Plaza Mayor)** and the time (15 minutes) and price **(1.200 pesetas)** on the other.

***Suggestions, Ex. G:*** Before dividing the class into pairs, you may want to model the dialogue: rider hails a taxi, driver asks the destination, rider indicates where and asks how long it takes, driver responds, rider asks how much, driver gives change, rider gives tip. At each point, ask the class to suggest appropriate expressions. Then divide the class into pairs and have each pair choose a card. Students playing the American tourist look at side 1 of the card for the address. Their partner then looks at side 2 for time and price.

***Suggestions, Ex. H:*** Brainstorm a list of cities, what they are noted for, and some descriptive adjectives. You may want to help students get started with these associations. Ask them what some of these cities are famous for: New Orleans (French/Cajun/Creole culture and cuisine, jazz, Mardi Gras), Miami (Cuban culture/arts, beaches), Denver (the "Mile-High City," ski resorts), San Antonio (history, missions, Mexican culture/arts/arquitecture), San Francisco (history, architecture, scenery), New York (monuments, museums, theatres, shopping places, size), Seattle (grunge music, coffee houses, scenery, commerce).

To round out the letter have students use expressions such as **Te va a gustar/Me gusta ________, porque es________ y porque tiene/es famosa por su/hay________.** You may suggest adjectives (and/or review them) and vocabulary expansion items such as music/art/architecture/industry/commerce/tourism/food, etc. Have students end the letter by asking a relevant question about a famous Spanish city. Bring a map or almanac in which students can research the distances of these cities from Washington. Have less-prepared students write about two cities, and more-prepared students three or more.

***Spanish speakers, Ex. H:*** Always have Spanish speakers fully carry out this activity. While many of them already speak and understand spoken Spanish, they may not know how to write it. This is a good place to start building the basic literacy skills in Spanish that they may lack.

# SEGUNDA ETAPA

## Preparación

>> Have you ever been to a travel agency?

>> When would you go to one?

>> Where would you want to go?

**Learning Strategies:**

*Previewing, brainstorming*

## En la agencia de viajes

| | | |
|---|---|---|
| **Agente:** | **¿En qué puedo servirles?** | How may I help you? |
| **Linda:** | Queremos planear un **viaje.** | trip |
| **Agente:** | ¿Adónde piensan ir? | |
| **Linda:** | **Esperamos** viajar a París. ¿Cuánto cuesta viajar a París **en avión**? | We hope / by plane |
| **Agente:** | Muchísimo. Un **viaje de ida y vuelta cuesta** 31.000 pesetas. | round trip / costs |
| **Julia:** | ¿Y **en tren**? | by train |
| **Agente:** | En tren es más barato. Un billete de ida y vuelta **sólo** cuesta 15.000 pesetas. | only |
| **Linda:** | **Es mucho**. Sólo tengo 10.000 pesetas y mi amiga tiene 9.000. | That's a lot. |
| **Agente:** | Entonces, por 7.000 pesetas pueden ir a Barcelona o a Málaga. | |
| **Julia:** | ¡Mm, Málaga tiene unas **playas hermosas**! | pretty beaches |
| **Linda:** | ¡Buena idea! Pero primero tenemos que **discutir** los planes con nuestros padres. | discuss |
| **Agente:** | Muy bien. **Aquí estoy para servirles.** | I'm here to help you. |
| **Linda y Julia:** | Muchísimas gracias. Hasta luego. | |



### Presentation: En la agencia de viajes

Play the Teacher Tape or read the dialogue for students (with books closed) and follow up by asking simple comprehension questions. Then play the Teacher Tape (or read) again and have students follow along in their books. Ask more comprehension questions and then have the students read the dialogue in groups of three, alternating the roles.

*Follow-up,* ***En la agencia de viajes:*** Find out the **peseta**/dollar exchange rate and have students calculate the dollar amounts of the costs discussed.

*Spanish speakers,* ***En la agencia de viajes:*** Ask Spanish speakers if they are familiar with the situation presented here. Ask them for variations. Again, help them with the spelling of the variations they provide.

*Support material,* ***En la agencia de viajes:*** Teacher Tape/CD #2 Track #8, transparency #53

## Etapa Support Materials

Workbook: **pp. 153–157**
Transparency: **#53**
Listening Activity masters: **p. 77**
Tapescript: **p. 116**
Teacher Tape

Quiz: **Testing Program, p. 133**
Chapter Test: **Testing Program, p. 135**

Support material, **En la agencia de viajes:**
**Teacher Tape** **, transparency #53**

**Ex. A:** pair work

***Suggestion, Ex. A:*** Have students ask their partners the question **¿Adónde esperas viajar?** and then answer, following the model. Then have students ask similar questions in the **Uds.** form.

**Ex. B:** pair work

***Answers, Ex. B:*** 1. Los Sres. Cano quieren viajar a México. 2. Raúl quiere viajar a París. 3. Bárbara quiere viajar a Quito. 4. Los estudiantes quieren viajar a Madrid. 5. Tú quieres viajar a Buenos Aires. 6. Yo quiero viajar a Caracas.

**Ex. C:** groups of four or more

***Suggestion, Ex. C:*** After students have circulated, ask follow-up questions to give them the opportunity to report back.

*Learning Strategy: Reading a graph*

***Follow-up, Ex. C:*** You might conduct a summative "tick mark" graph on the board to determine the most popular points of interest for travel for these students. Label your graph: **"Queremos más viajar a... ."**



# ¡Aquí te toca a ti!

**A. *¿Adónde esperas viajar?*** Tell where you hope to travel. Follow the model.

México
*Espero viajar a México.*

1. Barcelona
2. Lisboa
3. París
4. Nueva York
5. Quito
6. San Antonio
7. Seattle
8. Buenos Aires
9. Miami
10. Madrid

**B. *¿Adónde quiere viajar... ?*** Tell where the people in the drawings below want to travel.

1. Sr. y Sra. Cano

2. Raúl

3. Bárbara

4. los estudiantes

5. tú

6. yo

*Learning Strategy:*
*Polling*

**C. *Una encuesta*** (A survey) When your teacher gives the signal, circulate around the room and ask as many classmates as possible where they hope to travel.



## Exercise Progression

Exs. A and B provide controlled practice with the expressions for discussing plans along with different destinations. Ex. C offers more practice in a communicative open-ended format. The teacher may wish to present the **esperar** information in the **Estructura,** p. 285 before doing these exercises.

# Lectura cultural

## LA LLEGADA DEL CABALLO A AMÉRICA

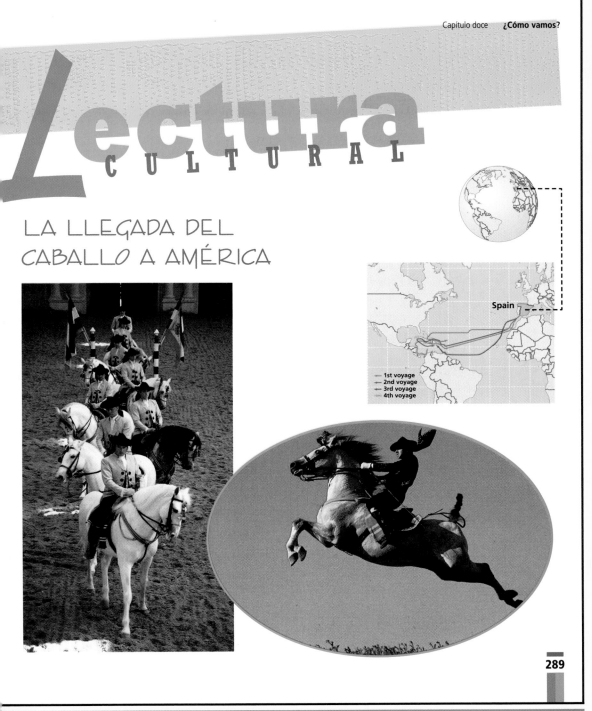





# Lectura cultural

*Spanish speakers:* Have the students go through each exercise in this section. Spanish-speaking students in foreign language classes probably already read English. Once these students have completed the activities, they might be asked to summarize the reading in Spanish in order to give them additional writing practice. They might also be required to keep a notebook with a special list of new vocabulary they might find in the reading selections.

# hapter ulminating ctivity

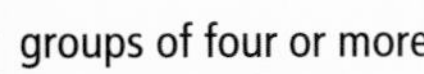

groups of four or more

ve students complete a transportation questionnaire, review- the vocabulary of this chapter and of Chapter 10. Ask a ies of questions, such as, **¿Tiene tu familia un coche? ¿Qué marca de coche tiene? ¿Quién conduce el coche? ¿Cómo vienes a la escuela? ¿Cuánto tardas en ir de tu casa a la escuela?** etc. After everyone has written the answers, you can then do a summary survey of the class by dividing the class into teams and assigning to each team a question or questions. Make sure students report their findings back to the class for a final tally.

***Answers, Guía para la lectura:*** **A.** Christopher Columbus **B.** Columbus discovered the Americas 500 years ago. His voyage lasted 33 days. **C.** second **D.** 4 voyages of Columbus; 1493: date of Columbus's second voyage; 17 ships; 1500 men **E.** Columbus was responsible for bringing the horse to the Americas.

*Learning Strategies:*

*Brainstorming, drawing inferences, skimming, reading for the main idea*

## Antes de leer

1. Years ago, how did people get around before they had modern modes of transportation?
2. Look at the pictures and the title of the reading on page 289. What do you think it will be about?
3. What are some of the uses people had for the horse?
4. Where do you think horses came from?

## Guía para la lectura

A. Skim the reading. What person is the reading talking about?

B. Scan the first paragraph for numbers. Did you find two? To what do they refer?

C. Scan the second paragraph for numbers. Did you find five? Did you find **segundo?** What do you think it means?

D. To what do the other numbers refer?

E. What does the writer want you to know about the person in the reading and the horse?

### La llegada del caballo a América

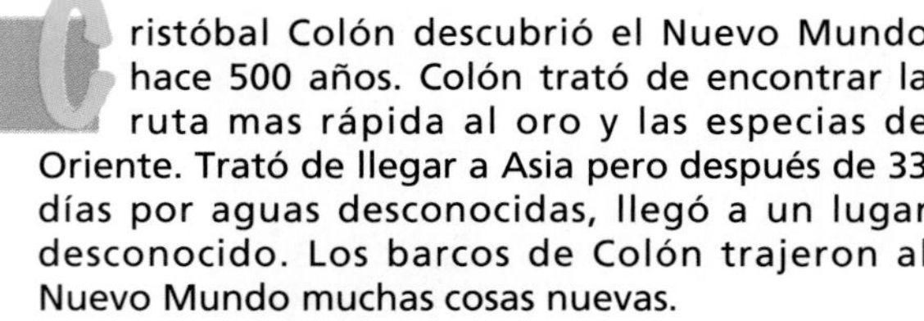

Cristóbal Colón descubrió el Nuevo Mundo hace 500 años. Colón trató de encontrar la ruta mas rápida al oro y las especias de Oriente. Trató de llegar a Asia pero después de 33 días por aguas desconocidas, llegó a un lugar desconocido. Los barcos de Colón trajeron al Nuevo Mundo muchas cosas nuevas.

Colón hizo cuatro viajes al Nuevo Mundo. En su segundo viaje en 1493, Colón volvió con 17 barcos, 1500 hombres y un Arca de Noé con animales del Viejo Mundo. Entre los animales que trajo Colón, el más importante fue el caballo. El caballo facilitó la vida de los nativos del Nuevo Mundo. Con el caballo fue más fácil cazar y más fácil llegar de un lugar a otro.

# Aquí leemos

## Estrategia para la lectura

You have learned to use the overall format of a reading passage to help you guess where important information can be found. Sometimes you need to find specific details you already know the passage contains. If you look over an entire passage very quickly but keep your attention focused on the kinds of specific information you want, you will find that names, dates, numbers, and key words will jump readily off the page. Just move your eyes quickly over the passage, picking out the type of information you are looking for. Then use the immediate context—words, expressions, or illustrations that surround a word you are trying to understand—to help you guess the meaning of any important words you don't know.

**Reading Strategies:**

*Use immediate context to help you make intelligent guesses about meanings.*

*Focus your attention when looking for specific information.*

## Antes de leer

Here are some examples of questions that involve locating specific details in a larger reading context. What would you read to find out...

- **The score for last night's ball game?**
- **What's on Channel 3 at 8:00 p.m.?**
- **The time of the earliest showing of a movie opening today?**
- **The price of a sweater on sale?**
- **The times when a discount coupon is valid at a local restaurant?**

The reading on page 292 helps you practice good reading techniques for this type of material. It is from a brochure advertising a special Youth Card that gives discounts on the Spanish rail system, RENFE. Look it over quickly. What do you think **días azules** are likely to be?



***Reading Strategy:*** The reading technique described here is sometimes known as scanning. Help students practice it informally by using materials in either Spanish or English that contain specific details of interest to them.

## Cultural Expansion

Explain that **RENFE** stands for **Red Nacional de los Ferrocarriles Españoles.** Point out that long distance trains (especially the **Talgo**) are fast and punctual. The new bullet trains built for Expo '92 that run between Sevilla and Madrid travel up to 180 m.p.h. Local trains (especially the **Exprés**) are slow but offer the opportunity to see a lot of the country. Mention also that there isn't much difference between first and second class accommodations on Spanish trains.

***Spanish speakers, Aquí leemos:*** Special attention should be paid to having Spanish-speaking students go through all of the exercises and activities that accompany this reading. Once they have completed the activities, they might be asked to write a summary, in Spanish, in order to give them additional writing practice. They might be asked to keep a notebook with a special list of new vocabulary they might find in the reading selections.

## Support Materials

Workbook: **pp. 158–160**
Unit Review Blackline Masters: **Unit 4 Review**
Listening Activity masters: **p. 82**
Tapescript: **p. 124**
Unit Exam: **Testing Program, p. 140**

**Atajo, Writing Assistant Software** 

## DÍAS AZULES

**MAYO**

| L | M | M | J | V | S | D |
|---|---|---|---|---|---|---|
| 1 | 2 | 3 | 4 | 5 | 6 | 7 |
| 8 | 9 | 10 | 11 | 12 | 13 | 14 |
| 15 | 16 | 17 | 18 | 19 | 20 | 21 |
| 22 | 23 | 24 | 25 | 26 | 27 | 28 |
| 29 | 30 | 31 | | | | |

**JUNIO**

| L | M | M | J | V | S | D |
|---|---|---|---|---|---|---|
| | | | 1 | 2 | 3 | 4 |
| 5 | 6 | 7 | 8 | 9 | 10 | 11 |
| 12 | 13 | 14 | 15 | 16 | 17 | 18 |
| 19 | 20 | 21 | 22 | 23 | 24 | 25 |
| 26 | 27 | 28 | 29 | 30 | | |

**JULIO**

| L | M | M | J | V | S | D |
|---|---|---|---|---|---|---|
| | | | | | 1 | 2 |
| 3 | 4 | 5 | 6 | 7 | 8 | 9 |
| 10 | 11 | 12 | 13 | 14 | 15 | 16 |
| 17 | 18 | 19 | 20 | 21 | 22 | 23 |
| 24 | 25 | 26 | 27 | 28 | 29 | 30 |
| 31 | | | | | | |

**AGOSTO**

| L | M | M | J | V | S | D |
|---|---|---|---|---|---|---|
| | 1 | 2 | 3 | 4 | 5 | 6 |
| 7 | 8 | 9 | 10 | 11 | 12 | 13 |
| 14 | 15 | 16 | 17 | 18 | 19 | 20 |
| 21 | 22 | 23 | 24 | 25 | 26 | 27 |
| 28 | 29 | 30 | 31 | | | |

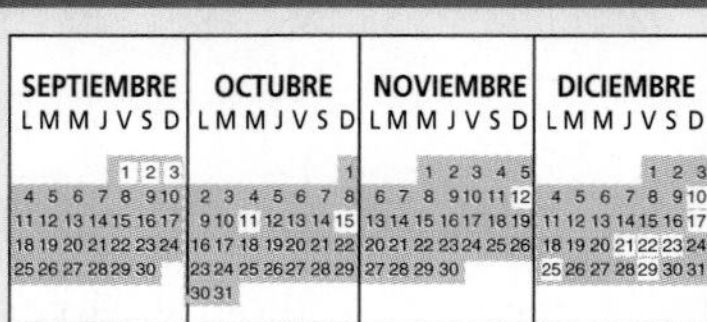

**SEPTIEMBRE**

| L | M | M | J | V | S | D |
|---|---|---|---|---|---|---|
| | | | | 1 | 2 | 3 |
| 4 | 5 | 6 | 7 | 8 | 9 | 10 |
| 11 | 12 | 13 | 14 | 15 | 16 | 17 |
| 18 | 19 | 20 | 21 | 22 | 23 | 24 |
| 25 | 26 | 27 | 28 | 29 | 30 | |

**OCTUBRE**

| L | M | M | J | V | S | D |
|---|---|---|---|---|---|---|
| | | | | | | 1 |
| 2 | 3 | 4 | 5 | 6 | 7 | 8 |
| 9 | 10 | 11 | 12 | 13 | 14 | 15 |
| 16 | 17 | 18 | 19 | 20 | 21 | 22 |
| 23 | 24 | 25 | 26 | 27 | 28 | 29 |
| 30 | 31 | | | | | |

**NOVIEMBRE**

| L | M | M | J | V | S | D |
|---|---|---|---|---|---|---|
| | | 1 | 2 | 3 | 4 | 5 |
| 6 | 7 | 8 | 9 | 10 | 11 | 12 |
| 13 | 14 | 15 | 16 | 17 | 18 | 19 |
| 20 | 21 | 22 | 23 | 24 | 25 | 26 |
| 27 | 28 | 29 | 30 | | | |

**DICIEMBRE**

| L | M | M | J | V | S | D |
|---|---|---|---|---|---|---|
| | | | | 1 | 2 | 3 |
| 4 | 5 | 6 | 7 | 8 | 9 | 10 |
| 11 | 12 | 13 | 14 | 15 | 16 | 17 |
| 18 | 19 | 20 | 21 | 22 | 23 | 24 |
| 25 | 26 | 27 | 28 | 29 | 30 | 31 |

La Tarjeta Joven va a cambiar tu vida. Con la Tarjeta Joven puedes viajar en tren por toda España con una reducción de 50% sobre el precio de la tarifa general, si viajas en días azules y haces un recorrido de más de 100 kms en viaje sencillo o de más de 200 kms si es de ida y vuelta. ¿Qué te parece? Puedes usar la tarjeta entre el 1 de mayo y el 31 de diciembre y recibes también un billete de litera gratis válido para recorridos nacionales.

¡Y hay más! Entre el 1 de junio y el 30 de septiembre con la Tarjeta Joven puedes viajar con un descuento entre el 30 y 50% por Alemania, Francia, Italia, Portugal y Marruecos. Antes de empezar el viaje a esos países tienes que pagar por la viñeta que corresponde a cada uno de los países. El precio de esta viñeta es de 1.500 pesetas para Francia y 1.200 para cada uno de los demás países.

Si tienes entre 12 y 26 años puedes comprar la Tarjeta Joven de RENFE. Está a la venta en RENFE

TARJETA joven

*litera:* sleeping compartment / *viñeta:* stamp

# Actividades

**A.** Although this passage is prose, it contains many details that spring to the eye. Focus your attention and look for the following types of information.

1. all the numbers
2. all the months mentioned
3. all the country names

**B.** Given the contexts in which they appear in the reading, guess the meaning of the following words and phrases.

1. **tarifa**
2. **recorrido**
3. **viaje sencillo**
4. **válido**
5. **descuento**
6. **autorizadas**

**C. La Tarjeta Joven** Answer these questions about details of **Tarjeta Joven** discounts.

1. During what months is the **Tarjeta Joven** valid?
2. Is the **Tarjeta Joven** valid every day of these months?
3. What is the minimum distance required for a one-way trip?
4. What is the minimum distance required for a round trip?
5. When can you get discounted travel to other countries?
6. How much does it cost to get a special discount travel stamp for France?
7. What age range is eligible for the **Tarjeta Joven**?
8. According to the testimonials of the young people in the photographs, what seems to be the most important benefit of the **Tarjeta Joven?**

"gracias a la Tarjeta Joven de RENFE encontré a mi príncipe azul"
"desde que descubrí la Tarjeta Joven tengo más novias que Elvis Presley"




*Answers, Ex. B:* 1. cost 2. distance 3. one way 4. valid 5. discount 6. authorized

*Answers, Ex. C:* 1. May to December 2. No, only on the blue days. 3. 100 kms 4. 200 kms 5. June 1st to September 30th 6. 1,500 pesetas 7. 12 to 26 yrs 8. girl or boyfriends

# Ya llegamos

*Spanish speakers, Actividades orales:* Most Spanish speakers already have a command of a variety of Spanish that is used in informal, very familiar contexts. Be sensitive and accept how the students say things the first time. What they have said may be totally appropriate in their speech community. Have them focus on the differences between how they say something and how the book is teaching them to express this. Remember, rather than "correcting" how they speak, your main objective is to expand the range of contexts in which these students can use Spanish.

**Exs. A, B, and C:**  pair work

*More-prepared students, less-prepared students, Ex. A, B, and C:* Pair a more-prepared student with a less-prepared student for student-to-student learning. Have different groups perform their role plays for the class.

*Variation, Ex. A:* Have each pair of students write the directions, then exchange them with another group, and try to follow the instructions received on the metro map.

*Spanish speakers, Actividades escritas:* Have Spanish speakers fully carry out this activity. Remember, while many of them already speak and understand spoken Spanish, they may not know how to write it. This is a good place to start building basic literacy skills in Spanish. Have them pay special attention to the spelling of the vocabulary that has been introduced in this unit; especially those words that may have more difficult spelling combinations. This is a good place to have them engage in peer-editing. Have them look at the written work of a partner and focus on the spelling and the basic grammatical structures that have been introduced in this unit.

## Actividades orales

*Cooperative Learning*

*Learning Strategies:* Negotiating, reading a map

*Critical Thinking Strategy:* Sequencing

**A. *Una visita corta* (short) *a Madrid*** You and a friend have a ten-hour layover in Madrid. Discuss how you will make use of the **metro** in order to see the following sights. Use expressions such as **Vamos a la estación…**, **Tomamos la dirección…**, **Cambiamos de trenes en…**, **Bajamos en…**, **Después vamos…** Begin and end your tour at the Plaza de Colón, which has buses connecting with the airport. Refer to your **metro** map on page 259.

1. la Plaza de España
2. la Plaza Mayor (near Sol)
3. el Parque del Retiro
4. la Plaza de Toros (near Ventas)

*Cooperative Learning*

*Learning Strategies:* Providing information, negotiating, reading a subway map

**B. *En un café*** You have just met a young traveler who speaks no English, but does speak Spanish. You and your new friend are in a café on the Paseo de la Castellana. Order something. As you get acquainted, share personal information about (1) where you are from, (2) your families, and (3) activities that you like. Then discuss (4) three places you each plan to visit while in Madrid and (5) two activities that you plan to do together. Finally, using the metro map on page 259, (6) explain to your new friend how to take the subway from the Cuzco Station to the Atocha Station.

*Cooperative Learning*

*Learning Strategies:* Organizing and revising a schedule, negotiating, persuading

**C. *¡Vamos al centro!*** You and a friend are making plans to spend Saturday downtown. Agree on (1) four activities to do together and (2) a place for lunch. Decide on (3) the best means of transportation to and from the downtown area and (4) how you will get around once there. Finally, (5) describe your itinerary to two of your friends and (6) invite them to join you. (7) Make any changes necessary to your plans to convince them to accompany you.

## Actividades escritas

**D. *La semana próxima*** Write a short note to a friend describing at least one thing that you will do (**ir** + **a**+ *infinitive*), have to do (**tener** + **que** + *infinitive*), or feel like doing (**tener ganas de** + *infinitive*) for each day next week.



**Ex. D:** writing

*More-prepared students, Ex. D:* Remind more-prepared students of alternative expressions, such as **necesitar** or **preferir**. Have them vary their writing.

*Variation, Ex. D:* Have students prepare short oral presentations and then give their talks to the class or in small groups.

**Exs. E and F:** writing

*Support material, Unidad 4:* Lab Manual Ya llegamos listening activities, Laboratory Program, Tapescript, and Teacher's Edition of the Workbook/Lab Manual

**E. *Una semana típica*** A friend writes to you from Spain and wants to know what you do in a typical weekend. Write a short note to him or her indicating what you do on Fridays, Saturdays, and Sundays. Include how you get around, where you go, what you do, and so on, for each day.

**F. *Mis planes*** Write a short paragraph about your plans for the future. Talk about next year (**el año próximo**) and the following years (**en dos, tres, etc. años**). Consider what you definitely *intend* to do (**pensar** + *infinitive*), what you would *like* to do (**querer** + *infinitive*), and what you *hope* to do (**esperar** + *infinitive*).

*Learning Strategies:*

*Providing information, organizing ideas in a letter*

*Learning Strategy:*

*Expressing plans for the future*

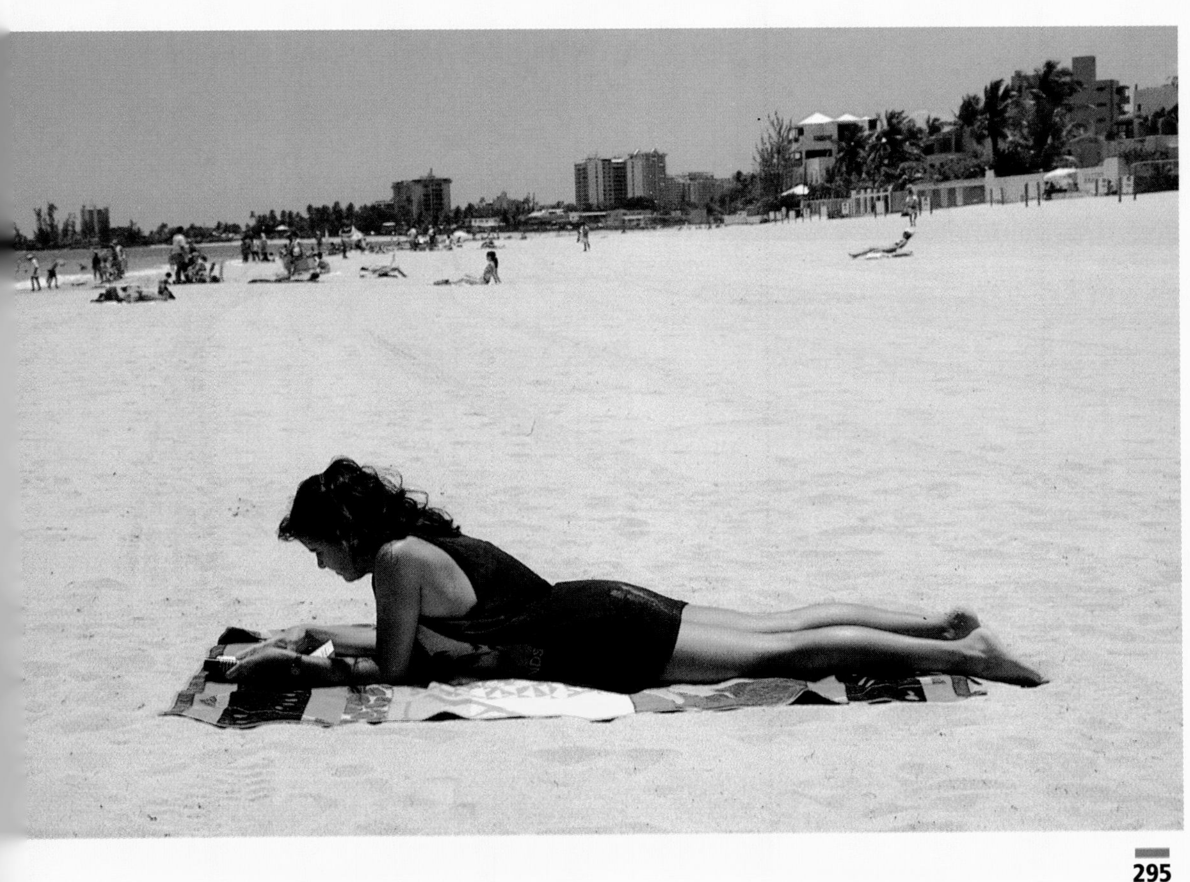



## Writing Activities

***Atajo** Writing Assistant Software* supports ATAJO

*Functional vocabulary:* Hypothesizing, sequencing events, etc.

*Topic vocabulary:* Arts, automobile, family members, money, professions, studies, trades, traveling, university, etc.

*Grammar:* Adverbs of time; verbs: future; verbs: **hacer, pensar, poder,** etc.

*ess-prepared students, Ex. E:* As a quick review, rainstorm a list of places, activities, and modes of transportaon with less-prepared students.

## Presentation: Activity A

You may have to explain that Spanish is a romance language. Therefore, Spanish literature will be found under Romance Literature.

# Conexión

- How do you find books in the library?
- What steps do you take?
- How are library books organized? By title? By subject?

### AL EMPEZAR

Most libraries use one of two systems of classification to organize their collection by subject—the Dewey Decimal system or the Library of Congress (LC) system. Do you know which system your school library uses? Which system does your local public library use?

Below is an abridged version of the LC subject headings in Spanish. Single letters indicate the major subject headings and the double letters indicate subcategories within each subject.

### *Clasificación de la Biblioteca del Congreso*

| | | |
|---|---|---|
| **A** | Obras generales | |
| | **AE** | Enciclopedias generales |
| | **AG** | Diccionarios |
| **B** | Filosofía--religión | |
| | **B** | Filosofía general |
| | **BF** | Psicología |
| | **BL** | Religiones, mitología |
| **D** | Historia y topografía (excepto continentes de América) | |
| | **DP** | España y Portugal |
| **E y F** | Historia (los continentes de América) | |
| **G** | Geografía y antropología | |
| | **G** | Mapas, átlases |
| | **GR** | Folklore |
| | **GV** | Recreación y tiempo libre |
| **J** | Ciencia política | |
| | **JK** | Historia constitucional (Estados Unidos) |
| | **JV** | Colonias y colonización |
| **M** | Música | |
| **N** | Bellas artes y artes visuales | |
| | **NA** | Arquitectura |
| | **NC** | Dibujo, diseño |
| | **ND** | Pintura |
| **P** | Lenguaje y literatura | |
| | **PQ** | Literatura romance |
| | **PR** | Literatura inglesa |
| | **PS** | Literatura de los Estados Unidos |
| **Q** | Ciencias puras | |
| | **QA** | Matemáticas |
| | **QB** | Astronomía |
| | **QC** | Física |
| | **QD** | Química |
| | **QE** | Geología |
| | **QK** | Botánica |
| **S** | Agricultura | |
| **T** | Tecnología | |

## ACTIVIDAD A

Imagine that you and your classmates all have to do oral presentations on a certain aspect of Spanish life. Under what call numbers will you find books on the following aspects of Spanish life? Write the letters of the classification.

*Modelo:* arquitectura de Barcelona <u>*NA*</u>

1. plantas que crecen en España
2. literatura española
3. pintores famosos
4. productos agrícolas
5. folklore
6. un mapa de España
7. música popular
8. la vida religiosa
9. historia general
10. deportes populares

## ACTIVIDAD B

You are a student library assistant at a school library in Mexico. Today library patrons have been forgetting to write down the first letters of the call numbers. Help them figure out the missing portions of the call numbers for the titles below.

*Modelo:* *Enciclopedia universal ilustrada* ***AE*** 61.E56 1905

1. *El ingenioso hidalgo Don Quijote de la Mancha* _ _6323 .A5A6 1935
2. *Goya en Andalucía* _ _813 .G7Z8 1989
3. *Mitología griega y romana* _ _725 .S62 1927
4. *Música y músicos en México* _ <u>*L*</u>106 .M6T3 1991
5. *Plantas de Costa Rica* _ _217 .P57 1978
6. *Planetas y satélites* _ _501 .S3
7. *Historia de España* _ _66 .H5572 1986
8. *Atlas geográfico de la República Argentina* _ _1755 .A77 1986

## ACTIVIDAD C

As library assistant you help people do research. Help your fellow students find books on the following topics by telling them what subject to look under and what letters will begin the call number.

| | *Tema* | *Cifra de clasificación* |
|---|---|---|
| **Ludwig von Beethoven** | ***música*** | ***M*** |
| 1. El Greco | | |
| 2. William Shakespeare | | |
| 3. Sigmund Freud | | |
| 4. Platón | | |
| 5. Albert Einstein | | |
| 6. Cristobal Colón | | |



### Presentation: Activity B

Read the titles aloud to the students before doing the activity. You may have to tell your students who Goya is.

*Answers, Activity B:* 1. PQ 2. ND 3. BL 4. M 5. QK 6. QB 7. DP 8. G

### Presentation: Activity C

You may have to explain who the famous people are. You can expand on this activity by asking students about other famous people or other topics of interest.

*Answers, Activity C:* 1. pintura, ND 2. literatura inglesa, PR 3. psicología, BF 4. filosofía general, B 5. física, QC 6. colonización, JV or historia, DP, E, and F

### Expansion Activity

Choose some titles in Spanish that are in the library. Have students go to the library to get the call numbers. If the school library doesn't use the Library of Congress system, a local university or public library might.

*Expansion, Ex. A:* Have students go to the library and find 4–5 references to be turned in on 3″ × 5″ cards on the topics listed in the text. You may want to have them give a short oral presentation as a follow up.

*Answers, Activity A:* 1. QK 2. PQ 3. ND 4. S 5. GR 6. G 7. M 8. BL 9. D 10. GV

*Activity B:* 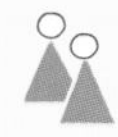 pair work  role play

## Cultural Context

Unit 5 does not feature any one student. Instead, it deals with a variety of sports and pastimes around the Spanish-speaking world. Chapter 13 centers on pastimes and extra-curricular activities. Chapter 14 deals with sports that students participate in, and Chapter 15 focuses on two international professional sports that include many Spanish-speaking stars: baseball and tennis.

Ask students about their favorite sports and pastimes. Do they like to participate in the same sports they watch regularly? Let them know that many of the same sports that are popular in the U.S. are also popular in the Spanish-speaking world. People in both cultures like to play baseball, tennis, and basketball and to go cycling. The most popular spectator sport in the U.S. is football, whereas soccer is the spectator and participatory favorite in Spanish-speaking countries.

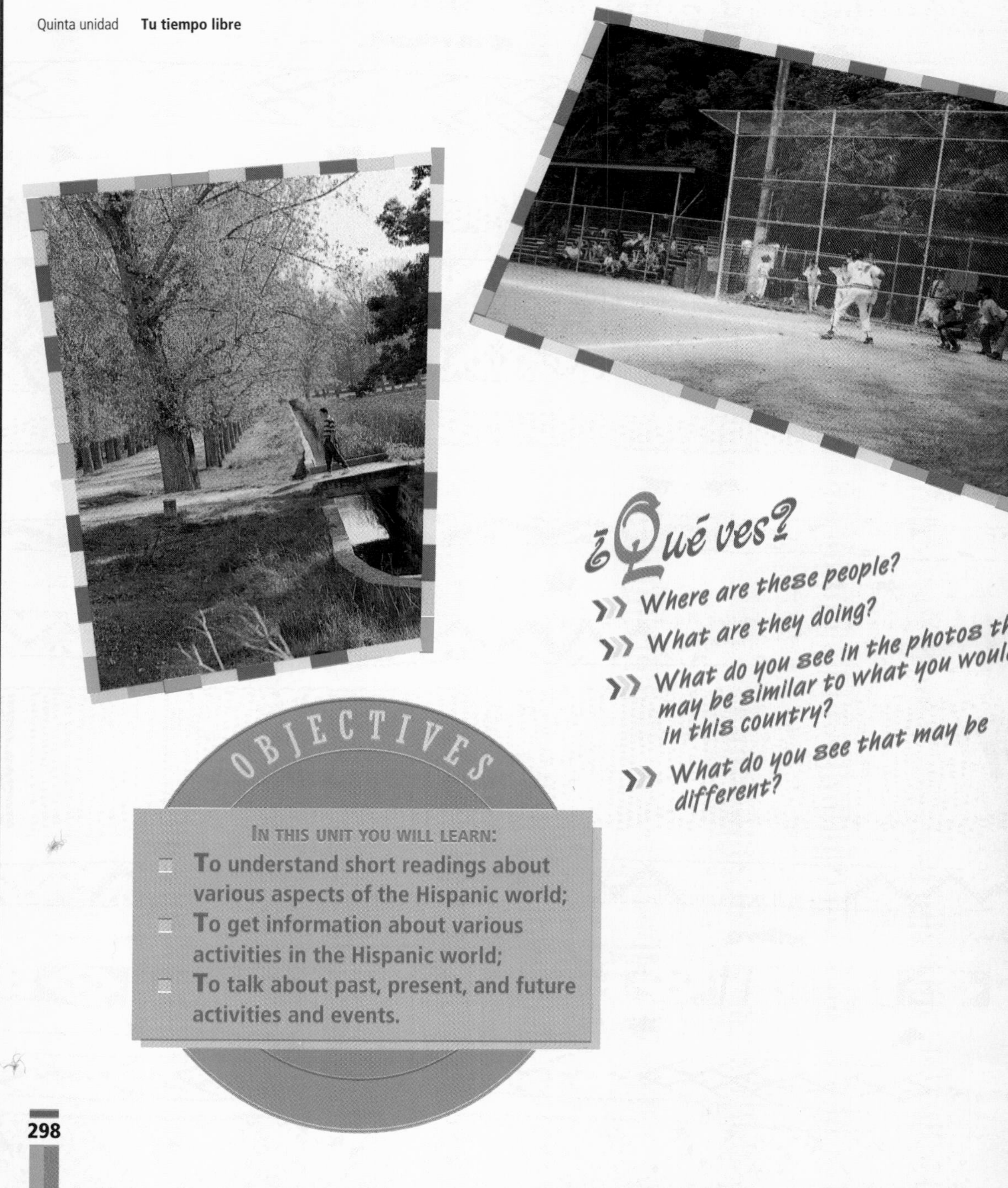

¿Qué ves?
» Where are these people?
» What are they doing?
» What do you see in the photos th
may be similar to what you woul
in this country?
» What do you see that may be different?
OBJECTIVES
IN THIS UNIT YOU WILL LEARN:
To understand short readings about various aspects of the Hispanic world;
To get information about various activities in the Hispanic world;
To talk about past, present, and future activities and events.
298

## *Capítulo trece: Los pasatiempos*

Primera etapa: **¿Qué te gusta hacer?**
Segunda etapa: **¿Adónde fuiste?**
Tercera etapa: **Una semana típica**

## *Capítulo catorce: Actividades deportivas*

Primera etapa: **Los deportes**
Segunda etapa: **Deportes de verano**

## *Capítulo quince: Dos deportes populares*

Primera etapa: **El béisbol**
Segunda etapa: **El tenis**

# Tu tiempo libre



## Planning Strategy

If you do not assign the Planning Strategy for homework (Workbook, p. 161) you may want to go over the items in class before beginning Chapter 13.

# Chapter Objectives

**Functions:** Talking about activities and events in the past; situating activities in the past
**Context:** Leisure time activities
**Accuracy:** Preterite of regular **-ar, -er, -ir** verbs; preterite of the irregular verbs **hacer, ir, andar, estar, tener;** adverbs and prepositions used for the past

## Cultural Context

**Now may be a good time to bring up the many professional tennis players from Spanish-speaking countries, as well as those of Hispanic descent who are from the U.S. Ask students if they can name any Hispanic tennis players, and if they know where the players are from. Possibilities include: Gabriela Sabatini from Argentina, Arantxa Sánchez Vicario from Spain, Mary Joe Fernández from the United States, Conchita Martínez from Spain, and Jaime Yzaga from Peru.**

CAPÍTULO 13

# LOS PASATIEMPOS

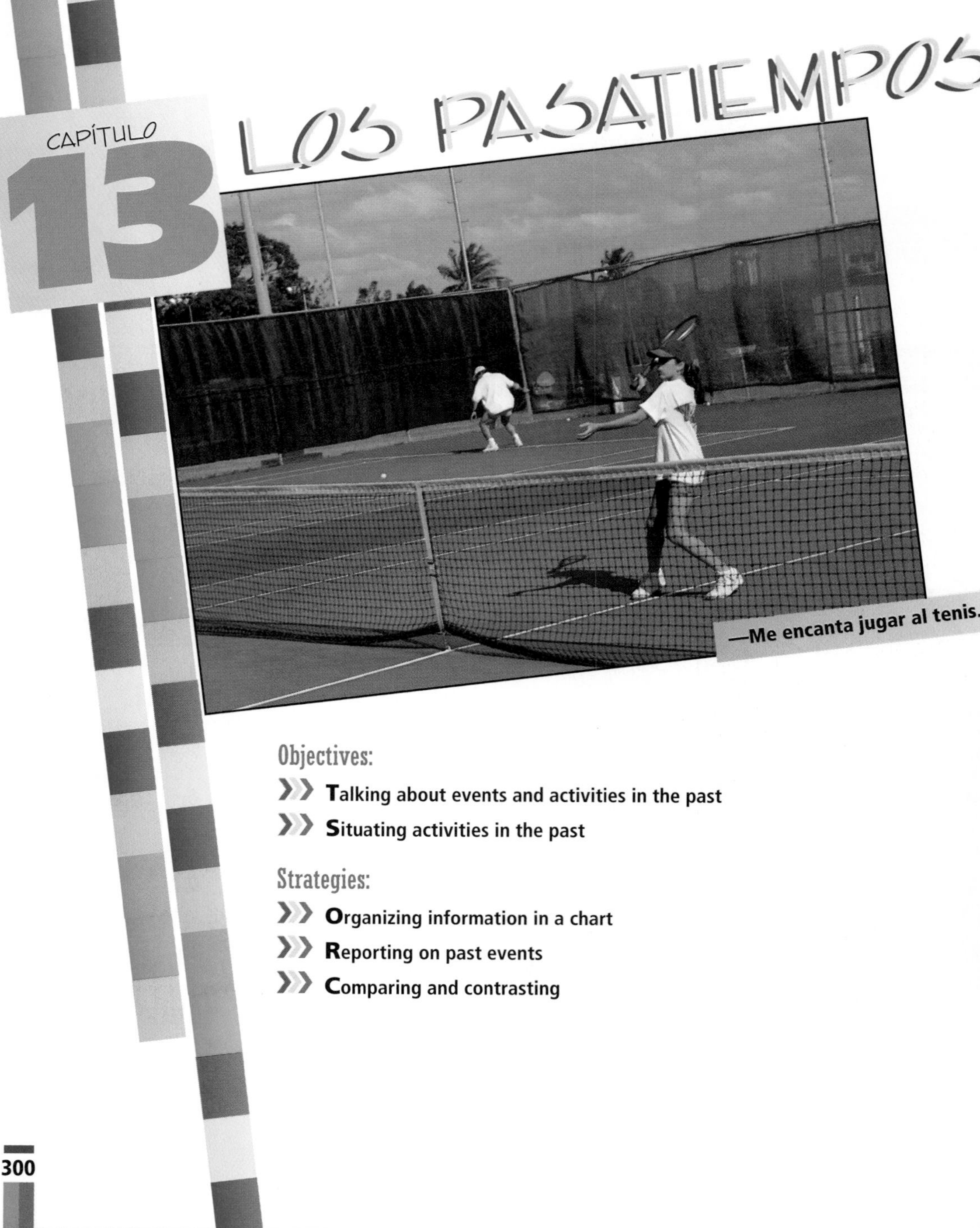

**—Me encanta jugar al tenis.**

### Objectives:

- **T**alking about events and activities in the past
- **S**ituating activities in the past

### Strategies:

- **O**rganizing information in a chart
- **R**eporting on past events
- **C**omparing and contrasting



## Video/CD-ROM

Chapter 13 Video Program
Chapter 13 CD-ROM Program

These can be used at the end of the chapter as expansion activities.

# Aquí practicamos

**C. *Anoche* (Last night)** Di *(say)* lo que *(what)* hicieron tu y tus amigos *(you and your friends did)* anoche. Sigue *(Follow)* el modelo.

**Modelo:** *Yo compré un disco compacto nuevo.*
*Roberto no compró un disco compacto nuevo.*

| A | B | C | D |
|---|---|---|---|
| yo | (no) | comprar | un programa de televisión |
| tú | | mirar | para un examen |
| Roberto | | estudiar | por teléfono |
| nosotros | | hablar | un disco compacto nuevo |
| Uds. | | escuchar | música rock |
| Elena y Juan | | | |

**D. *Por supuesto...*** Your parents have gone out to dinner and returned late at night. They ask what you've been up to while they were out. As they ask you questions, answer in the affirmative.

**Modelo:** ¿Terminaste tu tarea?
*Sí, por supuesto, yo terminé mi tarea.*

1. ¿Hablaste por teléfono con tu amigo?
2. ¿Cenaste aquí?
3. ¿Estudiaste para el examen de español?
4. ¿Miraste un programa de televisión?
5. ¿Tomaste alguna cosa?

**E. *El sábado pasado* (Last Saturday)** Pregúntales *(Ask)* a tus amigos lo que hicieron el sábado pasado. Usa preguntas *(questions)* de tipo sí/no. Sigue el modelo.

**Modelo:** —*¿Estudiaste el sábado pasado?*
—*No, no estudié el sábado pasado.* o:
—*Sí, estudié. Preparé mi examen de matemáticas.*

**Learning Strategy:**
*Requesting and providing specific information*

alquilar un vídeo
caminar al centro
cenar con un(a) amigo(a)
comprar un disco compacto
desayunar en un restaurante
escuchar tu estéreo
hablar por teléfono
mirar televisión
pasar tiempo con tu familia
visitar a un(a) amigo(a)



**Ex. E:** pair work

***More-prepared students, Ex. E:*** Have them construct follow-up questions using interrogative words. For example: **¿Qué programa miraste en la televisión? ¿Quién caminó al centro? ¿A qué hora cenaste con una amiga?** Then have them construct *yes/no* questions using the **Uds.** form, for example: **¿Miraron Uds. la televisión?** Next go on to information questions using **Uds.** as the subject, i.e., **¿Qué miraron Uds. en la televisión?**

***Less-prepared students, Ex. E:*** As extra reinforcement of forms, have students formulate their answers and write out the appropriate verb forms for the first half of the list, before starting the exercise orally. Have them follow a similar procedure with the question forms. You may wish to do a variation of this on the board or on a transparency, perhaps demonstrating the verb forms for only the even- or the odd-numbered sentences.

***Answers, Ex. E:*** ¿Alquilaste... ? ... alquilé ¿Caminaste... ? ... caminé... . ¿Cenaste... ? ...cené... . ¿Compraste... ? ...compré... . ¿Desayunaste... ? ...desayuné ¿Escuchaste... ? ... escuché mi estéreo. ¿Hablaste... ? ...hablé... . ¿Miraste... ? ... miré... . ¿Pasaste... ? ...pasé... con mi familia. ¿Visitaste... ? ...visité... .

## Exercise Progression

Ex. C provides mechanical practice with preterite forms in a personalized context. Ex. D is pair work in a question/answer format in which short but meaningful conversational exchanges occur.

***Suggestion, Ex. C:*** These column exercises are meant to provide controlled practice. One way to present these would be through the creation of a "word web." On a separate piece of paper, students would draw a web, then connect elements from the columns to form grammatically correct sentences. (They would have to write in the correct form of the verb in the middle column.) See the diagram below for a sample word web format. These will vary from exercise to exercise.

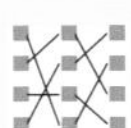

## Presentation: The preterite of the verb hacer

You may wonder why **hacer** is introduced here before the students have seen **-er** and **-ir** verbs in the preterite. By presenting **hacer** here, students can learn to ask meaningful questions at an early stage **(¿Qué hiciste anoche?, ¿Qué hizo María ayer?),** while continuing to answer with the many **-ar** verbs they know.

Introduce **hacer** by contrasting an action in the present and the past. For example: **Yo hago ejercicios todos los sábados. Yo hice ejercicios el sábado pasado.** (Gesture with your hands to indicate the past.) **También hice ejercicios ayer. ¿Hiciste tú ejercicios ayer?** Then summarize in the third person. **Él(Ella) (no) hizo ejercicios ayer.** Continue in the same manner with the plural forms. Then write the conjugation on the board and have students point out how it is different from the preterite of **-ar** verbs they have learned (no written accent marks, **i** instead of **a** predominant, etc.) Be sure to point out the spelling change in the third person singular if students do not notice it.

# Nota gramatical

## *The preterite of the verb hacer*

| | |
|---|---|
| —¿Qué **hizo** Tomás ayer? | What *did* Tomás *do* yesterday? |
| —Tomás **habló** con el profesor. | Tomás *talked* to the teacher. |
| —¿Qué **hicieron** ellos anoche? | What *did* they *do* last night? |
| —Ellos **estudiaron** mucho. | They *studied* a lot. |
| —¿Qué **hiciste** tú anoche? | What *did* you *do* last night? |
| —**No hice** nada. | I *didn't do* anything. |

The verb **hacer** is used in the preterite to talk about what was done in the past. Notice that when you are asked a question about the past with the verb **hacer**, you respond with a different verb that expresses what was done. Use **hacer** in your response only if you want to say that nothing was done, in which case you would say ***no hice nada, no hicimos nada,*** etc.

In the preterite, the verb **hacer** is conjugated as follows:

| *hacer* | | | |
|---|---|---|---|
| yo | **hice** | nosotros(as) | **hicimos** |
| tú | **hiciste** | vosotros(as) | **hicisteis** |
| él / ella / Ud. | **hizo** | ellos / ellas / Uds. | **hicieron** |

Here are some expressions with **hacer.**

| | |
|---|---|
| **hacer un viaje** | *to take a trip* |
| **hacer la cama** | *to make the bed* |
| **hacer las maletas** | *to pack* |
| **hacer ejercicio** | *to exercise* |
| **hacer un mandado** | *to run an errand* |

| | |
|---|---|
| Ellos **hicieron un viaje** a Bogotá, Colombia, el año pasado. | They *took a trip to* Bogota, Colombia, last year. |
| Ernestito **hizo la cama** ayer. | Ernestito *made the bed* yesterday. |
| **¿Hiciste las maletas** para tu viaje a México? | *Did you pack* for your trip to Mexico? |

*F.* Sustituye las palabras en cursiva *(italics)* con las palabras que estén entre paréntesis y haz *(make)* los otros cambios necesarios.

1. *Yo* no hice nada anoche. (nosotros / ella / ellos / tú / Ud. / vosotros)
2. ¿Qué hizo *Ud.* ayer? (tú / él / yo / Uds. / ellos / vosotras)
3. *Julio* hizo las maletas ayer. (yo / tú / María / nosotros / ellas)

*G.* ***¿Qué hicieron anoche?*** Un(a) amigo(a) quiere saber lo que hicieron tú y tus amigos anoche. Trabaja con un(a) compañero(a) *(partner)* y contesta *(answer)* según *(according to)* el modelo.

*—¿Qué hizo Roberto anoche?*
*—Roberto habló con María.*

**Roberto**

**Learning Strategy:**

*Reporting based on visual cues*

1. José

2. Marta y Ana

3. Melisa

4. Luis y Elena

5. Esteban

6. Sara



**Ex. G:** pair work

*Answers, Ex. G:* Students substitute the cues, using the forms of these verbs: 1. hizo / cenó 2. hicieron / escucharon 3. hizo / estudió 4. hicieron/ miraron 5. hizo / alquiló 6. hizo / habló

*Follow-up, Ex. G:* Have students create additional pictographs for their partners to identify and use in their answers. Draw pictographs of someone doing exercises/making their bed/doing their homework in one column; in another have students draw pictographs of someone walking/talking on the phone/watching TV, etc. Ask **¿Qué hizo Juan (María, etc.) anoche?** for each pictograph and have the whole class say what happened in each one. Point out and contrast very strongly cases where **hacer** is used in the answers versus cases where another verb is used.

Remind all students again of the spelling change from **c** to **z** in **hizo.**

*More-prepared students, Ex. G:* Have the pairs ask and answer about their real-life activities from last night.

*Less-prepared students, Ex. G:* Brainstorm with students about their real-life activities from yesterday or last night. Have them formulate how to ask their partners about yesterday. Then have them work in pairs asking and answering about last night.

## Exercise Progression

x. F provides mechanical practice with the preterite forms f **hacer** and their spelling changes. Ex. G follows a more neaningful question/answer format in which students nust respond without **hacer** in their answers. Ex. H, on the ollowing page, continues to reinforce this question/answer attern in structured pair work.

*Answers, Ex. F:* 1. nosotros no hicimos, ella no hizo, ellos no hicieron, tú no hiciste, Ud. no hizo, vosotros no hicisteis 2. hiciste tú, hizo él, hice yo, hicieron Uds., hicieron ellos, hicisteis vosotras 3. yo hice, tú hiciste, María hizo, nosotros hicimos, ellas hicieron

**Ex. H:**  pair work

*Answers, Ex. H:* Students substitute the cues, using the forms of these verbs: 1. visitaste / visité 2. estudiaste / estudié 3. hablaste / hablé 4. tomaste / tomé 5. escuchaste / escuché

*Suggestion Ex. H:* Have students create three additional items for each half of the exercise.

### Aquí escuchamos

After students have listened to the tape at least twice, ask volunteers to provide and write information for the chart (prepared ahead) on the board. You may wish to use part of this section for dictation practice as well.

*Answers, Aquí esuchamos:*

Juan: likes swimming and exercising
doesn't like listening to music

Eva: likes riding a bicycle
doesn't like talking on the phone

Esteban: likes renting videocassettes
doesn't like going to the movies

Elena: likes shopping
doesn't like exercising

*Support material, Aquí escuchamos:*
Teacher Tape/CD #2 Track #11 and Tapescript



**H. *¿Qué hiciste en casa de tu prima?*** Your parents were out of town, so you spent yesterday at your cousin Anita's house. Today, your friends want to know how you spent the day. Work with a partner and follow the model.

**Modelo:** hablar con María, Linda
—*¿Hablaste con María?*
—*No hablé con María, pero hablé con Linda.*

1. visitar a Julián, Alicia
2. estudiar con Teresa, Julia
3. hablar con los padres de Miguel, su hermana
4. tomar café, jugo de naranja
5. escuchar la radio, una cinta de Janet Jackson

## Aquí escuchamos:

### "¿Qué te gusta hacer?"

*Learning Strategies:*
*Previewing, listing*

### Antes de escuchar

**You will hear various students talking about what they like and don't like to do in their free time. What activities do you think they will mention? Make a list based on the leisure-time activities you have learned to discuss in Spanish. Then, before you listen, take a moment and copy the following chart on a separate piece of paper.**

| | Sí | No |
|---|---|---|
| Juan | | |
| Eva | | |
| Esteban | | |
| Elena | | |

*Learning Strategies:*
*Listening for details, taking notes in a chart*

### Después de escuchar

**Now listen to the tape again and indicate what each person likes to do and doesn't like to do.**

EJERCICIO ORAL

**I. *¿Qué hiciste tú durante* (during) *el fin de semana?*** It's Monday morning, and you and your friend are telling each other what you did and did not do over the weekend. Working in pairs, interview your partner to find out how he or she spent last weekend. Record your partner's responses in a chart like the one below.

When you are asking questions, use expressions like **¿Qué hiciste tú el viernes pasado por la tarde?** When you are answering questions, choose from among the suggestions provided here and be sure to use the preterite in your conversation. Possible activities: **trabajar mucho, mirar la televisión, bailar mucho, hablar por teléfono, estudiar,** etc.

| | |
|---|---|
| viernes por la noche | |
| sábado por la mañana | |
| sábado por la noche | |
| domingo por la tarde | |
| domingo por la noche | |

*Learning Strategies:*

*Interviewing, taking notes in a chart*

EJERCICIO ESCRITO

**J. *La semana pasada*** (1) Make a list of five things you did last week. For each activity on your list, tell on which day and at what time of day you did it. (2) When you have completed your list, work with a partner to fill out a chart like the one below. (3) For the activities that you both did, find out if you had a similar schedule **(¿Cuándo estudiaste para el examen de inglés?).**

| Mis actividades | Las actividades de nosotros(as) dos | Las actividades de mi compañero(a) |
|---|---|---|
| | | |
| | | |
| | | |

*Cooperative Learning*

*Learning Strategies:*

*Listing, organizing information in a chart*

*Critical Thinking Strategy:*

*Comparing and contrasting*



**Ex. I:** pair work

*Suggestion, Ex. I:* Have students add at least one time not included on the chart and at least one or two activities not listed in their text.

**Ex. J:** writing

*Follow-up, Ex. J:* Have students use information from their charts to write a short paragraph comparing and contrasting their week with their partner's. You may wish to have them read and edit each other's work.

## Preparación

Using the questions from **Preparación,** have students discuss their free time. Then ask them what they think students from the Hispanic world do in their free time. Do they think their activities will be the same or different, and in what ways? After this brief discussion, have students read out loud the conversation between Cristina and Carmen. As a follow-up to the dialogue and to present new expressions from p. 311 as well, ask *yes/no* questions about the girls' activities, using the new expressions. For example: **¿Cristina fue al médico? ¿Carmen fue de compras? ¿Cristina fue a la biblioteca? ¿No? ¿Quién fue a la biblioteca?,** etc.

*Support material, ¿Adónde fuiste?:*
Teacher Tape/CD #2 Track #12, transparency #54



# SEGUNDA ETAPA

**Learning Strategies:**
*Previewing, brainstorming*

### Preparación

- **Where do you go in your free time?**
- **What are some of the events you attend (games, concerts, and so on)?**

## ¿Adónde fuiste?

—¿Adónde fuiste anoche?
—A un partido de fútbol. ¿Y tú?
—Fui a un concierto.

It's Monday morning and before class begins, Carmen and her friend, Cristina, are talking about where they and some of their friends went last Saturday afternoon.

**Carmen:** Hola, Cristina, ¿cómo estás?
**Cristina:** Bien, y tú, ¿qué tal?
**Carmen:** Muy, muy bien. ¿Qué hiciste el sábado pasado? **¿Fuiste** al cine?
**Cristina:** No, no. No **fui** al cine. Roberto y yo **fuimos** al concierto. ¿Y tú?
**Carmen:** Yo **fui** a la biblioteca.
**Cristina:** **¿Fuiste** con tu novio?
**Carmen:** No, él **fue** al gimnasio.
**Cristina:** Y tu hermano, ¿qué hizo? **¿Fue** al gimnasio, también?
**Carmen:** No, mi hermano y su novia **fueron** al partido de fútbol.



## Etapa Support Materials

Workbook: **pp. 168–171**
Critical Thinking Masters: **p. 13**
Transparency: **#54**
Quiz: **Testing Program, p. 147**

Support material, **¿Adónde fuiste?:**
**Transparency #54**

a la biblioteca

a un restaurante

a la piscina

al cine

de compras

a una fiesta

a la playa

a un museo

al parque

al parque zoológico

al gimnasio

a casa de un(a) amigo(a)

al centro

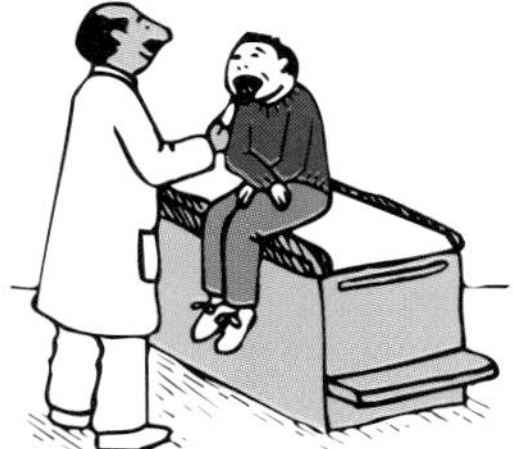

al médico

## Presentation: The preterite of ir

Begin by making statements in the present tense and then changing them to the past tense and asking follow-up questions. For example: **Yo siempre voy al cine los sábados. Yo fui al cine el sábado pasado.** (Gesture to show the past.) **¿Tú fuiste al cine también, Juan?** Summarize his answer in the third person. Continue with the plural forms. Then write the conjugations on the board and have students point out what they notice is different from the other verbs they have studied in the preterite (no accents, etc.).

**Ex. A:**  pair work

*Answers, Ex. A:* Students substitute the cues, using these verbs and articles: 1. fue / fue al 2. fue / fue al 3. fuiste / fui a la 4. fueron / fueron al 5. fueron / fueron al 6. fue / fue al 7. fueron / fueron al 8. fue / fue al

*Follow-up, Ex. A:* Ask different students where they went last night or last weekend. Add third-person follow-up questions occasionally to see if students have been listening. Try to practice all forms of the verbs.



## Nota gramatical

### The preterite of the verb *ir*

| | |
|---|---|
| Yo **fui** al cine anoche. | I *went* to the movies last night. |
| Ellos **fueron** a un concierto el sábado pasado. | They *went* to a concert last Saturday. |
| Nosotros **fuimos** al centro ayer. | We *went* downtown yesterday. |
| **¿Fuiste** tú a la fiesta de Julia el viernes pasado? | *Did you go* to Julia's party last Friday? |
| No, no **fui** a la fiesta. | No, I *did* not *go* to the party. |

In the preterite, the verb **ir** is conjugated as follows:

| *ir* | | | |
|---|---|---|---|
| yo | **fui** | nosotros(as) | **fuimos** |
| tú | **fuiste** | vosotros(as) | **fuisteis** |
| él / ella / Ud. | **fue** | ellos / ellas / Uds. | **fueron** |

## ¡Aquí te toca a ti!

**A. *¿Adónde fue...?*** Un(a) amigo(a) pregunta adónde fueron todos *(everyone went)* ayer por la tarde *(yesterday afternoon)*. Sigue el modelo.

David / cine
—*¿Adónde fue David?*
—*Fue al cine.*

1. Carmen / concierto
2. tu hermana / museo
3. tú / biblioteca
4. Jorge y Hernando / banco
5. Victoria y Claudia / restaurante
6. la profesora / médico
7. tus padres / centro
8. Mario / parque zoológico

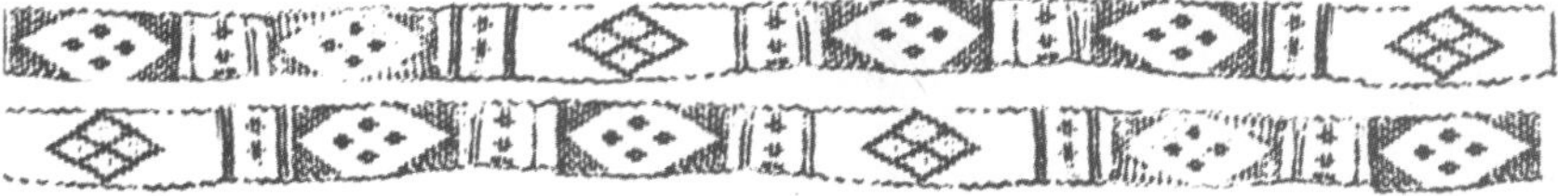



## Exercise Progression

Ex. A presents mechanical practice with preterite forms of **ir.** On the following page, Ex. B personalizes practice in a question/answer format; Ex. C reinforces the question/answer pattern in a whole-group communicative activity; Ex. D reviews and provides variations in the expression of likes and dislikes and allows students to create meaningful conversational exchanges.

**canciones, el libro/los libros, la casa/las casas,** etc. Then do a similar one using infinitives (**-r** forms), reminding students to use the singular in these cases. For example: **Me gusta bailar/estudiar/mirar la televisión/hacer la tarea/cenar en un restaurante,** etc.

**B. *¿Adónde fuiste?*** Ahora pregúntale a un compañero(a) adónde fue ayer. Sigue el modelo.

biblioteca /cine
—*¿Adónde fuiste ayer? ¿A la biblioteca?*
—*No, fui al cine.*

1. a la playa / a la piscina
2. a un restaurante / a casa de un(a) amigo(a)
3. al parque / al gimnasio
4. al partido de básquetbol / al concierto
5. a la biblioteca / de compras
6. a la piscina / a una fiesta

**C. *¿Adónde fuiste anoche?*** Now circulate around the room and ask at least eight of your classmates where they went last night. Create a chart of their responses like the one below, showing who went where. Be prepared to report your findings to the class.

**Learning Strategies:**

*Completing a chart, taking notes in a chart, reading a chart*

| | Nombre | Nombre | Nombre | Nombre |
|---|---|---|---|---|
| a un restaurante | *Luis* | *Carla* | | |
| al parque | | | | |
| al cine | *David* | | | |
| a una fiesta | | | | |
| a casa de un(a) amigo(a) | | | | |
| a un partido de básquetbol | | | | |
| al trabajo | | | | |
| ... | | | | |
| ... | | | | |

## Repaso

**D. *No, no me gusta..., prefiero...*** You are discussing what you like and do not like to do. When your partner asks you if you like to do something, you respond negatively and indicate what you prefer to do instead. Follow the model.

**Learning Strategy:**

*Expressing preferences*

estudiar
—*¿Te gusta estudiar?*
—*No, no me gusta estudiar. Prefiero ir al cine.*

**. B:** groups of four or more

*…uggestion, Ex. C:* You might want to brainstorm with the …ss to create a list on the board of some additional places they …ld include on their charts of places people went last night.

*…minder, Ex. C:* When the ellipses (...) appear as additional …s in a chart, it is intended that the students come up with and … in other personalized options that are appropriate for their …cussion.

*Follow-up, Ex. C:* Poll students informally to find out what activities were the most/least popular, how many students had the same activities, etc. You may also want to have students write up their information as a short report. You may want to have them read and edit each other's work before they turn it in.

*Reteaching, Ex. D:* Before doing Ex. D, review the verb **gustar** with students. Remind them that usually only 3rd person singular and plural forms are used, i.e., **gusta/gustan.** Do a short substitution drill orally or written on the board or transparency with items such as **Me gusta(n) la canción/las**

## Presentation: The preterite of -er and -ir verbs

After you have introduced the verbs using a monologue, write the forms on the board and have students point out how they are the same or different from the other preterite verbs they have studied. (You might want to write the conjugation of an **-ar** verb and the verb **hacer** on the board so they can compare them.) Ask them which form is the same in both the present and the preterite tenses (**nosotros** form of **-ir** verbs).

1. estudiar
2. leer
3. hacer ejercicio
4. ir al cine
5. caminar por el parque
6. mirar la televisión
7. correr
8. alquilar vídeos
9. ir de compras
10. ?

# ESTRUCTURA

## *The preterite of -er and -ir verbs*

| | |
|---|---|
| Yo **comí** en un restaurante anoche. | I *ate* in a restaurant last night. |
| Nosotros **escribimos** una carta ayer. | We *wrote* a letter yesterday. |
| Susana **no comprendió** la lección. | Susana *did not understand* the lesson. |
| **¿Recibieron** Uds. una invitación a la fiesta? | Did you *receive* an invitation to the party? |
| Ella **salió de** casa temprano ayer. | She *left* home early yesterday. |

To conjugate **-er** and **-ir** verbs in the preterite, drop the **-er** or **-ir** and add the following endings:

| *comer, vivir* | | | | | | | |
|---|---|---|---|---|---|---|---|
| yo | **com-** | ***í*** | ***comí*** | nosotros(as) | **com-** | ***imos*** | ***comimos*** |
| | **viv-** | ***í*** | ***viví*** | | **viv-** | ***imos*** | ***vivimos*** |
| tú | **com-** | ***iste*** | ***comiste*** | vosotros(as) | **com-** | ***isteis*** | ***comisteis*** |
| | **viv-** | ***iste*** | ***viviste*** | | **viv-** | ***isteis*** | ***vivisteis*** |
| él / ella / Ud. | **com-** | ***ió*** | ***comió*** | ellos / ellas / Uds. | **com-** | ***ieron*** | ***comieron*** |
| | **viv-** | ***ió*** | ***vivió*** | | **viv-** | ***ieron*** | ***vivieron*** |

Notice that the preterite endings for both **-er** and **-ir** verbs are identical and that the **yo** and the **él, ella, Ud.** forms have a written accent.

Other **-er** verbs

**aprender** *to learn*
**correr** *to run*
**perder** *to lose*
**vender** *to sell*
**volver** *to return*

Other **-ir** verbs

**asistir a** *to attend*
**compartir** *to share*
**salir con** *to go out with*
**salir de** *to leave*

# Aquí practicamos

**E. *Ayer* (Yesterday) *después de la escuela*** Di lo que hicieron tú y tus amigos ayer después de la escuela.

| A | B | C | D |
|---|---|---|---|
| yo | (no) | comer | pizza |
| Miguel | | escribir | dos cartas |
| tú | | recibir | los ejercicios del libro |
| Pedro y yo | | salir con | un(a) amigo(a) |
| Linda y Fernando | | asistir a | un partido |
| Ud. | | correr | un libro |
| | | perder | dos millas |

**F. *El fin de semana*** Compare notes with your partner about what you did over the weekend. Use the following expressions to begin asking each other questions. Find at least one activity that you both did.

comer en un restaurante
—*¿Comiste en un restaurante?*
—*Sí, comí en un restaurante.* o:
—*No, no comí en un restaurante.*

1. aprender información interesante
2. asistir a un concierto
3. perder la cartera
4. escribir una carta a tu amigo(a)
5. discutir algún problema con un(a) amigo(a)
6. recibir un regalo (*gift*)
7. correr un poco
8. comer en un restaurante
9. salir con un(a) amigo(a)
10. volver a casa tarde

Cooperative Learning

Learning Strategy:
*Asking questions*

Critical Learning Strategy:
*Comparing and contrasting*

**G. *Una tarde típica* (typical)** Using the drawings and verbs provided on page 316 as guides, explain to your parents how you and your boyfriend (girlfriend) spent the afternoon. Follow the model.

salir
*Salimos de la escuela.*

Learning Strategy:
*Reporting based on visual cues*



**Ex. F:** pair work

*Answers, Ex. F:*
1. aprendiste / aprendí
2. asististe / asistí
3. perdiste / perdí
4. escribiste / escribí
5. discutiste / discutí
6. recibiste / recibí
7. corriste / corrí
8. comiste / comí
9. saliste/salí
10. volviste / volví

*Follow-up, Ex. F:* Continue to ask questions with interrogative words to practice listening comprehension. Ask follow-up questions in the third person to practice all of the forms. Start out with **tú** questions and then practice **Uds.** questions. For example: **¿Qué hiciste anoche, Juan? (Yo estudié.) ¿Qué hizo Juan? ¿Miró la televisión?,** etc. **¿Qué hicieron tú y tus amigos/amigas el sábado pasado? (Asistimos a un partido de básquetbol.) ¿Qué hicieron ellos? ¿Estudiaron para un examen?,** etc.

**Ex. G:** pair work

## Exercise Progression

Ex. E is a mechanical drill designed to practice using the preterite forms of the verbs. Ex. F is a more personalized question/answer format, providing similar practice in a communicative format. Ex. G practices the contrasts between **-ar, -er,** and **-ir** verbs.

*Possible answers, Ex. G:*
1. Tomamos el autobús. 2. Estudiamos español. 3. Caminamos a su casa. 4. Escuchamos música y ella bailó. 5. Salimos de su casa. 6. Compramos un libro. 7. Comimos en un restaurante mexicano. 8. Miramos la televisión. 9. Escribimos una carta. 10. Bebimos un refresco en un café.

*Follow-up, Ex. G:* Now that students have additional verbs at their disposal, you can redo the **¡Adelante!** activities from the first **etapa** on p. 309. Have students use **-er** and **-ir** verbs along with **hacer** and **ir**. They can therefore give more details about their activities. It is often a good idea to brainstorm some possible verbs and expressions before beginning the activity. This also provides the opportunity to add expressions for things that students are anxious to know how to express.

## Aquí escuchamos

After students have listened to the tape at least twice, ask volunteers to provide and write information for the chart (prepared ahead) on the board. You may wish to use part of this section for dictation practice as well.

*Support material, Aquí escuchamos:*
Teacher Tape/CD #2 Track #13 and Tapescript

1. tomar

2. estudiar

3. caminar

4. escuchar

5. salir

6. comprar

7. comer

8. mirar

9. escribir

10. beber

# Aquí escuchamos:
## "¿Qué hiciste anoche?"

*Critical Thinking Strategy:*
*Predicting*

### Antes de escuchar

**You will hear a short conversation in which two students talk about what they did last night. Based on what you have been studying in this etapa, what do you think they will say?**

**Before you listen, take a moment and look at the chart on page 317. Copy it on a separate piece of paper.**

| | Olga | Esteban |
|---|---|---|
| estudiar | | |
| leer | | |
| mirar televisión | | |
| cenar con amigos | | |
| hablar por teléfono | | |
| escribir cartas | | |
| caminar | | |

**Learning Strategies:**

*Listening for details, taking notes in a chart*

## Después de escuchar

Now listen to the tape again and check off on your chart what each person did.

## ¡Adelante!

EJERCICIO ORAL

**H. *¿Adónde fuiste y qué hiciste el verano pasado?*** Talk to five of your classmates. (1) Find out one place they went and one activity that they did last summer. (2) Make a list of their responses. (3) Select the most interesting place and the most interesting activity and report them to the class.

**Learning Strategies:**

*Asking questions, listing*

**Critical Thinking Strategy:**

*Evaluating*

EJERCICIO ESCRITO

**I. *La semana pasada*** (Last week) Your pen pal in Argentina has reminded you that it is your turn to write. Write a note telling what you did and where you went last week. Indicate at least five things that you did and include at least two places that you went.

**Learning Strategies:**

*Listing, requesting personal information*



**Ex. H:**  groups of four or more

***Variation, Ex. H:*** You could have students write a paragraph with the information that they learned from their classmates, and then choose several students to read them to the class.

***Follow-up, Ex. H:*** Be sure to ask questions to give students the opportunity to report back to the class.

**Ex. I:** writing

***Follow-up, Ex. I:*** Have students read and then edit each other's letters and mark in pencil or different color ink possible errors to then point out to each other.

***Less-prepared students, Ex. I:*** Brainstorm possible vocabulary and expressions with them first. Have them recall the correct format of the verbs before they begin to write.

***More-prepared students, Ex. I:*** Allow them to write responses to their partners' letters, telling about their own invented activities and including questions about the activities mentioned in the original letters. (For more realistic responses, teacher could bring realia, i.e., photos, etc. from Buenos Aires or other Argentine cities to trigger these responses.)

***Answers, Aquí escuchamos:*** Olga—check: leer, escribir cartas; Esteban—check hablar por teléfono, mirar televisión

*Reteaching,* ***Una semana típica:*** Go back over the days of the week orally, and then write them on the board. Do a brief substitution review orally. For example: **Si hoy es lunes, ¿qué día es mañana? Si hoy es ________ , ¿qué día es mañana?** Then do the same with **pasado mañana.** Then shift to **ayer/anteayer,** i.e., **Si hoy es lunes, ¿qué día fue ayer?,** etc.

*Support material,* ***Una semana típica:*** Teacher Tape/CD #2 Track #14

# TERCERA ETAPA

## Preparación

**As you begin this etapa, think about what your routine was last week.**

- **Did you go to school everyday?**
- **Did you participate in any extracurricular activities?**
- **Did you study?**
- **Did you go out? Where?**

*Learning Strategy:*

*Previewing*

## Una semana típica

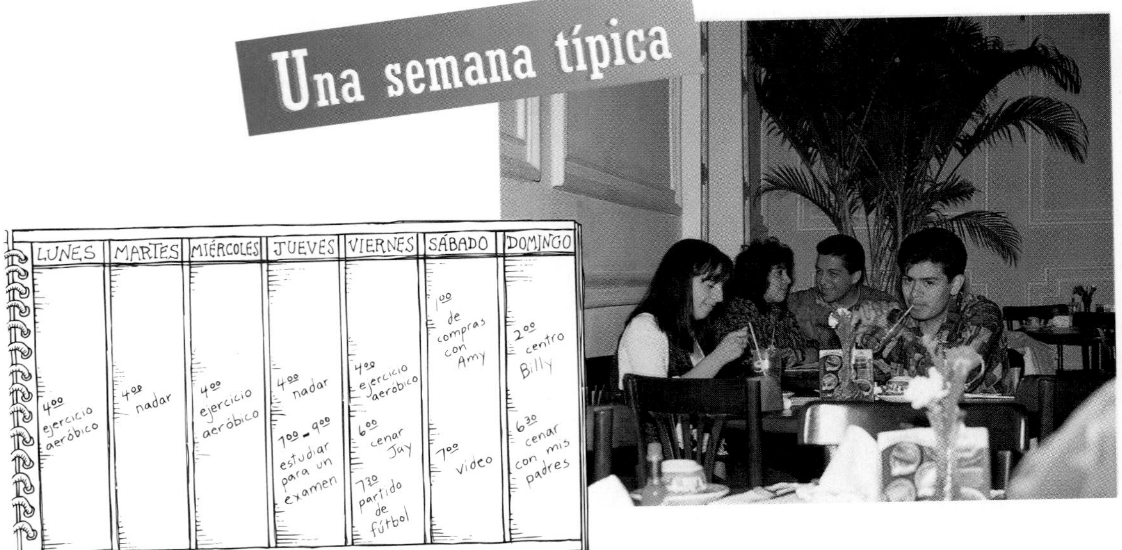


El lunes, miércoles y viernes asistí a mi clase de ejercicio aeróbico. El martes y jueves fui a la piscina y nadé por una hora. El jueves por la noche estudié para un examen por dos horas. El viernes después de mi clase de ejercicio aeróbico, cené con mi novio Jay. Comimos pizza en un restaurante italiano. Después fuimos a un partido de fútbol del equipo de nuestra escuela. Nuestro equipo perdió. El sábado a la una fui de compras con mi amiga Amy. Por la noche, alquilé un vídeo. Invité a mis amigos a mi casa y miramos el vídeo. El domingo fui al centro con mi amigo Billy. Compré dos discos compactos nuevos. Volví a casa a las 5:30 y cené con mis padres.



## Etapa Support Materials

Workbook: **pp. 172–177**
Critical Thinking Master: **p. 14**
Listening Activity masters: **p. 85**
Tapescript: **p. 127**
Quiz: **Testing Program, p. 150**
Chapter Test: **Testing Program, p. 153**

**Ex. A:** pair work

*Possible answers, Ex. B:*
1. El viernes pasado cenó con su novio. 2. El miércoles pasado estudió. 3. El sábado pasado miró la televisión. 4. El domingo pasado alquiló un vídeo. 5. El lunes pasado caminó en el parque. 6. El jueves pasado montó en bicicleta. 7. El martes pasado escuchó música. 8. El domingo pasado habló con sus padres.

# ¡Aquí te toca a ti!

**A. *¿Qué hizo Elisabeth?*** Con *(with)* un(a) compañero(a) di lo que hizo Elisabeth en los días específicos *(on the specific days)* de la semana pasada *(last week)*. Empieza *(Begin)* con el lunes pasado: ¿Qué hizo Elisabeth el lunes pasado?

1. lunes
2. martes
3. jueves
4. viernes
5. domingo

**B. *¿Qué hizo Elisabeth la semana pasada?*** Di lo que hizo Elisabeth la semana pasada. Basa *(Base)* tus respuestas *(answers)* en los dibujos *(drawings)*. Sigue el modelo.

**Learning Strategy:**
*Reporting based on visual cues*

**Modelo:** sábado
*El sábado pasado Elisabeth alquiló un vídeo.*

1. viernes

2. miércoles

3. sábado

4. domingo

5. lunes

6. jueves

7. martes

8. domingo



## Exercise Progression

Ex. A draws on information from the opening reading, and reinforces the question pattern with **hacer,** answers without **hacer.** It also practices time expressions. Ex. B continues this same pattern and reinforces vocabulary through the use of visual support.

*Possible answers, Ex. C:*
1. Marisol salió con su hermano. 2. Marrirosa y Juan fueron a un concierto de rock. 3. José escribió una carta.

*Follow-up, Ex. C:* Ask personalized questions based on the pictures using interrogative words. (You might want to use the **pregúntale** format.) Be sure to ask follow-up questions in the third person, to see if students are listening carefully.

## Presentation: Adverbs, prepositions, and other expressions used to designate the past

Write on the board today's date plus dates for last week, this year, and last year. Work backwards from **hoy** through **ayer, la semana pasada, el mes pasado** to **el año pasado.** Then introduce the notion of duration **(por).** As you introduce these lexical items, it would be useful to introduce the interrogative phrase **¿Por cuánto tiempo?** For example: **¿Por cuánto tiempo estudiaste anoche? Por cuánto tiempo corriste esta mañana?,** etc.

## Repaso

**C. ¿Qué hicieron?** Basándote en los dibujos, di lo que hizo cada *(each)* persona y cuándo.

**Modelo:** Martín y Catarina / el domingo por la tarde
*Martín y Catarina corrieron el domingo por la tarde.*

1. Marisol y su hermano / el lunes por la mañana

2. Marirrosa y Juan / el viernes por la noche

3. José / el miércoles por la tarde

## ESTRUCTURA

### Adverbs, prepositions, and other expressions used to designate the past

| | |
|---|---|
| **La semana pasada** compré un disco compacto. | *Last week* I bought a CD. |
| **El viernes pasado** comimos en un restaurante. | *Last Friday* we ate at a restaurant. |

The following time expressions are used to talk about an action or a condition in the past.

| | | | |
|---|---|---|---|
| **ayer** | *yesterday* | **la semana pasada** | *last week* |
| **ayer por la mañana** | *yesterday morning* | **el fin de semana pasado** | *last weekend* |
| **ayer por la tarde** | *yesterday afternoon* | **el mes pasado** | *last month* |
| **anoche** | *last night* | **el año pasado** | *last year* |
| **anteayer** | *the day before yesterday* | | |
| **el jueves (sábado, etc.) pasado** | *last Thursday (Saturday, etc.)* | | |

The preposition **por** will enable you to express how long you did something.

| | |
|---|---|
| Estudié **por** dos horas. | I studied *for* two hours. |
| Corrió **por** veinte minutos. | She ran *for* twenty minutes. |
| **por una hora (un día, tres años, cuatro meses, quince minutos,** etc.) | *for one hour (one day, three years, four months, fifteen minutes,* etc.) |

# Aquí practicamos

**D. *¿Qué hicieron recientemente* (recently)?** Di lo que hicieron tú y tus amigos recientemente.

| A | B | C | D |
|---|---|---|---|
| nosotros | (no) | cenar en un restaurante | la semana pasada |
| tú | | correr dos millas | ayer por la tarde |
| Margarita y Alicia | | no asistir a clase | el viernes pasado |
| Julián | | alquilar un vídeo | anteayer |
| yo | | hacer ejercicio | ayer por la mañana |
| Marta y yo | | caminar por el parque | el miércoles pasado |

**E. *¿Cuándo?*** Usa las expresiones entre paréntesis *(in parenthesis)* para decir cuándo hiciste las actividades que siguen *(that follow)*. Sigue el modelo.

¿Cuándo hablaste con María? (ayer por la mañana)
*Hablé con María ayer por la mañana.*

1. ¿Cuándo estudiaste francés? (el año pasado)
2. ¿Cuándo corriste? (ayer por la tarde)
3. ¿Cuándo hablaste con tu novia(o)? (el viernes pasado)
4. ¿Cuándo compraste tu bicicleta? (el mes pasado)
5. ¿Cuándo recibiste la carta de Julia? (el jueves pasado)
6. ¿Cuándo comiste pizza? (el domingo pasado)

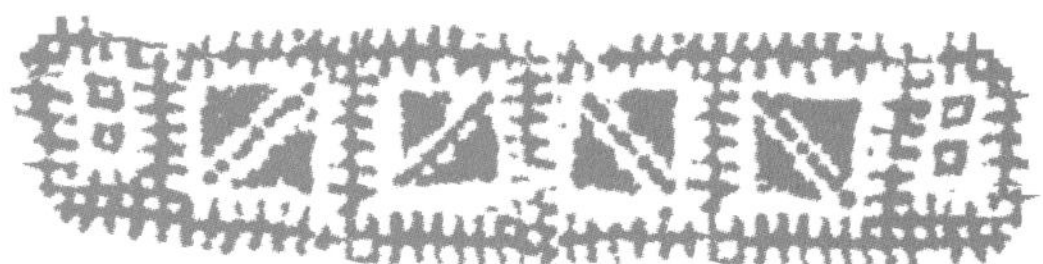

***Suggestion, Ex. D:*** These column exercises are meant to provide controlled practice. A possible way to present these would be through the creation of a "word web." On a separate piece of paper, students would draw a web, and then connect elements from the columns to form grammatically correct sentences. (They would have to write in the correct form of the verb in the middle column.) See the diagram below for a sample word web format. Word web formats will vary from exercise to exercise.

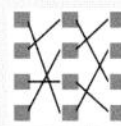

***Answers, Ex. E:*** Students substitute the cues using the following verbs: 1. estudié 2. corrí 3. hablé 4. compré 5. recibí 6. comí

***Follow-up, Ex. E:*** Continue to ask personalized questions using **cuándo.** Ask some **Uds.** questions also. **(¿Cuándo fueron tú y un amigo/una amiga al cine?)**

## Exercise Progression

Ex. D is a mechanical exercise designed to get students to focus on the new expressions. Ex. E offers meaningful practice with these expressions.

## Presentation: The preterite of the verbs **andar, estar,** and **tener**

Point out to students that learning irregular verbs in patterns is easier than learning each one individually. Follow the suggestions in the Teacher's Notes on p. 312.

*Answers, Ex. F:* 1. tú tuviste, Ud. tuvo, Ana y su novio tuvieron, yo tuve, nosotros tuvimos, vosotras tuvisteis 2. Uds. no estuvieron, Diego no estuvo, yo no estuve, tú no estuviste, nosotras no estuvimos, vosotros no estuvisteis 3. anduvo Ud., anduvieron Santiago y Enrique, anduvo Alicia, anduviste tú, anduvisteis vosotros

## Nota gramatical

### The preterite of the verbs *andar, estar,* and *tener*

| | |
|---|---|
| Yo **estuve** en casa de Pablo anteayer. | I *was* at Paul's house the day before yesterday. |
| **¿Anduviste** tú por el parque ayer? | *Did* you *walk* in the park yesterday? |
| Sí, yo **anduve** con mi amiga Paula. | Yes, I *walked* with my friend Paula. |
| Nosotros no **tuvimos** que estudiar anoche. | We *did* not *have* to study last night. |

Many common Spanish verbs are irregular in the preterite. However, some can be grouped together because they follow a similar pattern when conjugated. Note the similarities among the following three verbs when they are conjugated in the preterite.

| *andar, estar, tener* | | | |
|---|---|---|---|
| yo | **anduve**<br>**estuve**<br>**tuve** | nosotros(as) | **anduvimos**<br>**estuvimos**<br>**tuvimos** |
| tú | **anduviste**<br>**estuviste**<br>**tuviste** | vosotros(as) | **anduvisteis**<br>**estuvisteis**<br>**tuvisteis** |
| él<br>ella<br>Ud. | **anduvo**<br>**estuvo**<br>**tuvo** | ellos<br>ellas<br>Uds. | **anduvieron**<br>**estuvieron**<br>**tuvieron** |

*F.* Sustituye las palabras en cursiva con las palabras que están entre paréntesis y haz los otros cambios necesarios.

1. *Catarina* tuvo que estudiar mucho anoche. (tú / Ud. / Ana y su novio / yo / nosotros / vosotras)
2. *Juan y Roberto* no estuvieron en la fiesta de Sofía. (Uds. / Diego / yo / tú / nosotras / vosotros)
3. ¿Anduvieron *Uds.* a la escuela ayer? (Ud. / Santiago y Enrique / Alicia / tú / vosotros)



## Exercise Progression

Ex. F is a mechanical drill designed to focus on the preterite forms of the new verbs. On the following page, Ex. G offers a whole-group communicative exercise using these same forms.

**G. *La semana pasada*** Circulate around the room and ask several classmates the following questions. Have them (1) name three places where they were last week, (2) indicate three places they walked to, and (3) tell three things they had to do. Follow the model.

**Modelo:** *Estuve en la piscina el viernes por la tarde.*
*Anduve al parque el domingo por la mañana.*
*Tuve que estudiar el martes por la noche.*

1. ¿Dónde estuviste la semana pasada?
2. ¿Adónde anduviste la semana pasada?
3. ¿Qué tuviste que hacer la semana pasada?

Aquí escuchamos:
"¿Qué hiciste este fin de semana?"


## Antes de escuchar

**Think about what you did last weekend. You will hear a short conversation in which two students talk about what they did. What are some of the things you think they might talk about? Before you listen to the tape, copy the following chart.**

START

| | Olga | Juan |
|---|---|---|
| fue al parque | | |
| fue a la piscina | | |
| fue a la biblioteca | | |
| fue a cenar en un restaurante | | |
| fue a un concierto | | |
| fue a una fiesta | | |
| fue al gimnasio | | |
| fue de compras | | |
| fue al cine | | |
| estudió | | |
| descansó | | |

*Learning Strategies:*

*Previewing, brainstorming*



**Ex. G:** groups of four or more

*Follow-up, Ex. G:* Have students report back on their classmates' activities. Were there any activities, etc. in common? Was there anyone who did something completely different? Have students ask the teacher similar questions using the **Ud.** form.

### Aquí escuchamos

Have students make a list of their last weekend's activities. Then have them listen to the tape at least twice and complete the chart. Make a master chart on the board and have student volunteers fill in the information. Finally, have students compare their activities to those of Teresa and Juan. Are they similar or very different? Remember, too, that all or part of the **Aquí escuchamos** could be used for dictation practice.

*Support material,*
***Aquí escuchamos:***
Teacher Tape/CD #2 Track #15 and Tapescript

*Answers, Aquí escuchamos:* Olga—check: fue a un concierto, fue a una fiesta, fue al gimnasio, fue al cine, descansó Juan— check: fue a cenar en un restaurante, fue a la biblioteca, fue de compras, estudió, descansó

**Ex. H:** pair work

*Suggestion, Ex. H:* Have students create a questionnaire for this ahead of time. It should include different days of the week **(el lunes,** etc.), different amounts of time **(¿Por cuánto tiempo?),** and different periods during the day **(por la mañana,** etc.)

**Ex. I:** writing

*Less-prepared students, Ex. I:* Brainstorm a possible list of activities with them and have them recall the correct verb format before beginning.

*More-prepared students, Ex. I:* Remind them that a letter is a two-way street and that they need to show interest in their correspondent by asking about his or her activities, as well as telling their own.



*Learning Strategy:*

*Listening for details*

## Después de escuchar

**Listen to the tape again and check off each person's activities on your chart.**

## ¡Adelante!

*Learning Strategy:*

*Interviewing*

EJERCICIO ORAL

**H. *Intercambio*** Work with a partner and discuss what you did last week and for how long. Possible activities: **estudiar, comprar, hablar con amigos, comer, asistir a un concierto, andar, tener que hacer algo,** etc.

*Learning Strategies:*

*Listing, organizing information in a letter*

EJERCICIO ESCRITO

**I. *El fin de semana pasado*** Make a list of six things that you did last weekend. Write a postcard to a friend in Costa Rica, telling what you did.

# Vocabulario

## Para charlar

### Para hablar de una acción en el pasado

anoche
anteayer
el año pasado
ayer
ayer por la mañana
ayer por la tarde
el fin de semana pasado
el jueves (sábado, etc.) pasado
el mes pasado
por una hora (un día, tres años, cuatro meses, quince minutos, etc.)
la semana pasada

### Para hablar de las actividades

alquilar un vídeo
desayunar en un restaurante
montar en bicicleta
nadar

### Lugares adónde vamos

el concierto
el gimnasio
el museo
el parque zoológico

## Vocabulario general

### Verbos

andar
asistir a
caminar
cenar
comprar
no hacer nada
pasar tiempo
perder
salir de
visitar
volver

### Otras expresiones

hacer la cama
hacer ejercicio
hacer las maletas
hacer un viaje
una milla
nada
por un año
por una hora
por un mes
por unos minutos

*…upport material, **Capítulo 13:*** Improvised Con-…sation, Teacher Tape/CD #2 Track #16 and Tapescript; …Manual listening activities, Laboratory Program, …escript, and Teacher's Edition of the Workbook/Lab Manual

*Additional activity, add-on chain:* The first person begins by stating what he or she did last evening. The next person repeats this and adds their activity. The next repeats those two and then adds on, and so on. Students may not repeat verb forms. For example: **Juan cenó en un restaurante, María miró la tele y yo escuché un disco compacto.** This is very good memory and vocabulary practice. If a student gets stuck, try coaching with non-verbal signals. If the class is large, it is possible to divide it into groups and do two or three chains so that they don't become too long or unmanageable.

# Chapter Culminating Activities

groups of four or more

Students take a survey of how their classmates spent last evening. The teacher assigns one or two questions to each student. Students then ask their classmates if they did these things last evening. Students record the number who say *"yes"* and the number who say *"no"* and report to the class. Some possible activities include **mirar la televisión, estudiar, mirar un vídeo, hablar con mis amigos, estudiar para un examen, trabajar, hablar por teléfono con _____, escuchar música, comer pizza, comer chocolate, ir de compras, bailar, correr, salir de casa,** etc.

Working in pairs, students ask each other when they last did the above activities. Insist that they be exact in their answer (**ayer por la mañana, la semana pasada, el año pasado,** etc.) Remind them to use the expression **nunca** for situations where they have never done something. When students have finished questioning each other, have some pairs report back to the class, each person telling about his or her partner.

groups of four or more

Any version of vocabulary charades or bingo are also good ending activities.

# Lectura cultural

## Reading Strategies

In order to develop reading skills, students should approach the text with the goal of general comprehension. If you time the reading (i.e., only allowing a limited amount of time to read the selection), students become accustomed to reading without understanding every single word, thus increasing their reading rate. It might be helpful to point out to students that they should not be trying to decipher (i.e., translate) every word, but should look at the meaning of a whole sentence or paragraph with help provided by the context (photos, headings, known vocabulary, prior knowledge of the topic, etc.).



# Lectura cultural

## ESPAÑA JOVEN

## Antes de leer

In this chapter you have been talking about what young people like to do in their free time. Look at the pictures on page 326. What are the people doing? Look at the title of the reading. What do you think the reading will be about?

## Guía para la lectura

A. What is the main idea of each paragraph?
B. List some things Spanish young people do during the week.
C. List some things Spanish young people do during the weekend.
D. List some things Spanish young people worry about.

**Learning Strategy:**

*Brainstorming*

**Critical Thinking Strategy:**

*Predicting*

**Learning Strategies:**

*Reading for main idea, listing, reading for details*

### España joven

Durante la semana los adolescentes españoles casi no salen, dividen su tiempo entre la casa y la escuela. Cuando están en casa pasan mucho tiempo hablando por teléfono y escuchando música. La mayoría de los chicos y chicas dedican gran parte de su tiempo libre a mirar la televisión. Más de la mitad pasa más de cuatro horas frente al televisor.

Los fines de semana son diferentes. Los jóvenes no se quedan en casa, todos salen con sus amigos, sobre todo a bailar. Por lo general, los más jóvenes deben regresar a casa antes de las 10:30 de la noche. En este sentido, los padres son más estrictos con las chicas que con los chicos.

A pesar de su juventud, les preocupa la crisis económica. Saben que hay mucha gente sin trabajo. En 1994, el desempleo en España subió a 22%. Muchos temen que la situación vaya a afectar su futuro. No están muy interesados en la política, pero muchos se preocupan por la ecología. Dicen que alguien tiene que preocuparse por salvar el planeta.

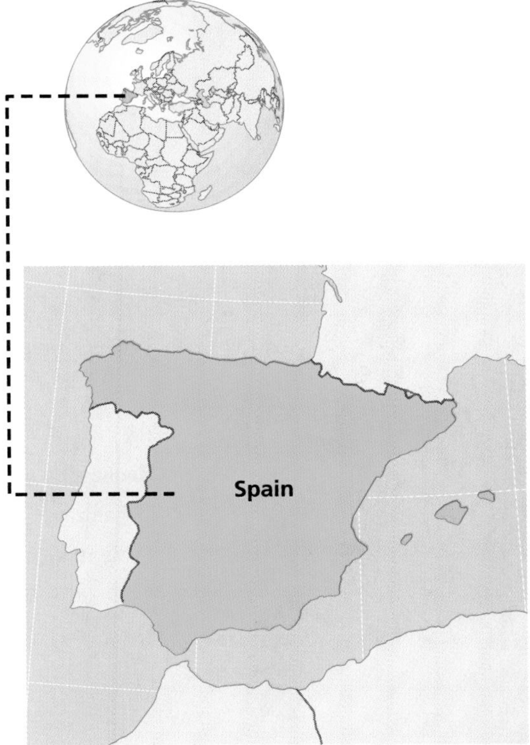




*Answers, Guía para la lectura:* **A.** Paragraph 1: Spanish teens stay in during the week and watch a lot of television. Paragraph 2: On weekends, teens go out with their friends, often to dance. Paragraph 3: Teens are worried about Spain's economic situation. **B.** School, talking on the phone, listening to music, watching TV **C.** go out with friends, dance **D.** the economy, the ecology

## Chapter Objectives

**Functions:** Talking about and situating activities and events in the past
**Context:** Sports and leisure time activities
**Accuracy:** **Hace** and **hace que;** preterite of verbs ending in **-gar** and **-car;** expressions used to talk about a series of actions

## Cultural Context

Let students know that Spain is one of several European countries where basketball has become very popular. It is played in gyms and playgrounds across the country. The presence of the United States "Dream Team" caused particular excitement in Spain during the Olympics in Barcelona. The Spanish national team also did better than ever before during the Barcelona Olympics. Many U.S. basketball players go to Spain to play professionally, and the professional basketball leagues there are pulling increasingly larger audiences.

CAPÍTULO 14

# ACTIVIDADES DEPORTIVAS

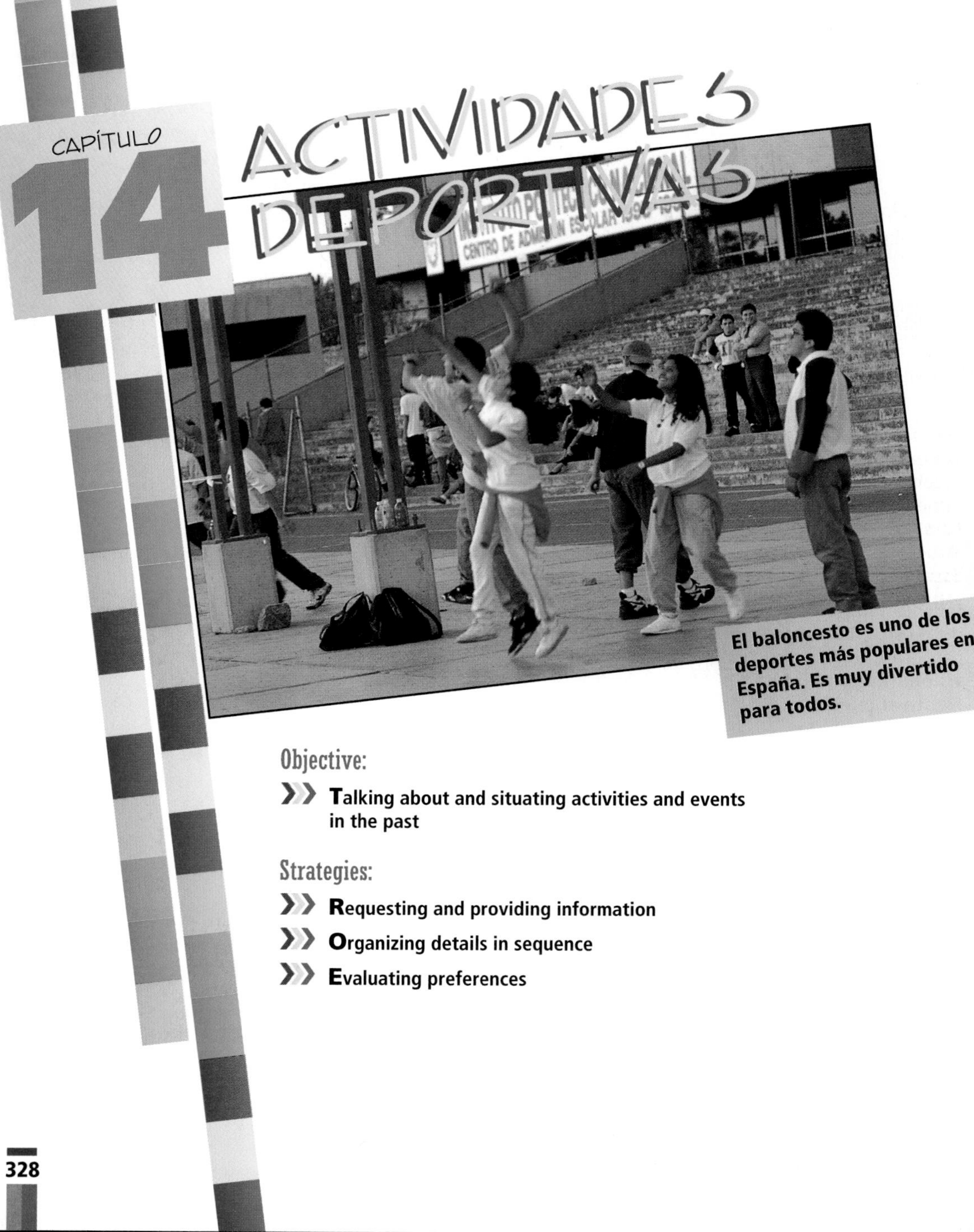

El baloncesto es uno de los deportes más populares en España. Es muy divertido para todos.

**Objective:**

- Talking about and situating activities and events in the past

**Strategies:**

- Requesting and providing information
- Organizing details in sequence
- Evaluating preferences

328

## Video/CD-ROM

Chapter 14 Video Program
Chapter 14 CD-ROM Program

These can be used at the end of the chapter as expansion activities.

Notice that when **hace** is placed at the beginning of the sentence, you must insert **que** before the subject.

| | |
|---|---|
| —**¿Cuánto hace que hablaste** con tu amigo? | *How long ago did you talk* to your friend? |
| —**Hace una semana que hablé** con él. | I *spoke* to him *a week ago.* |

To ask a question with this time expression, use the following model:

**¿Cuánto + hace + que +** *verb in the preterite?*

Some expressions you have already learned for expressing length of time are:

| | |
|---|---|
| **un minuto, dos minutos, tres minutos,** etc. | **una semana, dos semanas, tres semanas,** etc. |
| **una hora, dos horas, tres horas,** etc. | **un mes, dos meses, tres meses,** etc. |
| **un día, dos días, tres días,** etc. | **un año, dos años, tres años,** etc. |

## Aquí practicamos

*D.* Sustituye las palabras en cursiva con las palabras que están entre paréntesis y haz los otros cambios necesarios.

1. Hace *2 días* que Juan habló con su novia. (5 horas / 4 meses / 6 días / 1 mes / 3 semanas)
2. Marirrosa vendió su bicicleta hace *3 meses.* (8 días / 1 año / 6 semanas / 2 horas / 3 meses)

*E.* ***Hablé con ella hace...*** Un(a) amigo(a) quiere saber *(wants to know)* cuánto tiempo hace que hiciste algo *(how long ago you did something)*. Habla con un(a) compañero(a) y sigue el modelo.

**Modelo:** hablar con ella / 2 horas
—*¿Cuánto hace que hablaste con ella?*
—*Hablé con ella hace 2 horas.*

1. vivir en Indiana / 10 años
2. estudiar francés / 2 años
3. comprar la bicicleta / 3 meses
4. recibir la carta de Ana / 5 días
5. comer en un restaurante / 2 semanas
6. ir al cine / 3 semanas



### Exercise Progression

Ex. D is a mechanical substitution drill designed to practice the *"ago"* structures with different periods of time. Ex. E offers practice in a controlled question/answer format.

**Ex. E:** pair work

*Reteaching:* Some students may benefit from handling, sorting, and arranging 3 x 5 cards that have the *"ago"* formula written on them. Have them manipulate groups of five cards: 1. **Hace;** 2. (time); 3. **que;** 4. (person or persons); 5. (verb in the preterite). Students could also be given blank cards on which to write their own *"ago"* sentence for another student to unscramble.

A possible listening exercise would be the teacher making true/false statements about recent school activities: **Nuestro equipo de fútbol ganó hace tres días.** Students answer **sí** or **no.**

*More-prepared students, Exs. E and F:* The teacher could ask students oral questions similar to those in Exs. E and F.

*Less-prepared students, Exs. E and F:* Students could review expressions of length of time by listing common events and about how long they take. They could then list favorite/most interesting things they have done in their lives, and how long ago they did them.

*Answers, Exs. E and F:* Students substitute the cues following the models, using these verb forms: 1. viviste / viví 2. estudiaste / estudié 3. compraste / compré 4. recibiste / recibí 5. comiste / comí 6. fuiste / fui

**Ex. F:** pair work

*Follow-up, Exs. E and F:* Ask **Uds.** questions (with books closed) similar to those in the exercise. For example: **¿Cuánto hace que comieron Uds.?,** etc.

**Ex. G:** pair work

*Suggestion, Ex. G:* Encourage students to go beyond simply telling how long ago they did the activity pictured, perhaps telling where, with whom, and what it was like.

*Possible answers, Ex. G:*
All of the questions will begin with **¿Cuánto hace que... ?**
1. ...comiste pizza? / Comí pizza hace... 2. ...fuiste al cine? / Fui al cine hace... 3. ...fuiste a la oficina de correos? / Fui a la oficina de correos... 4. ...corriste? / Corrí hace... 5. ...visitaste a tus abuelos? / Visité a mis abuelos hace... 6. ...compraste una mochila? / Compré una mochila hace... 7. ...miraste la televisión? / Miré la televisión hace... 8. ...alquilaste un vídeo? Alquilé un vídeo hace...

**F. Hace...** Now ask your partner each of the questions in Activity E on page 333. He or she will answer, using the alternate construction below.

**Modelo:** hablar con ella / 2 horas
—*¿Cuánto hace que hablaste con ella?*
—*Hace 2 horas que hablé con ella.*

**Learning Strategy:**
*Requesting and providing information based on visual cues*

**G. ¿Cuánto hace que... ?** Basándote en los dibujos, hazle preguntas a un(a) compañero(a).

1.

2.

3.

4.

5.

6.

7.

8.



## Exercise Progression

Ex. F offers more practice in a controlled question/answer format. Ex. G provides a visual context and requires students to provide the entire discourse themselves.

## Nota gramatical

### The preterite of verbs ending in -gar

| | |
|---|---|
| —¿A qué hora **llegaste** a la escuela ayer? | What time *did* you *arrive* at school yesterday? |
| —**Llegué** a las 8:00 de la mañana. | I *arrived* at 8:00 a.m. |
| —¿**Jugaron** al tenis tú y Julián el domingo pasado? | *Did* you and Julián *play* tennis last Sunday? |
| —Yo **jugué**, pero Julián no **jugó.** | I *played*, but Julián *did* not *play.* |
| —¿Cuánto **pagaste** tú por la bicicleta? | How much *did* you *pay* for the bicycle? |
| —Yo **pagué** 150 dólares. | I *paid* 150 dollars. |

In the preterite, verbs that end in **-gar** are conjugated as follows:

| *llegar* | | | |
|---|---|---|---|
| yo | **llegué** | nosotros(as) | **llegamos** |
| tú | **llegaste** | vosotros(as) | **llegasteis** |
| él / ella / Ud. | **llegó** | ellos / ellas / Uds. | **llegaron** |

Notice that in the **yo** form of these verbs, the **g** of the stem changes to **gu** before you add the **é**. The other forms of the verb are just like those you studied in Chapter 13. Two common verbs that end in **-gar** are:

**pagar por** *to pay*
**jugar a** *to play (a game or sport)*

H. Sustituye las palabras en cursiva con las palabras que están entre paréntesis y haz los otros cambios necesarios.

1. El año pasado, *nosotros* pagamos 150 dólares por la bicicleta. (Marisol / yo / Ud. / Ángela y su mamá / él / vosotros)
2. *Julián* no jugó al tenis ayer por la tarde. (nosotros / Uds. / yo / tú / Mario y David / vosotros)
3. ¿Llegaste *tú* tarde a la clase ayer? (Juan / yo / Bárbara y yo / Linda y Clara / Ud. / vosotros)



### Presentation: The preterite of verbs ending in -gar

Begin by asking **tú** questions with **llegar,** since students will automatically answer correctly in the **yo** form of the preterite. Then write **llegué** on the board and ask students why the **g** of verbs ending in **-gar** must change to **gu** before **e** or **i.** You might want to review the **Pronunciación** sections on pp. 160, 167, and 175 where the sounds of **g** are discussed.

*Answers, Ex. H:* 1. Marisol pagó, yo pagué, Ud. pagó, Ángela y su mamá pagaron, él pagó, vosotros pagasteis 2. nosotros no jugamos, Uds. no jugaron, yo no jugué, tú no jugaste, Mario y David no jugaron, vosotros no jugasteis 3. llegó Juan, llegué yo, llegamos Bárbara y yo, llegaron Linda y Clara, llegó Ud., llegasteis vosotros

## Exercise Progression

Ex. H is a simple substitution drill. On the following page, Exs. I, J, and K provide opportunities for real communication using past tense among classmates.

**Ex. I, J, and K:**  groups of four or more

*Suggestion, Ex. I:* You can also have students say when and where they bought the item.

*Variation, Ex. J:* This exercise could also be a short writing activity where students describe a trip they have taken—where and when they went, when they arrived, and what they did there.

*Answers, **Aquí escuchamos:*** 1. the school basketball team 2. She practiced for 3 hours. 3. on Friday 4. to her aerobics class 5. She was late two days ago.

*Support material, **Aquí escuchamos:*** Teacher Tape/CD #2 Track #18 and Tapescript



*Learning Strategy:*

*Requesting and providing information*

**I. ¿Cuánto pagaste por... ?** Circulate around the room and ask classmates how much they paid for something they bought recently. Suggestions: **una mochila, un disco compacto, una pizza,** etc.

**J. ¿Cuándo llegaste a... ?** Circulate around the room and ask classmates when they arrived at some place they went to recently. Suggestions: **el partido, la escuela, a casa,** etc.

**K. ¿A qué deporte jugaste y cuándo?** Circulate around the room and ask classmates what sport they played recently and when.

## Aquí escuchamos: "Los deportes"

*Critical Thinking Strategy:*

*Predicting*

### Antes de escuchar

**Think about the sports activities that you and/or your classmates participate in after school. In this short conversation, Sonia and Mari run into each other after school.**

1. What do you think they might talk about?
2. Where do you think they might be going?

**Look at the following questions before your teacher plays the tape.** START

*LearningStrategy:*

*Listening for details*

### Después de escuchar

1. What team is Sonia on?
2. Why is she tired?
3. When is the big game?
4. Where is Mari going?
5. Why is she going so early?

EJERCICIO ORAL

**L. ¿Qué pasó?** Work in pairs within groups of four. Ask your partner when was the last time he (she) went to a store **(tienda),** what he (she) bought, and how much he (she) paid for it. Your teacher will be available to provide words you don't know. As a group, compile your responses. Your teacher will then record all the groups' responses on the board to determine the most popular purchases and their price ranges.

Cooperative Learning

*Learning Strategies:*

*Requesting and providing information, recording information*

EJERCICIO ESCRITO

**M. Querido...** A friend from Argentina wants to know what sorts of sports are popular in this country and which ones you like. Write a short note to him (her). (1) Name some popular sports. (2) Tell which ones you prefer, (3) mentioning whether you like to attend the games **(asistir a los partidos),** watch them on television, or participate **(practicar).** (4) In a second paragraph, tell whether you are on a team, if you do these sports in competition **(para la competición),** or if you prefer to do sports simply for exercise (running, swimming, bicycling, weightlifting, and aerobic exercises are often done mainly for this purpose). (5) Chat a little about a sport that you do, when you last did it and where.

*Learning Strategies:*

*Organizing ideas, selecting and providing personal information*

*Critical Thinking Strategies:*

*Evaluating, categorizing*



**Ex. L:** pair work

 writing

*Learning Strategies: Polling, reading a graph*

*Suggestions, Ex. L:* Option A: Students can create grids to organize their information. When the grids have been filled out by the small groups, write the labels for the categories **(diversión, cursos, ropa, regalos,** and any others the class came up with) on the board and then poll the various groups to find out which of the categories figure on their grids, and how many times each one figures. **(¿Qué categorías tiene su grupo? ¿Y cuántas personas compraron algo para cada categoría?)** Keep count on the board using tick marks. When all groups have been polled, have the students rank the categories in order of their frequency (from least to most) in this exercise.

*(cont. from bottom of page)*

*Ex. L:* Option B: When the grids have been filled out by the small groups, have each group figure the total amount they have indicated spent for each category. Write the categories on the board. Then, working your way through category-by-category, poll the groups to find out how much money they spent on each one **(¿Cuánto dinero pagó su grupo para esta categoría?).** Students can practice using numbers in Spanish if you let them do the addition and report the total for you to write. When you have totals for each category, have students rank them in order of the amount spent (from least to most).

*Expansion, Options A & B:* If your class has participated in both suggested follow-up options, it may be interesting to compare the frequency of the categories (i.e., the number of items attributed to each category) to the amount of money spent in each. For a number of reasons (the greater cost of clothing, a holiday season), these may not correspond. This contrast is sometimes enlightening.

*Follow-up, Ex. L:* Interested students could take this opportunity to analyze the class responses and write up a description of buying habits of their classmates, perhaps categorizing students by gender or age.

**Ex. M:** writing

*Follow-up, Ex. M:* Students could also provide the friend from Argentina with a magazine article-style account of popular sports in their state, complete with written copy and photos.

## Presentation: Deportes de verano

To practice vocabulary, put up pictures of various summer sports around the room. Have students discuss the summer sports they participate in. Then ask them what they think students from the Hispanic world do in the summer time (or when the weather is warm, regardless of the season). Do they think their activities will be the same or different, and in what ways? You can have students do a human graph of the most popular sports by asking them to line up in front of their favorite sport, and then counting the number of people in each line. Younger students might then enjoy graphing the results on paper.



# SEGUNDA ETAPA

## Preparación

**Learning Strategies:**

*Previewing, brainstorming*

**As you begin this etapa, think about sports or activities you like to do in the summer.**

- **Are you close to the beach?**
- **Do you go to a pool?**
- **Do you go camping?**
- **Do you go fishing?**

## Deportes de verano

practicar el esquí acuático

practicar el surfing

tomar el sol

practicar el windsurf

practicar la vela

ir de camping



## Etapa Support Materials

Workbook: **pp. 183–188**
Transparency: **#55**
Listening Activity masters: **p. 92**
Tapescript: **p. 139**
Quiz: **Testing Program, p. 161**
Chapter Test: **Testing Program, p. 163**

**Ex. A:** pair work

*Suggestion, Ex. A:* For more speaking practice, have students explain to their partners why they prefer the second sport.

la natación / nadar

practicar el alpinismo

la pesca / ir de pesca

practicar el ciclismo

el buceo / bucear

caminar en la playa

## ¡Aquí te toca a ti!

**A. *¿Qué actividad prefieres?*** Pregúntale a un(a) amigo(a) acerca de *(about)* las actividades de verano que prefiere. Sigue el modelo.

el ciclismo / el alpinismo
—*¿Te gusta practicar el ciclismo?*
—*No, no me gusta practicar el ciclismo, prefiero practicar el alpinismo.*

1. ir de pesca / nadar
2. la vela / el windsurf
3. el esquí acuático / el buceo
4. el alpinismo / ir de camping
5. el ciclismo / tomar el sol
6. el surfing /caminar en la playa



### Exercise Progression

Ex. A is a controlled question/answer activity in which students practice chapter vocabulary and **gustar** and **preferir**. On the following page, Ex. B provides drawings, students provide descriptions; Ex. C is a communicative exercise that allows students to interview each other about their interests in summer sporting activities.

*Variation, Ex. B:* You can provide students with similar descriptions using chapter vocabulary and have them draw their own pictures of the activity. Then collect the pictures and pin one on the back of each student. Students must then circulate and ask **sí/no** questions about the drawing. When they think they know what it depicts, they can come to you and describe the picture. When they are correct, they can remove the picture and put it on the board, writing a description of it.

**Ex. C:**  pair work

*More-prepared students, Ex. C:* Have these students play the role of travel agents, taking their information from Ex. C and writing up a summer vacation itinerary for their partners. Have them refer to Chapter 13 vocabulary for more ideas.

*Less-prepared students, Ex. C:* These students can practice all sports/activity vocabulary by giving clues to a partner (key words, famous people associated with activity, etc), who will then guess the sport being described.

*Learning Strategy: Organizing information in a report, team writing*

*Critical Thinking: Comparing and contrasting*

*Variation, Ex. C:* You may want to have the students do a team writing project in which they write a three-paragraph report, naming their shared preferences in the first paragraph, the activities neither of them likes in the second, and pointing out their differences in the third.

*Learning Strategy:*

*Reporting based on visual cues*

**B. ¿Qué hacen?** Basándote en los dibujos, di lo que hace cada persona.

**Modelo:** Julián
*Julián practica el esquí acuático.*

1. Isabel

2. Juan

3. Mario y Julia

4. Elena

5. Pedro

6. Tomás y Laura

7. Esteban y Roberto

8. Regina y Mari

*Cooperative Learning*

*Learning Strategies:*

*Interviewing, taking notes in a chart*

*Critical Thinking Strategy:*

*Comparing and contrasting*

**C. ¿Qué actividad de verano te gusta?** Compare your attitude with that of your partner about summer sports and activities. (1) Make a list like the one on page 341 and indicate your opinions of each in the left column. (2) Then interview your partner, writing the appropriate number to indicate his (her) preferences in the right column. Use the following scale to indicate how much each of you likes each activity:

**no = 0, poco = 1, bastante bien = 2, mucho = 3, muchísimo = 4, No tengo experiencia con esta actividad = X**

**Modelo:** —*¿Te gusta practicar el surfing?*
—*No, no me gusta practicar el surfing, pero me gusta mucho caminar en la playa.*



*Learning Strategies: Polling, tallying results, reading a graph*

*Critical Thinking: Drawing inferences from a graph*

*Follow-up, Ex. C:* Have student pairs tally their points allotted for each sport and report out those totals (recycling numbers) while a selected student enters them on a calculator. Record the total for each sport on the board and then conduct an expansion discussion based on reading the results of the poll while practicing the targeted vocabulary and structures, i.e.: **¿Qué deporte(s) le gusta(n) más a la clase? ¿Cuál(es) le gusta(n) menos? ¿Con qué actividad(es) no tenemos mucha experiencia?** Then lead them to draw inferences: **¿Por qué no? (No tenemos playa; no estamos cerca del océano.)**

| Yo | | Mi amigo(a) |
|---|---|---|
| | practicar el surfing | 0 |
| | tomar el sol | |
| | caminar en la playa | 3 |
| | practicar el esquí acuático | |
| | ir de pesca | |
| | nadar | |
| | practicar la vela | |
| | ir de camping | |
| | practicar el ciclismo | |
| | practicar el windsurf | |
| | bucear | |
| | jugar al golf | |
| | jugar al tenis | |

(3) Go over the results with your partner. Name the activities about which your attitudes are the same and those where your opinions are the most different.

—*A los (las) dos nos gusta tomar el sol y nadar.*
—*A los (las) dos no nos gusta ir de pesca.*
—*Tenemos opiniones diferentes de practicar el surfing.*
—*No tenemos experiencia con el windsurf.*

*Support material, Ex. D:* Transparency #55

*Suggestion, Ex. D:* To check spelling and review the alphabet, have students spell the verbs they use in items 1–6.

*Possible answers, Ex. D:* 1. Anduvo al parque. 2. Llegó a las 2:00 de la tarde. 3. Jugó al fútbol. 4. Compró un refresco. 5. Pagó por el refresco. 6. Volvió a casa a las 5:30.

**Ex. E:**  pair work

*More- and less-prepared students, Ex. E:* After Ex. E, students could prepare and present "A Day in the Life of . . . " as if on television. Students could interview each other about the most interesting/unbelievable/unforgettable day of their lives. More-prepared students could use a wider range of activities, while less-prepared students could limit their descriptions to a day of sports/leisure activities.

*Answers, Ex. E:* 1. anduve 2. llegué 3. jugué 4. compré 5. pagué 6. volví

**Ex. F:** writing

*Suggestion, Ex. F:* Students can test their memories in this exercise by saying what they remember about each specific activity. This is also an opportunity to discuss observation and memory and perhaps introduce some memory games.

*Follow-up, Ex. F:* Be sure to ask follow-up questions, to give students the opportunity to report back what they found out from their classmates.



# Repaso

*Learning Strategy:*

*Reporting based on visual cues*

**D. *¿Qué hizo Esteban ayer?*** Basándote en los dibujos, di lo que hizo Esteban ayer.

**1.** andar

**2.** llegar

**3.** jugar

**4.** comprar

**5.** pagar

**6.** volver

**E. *¿Qué hiciste tú ayer?*** Ahora imagina que eres Esteban. Di lo que hiciste ayer usando *(using)* las actividades del Ejercicio D.

*Learning Strategies:*

*Interviewing, taking notes*

**F. *¿Cuánto hace que... ?*** Go around the room and ask your classmates when they last did a specific activity: for example, when they played tennis, when they ate at a restaurant, walked in the park, etc. Take notes on their responses and be prepared to report back to the class.

### *The preterite of verbs ending in -car*

| | |
|---|---|
| —¿Quién **buscó** el libro? | Who *looked* for the book? |
| —Yo **busqué** el libro. | I *looked for* the book. |

## Exercise Progression

Ex. D practices regular and irregular verbs (3rd person singular), as does Ex. E (same activity using 1st person singular). Ex. F is an open-ended communicative activity using **¿Cuánto tiempo hace que... ?** and appropriate responses.

—**¿Tocó** Julián la guitarra en la fiesta anoche?
—No, yo **toqué** la guitarra anoche.

*Did* Julián *play* the guitar at the party last night?
No, I *played* the guitar last night.

Verbs that end in **-car** are conjugated in the preterite as follows:

| *buscar* | | | |
|---|---|---|---|
| yo | **busqué** | nosotros(as) | **buscamos** |
| tú | **buscaste** | vosotros(as) | **buscasteis** |
| él / ella / Ud. | **buscó** | ellos / ellas / Uds. | **buscaron** |

You will note that in the **yo** form of these verbs, the **c** of the stem changes to **qu** before you add the **é**. The other forms of the verb are conjugated exactly like those you studied in Chapter 13. Some common verbs that end in **-car** are:

| | |
|---|---|
| **tocar** | *to play (a musical instrument); to touch* |
| **sacar** | *to take out, remove* |
| **practicar** | *to practice* |

## Aquí practicamos

**G.** Sustituye las palabaras en cursiva con las palabras que están entre paréntesis y haz los cambios necesarios.

1. *Elena* buscó la casa de Raúl. (tú / Ud. / Lilia y su novio / yo / vosotros)
2. *Olga* no tocó el piano anoche. (Uds. / Diego / yo / tú / nosotras)
3. ¿Practicaron *Uds.* ayer por la tarde? (nosotros / Santiago y Enrique / tú / yo / vosotras)

**H. *¿Qué deporte practicaste el verano pasado?*** Un(a) amigo(a) quiere saber acerca de *(wants to know about)* los deportes que practicaste el verano pasado. Contesta según el modelo.

el windsurf
—*¿Practicaste el windsurf el verano pasado?*
—*No, no practiqué el windsurf, practiqué el buceo.*

1. el buceo
2. el surfing
3. el esquí acuático
4. la vela
5. el alpinismo
6. el ciclismo



### Vocabulary Expansion

trompeta, violín, órgano, flauta, clarinete, guitarra, piano, tambores

***Answers, Ex. G:*** 1. tú buscaste, Ud. buscó, Lilia y su novio buscaron, yo busqué, vosotros buscasteis 2. Uds. no tocaron, Diego no tocó, yo no toqué, tú no tocaste, nosotras no tocamos 3. practicamos nosotros, practicaron Santiago y Enrique, practicaste tú, practiqué yo, practicasteis vosotras

***Suggestion, Ex. G:*** This exercise lends itself to the use of a small, soft ball, which you can toss to a student as you say the new subject. The student substitutes the correct verb and tosses the ball back.

**Ex. H:** pair work

***Suggestion, Ex. H:*** You can tell students that if they have not actually participated in any of these sports, they can say that the sport interests them and tell why. This is an opportunity to review **Me interesa** and **Me fascina.**

### Presentation: Verbs ending in -car

tart out by asking **tú** questions in the preterite with **prac-car.** Students will automatically answer with the correct form f the verb. After a few questions, write the **yo** form of the erb on the board and ask students why the **c** of verbs ending n **-car** must change to **qu** before **e** and **i.** You might want to eview the **Pronunciación** sections on p. 93 where **que** and **ui** are discussed and on p. 195 where **ce** and **ci** are disussed. Point out that **tocar** also means *to touch* or *to knock.*

### Exercise Progression

Ex. G is a mechanical drill to practice the preterite forms of verbs ending in **-car.** Ex. H offers meaningful practice of the verb **practicar** and chapter vocabulary.

## Presentation: Expressions used to talk about a series of actions

The purpose of introducing these lexical items is to lead students to string sentences together and produce extended discourse, i.e., to begin to talk in paragraphs. These time indicators will be expanded throughout Unit 5. You may wish to begin this presentation by enumerating things you did yesterday. Students may imitate your model before they go on to the exercises.

To make the idea of time transpositions clearer to students, have them generate examples in English.

*Reteaching, visual orientation:* Some students may benefit from actually seeing a series of actions performed on videotape. Have students watch a short selection, and then report the order in which each action occurred. If there is some debate about the order, rerun the video and determine which students made the best eye-witnesses.

*Suggestion, Ex. I:* You might want to practice this as a listening/memory exercise, with students listening to the sequence and then attempting to retell what was done.



# Palabras útiles

### *Expressions used to talk about a series of actions*

**Primero,** yo estudié en la biblioteca. **Entonces,** caminé al parque y visité a un amigo. **Por fin,** volví a casa.

When talking about a series of actions in the past, you will find the following expressions useful:

| | |
|---|---|
| **primero** | *first* |
| **entonces (luego)** | *then* |
| **por fin (finalmente)** | *finally* |

These expressions are also useful when talking about future actions:

**Primero,** voy a estudiar en la biblioteca. **Entonces,** voy a caminar al parque y voy a visitar a un amigo. **Por fin,** voy a volver a casa.

You can also use them to talk about daily routines:

Todos los días después de la escuela, llego a casa a las 4:00. **Primero,** como un sándwich y bebo un vaso de leche. **Entonces,** saco la basura. **Por fin,** estudio un rato.

*I.* ***¿Qué hizo Felipe?*** Use the expressions in parentheses to tell what Felipe did in the past and in what order. Follow the model.

**Modelo:** Felipe tomó el autobús al centro. (el domingo pasado)
*El domingo pasado, Felipe tomó el autobús al centro.*

1. Comió en un restaurante. (primero)
2. Compró un disco compacto. (entonces)
3. Visitó a una amiga en el parque. (luego)
4. Volvió a su casa a las 5:00 de la tarde. (finalmente)

Now tell what Felipe did last Saturday.

**Felipe fue a la playa el sábado pasado.**

5. Practicó el windsurf. (primero)
6. Nadó en el mar. (entonces)
7. Tomó el sol. (luego)
8. Caminó a casa. (finalmente)



## Exercise Progression

Ex. I illustrates the use of these sequencing expressions, telling what was done and in what order, and what will be done. Exs. J and K on the following pages review a variety of verbs from all conjugations and provide practice telling the order of activities.

Now tell what he is going to do at some point in the future.

9. Felipe va a viajar a España. (el mes próximo)
10. Va a ir a Madrid. (primero)
11. Va a visitar la ciudad de Valencia. (entonces)
12. Va a volver el 5 de junio. (por fin)

**J. *Primero... entonces... finalmente...*** Describe the order of each set of three activities. Choose logical verbs to go with the words provided. Follow the model.

nosotros / piscina / en casa / programa de televisión
*Primero nosotros fuimos a la piscina. Entonces estudiamos en casa. Finalmente miramos un programa de televisión.*

1. ellos / escuela / sándwich / televisión
2. yo / biblioteca / centro / disco compacto
3. nosotros / casa / jugo de naranja / estéreo
4. ella / café y pan tostado / autobús / un amigo
5. él / sándwich de jamón con queso / metro / centro
6. ellas / parque / refresco / casa

# *Aquí escuchamos:*
## "¡Qué bien lo pasaste!"

### Antes de escuchar

**Have you ever been to the beach? Roberto has just spent a weekend at the beach. What do you think he did there?**

*Learning Strategies:*

*Previewing, brainstorming*



***Less-prepared students, Ex. J:*** These students might benefit from writing this challenging exercise. You can check their work, and then have them try the exercise orally.

***More-prepared students, Ex. J:*** These students might like to write additional, original dehydrated sentences for their partners to try.

***Possible answers, Ex. J:*** Students substitute the cues and add the expressions following the model, using the verbs and other words in these forms: 1. fueron a la, comieron un, miraron la 2. fui a la, fui al, compré un 3. estuvimos en, tomamos (bebimos) un, escuchamos el 4. desayunó, tomó el, visitó a 5. comió un, tomó el, fue al 6. fueron/anduvieron al, tomaron un, volvieron a

***Suggestion, Aquí escuchamos:*** Prepare a brief dictation based on the list of activities on p. 346.

***Support material, Aquí escuchamos:*** Teacher Tape/CD #2 Track #19 and Tapescript

*Answers, **Aquí escuchamos:*** nadar, bucear, practicar el windsurf, cenar

**Ex. K:** pair work

*Suggestion, Ex. K:* Encourage your students to organize this activity using a calendar, and to select the most interesting or unusual events of the summer. This should lead to increased conversation among partners. This activity provides preparation for the **Ya llegamos** section at the end of Unit 5.

**Ex. L:** writing

*Suggestion, Ex. L:* Remind students that they can use information from the preceding exercise to organize their letter. You can also have them include questions for the pen pal about his or her school and vacation schedule, and what the "winter" months of June, July, and August are like in Chile. This activity provides preparation for the **Ya llegamos** section at the end of Unit 5.



**Before you listen to the tape, look at the list of activities in the next section.**

*Learning Strategy:*

*Listening for details*

## Después de escuchar

**Indicate the order in which Roberto did some of his activities. Be careful: some of the following activities are not mentioned in the conversation.**

| | |
|---|---|
| bucear | nadar |
| caminar en la playa | practicar el windsurf |
| cenar | tomar el sol |

EJERCICIO ORAL

*Cooperative Learning*

*Learning Strategy:*

*Organizing details in sequence*

K. ***El verano pasado*** Both you and your partner were very busy last summer, participating in many summer sports and activities. To make an accurate report to each other about your activities, organize them in the order in which you did them. (Use time expressions to list your activities in order.) Include at least five activities each. Find at least one activity that you both participated in.

EJERCICIO ESCRITO

*Learning Strategy:*

*Organizing details in sequence*

L. ***Durante las vacaciones...*** You've just come back to school from summer vacation and want to tell your pen pal in Chile what you did during the summer. Write your friend a note and indicate what you did, including at least five of the activities that you were involved in. (Use time expressions to give an idea of the order of your summer activities.)

# Vocabulario

## Para charlar

*Para hablar de una serie de acciones*

entonces
finalmente
luego
por fin
primero

*Para hablar del tiempo*

un año
un día
una hora
un mes
un minuto
una semana

## Vocabulario general

*Verbos*

buscar
jugar
sacar

*Sustantivos*

una guitarra

*Otras expresiones*

¿Cuánto hace que + *verb in the preterite?*
Hace + *length of time* + que + *subject* + *verb in the preterite.*
*Subject* + *verb in the preterite* + hace + *length of time.*

*Deportes*

hacer ejercicio aeróbico
jugar...
al baloncesto
al golf
al hockey
al hockey sobre hierba
levantar pesas
patinar
patinar en ruedas

*Deportes de verano*

el buceo / bucear
caminar en la playa
ir de camping
la natación / nadar
la pesca / ir de pesca
tomar el sol

practicar...
el alpinismo
el ciclismo
el esquí acuático
el surfing
la vela
el windsurf

# Chapter Culminating Activity

*Learning Strategies: Planning an itinerary, organizing details in sequence, negotiating, describing in different time frames*

 groups of three

Divide the class into groups of three students. Have them use the maps in the front matter to plan a trip to Latin America. Ask them to decide where they are going to go, what they are going to visit, where the sites are located, and how they will get there. Once they have figured out their itinerary, they can explain it, using the immediate future, to another group (who, in turn will describe their itinerary). Then mix up the groups so that each group can now describe its trip (or that of the group with which it was just talking) to a third group, this time using the preterite. Encourage students to use **primero, entonces, luego, por fin, finalmente,** as well as other time expressions. This activity provides preparation for the **Ya llegamos** section at the end of Unit 5.

***Support material, Capítulo 14:*** Improvised Conversation, Teacher Tape/CD #2 Track #20 and Tapescript; Lab Manual listening activities, Laboratory Program, Tapescript, and Teacher's Edition of the Workbook/Lab Manual

# Lectura cultural

## Prereading

In order to orient students to the geography of the reading, you might want to begin with a map of Mexico and Central America. You might also show students a collection of Mexican coins and the Mexican flag, recounting the legend of Tenochtitlán depicted on those items. You could also briefly describe the legend of the feathered serpent, ***Quetzalcóatl.***

# Lectura cultural

**Learning Strategy:**

*Reading for cultural information*

## LA LEYENDA DEL QUETZAL: UN PÁJARO MITOLÓGICO

### Antes de leer

**Learning Strategies:**

*Brainstorming, using cognates and context for meaning and theme*

1. Do you know what a legend is? What does it make you think of? Can you name a well-known character from a legend?
2. Look at the title. Can you find the word in the title that means legend?
3. Look at the title again and identify the word that refers to an animal.
4. Look at the drawings that accompany this reading on page 349. What do they suggest to you about the reading's theme?

### Guía para la lectura

**Learning Strategy:**

*Reading for details*

**A.** Read the first paragraph and answer the following questions.

1. Who was Quetzal?
2. What did someone say about him on his 18th birthday?

**B.** Read the second paragraph and decide what happened to Quetzal. More than one answer is correct.

1. Quetzal was in a fierce battle.
2. Quetzal's father was captured by the enemy.
3. An arrow struck Quetzal and he became a sacred bird.
4. Quetzal fell out of a tree and broke his leg.

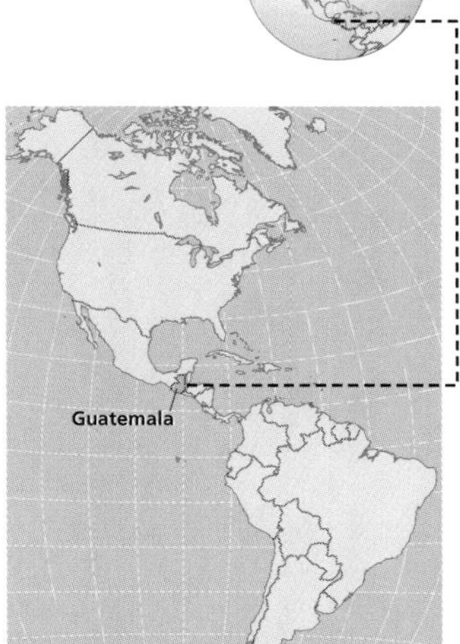


## La leyenda del quetzal: un pájaro mitológico

*os nativos de Guatemala son descendientes de los mayas y los quichés, dos grupos indígenas de las Américas. Cuentan una leyenda de Quetzal, un joven muy valiente.*

Quetzal era el hijo de uno de los caciques, un líder importante. Cuando Quetzal cumplió dieciocho años, un adivino leyó su suerte y anunció: "Quetzal nunca va a morir; va a vivir eternamente."

Quetzal era un joven muy valiente y siempre luchaba contra los enemigos de su tribu. Un día en una batalla, una flecha le dio en el corazón y el joven cayó a tierra. Cuando Quetzal cerró los ojos, se transformó en un pájaro hermoso de larga cola. Desde entonces en Guatemala, el quetzal es un pájaro sagrado y el símbolo nacional.

***Answers, Guía para la lectura:*** **A.** 1. an important leader 2. that he would live forever **B.** 1 and 3

# Chapter Objectives

**Functions:** Talking about sports and popular sports personalities in the Spanish-speaking world, including the United States; using sports-related vocabulary to talk about actions in the past, present and future time.
**Context:** Different popular sports
**Accuracy:** The present progressive tense; past, present, and future time.

## Cultural Expansion

Have students study the photo on this page. What are the people in the photo doing, how are they dressed, how old are they? How are these people similar or different from ones they know? What sports do they think are popular in the Spanish-speaking world and why? Do they think they are the same as ones played in the United States? Have students write down their answers to these questions. After studying this chapter, have them compare what they wrote originally with what they learned here. Is it the same or different, were they on target or not? Have them exchange this information with their classmates. Were they on target or not? Open discussion about cultural similarities and differences. Did they expect baseball or tennis to be so popular? Does tennis attract the same crowd as baseball? Why isn't soccer, the most popular game in the Spanish-speaking world, popular here? Is this changing? Did they know the World Cup Soccer Championship was played in the United States in 1994? Were any games played in your city or state?

CAPÍTULO 15

# DOS DEPORTES POPULARES

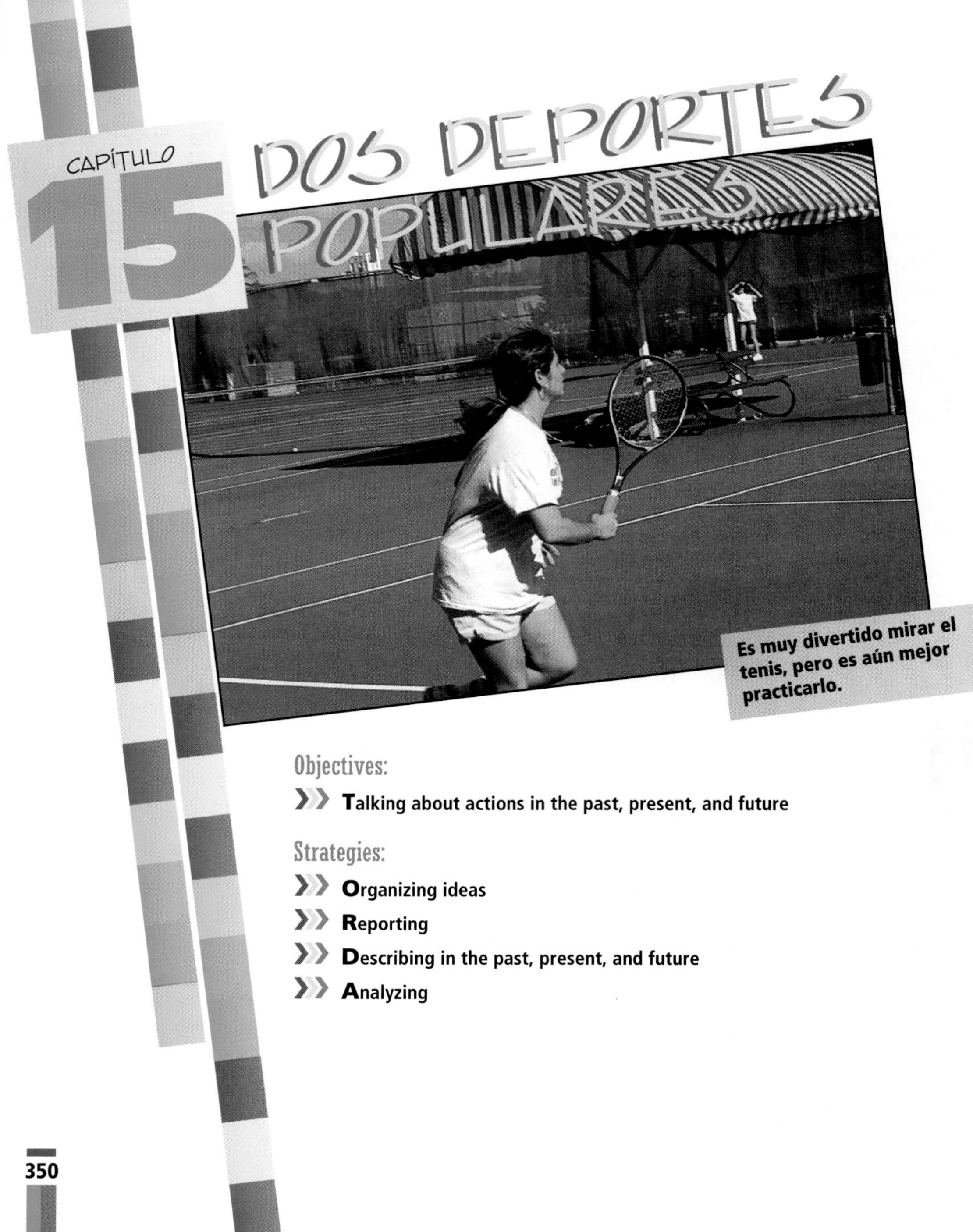

**Es muy divertido mirar el tenis, pero es aún mejor practicarlo.**

### Objectives:

- **Talking about actions in the past, present, and future**

### Strategies:

- **Organizing ideas**
- **Reporting**
- **Describing in the past, present, and future**
- **Analyzing**

## PRIMERA ETAPA

### Preparación

>> **Think about the importance we give to sports in this country. When you think about sports in Latin America, what do you think of? This etapa begins with a short reading about a sport that is very popular in several Latin American countries.**

*Learning Strategy:*
*Previewing*

## El béisbol

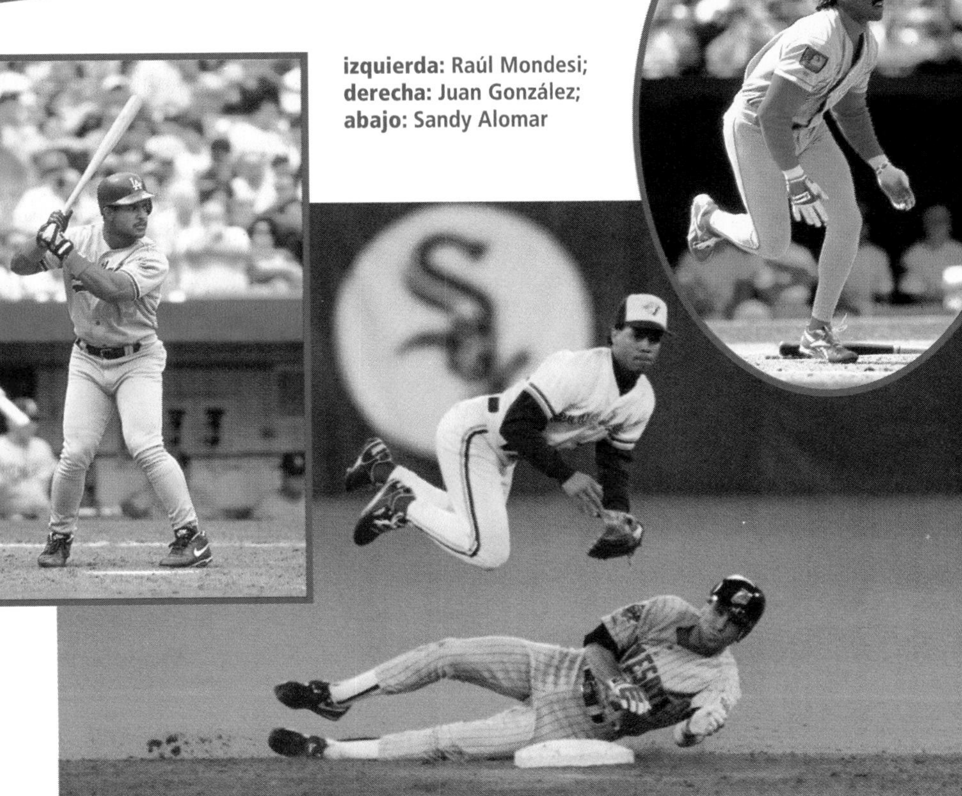

**izquierda:** Raúl Mondesi;
**derecha:** Juan González;
**abajo:** Sandy Alomar



### Prereading

Have students try to guess the countries where baseball is popular. List them on the board. Also ask students for the names of Hispanic ball players and list them on the board. See if any of the countries or names appear in the reading.

### Cultural Context

Students may already know that soccer is very popular in the Spanish-speaking world, both as a spectator and a participatory sport. They may not be quite as aware of the popularity of baseball in Spanish-speaking countries. Let them know that the Caribbean countries, Mexico, and Central America all have thriving baseball leagues. Many of the best players in the U.S. leagues come from these countries.

*Support material,*
Transparencies #4, #4a, #5, #5a, #6, #6a

### Etapa Support Materials

Workbook: pp. 189–193
Transparency: #56
Quiz: Testing Program, p. 168

Support material, **El béisbol:** Transparencies #4, #4a

### Video/CD-ROM

Chapter 15 Video Program
Chapter 15 CD-ROM Program

These can be used at the end of the chapter as expansion activities.

## Reading Strategies

Before they read, ask students to think about what they already know about the game of baseball—how it's played, what makes a good player, when and where it's played here, for example. Instruct them to use this knowledge as they read in Spanish. This is a good lead-in to Exs. A (vocabulary) and B (comprehension) after the reading as well.

## Cultural Expansion

Refer back to the list of Hispanic ball players on the board. Which ones did not appear in the reading? Of those that did, what position does each one play and on which major league team? You may wish to tell students that since baseball originated in the United States, most of its vocabulary in Spanish is borrowed from English, with a few modifications in spelling and pronunciation. Have students generate a vocabulary list and then do equivalents in Spanish. For example, a *home run* becomes a **jonrón;** a *bat,* **bate;** *first, second, third base,* **primera, segunda, tercera base;** a *pitcher* is either **lanzador** or **pícher.**

After finishing the list, the teacher may wish to ask simple, name comprehension questions with this vocabulary in Spanish. For example: **¿En qué puesto/posición juega _______? ¿En qué liga juega _______? ¿En qué equipo juega _______?**



Andrés Galarraga

**Learning Strategies:**

*Reading for details, using cognates for meaning*

## EL BÉISBOL

El béisbol es el deporte nacional de los Estados Unidos. También es muy popular en varios países del mundo hispánico, principalmente Cuba y la República Dominicana. En Canadá no es tan popular, pero hay dos equipos en las **ligas** mayores—un equipo en Montreal y otro en Toronto. El deporte también es muy popular en México, Puerto Rico, las naciones de Centroamérica, Venezuela y Colombia. También se juega en el Japón, Taiwan y en Corea del Sur.

Hay muchos beisbolistas de origen hispano que juegan en las ligas mayores. Por ejemplo, Juan González de los Texas Rangers, Andrés Galarraga de los Colorado Rockies, Raúl Mondesi de los Los Angeles Dodgers y Sandy Alomar de los Toronto Blue Jays. Hay ciertas **cualidades** que tienen todos estos beisbolistas en común: fuerza física, rapidez, **reflejos. Lanzar** la pelota y **golpear**la con el bate son actividades que requieren mucha práctica y preparación. ¿Te gusta el béisbol? ¿Cuál es tu equipo favorito?

## ¡Aquí te toca a ti!

**A. Estudio de palabras** ¿Qué crees que significan las siguientes palabras que están en negritas en la lectura? *(What do you think the following words in boldface in the reading mean?)*

1. ligas
2. cualidades
3. reflejos
4. lanzar
5. golpear

**B. Comprensión** Contesta las siguientes preguntas sobre la lectura.

1. In what Latin American countries is baseball popular?
2. Is it popular in Canada?
3. Where else, besides the Americas, is baseball played?
4. What are some of the characteristics of good baseball players?
5. Why are the players mentioned in the reading significant?

# Repaso

**Learning Strategy:**

*Reporting based on visual cues*

## C. *¿Qué hizo Alicia ayer?* 

Basándote en los dibujos, di lo que hizo Alicia por la tarde.

**1.** salir de

**2.** practicar

**3.** llegar

**4.** primero / sacar

**5.** entonces / practicar

**6.** luego / cenar

**7.** finalmente / mirar

## D. *¿Qué hiciste tú ayer?* 

Ahora imagina que tú eres la persona en los dibujos. Di lo que hiciste ayer.

# ESTRUCTURA

### *The present progressive*

| | |
|---|---|
| —¿Qué **estás haciendo** ahora mismo? | What *are* you *doing* right now? |
| —**Estoy estudiando.** | I *am studying.* |
| —¿Qué **está haciendo** Catarina ahora? | What *is* Catarina *doing* now? |
| —**Está hablando** por teléfono. | She *is talking* on the phone. |
| —¿Qué **están haciendo** tus padres en este momento? | What *are* your parents *doing* at this moment? |
| —**Están mirando** la tele. | They *are watching* TV. |

may wish to do a few more examples using these verbs.

*Suggestions, Ex. D:* Have each student write a paragraph contrasting what he or she did compared to another student in order to reinforce spelling changes. For example: **Yo practiqué el fútbol pero mi amigo, ________ , practicó el béisbol.** You may wish to divide the class into small groups and have each group write its paragraph on the board. If students do board work, have them underline all the verbs in their paragraph for extra emphasis on spelling contrasts.

## Presentation: The present progressive

Introduce this structure by making statements in Spanish in the present progressive. Since students already know the verb **estar** and the action verbs you will be using, they should be able to understand the idea of an action in progress. For example: **Estoy hablando en este momento. Estoy presentando el presente progresivo de los verbos. Uds. están escuchando. Uds. están aprendiendo una estructura nueva.** Emphasize that this tense underscores the fact that an action is going on at the moment of speaking. Have students generate, in complete sentences, the present participle of other regular verbs that they have studied **(cantar, cenar, descansar, esperar, esquiar, mirar, tomar, trabajar, viajar, aprender, beber, vender, abrir, asistir, subir, vivir).** Make a few statements in Spanish using the three expressions used with the present progressive. Then ask questions such as: **¿Qué estás haciendo en este momento? ¿Qué están haciendo tus compañeros de la clase de español ahora mismo? ¿Qué está haciendo tu mamá/papá/hermano/hermana ahora?** etc.

*teaching, Ex. C:* Before doing Ex. C, remind students of ently learned preterite forms. To review orally, state a subject **), tú, ella, Uds.,** etc.) and have students say the correct m. This may be written out on the board or on a transrency as well.

*llow-up, Ex. C:* Have students re-do Ex. C with different bjects, such as **los niños, nosotros, Juan y María, la ofesora.** You may wish to divide students into groups of ee and have each group be responsible for one subject and y orally what the subject did. For example, **Los niños lieron de la escuela, practicaron el fútbol, llegaron casa,** etc.

*Reteaching, Ex. D:* As students do Ex. D, be sure to suggest verbs such as **llegar, practicar, sacar,** etc. as examples. Have them repeat out loud **yo practiqué, yo saqué,** and **yo llegué** in order to reinforce the same sound pattern, then remind them of the recently learned spelling changes between **practicó** and **practiqué, sacó** and **saqué, llegó** and **llegué.** Remind them that **ce** or **ci, ge** or **gi (cielo** or **cero, geografía** or **gitano)** has a different sound than **ca, co, cu** or **ga, go, gu.** Write "baby talk," **ca, que, qui, co, cu** or **ga, gue, gui, go, gu** on the board and have them pronounce it in order to reinforce the sound pattern while noting spelling changes. Remind them that this pattern is true for any verb ending in **-gar** or **-car (pagar, jugar, tocar, buscar,** etc.). You

*Suggestion, Ex. E:* These column exercises are meant to provide controlled practice. A possible way to present these would be through the creation of a "word web." On a separate piece of paper, students would draw a web, and then connect elements from the columns in ways that form grammatically correct sentences. (They would have to write in the correct form of the verb in the middle column.) See the drawing below for a sample word web format. Word web formats will vary from exercise to exercise.

In Spanish, when you want to show that an action is in progress at the time you are speaking, you use the *present progressive.* You will notice that the examples given on page 353 all include a form of the verb **estar** plus a form of another verb that ends in **-ndo**. This form of the verb that ends in **-ndo** is known as the *present participle.* To form the present participle of **-ar** verbs, drop the **-ar** and add **-ando**.

| | | | |
|---|---|---|---|
| habl**ar** | habl**ando** | compr**ar** | compr**ando** |
| bail**ar** | bail**ando** | estudi**ar** | estudi**ando** |
| toc**ar** | toc**ando** | nad**ar** | nad**ando** |

To form the present participle of **-er** and **-ir** verbs, drop the **-er** or **-ir** and add **-iendo.**

| | | | |
|---|---|---|---|
| com**er** | com**iendo** | sal**ir** | sal**iendo** |
| corr**er** | corr**iendo** | escrib**ir** | escrib**iendo** |

The present participles of **leer** and **dormir** (two frequently used verbs you already know) are irregular.

| | | | |
|---|---|---|---|
| leer | **leyendo** | dormir | **durmiendo** |

Julia **está leyendo** una revista. — Julia *is reading* a magazine.
José **está durmiendo** ahora mismo. — José *is sleeping* right now.

Notice that in the above examples of the present progressive, **estar** agrees with the subject, while the present participle (the **-ndo** form of the verb) stays the same.

Some expressions you can use with the present progressive to stress that the action is in progress while you are speaking are:

**ahora** *now* **ahora mismo** *right now* **en este momento** *at this moment*

## Aquí practicamos

**E. *Ahora mismo*** Di lo que tú y tus amigos están haciendo ahora mismo *(are doing right now).*

| A | B | C | D |
|---|---|---|---|
| ahora mismo | yo<br>[nombre de tu amigo(a)] y yo<br>[nombre de tu amigo(a)]<br>tú<br>[un(a) amigo(a)] y [otro(a) amigo(a)] | estar | estudiar<br>comer<br>escribir<br>dormir<br>leer |



## Exercise Progression

Ex. E is a mechanical drill designed to practice the different forms of the present progressive. Ex. F on the following page provides meaningful practice in a communicative format.

**F. *¿Qué están haciendo en este momento?*** Di lo que están haciendo en este momento las personas en los dibujos.

> **Learning Strategy:**
> *Reporting based on visual information*

1. Jaime

2. Julia

3. Marirrosa y Juan

4. Alberto

5. Carmen y Cristina

6. Juanito

## *Aquí escuchamos:*

### "¿Vienes a la fiesta?"

#### Antes de escuchar

**Marta calls Luis to tell him that she can't come to a party that Luis is hosting. The party is in full swing while they are talking on the phone. Marta will ask Luis about what her friends are doing. How do you think she will ask him? How will he describe what everyone is doing?**

**Before you listen to the tape, copy the following list on a separate sheet of paper.**

| | |
|---|---|
| está preparando comida | está tocando la guitarra |
| está bailando | está comiendo |
| está trabajando | está cantando |

> **Critical Thinking Strategy:**
> *Predicting*



*Possible answers, Ex. F:*
1. Jaime está comprando algo. 2. Julia está corriendo. 3. Marirrosa y Juan están mirando la televisión. 4. Alberto está comiendo un bocadillo. 5. Carmen y Cristina están caminando en el parque. 6. Juanito está tomando/bebiendo leche.

### Aquí escuchamos

Create a master chart on the board, and call on student volunteers to write the information on the board as they listen to the tape. Divide the tape into sections, stop after each, and ask for a new volunteer. Play the tape again in the same fashion and have new volunteers either place a check if they agree with what's on the board, or write a new name, etc. Be sure to correct with the whole class afterwards.

*Answers, **Aquí escuchamos:***
Marta: está trabajando
Marcos y Carmen: están bailando
Felipe: está comiendo
Sara: está tocando la guitarra y cantando
María: está preparando comida

*Support material, **Aquí escuchamos:***
Teacher Tape/CD #2 Track #21 and Tapescript

*Follow-up, Ex. F:* As a variation, divide the class into pairs and have them do a charade of one of the actions in the exercise. Have the rest of the class guess which action is being performed. (e.g., **Están tomando leche.**) You may wish to expand the exercise by having student pairs do charades of other actions, not included in the exercise. You may want to create a master list ahead of time on the board to avoid confusion.

**Ex. G:** 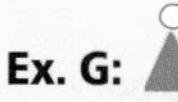 pair work

**Ex. H:** pair work

 writing

***Support material, Ex. H:*** **Transparency #56**

***Less-prepared students, Ex. H:*** Have students number each of the activities. Then point to each different activity and have them recall the verb (activity) and write each one down. These students can then go back on their own and write their sentences.

***More-prepared students, Ex. H:*** Brainstorm a list of adverbial expressions such as **debajo del árbol, cerca de la piscina, en el sol, en la sombra, en el suelo** to round-out their sentences (this also serves as a lead-in to the cohesion element in the second stage of this writing exercise). When doing the second part, pair up a more-prepared student with a less-prepared one to write the composition. Have student pairs read and edit each other's work.

***Suggestion, Ex. H:*** Have students recall different expressions to express *"now"* before they begin **(en este momento, ahora mismo, ahora).** Encourage them to vary their time expressions in their discussion.



*Learning Strategy:*

*Listening for details*

## Después de escuchar

**Now listen to Marta and Luis's conversation again and indicate who is doing what by writing the name of the person next to the appropriate activity on your list.**

# ¡Adelante!

*Learning Strategy:*

*Reporting based on personal knowledge*

*Cooperative Learning*

*Learning Strategies:*

*Listing, describing based on visual information, organizing ideas in a paragraph*

### EJERCICO ORAL

**G. *En este momento*** Think about various people in your life whose daily schedules are familiar to you. Make a list of four people who have different schedules—parents, brothers, sisters, boy/girl friends, best friends. Discuss with a partner what the people you each know are doing right now.

### EJERCICO ESCRITO

**H. *¿Qué está(n) haciendo?*** (1) Look at the drawing on page 357 of people enjoying a weekend afternoon in the park. (2) Write at least six sentences telling what they are doing. Identify a different activity in each of your sentences. (3) Then, working with a partner, create a composite list of activities from which the two of you can write a brief composition describing how the people in the park are spending their afternoon. (4) Remember to give your composition an introductory sentence and a closing sentence that briefly summarizes the point of the composition. Take care to organize the sentences between the beginning and end so that you guide your readers smoothly from one activity to the next.

**Modelo:** (first sentence)
*Hoy es domingo y hay muchas personas en el parque. Ellos están haciendo muchas cosas.* (o: *Hay muchas actividades también.) Por ejemplo, hay una mujer que...*
(last sentence)
*Siempre hay mucho para hacer en el parque el fin de semana.*

### *Learning strategy: Using cohesive devices to organize ideas in a paragraph*

*Variation, Ex. H:* You may want to take this opportunity to encourage flexibility in paraphrasing. Have students notice the different interpretations possible for many of the actions in the drawing. For example, they may say of the woman using the telephone: **está hablando** or **está llamando (a un amigo);** of the woman at the refreshment stand: **está comprando** or **está pagando;** of the seated couple with the dancers: **están escuchando** or **están mirando;** of the person under the tree with a book: **está leyendo, está estudiando,** or even **está pensando;** of the people with the guitar player: **están escuchando** or **están cantando;** of the person napping: **está durmiendo** or **está descansando.**

Point out to students that it may be appropriate to use two such options together for a more interesting sentence, and one that might help them achieve cohesion (flow) in their compositions. Brainstorm with them to create a list of "linking" expressions they know that might accomplish this. Some ideas are: **Mientras que...** (While . . .); **También,... ; En otro lugar,... ; Cerca del árbol,... ; Al quiosco de refrescos... ; A la cabina telefónica,... ; No muy lejos,... .**

Encourage students to include a summative paragraph in their composition mentioning activities they personally enjoy doing in the park.

## SEGUNDA ETAPA

### Preparación

*Learning Strategies:*

*Previewing, brainstorming*

- Have you ever played tennis?
- Have you ever watched a match on television?
- Who are some of the great players that you know about?
- What are some of the major tournaments that are played around the world?

# El tenis

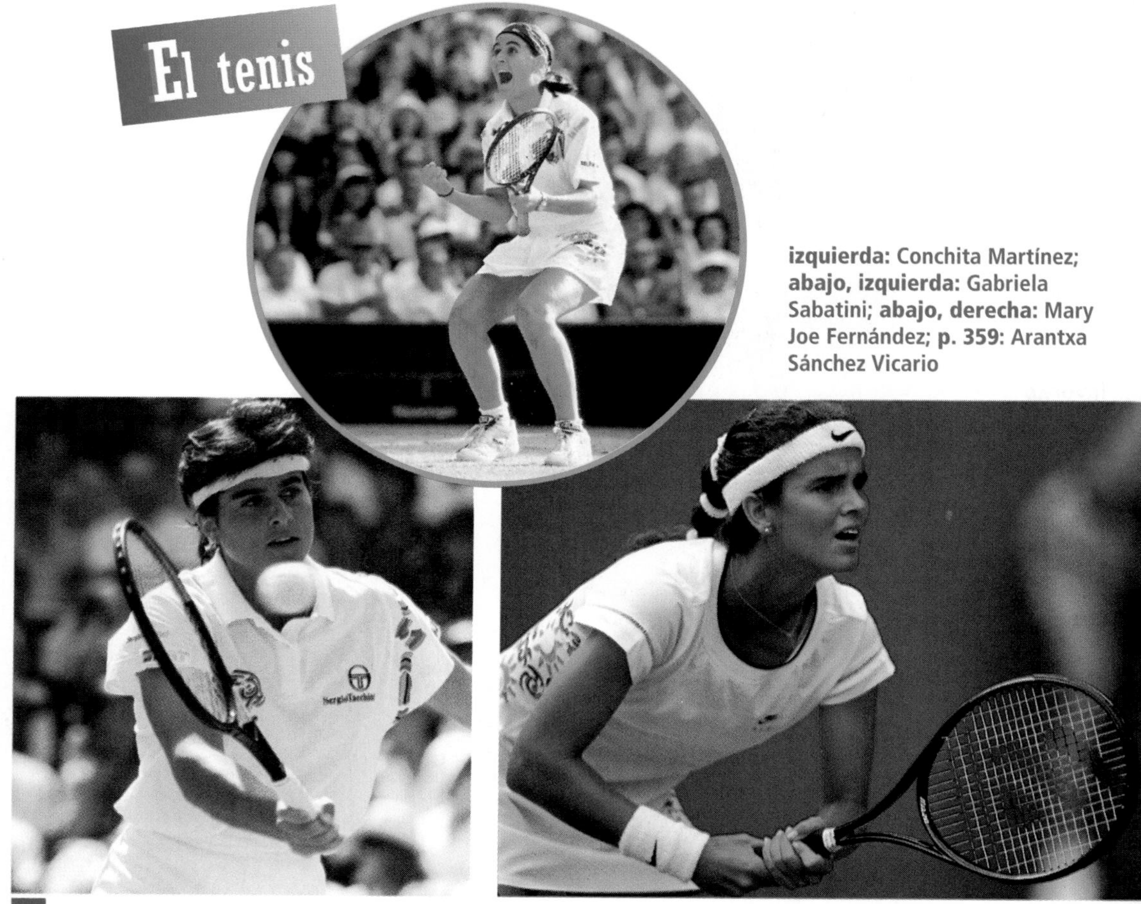

**izquierda:** Conchita Martínez; **abajo, izquierda:** Gabriela Sabatini; **abajo, derecha:** Mary Joe Fernández; **p. 359:** Arantxa Sánchez Vicario



## Etapa Support Materials

Workbook: **pp. 194–200**
Transparency: **#57**
Listening Activity masters: **p. 99**
Tapescript: **p. 146**
Quiz: **Testing Program, p. 171**
Chapter Test: **Testing Program, p. 174**

## Las tenistas hispanas

El tenis requiere **agilidad** y control del cuerpo, pero no gran fuerza. Por eso es un deporte que pueden jugar personas de **diversas** edades y condiciones físicas. Al nivel profesional, se necesita una combinación de **habilidad,** buena técnica y una excelente condición física.

Entre las mejores tenistas femeninas del mundo, hay un grupo de hispanas: Gabriela Sabatini de Argentina, Mary Joe Fernández de Estados Unidos, Arantxa Sánchez Vicario y Conchita Martínez de España. Todas juegan en los grandes **torneos** que se juegan en Inglaterra, en Francia y en los Estados Unidos. En 1994, Conchita ganó el prestigioso torneo en Wimbledon y Arantxa ganó el U.S. Open y el French Open. Arantxa es tan popular en España que tiene que vivir en Andorra, un pequeño país entre Francia y España, para **evitar** a los **admiradores** y periodistas. ¿Te gusta el tenis? ¿Te gusta jugarlo o mirarlo? ¿Quién es tu tenista favorito?

**Learning Strategies:**

*Reading for cultural information, reading for details*

## ¡Aquí te toca a ti!

**A. *Estudio de palabras*** ¿Qué crees que significan las siguientes palabras que están en negritas en la lectura?

1. agilidad
2. diversas
3. habilidad
4. torneos
5. evitar
6. admiradores

**B. *Comprensión*** Contesta las siguientes preguntas sobre la lectura.

1. What characteristics are required of a tennis player?
2. Where are the tennis players featured in the reading from?
3. What did Martínez do in 1994?
4. What did Sánchez Vicario do in 1994?
5. Why does Sánchez Vicario live in Andorra?



### Prereading

Remind students to focus on cognates by having them skim the text and make a list of cognates. Have them tell the meaning of each word. Then brainstorm about how this information can help them understand the reading. This can also serve as a lead-in to Ex. A after the reading.

## Cultural Expansion

You may wish to point out that Sabatini is an Italian name and that in the late 19th century, there was a large wave of Italian immigration to Argentina, very similar to that in the U.S. Because of the Italian influence in Argentina, pizza is a common (as well as popular) dish there. In the case of Mary Joe Fernández you may wish to point out the long Hispanic presence in what is now the U.S. and the large Hispanic population (around 20 million) in our country. You may also wish to contrast the first names of the two Spanish players, and point out that Arantxa is a Basque, not a Spanish name. Use a map of Spain and point out the Basque region as well as Andorra.

***Suggestion, Ex. A:*** This short exercise provides a good opportunity to discuss cognates and word families. After students have guessed and explained the meaning of each word, have them identify other words in the same family in English, and look them up in Spanish (agility, agile; diverse, diversity, etc.).

*Suggestion, Ex. C:* Ask for as many variations or paraphrases of each drawing as students can think of in order to expand vocabulary usage. For example, the first one could be **llamando a un amigo/hablando con un amigo/hablando por teléfono.** The exercise can be done quickly as oral work or may be written out individually or in pairs.

*Possible answers, Ex. C:*
1. Roberto está hablando por teléfono. 2. Esteban y Carmen están estudiando. 3. Marirrosa y su amigo están comiendo pizza.
4. Carlos está haciendo la maleta.
5. Cristina está leyendo. 6. José y Patricio están jugando al tenis.
7. Mi papá está haciendo la cama.

## Presentation: Past, present, and future time

There is no new material presented in this **Estructura.** It is designed to review and contrast the four time frames (preterite, present, present progressive, future) that students have already learned. Make statements and then ask students simple questions that contrast the four tenses. For example: **Siempre hablo español en la clase. Ahora mismo estoy hablando español. Ayer hablé español y mañana voy a hablar español también. ¿Qué haces todos los días? ¿Qué estás haciendo ahora? ¿Qué hiciste ayer? ¿Qué vas a hacer mañana?,** etc.

## Repaso

*Learning Strategy:*

*Reporting based on visual cues*

**C. *En este momento...*** Di lo que está haciendo cada persona en este momento en los dibujos que siguen.

**1.** Roberto

**2.** Esteban y Carmen

**3.** Marirrosa y su amigo

**4.** Carlos

**5.** Cristina

**6.** José y Patricio

**7.** mi papá

## ESTRUCTURA

### *Past, present, and future time*

Pasado: Ayer hablé por teléfono con mi abuelo.
Presente: Hoy hablo con mis amigos en la escuela.
Progresivo: Ahora mismo estoy hablando con mi amigo.
Futuro: Mañana voy a hablar con mi profesor.

Pasado: Esta mañana caminé a la escuela.
Presente: Camino por el parque los sábados por la tarde.
Progresivo: Estoy caminando al parque ahora mismo.
Futuro: Tengo ganas de caminar al centro más tarde.

Pasado: El año pasado viajamos a México.
Presente: Cada año viajamos a México.
Progresivo: En este momento estamos viajando a México.
Futuro: El año próximo esperamos viajar a España.

In this unit, you have learned to form the preterite so that you can talk about events in the past. You have also learned the present progressive, so that you can talk about events taking place at the moment you are speaking. You have also learned certain expressions that help situate events in the past, present, and future. Now it is important to review the verb structures and expressions that allow you to express yourself in past, present, and future time.

### *Past time:*

**preterite tense**

—¿Qué **hiciste** tú anoche?
—Yo **comí** en un restaurante y **fui** al cine.

### *Present time for routine activities:*

**present tense**

—¿Qué **haces** tú después de la escuela todos los días?
—Yo **visito** a mis amigos.

### *Present time for actions going on at the moment of speaking:*

**present progressive**

—¿Qué **estás haciendo**?
—**Estoy buscando** mis llaves.

### *Future time:*

**ir** + **a** + *infinitive*
**querer** + *infinitive*
**quisiera** + *infinitive*
**esperar** + *infinitive*
**pensar** + *infinitive*
**tener ganas de** + *infinitive*

—¿Qué **van a hacer** Uds. durante las vacaciones?
—Yo **voy a visitar** a amigos en California.
—Yo **quiero ir** a Nuevo México.
—Y yo **quisiera viajar** a Europa.
—Pablo **espera volver** a la Argentina.
—La profesora de español **piensa viajar** a Bolivia.
—Mis padres **tienen ganas** de viajar a Florida.

*Suggestion, Ex. D:* These column exercises are meant to provide controlled practice. A possible way to present these would be through the creation of a "word web." On a separate piece of paper, students would draw a web, and then connect elements from the columns in ways that form grammatically correct sentences. See the diagram below for a sample word web format. Word web formats will vary from exercise to exercise.

## Cooperative Learning

The student pairs could create a small composition together comparing and contrasting their habits based on the information they record on charts (as a variation of Ex. D). This activity provides preparation for the **Ya llegamos** section at the end of Unit 5.

*Learning strategy: Team writing*

*Critical Thinking: Comparing and contrasting*

*Reteaching, Exs. E–G:* Because these exercises require frequent use of questions, you can review interrogatives by preparing a set of question cards and a corresponding set of answer cards. Distribute one card to each student, and have them move around the room finding their match. Have students read their questions and answers aloud.



# Aquí practicamos

**D. *Hoy, ayer y mañana*** Di lo que tú y tus amigos están haciendo, hacen, hicieron y van a hacer.

| A | B | C |
|---|---|---|
| ayer | yo | hablar por teléfono con sus amigos |
| de costumbre | ? | mirar un programa de televisión |
| ahora mismo | tú y ? | estudiar para un examen |
| todos los días | ? y yo | comer en un restaurante |
| anoche | ? y ? | salir con sus amigos |
| el fin de semana próximo | | ? |

**E. *Quisiera saber...*** Hazle las preguntas a un(a) compañero(a).

1. ¿Estás en la escuela todos los días? ¿Estuviste en la escuela el sábado pasado? ¿Vas a estar en la escuela el verano próximo?
2. ¿Haces un viaje cada verano? ¿Hiciste un viaje el año pasado? ¿Vas a hacer un viaje el año próximo?
3. ¿Desayunas todos los días? ¿Desayunaste ayer por la mañana? ¿Vas a desayunar mañana por la mañana?
4. ¿Miras algún programa de televisión los viernes? ¿Miraste un programa de televisión el domingo por la noche? ¿Vas a mirar un programa de televisión mañana por la noche?
5. ¿Hablas por teléfono con alguien cada noche? ¿Hablaste por teléfono con alguien anoche? ¿Vas a hablar por teléfono con alguien esta noche?

*Learning Strategies:*

*Reporting based on visual cues, describing in the present, past, and future*

**F. *De costumbre...*** For each of the drawings on page 363, explain what the people do normally **(de costumbre)**, what they did in the past, and what they'll do in the future. Begin each explanation with **De costumbre...**, continue it with **Pero...**, and finish it with **Y...** .

*Modelo:* ¿Qué hace José Luis durante *(during)* las vacaciones de verano?
*De costumbre él está escuchando música. Pero el año pasado estuvo en la playa. Y el año próximo piensa viajar a México.*

de costumbre

el año pasado

el año próximo

## Exercise Progression

Ex. D practices sentence construction and time frames using columns of word cues. Ex. E practices the same tenses in a personalized question/answer format. Ex. F on the following page displays visual stimuli to give students practice recognizing time signals, and Ex. G on page 364 offers question/answer practice in a controlled format.

**Ex. E:**  pair work

*Suggestion, Ex. E:* Because each of these questions is a **sí/no** question, you will want to have students provide more information in their answers than simply **sí** or **no.** Have students practice doing so as a class before putting them in groups. You might want students to suggest additional questions of an open-ended nature for this exercise.

1. ¿Qué hace Vera durante el fin de semana?

de costumbre

el fin de semana pasado

el fin de semana próximo

2. ¿A qué hora llega Marcos a la escuela?

de costumbre

anteayer

el viernes próximo

3. ¿Qué comen Sabrina y Carolina cuando van al centro?

de costumbre

el sábado pasado

el sábado próximo

4. ¿Qué hace Oscar los viernes?

de costumbre

el viernes pasado

el viernes próximo



*More-prepared students, Ex. F:* Students who are more prepared can write their own questions following this model and interview another student, and then write up a short biography of that person. Some suggested questions: **¿Qué haces durante las vacaciones? ¿Qué haces durante el fin de semana? ¿Qué comes cuando estás en la escuela? ¿Qué haces el sábado por la mañana?**

*Less-prepared students, Ex. F:* These students can use Ex. F questions and/or generate more examples only in the **yo** form by saying or writing what they usually do during the week or on weekends. They can then tell what they did differently at some time in the past, and then what they will do in the future, working vertically with the Ex. F chart, rather than horizontally.

*Possible answers, Ex. F:* Students substitute the cues and add the following information: 1. ...mira la televisión. / ...fue al museo. / ...piensa ir a una fiesta. 2. ...llega a las ocho menos cuarto. / ...llegó a las ocho y media. / ...va a llegar a las siete y cuarto. 3. ...comen sándwiches. / ...comieron ensalada. / ...van a comer pizza. 4. ...va al cine. / ...estudió. / ...va a ir a un restaurante con su novia.

*Learning strategy: Organizing information, describing*

*nswers, Ex. E:* Answers will vary, but the verbs will be the following forms: 1. estoy, estuve, voy a estar 2. hago, ce, voy a hacer 3. desayuno, desayuné, voy a desayunar miro, miré, voy a mirar 5. hablo, hablé, voy a hablar

*ollow-up, Ex. E:* Ask follow-up questions in the third erson, giving students the opportunity to report back some of e information they found out when questioning their parters. This activity provides preparation for the **Ya llegamos** ction at the end of Unit 5.

*Variation, Ex. F:* You can personalize this exercise by having students give information about themselves, their family, or their friends using the same questions as provided in Ex. E.

**Ex. G:** role play

*Possible answers, Ex. G:* Students substitute the cues, using the following forms of the verbs: 1. No, voy a ir... 2. No, pienso viajar... 3. No, fui... 4. Sí, voy a visitar... 5. No, fui... 6. No, viajé a...

*Follow-up, Ex. G:* To proceed from this controlled interview to a more creative one, have students who have done some traveling abroad or in this country volunteer to bring in souvenirs and be interviewed by classmates, who will organize the question and answer format themselves. Students often enjoy watching these activities on videotape.

## Aquí escuchamos

If you choose to practice this exercise as a telephone conversation, it is an opportunity to stress the importance of good listening skills. Have students sit back-to-back and practice inviting each other somewhere, turning each other down, and making alternate plans.

*Answers, Aquí escuchamos:* 1. to buy a new CD 2. immediately 3. he has to study 4. he will be working at 1 p.m. 5. tomorrow morning

*Support material, Aquí escuchamos:* Teacher Tape/CD #2 Track #22 and Tapescript



**G. *Una entrevista*** You are being interviewed by a reporter from your school newspaper about your many travels. Answer the questions using the cues given in parentheses. Follow the models.

**Modelos:** ¿Esperas viajar a España este año? (no, el año próximo)
*No, voy a viajar a España el año próximo.*

¿Piensas ir a México? (no, el año pasado)
*No, fui a México el año pasado.*

1. ¿Piensas ir de vacaciones mañana? (no, hoy)
2. ¿Viajaste a Costa Rica el verano pasado? (no, el mes próximo)
3. ¿Esperas viajar a Madrid? (no, el año pasado)
4. ¿Quisieras visitar la ciudad de México? (sí, el año próximo)
5. ¿Piensas ir a Santa Fé este año? (no, el año pasado)
6. ¿Quieres viajar a Europa el año próximo? (no, el verano pasado)

# Aquí escuchamos:
## "¿Para qué vas al centro?"

**Learning Strategy:** *Previewing*

### Antes de escuchar

Isabel will invite Pedro to go downtown. How do you think she will say this? How will Pedro say he can or can't accompany her? Before you listen, take a moment to preview the following questions.

START

**Learning Strategy:** *Listening for details*

### Después de escuchar

1. Why does Isabel want to go downtown?
2. When does Isabel want to go?
3. Why can't Pedro go?
4. Why can't Pedro go tomorrow afternoon?
5. When do they decide to go?

# Aquí leemos

## Estrategia para la lectura

Sometimes when you read something you run your eyes over the text and pull out key bits of information. This is called *scanning.* For example, if you were reading an advertisement for certain movies currently showing in your town or city, you might run your eyes over the ad and look for titles and names of theatres. Next, you might look for times and days. Finally, you might look for prices. Then, you would use this information to decide what movie you will see, where you will see it, and how much it will cost.

*Reading Strategies:*

*Begin by seeing how the reading is organized.*
*Use familiar words to help you guess meaning.*
*Use photos to help decide what the content will be*
*Use the format and layout for clues.*

## Antes de leer

What sorts of things do you do in the summer to cool off?
Do you like to swim? Where do you swim?

Look at the ads on page 370. What do you think they are advertising?

Here is some information to use for this reading. The summers in Madrid, especially the months of July and August, can be very hot. The temperatures can go as high as 42° C (about 107° F) every day. This is the reason why the largest waterpark in Europe, **Aquopolis,** is located just outside of Madrid. **Aquopolis,** along with many of the other waterparks, provides free bus transportation to the park from various points in Madrid on a daily basis.



## Presentation: Aquí leemos

Have students read the **Estrategia para la lectura** and the **Antes de leer.** Then give them a little while to look over these ads (a minute at most). Move right on to the **Actividades.** Reassure students that they are not expected to read everything from start to finish, but rather to extract specific bits of information, just as they would when reading ads in English.

## Support Materials

Workbook: **pp. 201–204**
Unit Review Blackline Masters: **Unit 5 Review**
Listening Activity masters: **p. 105**
Tapescript: **p. 154**
Unit Exam: **Testing Program, p. 179**

**Atajo,** Writing Assistant Software 

Este verano, empápate de agua, sol y diversiones a mares en AQUOPOLIS.
Deslízate por el Río Rápido, el Lago de la Aventura, etc...
Sigue la corriente de AQUOPOLIS,
será el verano más fresco y divertido de tu vida.

Aquopolis

**EL PARQUE ACUATICO MAS GRANDE DE EUROPA**

En Villanueva de la Cañada, a 20 minutos de Madrid.

Autobuses gratuitos desde:

| | Horarios de salida Laborables | Sábados y festivos |
|---|---|---|
| PZA. ESPAÑA C/ Reyes (junto cine Coliseum) | 11,00-12.00 | 11,00-12.00-13,00 |
| ALCORCON (Estación RENFE) | 11,00 | 11,00-12,00 |

## Parques acuáticos

• **El Acuatico de San Fernando de Henares**. Crtra. de Barcelona, Km. 15,500. Tel. 673 10 13. Abierto durante el día a partir del 7 de junio. Desde el día 11 de junio, también por la noche. Horario: Diurno, de 11 a 20h. Nocturno, de 23 a 8h. Precios: Laborables: niños 850 pts., adultos 1.100 pts. Sábados y festivos: niños 1.100 pts., adultos 1.500 pts. Media jornada: laborables 850 pts., sábados y festivos, 1.200 pts. Bonos 30 días: 6.500 pts.

• **Aquapalace**. PºErmita del Santo, 48. Tel. 526 17 79. Horario: Todos los días, de 11 a 20h. Precios: De lunes a viernes: 950 pts, todo el día, 650 pts., 4 horas. Sábados, domingos y festivos: niños 800 pts, adultos 1.100 pts.

• **Aquopolis**. Villanueva de la Cañada. Crtra. de la Coruña. Tel. 815 69 11/86. Abierto hasta el 11 de septiembre. Horario: Junio y septiembre: laborables de 12 a 19h., sábados y festivos de 11 a 19h. Julio y agosto: laborables de 12 a 20h., sábados y festivos de 11 a 19h. Precios: De lunes a viernes: niños 1.000 pts. adultos 1.500 pts. Sábados y festivos: niños 1.100 pts, adultos 1.700 pts.

• **Lagosur**. Autovía Madrid – Toledo, Km. 9 (Parquesur). Tel. 686 70 00. Hasta el 11 de septiembre. Junio: de 11 a 19h. Julio, agosto y septiembre: 11 a 20 h. Precios: de lunes a viernes: 700 pesetas., niños y 950, adultos; sábados: 700, niños y 1.100, adultos; domingos y festivos: 800, niños y 1.400, adultos.

370

## Actividades

A. What are the names of the four waterparks advertised?

B. Run your eyes over the ad for **El Acuático de San Fernando de Henares.** What is the telephone number for this park?

C. Run your eyes over the four ads again to look for other numbers. What do you think they refer to?

D. Now scan the four ads to look for the names of months. How late in the year are **Aquopolis** and **Lagosur** open?

E. Finally, scan the four ads and look for days of the week. What do you think the word **festivos** means? What about **laborales?**

F. With a partner, make a chart with the prices for adults on Saturdays at the four parks.

G. Of the four, which is the most expensive for adults on Saturdays?

H. Of the four, which is the cheapest for adults on Saturdays?

*Learning Strategies:*

*Scanning for details, using cognates for meaning*

*Critical Thinking Strategies:*

*Drawing inferences, comparing and contrasting*

*Answers, Actividades:*
**A.** El Acuático de San Fernando de Henares; Aquopolis; Aquapalace; Lagosur **B.** 673-10-13 **C.** dates, hours, prices **D.** 11 de septiembre **E.** holidays; workdays **F.** El Acuático de San Fernando de Henares—1.500 ptas.; Aquopolis—1.700 ptas.; Aquapalace—1.100 ptas.; Lagosur—1.100 ptas. **G.** Aquopolis—1.700 ptas. **H.** Aquapalace—1.100 ptas. and Lagosur—1.100 ptas.

**Ex. A:** groups of four or more

***Suggestions, Exs. A and B:*** Give students time to write out what they are going to say. You might want to assign these activities for homework. Then have some volunteers tell about their past week to the class and have students ask follow-up questions.

**Ex. B:** pair work

***Support material, Unidad 5:*** Lab Manual Ya llegamos listening activities, Laboratory Program, Tapescript, and Teacher's Edition of the Workbook/Lab Manual

# Ya llegamos

## Actividades orales

**A. *La semana pasada*** Explain to your classmates what you did last week and in what order. They will ask you questions for clarification. Don't forget to use a variety of verbs to talk about the past and be sure to use appropriate time indicators.

*Cooperative Learning*

*Learning Strategies:*

*Organizing and revising a schedule, negotiating, organizing and delivering a group presentation, persuading*

*Critical Thinking Strategies:*

*Sequencing, evaluating*

**B. *¡Vivan las vacaciones!*** Imagine that your Spanish class has just won the lottery together. The money will be used for a class trip this coming summer which will be a tour of some Spanish-speaking countries. It has been decided to have a competition to decide the itinerary the class will adopt. The team with the winning itinerary will get to travel first class.

With a partner, agree on an itinerary that includes at least (1) two different places to visit, and (2) four activities to do at each place, in the order you suggest doing them. (Don't forget to use the expressions for talking about a series of actions that you learned on page 344.) Decide on (3) the means of transportation you will take to and from the different places, and (4) how you will get around once there. Then, (5) describe your itinerary to two of your friends, using the different techniques you learned for expressing actions in the future (See box below and page 361.). (6) After listening to the suggested itineraries, create one travel plan, taking the most interesting ideas from each pair. Make any changes necessary to your plans to convince the class to select your proposal. Finally, (7) organize a presentation to the class in which the four of you try to persuade them to adopt your itinerary. Be convincing; you want to travel first class. You may even want to prepare a publicity poster.

**Expressions to talk about actions in the future**

**esperar** + *infinitive*
**ir + a** + *infinitive*
**pensar** + *infinitive*
**querer** + *infinitive*
**quisiera** + *infinitive*
**tener ganas de** + *infinitive*

*C. ¿Qué quieres hacer?* Look at the expressions in the box on page 372 and talk with a partner about your plans for the future. Try to use all of the expressions in your conversation.

## Actividades escritas

*D. Una semana típica* Write a short paragraph indicating what you do in a typical week.

*E. Mis últimas vacaciones* Write a short paragraph about what you did during your last vacation.

*F. El verano próximo* Write a short paragraph in which you indicate what you will do next summer.



**Ex. C:**  pair work

*Variation, Ex. C:* If you feel students need more practice with the preterite, have students pretend that they have already taken a trip and have them say what they did. For example: **Fuimos a Segovia y visitamos el acueducto romano.** Tell them to try to impress you and the rest of the class with their knowledge of culture by mentioning what they saw in each of the places they visited.

**Exs. D, E, and F:**  writing

### Writing Activities

*Atajo, Writing Assistant Software*

supports ATAJO

*Functional vocabulary:* Expressing time relationships, linking ideas, planning a vacation, sequencing events, talking about daily routines, writing a news item, etc.

*Topic vocabulary:* Calendar, classroom, clothing, cooking, days of the week, household chores, leisure, time expressions, time of day, etc.

*Grammar:* Verb summary; verbs: preterite; verbs: **ser** and **estar;** verbs: **tener** and **haber;** adverbs of time; verbs: **hacer;** verbs: participles; etc.

## Warm-up Activities

***Paso 1:*** Ask students, **¿Te gusta hacer ejercicios en tu tiempo libre?** Then tell them that the following passage discusses aerobic exercises and the amount of energy we use (how many calories we burn) when we do certain activities. You may want to ask questions such as:

- Do you know what "aerobic" means?
- Can you think of any common activities that are aerobic?

***Paso 2:*** Ask students to work with a partner to complete the following activity: **¿Qué hiciste el fin de semana pasado?** Ask your partner if he or she did the following activities last weekend. Be sure to record all responses in a notebook for group discussion. Place an asterisk (*) next to activities you think are aerobic. Do your classmates agree with your choices?

bailar

Student 1: **¿Bailaste el fin de semana pasado?**

Student 2: **Sí. Bailé en la fiesta de Martín.**

**Actividad:**  pair work

***Answers, Actividad:***

**Paso 1.** 1. E 2. A. 3. B 4. F 5. G 6. D 7. C

**Paso 2.** 1. 105 2. 54.9 3. Pedro

# Conexión

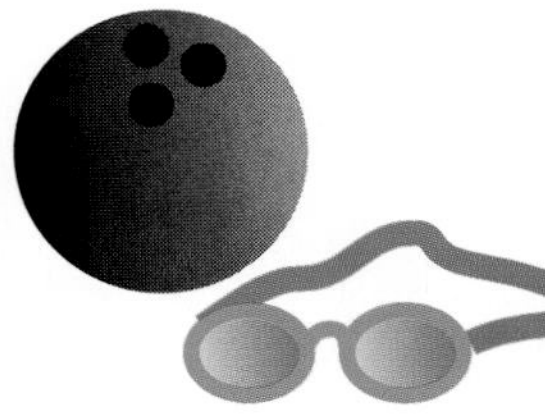

- Do you know what "aerobic" means?
- Can you think of any common activities that are aerobic?

## Los ejercicios aeróbicos y la utlilización de energía

### AL EMPEZAR

The following passage discusses aerobic exercises and the amount of energy we use (how many calories we burn) when we do certain activities.

### LOS EJERCICIOS AERÓBICOS Y LA UTILIZACIÓN DE ENERGÍA

El término aeróbico significa "vivir en la presencia del oxígeno". Los ejercicios aeróbicos, la natación, el ciclismo y el correr, por ejemplo, estimulan el **corazón** y los **pulmones** con el objetivo de aumentar la cantidad de oxígeno que el **cuerpo** pueda utilizar dentro de un período de tiempo. Los ejercicios aeróbicos también son ideales para quemar calorías y **bajar de peso**, ya que **el coeficiente de utilización de energía** (CUE) de estas actividades es muy alto. Esto quiere decir que utilizamos mucha energía cuando los practicamos.

heart / lungs
body
to lose weight / energy use quotient

Cuanto más tiempo se pase haciendo ejercicios aeróbicos, más energía se utiliza. Y las personas de mayor peso suelen utilizar más energía que las de menor peso haciendo la misma actividad. La primera columna del siguiente **esquema** nos da el CUE de varias actividades, algunas aeróbicas y otras no. Se multiplica el CUE por el peso de una persona—en kilogramos—para determinar el número de calorías que se queman haciendo una actividad. ¿Cuánto pesas tú en kilogramos? La fórmula para convertir las **libras** en kilogramos no es muy complicada.

chart
pounds

| Fórmula: | libras | X | 0,45 | = | kilogramos |
|---|---|---|---|---|---|
| | Ana pesa 100 lbs | X | 0,45 | = | Ana pesa 45 kilogramos |
| | Pedro pesa 150 lbs | X | 0,45 | = | Pedro pesa 68 kilogramos |

Ya mencionamos que las personas de mayor peso queman más calorías que las de menor peso haciendo la misma actividad. ¿Quién utiliza más energía haciendo las actividades de la lista, Pedro o Ana?

| Actividad | CUE | X (se multiplica por) | El peso | | | Calorías por minuto |
|---|---|---|---|---|---|---|
| El boliche | 0,0471 | X | (Ana) | 45kg | = | 2,1 |
| | | | (Pedro) | 68kg | = | 3,2 |
| Caminar 1 milla en 17 minutos | 0,0794 | X | (Ana) | 45kg | = | 3,5 |
| | | | (Pedro) | 68kg | = | 5,4 |
| El ciclismo 1 milla en 6,4 minutos | 0,0985 | X | (Ana) | 45kg | = | 4,4 |
| | | | (Pedro) | 68kg | = | 6,7 |
| La natación | 0,1333 | X | (Ana) | 45kg | = | 6,0 |
| | | | (Pedro) | 68kg | = | 9,1 |
| Correr 1 milla en 10 minutos | 0,1471 | X | (Ana) | 45kg | = | 6,6 |
| | | | (Pedro) | 68kg | = | 10,0 |

## meta final

ACTIVIDAD

*Paso 1:* Work with a partner to match the term in column A with its definition in column B. Record your choices on a separate sheet of paper. Prepare for class discussion!

| A | B |
|---|---|
| _____1. el kilogramo | A. unidad de energía |
| _____2. la caloría | B. montar en bicicleta |
| _____3. el ciclismo | C. nadar |
| _____4. aeróbico | D. gas que respiramos |
| _____5. los pulmones | E. unidad de peso del sistema métrico |
| _____6. el oxígeno | F. en la presencia del oxígeno |
| _____7. la natación | G. órganos internos que usamos para respirar |

*Paso 2:* Refer to the chart to answer the following questions.

1. Ana caminó por 30 minutos ayer por la tarde (velocidad = 1 milla en 17 minutos). ¿Cuántas calorías quemó ella?
2. Pedro comió una pizza que contenía unas 500 calorías el viernes por la noche. ¿Cuántos minutos tiene que nadar para quemar esas calorías?
3. Una persona misteriosa corrió en el parque por 45 minutos. Sabemos que la persona quemó 450 calorías. ¿Quién fue al parque? ¿Pedro o Ana?



*Paso 2:* Ask students to fold a piece of paper in half to make two columns. In Column 1, have them list the 5 most aerobically challenging activities included on the chart above. In Column 2, have them list their 5 favorite activities from the list.

*Paso 3:* Now have students compare their lists with those of a partner. Can they comment during class discussion on how their lists are alike or different? Have them use the following models as a guide:

**A mi compañero(a) le gusta_______. Pero yo prefiero______.**
**Yo pienso que correr es más difícil que jugar al billar. Correr requiere más energía.**
**Mi compañero(a) piensa que caminar es más fácil que nadar. Caminar requiere menos energía.**

### Expansion Activity

Using the lists of activities and body weights (kg) they completed earlier, ask students to calculate how many calories they would use per minute for each of the activities on the lists they made. Remind them to *multiply* the **CUE** of the activity by body weight (kg). Have them share their findings with the class.

**CUE**
**Me gusta correr.**

| **Yo peso...** | **Calorías por minuto** |
|---|---|
| 0.1856 × 40kg = | 7.4 **calorías** |

**Yo quemo 7.4 calorías por minuto corriendo en mi vecindario.**

## Presentation: Los ejercicios aeróbicos

In order to help students become more familiar with the metric system, you may want to do the following activities with them. Keep in mind that the issue of weight can be very delicate, and students may not want to share their weight. Tell them that it's OK to use approximate weights for these exercises.

*Paso 1. El sistema métrico:* With the notable exception of the United States, most countries of the world use the metric system of weights and measures. Ask students to use the formula provided in the passage to determine the weight (in kilograms) of the following people.

| | | | |
|---|---|---|---|
| Marcos pesa 105 libras | × 0.45 | = | 47 kilogramos (kg). |
| Mi compañero pesa_____libras | × 0.45 | = | _____kg. |
| La profesora pesa_____libras | × 0.45 | = | _____kg. |
| Mi mejor amigo pesa_____libras | × 0.45 | = | _____kg. |
| Mi madre pesa_____libras | × 0.45 | = | _____kg. |
| Yo peso_____libras | × 0.45 | = | _____kg. |

# Cultural Context

Unit 6 features Alicia Sánchez, a young woman from Mexico. The unit centers around shopping. In Chapter 16, we read about people going to specialty stores—a record shop, a stationery store, and a sporting goods store. In Chapter 17, we read about people shopping for food at an open-air market, as well as a supermarket. Finally, in Chapter 18, we read about people visiting a clothing boutique and a shoe store.



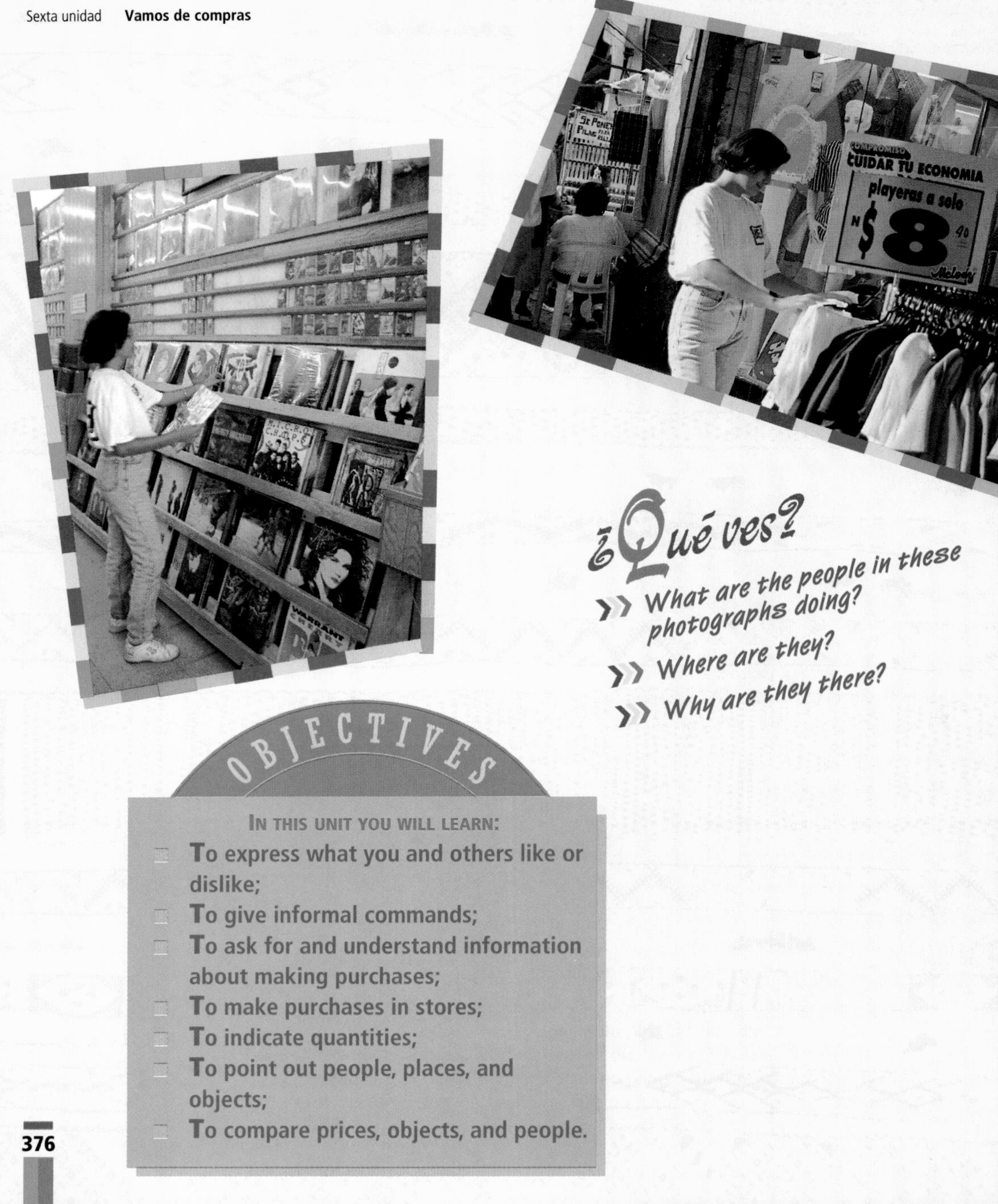


## ¿Qué ves?

- What are the people in these photographs doing?
- Where are they?
- Why are they there?

## Objectives

IN THIS UNIT YOU WILL LEARN:

- To express what you and others like or dislike;
- To give informal commands;
- To ask for and understand information about making purchases;
- To make purchases in stores;
- To indicate quantities;
- To point out people, places, and objects;
- To compare prices, objects, and people.

# Unidad seis

## Capítulo dieciséis: Vamos al centro comercial

**Primera etapa:** En la tienda de música
**Segunda etapa:** En la papelería
**Tercera etapa:** La tienda de deportes

## Capítulo diecisiete: ¿Cuánto cuesta... ?

**Primera etapa:** Día de feria
**Segunda etapa:** En el supermercado

## Capítulo dieciocho: ¿Qué quieres comprar?

**Primera etapa:** Tienda "La Alta Moda"
**Segunda etapa:** Zapatería "El Tacón"

If you do not assign the Planning Strategy for homework (Workbook, p. 205), you may want to go over the questions in class before beginning Chapter 16.

# Chapter Objectives

Functions: Making purchases and choices; expressing quantity; asking for prices

Context: **Tienda de música; papelería; tienda de deportes**

Accuracy: The verb **gustar** (presented with all of the indirect object pronouns); familiar commands (both affirmative and negative)

# Cultural Observation

Ask students to study the photo on this page. Where are Alicia and her friend? Modern shopping malls can be found in all the capital cities as well as other larger cities in Latin America. Just like in the U.S., many people enjoy going to the malls to window-shop, to see what is new, and to have something to do.

## Chapter Warm-up: Birthday Lineup

- Tell the students that when you give the signal, they are to attempt to find everyone whose birthday falls in the same month as theirs.
- Instruct the students to line up in chronological order of birth.
- When they are all lined up, have them tell the dates of their birthdays from January to December.

CAPÍTULO 16

# VAMOS AL CENTRO COMERCIAL

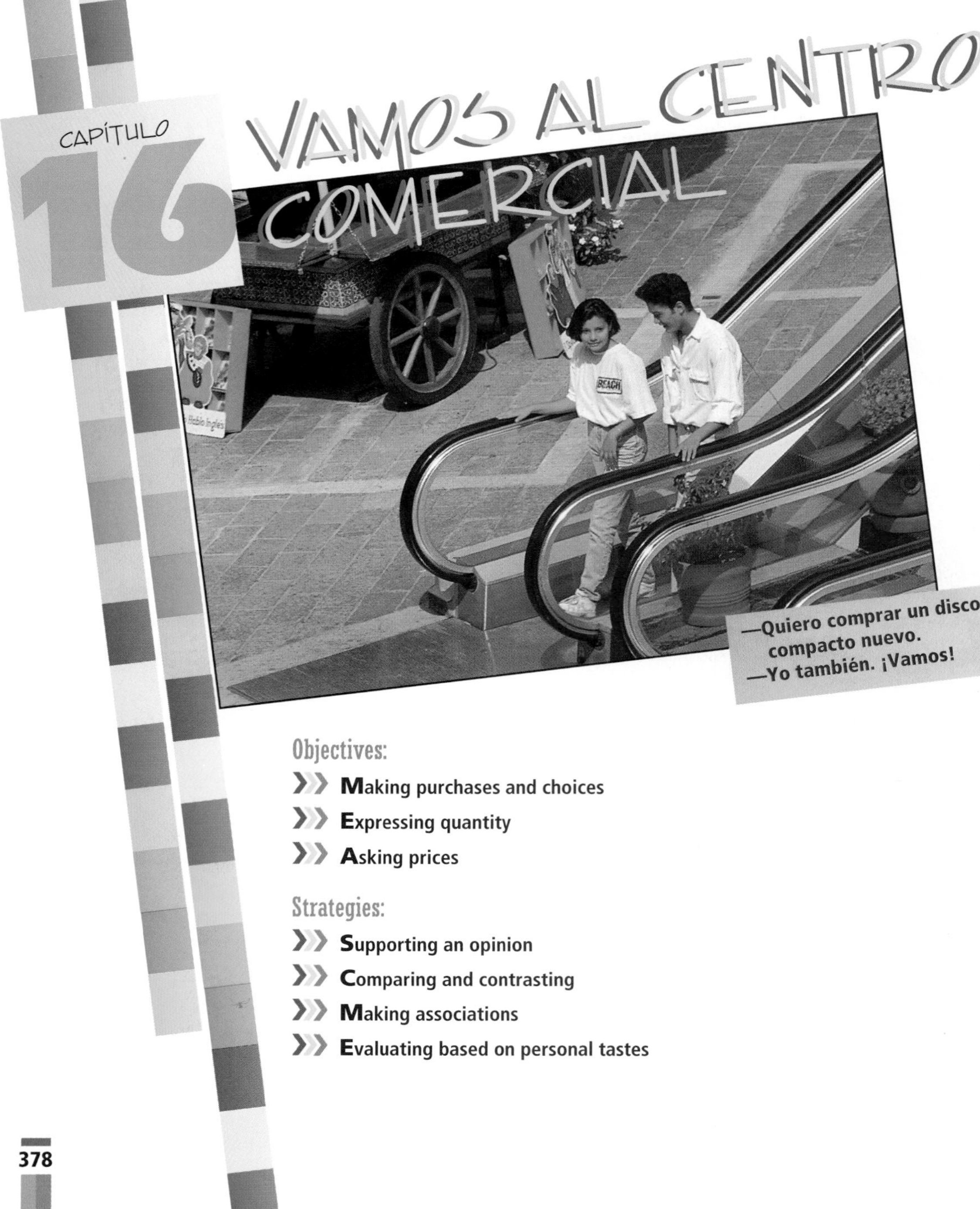

—Quiero comprar un disco compacto nuevo.
—Yo también. ¡Vamos!

Objectives:

- **M**aking purchases and choices
- **E**xpressing quantity
- **A**sking prices

Strategies:

- **S**upporting an opinion
- **C**omparing and contrasting
- **M**aking associations
- **E**valuating based on personal tastes



## Video/CD-ROM

Chapter 16 Video Program
Chapter 16 CD-ROM Program

These can be used at the end of the chapter as expansion activities.

# PRIMERA ETAPA

## Preparación

- **D**o you like to go shopping? Why, or why not?
- **W**here do you usually go to buy the things you need?
- **W**hat kinds of questions do you normally need to ask when you are shopping?
- **D**o you do your grocery shopping at the same place where you buy such items as records, clothes, shoes, and sporting goods?

*Learning Strategy:*
*Previewing*

## En la tienda de música

Anoche Beatriz y Mónica **fueron** a un concierto de rock en el Parque Luna. **A ellas les encantó** escuchar a su grupo favorito Juan Luis Guerra y los 440. Hoy Mónica quiere comprar uno de sus discos compactos. **Por eso**, van a la tienda de música "La Nueva Onda". Beatriz quiere comprar un disco compacto de Jon Secada, pero es muy **caro.**

went / They loved
Because of this
expensive

**Beatriz:** ¡**Qué pena!** No tengo **suficiente** dinero para comprar el disco compacto.
**Mónica:** Mira, yo encontré la cinta de Juan Luis Guerra y los 440 que me gusta y es muy **barata.**
**Beatriz:** **A ver.** ¿Dónde están las cintas?
**Mónica:** **Allí**, al lado de los vídeos.
**Beatriz:** ¡Super! Aquí está la cinta que me gusta a mí.

What a shame! / enough
inexpensive
Let's see.
There

## ¡Aquí te toca a ti!

**A. *Para mi cumpleaños...*** Complete the following sentences that make up your "wish list" for your next birthday.

1. Yo quiero...
2. Quisiera...
3. Necesito...
4. Por favor, compre...
5. ¿Tienes suficiente dinero para comprar... ?

*Critical Thinking Strategy:*
*Evaluating based on personal taste*

379

## Etapa Support Materials

Workbook: **pp. 206–210**
Teacher Tape
Quiz: **Testing Program, p. 184**

Support material, **En la tienda de música:**
**Teacher Tape**

## Exercise Progression

Exs. A and B both provide meaningful open-ended activities designed to give students the opportunity to practice the vocabulary in a realistic way.

## Preparación

Introduce this topic by asking general questions about shopping: Do you like to go shopping? Why, or why not? Where do you usually go to buy the things you need? Do you go more out of necessity or for fun and browsing? Do you generally prefer the bigger stores where you can buy groceries as well as records, clothes, and sporting goods all at once, or do you prefer smaller specialty stores? Why? What are the favorite shopping places locally? Where do you spend the majority of your money? On what? Do you think you are treated well when you go out shopping with friends? Do you think the customer is always right? What kinds of questions do we normally ask in a shopping situation?

## Presentation: En la tienda de música

You can begin by playing the dialogue from the Teacher Tape (with books closed). You may want to play it twice before having students answer general comprehension questions. For example: **¿Dónde están las dos amigas? ¿Adónde fueron anoche? ¿Qué quieren comprar?** etc. Then have students open their books and read the dialogue. Follow up by asking personalized questions. If you do not use the Teacher Tape, you might want to choose a student (maybe a Spanish-speaker) and model the dialogue while students listen with books closed. Then proceed as above.

**Ex. A:** writing

*Support material, En la tienda de música:*
Teacher Tape/CD #2 Track #24

**Ex. B:** pair work

writing

## Pronunciation

Additional activities appear in the Laboratory Tape Program.

***Support material, Pronunciación:***
Pronunciation Tape



**B. *Los regalos*** You are at **"La Nueva Onda",** buying presents for your family and friends. (1) Decide which tapes or CDs you will get for whom. (2) Put together a list (of at least four people and gifts) as you make your decisions. When you have made your choices, (3) discuss them with your partner. As you go through your list, (4) make some comment explaining each choice.

*Modelo:* **Student 1:** *Pienso comprar este disco compacto para mi prima. [X] es su cantante favorito. Y esta cinta es para papá. Escucha siempre la música de [X].*
**Student 2:** *Buena idea. Yo voy a comprar esta cinta para mi hermano. Le gusta mucho el jazz latino. Quisiera comprar el disco compacto pero es muy caro.*

# *Pronunciación: The consonant r*

A single **r** within a word is pronounced like the *dd* in the English words *daddy* and *ladder*, that is, with a single tap of the tip of the tongue against the gum ridge behind the upper front teeth.

## Práctica

C. Escucha a tu maestro(a) cuando lee las siguientes palabras y repítelas después para practicar la pronunciación.

1. cámara
2. pájaro
3. farmacia
4. cuatro
5. pintura
6. estéreo
7. libro
8. hermano
9. parque
10. serio

# ESTRUCTURA

### *The verb gustar*

You are already familiar with the verb **gustar** and its use in the following expressions:

| | |
|---|---|
| **Me gusta** la música rock. | *I like* rock music. |
| **Te gusta** bailar. | *You like* to dance. |

**Ex. D:**  groups of 3

writing

*Answers, Ex. D:* While personalized responses will vary, grammatical forms will be: 1. ...gustan más los discos compactos; ...gustan más las cintas 2. ...gusta más el concierto; ... gusta más la película 3. ...gusta más ir de compras; ...gusta más hablar por teléfono 4. ...gusta más la computadora; ...gusta más la máquina de escribir 5. ...gusta más el jazz; ...gusta más la música clásica 6. ...gustan más las fotografías; ...gustan más los vídeos 7. ...gusta más la televisión; ... gusta más el cine 8. ...gusta más la radio; ...gusta más la grabadora 9. ...gusta más bailar; ...gusta más mirar la televisión

In order to express what someone else likes or dislikes, the pronouns **le** (singular) and **les** (plural) are used. The pronoun **nos** is used for **nosotros(as).**

| | |
|---|---|
| **Le gusta** Jon Secada. | *You (formal) / He / She like(s)* Jon Secada. |
| **Les gusta** el concierto. | *You (plural) / They like* the concert. |
| **Nos gusta** la música latina. | *We like* Latin music. |

If you want to clarify who likes something, the preposition **a** must be placed before the noun or pronoun that identifies the person(s).

| | |
|---|---|
| **A Luis** le gusta el jazz. | *Luis* likes jazz. |
| **A Ana y Javier** les gusta el disco compacto. | *Ana and Javier* like the CD. |
| **A Ud.** le gusta el disco compacto. | *You* like the CD. |
| **A Uds.** les gusta la cinta. | *You (plural)* like the tape. |
| **A Lucy y a mí** nos gusta bailar. | *Lucy and I* like to dance. |

Remember that **gusta** (singular) and **gustan** (plural) agree in number with the words that follow them (the subject).

| | |
|---|---|
| A mi hermana le **gusta la tienda.** | My sister *likes the store.* |
| A mi hermana le **gustan los discos compactos.** | My sister *likes CDs.* |

The verb **encantar** (*to like very much, to love*) follows the same pattern as **gustar.**

## Aquí practicamos

*D.* ***Los gustos*** Ask two classmates what they like most. After they answer, indicate what the two of them like in common. If they don't like the same thing, indicate what each of your classmates likes. Follow the model.

*Learning Strategies:*

*Interviewing, reporting*

*Critical Thinking Strategies:*

*Evaluating based on personal tastes, comparing and contrasting*

**Modelo:**

**Tú:** *¿Les gusta más la radio o la grabadora?*
**Estudiante A:** *Me gusta más la grabadora.*
**Estudiante B:** *Me gusta más la grabadora.* o: *Me gusta la radio.*
**Tú:** *Ah, a los dos les gusta la grabadora.* o: *Ah, a él/ella le gusta la grabadora y a él/ella le gusta la radio.*

1. los discos compactos o las cintas
2. el concierto o la película
3. ir de compras o hablar por teléfono
4. la computadora o la máquina de escribir
5. el jazz o la música clásica
6. las fotografías o los vídeos
7. la televisión o el cine
8. la radio o la grabadora
9. bailar o mirar la televisión



## Exercise Progression

Ex. D provides practice with the forms of the verb **gustar** and the indirect object pronouns while allowing students to use the expression in meaningful communication. Organizing their notes on a chart allows students to use the chart as an outline of the information they are discussing while practicing control of the appropriate grammatical structures. On the following page, Ex. E offers meaningful practice in a personalized context; Ex. F provides more meaningful practice in a controlled situation; Ex. G affords students the opportunity to express themselves with the structure in a personalized communicative format.

**Ex. E:** writing

*Suggestions, Ex. E:* Have students write out sentences and then do peer editing. You might also want to have students write out the answers on the board and then have the class point out any errors.

*Answers, Ex. F:* 1. A Benito y a mí nos encantó... 2. A Laura no le gustó... 3. A mi prima no le gustó... 4. A mí me encantó... 5. A ellos no les gustó... 6. A Ud. le encantó... 7. A nosotros nos encantó... 8. A Uds. les encantó... 9. A ella no le gustó... 10. A Eduardo y a mí nos encantó...

**Ex. G:** pair work

*Variation, Ex. G:* Write the following categories on the board: **Comida, Lugares, Música, Cosas para hacer**. As students report on what their classmates like to do, write each classmate's name under the appropriate heading(s). You can then make statements like **A Ana y a Susy les gusta...** etc.

*Learning Strategy: Categorizing*

*Answers, Aquí escuchamos:* 1. Isabel 2. la música latina; la música clásica 3. los CDs son muy caros 4. Isabel 5. Los Lobos 6. a la tienda de música

*Support material, Aquí escuchamos:* Teacher Tape/CD #2 Track #25 and Tapescript

Learning Strategy:

*Reporting based on personal knowledge*

**E. *¿Qué les gusta hacer?*** Do you know your friends and family well? What is the one thing they most like to do? Follow the model.

Modelo: mi hermana
*A mi hermana le gusta estudiar.*

1. mi mejor amigo(a)
2. mi madre
3. mis abuelos
4. mis compañeros de clase
5. mis primos
6. mi padre
7. mi hermano(a)
8. mis profesores

**F. *El concierto de rock*** Explain who really liked the concert and who did not like it. Follow the models.

Modelos: a mi hermano / sí
*A mi hermano le encantó el concierto.*

a mis padres / no
*A mis padres no les gustó el concierto.*

1. a Benito y a mí / sí
2. a Laura / no
3. a mi prima / no
4. a mí / sí
5. a ellos / no
6. a Ud. / sí
7. a nosotros / sí
8. a Uds. / sí
9. a ella / no
10. a Eduardo y a mí / sí

**G. *¿Qué le encanta a tu compañero(a)?*** Find out from a classmate the things that he or she likes and loves to do and eat, the places that he or she likes to go, and the music or group **(grupo)** that he or she likes to listen to. Then report that information to the class. Work with a partner and follow the model.

Modelo:
**Tú:** *¿Qué te gusta hacer?*
**Compañera:** *A mí me gusta... y me encanta...*
**Tú:** *A Anita le gusta... y le encanta...*

## Aquí escuchamos:

### "Me gusta la música..."

Critical Thinking Strategy:

*Predicting*

### Antes de escuchar

**Isabel and Miguel are giving information about their likes and dislikes. Based on what you've learned in this etapa, what are some of the likes and dislikes you expect them to talk about?**

## Después de escuchar

**Make a list of the things that Isabel likes and another of the things that Miguel likes. Be prepared to indicate in Spanish which preferences they have in common.**

**Contesta las preguntas sobre la conversación entre Isabel y Miguel.**

1. **¿A quién le gustan muchos tipos de música?**
2. **¿Qué música le gusta más a Isabel? ¿y a Miguel?**
3. **¿Por qué le gustan más a Miguel las cintas que los discos compactos?**
4. **¿A quién le gusta Jon Secada?**
5. **¿Quiénes le gustan más a Miguel?**
6. **¿Adónde van a ir los dos?**

*Learning Strategies:*

*Listing , listening for details*

## ¡Adelante!

EJERCICIO ORAL

**H. *¿Qué te gusta hacer los fines de semana?*** Work in pairs and (1) tell your partner the things that you like to do on weekends. (2) Find out if there are activities that you both like. (3) Then report back to the class.

—*¿Qué te gusta hacer los fines de semana?*
—*A mí me gusta charlar con mis amigos.*
—*A mí también me gusta charlar con mis amigos.*
(To the class) —*A nosotros nos gusta charlar con nuestros amigos.*

*Cooperative Learning*

*Learning Strategy:*

*Reporting based on personal tastes*

*Critical Thinking Strategy:*

*Comparing*

EJERCICIO ESCRITO

**I. *Un diálogo de contrarios*** Imagine that you and another student have a relationship that is based on opposites. The two of you are friends, despite great differences in likes, dislikes, interests, and possessions. Make up some details about your two lives and write a dialogue together of about twelve sentences in length (or about six to eight comments from each individual).

*Cooperative Learning*

*Critical Thinking Strategy:*

*Comparing and contrasting*

**Ex. H:** pair work

*Suggestion, Ex. H:* Be sure to ask follow-up questions to give students the opportunity to report back. This activity provides preparation for the **Ya llegamos** section at the end of Unit 6.

*Variation, Ex. H:* In their discussion you may want to guide them to: (1) Talk about what they like to do with their families, with friends, for relaxation, for amusement, where they like to eat, where they like to go. As they learn about their partners' favorite weekend activities, (2) mention whether or not they like to do these things. (3) Record the gist of their discussion in charts with four columns labeled as follows: **Los gustos de mi compañero(a), Mi opinión, Mis gustos, Su opinión.** Each student should mention at least four activities. (4) During their discussion, students should decide on something they would like to do next weekend.

*Reteaching:* Some students may have difficulty with the concept of **gustar** beyond **Me gusta** and **Me gustan.** These students could benefit from the following visual reinforcement:

The teacher will name categories from previous chapters (for example sports) asking **¿A quiénes les gusta... ?** Those students will stand up and confirm, **Sí. A mí me gusta... .** Other students keep notes: **A Kristin y a Benjamín les gusta el fútbol.**

**Ex. I:** pair work

writing

*More-prepared students, Ex. I:* More-prepared students could memorize and present their dialogues, complete with props, music, etc. To give students a sense of definition for their dialogues, it is useful to give them a task to complete (e.g., a conflict to present and resolve, a lesson to teach, a surprise ending, etc.).

*Less-prepared students, Ex. I:* Less-prepared students could work with more concrete examples. Have these students identify two very different people (a rock star and an Olympic athlete, for example), and write about them.

## Presentation: En la papelería

Introduce the topic by asking the following questions: Where do you go to buy materials for school? What other stationery stores are in the area? What kinds of goods do you find in a stationery store other than paper? Do you think that the rising popularity of computers at home and at school has hurt sales of paper and pens?

Have students listen to the dialogue on the Teacher Tape (with books closed). Proceed by asking students whether they can give the names of some of the items mentioned. Emphasize the use of **¿En qué puedo servirles?** Then have students practice reading the dialogue with their partners. If you do not use the Teacher Tape, model the dialogue with a student (maybe one of your Spanish-speaking students) with students' books closed, and then proceed as above.

## Vocabulary Expansion

**tarjeta postal**

***Support material, En la papelería:***
Teacher Tape/CD #2 Track #26, transparency #58



# SEGUNDA ETAPA

### Preparación

**Learning Strategies:**
*Previewing, brainstorming*

- **What are some of the items that you will find at a stationery store or in the paper goods section of a department store?**
- **What are some of the questions that a person who works in a store usually asks a customer?**

## En la papelería

*En la papelería:* At the stationery store

| | |
|---|---|
| How may I help you? | —Buenos días, muchachos. **¿En qué puedo servirles?** |
| typewriter paper | —Necesitamos **papel para escribir a máquina.** ¿Tiene? |
| sheets | —¡Cómo no! ¿Cuántas **hojas** quieren? |
| airmail paper | —Diez, por favor. ¿Y **papel de avión?** |
| Here you are. / Anything else? | —**Aquí tienen. ¿Algo más?** |
| birthday cards / Mother's Day card | —Sí, yo necesito tres **tarjetas de cumpleaños** y una **tarjeta del Día de la Madre.** |
| | —Acabamos de recibir unas muy bonitas. Mira aquí. |
| envelopes | —Mm... Sí, son muy bonitas. ¿Vienen con **sobres?** |
| | —¡Pues, claro! |
| That's all for today. | —Bien. **Es todo por hoy.** |

## ¡Aquí te toca a ti!

**A. *¿Qué compraron en la papelería?*** Mira las fotos en la página 385 y di qué compró cada persona. Sigue el modelo.

Estela
*Estela compró una tarjeta de cumpleaños.*



## Etapa Support Materials

Workbook: **pp. 211–215**
Transparency: **#58**
Teacher Tape
Quiz: **Testing Program, p. 187**

Support material, **En la papelería:**
**Teacher Tape**
**Transparency: #58**

Estela

1. La Srta. Balboa

2. Ignacio



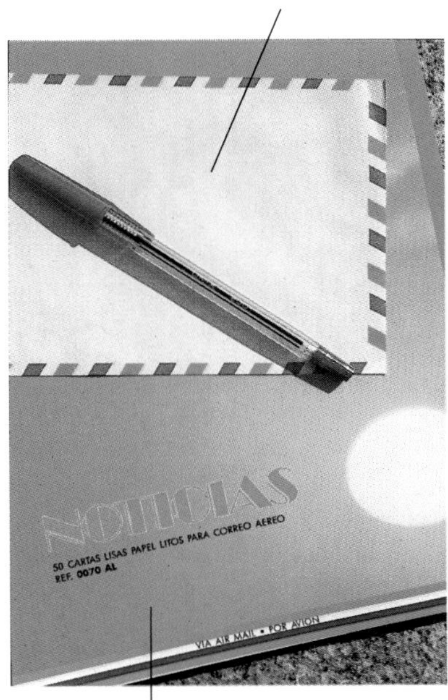


4. Cristina

3. Inés

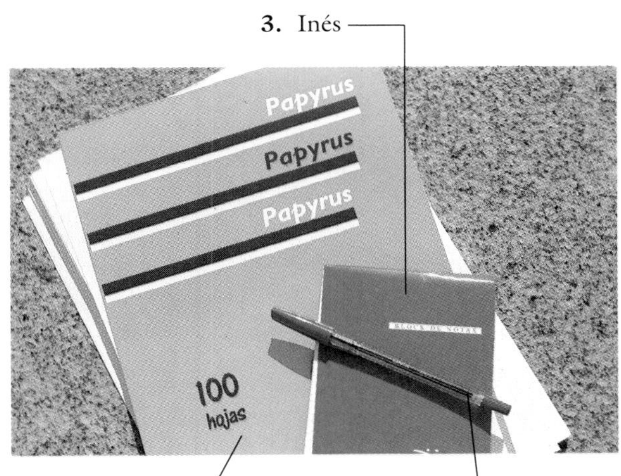

5. el Sr. Rodríguez

6. Roberto



*Answers, Ex. A:* Answers may vary in some cases. 1. La Srta. Balboa compró papel de avión. 2. Ignacio... unos sobres. 3. Inés... un cuaderno. 4. Cristina... unas hojas de papel. 5. El Sr. Rodríguez... papel para escribir a máquina. 6. Roberto... un bolígrafo.

*Variation, Ex. A:* Have students role play the clerk and the customer using the expressions **¿En qué puedo servirles? / Yo quisiera...**

## Exercise Progression

Exs. A and B offer meaningful practice with new and old vocabulary in controlled situations.

*Support material, Ex. B:*
Transparency #58

*Answers, Ex. B:* 1. ... papelería... un bolígrafo y papel de avión 2. ... tienda de música... discos compactos 3. ... papelería... una tarjeta de cumpleaños 4. ... papelería... lápices 5. ... tienda de música... cintas 6. ... papelería... sobres 7. ... papelería... una goma

**Ex. C:** pair work

role play

*More-prepared students, Ex. C:* For a more challenging variation of written and memorized dialogues for more-prepared students, give them individual situation cards that tell them what roles they will play at the store. For example, Student 1 would have a card reading, "You have picked out exactly the pen and paper you need, but at the register, you come up a dollar short. Assure the clerk you'll come back later with the money." Student 2's card: "You just started this new job as clerk and like it a lot, but your boss is very strict. You must be friendly to customers, but not give in to unreasonable demands." Student 3: "You are in a hurry to check out but there is some problem with the customer ahead of you. See if you can be of help. By the way, you are carrying no cash." This is particularly good for developing listening, as well as speaking skills. If students enjoy the activity, enlist them to write ideas for more situation cards.

*Less-prepared students, Ex. C:* Ask less-prepared students to work out a dialogue and then switch roles. Have volunteers present their dialogues to the class.

**B. *¿Adónde vas para comprar... ?*** Mira los dibujos y di adónde vas para comprar cada cosa. Sique el modelo.

**Modelo:** discos compactos
*Voy a la tienda de música para comprar discos compactos.*

1.

2.

3.

4.

5.

6.

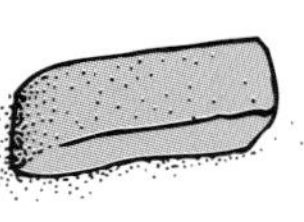
7.

## Repaso

**Learning Strategies:**

*Describing personal tastes, making recommendations*

**Critical Thinking Strategy:**

*Making associations*

**C. *En la tienda de música*** You are shopping for presents for three of your friends at **"La Nueva Onda."** Together with another student, (1) play the role of the clerk and the customer at a record store. (2) Tell the clerk the music your friends like. The clerk will make suggestions for each gift. (3) Buy two CDs and a tape. (4) Pay and leave.

**Modelo:** *—¿En qué puedo servirle?*
*—A mi amiga Claudia le gusta la música clásica. Quiero comprar un disco compacto para ella. ¿Qué tiene Ud.?*

## Pronunciación: The consonant *rr*

An **rr** (called a trilled *r)* within a word is pronounced by flapping or trilling the tip of the tongue against the gum ridge behind the upper front teeth. When an **r** is the first letter of a Spanish word, it also has this sound.



### Presentation: Pronunciation

Since many students find it difficult to produce the trilled **r,** point out that it is usually easier for a native English speaker to produce a trilled **r** after the letter **p.** Have them invent little phrases in English with *pr* words and encourage them to practice them until they can produce the trilled **r** sound. *(The princess is pretty.)*

Additional activities appear in the Laboratory Tape Program.

*Support material, Pronunciación:* Pronunciatio
Tape 

Answers, Ex. E: 1. habla 2. come 3. haz 4. mira 5. lee 6. sal 7. dobla 8. compra 9. di 10. corre 11. descansa 12. sé 13. escucha 14. escribe 15. ten

## Práctica

*D.* Escucha a tu maestro(a) cuando lee las siguientes palabras. Después repítelas para practicar la pronunciación.

1. borrador
2. perro
3. correo
4. barrio
5. aburrido
6. radio
7. Roberto
8. rubio
9. río
10. música rock

## ESTRUCTURA

### *The imperative with tú: familiar commands*

| | |
|---|---|
| —Luis, **mira** las tarjetas de cumpleaños. | Luis, *look* at the birthday cards. |
| —Son muy bonitas. **Compra** dos. | They are very pretty. *Buy* two. |

In Chapter 8, you learned to give orders, directions, and suggestions using the formal command forms (**Ud.** and **Uds.**). Here you will learn the informal command form **(tú)**, used to make requests of family members, peers, or younger people.

#### Regular Familiar Command

| Affirmative | | |
|---|---|---|
| Verbs ending in **-ar: bailar** | Verbs ending in **-er: beber** | Verbs ending in **-ir: escribir** |
| **baila** | **bebe** | **escribe** |

1. The *regular affirmative **tú** command* has the same ending as the third-person singular **(él, ella)** of the present tense.

2. The verbs **decir, hacer, ir, poner, salir, ser, tener,** and **venir** have irregular affirmative command forms.

| | | | | | | | |
|---|---|---|---|---|---|---|---|
| decir | **di** | ir | **ve** | salir | **sal** | tener | **ten** |
| hacer | **haz** | poner | **pon** | ser | **sé** | venir | **ven** |

## Aquí practicamos

*E.* Da la forma del mandato con *tú* de los siguientes verbos.

1. hablar
2. comer
3. hacer
4. mirar
5. leer
6. salir
7. doblar
8. comprar
9. decir
10. correr
11. descansar
12. ser
13. escuchar
14. escribir
15. tener



### [Pr]esentation: Familiar commands

[To] introduce the command form you could use TPR. (For a more [co]mplete description of TPR, see **Etapa preliminar E.)** For [ex]ample, you might say: **Ven aquí, María, por favor. [Es]cribe en la pizarra, Juan. Mira este libro, Ramón. Sal [de] la clase, Estela.,** etc. Then write a few verbs on the board [an]d explain how the commands are formed. Point out the [irr]egular command forms.

[Th]e formation of the negative **tú** command will be presented [in] the next **etapa**.

### Exercise Progression

Ex. E is designed to give students ample practice forming the familiar commands of both regular and irregular verbs. On the following page, Ex. F offers meaningful practice in a realistic context; Ex. G provides more practice in a personalized communicative activity.

**Answers, Ex. F:** 1. ven 2. sé 3. haz 4. pon 5. sal 6. ve 7. compra 8. usa 9. ten 10. di

**Ex. G:** pair work

**Suggestion, Ex. G:** Tell students to be creative in their advice. Have volunteers give some creative advice to their partners in front of the class.

**Answers, Aquí escuchamos:** 1. disquetes y una cinta 2. en paquetes de cinco o diez disquetes 3. dos cintas 4. papel 5. "No gracias. Ya tengo mucho papel." 6. sobres

**Support material, Aquí escuchamos:** Teacher Tape/CD #2 Track #27 and Tapescript

**F. A tu hermano** Use the command form to get your younger brother to do what you want. Follow the model.

caminar al quiosco de la esquina
*Camina al quiosco de la esquina.*

1. venir aquí
2. ser bueno
3. hacer la tarea
4. poner la radio
5. salir de mi cuarto
6. ir al quiosco de periódicos
7. comprar mi revista favorita
8. usar tu dinero
9. tener paciencia
10. decir la verdad

*Learning Strategy:* Making recommendations

*Critical Thinking Strategy:* Associating school success and personal habits

**G. Consejos** Your best friend has problems at school. Give him or her some pieces of advice on what to do to improve the situation. Use these verbs in complete sentences. Follow the model.

**estudiar escuchar trabajar hablar hacer practicar ir venir escribir leer llegar decir salir**

Modelo: *Haz la tarea todos los días.*
*Llega a clase temprano.*

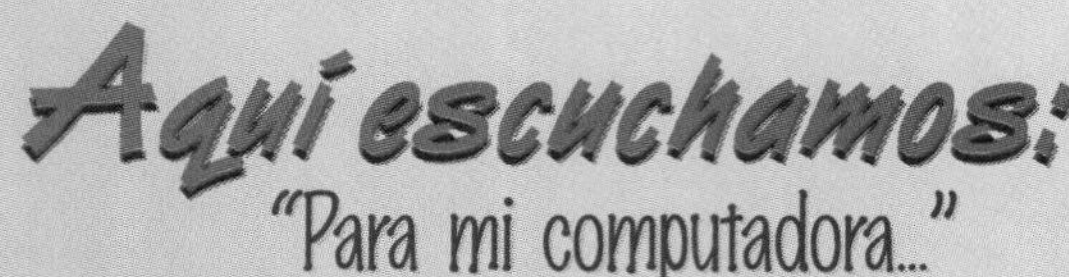


"Para mi computadora..."

*Learning Strategies:* Previewing, brainstorming

## Antes de escuchar

**In preparation for this conversation between a clerk and a customer, think about some of the items you would buy for use with a computer. Some of the same vocabulary that you already know in Spanish applies. Can you give some examples?**

**Now read the following questions to get an idea of what to listen for in the conversation.**

*Learning Strategy:* Listening for details

## Después de escuchar

1. ¿Qué necesita el señor que va a la papelería?
2. ¿Cómo se venden los disquetes para la computadora?
3. ¿Cuántas cintas compra el señor?
4. ¿Qúe le pregunta la empleada si necesita el señor?
5. ¿Qué dice él cuando ella le pregunta eso?
6. ¿Qué recuerda el hombre que necesita comprar para su esposa?

EJERCICIO ORAL

**Learning Strategy:** *Negotiating*

**H. *Ve a la papelería*** You need computer disks from the stationery store, but you have to prepare for a major test. (1) Call your friend and explain the situation. (2) Ask him or her to do you a favor and go to the store to buy the disks for you. (3) Tell him or her one other thing that you need from the stationery store. (4) After your friend agrees to do this errand, tell him or her when and where to meet you to deliver the purchases. (5) Remember to thank your friend for the help. Here is the beginning of your conversation. Work with a partner and finish the conversation. Use informal commands as needed to make your requests.

**Modelo:**

**Tú:** *¡Hola, Ester!*
**Amiga:** *¡Hola! ¿Qué tal?*
**Tú:** *Bien, pero tengo mucho que hacer.*
**Amiga:** *¿Qué tienes que hacer?*
**Tú:** ...

EJERCICIO ESCRITO

**Learning Strategies:** *Listing, making recommendations*

**Critical Thinking Strategies:** *Evaluating, prioritizing*

**I. *Consejos*** One of your friends has some problems with school work. He or she has asked you what to do in order to be more successful. Try to help by writing a list of eight suggestions for improving the situation. Use the informal command forms of the following verbs in the sentences you write: **estudiar, trabajar, hablar, hacer, practicar, escribir, decir, tener, salir, ver.** Then rearrange your sentences in order of priority, starting with the three most effective suggestions for ensuring your friend's success.



**Ex. H:**  pair work

***Suggestion, Ex. H:*** Have your Spanish-speaking students model a dialogue for the class before students begin to work in pairs. Then ask two or three pairs to present their dialogues in front of the class.

**Ex. I:** writing

***Less-prepared students, Ex. I:*** Less-prepared students may need more practice with familiar commands. Give them a list of choices an indecisive person has to make: Shall I stay home tonight and study or shall I go to the baseball game for an hour? The students will respond (orally or in writing) by selecting one option and forming the **tú** command with it: Go to the baseball game and study in the morning.

***More-prepared students, Ex. I:*** More-prepared students could do the same activity, adding reasons for selecting what they did.

***Reteaching:*** Recall vocabulary from previous chapters with this listening exercise: Read to the class (or prepare a tape of) a list of plausible bits of conversations we could overhear in a variety of places—at the pool, in science class, at the stationery store, at a football game, at the beach, in the metro, etc. Each example should include key vocabulary words and a familiar command: **"¡Alicia, dame ese disco compacto! ¿Sabes cuánto cuesta? Tengo que comprármelo".** Students write **en la tienda de música.**

## Presentation

To get students thinking about this topic you may want to ask them questions like the following: What are some examples of sports equipment? Where do you go to shop for sports equipment of all kinds? What items do you usually buy in a sporting goods store? What sports require the most expensive equipment? the least expensive equipment? Have you ever been to a store that sells used equipment?

## Presentation: La tienda de deportes

Play the Teacher Tape twice (with books closed) to introduce the dialogue. Then ask simple comprehension questions such as, **¿Qué compró la chica en la tienda de deportes? ¿Está en oferta la raqueta en el escaparate? ¿Tienen esquíes para vender? ¿Por qué no?** Then have students practice reading the dialogue with their partners, telling them to switch roles. If you do not use the Teacher Tape, read the dialogue twice with one of your Spanish-speaking students or another student (with books closed). Then proceed as above.

Students should learn the question **¿Cuánto cuesta/cuestan... ?** You may point out that **costar** follows the same pattern as **poder.** Students do not need to know the complete conjugation because they are only going to use the third-person forms of the verb.

## Vocabulary Expansion

**un balón (de baloncesto, de fútbol)**

*Support material, La tienda de deportes:*
Teacher Tape/CD #2 Track #28, transparencies #59, #60

# TERCERA ETAPA

## Preparación

*Learning Strategies:* Previewing, brainstorming

- **Where do you go to shop for sports equipment of all kinds?**
- **What are some examples of sports equipment?**
- **What items do you usually buy when you go to a sporting goods store?**
- **Which sports require the most expensive equipment? the least expensive?**

*La tienda de deportes:* The sporting goods store

## La tienda de deportes

Elsa y Norma entran en una tienda de deportes.
—Sí, señoritas, ¿qué necesitan?
—Quisiera saber **cuánto cuesta la raqueta** en el **escaparate.** (how much the racket costs / display window)
—¡Ah! **Buen ojo**. Es una raqueta muy buena y cuesta 120 dólares. (Good eye.)
—¿Cómo? ¿No está **en oferta?** (on sale)
—No, señorita. La oferta terminó ayer.
—¡Qué pena! Bueno. Y las **pelotas de tenis, ¿qué precio tienen?** (tennis balls / what price are they?)
—Mm... tres dólares.

—Bueno, **voy a llevar** tres. Puedo ver los **zapatos de tenis** también, por favor. (I'll take / tennis shoes)
—Por supuesto. ¿Algo más?
—Sí. ¿Venden **esquíes?** (skis)
—Sí, pero no hay más. Vendimos todos los esquíes en la oferta.
—Mm... bueno. Gracias.
—**A sus órdenes.** (At your service.)

## ¡Aquí te toca a ti!

**A. *Necesito comprar...*** You are in a sporting goods store and you want to examine some items (p. 391) before you buy. Ask to see them.

*Modelo:* pelotas de tenis
*Quisiera ver las pelotas de tenis, por favor.*



## Etapa Support Materials

Workbook: **pp. 216–219**
Transparencies: **#59, #60**
Teacher Tape
Listening Activity masters: **p. 107**
Tapescript: **p. 157**

Quiz: **Testing Program, p. 189**
Chapter Test: **Testing Program, p. 191**
Support material, **La tienda de deportes:**
**Teacher Tape**
**Transparencies: #59, #60**

1.

2.

3.

4.

5.

6.

**B. *¿Cuánto cuesta... ?*** Now you want to know the price of different items in the sporting goods store. Ask the clerk. In pairs, play the role of the customer and clerk. The person playing the clerk should make up reasonable prices for each item in Activity A. Follow the model.

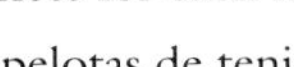

pelotas de tenis
—*Buenos días. ¿Cuánto cuestan las pelotas de tenis en el escaparate?*
—*Cuestan 3 dólares por tres.*
—*Mm... bien. Voy a llevar seis. Aquí tiene 6 dólares.*

**¿Qué crees?**

**The site of the 1992 Olympic Games:**

**a) Spain**
**b) Korea**
**c) Mexico**
**d) U.S.A.**

**respuesta** 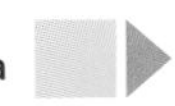

## Repaso

**C. *Mis libros favoritos*** You need to buy a present for a friend. You have decided to get something from a bookstore, but you need some advice. Ask a classmate to suggest three books that you could buy as a present. (He or she should use the **tú** command to make the suggestions.)

**Learning Strategy:**

*Making recommendations*

## ESTRUCTURA

### *The imperative with tú: negative familiar commands*

| | |
|---|---|
| **No compres** los esquíes. | *Don't buy* the skis. |
| **No lleves** la raqueta. | *Don't take* the racket. |



**Ex. B:**  pair work

 role play

***Suggestions, Ex. B:*** You might want to use the transparency for this exercise. Have students ask for at least four items and alternate roles (of clerk and customer) after each one. Encourage them to add other expressions and to vary the language any way they wish. Have volunteers present their mini-dialogues to the class. You could then ask follow-up questions in the third person to test listening comprehension.

**Ex. C:** pair work

***Suggestion, Ex. C:*** Brainstorm with the class to come up with a list of personal interests that might suggest choices of reading material: **los deportes, la moda, la aventura, la vida de personas famosas, la historia de... ; la gastronomía, los viajes, el romance, el misterio, la ficción científica, los animales, las colecciones.**

## Cultural Expansion

Since Ex. C involves buying books, it might be a good time to mention some of the famous Spanish and Latin American writers of the twentieth century. Ten Hispanics have won the Nobel Prize in Literature. Recently it was won in two consecutive years—1990 and 1991—by a Spaniard, Camilo José Cela, for his novels *La familia de Pascual Duarte* and *La colmena,* among others, and by the Mexican Octavio Paz, for his poetry and essays. He is most famous for his collection of essays called *El laberinto de la soledad.* Gabriel García Márquez is another famous Nobel prize winner. He is most famous for his book *Cien años de soledad.*

## Exercise Progression

Ex. A is designed to give students the opportunity to practice the vocabulary in a controlled situation. Ex. B provides more practice in an open-ended communicative activity.

***Support material, Ex. A:*** Transparency #59

**Ex. A:**  pair work

***Suggestion, Ex. A:*** Have students role play the clerk and the customer using the question **¿Qué necesitan?** Have them alternate roles after each item.

***Answers, Ex. A:*** Students add the following cues to the model: 1. la raqueta de tenis 2. los zapatos de tenis 3. los esquíes 4. la pelota (el balón) de baloncesto 5. la pelota (el balón) de fútbol 6. la bicicleta

## Presentation: Negative familiar commands

Tell students that you will ask them to do something, but that you may change your mind in the middle of the action so they need to listen carefully. Ask two students to do something and then ask one of them not to do it. For example: **María y Juan, vengan aquí.** (Students get up.) **No, Juan, no vengas. María, ven aquí. José y Alicia, vayan afuera. No, José, no vayas afuera. José, pon este libro en mi escritorio/mesa. No, José, no lo pongas en mi escritorio/mesa.** etc.

Write the **yo** form of several verbs (include spelling change verbs) on the board and show students how the negative familiar commands are formed. Point out the irregular commands for **ir** and **ser**.

*Answers, Ex. D:* 1. no esquíes 2. no lleves 3. no vayas 4. no comas 5. no seas 6. no vendas 7. no compres 8. no salgas 9. no cruces 10. no tengas

**Ex. E:** pair work

*Answers, Ex. E:* 1. no seas 2. no llegues 3. no tengas 4. no dobles 5. no escribas 6. no busques 7. no mires 8. no vengas 9. no pongas 10. no digas

*Variation, Ex. E:* Have students write a list of do's and don'ts for students coming to their school next year. Students can then compare suggestions and rank order them from most to least important.

The negative **tú** command is different from the affirmative **tú** command. Study the chart.

*Regular Familiar Command*

| *Negative* | | |
|---|---|---|
| Verbs ending in -**ar: bailar** | Verbs ending in -**er: beber** | Verbs ending in -**ir: escribir** |
| **no bailes** | **no bebas** | **no escribas** |

1. To form the *regular negative **tú** command,* drop the **o** from the **yo** form of the present tense and add **es** for **-ar** verbs and **as** for **-er** and **-ir** verbs:

| | | |
|---|---|---|
| **yo bailo** | → **bail-** | → **no bailes** |
| **yo bebo** | → **beb-** | → **no bebas** |
| **yo escribo** | → **escrib-** | → **no escribas** |

2. Verbs that end in **-car, -gar,** or **-zar** such as **practicar, llegar,** and **cruzar** change the spelling in the negative **tú** command: **c → qu — no practiques, g → gu — no llegues,** and **z → c — no cruces.**

3. The negative **tú** command of the eight irregular verbs you learned in the last **etapa** follow the same rule as the regular negative **tú** commands, except for **ir** and **ser.**

| | | | | | |
|---|---|---|---|---|---|
| decir | **no digas** | poner | **no pongas** | tener | **no tengas** |
| hacer | **no hagas** | salir | **no salgas** | venir | **no vengas** |
| ir | **no vayas** | ser | **no seas** | | |

a

## Aquí practicamos

*D.* Da la forma negativa del mandato con *tú* de los siguientes verbos.

1. esquiar aquí
2. llevar los libros
3. ir al parque
4. comer en tu casa
5. ser antipático
6. vender tus pelotas de tenis
7. comprar los zapatos allí
8. salir de la tienda
9. cruzar la calle
10. tener miedo *(be afraid)*

*E.* Tell your friend not to do these things. Work in pairs. Then reverse roles and repeat.

1. ser malo
2. llegar tarde
3. tener problemas
4. doblar a la derecha
5. escribir en el libro
6. buscar tus cuadernos
7. mirar mucho la TV
8. venir solo a la fiesta
9. poner la radio en clase
10. decir malas palabras



### Exercise Progression

Exs. D and E provide controlled practice with the structure. On the following pages, Ex. F offers more practice in a controlled yet communicative activity; Ex. G affords the opportunity for further practice in a personalized context.

**F. Consejos** You are new in the neighborhood and don't know where to go for the best buys. Your friend will direct you to various shops in town to get good prices and good quality. Work with a partner and follow the model.

**Modelo:** —*Voy a comprar carne en la Carnicería Montoya.*
—*No compres allí. Compra en la Carnicería Martín. Es mejor* (better).

1. Como en el restaurante La Estancia.
2. Hago compras en la Frutería la Sevillana.
3. Voy a la Panadería López.
4. Escucho discos compactos en la tienda de música Cantar y Bailar.
5. Busco lápices y borradores en la Papelería Mollar.
6. Miro las flores en la Florería La Rosa Roja.

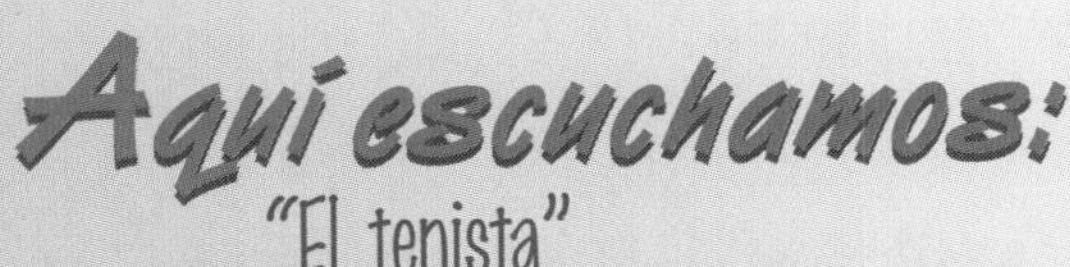

## Aquí escuchamos: "El tenista"

### Antes de escuchar

**Read the statements on page 394 to get an idea of the content of the conversation before listening.**

**Learning Strategy:**
*Previewing*



*Support material, Ex. F:*
Transparency #60

**Ex. F:** pair work

role play

*Answers, Ex. F:* 1. No comas... . Come en el Restaurante La Cabaña. 2. No hagas... . Haz compras en el Mercado Popular. 3. No vayas... . Ve a la Panadería la Oriental. 4. No escuches... . Escucha discos compactos en la Tienda de Música. 5. No busques... . Busca... en la Papelería los Amigos. 6. No mires... . Mira las flores en la Florería Arónica.

*Support material, Aquí escuchamos:*
Teacher Tape/CD #2 Track #29 and Tapescript

*Answers, Aquí escuchamos:* 1. F, tennis racket 2. T 3. T 4. F, but they are not very expensive 5. F, $99 6. T 7. F

**Ex. G:** pair work

This activity provides preparation for the **Ya llegamos** section at the end of Unit 6.

*Suggestions, Ex. G:* Give students time to prepare, practice, and then reverse roles. Then ask some volunteers to present their mini-situations to the class. Ask follow-up questions in the third person to test listening comprehension. For students who have no interest or involvement with sports, have them select another activity they enjoy and modify the exercise accordingly.

**Ex. H:** writing

*Suggestion, Ex. H:* As suggested above, modify the writing exercise for those students having no personal interest in sports. These students could, for example, write about a family member or friend who is a sports fanatic, pretend to be a popular sports figure doing this exercise, or choose another interest entirely.



*Learning Strategy:*

*Listening for details*

## Después de escuchar

**Decide whether the following statements are true or false. If something is false, indicate what the correct information should be, based on the conversation.**

1. The customer wants to buy some tennis shoes.
2. The customer indicates that he already has a tennis racket.
3. The customer wants a larger tennis racket.
4. The saleswoman says that the large rackets are still on sale.
5. The price of the racket is $199.
6. The offer comes with a free can of tennis balls.
7. The man decides not to buy the racket because it is too expensive.

*Learning Strategies:*

*Interviewing, making recommendations, supporting opinion*

*Critical Thinking Strategies:*

*Analyzing, making associations between personal preferences and sports*

## ¡Adelante!

### EJERCICIO ORAL

**G. *¿Qué deporte?*** Your friend wants to take up a new sport and asks you for advice because you are familiar with a number of sports. (1) Ask your friend about his or her preferences for season, team, or individual sports. Find out if your friend likes to play sports for competition or pleasure, and about any equipment to which he or she has access. (2) Choose a sport and advise your friend to take it up. Explain why, basing your decisions on your friend's talents and preferences. (3) Tell him or her what to buy in order to start practicing.

*Learning Strategies:*

*Organizing ideas in a paragaraph, supporting opinion*

*Critical Thinking Strategy:*

*Evaluating*

### EJERCICIO ESCRITO

**H. *Mi deporte preferido*** Write six to eight sentences about your favorite sport, indicating why you like it, how often you participate in that sport, where, and with whom.

# Vocabulario

## Para charlar

### Para expresar gustos

me / te / le / les / nos encanta(n)
me / te / le / les / nos gusta(n)

### Lugares para comprar

una papelería
una tienda de deportes
una tienda de música

### Expresiones para comprar

¿Algo más?
A sus órdenes.
Aquí tiene(n).
¿En qué puedo servirle(s)?
Es todo por hoy.
No hay más.
¿Qué necesita(n)?
Voy a llevar…

### Para preguntar el precio

¿Cuánto cuesta(n)?
¿Qué precio tiene(n)?
¿No está(n) en oferta?

## Temas y contextos

### Una tienda de música

una cinta
un disco compacto
un vídeo

### Una papelería

una hoja
el papel de avión
el papel para escribir a máquina
un sobre
una tarjeta de cumpleaños
una tarjeta del Día de la Madre

### Una tienda de deportes

unos esquíes
una pelota de tenis
una raqueta
unos zapatos de tenis

## Vocabulario general

### Sustantivos

un centro comercial
un escaparate
el precio

### Adjetivos

barato(a)
bonito(a)
caro(a)
favorito(a)
suficiente

### Otras expresiones

A ver.
Buen ojo.
fueron
por eso
¡Qué pena!
¡Super!

*Support material, Capítulo 16:* Improvised Conversation, Teacher Tape/CD #2 Track #30 and Tapescript; Lab Manual listening activities, Laboratory Program, Tapescript, and Teacher's Edition of the Workbook/Lab Manual

# Chapter Culminating Activities

pair work

Have students work in pairs and write out a list of sports and the equipment that is needed for each one. Then have them discuss with their partners which sports are cheaper and which are more expensive to play. You could follow up with a class discussion of sports (in Spanish), giving students the opportunity to share the ideas they talked about with their partners.

writing

Have students write out lists giving advice to a friend on how to maintain a healthy lifestyle. Set a time limit and encourage them to be creative. Then have the students with the longer lists read their advice to the class. Lead a class discussion on fitness, talking about the advice given.

groups of four or more

*More-prepared students:* More-prepared students might like to plan to debate an issue relevant to most schools—the elimination of sports as school-sponsored programs. If your school has no sports program, have students argue for/against beginning one (or reinstating it), or have them argue for/against removing it.

*Less-prepared students:* Less-prepared students could participate voluntarily, as if at an open forum for students, parents, and staff.

# Lectura cultural

## Prereading

Spanish-speaking youth around the world have access to a wide variety of music. You can remind students that although American music is very popular in Latin America and Spain, the favorite groups are usually local and national. Because many students in Latin America and Spain begin learning English at an early age, they are able to understand some of the lyrics of the American songs. You can also point out the influence of Hispanic music in the United States.



# Lectura cultural

## ESTRELLAS MUSICALES LATINAS

Celia Cruz

Rubén Blades

Gloria Estefan

*Learning Strategies:*

*Previewing, brainstorming*

*Critical Thinking Strategy:*

*Making associations*

### Antes de leer

1. Look at the photos to see if you recognize these people. What do they do?
2. Do you know the names of any other Spanish-speaking representatives of this profession? Where are they from?

### Guía para la lectura

A. Read the first sentence of each paragraph of the reading passage on page 397 to decide who is described there. Where is each person from?

**B.** Read each paragraph quickly and make a list of some of the key words that are related to what these people do. Were you able to find at least six?

**C.** Now answer the following questions about the entire passage according to the information you find in it.

1. Which person studied at a university in the U.S.?
2. Who performs in two languages?
3. Which one often appears with another famous person?
4. Who is particularly concerned about social problems?

**Learning Strategies:**

*Scanning for specific details and key words, reading for details*

## Estrellas musicales latinas

Varios cantantes del mundo hispano tienen fama internacional. Son verdaderas estrellas de la música latina y las tiendas de música venden sus cintas y discos compactos como tortillas calientes. Aquí presentamos información sobre cuatro de los cantantes más populares.

Juan Luis Guerra

Celia Cruz, "la reina de la salsa", es cubana y tiene una voz potente, con toda la gracia y el color de los trópicos. Embajadora de la música del Caribe, viaja constantemente por el mundo, actuando en compañía de Tito Puente, otro salsero legendario. Muchas personas que van a los conciertos de Celia Cruz se ponen a bailar porque es imposible resistir el ritmo.

Gloria Estefan vive en Miami desde hace años. En su vida y en su música es completamente bilingüe, o sea, habla y canta en español y en inglés. Aunque sus canciones más conocidas son en inglés con el grupo *Miami Sound Machine,* Gloria Estefan confiesa que las emociones le vienen en español. En el álbum "Mi tierra" canta doce canciones nuevas exclusivamente en español.

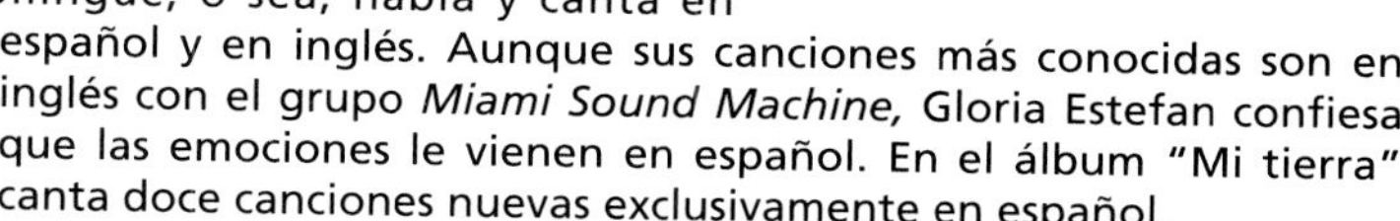

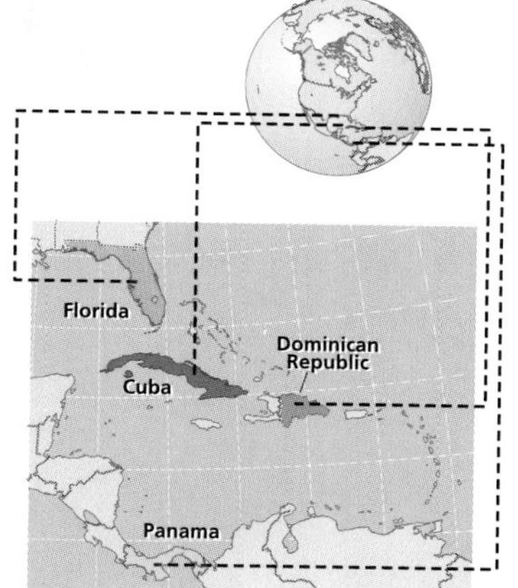


Rubén Blades, panameño educado en la universidad de Harvard, trae una dimensión social y panamericana a la salsa. Escribe muchas de sus canciones y cuenta historias como nadie. Canciones como "Decisiones" y "Buscando América" reflejan la vida y la realidad latinoamericana.

Juan Luis Guerra, de la República Dominicana, pone de moda otra vez el merengue, la música de su país. Canta sobre los problemas sociales y económicos de su gente mientras que los invita a desahogarse de la mejor manera que saben: bailando. Con canciones como "Ojalá que llueva café" y "Burbujas de Amor" este cantante dinámico le da al merengue una nueva popularidad.



***Answers, Guía para la lectura:*** **A.** Celia Cruz: Cuba, Gloria Estefan: Miami, Rubén Blades: Panama, Juan Luis Guerra: Dominican Republic **B.** música latina, cintas, discos compactos, salsero, voz potente, bailar, ritmo, canciones, álbum, salsa, merengue **C.** 1. Rubén Blades 2. Gloria Estefan 3. Celia Cruz 4. Juan Luis Guerra

## Chapter Objectives

**Functions:** Making purchases and choices; expressing quantity; asking for prices

**Context:** **Mercado al aire libre; supermercado**

**Accuracy:** Demonstrative adjectives and pronouns; expressions of quantity; the interrogative words **cuál/cuáles**

## Cultural Observation

Have students study the photo on this page. Ask them where Alicia Sánchez is and what she is doing. Ask them to consider whether or not one could take a similar photo in the places they shop for fresh produce. How many items are similar to the produce they see in their local supermarkets? How many are different? Help students identify as many of the different items as possible.

# CAPÍTULO 17 ¿CUÁNTO CUESTA...?

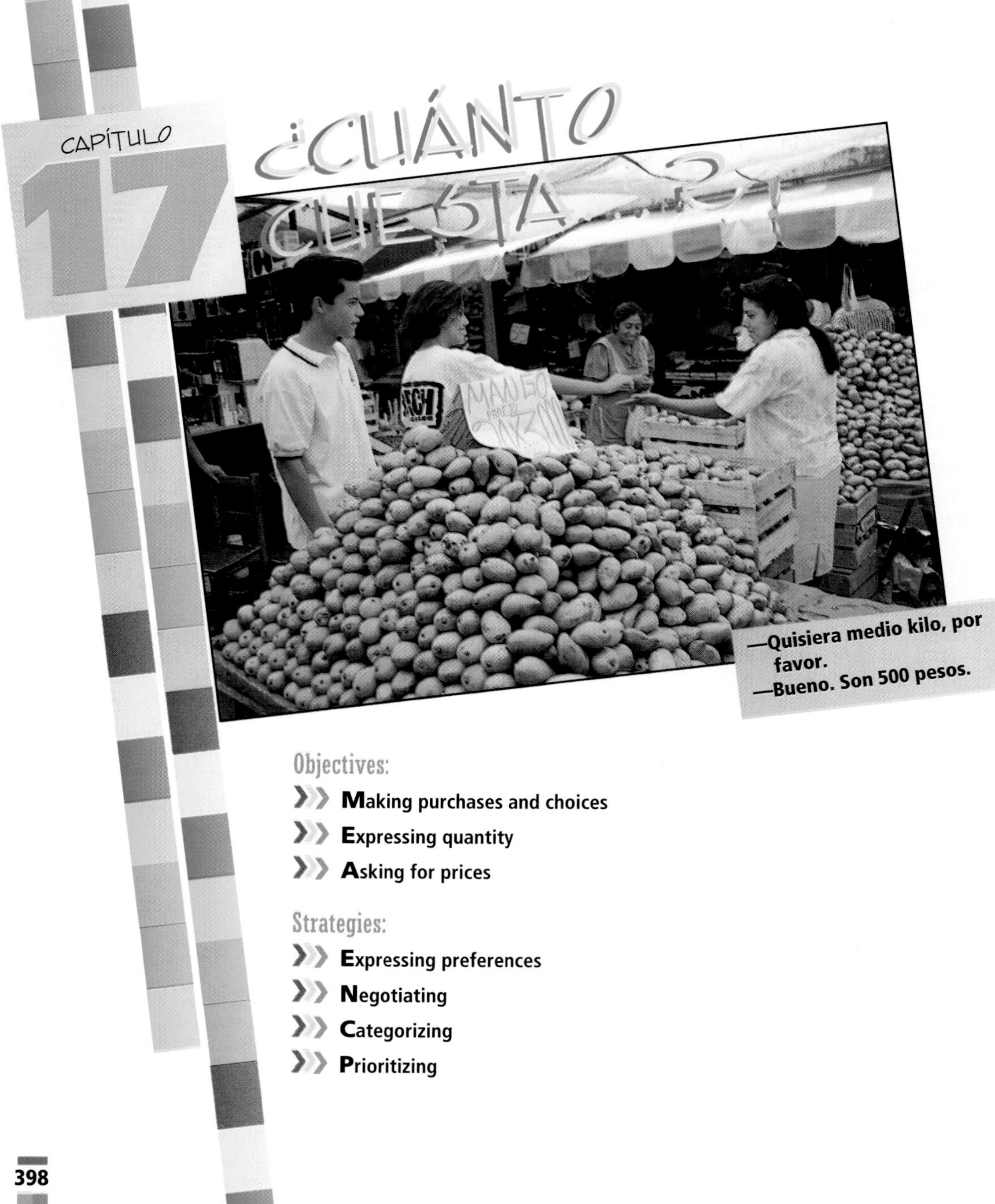

—Quisiera medio kilo, por favor.
—Bueno. Son 500 pesos.

### Objectives:

- **M**aking purchases and choices
- **E**xpressing quantity
- **A**sking for prices

### Strategies:

- **E**xpressing preferences
- **N**egotiating
- **C**ategorizing
- **P**rioritizing



## Video/CD-ROM

**Chapter 17 Video Program**
**Chapter 17 CD-ROM Program**

**These can be used at the end of the chapter as expansion activities.**

## PRIMERA ETAPA

### Preparación

›› **H**ave you ever been to an open-air market? If so, where? when?

›› **W**hat kinds of products can you buy in a market?

›› **H**ow is the shopping experience in a place like this different from going to a regular grocery store?

*Learning Strategy:*
*Previewing*

## Día de feria

Ayer jueves fue **día de feria** en Oaxaca. La señora Fernández caminó **hasta** la plaza cerca de su casa donde **cada** semana hay un **mercado al aire libre.** A la señora Fernández le gusta comprar las frutas y los **vegetales** que **ofrecen** los **vendedores** porque son productos **frescos** y baratos. **Además** a ella le encanta **regatear**. Hoy, piensa comprar vegetales para una **ensalada.**

market day / as far as
each / open-air market
vegetables / offer
sellers / fresh / Besides
to bargain / salad

**Sra. Fernández:** ¿Cuánto cuesta el **atado** de zanahorias?
**Vendedora:** 1.300 pesos.
**Sra. Fernández:** Bueno, 2.000 pesos por **estos** dos atados.
**Vendedora:** Tenga, 2.100.
**Sra. Fernández:** Está bien.

bunch

these



## Etapa Support Materials

Workbook: **pp. 220–226**
Transparencies: **#61, #62, #63**
Teacher Tape
Quiz: **Testing Program, p. 195**

Support materials, Día de feria:
**Teacher Tape** **Transparency #62**

## Chapter Warm-up: Corners

- Announce corners: green vegetables, non-green vegetables, red fruits, and other fruits.
- Tell students to go to the corner for their favorite kind of fruit and vegetable, and have them discuss with another student all of the vegetables or fruits that might fit their category.
- Then have each pair team up with another pair and paraphrase what they discussed together as a pair.
- Ask one student at random from each team of four to report to the class.

## Preparación

In order to draw on students' prior knowledge, you may want to ask them questions such as: Have you ever been to an open-air market? If so, where and when? What kinds of products are sold in a market? How is the shopping experience in a place like this different from going to a regular grocery store?

## Presentation: Día de feria

You might want to start with the **Comentarios culturales** on p. 400 and tell students about the open-air markets. Explain **el regateo.** Then use the transparency to present the new vocabulary of fruits and vegetables. Ask students about their likes and dislikes. Then go on to the dialogue, using any of the techniques described in previous **etapas.** This chapter contains a large amount of vocabulary. It is important to remember that students do not need to learn all of the vocabulary for the food items. When you test vocabulary, it should be open-ended enough so that students can work with their favorite foods.

*Support material, **Día de feria:*** Teacher Tape/CD #2 Track #31, transparency #61

## Vocabulary Expansion

**Maíz** is the generic word for *corn* and is used in such expressions as **tortillas de maíz,** etc.; **choclo** refers to whole kernels of corn (in Chile, Argentina, Uruguay, and Paraguay); **elote** is widely used for an ear of corn; **chícharos** (*peas* in Mexico); **arvejas** (*peas* in South America); **ejotes** (*green beans*) or **judías verdes** (in Spain); **plátanos** (*bananas* in Spain and Mexico); **cerezas** (*cherries*); **duraznos** or **melocotones** (*peaches*); **piña** (*pineapple*); **jitomate** (*tomato* in Mexico).

## Cultural Expansion

You might also want to have students look again at the photo on p. 398. This is a picture of a typical indoor market. Another typical indoor market is **La Merced** in Mexico City. It is one of the largest markets in the Americas and is over 400 years old. It extends over several city blocks and offers the widest selection of produce at very low prices. Like other markets, it also offers a wide array of other household articles, such as clothing, etc.

**Ex. A:** pair work

*Support material, Ex. A:*
Transparency #62

*Answers, Ex. A:*
1. guisantes/chícharos 2. cebollas 3. zanahorias 4. manzanas 5. uvas 6. naranja 7. maíz/elote 8. peras 9. limones 10. tomates/jitomates 11. lechuga 12. papas/patatas

*Suggestion, Exs. A and B:*
Use the transparencies with books closed. You might want to ask students if they like the fruits or vegetables after they identify them.

*Learning Strategy:*

*Reading for cultural information*

# COMENTARIOS CULTURALES

## Los mercados al aire libre

Open-air markets are characteristic of all Hispanic countries. In rural areas, these markets are particularly important since they offer a place where people from the surrounding communities can meet to buy, sell, and socialize. Once a week, vendors and shoppers gather in a designated location, often the main plaza of a small town. Farmers come from all over the local countryside, bringing vegetables and fruit they have grown on small plots of land. One can also buy pots, pans, brooms, soap, and other household items at the markets, as well as regional handicrafts such as brightly woven cloth, colorful shirts, embroidered dresses, musical instruments, wooden carvings, and so on. More and more commonly, there are even manufactured goods and high-tech equipment such as radios and televisions for sale.

## ¡Aquí te toca a ti!

**A. *¿Qué son?*** Identifica las frutas y los vegetales abajo y en la página 401.

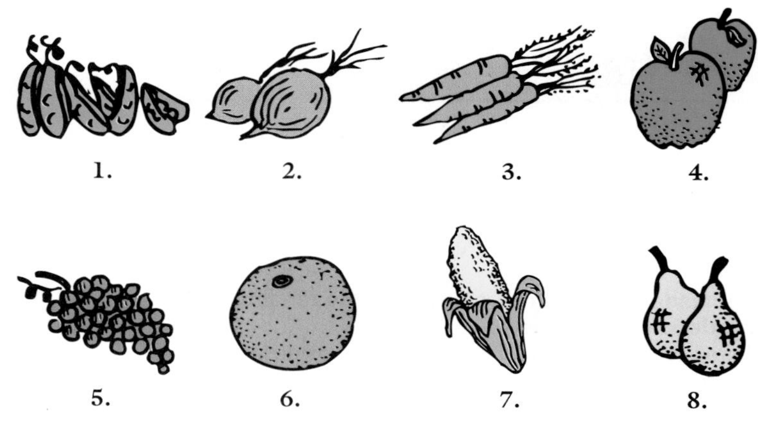




## Exercise Progression

The goal of this series of exercises is to have students order what they want in a market. Exs. A and B on this page and the following associate the names of the new vocabulary with a picture. Ex. C provides a situational context for buying fruits and vegetables.

9.

10.

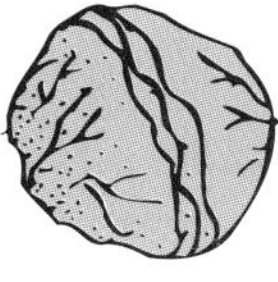
11.

12.

**B. *Preparando una ensalada*** You and your friend are making a salad for a class party. Decide whether you will make a fruit salad or a green salad. Then, as you examine the contents of the refrigerator (shown in the following drawings), take turns identifying what there is. Together make a list of the items you want for your salad and a list of those which you don't. Follow the model.

> **Learning Strategy:**
> Expressing preferences
>
> **Critical Thinking Strategy:**
> Categorizing

*Modelo:*

**Student 1:** *Hay maíz. ¿Quieres maíz?*
**Student 2:** *Sí, quiero maíz. Me gusta el maíz.*
o:
*No, no me gusta mucho el maíz.*
o:
*¡Claro que no! ¡Es una ensalada de frutas!*

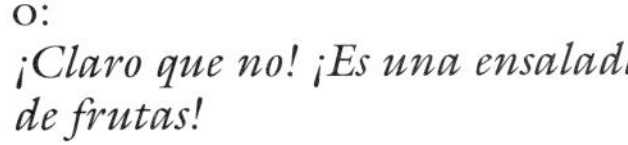

1.

2.

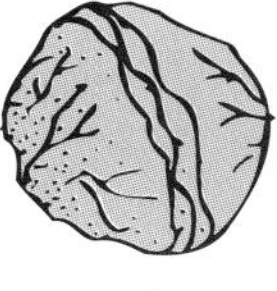
3.

4.

5.

6.

7.

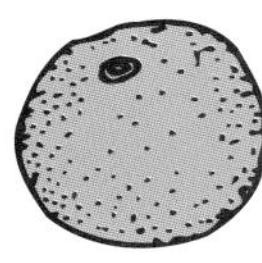
8.

9.

10.

## Repaso

**C. *La oferta*** You and your friend have saved some money to shop for sporting goods at a flea market. One of you is attracted to the newer, more expensive items. The other is always looking for bargains. Take turns trying to persuade each other as in the model on page 402. (Note that the first item in each pair is the more expensive one.)

> **Learning Strategy:**
> Negotiating



*Reteaching:* Before beginning the **Repaso** section, review the forms and uses of affirmative and negative **tú** commands. A fast-paced game of **"Simón dice"** is usually appreciated by older and younger students. Begin with **tocar** and move to other verbs (hop, stand, point, sing, sit down, etc.) Then ask for student volunteers to be Simón.

**Ex. C:**  pair work

*Suggestion, Ex. C:* After looking at the directions and model for this exercise, ask students what reasons they might have for accepting or rejecting their friend's advice. Brainstorm with them to help them integrate familiar vocabulary into this context. Some examples include: **Sí, es verdad, y yo no tengo mucho dinero./...y yo necesito pelotas de tenis./...y quiero comprar otras cosas también./Sí, y las pelotas de tenis son buenas también./Pero no quiero las pelotas de tenis; quiero la pelota de fútbol./Pero no me gustan las pelotas de tenis./Pero ya tengo pelotas de tenis.**

*Support material, Ex. B:* Transparency #63

**Ex. B:** pair work

*Answers, Ex. B:* 1. peras 2. cebollas 3. lechuga 4. manzanas 5. uvas 6. guisantes/chícharos 7. tomates/jitomates 8. naranja 9. zanahorias 10. fresas

*Follow-up, Ex. B:* Write the words from the Vocabulary Expansion (p. T400) on the board and ask students personalized questions to give them a chance to use the new vocabulary. For example: **¿Qué fruta te gusta más? ¿Qué ingredientes te gusta poner en una ensalada?,** etc. You might prefer to ask questions using the **pregúntale** format.

## Presentation: Pronunciation

Point out that the consonant combination *ph* does not exist in Spanish. Therefore, cognates that have a *ph* in English will have an **f** in Spanish. For example: **filosofía, farmacia, fotografía.**

Additional activities appear in the Laboratory Tape Program.

***Support material, Pronunciación:***
Pronunciation Tape

**Student 1:** *Voy a comprar la pelota de fútbol.* o: *Mira la pelota de fútbol.* o: *¡Qué buena pelota de fútbol!*
**Student 2:** *Pero no compres la pelota de fútbol. Compra las pelotas de tenis. Son más baratas.*
**Student 1:** *Tienes razón* (You're right). *Voy a llevar las pelotas de tenis.* o: *No, yo prefiero la pelota de fútbol.*

1. raqueta grande / pequeña
2. zapatos nuevos / usados
3. esquíes para la nieve / esquíes para el agua
4. fútbol nuevo / viejo
5. bicicleta Cinelli / Sprint
6. pelota de básquetbol / pelota de fútbol

## Pronunciación: *The consonant f*

The consonant **f** in Spanish is pronounced exactly like the *f* in English.

### Práctica

*D.* Escucha a tu maestro(a) cuando lee las siguientes palabras. Después repítelas para practicar la pronunciación.

1. fútbol
2. flor
3. ficción
4. frente
5. final
6. farmacia
7. favorito
8. fresco
9. alfombra
10. suficiente

## ESTRUCTURA

### Demonstrative adjectives

¿Quieres **estas** manzanas verdes o **esas** manzanas rojas?
Do you want *these* green apples or *those* red apples?

Quiero **aquellas** manzanas **allá**.
I want *those* apples *over there*.

Demonstrative adjectives are used to point out specific people or things. They agree in number and gender with the nouns that follow them. There are three sets of demonstrative adjectives:

**este** *this* **ese** *that* **aquel** *that over there*

*To point out people or things...*

| | a. near the speaker | b. near the listener | c. far from both speaker and listener |
|---|---|---|---|
| Sing. masc. | **este** limón | **ese** limón | **aquel** limón |
| Sing. fem. | **esta** manzana | **esa** manzana | **aquella** manzana |
| Plural masc. | **estos** limones | **esos** limones | **aquellos** limones |
| Plural fem. | **estas** uvas | **esas** uvas | **aquellas** uvas |

## Aquí practicamos

*E.* Replace each definite article with the correct demonstrative adjective, according to its column heading. Follow the model.

la papa
**a. near the speaker:** *esta papa*
**b. near the listener:** *esa papa*
**c. far from both:** *aquella papa*

| a. near the speaker | b. near the listener | c. far from both |
|---|---|---|
| 1. la manzana | 4. el limón | 7. el maíz |
| 2. el limón | 5. los tomates | 8. las peras |
| 3. los pasteles | 6. las fresas | 9. el queso |

*F.* ***¿Prefiere estas manzanas o esos tomates?*** You are the checkout person at a grocery store. Your customer is undecided about what to buy. Offer him or her choices according to the cues. Work in pairs.

fresas / uvas
—*¿Prefiere Ud. estas fresas o esas uvas?*
—*Prefiero estas uvas, por favor.*

1. naranjas / manzanas
2. banana / pera
3. limón / papas
4. maíz / guisantes
5. tomates / lechuga
6. cebollas / bananas
7. uvas / fresas
8. zanahorias / naranjas



*Suggestions, Ex. E:* Have students write out the exercise and then edit their partners' work. Write **aquí, ahí,** and **allá** on the board. Then say the cues from the book and add one of the adverbs. The students will repeat the noun with its corresponding demonstrative adjective.

*Answers, Ex. E:* 1. esta manzana 2. este limón 3. estos pasteles 4. ese jamón 5. esos tomates 6. esas fresas 7. aquel maíz 8. aquellas peras 9. aquel queso

**Ex. F:**  pair work

 role play

*Answers, Ex. F:* Answers will vary according to students' preferences, but they will be using the demonstrative adjectives in one or the other of the following forms: 1. estas naranjas / esas manzanas / estas manzanas 2. esta banana / esa pera / esta pera 3. este limón / esas papas / estas papas 4. este maíz / esos guisantes / estos guisantes 5. estos tomates / esa lechuga / esta lechuga 6. estas cebollas / esas bananas / estas bananas 7. estas uvas / esas fresas / estas fresas 8. estas zanahorias / esas naranjas / estas naranjas

### resentation: Demonstrative djectives

troduce the demonstrative adjectives inductively by using assroom objects. Point to different items as you say, **Este uaderno es de Juan. Ese libro es de Estela. Aquel bro es de José.** etc. After pointing out various objects using oth the singular and plural demonstratives, write them on the oard and explain their differences. You might want to teach em *"This and these have the t's"* to help them remember hich ones are used close to the speaker. Point out that these djectives are often clarified by **aquí, ahí,** and **allá (este quí, ese ahí, aquel allá).** You may also want to associate **allá** with *yonder* in English, in order to stress the distance from the speaker. Remind students that since demonstratives are adjectives, they must agree in both gender and number with the nouns they modify.

### Exercise Progression

Ex. E is designed to coordinate the forms of the demonstratives with the nouns they modify, as well as with their location to the speaker. Ex. F provides meaningful practice in a personalized open-ended context.

## Presentation: Expressions of specific quantity

Introduce the expressions by indicating the quantity of food that would be required for different numbers of people. You could do this by presenting a monologue about a party you are going to have. For example: **Voy a tener una fiesta el sábado y 16 personas van a asistir. Necesito comprar 10 litros de refresco y 4 botellas de sidra para tomar. Para los bocadillos necesito dos kilos de queso y un kilo de jamón.** etc.

Point out that the metric system is used all over the world, including those countries where Spanish is spoken. One liter is approximately equivalent to one quart (1 liter = 1.057 quarts). One kilogram is a little more than two pounds (1 kilogram = 2.205 pounds). One gram is 0.035 ounce. There are 1,000 grams in a kilogram.

# Palabras útiles

### Expressions of specific quantity

¿Cuánto cuesta **un litro** de leche? — How much is *a liter* of milk?
Quisiera **medio kilo** de uvas. — I would like *a half kilo* of grapes.

The following expressions are used to indicate quantities.

| | |
|---|---|
| **un kilo de** | a kilogram of |
| **medio kilo de** | a half kilogram of |
| **una libra de** | a pound of |
| **50 gramos de** | 50 grams of |
| **un litro de** | a liter of |
| **una botella de** | a bottle of |
| **una docena de** | a dozen of |
| **un pedazo de** | a piece of |
| **un atado de** | a bunch of |
| **un paquete de** | a package of |

**G.** Usa la información entre paréntesis para contestar las preguntas de los vendedores. Sigue el modelo.

**Modelo:** ¿Qué desea? (2 kilos de tomates / 1 kilo de uvas)
*Necesito dos kilos de tomates y un kilo de uvas.*

1. ¿Qué necesita hoy? (1/2 kilo de lechuga / un atado de zanahorias)
2. ¿Qué quisiera? (200 gramos de jamón / 2 docenas de peras)
3. ¿Qué desea? (1/2 litro de leche / 1 botella de agua mineral)
4. ¿En qué puedo servirle? (1/2 docena de naranjas / 2 kilos de uvas)
5. ¿Necesita algo? (3 botellas de limonada / 1 paquete de mantequilla)

*Learning Strategy:*
*Reporting based on visual information*

**H. ¿Cuánto compraron?** Mira los dibujos en la página 405 y di cuánto de cada cosa compró la persona indicada.

**Modelo:** ¿Qué compró Juanita?
*Ella compró cincuenta gramos de queso.*

50g

## Exercise Progression

Exs. G and H provide controlled and meaningful practice with the expressions of specific quantity. Ex. I on the following page offers a realistic context to practice the vocabulary in a communicative activity.

1. ¿Qué compró Mercedes?

2. Qué compró el señor González?

3. ¿Qué compró Antonio?

4. ¿Qué compró Maribel?

5. ¿Qué compró la señora Ruiz?

6. ¿Qué compró Francisco?

### I. En el mercado

You are shopping in an open-air market in Puerto Rico. Ask the seller the price of each item, and then say how much you want to buy. Work with a partner, playing the roles of buyer and seller. Use the cues provided and follow the model.

zanahorias: 2 dólares el atado / 2 atados
*—¿Cuánto cuestan estas zanahorias?*
*—Dos dólares el atado.*
*—Quiero dos atados, por favor.*
*—Aquí tiene. Cuatro dólares, por favor.*

1. leche: 2 dólares la botella / 3 botellas
2. naranjas: 3 dólares la docena / 1/2 docena
3. papas: 2 dólares el kilo / 500 gramos
4. cebollas: 1.50 dólares el kilo / 1/2 kilo
5. mantequilla: 2.50 dólares el paquete / 2 paquetes
6. pastel: 1 dólar el pedazo / 2 pedazos



*Answers, Ex. H:* 1. dos litros de leche 2. un kilo de azúcar 3. un kilo de jamón 4. una docena de naranjas 5. un kilo de plátanos/bananas 6. una libra de manzanas

**Ex. I:**  pair work

role play

*Suggestion, Ex. I:* Do one or two examples with the class before having students work in pairs. Encourage them to incorporate greetings and leave-taking expressions into their mini-dialogues. This activity provides preparation for the **Ya llegamos** section at the end of Unit 6.

*Answers, Ex. I:* Students substitute the cues, following the model and adding expressions of their choice. They will use **cuesta** in numbers 1, 5, and 6. They will use **cuestan** in 2, 3, and 4.

*Answers, Aquí escuchamos:* papas, cebollas, mangos, lechuga, tomates

**Ex. J:** 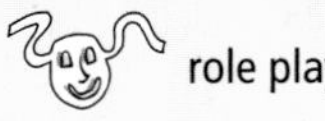 pair work

role play

*Suggestion, Ex. J:* Do the exercise first with the whole class. You play the role of the salesperson and the class is the customer. After they see how the exercise works, have them work in pairs.

*Follow-up, Ex. J:* Additional role playing situation: You've been sent to the market to buy a variety of things. However, as you're doing the shopping, you buy only things you like. Tell the vendor what you want to buy and how much. Be sure to ask for the price, to thank the vendor, and to give an appropriate leave-taking expression.

*Support material, Aquí escuchamos:* Teacher Tape/CD #2 Track #32 and Tapescript

# Aquí escuchamos:

## "De compras en el mercado"

*Critical Thinking Strategy:*

*Predicting*

### Antes de escuchar

**You will hear a conversation between Mr. Estévez and a vendor at the market.**

1. What kind of products are sold in an open-air market?
2. What do you expect the conversation between the shopper and the vendor will be about?
3. What are some of the questions a shopper and a vendor usually ask each other?

*Learning Strategy:*

*Listening for details*

### Después de escuchar

**Mira la lista de palabras que hay a continuación. Haz una lista de las cosas que compró el Sr. Estévez.**

| | |
|---|---|
| cebollas | fresas |
| plátanos | maíz |
| guisantes | uvas |
| mangos | zanahorias |
| tomates | manzanas |
| aguacates | lechuga |
| papas | melón |

EJERCICIOS ORALES

*J.* ***El postre*** (dessert) Your mother has put you in charge of buying some fruit for dessert. Work in pairs and follow the directions.

| Sales person | Customer |
|---|---|
| 1. Greet the customer. | a. Greet the salesperson. |
| 2. Ask what he or she needs to buy. | b. Say that you need some fruit for dessert **(para el postre).** |
| 3. Offer a choice of fruits. | c. Decide what you are going to buy. Ask how much the fruit(s) cost(s). |
| 4. Tell him or her the price(s). | d. Bargain over the price. |
| 5. Agree on the price. Ask if he or she needs something else. | e. Answer. |
| 6. Respond if necessary; then end the conversation. | f. End the conversation. |

**K. *¿Te gusta más... ?*** You and your friend have just won the lottery and you want to buy a number of things. (1) Bring to class pairs of magazine pictures of at least five objects (two different versions of each) whose names you know in Spanish and that you would like to own. (Catalogs will be a good source for finding multiples of objects.) (2) Following the model, get each other's opinion about which items you each like better. (Remember to make the agreement with **este** and **ese.**) (3) Make a list of the first five things you plan to buy together with your winnings.

Cooperative Learning
Learning Strategy: Negotiating
Critical Thinking Strategy: Prioritizing

**Student 1:** *¿Te gusta más esta bicicleta americana o esta bicicleta italiana?*
**Student 2:** *Prefiero esa bicicleta italiana. Y tú, ¿prefieres este viaje a Madrid o este viaje a Barcelona?*
**Student 1:** *A mí me gusta más ese viaje a Madrid.*

## EJERCICIO ESCRITO

**L. *¿Qué comemos?*** Your family has invited an exchange student from Spain, who is your friend at school, to join you for dinner. His parents are in town and are also invited. Work with a classmate to write up a shopping list of eight food items that you need to buy for the dinner, indicating the quantity or amount of each. (Look at p. 404 to review the vocabulary for amounts.) Consider drinks, salads, vegetables, meat, and desserts.

Cooperative Learning
Learning Strategy: Listing
Critical Thinking Strategy: Categorizing

**Ex. K:** pair work

***Suggestion, Ex. K:*** This exercise requires that students bring magazine pictures to class. Unless you can supply these props at class time, students will need to be aware of this assignment in advance.

**Ex. L:** pair work

## Preparación

In order to activate students' prior knowledge about this topic, you may want to ask questions such as the following: What are some of the differences between shopping at a supermarket and an open-air market? What products or services can you find at a supermarket that you could not get at an open-air market? Who goes shopping for food in your family? Where? Do you like to go along?

## Presentation: En el supermercado

Use the transparency to introduce the new vocabulary. Then describe Roberto's and Ricardo's shopping with books closed. As you narrate, use the transparency to illustrate new vocabulary. Continue by asking general questions: **¿Dónde están Roberto y Ricardo? ¿Qué compran?,** etc. The whole class can make the list of items mentioned.

## Vocabulary Expansion

**carne molida, catsup, mostaza, mayonesa, pepinillos**
(useful hamburger language)

Point out that Spanish-speakers say **galletas** when the meaning would be understood from context, but that they would specify **galletas saladas** *(crackers)* and **galletas dulces** *(cookies)* for clarification.

***Support material, En el supermercado:***
Transparency #64



# SEGUNDA ETAPA

## Preparación

- What are some of the differences between shopping at a supermarket and an open-air market?
- What products can you find at a supermarket that you could not get at an open-air market?
- When you go shopping for food, where do you prefer to go? Why?

*Learning Strategies:*
*Previewing, brainstorming*

## En el supermercado

**Una vez** por semana Ricardo hace las compras en el supermercado **para** su mamá. Hoy Roberto también tiene que ir al supermercado para comprar **alimentos** para su familia. Los dos amigos van **juntos.** Primero, van a la sección de los **productos lácteos** porque Ricardo tiene que comprar mantequilla, leche, yogur, crema y queso. También van a la sección de las **conservas** porque necesitan tres **latas** de **sopa** y una lata de **atún,** una botella de **aceite** y un paquete de **galletas.**

Once / for
food
together
dairy products
packaged goods
cans / soup / tuna / oil
cookies

## Etapa Support Materials

Workbook: **pp. 227–234**
Transparencies: **#64, #65, #66**
Listening Activity masters: **p. 113**
Tapescript: **p. 168**

Quiz: **Testing Program, p. 198**
Chapter Test: **Testing Program, p. 201**
Support material, En el supermercado:
**Transparency #64**

**Luego pasan por** la sección de los productos **congelados** porque Roberto tiene que comprar **pescado**, una pizza, un pollo y también: ¡**helado** de chocolate, por supuesto! A Roberto le encanta el helado.

Then they pass by / frozen fish / ice cream

Para terminar, ellos compran pastas, **harina**, azúcar, **sal**, **pimienta**, arroz y mayonesa. El **carrito** de Roberto está muy **lleno.**

flour / salt / pepper shopping cart / full

## COMENTARIOS CULTURALES

### Las frutas y los vegetales tropicales

In the tropical parts of Central and South America, Mexico, and the Caribbean, many kinds of delicious vegetables and fruits are commonly available for everyday consumption. You may be familiar with the **aguacate** (avocado) and the **chile** (hot green or red pepper). Fruits such as **papayas** (small melon-like fruit) and **mangos** (peach-like fruit) can be found fresh as well as in fruit juices in many supermarkets in the U.S. The **plátano** (a large green banana) is eaten frequently with meals in a number of Hispanic countries. It is generally served fried or boiled. The **mamey** (coconut-like fruit) and the **zapote** (fruit shaped like an apple with green skin and black pulp inside) can often be found on the Mexican table as a much appreciated dessert. Another popular dessert is guava paste, served with fruit or cheese.

*Learning Strategy:*

*Reading for cultural information*

## ¡Aquí te toca a ti!

**A. *En el carrito de Lidia hay...*** Lidia's mother sent her to the store. But since Lidia forgot the shopping list, the shop assistant helps her to remember by mentioning some items. Work with a partner playing the roles of the shop assistant and Lidia. Look at the drawings on page 410 and indicate what she's buying. Follow the model.

**Clerk:** *¿Necesitas arroz?*
**Lidia:** *No, pero necesito pasta.*



## Cultural Expansion

After reading the **Comentarios culturales,** ask students which fruits and vegetables they have tasted. Remind them that **plátano** means *banana* in Mexico and Spain. The banana that is usually eaten fried with rice is called a **plátano macho** in Mexico. Explain that the **mamey,** while having a coconut-like flavor, is a soft fruit (unlike the coconut) and its pulp is used to make a delicious **licuado** with milk or to make a favorite Mexican dessert: **dulce de mamey** (made with sugar, milk, mamey pulp, and vanilla). The **zapote** is also used to make another Mexican dessert favorite: **dulce de zapote.** It is made with the **zapote** pulp, orange juice, and sugar. It has a creamy texture and a tangy flavor. They enjoy it much the way we do applesauce. **Pasta de guayaba** has a firm texture that can be cut into pieces, and it is almost always served with a fresh white cheese.

**Ex. A:** 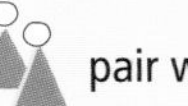 pair work

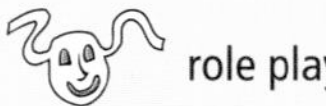 role play

*Support material, Ex. A:* Transparency #65

## Exercise Progression

Ex. A provides practice associating vocabulary words with drawings of the items they represent. Ex. B on the following page offers more practice in a personalized question/answer format.

*Answers, Ex. A:* Students follow the model, substituting the following cues: 1. pizza 2. sal 3. pescado 4. helado 5. leche 6. atún

**Ex. B:**  pair work

*Follow-up, Ex. B:* You may want to continue practicing the vocabulary by asking additional personalized questions. **¿Prefieres sándwiches de pollo o de atún? ¿Pones mayonesa en tus sándwiches de atún? ¿Qué te gusta poner en las hamburguesas?** etc. You might prefer to ask questions using the **pregúntale** format.

*Reteaching:* Review days of the week by having students fill out a calendar for a typical week of dinners at their house—**Los lunes, tenemos una cena grande con... porque todos están en casa.** They could also predict what meals each family member would cook on various days if they could make anything they wanted.

*More-prepared students:* Give students an opportunity to review **tú** commands, chapter vocabulary, and pronunciation by creating commercials for grocery items. Perhaps more-prepared students would be interested in writing and producing (and video-taping) these commercials.

*Less-prepared students:* In addition to participating in the creation of commercials, less-prepared students could act as at-home TV viewers making (constructive) comments about the commercials.

1. ¿Necesitas harina? 2. ¿Necesitas pimienta? 3. ¿Necesitas pollo?

4. ¿Necesitas galletas? 5. ¿Necesitas yogur? 6. ¿Necesitas mayonesa?

*Cooperative Learning*

*Learning Strategies:*

*Brainstorming, negotiating*

*Critical Thinking Strategy:*

*Expressing preferences*

**B. *Preferencias personales*** Your father always likes to give you a choice when he prepares meals. He is preparing this week's menu. Tell him what you would like each day from the choices given. Then, with your partner, set up a different menu for the following week, agreeing on what to serve each day. Follow the model.

**Modelo:** ¿Quisieras carne o pescado hoy?
*Quisiera carne, por favor.*

1. ¿Quisieras pollo o atún el lunes?
2. ¿Quisieras yogur o helado el martes?
3. ¿Quisieras pizza o pescado el miércoles?
4. ¿Quisieras pasta o papas el jueves?
5. ¿Quisieras pollo o sopa el viernes?
6. ¿Quisieras mayonesa o aceite en la ensalada el sábado?
7. ¿Quisieras fruta o helado el domingo?

## Repaso

*Cooperative Learning*

*Learning Strategies:*

*Brainstorming, negotiating*

*Critical Thinking Strategy:*

*Prioritizing*

**C. *¿Preparamos una sopa de vegetales?*** Your favorite aunt and uncle are coming for dinner tonight. They are strict vegetarians; so you have to plan the meal carefully. You've decided to serve vegetable soup and fruit salad. With a classmate, write a double shopping list, one of fruits and one of vegetables. Include at least five items on each list. Then, since your budget may not allow you to purchase all the items, rewrite the two lists, naming the fruits and vegetables in the order in which you would prefer to include them in the menu.

**Modelo:** *En la sopa podemos poner ________.*
*En la ensalada de frutas podemos poner ________.*

## ESTRUCTURA

### *The interrogative words cuál and cuáles*

The words **¿cuál?** *(which)* and **¿cuáles?** *(which ones)* are used when there is the possibility of a choice within a group.

| | |
|---|---|
| **¿Cuáles** prefiere, las manzanas verdes o las manzanas rojas? | *Which ones* do you prefer, the green apples or the red apples? |

In some cases, in English you use the question word *what,* while in Spanish you use **cuál,** as in the examples above. Notice the idea of a choice within a group: *Of all possible addresses / names, which one is yours?*: **¿Cuál es tu dirección / nombre?**

| | |
|---|---|
| **¿Cuál** es tu nombre? | *What* is your name? |
| **¿Cuál** es tu dirección? | *What* is your address? |

## Aquí practicamos

**D. *¿Cuál quieres?*** You are babysitting for a young child who doesn't speak very clearly yet. You are trying to guess what he wants by offering him some choices. Follow the model.

**Modelo:** este libro grande / aquel libro pequeño
*¿Cuál quieres, este libro grande o aquel libro pequeño?*

1. el vídeo de Mickey Mouse / el vídeo de Blanca Nieves *(Snow White)*
2. esta fruta / ese pan dulce

**¿Qué crees?**

**Chocolate is a product that originally came from:**

**a) Switzerland**
**b) Europe**
**c) Mexico**
**d) South America**

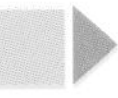

**respuesta**



**Ex. C:** pair work

*Suggestion, Ex. C:* Have a few students give the ingredients of their soup or salad. Ask follow-up questions to see if other students were listening carefully.

### Presentation: The interrogative words cuál and cuáles

Since students have already seen and used these interrogative words, you might want to introduce them simply by asking questions such as, **¿Cuál es tu apellido? ¿Cuál es tu número de teléfono?** etc. Point out that **cuál/cuáles** is usually followed by a verb rather than a noun. It is generally used with the verb **ser,** except when asking for a definition: **¿Qué es el mamey?** etc.

*Answers, Ex. D:* Students form questions by following the model and substituting the cues. Each question begins with **cuál,** except number 5, which starts with **cuáles.**

### Exercise Progression

Ex. D provides meaningful practice with the interrogative words as well as with the demonstrative adjectives learned in the previous **etapa.** Ex. E on the following page offers students the opportunity to use the interrogative word **cuál** in a personalized communicative format.

**Ex. E:**  pair work

role play

*Answers, Ex. E:* Students add **¿Cuál es... ?** each time, substituting the cues. Their partners' responses will vary.

*Follow-up, Ex. E:* Have a few students tell the class what they found out about their classmates.

## Presentation: Demonstrative pronouns

Since students have already used the demonstrative adjectives, they will understand when you introduce the pronouns inductively. Make statements using students' possessions and classroom objects. Then write a statement on the board and have students point out the difference between the adjectives and the pronouns (the written accent).

3. este sándwich de queso / aquél de jamón
4. este chocolate / ese jugo
5. estas uvas / esas fresas
6. este helado de chocolate / esa botella de leche

Learning Strategies:

*Interviewing, requesting and providing information*

**E. *Preguntas personales*** When you are applying for a part-time job in the local grocery store, the interviewer asks you a series of personal questions. With your partner role play the interview, switching roles after completing the first interview. (Use **cuál** and **cuáles** in your questions.)

 tu nombre
*¿Cuál es tu nombre?*

1. tu nombre
2. tu dirección
3. tu número de teléfono
4. tus días preferidos para trabajar
5. tu modo de transporte

## Nota gramatical

### Demonstrative pronouns

Ese yogur no es muy bueno. **Éste** aquí es mejor. — That yogurt is not very good. *This one* here is better.

1. Demonstrative pronouns are used to indicate a person, object, or place when the noun itself is not mentioned.
2. Demonstrative pronouns have the same form as demonstrative adjectives, but they add an accent mark to show that they have different uses and meanings.

| | | | |
|---|---|---|---|
| **éste** / **ésta** | *this one* | **éstos** / **éstas** | *these* |
| **ése** / **ésa** | *that one* | **ésos** / **ésas** | *those* |
| **aquél** / **aquélla** | *that one (over there)* | **aquéllos** / **aquéllas** | *those (over there)* |

 c

3. Demonstrative pronouns agree in gender and number with the nouns they replace.

| | |
|---|---|
| Esta manzana es roja, **ésa** amarilla y **aquélla** verde. | This apple is red, *that one* yellow, and *that one over there* green. |
| Me gusta más esta naranja que **ésa** o **aquélla.** | I like this orange better than *that one* or *that one over there.* |

4. When using demonstrative pronouns, it is helpful to use adverbs of location to indicate how close to you an object is. The location helps you decide whether you should refer to the object using **éste(a), ése(a),** or **aquél(la).**

You have already learned **aquí** *(here)*. Here are two other adverbs you can use to talk about location:

**allí** *there* **allá** *over there*

| | |
|---|---|
| ¿Quieres **esta** lechuga **aquí, ésa allí** o **aquélla allá?** | Do you want *this* lettuce *here, that one there,* or *that one over there?* |

# Aquí practicamos

**F. ¿Cuál?** You are doing some shopping with a friend. Because there are so many items to choose from, you have to explain which objects you are discussing. Use **éste(a)**, **ése(a)**, or **aquél(la)** in your answer, according to the cue in parentheses. Follow the model.

¿Qué libros vas a comprar? **(those)**
*Voy a comprar ésos.*

1. ¿Qué calculadora vas a comprar? **(this one)**
2. ¿Qué frutas vas a comprar? **(those over there)**
3. ¿Qué galletas quieres? **(those)**
4. ¿Qué paquete de arroz quieres? **(this one)**
5. ¿Qué pescado vas a comprar? **(that one)**
6. ¿Qué jamón quieres? **(that one over there)**

**G. ¿Cuál prefieres?** Use the cues provided on page 414 to tell what you prefer. Remember to make the pronoun agree with the noun provided. Work with a partner and follow the model.

queso / allí
—*¿Cuál prefieres?*
—*Prefiero ése allí.*



## Exercise Progression

Exs. F and G both provide meaningful practice with the demonstrative pronouns as well as with the new vocabulary.

*Answers, Ex. F:* 1. ésta 2. aquéllas 3. ésas 4. éste 5. ése 6. aquél

*Answers, Ex. G:* 1. ése 2. aquélla 3. éste 4. aquélla 5. ése 6. aquélla 7. éste

## Cultural Expansion

Although supermarkets are becoming ever more popular in the large cities of Latin America, many people still prefer to buy their produce, meats, eggs, and poultry at the markets, for reasons of freshness and selection. They go to supermarkets to stock up on staple articles such as cooking oil, rice, etc., because they find lower prices there.

*Answers, Aquí escuchamos:* 1. Teresa 2. the supermarket 3. chicken, rice, black beans, oil, ice cream 4. chicken 5. mangos, papaya, bananas 6. ice cream

**Ex. H:** 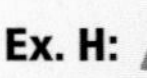 pair work

 role play

*Ex. H:* This activity provides preparation for the **Ya llegamos** section at the end of Unit 6.

*Support material, Aquí escuchamos:* Teacher Tape/CD #2 Track #33  and Tapescript





1. paquete de mantequilla / allí
2. botella de aceite / allá
3. paquete de arroz / aquí
4. lata de sopa / allá
5. paquete de galletas / allí
6. lata de atún / allá
7. paquete de harina / aquí

## Aquí escuchamos: "Por favor, compra..."

*Learning Strategy:* Previewing

### Antes de escuchar

**Review the vocabulary in this chapter to prepare for the conversation between Teresa and her mother about which grocery items to buy. Also read the following questions to help you anticipate what you will hear.**

START

*Learning Strategy:* Listening for details

### Después de escuchar

**Complete the following sentences in English based on information provided in the conversation.**

1. The person who is going to do the shopping is . . .
2. The shopping will be done at . . .
3. Three of the items on the shopping list are . . .
4. The kind of meat that will be served for dinner is . . .
5. Some of the fruit to be bought is . . .
6. The dessert will be . . .

## ¡Adelante!

EJERCICIO ORAL

*Cooperative Learning*

*Learning Strategy:* Negotiating

H. ***Un picnic*** You and your friend are planning a picnic. At the delicatessen you have to decide what you want to buy, but you don't always agree with each other. For each suggestion you make, your friend disagrees and tells you to buy something else. Work with a partner. Use the cues provided and follow the model on page 415. Finally, decide on five items that you both are willing to take to the picnic.

estos sándwiches de atún / esos sándwiches de pollo

*—¿Vamos a llevar estos sándwiches de atún?*
*—No, no lleves ésos de atún. Lleva ésos de pollo.*

1. esa ensalada de frutas / aquella ensalada verde
2. esos tacos de carne / aquellos tacos de queso
3. estos licuados de banana / esos licuados de fresa
4. este helado de fresas / ese yogur de fresas
5. aquella tortilla de jamón / esa tortilla de papas
6. este pastel de fresas / aquel pastel de manzanas
7. esa salsa de tomate / esta salsa de chile
8. esa sopa de pollo / esta sopa de pescado

## EJERCICIO ESCRITO

**I. ¿Cuánto cuesta todo esto?** You and two friends are planning a dinner for some classmates. You are on a tight food budget. You have only $16 to spend—$3 for beverages, $3 for dessert **(el postre),** and $10 for the main course **(el plato principal).** Compare the prices on the lists and decide how much you can buy of each thing without going over the limit. After you decide, write down what you will buy and how much you will have spent. Work with two classmates and follow the model. Be prepared to report to the class on your final menu and its cost.

*Cooperative Learning*

*Critical Thinking Strategy:*

*Analyzing*

**PRODUCTOS CONGELADOS**

|  |  |
|---|---|
| Pescado | 1 kilo/$5 |
| Pizza | $5 |
| Papas fritas *(fried)* | $2 |
| Pollo | 2/$5 |
| Vegetales | $2 |
| Helado | $4 |

**PRODUCTOS LÁCTEOS**

|  |  |
|---|---|
| Yogur | 3/$2 |
| Leche | 1 litro/$1 |
| Mantequilla | $1 |
| Crema | 2/$1 |
| Queso | $2 |

**OTROS PRODUCTOS**

|  |  |
|---|---|
| Pan | $1 |
| Galletas | $2 |
| Arroz | $2 |
| Pastas | $2 |
| Lechuga | $1 |
| Tomates | 1 kilo/$2 |

**BEBIDAS**

|  |  |
|---|---|
| Café | 1 kilo/$5 |
| Refrescos | 2 litros/$2 |
| Agua mineral | 1 litro/$2 |
| Limonada | 2 litros/$3 |

**CONSERVAS**

|  |  |
|---|---|
| Sopa | 2/$1 |
| Atún | 2/$2.50 |
| Salsa de tomate | 2/$1.50 |
| Aceitunas | 2/$1.50 |

*—¿Qué vamos a servir?*
*—Bueno, para el plato principal, ¿por qué no preparamos pollo con papas fritas y vegetales?*
*—A ver. El pollo cuesta...*



*Support material, Ex. I:* Transparency #66

**Ex. I:** groups of three

*Follow-up, Ex. I:* Have a few students present their dialogues, telling the class what they will serve. Then ask follow-up questions to see if the other students were listening carefully. This activity provides preparation for the **Ya llegamos** section at the end of Unit 6.

# Chapter Culminating Activities

Since this chapter is heavily oriented toward useful vocabulary, this would be a good time to assign student projects. Individuals or groups of students could be asked to prepare bulletin board displays of bakery products, meats, delicatessen items, etc. They can use pictures cut out of magazines and then write their own labels in Spanish.

Have students write out a well-balanced menu of what they would like to eat at each of the three meals for every day of the following week. Then have them compare their menus with those of their partners and discuss their likes and dislikes.

You might want to play a vocabulary game. See the suggestions given in the **Vocabulario** of Chapters 1–5.

*Support material, Capítulo 17:* Improvised Conversation, Teacher Tape/CD #2 Track #34 and Tapescript; Lab Manual listening activities, Laboratory Program, Tapescript, and Teacher's Edition of the Workbook/Lab Manual

## Para charlar

### Para preguntar sobre preferencias

¿Cuál prefieres... ?
¿Cuál quieres... ?

## Temas y contextos

### Cantidades

un atado de
una botella de
una docena de
50 gramos de
un kilo de
una libra de
un litro de
medio kilo de
un paquete de
un pedazo de

### Productos congelados

el helado
el pescado
el pollo

### Productos lácteos

la crema
un yogur

### Productos varios

el azúcar
una galleta
el harina
la mayonesa
la pasta
la pimienta
la sal

## Vocabulario general

### Sustantivos

los alimentos
un carrito
una feria
un mercado al aire libre
un(a) vendedor(a)

### Otras palabras y expresiones

además
allá
allí
aquél(la) / aquéllos(as)
cada
ése(a) / ésos(as)
éste(a) / éstos(as)
hasta
juntos
luego
para
una vez

### Verbos

ofrecer
pasar
regatear

### Adjetivos

amarillo(a)
aquel(la)
ese(a)
este(a)
fresco(a)
lleno(a)
rojo(a)
verde

*Conservas*

el aceite
una lata de atún
una lata de sopa

*Frutas*

una banana
una ensalada de frutas
la fresa
un limón
una manzana
una naranja
una pera
una uva

*Vegetales*

una cebolla
una ensalada de vegetales (verde)
un guisante
la lechuga
el maíz
una papa
un tomate
una zanahoria

# Lectura cultural

*Prereading notes:* Review differences between open-air markets and supermarkets, perhaps by describing a scene and having students say which place you are describing. Discuss advantages and disadvantages of each, and have students think of some possible constraints people in ancient times had in terms of providing and preparing food for their families.



# Lectura CULTURAL

## EL MERCADO DE LOS AZTECAS QUE VIO HERNÁN CORTÉS

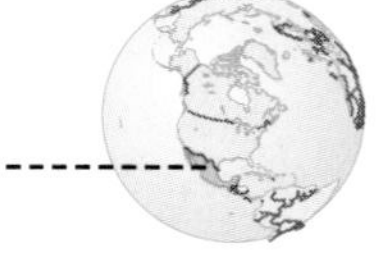

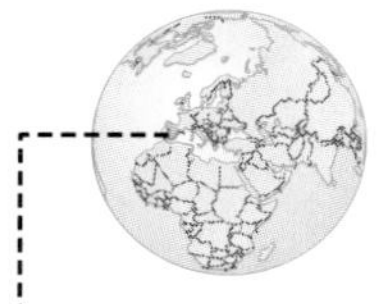

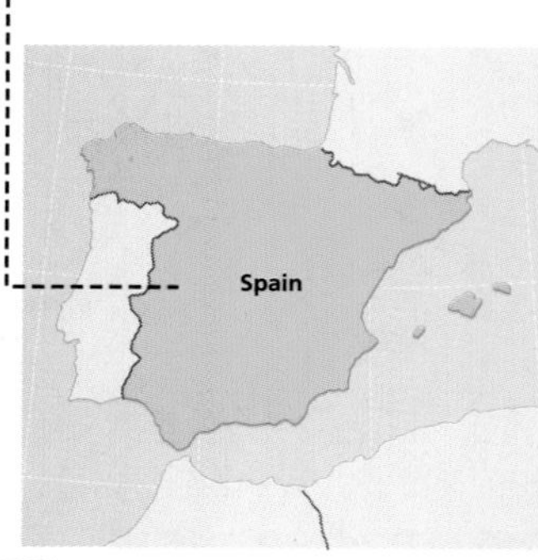

*Answers, **Guía para la lectura:*** **A.** 1. Hernán Cortés 2. a description 3. the city of Tenochtitlán **B.** 1. Tenochtitlán and Granada 2. 30,000 **C.** bread, meat, poultry, vegetables, clothing, shoes, jewelry

## Antes de leer

1. Look at the picture on page 418 and the title of the passage. What do you think it is going to be about?
2. Who are some of the first people from Europe to explore the New World?
3. What do you know about Spain's role in this exploration?

## Guía para la lectura

**Learning Strategies:**

*Reading for cultural information, reading for details, listing*

**Critical Thinking Strategy:**

*Predicting*

A. Read the first paragraph to determine . . .
   1. who is being talked about.
   2. what this person sent to the emperor of Spain.
   3. what the next two paragraphs will be about.

B. Read the second paragraph and find . . .
   1. the names of two cities.
   2. the number of people who went to the Aztec market.

C. Now read the last paragraph and make a list of things sold at the market. Did you find at least five items?

### El mercado de los aztecas que vio Hernán Cortés

En 1519, cuando el conquistador Hernán Cortés y sus hombres llegaron a Tenochtitlán, una ciudad de 300.000 habitantes, vieron maravillosos edificios de piedra, pirámides, templos, palacios y torres. Ésta era la capital del imperio azteca. En sus cartas al emperador de España, Cortés describió la gran ciudad. Esta descripción del mercado que vio Cortés viene en parte de una de estas cartas.

*La ciudad de Tenochtitlán es grande y admirable. Es más grande que Granada en España, cuando tomamos esa ciudad en 1492. Tiene muchos edificios más y mucha más gente. Hay en la ciudad de los aztecas un mercado en que todos los días hay 30.000 personas o más que venden y compran.*

*Este mercado tiene muchas cosas de la tierra como pan, carne, aves, y muchos vegetales y muchas otras cosas buenas que los aztecas comen. También hay cosas como ropa y zapatos. Hay joyerías de oro y plata, piedras preciosas y plumas. Todas las cosas son de tan buena calidad como puede ser en todas las plazas y mercados del mundo y las personas que van allí son gente de toda razón y buena conducta.*

## Chapter Objectives

**Functions:** Making purchases and choices; comparing things
**Context:** **Tienda de ropa; zapatería**
**Accuracy:** Comparisons of inequality and equality

## Cultural Observation

Ask students to study the photo on this page. Point out that it is easy to find what you want at a market. For example, if you're looking for shoes, you simply go to the shoe section and there will be many little stalls selling shoes all in one area.

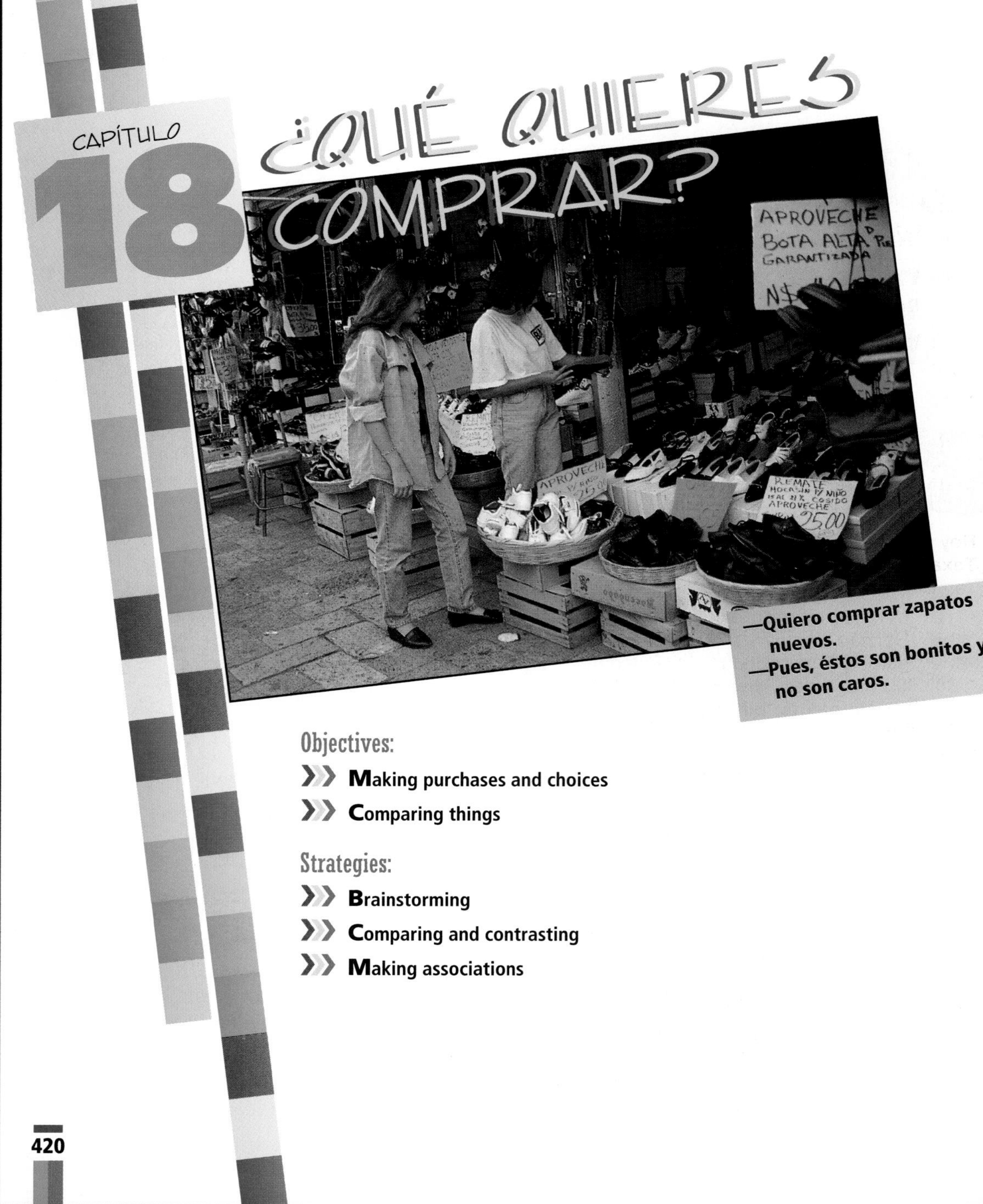


—Quiero comprar zapatos nuevos.
—Pues, éstos son bonitos y no son caros.

### Objectives:

- Making purchases and choices
- Comparing things

### Strategies:

- Brainstorming
- Comparing and contrasting
- Making associations

420

## Video/CD-ROM

**Chapter 18 Video Program**
**Chapter 18 CD-ROM Program**

**These can be used at the end of the chapter as expansion activities.**

# PRIMERA ETAPA

## Preparación

**Look at the title and the drawings.**

- **What do you think the name of the store below means?**
- **What are some of the clothing items that are missing in the drawings? Do you know how to say *hat* in Spanish?**
- **What kinds of things do you say when you make comparisons?**

*Learning Strategy:*
*Previewing*

*Critical Thinking Strategy:*
*Drawing inferences*

## Tienda "La Alta Moda"

Hoy sábado Mercedes y Sarita van de compras al centro comercial en El Paso, Texas. Ellas necesitan comprar un **regalo** para el cumpleaños de Rosa. También a ellas les gusta **ir de escaparates.**

gift
to window-shop

—Aquí tienen **ropa** muy moderna. — clothes
—¡Mira esta **falda azul**! ¡Qué linda! — blue skirt
—A Rosa le va a gustar ese color. Con este **cinturón negro** es muy bonita. Creo que le va a gustar. — black belt
—Sí, tienes razón. Perfecto. Ahora yo necesito un **vestido** para mí. — dress
—Aquí al frente hay una boutique muy elegante.
—Mm... entonces, **seguro** que es cara. — surely
—Vamos a ir de escaparates.

### Presentation: Tienda "La Alta Moda"

Use the transparency to present the vocabulary. Ask students about their favorite articles of clothing. Have students listen to the dialogue on the Teacher Tape. Then continue by using techniques described in previous **etapas.**

### Vocabulary Expansion

*Jeans* are usually just called **jeans** in most Spanish-speaking countries. Other words still in use are **pantalones de vaquero, vaqueros,** or **pantalones de mezclilla.** Other useful words that students may ask about are **traje de baño, pantalones cortos, corbata, chaleco, traje,** and **traje deportivo.**

*Support material, Tienda "La Alta Moda":*
Teacher Tape/CD #2 Track #35
, transparencies #67, #67a

## Etapa Support Materials

Workbook: **pp. 235–241**
Transparencies: **#67, #67a, #68, #69**
Teacher Tape
Quiz: **Testing Program, p. 205**

Support materials, **Tienda "La Alta Moda":**
**Transparencies #67, #67a**

*Reteaching:* Briefly remind students about noun-adjective agreement in Spanish before introducing the color words. You may wish to write a noun-adjective pair, such as **la casa bonita,** on the board. Have students give the plural, then change from **casa** to **libro,** then to **libros,** making the necessary agreement adjustments. Use this as a lead-in to the colors. Point out that the color words are also adjectives. Use the transparency or drawings in the text to illustrate the point.

## Presentation: Los colores

Ask **¿De qué color es la camisa?** and answer according to the color in the transparency. Then have students answer the same question as you point to different items. Continue by asking students about the colors they're wearing. If you do not use the transparency, point out the colors of different students' clothing and then ask follow-up questions. As students answer questions about the color of their clothing, repeat for emphasis the correct noun-adjective agreements, for example, **Sí, Roberto lleva una camisa blanca.**

## Vocabulary Expansion

Write the other colors on the board for classroom use: **anaranjado, violeta, rosa (rosado), gris, café (marrón).** You might also want to add the adjectives **claro** and **oscuro** and give examples of their use. Another useful color is **azul marino** *(navy blue).* Write the verb **llevar** on the board and tell students this is the most common one to use with clothing, but that **tener** or **usar** as paraphrases or variations are also acceptable.



### LOS COLORES

una camisa roja

un suéter azul

una chaqueta verde

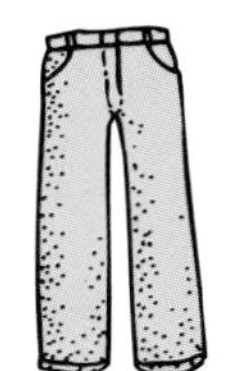
pantalones amarillos

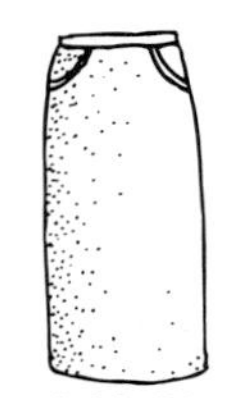
una falda blanca

un impermeable negro

## ¡Aquí te toca a ti!

*Learning Strategy:*

*Reporting based on visual cues*

**A. *¿Qué llevan hoy?*** In your job as fashion reporter for the school newspaper, you need to know what everyone is wearing. Describe each person's outfit in the drawings shown below and on page 423, following the model.

*Luis lleva una camisa roja con unos pantalones blancos.*

Luis

1. Roberta

2. Nadia

3. Alfonso



***Support material, Los colores:*** Transparency #68

***Support material, Ex. A:*** Transparency #69

***Ex. A:*** This activity provides preparation for the **Ya llegamos** section at the end of Unit 6.

### Exercise Progression

Ex. A is designed to associate the pictures with the vocabulary word and its color. Exs. B and C on the following page provide meaningful practice with the new vocabulary.

4. Arturo

5. Olga

6. Esteban

**B. *¿Dónde trabajas durante (during) las vacaciones?*** You have decided to get a sales job this summer at a store in the local shopping center. Explain where you are working and what you sell. Follow the model.

tienda de música
*Voy a trabajar en la tienda de música, y voy a vender discos compactos y cintas.*

1. papelería
2. tienda de deportes
3. tienda de música
4. tienda de ropa para mujeres
5. tienda de ropa para hombres
6. tienda de ropa para niños

Critical Thinking Strategy:
*Making associations*

**C. *¿Qué ropa llevas a la fiesta?*** You are trying to decide what to wear to the party tonight. Using the items of clothing on page 421 and your favorite colors, put together your outfit. Work with a partner. Be prepared to report back to the class. Follow the model.

*—¿Qué vas a llevar a la fiesta?*
*—Voy a llevar unos patalones negros y un suéter rojo.*

Learning Strategy:
*Describing based on personal information*

## Repaso

**D. *En el mercado*** You need to get fruits and vegetables to accompany your dinner. In pairs, play the role of the shopkeeper and the customer. Remember that all the produce is not available all year round. Before you begin, (1) make a list of what you want to buy. (2) Your partner will make a list of what is available. (3) Then create your own conversation, following the model.

*—Buenos días, señorita (señor). ¿Qué desea?*
*—¿Tiene fresas?*
*—Sí, ¿cuánto quiere?*
*—Medio kilo, por favor.*
*—Aquí tiene. ¿Algo más?*

Cooperative Learning

Learning Strategies:
*Listing, negotiating*

Critical Thinking Strategy:
*Comparing*



**Ex. C:** pair work

*Ex. C:* This activity provides preparation for the **Ya llegamos** section at the end of Unit 6.

**Ex. D:** 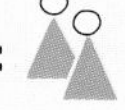 pair work

 role play

*Suggestions, Ex. D:* Encourage students to use other appropriate greetings or leave-taking expressions. Ask them to buy at least four different items and to alternate roles. Then have a few pairs of students present their mini-dialogues to the class.

*ss-prepared students, Ex. A:* Play **¿Quién es?** ve students write out descriptions of their classmates based what they're wearing (articles of clothing and colors). Then ve them read the descriptions to the class and have the class ess who it is.

*ore-prepared students, Ex. A:* Have them write nilar descriptions, using school-wide personalities, perhaps ner teachers or the principal, or perhaps TV or sports personties, noted for their clothing. You may need to brainstorm ditional vocabulary with students first. The descriptions could gin like this, **Esta persona es famosa por sus** ________ (article of clothing) __________ (color), or **esta persona siempre lleva** _______________. Have the class guess who they are.

*Answers, Ex. A:* 1. Roberta lleva un vestido blanco y negro. 2. Nadia lleva una blusa azul y unos pantalones amarillos. 3. Alfonso lleva una camisa blanca, un suéter amarillo y unos pantalones verdes. 4. Arturo lleva una camiseta azul (claro) y unos jeans/pantalones azul marino. 5. Olga lleva una blusa amarilla y una falda verde. 6. Esteban lleva un traje deportivo rojo.

## Pronunciation

Additional activities appear in the Laboratory Tape Program.

## Presentation: Expressions of comparison

Begin by giving students different numbers of objects (pencils, pens, etc.) to illustrate the comparative with quantity. Then make statements such as, **Julia tiene más lápices que Felipe. Felipe tiene menos lápices que Julia.** To make the meaning clear, first count the number of objects each student has. Continue by using adjectives to compare different people. For example: **Mi mamá es más simpática que mi tía. Mi papá es más alto que sus hermanos. Mis hermanas son más altas que yo.** etc. Then present the irregular comparatives by making sentences that illustrate their use. For example: **Mi abuelo tiene 78 años y mi abuela tiene 75 años. Mi abuelo es mayor que mi abuela. Mi abuela es menor que mi abuelo. El equipo de baloncesto de Duke es mejor que el equipo de Yale.** etc. Then write a few examples on the board and point out that the adjectives must agree with the noun/person to which they refer.

**Support material, Pronunciación:** Pronunciation Tape

# Pronunciación: The consonant *l*

The consonant **l** in Spanish is pronounced like the *l* in the English word *leak*.

## Práctica

E. Escucha a tu maestro(a) cuando lee las siguientes palabras. Después repítelas para practicar la pronunciación.

1. lápiz
2. leche
3. listo
4. inteligente
5. papel
6. libro
7. luego
8. malo
9. abuela
10. fútbol

# ESTRUCTURA

## Expressions of comparison

| | |
|---|---|
| Hoy hay **menos** clientes **que** ayer. | Today there are *fewer* customers *than* yesterday. |
| Estos discos compactos son **más** caros **que** ésos. | These CDs are *more* expensive *than* those. |

1. To establish a comparison in Spanish, use these phrases:

| | |
|---|---|
| **más... que** | *more . . . than* |
| **menos... que** | *less . . . than* |

2. A few adjectives have an irregular comparative form and do not make comparisons using **más** or **menos.**

| | | |
|---|---|---|
| **bueno / buen** *(good)* | → | **mejor(es)** *(better)* |
| **malo / mal** *(bad / sick)* | → | **peor(es)** *(worse)* |
| **joven** *(young)* | → | **menor(es)** *(younger)* |
| **viejo** *(old)* | → | **mayor(es)** *(older)* |

| | |
|---|---|
| Estos vestidos son **mejores que** esas blusas. | These dresses are *better than* those blouses. |
| Yo soy **menor que** mi hermano. | I am *younger than* my brother. |

# Aquí practicamos

**F. *¿Qué tienes?*** You are in a bad mood today and disagree with everyone. Say the opposite of what you hear.

Pedro tiene más cintas que Juan.
*No, Pedro tiene menos cintas que Juan.*

1. Rafael tiene más dinero que José.
2. Anita tiene más amigas que Pilar.
3. Yo tengo más paciencia que tú.
4. Tomás tiene más camisas que Alfonso.
5. Tú tienes más faldas que yo.
6. Mi familia tiene más niños que tu familia.

**Critical Thinking Strategy:**
*Contrasting*

**G. *¿Cuál es mejor?*** Express which one of the two items shown in the drawings would be a better addition to your wardrobe. Follow the model.

falda roja / chaqueta negra
*Para mí, una falda roja es mejor que una chaqueta negra.*

**Learning Strategy:**
*Expressing preferences*

***More-prepared students, Ex. G:*** Have students give a reason for their choices. For example, **Para mí, una falda roja es mejor que una chaqueta negra porque no me gusta el negro/porque no tengo mucha ropa negra/porque nunca llevo chaqueta/porque ya tengo una chaqueta negra.**

***Answers, Ex. G:*** Students' preferences will vary but they will be using the following articles of clothing and colors: 1. una blusa/chaqueta verde, unos pantalones azules 2. una falda negra, un suéter amarillo 3. una chaqueta verde, un impermeable rojo 4. una camisa blanca, una camiseta azul 5. una blusa verde, una camiseta blanca 6. un vestido negro y blanco, unos pantalones negros 7. un cinturón rojo/azul 8. un suéter negro, una blusa amarilla

## Exercise Progression

Exs. F and G provide practice with the new structure as well as the new vocabulary. Ex. H on the following page offers a personalized context for students to compare different people and things.

**Ex. H:** pair work

*Suggestion, Ex. H:* Have students work in groups of four. First have them interview each other to find out how many of the items in the exercise each one has, i.e., **¿Cuántos/as ____________ tienes?** Then have them split into pairs and write up their comparisons, e.g., **Yo tengo menos hermanas que mi amiga Ana, pero ella tiene más hermanos que Susana.** Be sure to have different pairs report back to the class with their findings.

*Variation, Ex. H:* Have different students make three comparative statements to the class. Then ask follow-up questions to give students the opportunity to say what they heard.

## Aquí escuchamos

*Suggestion:* After students listen to the tape, have them prepare some of the comparisons in Spanish. This can provide a quick review and serve as a lead-in to the next exercises.

*Answers, Aquí escuchamos:* 1. F, $45 2. T 3. F, the blue one is prettier 4. F, she doesn't have enough money for the blue one and will look for a less expensive one 5. T 6. F, she likes it 7. F, she already has one

*Support material, Aquí escuchamos:* Teacher Tape/CD #2 Track #36 and Tapescript

Critical Thinking Strategy:
*Comparing and contrasting*

**H. *Mis amigos y yo*** Use the nouns provided to compare yourself to your friends. Use the expressions **más... que** and **menos... que.** Follow the model.

**Modelo:** hermanas
*Yo tengo menos hermanas que mi amiga Ana.*

1. hermanos
2. tíos
3. amigos
4. radios
5. cintas
6. libros
7. dinero
8. bicicletas

# Aquí escuchamos:
## "¿Más o menos?"

Learning Strategy:
*Previewing*

### Antes de escuchar

**Review the expressions for making comparisons found in this etapa. Now look at the true/false statements in preparation for listening to the conversation.**

START

Learning Strategy:
*Listening for details*

### Después de escuchar

**Decide whether the following statements are true or false. If something is false, provide the correct information according to the conversation.**

1. Patricia sees a blue blouse that costs $55.
2. The blue blouse is more expensive than the green one.
3. The green blouse is prettier than the blue one.
4. Patricia has a lot of money and doesn't care about the cost of the blouses.
5. Elena sees some blouses on sale that cost less than the other blouses.
6. Patricia doesn't like the white blouse.
7. Patricia says that she is going to buy a black skirt.

EJERCICIO ORAL

**I. Mis parientes** (relatives) Using the vocabulary that you have learned in earlier chapters, tell your classmates how many grandparents, aunts, uncles, cousins, brothers, and sisters you have. As you mention the different numbers, a classmate says that he or she has more or fewer than you. Follow the model.

**Critical Thinking Strategy:**
Comparing and contrasting

**Modelo:**
**Tú:** *Yo tengo tres hermanos.*
**Compañero(a):** *Yo tengo menos hermanos que tú. Tengo un hermano.*

EJERCICIO ESCRITO

**J. La vida de la gente famosa** You are a reporter for the school paper and are responsible for this month's gossip column. Imagine that you have interviewed several celebrities and are comparing their lifestyles. Choose your own celebrities and write a series of eight comparisons in all. Be prepared to read them back to the class.

**Learning Strategies:**
Listing, describing

**Critical Thinking Strategies:**
Evaluating, analyzing, comparing and contrasting

**Modelo:** *Jay Leno tiene más* ___________ *que David Letterman. Paula Abdul es menos* ___________ *que Diana Ross.*

**Ex. I:** pair work

***Suggestion, Ex. I:*** There are several follow-up exercises that can be done with this. You can have students total the number of people in their families, then determine who in class has the largest/smallest family. Alternatively, you may want to draw attention to the different generations in families, having students tell how large each generation is in his/her family, and making class comparisons of these.

***Follow-up, Ex. I:*** Have several students report back to the class.

**Ex. J:** writing

***Less-prepared students, Ex. J:*** First, brainstorm with students a list of famous people and items to be compared to facilitate the exercise.

***More-prepared students, Ex. J:*** Have more-prepared students exchange papers and edit each other's work.

## Presentation: Zapatería "El Tacón"

Use the transparency to point out the different items in the **zapatería.** Ask questions such as, **¿Qué llevas hoy—zapatos o botas? ¿zapatos de tenis o sandalias? ¿zapatos de tacón o botas? ¿calcetines o medias? ¿una bolsa de cuero o una mochila?**

If you do not use the transparencies, introduce the vocabulary by pointing to what different students are wearing. Then ask general questions using the new words.

***Support material, Zapatería "El Tacón":*** Transparencies #70, #70a

# SEGUNDA ETAPA

*Learning Strategy:*

*Previewing*

### Preparación

- Where do you usually go to buy shoes?
- What kind of shoes do you like to wear most?
- What questions do you usually ask at a shoestore?

## Zapatería "El Tacón"

## Etapa Support Materials

Workbook: **pp. 242–246**
Transparencies: **#70, #70a, #71**
Listening Activity masters: **p. 119**
Tapescript: **p. 176**

Quiz: **Testing Program, p. 208**
Chapter Test: **Testing Program, p. 210**

Support material, **Zapatería "El Tacón":**
**Transparencies #70, #70a**

# ¡Aquí te toca a ti!

**A. *En la zapatería*** You need to get some new shoes. When the clerk asks you, tell him or her what you want to see. Take turns with your partner in playing the role of the clerk. Follow the model.

**Modelo:** —*¿En qué puedo servirle?*
—*Quisiera ver unos zapatos de tacón.*

**B. *¿Qué número?*** Now go back to Activity A and give your shoe size to the clerk. Use your European size. Refer to the chart on page 431 for sizes.

**Modelo:** —*¿En qué puedo servirle?*
—*Quisiera ver unos zapatos de tenis.*
—*¿Qué número?*
—*Cuarenta y tres, por favor.*

**Learning Strategy:**
*Reading a chart*

# Repaso

**C. *La ropa de María y Marta*** Use the information provided in the following chart to make comparisons about María's and Marta's clothes. Remember the expressions for comparison **más... que** and **menos... que.** Follow the model.

**Modelo:** *María tiene menos camisetas que Marta.*

**Critical Thinking Strategy:**
*Comparing*

| | *María* | *Marta* |
|---|---|---|
| CAMISETAS | 5 | 6 |
| FALDAS | 2 faldas cortas<br>1 falda larga<br>2 faldas negras | 1 falda azul<br>1 falda amarilla |
| VESTIDOS | 1 vestido de fiesta<br>1 vestido rojo<br>1 vestido verde | 1 vestido de fiesta<br>4 vestidos rojos<br>1 vestido verde |
| SUÉTERES | 5 | 4 |
| CINTURONES | 1 | 3 |
| PANTALONES | 4 | 2 |



## Exercise Progression

Exs. A and B provide practice with the new vocabulary in personalized open-ended activities. Ex. C offers meaningful practice in a controlled situation.

**Exs. A and B:**  pair work

 role play

***Reteaching:*** Quickly review numbers 10–100, counting by 10s and then by 5s, before doing Ex. B.

***More-prepared students, Exs. A and B:*** Have students combine Exs. A and B for a more complete and logical dialogue situation. Have them ask for at least three different items.

***Less-prepared students, Exs. A and B:*** After students have done both A and B separately, have them combine the exercises, asking for at least two items.

***Less-prepared students, Ex. C:*** Remind students that there may be more than one possible comparison in some of the categories and have them find as many as they can.

**Ex. C:**  pair work

***More-prepared students, Ex. C:*** After students have made all possible comparisons, have them work with a partner to make conclusions about each of the girls, e.g., **A Marta no le gustan los pantalones, le gustan los vestidos, especialmente los vestidos rojos.**

### Ex. C: Think, Pair, Share

- Tell each student to think independently of the conclusions that could be drawn about María's and Marta's clothes.
- Direct students to form pairs.
- Then tell the pairs to compare their conclusions until they agree. Tell them to take turns answering first.
- Ask different students at random to make statements about which person has more or less than the other.

## Presentation: Expressing equality

Begin by making statements and asking questions comparing different students and objects in the classroom. For example: **José es alto. Enrique es alto también. José es tan alto como Enrique. María tiene tres cuadernos y Alicia tiene tres cuadernos. María tiene tantos cuadernos como Alicia.** etc. Then write a few examples on the board and point out agreement between **tantos/tantas** and the nouns they modify.

*Follow-up, Ex. D:* Remind students of noun-adjective agreement (especially because all examples in the exercise are masculine singular) and ask personal follow-up questions illustrating different agreement possibilities. For example: **¿Las enchiladas son tan buenas como las hamburguesas? ¿Gloria Estefan es tan guapa como Paula Abdul? ¿Los estudiantes de esta clase son tan inteligentes como los estudiantes de la otra clase de español?**, etc.

*Less-prepared students, Ex. E:* Have them scan the exercise and note whether items are masculine or feminine, singular or plural and make a note of what form of **tanto** to use in each case. Then have them do the exercise.

# ESTRUCTURA

### Expressing equality

To express equality in Spanish, use the phrase **tan** + adjective / adverb + **como** = *as . . . as.*

| | |
|---|---|
| El carrito de Roberto está **tan** lleno **como** el de Ricardo. | Robert's shopping cart is *as* full *as* Richard's. |
| Margarita compra **tan** frecuentemente **como** Linda. | Margarita shops *as* frequently *as* Linda. |

Another way to make comparisons in Spanish is with the words **tanto** and **como. Tanto** and **como** are used with nouns, as in these examples.

| | |
|---|---|
| Este señor compró **tanta** mercadería **como** esa señora. | This man bought *as* much merchandise *as* that woman. |
| Laura compró **tantos** huevos **como** Sonia. | Laura bought *as* many eggs *as* Sonia. |

**tanto(a)** + noun + **como** = *as much* + noun + *as*
**tantos(as)** + noun + **como** = *as many* + noun + *as*

The words **tanto(a)/tantos(as)** agree in gender and number with the nouns that follow.

## Aquí practicamos

Critical Thinking Strategy: Comparing

**D. Los gemelos** Because they are identical twins, Nicolás and Andrés are the same in almost every way. Compare them using the cues given. Follow the model.

**Modelo:** alto
*Nicolás es tan alto como Andrés.*

1. inteligente
2. gordo
3. bueno
4. energético
5. bajo
6. simpático
7. guapo
8. divertido

Critical Thinking Strategy: Comparing

**E. Nicolás come tanta comida como Andrés.** The twins' mother is always careful to serve them exactly the same amount of food. Describe what they have on their plates, using the cues on page 431. **¡OJO!** *(Watch out!)* Don't forget to use the correct form of **tanto.**

**Modelo:** helado
*Nicolás tiene tanto helado como Andrés.*



## Exercise Progression

Exs. D and E provide controlled practice with the new structure. Ex. F on the following page offers meaningful practice in a personalized communicative-type format.

1. papas fritas
2. pescado
3. carne
4. galletas
5. queso
6. fruta
7. pastas
8. pollo

F. **¡Yo soy mejor que tú!** Some people always think that they are the best. With a classmate, have a bragging contest. Use the cues and your imagination. Follow the model.

**Modelo:** mi casa / bonita
—*Mi casa es tan bonita como la casa del presidente.*
—*No importa.* (That doesn't matter.) *Mi casa es más bonita que la casa del presidente.*

1. mis notas / altas
2. mi madre / inteligente
3. mi hermana / bonita
4. mi padre / importante
5. mi tío / rico
6. mi hermano / divertido

Critical Thinking Strategy:
Comparing

## COMENTARIOS CULTURALES

### Tallas internacionales

Shoe sizes are different in Spain and Latin America than they are in the U.S.

Men's shoes

| U.S. | 8 | 9 | 10 | 11 | 12 | 13 |
|---|---|---|---|---|---|---|
| Spain | 41 | 42 | 43 | 44 | 45,5 | 47 |

Women's shoes

| U.S. | 4 1/2 | 5 1/2 | 6 1/2 | 7 1/2 | 8 1/2 | 9 1/2 |
|---|---|---|---|---|---|---|
| Spain | 35,5 | 36,5 | 38,5 | 39,5 | 40,5 | 42 |

¿Qué crees?

If you go shopping in Mexico City, in which place would you bargain?

a) supermarket
b) drug store
c) open-air market
d) department store

respuesta



*More-prepared students, Ex. E:* After students are done, have them create personalized comparison questions to ask each other or the class. Check their work for accuracy, or have them check each other, before having them ask their questions.

*Answers, Ex. E:* 1. tantas papas fritas como 2. tanto pescado como 3. tanta carne como 4. tantas galletas como 5. tanto queso como 6. tanta fruta como 7. tantas pastas como 8. tanto pollo como

**Ex. F:**  pair work

*Less-prepared students, Ex. F:* Help students establish or brainstorm with them terms of comparison for each item before beginning the exercise. For example, for **notas altas,** they could compare with a known school "genius" or TV figure, etc.

*More-prepared students, Ex. F:* Have more-prepared students create at least three additional situations and compare them.

## Aquí escuchamos

*Suggestion:* Have students look at the comprehension questions and take notes, or write key words they hear in the Spanish text for each item. Call on volunteers after listening twice (or three times) to give the information.

*Support material, Aquí escuchamos:* Teacher Tape/CD #2 Track #37  and Tapescript



# Aquí escuchamos:

## "¿De qué talla?"

**Learning Strategy:**

*Previewing*

### Antes de escuchar

**Review the expressions of equality found in this etapa. Now look at the questions to anticipate the content of the conversation you will hear between a shoe salesman and a customer.**

START

c

## Después de escuchar

**Choose the statement that best matches the information provided in the conversation.**

1. Francisco wants to buy . . .
   a. a pair of brown shoes.
   b. a pair of black shoes.
   c. a pair of white shoes.
2. Francisco's shoe size is . . .
   a. 10 to 10 1/2.
   b. 9 to 9 1/2.
   c. 11 to 11 1/2.
3. The price of the first pair of shoes that the salesman brings out is . . .
   a. $85.
   b. $65.
   c. $75.
4. The problem with the first pair of shoes is that . . .
   a. they are the wrong color.
   b. they are not the right size.
   c. they are too expensive.
5. The second pair of shoes costs . . .
   a. more than the first pair.
   b. the same as the first pair.
   c. less than the first pair.
6. Francisco is most concerned about . . .
   a. the price of the shoes.
   b. the style of the shoes.
   c. the brand name of the shoes.

*Learning Strategy:*

*Listening for details*

EJERCICIO ORAL

**G. *¿Cuánto cuesta todo esto* (all this)?** Work with a partner. You need new shoes, socks, and a bag for this season. You have $40 to spend. On page 434 are the ads for two different shoe stores. Compare their prices and decide where you can get the best deals and what you can buy without going over the limit. Follow the model.

*Cooperative Learning*

*Learning Strategy:*

*Brainstorming*

*Critical Thinking Strategies:*

*Comparing and contrasting, prioritizing*



*Support material, Ex G:* Transparency #71

**Ex. G:** pair work

*Variation, Ex. G:* Before students do this activity, brainstorm with them to come up with factors they consider in making purchases and write them on the board, such as: price **(el precio);** color **(los colores);** size **(la talla);** quality **(la calidad);** brand name **(la marca de fábrica);** style **(la moda);** current possessions **(lo que ya tengo);** condition of current possessions **(condición de lo que ya tengo);** popularity among friends **(lo que es popular con mis amigos).**

*Learning Strategy: Brainstorming*

*Follow-up, Ex. G:* After students have done the activity with their partner, create a "tick mark" graph on the board. Enter the two most important factors from each pair to determine the overall most important factors to students in the class when making purchases.

## Cooperative Learning

**Learning Strategy: Reading a graph**

*Critical Thinking Strategies: Prioritizing, comparing and contrasting*

*Answers, Aquí escuchamos:* 1. b 2. a 3. b 4. b 5. c 6. a

**Ex. H**  writing

*Less-prepared students, Ex. H:* Remind students to set up their discussion in terms of **más/menos/tanto como** for each of the categories listed.

*More-prepared students, Ex. H:* Have them include their reasons for making purchases. For example, **Compro/voy a comprar pantalones vaqueros en (nombre de la tienda) porque tiene más tallas y modas que en (nombre de la tienda).**

**¡"La Casa del Zapato" anuncia una gran oferta de zapatos!**

| | |
|---|---|
| zapatos de tacón | $50 |
| zapatos negros | $25 |
| zapatos de tenis | 2 pares por $30 |
| bolsas de cuero | desde $5 hasta $15 |
| medias | 5 pares por $10 |
| calcetines | $2 el par |
| botas | $50 |
| sandalias | $35 |
| zapatos de fiesta | $75 |

**Zapatería "El Tacón" tiene los mejores precios de la ciudad.**

| | |
|---|---|
| zapatos de tacón | $45 |
| zapatos negros | $20 |
| zapatos de tenis | $30 el par |
| bolsas de cuero | $25 |
| medias | 5 pares por $10 |
| calcetines | $2 el par |
| botas | $50 |
| sandalias | $35 |
| zapatos de fiesta | $75 |

**Modelo:** *Los zapatos de tacón son más caros en "La Casa del Zapato". Los zapatos de fiesta cuestan tanto en "La Casa del Zapato" como en la zapatería "El Tacón".*

**Cooperative Learning**

**Learning Strategies:**

*Brainstorming, listing*

**Critical Thinking Strategy:**

*Comparing and contrasting*

## EJERCICIO ESCRITO

**H. *Comparaciones*** With your partner, (1) discuss the differences between two quite different stores with which you are both familiar. Consider such factors as location **(la localidad),** prices **(los precios),** service **(el servicio),** merchandise quality **(la calidad),** brand names **(las marcas),** sizes **(las tallas),** variety of departments or offerings **(la variedad disponible),** customers **(la clientela),** background music **(la música de fondo),** etc. (2) Make a list of at least four differences between the two stores. (3) Then decide on three items that you would prefer to purchase in each store.

# Vocabulario

## Para charlar

### Para hacer comparaciones

mayor
más… que
mejor
menor
menos… que
peor

### Para establecer igualdad

tan / tanto… como

## Temas y contextos

### Una tienda de ropa

un abrigo
una blusa
una camisa
una camiseta
una chaqueta
un cinturón
una falda
un impermeable
unos pantalones
un suéter
un vestido

### Una zapatería

una bolsa de cuero
una bota
unos calcetines
unas medias
unas sandalias
un zapato
un zapato de tacón
un zapato de tenis

## Vocabulario general

### Sustantivos

una boutique
la moda

### Verbos

llevar

### Adjetivos

azul
blanco
moderno(a)
negro
seguro(a)

*Support material, Capítulo 18:* Improvised Conversation, Teacher Tape/CD #2 Track #38 and Tapescript; Lab Manual listening activities, Laboratory Program, Tapescript, and Teacher's Edition of the Workbook/Lab Manual

# Chapter Culminating Activity

Set up a "shopping extravaganza" in the classroom. Choose several students to be salespersons in different stores (clothing store, shoe store, stationery store, sporting goods, etc.); give each salesperson a list of items and prices. These students set up the stores around the rim of the classroom; other students then go shopping. Everyone is required to make a certain number of purchases or, if you prefer, each person starts out with a specific amount of money. After a certain time for shopping, students report to the class (or to small groups) on what they bought where.

## Vocabulario: Team Project

Part I

- Assign the students to at least five teams to make a **centro comercial.** Each team will represent a different store. You will need two days, preferably three, for this activity.
- Have the class brainstorm to plan where they would like to put all the stores in their classroom.
- Instruct teams to get together to plan the design of their store, which items to include, and who will furnish them. A combination of drawings for the store backdrop and real items work well.
- Tell the teams to be ready to set up their stores the following day.

Part II

- **En el centro comercial.** Students will alternately play the roles of storekeepers and shoppers.
- Prizes may be given for the best salesperson, the most difficult customer, the most beautiful store, etc.

# Lectura CULTURAL

## INÉS SASTRE, SUPERMODELO ESPAÑOLA

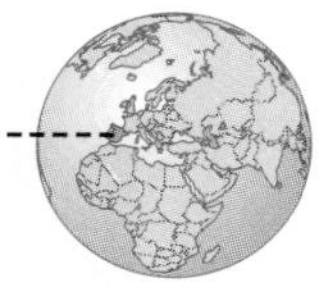

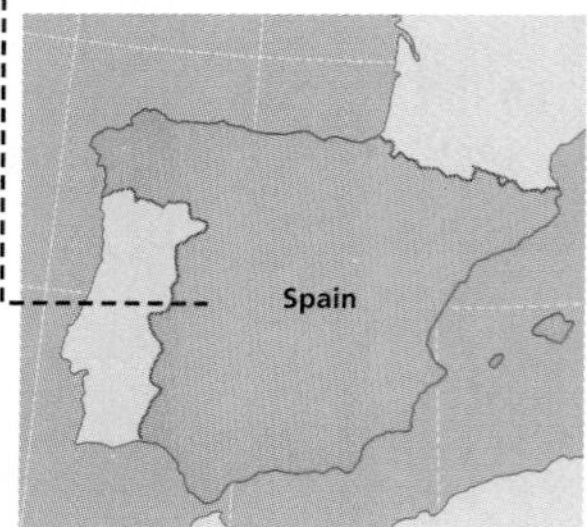

**Learning Strategies:**

*Previewing, brainstorming, reading for main ideas, using cognates and context for meaning*

### Antes de leer

1. Look at the photos that accompany this reading. What do you think it will be about?
2. Are you familiar with names of some of the famous people who do this sort of work?
3. Now look at the title. What is the person's name and what country is she from?

**izquierda: Claudia Schiffer; derecha: Naomi Campbell**

## Guía para la lectura

*A.* Look at the subtitles of the text. Make a prediction about what you think will be the topic of each subdivision.
# 1. # 2. # 3.

*B.* Read the first paragraph and find three names. Where are these women from?

*C.* Now read the second paragraph to determine . . .
1. why Inés Sastre is so famous.
2. what three countries are mentioned.

*D.* Read the third paragraph and answer the following questions.
1. How old is Inés Sastre?
2. Where was she born?
3. What movie did she appear in?

**Learning Strategies:**

*Scanning and reading for details, reading for main idea*

**Critical Thinking Strategy:**

*Predicting*

### Inés Sastre, supermodelo española

**Club de famosas**

Hoy día, las supermodelos son tan universalmente famosas como las estrellas de cine y los músicos "pop". En las revistas de todo el mundo vemos las fotos de la alemana Claudia Schiffer, la estadounidense Cindy Crawford y la inglesa Naomi Campbell. Muy pronto, una modelo española va a formar parte de este "club de famosas" en el mundo de la moda.

**Una entre mil**

Recientemente, la compañía cosmética Max Factor seleccionó a Inés Sastre entre más de mil modelos para representar su nueva línea de productos de belleza en Europa, Estados Unidos y Japón. Nos dice: "Me llamaron en París para hacer la primera prueba. Al poco tiempo me invitaron a hacer el primer anuncio en Nueva York. Obviamente éste es un momento muy importante en mi carrera".

**Éxito**

¿Quién es esta española que tan joven tiene tanto éxito? Inés Sastre sólo tiene 19 años. Nació en Madrid, que todavía es su ciudad preferida. A la edad de 13 años fue actriz en la película *El dorado.* Empezó a trabajar como modelo y a los 16 años recibió un prestigioso premio internacional: "The Look of the Year", de la agencia de modelos Elite. Ahora participa en los más importantes desfiles de moda en su país y en el resto de Europa.



***Answers, Guía para la lectura:*** **A.** Answers will vary. **B.** Claudia Schiffer: Germany, Cindy Crawford: U.S., Naomi Campbell: England **C.** 1. She represents Max Factor in Europe. 2. U.S., Japan, France (Paris) **D.** 1. 19 2. Madrid 3. "El dorado"

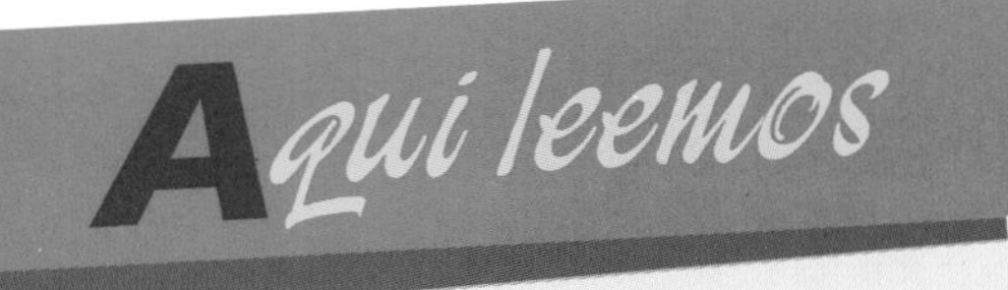

# Aquí leemos

## Presentation, Aquí leemos

Ask students where they like to shop. Why do they like it there? How do they know where to find the articles they need? Do they read the store directory or do they browse until they find what they need? This activity can be done in English and is intended to set the context of the reading. As students talk about their favorite shopping places and stores, you can insert some words that appear in the reading.

## Presentation: Lectura

This directory is not intended to be read in detail from top to bottom. Here students can practice skimming and scanning skills. The exercise that corresponds to this reading is designed for using the directory in the same way that a tourist might when walking into **El Corte Inglés.**

**Reading Strategies:**

*Keep your reading purpose in mind.*
*Notice overall organization and main ideas.*
*Always base guesses on context and background knowledge, not on just a single word.*
*Use cognates carefully.*
*Read for details only when you know what you need.*

## Estrategia para la lectura

In this unit you can practice all your reading skills. Any piece of writing is designed to be read for a particular purpose. If you keep the purpose in mind, you can use your background knowledge and the context to help you predict and understand the content. As you know, cognates are very helpful to English readers of Spanish. But good readers use them carefully because false cognates can mislead you. By combining all your sources of information, you can make the best guesses about content.

## Antes de leer

The reading in this unit is related to shopping. Before looking at it, think about your own shopping experiences and answer these questions.

- **When you go into a department store, how do you know where to find the articles you need? By browsing? By looking at a store directory?**
- **How are store directories organized? What are four or five categories you expect on a store directory?**
- **What store departments are most familiar to you? What Spanish words do you know that are related to those departments?**

On page 439, you'll see a directory from **El Corte Inglés,** a famous department store in Madrid. You can read it just like anyone else who would be shopping in the store. But, like anyone else, you would probably have particular items in mind that you want to look for. No one ever reads such a directory in detail from top to bottom! So on the first reading, just try to get a general idea of what is offered in this store and of how the store is organized. Look for cognate words that can help you understand the directory. Then do the **Actividades**, which will instruct you to find particular information.



## Support Materials

Workbook: **pp. 247–252**
Unit Review Blackline Masters: **Unit 6 Review**
Listening Activity masters: **p. 124**
Tapescript: **p. 183**
Unit Exam: **Testing Program, p. 214**

**Atajo,** Writing Assistant Software 

**Departamentos:**
**Tejidos.** Boutique. Mercería. Sedas. Lanas. **Supermercado.** Alimentación. Limpieza. **Imagen y Sonido.** Hi-Fi. Ordenadores. Radio. TV. Videos. Librería. Palelería.

**Servicios:**
Patrones de moda. Revelado rápido de Fotografías. Consultorio Esotérico.

**Departamentos:**
**Complementos de Moda.** Perfumería y Cosmética. Joyería. Bisutería. Bolsos. Fumador. Marroquinería. Medias. Pañuelos. Relojería. Sombreros. Turismo. Fotografía.

**Servicios:**
Reparación relojes y joyas. Estanco. Quiosco de Prensa. Información. Servicio de Intérpretes. Objetos perdidos. Optica 2000. Filatelia y Numismática. Empaquetado de Regalos.

**Departamentos:**
**Hogar Menaje.** Artesanía. Cerámica. Cristalería. Cubertería/ Accesorios Automóvil. Bricolaje. Loza. Orfebrería. Porcelanas (Lladró, Capodimonte). Platería. Regalos. Vajillas. Saneamiento. Electrodomésticos. Muebles de Cocina.

**Servicios:**
Reparación de Calzado. Plastificado de Carnet. Duplicado de llaves. Grabación de objetos. Floristería. Listas de Boda.

**Departamentos:**
**Niños/as.** (4 a 10 años) Confección. Boutiques. Complementos. Juguetería. **Chicos/as.** (11 a 14 años) Confección. Carrocería. Canastillas. Regalos bebé. Zapatería bebé. **Zapatería.** Señoras, Caballeros y Niños.

**Servicios:**
Estudio Fotográfico y realización de retratos.

**Departamentos:**
**Confección Caballeros.** Confección. Ante y Piel. Boutiques. Ropa Interior. Sastrería a Medida. Artículos de Viajes. Complementos de Moda. Zapatería. Tallas Especiales.

**Servicios:**
Unidad Administrativa (Tarjeta de compra El Corte Inglés. Venta a plazos. Envíos al extranjero y nacionales. Devolución I.V.A. Post-Venta). Peluquería Caballeros y Niños. Centro de Seguros. Agencia de Viajes.

**Departamentos:**
**Señoras.** Confección. Punto. Peletería. Boutiques Internacionales. Lencería y Corsetería. Futura Mamá. Tallas Especiales. Complementos de Moda. Zapatería. Pronovias.

**Servicios:**
Peluquería Señoras. Conservación de pieles.

*Answers, Ex. A:* Both words refer to accessories. Point out how many times each occurs and the evidence that the meanings overlap somewhat.

*Answers, Ex. B:* 1. They are all intended to be used by women. 2. They are intended to relate to children. (Point out that parents often buy children's portraits in department stores.) 3. Levels 2, 3, 4 4. Levels 3 and 4 have separate **peluquerías** for men and women.

*Answers, Ex. C:* 1. Zapatería, Segunda Planta 2. Revelado rápido de Fotografías, Sótano 3. Servicio de Intérpretes, Planta Baja 4. Regalos de bebé/Juguetería, Segunda Planta 5. Supermercado, Sótano

## Actividades

*A.* Look for these familiar-looking words in the department headings on page 439. Examine the list of merchandise included under each one and guess the best English equivalent for the heading. The best one will not be the English word it most resembles!

1. **complementos**
2. **confección**

*B.* Look more carefully at the lists of departments and services offered on each floor, or **planta.** Then, answer the questions.

1. What do the services and merchandise on the **cuarta planta** have in common?
2. What do the services and merchandise on the **segunda planta** have in common?
3. On which levels can you buy shoes?
4. How many hair salons **(peluquerías)** are there? Why are they located where they are?

*C.* Imagine that you have come to **El Corte Inglés** to buy the following items. Where do you go? For each item, write the name of the department and the **planta** on which it is located.

1. **Necesitas un par de zapatos nuevos.**
2. **Quieres revelar tus fotografías.**
3. **No sabes cómo explicarle al dependiente que quieres las fotografías en colores. Necesitas un intérprete.**
4. **Quieres un regalo para tu hermano de 5 años.**
5. **Necesitas comprar fruta para el viaje en tren.**

# Ya llegamos

## Actividades orales

**A. *Mi ropa*** You and your mother go shopping. Tell her what you hope to buy and the colors and combinations you like. Work in pairs and take turns playing each role.

**B. *La música*** Explain to your partner the type of music you like, the singers or groups you like to listen to, and whether you prefer cassettes or CDs. Find out your partner's preferences, too.

**C. *¡Celebremos con fiesta!*** You and your classmates are organizing a Spanish Club party to celebrate the end of the school year. The class should form planning teams of three to five students each, and the team coming up with the proposal accepted by the entire class will have their tickets to the party paid for by the class.

You should plan: (1) the location of the party (private home, park, local youth club or camp); (2) the menu (snacks, picnic, or seated meal, as well as drinks); (3) the activities (team sports, swimming, sing-a-long, dancing); (4) the music (types of music represented, how delivered); and (5) what you recommend people wear (based on planned activities). Consider the maximum amount per student you will need to charge. Don't forget to allow enough in your budget to pay for the winning team members!

First, (1) discuss your group's general preferences in the five categories mentioned above; then, (2) come to an agreement and (3) set a budget for each area; and finally, (4) assign a student to be in charge of each category. Each of these students should take notes about the group's preferences and develop a list of things that need to be done or purchased. If appropriate, estimate the cost for your area(s) of responsibility.

Refine your plans as a group in the form of a presentation to the whole class. Make your presentation appealing and convincing . . . you want your team's proposal to win!

**Cooperative Learning**

**Learning Strategies:**

*Organizing and revising a project, negotiating, budgeting, estimating, organizing and delivering a group presentation*

**Critical Thinking Strategy:**

*Persuading*



**Ex. A:**  pair work

role play

***Variation, Ex. A:*** Tell students to pretend that they are going shopping with their best friend instead of their mother. Have several students report back on their friends' preferences in clothes.

**Ex. B:** pair work

role play

**Ex. C:**  groups of three

***Suggestion, Ex. C:*** In each group, designate, or have students choose, (1) a leader who initiates discussion, (2) a recorder(s) who takes notes, and (3) a participant(s) who asks questions and clarifies information.

***Support material, Unidad 6:*** Lab Manual Ya llegamos listening activities, Laboratory Program , Tapescript, and Teacher's Edition of the Workbook/Lab Manual

## Writing Activities

### *Atajo, Writing Assistant Software*

*Functional vocabulary:* Agreeing and disagreeing; asking for/giving advice; asking for information; asking for help; expressing an opinion; etc.

*Topic vocabulary:* Bread; cheeses; cooking; drinks; fish and seafood; fruits; legumes and vegetables; meat; money; musical instruments; pastry; quantity; stores; etc.

*Grammar:* Verbs: **gustar** type; **encantar**; verbs: imperative; comparatives; adjectives: demonstrative; pronouns: interrogatives; etc.

**Ex. D:** groups of four or more

*Variation, Ex. D:* Tell students to use only Spanish and to act out the situation as if they were going to present it as a skit. Set a time limit and then have a few groups of students present their mini-situations to the class. Ask follow-up questions to test students' listening comprehension. For example: **¿Qué comida van a llevar?** etc.

*Reteaching, Ex. E:* Have students identify the past time context and need for the use of the preterite. Review/brainstorm preterite verbs and forms with students before going on to the exercise.

# Actividades escritas

**D. *Vamos de picnic*** You are planning a picnic with four friends. Plan what you want to eat and drink. Decide which person will buy what. Write up the shopping list.

**E. *Fui de compras*** Write a note to a Spanish-speaking friend describing a recent shopping trip and the various purchases you made.

**F. *¿Qué vas a comprar?*** Plan a shopping trip to four different stores, writing down the items that you would like to purchase at each store.

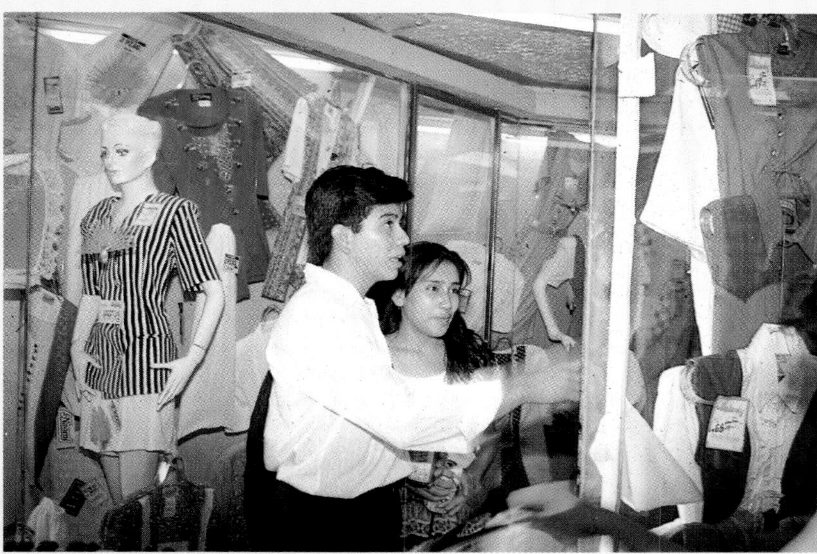

—A mí me gustan estos pantalones. ¿Qué te parece?
—Me gustan, pero no quiero comprarlos ahora.

## Additional Warm-up Activity

Ask students to work with a partner. Ask students how much they know about the countries shown on the chart on page 445 and ask them to associate: a) a capital city, b) a monetary unit, and c) a language with each country and then record their answers in a notebook. Tell them to be prepared for classroom discussion.

***Answers, Actividad:***
**Paso 1.** 1. El tipo de cambio 2. país y moneda, cantidad, tipo de cambio, valor en dólares (U.S.) 3. Sí, hay que multiplicarlas.
**Paso 2.** 1. $73.80 2. $44.44 3. 100 pesos 4. 100 pesetas 5. Venezuela

## Expansion

Here are some additional activities that you can do with students to expand on this topic.

***Paso 1. ¿Qué significan los términos?:*** Work with a partner to match the term in column A with its definition in column B (below). Prepare for class discussion!

***Paso 2. Vamos de compras:*** These American tourists (p. T445, bottom) want to go shopping while on vacation, but they don't know anything about changing money. Let's help them, using the exchange rates listed on the chart on page 445.

# Conexión

> What do you know about exchange rates before reading the passage?
>
> For whom are exchange rates important? When do we need to know about exchange rates?
>
> The basic monetary unit in the United States is the dollar. What is the basic monetary unit of England? Spain? France? Germany? Japan?

## El tipo de cambio

### AL EMPEZAR

Shopping in another country requires knowledge of that country's currency, or monetary system. The following passage discusses el **tipo de cambio**, or the exchange rate.

### EL TIPO DE CAMBIO

Cuando la gente quiere comprar algo en otros países es necesario cambiar la **moneda** (money; currency) de su país por la moneda del otro. El tipo de cambio determina el valor de la moneda de un país respecto a la moneda del otro, indicando la cantidad que se puede comprar. Por ejemplo, si se pueden cambiar 125 pesetas españolas por un dólar ($1) estadounidense, un español que viaja a Nueva York con 400 pesetas tiene tres dólares estadounidenses para **gastar** (spend) durante su visita. También el norteamericano que llega a Madrid con $3 sale de la casa de cambio con 400 pesetas.

El tipo de cambio varia de día en día, basándose en la demanda internacional de las monedas. El siguiente esquema indica el tipo de cambio en dólares estadounidenses del 29 de abril de 1995. Se multiplica la cantidad de moneda extranjera por el tipo de cambio del mismo país para determinar el valor en dólares (U.S.).

| A | B |
|---|---|
| ______ 1. la peseta | a. todas las cosas que compramos. |
| ______ 2. el tipo de cambio | b. la moneda de Perú |
| ______ 3. la casa de cambio | c. el dinero que se usa en un país |
| ______ 4. el sol | d. la moneda de España |
| ______ 5. el bolívar | e. nos indica el valor de una moneda. |
| ______ 6. la moneda | f. la moneda de Venezuela |
| ______ 7. el peso | g. un lugar donde cambiamos una moneda por otra |
| ______ 8. la mercancía | h. el nombre más popular de monedas en el mundo hispano |

# con la economía

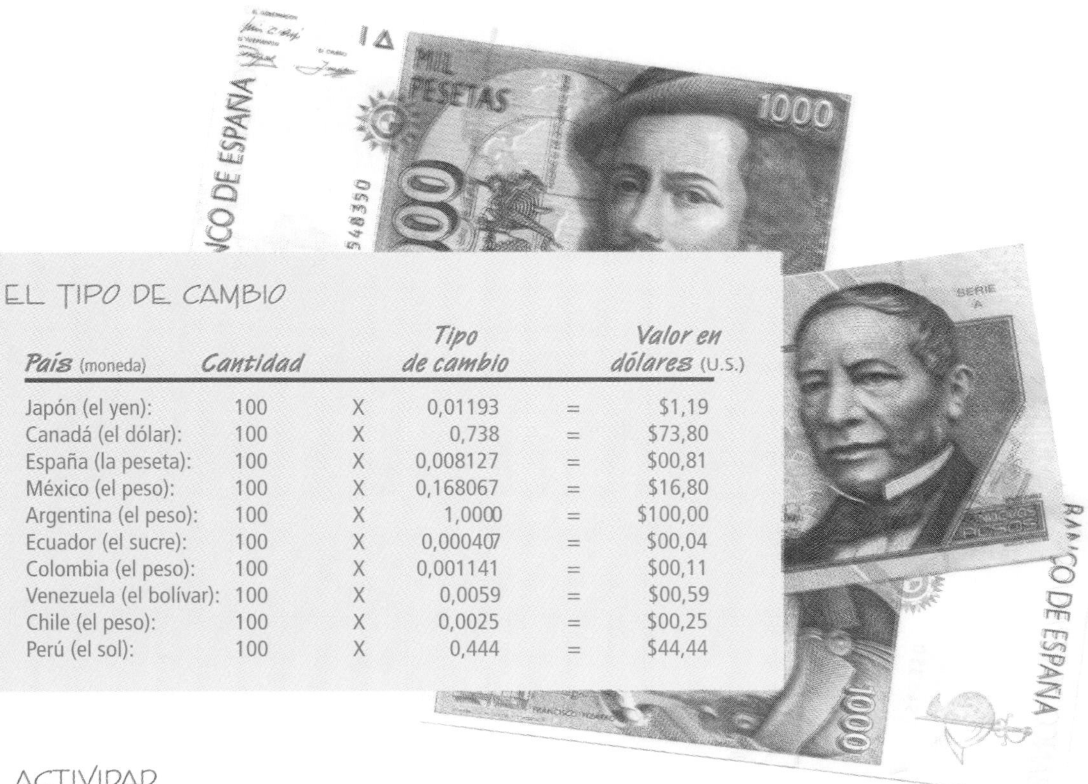


EL TIPO DE CAMBIO

| *País* (moneda) | *Cantidad* | | *Tipo de cambio* | | *Valor en dólares* (U.S.) |
|---|---|---|---|---|---|
| Japón (el yen): | 100 | X | 0,01193 | = | $1,19 |
| Canadá (el dólar): | 100 | X | 0,738 | = | $73,80 |
| España (la peseta): | 100 | X | 0,008127 | = | $00,81 |
| México (el peso): | 100 | X | 0,168067 | = | $16,80 |
| Argentina (el peso): | 100 | X | 1,0000 | = | $100,00 |
| Ecuador (el sucre): | 100 | X | 0,000407 | = | $00,04 |
| Colombia (el peso): | 100 | X | 0,001141 | = | $00,11 |
| Venezuela (el bolívar): | 100 | X | 0,0059 | = | $00,59 |
| Chile (el peso): | 100 | X | 0,0025 | = | $00,25 |
| Perú (el sol): | 100 | X | 0,444 | = | $44,44 |

ACTIVIDAD

*Paso 1:* Reading a chart is not difficult if you approach the task in an organized way. Refer to the chart above.

1. ¿Cuál es el título del esquema?
2. ¿Qué hay en la primera columna? ¿la segunda? ¿la tercera? ¿la cuarta?
3. ¿Es importante el orden de las columnas? ¿Por qué?

*Paso 2:* Use the chart to answer the following questions.

1. ¿Cuánto valen 100 dólares canadienses en los Estados Unidos?
2. ¿Cuánto valen 100 soles peruanos en los Estados Unidos?
3. ¿Cuánto valen $16,80 (U.S.) en México?
4. ¿Cuánto valen 81 **centavos** (U.S.) en España? — cents
5. Jaime quiere gastar los 200 bolívares que tiene. ¿Dónde está Jaime?



*Paso 3: Para pensar:* Trabaja con un(a) compañero(a) para contestar las siguientes preguntas. Usa una calculadora.

**a. Es el 29 de abril. Toru Suzuki, estudiante japonés, llega a Los Ángeles, California con 900 yen. A Toru le gusta la cocina norteamericana y quisiera almorzar una hamburguesa con queso en un restaurante de comida rápida. ¿Tiene dinero suficiente? ¿Cuántos dólares (U.S.) tiene Toru después de cambiar los yen. [Pista:** 900 × .01193 = ?]

**b. Linda Piana, profesora chilena, necesita mandarle 50 dólares (U.S.) a su hija, Cristina, que vive en Nueva York porque Cristina quiere comprar un traje de baño para el verano. ¿Cuántos pesos chilenos necesita cambiar?**

## Extension Activity

Information on foreign exchange rates is available in the financial section of most major newspapers. Many banks and travel agencies can also supply potential tourists and business people with current exchange rates. Using the sources mentioned above, have students update the chart included in this lesson. Have the currency values changed significantly? Have they risen? Fallen?

**ime está en Canadá. Quiere comprar una camisa negra que cuesta 40 dólares canadienses.**
× .738 = 29.52 **Jaime necesita cambiar $29.52 dólares (US).**

| **rista** | **está en** | **quiere comprar** | **cuesta** | **necesita $___ (US)** |
|---|---|---|---|---|
| gina | Venezuela | una raqueta | 9323 bolívares | ______ |
| niel | Argentina | un disco compacto | 14 pesos | ______ |
| istina | Colombia | una botella de agua | 2630 pesos | ______ |
| a | Ecuador | una libra de azúcar | 17200 sucres | ______ |
| cia | Japón | una falda azul | 25.50 yen | ______ |
| drés | España | una bicicleta verde | 24610 pesetas | ______ |

# Critical Thinking Strategies

*The numbers in parentheses on pages 446–448 refer to the chapter in which the strategy is found.*

## Analysis

*The separation of a whole into its identifiable parts*

### Analyzing

*Examining an object or an idea, studying it from every angle to see what it is, how it works, how many similarities and differences it has from other objects or ideas, and how its parts relate or fit together.*

*Analyzing (3, 7, 9, 13, 16, 17, 18)*
*Analyzing differences (7)*
*Analyzing degrees of commonality and difference (15)*

### Categorizing

*Organizing information into groups with similar qualities or attributes.*

*Categorizing (5, 8, 14, 17)*
*Classifying (3, 7)*

### Comparing and contrasting

*Looking for similarities and/or differences between ideas, people, places, objects, and situations.*

*Comparing and contrasting (1, 2, 3, 4, 5, 6, 7, 8, 9, 10, 11, 12, 13, 14, 16, 18)*
*Comparing and contrasting results from different samplings (5)*
*Distinguishing between different number sets (7)*

### Making associations

*Using an idea, person, event, or object to trigger the memory of another. Seeing relationships between two or more things.*

*Making associations (3, 4, 6, 7, 9, 10, 16, 18)*
*Associating personal likes and sports (16)*
*Associating possessions with activities (4)*

### Sequencing

*Arranging details in order according to specified criteria.*

*Sequencing (8, 11, 12)*

## Synthesis

*The combining of separate elements to form a unified, coherent whole*

### Drawing inferences

*Conjecturing logical, possible explanations or reasons for choices, actions, events, or situations.*

*Drawing inferences (3, 4, 18)*

### Hypothesizing

*Making an assertion as a basis for reasoning or argument*

*Hypothesizing (7)*

### Predicting

*Expecting behavior, actions, or events based on prior experience and/or available facts.*

*Predicting (1, 4, 5, 10, 11, 12, 13, 14, 15, 16, 17)*

### Seeing cause-and-effect relationships

*Anticipating a logical result from an action or event.*

*Seeing cause-and-effect relationships (6, 7, 9)*

### Synthesizing

*Pulling together pieces of information and ideas to create a new whole.*

*Synthesizing (4, 9)*

## Evaluation

*Determination of worth; judgment; appraisal.*

### Determining preferences

*Making personal value judgments.*

*Determining preferences (4, 5)*
*Expressing preferences (7, 16, 17, 18)*
*Expressing opinion (17)*

### Evaluating

*Determining worth; judging.*

*Evaluating (3, 4, 7, 9, 11, 12, 13, 14, 15, 16, 17, 18)*
*Evaluating based on personal taste (16)*
*Evaluating preferences (14)*
*Making judgments (2, 10)*

### Prioritizing

*Establishing precedence in order of importance or urgency; determining relative value.*

*Prioritizing (1, 4, 5, 8, 9, 10, 11, 12, 16, 17, 18)*

# Learning Strategies

# Reading Strategies

## Predicting

*When you predict, you use what you already know about a topic, person, or event. Using what you already know helps you make a logical prediction which, in turn, helps you to focus on the material you are reading. You make a prediction and then you read to check if your prediction is correct. (1, 2, 6, 10, 13, 17, 18; Unit 1, 2)*

## Previewing

*By looking over the whole reading before you start to read it, you begin to get a sense of what it may be about. There are several ways to do this.*

### Using the title to predict meaning

*Look at the title and ask yourself questions about it. Then predict answers to your questions. (1, 2, 3, 4, 5, 6, 7, 8, 9, 10, 12, 13, 14, 17; Unit 1, 5)*

### Activating background knowledge

*Recall what you already know about the topic. (1, 5, 8, 9, 11, 12, 14, 16, 17, 18; Unit 3, 6)*

### Using photos, art work, and illustrations to predict meaning

*Look at the pictures and predict what the reading is about. (1, 2, 3, 4, 5, 6, 7, 8, 9, 10, 11, 12, 13, 14, 15, 16, 17, 18; Unit 1, 3, 5)*

### Skimming

*Look quickly at the reading to get the gist of its content, determining what kind of text it is. It may be a description, a narration, a comparison, a characterization, etc. (2, 5, 6, 10, 12; Unit 1, 5, 6)*

### Scanning

*Look quickly for specific information, letting your eyes move quickly down the page. Don't worry about every word. Slow down when you see words or phrases that might be important to you. Look for clues in the text, such as names, dates, numbers, etc., to help you see what kind of information is being presented. (1, 4, 5, 6, 7, 8, 9, 10, 11, 12, 15, 16, 18; Unit 1, 3, 4, 5, 6)*

## Cognate recognition

*Cognates are words that look alike in two languages, for example,* ***hospital, universidad, moderno,*** *etc., shared by Spanish and English. There are cognates, however, whose meaning is not what it at first appears to be, for example* ***lectura*** *does not mean* lecture *but* reading. (3, 4, 7, 11, 14; Unit 2, 3, 5, 6)

## Finding main ideas

*Main ideas are the central or most important ideas contained in a reading. It may have many related ideas, but one or two ideas are usually the most important of all. (4, 12, 13, 18; Unit 2)*

## Using context to guess meaning

*Sometimes you can figure out the meaning of a difficult word by looking at the context, —the other words and expressions in the sentence or nearby sentences. Look at these cues to help you. (18; Unit 1, 2, 4, 6)*

## Paraphrasing

*When you paraphrase, you put information and ideas into your own words. If you stop and paraphrase while you are reading, you can check your comprehension as you go along. Paraphrasing after you finish reading is a good way to check your understanding and help you to remember ideas and information. (9, 15; Unit 2)*

## Taking notes in a chart

*Taking notes as you read helps you organize and remember important information. When you take notes, write down the most important information only. One type of chart you might use may have the main ideas in one column and the details in another column. (1; Unit 5)*

# Glossary of Functions

*The numbers in parentheses refer to the chapter in which the word or phrase may be found.*

**Greeting / taking leave of someone**

*¡Hola!* (1)
*Buenos días.* (1,2)
*Buenas tardes.* (1)
*Buenas noches.* (1)
*¿Cómo estás?* (1)
*¿Cómo está(n) Ud(s).?* (2)
*¿Cómo te va?* (1)
*¿Qué tal?* (1)
*Muy bien, gracias.* (1,2)
*Bien gracias. ¿Y tú?* (1)
*(Estoy) bien, gracias. ¿Y Ud.?* (2)
*Más o menos.* (1)
*Adiós.* (1)
*Chao.* (1)
*Hasta luego.* (1)
*Saludos a tus padres.* (2)

**Introducing someone**

*Te presento a…* (1)
*Quisiera presentarle(les) a…* (2)
*Mucho gusto.* (1)
*Encantado(a).* (2)
*Me llamo…* (4)
*Se llama…* (6)

**Being polite**

*Por favor…* (1)
*(Muchas) gracias.* (1)
*De nada.* (1)
*Sea(n) Ud(s). …* (8)
*Vaya(n) Ud(s). …* (8)

**Talking about preferences**

*(No) me / te / le / les / nos gusta(n).* (1,16)
*Me / te / le / les / nos encanta(n).* (16)
*¿Cuál quieres?* (17)
*¿Cuál prefieres?* (17)
*¿Qué te gusta más?* (5)
*Me gusta más…* (5)
*Prefiero…* (11)
*Sí, tengo ganas de…* (10,15)

**Ordering / taking orders for food or drink**

*Vamos al café.* (1)
*Vamos a tomar algo.* (1)
*¿Qué van a pedir?* (3)
*¿Qué desea(n) tomar?* (1)
*¿Y Ud.?* (1)
*Yo quisiera…* (1)
*Voy a comer…* (1)
*Para mí…* (1)
*Aquí tiene(n).* (1)
*¡Un refresco, por favor!* (1)

**Commenting about food**

*¡Qué bueno(a)!* (3)
*¡Qué comida más rica!* (3)
*¡Qué picante!* (3)
*¡Es riquísimo(a)!* (3)
*¡Es delicioso(a)!* (3)

**Identifying personal possessions**

*¿De quién es / son?* (4)
*Es / Son de…* (4)

**Getting information about other people**

*¿De dónde eres / es?* (3)
*¿Dónde vive?* (6)
*¿Cuántos(as)… ?* (6)
*¿Por qué… ?* (6)
*¿Qué… ?* (6)
*¿Quién… ?* (3,6)
*¿Cómo es / son?* (6)
*Está casado(a) con…* (6)
*¿Cuántos años tienes?* (7)
*Tiene… años.* (7)
*Vive en…* (4)
*Es de…* (3)
*Pregúntales a los otros.* (12)

**Expressing frequency / time**

*a menudo* (7)
*de vez en cuando* (7)
*en otra oportunidad* (7)

*nunca (7)*
*rara vez (7)*
*una vez al año (9)*
*algún día (12)*
*como de costumbre (11)*
*una vez (17)*
*cada domingo (6)*
*todos los días (6)*
*la semana entera (11)*
*por unos minutos (13)*
    *una hora (13)*
    *un día (13)*
    *dos meses (13)*
    *tres años (13)*

**Telling time**

*¿Qué hora es? (9)*
*¿A qué hora? (9)*
*¿Cuándo? (9)*
*a las cinco de la mañana (9)*
*a la una de la tarde (9)*
*desde… hasta… (9)*
*entre… y… (9)*
*al mediodía (9)*
*a la medianoche (9)*
*ahora (9)*

**Asking for / giving directions**

*¿Cómo llego a… ? (8)*
*¿Dónde está… ? (8)*
*¿Está lejos / cerca de aquí? (8)*
*Allí está… (3)*
*Cruce la calle… (8)*
*Doble a la derecha. (8)*
    *a la izquierda. (8)*
*Está al final de… (8)*
    *al lado de… (8)*
    *cerca de… (8)*
    *delante de… (8)*
    *detrás de… (8)*
    *entre… y… (8)*
    *en la esquina de… (8)*
    *frente a… (8)*
    *lejos de… (8)*
*Tome la calle… (8)*
*Siga derecho por… (8)*

**Making plans to go out / to go into town**

*¿Quieres ir conmigo? (10)*
*¿Para qué? (10)*
*Tengo que… (10)*
*¿Cuándo vamos? (10)*
*¿Cómo vamos? (12)*
*¿Adónde vamos? (7)*
*Vamos a dar un paseo. (10)*
    *hacer un mandado. (10)*
    *ir de compras. (10)*
    *ver a un amigo. (10)*
*Vamos en autobús. (10)*
    *a pie. (10)*
    *en bicicleta. (10)*
    *en coche. (10)*
    *en metro. (10)*
    *en taxi. (10)*
*Vamos hoy. (10)*
    *esta mañana / tarde / noche. (10)*
    *mañana. (10)*
    *mañana por la mañana. (10, 11)*
    *el sábado por la noche. (10, 11)*
*¿Cuánto tarda en llegar a… ? (12)*
*Tarda diez minutos, como máximo. (12)*

**Taking the subway**

*Por favor, un billete sencillo. (11)*
    *un billete de diez viajes. (11)*
    *un metrotour de tres días. (11)*
    *un metrotour de cinco días. (11)*
    *una tarjeta de abono transportes. (11)*
    *un plano del metro. (11)*
*¿Dónde hay una estación de metro? (11)*
*¿Dónde bajamos del tren? (11)*
*Bajamos en… (11)*
*Cambiamos en… (11)*
*¿En qué dirección… ? (11)*
*¿Qué dirección tomamos? (11)*
*una línea (11)*

**Making travel plans**

*Quiero planear un viaje. (12)*
*Aquí estoy para servirles. (12)*
*¿En qué puedo servirles? (12)*
*¿Cuánto cuesta un viaje de ida y vuelta? (12)*
    *en avión? (12)*
*Es mucho—sólo tengo… pesetas. (12)*
*Tengo que hacer las maletas. (13)*

**Talking about the past**

*el año pasado (13)*

*el mes pasado (13)*
*la semana pasada (13)*
*el fin de semana pasado (13)*
*el jueves pasado (13)*
*ayer por la mañana (13)*
*por la tarde (13)*
*ayer (13)*
*anoche (13)*
*anteayer (13)*
*¿Cuánto hace que (no te veo)? (14)*
*Hace (5 años) que (no te veo). (14)*
*(José,) (no te veo) hace (5 años). (14)*

**Talking about the present**

*Nos vamos ahora. (15)*
*ahora mismo. (15)*
*en este momento. (15)*
*Estoy comiendo (estudiando, etc.). (15)*

**Talking about the future**

*Pienso ir a... (11, 15)*
*Espero hacer un viaje a... (13)*
*Quiero... (15)*
*Quisiera... (15)*
*Tengo ganas de... (15)*
*Voy a... (7)*
*Vamos a ir de viaje esta semana. (11)*
*este año. (11)*
*este mes. (11)*
*la semana próxima. (11)*
*el mes próximo. (11)*
*el año próximo. (11)*
*mañana por la tarde. (10, 11)*

**Expressing wishes and desires**

*Quiero... (11, 15)*
*Tengo ganas de... (10, 15)*
*Espero... (12, 15)*
*Quisiera... (15)*

**Making purchases**

*¿Cuánto cuesta(n)? (16)*
*¿Qué precio tiene(n)? (16)*
*¿No está en oferta? (16)*
*A ver. (16)*
*¡Super! (16)*
*A sus órdenes. (16)*
*Aquí tiene(n). (16)*
*¿Cuántos hay? (4)*
*¿Dónde hay... ? (4)*
*Aquí hay otro(a)... (3)*
*No hay más. (16)*
*¡Qué pena! (16)*
*Voy a llevar... (16)*
*(Tiene Ud.) buen ojo. (17)*
*¿Qué necesita(n)? (16)*
*Necesito(amos) un atado de... (17)*
*una botella de... (17)*
*una docena de... (17)*
*50 gramos de... (17)*
*un (medio) kilo de... (17)*
*una libra de... (17)*
*un litro de... (17)*
*un paquete de... (17)*
*un pedazo de... (17)*
*¿Algo más? (16)*
*Es todo por hoy. (16)*

**Making comparisons**

*mayor que... (18)*
*peor que... (18)*
*mejor que... (18)*
*menor que... (18)*
*menos... que... (18)*
*más... que... (18)*
*tan / tanto... como... (18)*

**Expressing disbelief**

*¿Verdad? (2)*
*¿No? (2)*

**Making plans to meet**

*¿Dónde nos encontramos? (9)*
*¿A qué hora nos encontramos? (9)*
*De acuerdo. (9)*
*¡Claro (que sí)! (5, 10)*
*Sí, puedo. (10)*
*No, no puedo. (10)*
*Lo siento. (7)*
*Es imposible. (10)*

**Answering the telephone**

*¡Bueno! (7)*
*¡Hola! (7)*
*¡Diga! (7)*
*¡Dígame! (7)*

# Verb Charts

## Regular Verbs

### SIMPLE TENSES

| Infinitive | Present Indicative | Preterite | Commands |
|---|---|---|---|
| **hablar**<br>*to speak* | hablo<br>hablas<br>habla<br>hablamos<br>habláis<br>hablan | hablé<br>hablaste<br>habló<br>hablamos<br>hablasteis<br>hablaron | habla<br>(no hables)<br>hable<br>hablen |
| **vivir**<br>*to live* | vivo<br>vives<br>vive<br>vivimos<br>vivís<br>viven | viví<br>viviste<br>vivió<br>vivimos<br>vivisteis<br>vivieron | vive<br>(no vivas)<br>viva<br>vivan |

| Infinitive | Present Indicative | Preterite | Commands |
|---|---|---|---|
| **aprender**<br>*to learn* | aprendo<br>aprendes<br>aprende<br>aprendemos<br>aprendéis<br>aprenden | aprendí<br>aprendiste<br>aprendió<br>aprendimos<br>aprendisteis<br>aprendieron | aprende<br>(no aprendas)<br>aprenda<br>aprendan |

### COMPOUND TENSES

| | | | | | |
|---|---|---|---|---|---|
| *Present progressive* | estoy<br>estás<br>está | estamos<br>estáis<br>están | hablando | aprendiendo | viviendo |

## Stem-Changing Verbs

SIMPLE TENSES

| Infinitive<br>Present Participle<br>Past Participle | Present Indicative | Commands |
|---|---|---|
| pensar<br>*to think*<br>**e → ie**<br>pensando<br>pensado | **pienso**<br>**piensas**<br>**piensa**<br>pensamos<br>pensáis<br>**piensan** | **piensa**<br>**no pienses**<br>**piense**<br>**no penséis**<br>**piensen** |

## Change of Spelling Verbs

SIMPLE TENSES

| Infinitive<br>Present Participle<br>Past Participle | Present Indicative | Preterite | Infinitive<br>Present Participle<br>Past Participle | Present Indicative | Preterite | Infinitive<br>Present Participle<br>Past Participle | Preterite |
|---|---|---|---|---|---|---|---|
| comenzar<br>(e → ie)<br>*to begin*<br>**z → c**<br>**before e**<br>comenzando<br>comenzado | comienzo<br>comienzas<br>comienza<br>comenzamos<br>comenzáis<br>comienzan | **comencé**<br>comenzaste<br>comenzó<br>comenzamos<br>comenzasteis<br>comenzaron | pagar<br>*to pay*<br>**g → gu**<br>**before e**<br>pagando<br>pagado | pago<br>pagas<br>paga<br>pagamos<br>pagáis<br>pagan | **pagué**<br>pagaste<br>pagó<br>pagamos<br>pagasteis<br>pagaron | tocar<br>*to play*<br>**c → que**<br>**before e**<br>tocando<br>tocado | **toqué**<br>tocaste<br>tocó<br>tocamos<br>tocasteis<br>tocaron |

# Irregular Verbs

SIMPLE TENSES

| Infinitive<br>Present Participle<br>Past Participle | Preterite | Infinitive<br>Present Participle<br>Past Participle | Present Indicative | Preterite | Commands | Infinitive<br>Present Participle<br>Past Participle | Present Indicative | Preterite | Commands |
|---|---|---|---|---|---|---|---|---|---|
| andar<br>*to walk*<br>andando<br>andado | **anduve**<br>**anduviste**<br>**anduvo**<br>**anduvimos**<br>**anduvisteis**<br>**anduvieron** | estar<br>*to be*<br>estando<br>estado | **estoy**<br>**estás**<br>**está**<br>estamos<br>estáis<br>**están** | **estuve**<br>**estuviste**<br>**estuvo**<br>**estuvimos**<br>**estuvisteis**<br>**estuvieron** | **está (no estés)**<br>**esté**<br>**estén** | ir<br>*to go*<br>**yendo**<br>ido | **voy**<br>**vas**<br>**va**<br>**vamos**<br>**vais**<br>**van** | **fui**<br>**fuiste**<br>**fue**<br>**fuimos**<br>**fuisteis**<br>**fueron** | **ve (no vayas)**<br>**vaya**<br>id **(no vayáis)**<br>**vayan** |
| | | hacer<br>*to make, do*<br>haciendo<br>**hecho** | **hago**<br>haces<br>hace<br>hacemos<br>hacéis<br>hacen | **hice**<br>**hiciste**<br>**hizo**<br>**hicimos**<br>**hicisteis**<br>**hicieron** | **haz (no hagas)**<br>**haga**<br>**hagan** | | | | |

| Infinitive<br>Present Participle<br>Past Participle | Present Indicative | Infinitive<br>Present Participle<br>Past Participle | Present Indicative | Commands | Infinitive<br>Present Participle<br>Past Participle | Present Indicative | Preterite | Commands |
|---|---|---|---|---|---|---|---|---|
| poder<br>*can, to be able*<br>**pudiendo**<br>podido | **puedo**<br>**puedes**<br>**puede**<br>podemos<br>podéis<br>**pueden** | ser<br>*to be*<br>siendo<br>sido | **soy**<br>**eres**<br>**es**<br>**somos**<br>**sois**<br>**son** | **sé (no seas)**<br>**sea**<br>**sean** | tener<br>*to have*<br>teniendo<br>tenido | **tengo**<br>**tienes**<br>**tiene**<br>tenemos<br>tenéis<br>tienen | **tuve**<br>**tuviste**<br>**tuvo**<br>**tuvimos**<br>**tuvisteis**<br>**tuvieron** | **ten (no tengas)**<br>**tenga**<br>tened **(no tengáis)**<br>**tengan** |
| querer<br>*to like*<br>queriendo<br>querido | **quiero**<br>**quieres**<br>**quiere**<br>queremos<br>queréis | | | | | | | |

## Spanish-English

*The numbers in parentheses refer to the chapters in which active words or phrases may be found.*

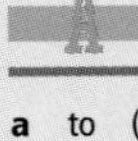


**a** to (1)
**a menudo** frequently, often (7)
**a pesar de** in spite of
**a pie** on foot, walking (10)
**¿A qué hora?** At what time? (9)
**a veces** sometimes (1)
**A ver.** Let's see. (16)
**al** to the (7)
**al lado de** beside, next to (8)
**abrigo** *m.* coat (18)
**abogado(a)** *m. (f.)* lawyer (3)
**abuela** *f.* grandmother (6)
**abuelo** *m.* grandfather (6)
**aburrido(a)** bored, boring (6)
**acabar de...** to have just . . . (2)
**acción** *f.* action (15)
**aceite** *m.* oil (17)
**aceite de oliva** *m.* olive oil
**aceituna** *f.* olive (2)
**acontecimiento** *m.* event
**¡adelante!** go ahead!
**además** besides (17)
**adiós** good-bye (1)
**adivino(a)** *m. (f.)* fortune-teller
**¿adónde?** where? (7)
**aeropuerto** *m.* airport (7)
**aficionado(a)** *m. (f.)* (sports) fan
**agua** *f.* water (1)
**ahora** now (9)
**ahora mismo** right now (15)
**alcanzar** to reach
**alemán (alemana)** *m. (f.)* German (3)
**Alemania** Germany (3)
**alfombra** *f.* rug, carpet (4)
**algo** something (1)
**alguno(a)** some, any
**algún día** someday (12)
**alimento** *m.* food (17)
**alpinismo** *m.* mountain climbing; hiking (14)
**alquilar un vídeo** to rent a video (13)
**alrededor** around
**alto(a)** tall (6)
**alumno(a)** *m. (f.)* student (4)
**allá** over there (17)
**allí** there (4)
**amarillo(a)** yellow (17)
**americano(a)** *m. (f.)* American (3)
**amigo(a)** *m. (f.)* friend (2)
**andar** to go along, walk (13)
**animal** *m.* animal (5)
**anoche** last night (13)
**antes** before
**antipático(a)** disagreeable (6)
**anunciar** to announce (9)
**anuncio** *m.* advertisement
**año** *m.* year (14)
**apartamento** *m.* apartment (4)
**apellido** *m.* last name (6)
**aprender** to learn (5)
**aquel(la)** that (17)
**aquél(la)** *m. (f.)* that one (17)
**aquí** here (4)
**Argentina** Argentina (3)
**argentino(a)** *m. (f.)* Argentine (3)
**arquitecto(a)** *m. (f.)* architect (3)
**arroz** *m.* rice (3)
**arte** *m.* or *f.* art (5)
**asistir a** to attend (13)
**atado** *m.* bunch (17)
**atún** *m.* tuna (17)
**aunque** although
**autobús** *m.* bus (4)
**estación de autobuses** *m.* bus terminal (7)
**ave** *f.* bird, fowl
**avión** *m.* plane (12)
**ayer** yesterday (13)
**ayudar** to help
**azúcar** *m.* sugar (17)

### B

**bailar** to dance (1)
**baile** *m.* dance (9)
**baile folklórico** *m.* folk dance (9)
**baile popular** *m.* popular dance (9)
**bajar** to go down, to lower (11)
**bajo(a)** short (6), *prep.* under
**banana** *f.* banana (17)
**banco** *m.* bank (7)
**barato(a)** cheap (16)
**barco** *m.* boat
**barrio** *m.* neighborhood (7)
**barro** *m.* clay
**básquetbol** *m.* basketball (5)
**bastante** enough
**Bastante bien.** Pretty good. (1)
**batalla** *f.* battle
**bebida** *f.* drink (1)
**béisbol** *m.* baseball (5)
**belleza** *f.* beauty
**beso** *m.* kiss (5)
**biblioteca** *f.* library (7)
**bicicleta** *f.* bicycle (4)
**bien** well, fine; very (1)
**billete** *m.* ticket (11)
**billete de diez viajes** *m.* ten-trip ticket (11)
**billete de ida y vuelta** *m.* round-trip ticket (12)
**billete sencillo** *m.* one-way ticket (11)
**biología** *f.* biology (5)
**blusa** *f.* blouse (18)
**bocadillo** *m.* sandwich (French bread) (1)
**bolígrafo** *m.* ball point pen (4)
**Bolivia** Bolivia (3)
**boliviano(a)** *m. (f.)* Bolivian (3)
**bolsa** *f.* purse (18)
**bonito(a)** pretty (6)
**borrador** *m.* eraser (4)
**bota** *f.* boot (18)
**botella** *f.* bottle (17)
**boutique** *f.* boutique (18)
**bucear** to snorkel, dive (14)
**buceo** *m.* snorkeling, diving (14)
**bueno(a)** good, well (1)
**Buenas noches.** Good evening. / Good night. (1)
**Buenas tardes.** Good afternoon. (1)

**¡Bueno!** Hello! (answering the phone) (7)
  **Buenos días.** Good morning. (1)
**burbuja** *f.* bubble
**buscar** to look for (14)

## C

**caballo** *m.* horse
**cacahuete** *m.* peanut (2)
**cada** each, every (17)
**caer** to fall
**café** *m.* café, coffee (1)
**calamares** *m.* squid (2)
**calcetín** *m.* sock (18)
**calculadora** *f.* calculator (4)
**calidad** *f.* quality
**caliente** hot (3)
**calle** *f.* street (8)
**cama** *f.* bed (4)
**cámara** *f.* camera (4)
**camarero(a)** *m. (f.)* waiter (waitress) (1)
**cambiar** to change (11)
**cambio** *m.* change, alteration (12)
**caminar** to walk (13)
  **caminar en la playa** to walk on the beach (14)
**camisa** *f.* shirt (18)
**camiseta** *f.* T-shirt (18)
**campaña** *f.* campaign
**campo** *m.* country (vs. city)
**Canadá** Canada (3)
**canadiense** *m.* or *f.* Canadian (3)
**canción** *f.* song
**cansado(a)** tired (9)
**cantante** *m.* or *f.* singer
**cantar** to sing (1)
**cantidad** *f.* quantity (17)
**carne** *f.* meat (3)
**carnicería** *f.* butcher shop (7)
**caro(a)** expensive (16)
**carrera** *f.* career
**carril-bici** *m.* bike path
**carrito** *m.* shopping cart (17)
**carta** *f.* letter
**cartera** *f.* wallet (4)
**casa** *f.* house (4)
**casado(a)** married (6)
**casi** almost
**catedral** *f.* cathedral (7)
**cazar** to hunt
**cebolla** *f.* onion (17)
**celebrar** to celebrate (9)
**cenar** to have supper (13)
**centro** *m.* center (16)
  **centro comercial** shopping center (16)
**cerca (de)** near, close to (8)
**cerrar** to close
**¡Chao!** Good-bye! (1)
**chaqueta** *f.* jacket (18)
**charlar** to chat (1)
**chico(a)** *m. (f.)* boy (girl)
**chile** *m.* hot pepper (3)
**Chile** Chile (3)
**chileno(a)** *m. (f.)* Chilean (3)
**China** China (3)
**chino(a)** *m. (f.)* Chinese (3)
**chocolate** *m.* chocolate (1)
**chorizo** *m.* sausage (2)
**ciclismo** *m.* cycling (14)
**cien** one hundred (7)
**ciencia** *f.* science (5)
**ciento** a hundred (12)
**cincuenta** fifty (7)
**cine** *m.* movie theater (7)
**cinta** *f.* tape (cassette) (4)
**cinturón** *m.* belt (18)
**cita** *f.* date, appointment (10)
**ciudad** *f.* city
**¡Claro!** Of course! (5)
  **¡Claro que sí!** Of course!! (reaffirmed) (10)
**club** *m.* club (7)
**coche** *m.* car (4)
**cola** *f.* tail
**colegio** *m.* school (7)
**Colombia** Colombia (3)
**colombiano(a)** *m. (f.)* Colombian (3)
**comedor** *m.* dining room
**comentar** to comment (3)
**comentario** *m.* commentary
**comer** to eat (1)
**comida** *f.* meal (1)
  **comida mexicana** Mexican food (3)
**como** how, as, like (11)
  **como de costumbre** as usual (11)
**¿cómo?** how?, what? (1)
  **¿Cómo es? / son?** How is it / are they? (6)
  **¿Cómo está Ud.?** How are you? (formal) (2)
  **¿Cómo estás?** How are you? (informal) (1)
  **¿Cómo te llamas?** What's your name? (4)
  **¿Cómo te va?** How is it going? (1)
**cómoda** *f.* dresser (4)
**compañía** *f.* company (3)
**comparación** *f.* comparison (18)
**compartir** to share (5)
**comprar** to buy (13)
**comprender** to understand (5)
**computadora** *f.* computer (4)
**concierto** *m.* concert (13)
**concurso de poesía** *m.* poetry contest (9)
**congelado(a)** frozen (17)
**conmigo** with me (10)
**conserva** *f.* preserve, canned good (17)
**construir** to build
**contador(a)** *m. (f.)* accountant (3)
**contar** to tell, to count
**contento(a)** happy (9)
**contestar** to answer (1)
**continuar** to continue (9)
**contra** against
**conversación telefónica** *f.* telephone conversation (7)
**corazón** *m.* heart
**correr** to run (5)
**corto** short (in length)
**cosa** *f.* thing (11)
**Costa Rica** Costa Rica (3)
**costarricense** *m. or f.* Costa Rican (3)
**costumbre** *f.* custom
**crema** *f.* cream (17)
**croissant** *m.* croissant (1)
**cruzar** to cross (8)
**cuaderno** *m.* notebook (4)
**cuadrado** *m.* square
**¿cuál?** which? (17)
**cualquier** any (13)
**¿cuántos(as)?** how many? (6)
  **¿Cuántos años tienes?** How old are you? (7)
  **¿Cuánto cuesta(n)?** How much is it (are they)? (16)
  **¿Cuántos hay?** How many are there? (4)
**cuarenta** forty (7)
**cuarto** *m.* room (4)
**cuatrocientos(as)** four hundred (12)
**Cuba** Cuba (3)
**cubano(a)** *m. (f.)* Cuban (3)
**cuero** *m.* leather (18)
**cuerpo** *m.* body

## D

**de** of (3)

**de acuerdo** OK (we are in agreement) (9)

**¿De dónde es (eres)?** Where are you from? (3)

**de la / del** of the (8)

**de nada** you're welcome (3)

**¿De quién es… ?** Whose is it? (4)

**de vez en cuando** from time to time (7)

**deber** to owe, must, should (10)

**decir** to say (10)

**dejar** to leave, to relinquish

**delante de** in front of (8)

**delgado(a)** thin (6)

**delicioso(a)** delicious (3)

**demás** rest, remaining

**dentista** *m.* or *f.* dentist (3)

**dentro** inside

**deporte** *m.* sport (5)

**deportista** sportsman, sportswoman

**derecha** right (8)

**desahogar** to ease pain

**desayunar** to eat breakfast (13)

**desayuno** *m.* breakfast (1)

**descansar** to rest (9)

**desconocido(a)** unknown

**desde** from (9)

**desear** to want, wish for (1)

**desempleo** *m.* unemployment

**desfile** *m.* parade (9)

**desierto** *m.* desert

**despacio** slow (8)

**despedirse** to say good-bye (1)

**después** after (1)

**detrás de** behind (8)

**día** *m.* day (14)

**Día de la Independencia** *m.* Independence Day (9)

**dibujo** *m.* drawing

**dibujos animados** animated film, cartoon

**¡Diga! / ¡Dígame!** Hello! (answering the phone) (7)

**dinero** *m.* money (2)

**disco compacto** *m.* compact disc (4)

**discoteca** *f.* discotheque (7)

**disculparse** to apologize (7)

**discutir** to argue (12)

**disfrutar** to enjoy

**divertido(a)** fun, amusing (6)

**divorciado(a)** divorced (6)

**doblar** to turn (8)

**docena** *f.* dozen (17)

**doctor(a)** *m. (f.)* doctor (3)

**domingo** *m.* Sunday (10)

**dominicano(a)** *m. (f.)* Dominican (3)

**¿dónde?** where? (6)

**¿Dónde está… ?** Where is . . . ? (8)

**¿Dónde hay… ?** Where is / are there . . . ? (4)

**doscientos(as)** two hundred (12)

**dueño(a)** *m. (f.)* owner

## E

**Ecuador** Ecuador (3)

**ecuatoriano(a)** *m. (f.)* Ecuadoran (3)

**edad** *f.* age (7)

**edificio** *m.* building (7)

**ejemplo** *m.* example

**por ejemplo** for example

**el** *m.* the (2)

**él** he (2)

**El Salvador** El Salvador (3)

**ella** she (2)

**ellos(as)** *m. (f.)* they (2)

**embajador(a)** *m. (f.)* ambassador, ambassadress

**empezar** to begin

**en** in (1)

**en este momento** at this moment (15)

**en otra oportunidad** at some other time (7)

**¿En qué dirección?** In which direction? (11)

**¿En qué puedo servirle(s)?** How can I help you (plural)? (12)

**encantado(a)** delighted (2)

**enchilada** *f.* soft, corn tortilla filled with cheese, meat, or chicken (3)

**encontrar** to find (9)

**encuesta** *f.* survey (12)

**enemigo(a)** *m. (f.)* enemy

**enfermero(a)** *m. (f.)* nurse (3)

**enfermo(a)** sick (9)

**enojado(a)** angry, mad (9)

**ensalada** *f.* salad (17)

**ensalada de frutas** *f.* fruit salad (17)

**ensalada de vegetales (verduras)** *f.* vegetable salad (17)

**entero** whole (11)

**entonces** then (9)

**entrada** *f.* entrance ticket (11)

**entre** between (8)

**equipo** *m.* team

**escaparate** *m.* shop window (16)

**escribir** to write (5)

**escrito** written

**escritorio** *m.* desk (4)

**escuchar** to listen (to) (1)

**escuela** *f.* school (4)

**escuela secundaria** *f.* high school (7)

**escultura** *f.* sculpture (5)

**ese(a)** that (17)

**ése(a)** *m. (f.)* that one (17)

**espacio** *m.* space

**España** Spain (3)

**español(a)** *m. (f.)* Spaniard, Spanish (3)

**especia** *f.* spice

**especial** special (11)

**especie** *f.* species

**esperar** to hope, to wait (12)

**espíritu** *m.* spirit

**esposa** *f.* wife (6)

**esposo** *m.* husband (6)

**esquema** *m.* chart, diagram

**esquí** *m.* ski (16)

**esquí acuático** *m.* water ski (14)

**esquina** *f.* corner (8)

**en la esquina de** on the corner of (8)

**esta** this (11)

**ésta** this one (3)

**establecer** to establish (18)

**estación** *f.* station (7)

**estadio** *m.* stadium (7)

**Estados Unidos** United States (3)

**estadounidense** *m.* or *f.* American, from the United States (3)

**estante** *m.* book shelf (4)

**estar** to be (8)

**Está a(l) final de…** It's at the end of . . . (8)

**estar en forma** to be in shape

**este(a)** this (17)

**éste(a)** *m. (f.)* this one (17)

**estéreo** *m.* stereo (4)

**estrella** *f.* star

**estudiante** *m.* or *f.* student (3)

**estudiar** to study (1)

**etapa** *f.* stage, phase

**éxito** *m.* success

**expresar** to express (1)

**expresión** *f.* expression (6)

**fácil** easy

**falda** *f.* skirt (18)
**familia** *f.* family (6)
**famoso(a)** famous (12)
**farmacia** *f.* pharmacy, drugstore (7)
**favorito(a)** favorite (16)
**feo(a)** ugly, plain (6)
**feria** *f.* fair (9)
**fiesta** *f.* party (9)
**Fiesta del pueblo** *f.* religious festival honoring a town's patron saint (9)
**fin de semana** *m.* weekend (10)
**finalmente** finally (14)
**firmar** to sign
**flan** *m.* caramel custard (3)
**flecha** *f.* arrow
**florería** *f.* flower shop (7)
**francés (francesa)** *m. (f.)* French (3)
**Francia** France (3)
**frecuentemente** frequently (10)
**frente a** across from, facing (8)
**fresa** *f.* strawberry (17)
**fresco(a)** cool (17)
**frío(a)** cold
**frijoles** *m.* beans (3)
**fruta** *f.* fruit (17)
**fuegos artificiales** *m.* fireworks (9)
**fuerza** *f.* strength
**fútbol** *m.* soccer (5)
**fútbol americano** *m.* football (5)
**futuro** *m.* future (15)

## G

**gafas** *f. pl.* eyeglasses
**galleta** *f.* biscuit, cookie (17)
**ganar** to earn (2)
**garaje** *m.* garage (3)
**gastar** to spend, to waste
**gato** *m.* cat (5)
**gente** *f.* people
**gimnasio** *m.* gym (13)
**globo** *m.* globe, sphere, balloon (1)
**gordo(a)** fat (6)
**grabadora** *f.* tape recorder (4)
**gracia** *f.* grace
**gracias** thank you (1)
**la misa de Acción de Gracias** *f.* Thanksgiving Day mass (9)
**gramo** *m.* gram (17)
**granadina** *f.* grenadine (1)
**gratis** free
**grupo** *m.* group (1)
**guapo(a)** handsome (6)
**Guatemala** Guatemala (3)
**guatemalteco(a)** *m. (f.)* Guatemalan (3)
**guisante** *m.* pea (17)
**guitarra** *f.* guitar (14)
**gustar** to like (5)
**gusto** *m.* taste (5)
**con mucho gusto** with pleasure (1)

## H

**habilidad** *f.* ability
**hablar** to talk (1)
**hacer** to do, to make (9)
**hacer la cama** to make the bed (13)
**hacer ejercicio** to exercise (13)
**hacer las maletas** to pack (13)
**hacer un mandado** to do an errand (10)
**hacer un viaje** to take a trip (13)
**hamburguesa** *f.* hamburger (3)
**harina** *f.* flour (17)
**hasta** until (17)
**Hasta luego.** See you later. (1)
**hay** there is / are (4)
**helado** *m.* ice cream (17)
**hermana** *f.* sister (6)
**hermano** *m.* brother (6)
**hermoso(a)** beautiful (12)
**hija** *f.* daughter (6)
**hijo** *m.* son (6)
**hispano(a)** *m. (f.)* Hispanic (9)
**historia** *f.* history, story
**hoja** *f.* leaf, piece of paper (16)
**¡Hola!** Hello! (1)
**hombre** *m.* man (3)
**Honduras** Honduras (3)
**hondureño(a)** *m. (f.)* Honduran (3)
**hora** *f.* hour (9)
**horario** *m.* schedule (11)
**horrible** horrible (3)
**hospital** *m.* hospital (7)
**hotel** *m.* hotel (7)
**hoy** today (10)

## I

**ida y vuelta** round trip
**iglesia** *f.* church (7)
**igual** equal
**igualdad** *f.* equality (18)
**impermeable** *m.* raincoat (18)
**imposible** impossible (10)
**indígena** native
**ingeniero(a)** *m. (f.)* engineer (3)
**Inglaterra** England (3)
**inglés (inglesa)** *m. (f.)* English (3)
**inteligente** intelligent (6)
**interesante** interesting (6)
**invierno** *m.* winter
**invitación** *f.* invitation (12)
**ir** to go (7)
**ir a...** to be going to . . . (10)
**ir de camping** to go camping (14)
**ir de compras** to go shopping (10)
**ir de pesca** to go fishing (14)
**Vamos a...** Let's go . . . (1)
**Italia** Italy (3)
**italiano(a)** *m. (f.)* Italian (3)
**izquierda** left (8)

## J

**jamón** *m.* ham (1)
**Japón** Japan (3)
**japonés (japonesa)** *m. (f.)* Japanese (3)
**jazz** *m.* jazz (5)
**joven** young (18)
**joya** *f.* jewel
**jueves** *m.* Thursday (10)
**jugador(a)** *m. (f.)* player
**jugar** to play (a sport or game) (11)
**jugar al baloncesto** to play basketball (14)
**jugar al hockey** to play hockey (14)
**jugar al hockey sobre hierba** to play field hockey (14)
**jugar al golf** to play golf (14)
**jugo** *m.* juice (1)
**juguete** *m.* toy
**junto** together (17)
**juventud** *f.* youth

## K

**kilo** *m.* kilogram (17)
**medio kilo** half kilo (17)
**kilómetro** *m.* kilometer (17)

## L

**la** *f.* the (4)
**lácteo(a)** dairy (17)
**producto lácteo** *m.* dairy product (17)

**lápiz** *m.* pencil (4)
**largo** long
**las** *f.* the (plural) (4)
**lata** *f.* can, tin (17)
**leche** *f.* milk (1)
**lechuga** *f.* lettuce (17)
**leer** to read (5)
**lejos (de)** far (from) (8)
**lengua** *f.* language, tongue (5)
**levantar pesas** to lift weights (14)
**leyenda** *f.* legend
**libra** *f.* pound (17)
**librería** *f.* bookstore (7)
**libro** *m.* book (4)
**licuado** *m.* milkshake (1)
**limón** *m.* lemon (17)
**limonada** *f.* lemonade (1)
**línea** *f.* line (11)
**listo(a)** ready (9)
**litro** *m.* liter (17)
**llamarse** to be called (4)
  **Me llamo...** My name is . . . (4)
  **Se llama...** His or her name is . . . (6)
**llave** *f.* key (4)
**llegar** to arrive (8)
**lleno(a)** full (17)
**llevar** to take, carry (4)
**llover** to rain
**los** *m.* the (plural) (4)
**luchar** to fight
**luego** then, afterwards (14)
**lugar** *m.* place, location (7)
**lunes** *m.* Monday (10)
**luz** *f.* light

**madre** *f.* mother (6)
**maíz** *m.* corn (17)
**mal** poorly (1)
**malo(a)** bad (6)
**mantener** to maintain
**mantequilla** *f.* butter (1)
**manzana** *f.* apple (17)
**mañana** *f.* morning, tomorrow (10)
**martes** *m.* Tuesday (10)
**máquina** *f.* machine (4)
  **máquina de escribir** *f.* typewriter (4)
**más** more (1)
  **más o menos** so-so (1)
  **más... que** more . . . than (18)
**mayonesa** *f.* mayonnaise (17)
**mayor** older (18)
**mayoría** *f.* majority
**mecánico(a)** *m. (f.)* mechanic (3)
**media** *f.* stocking (18)
**medianoche** *f.* midnight (9)
**médico** *m.* doctor (3)
**medio(a)** half (17)
**medio** *m.* middle, means (4)
  **medio de transporte** *m.* means of transportation (4)
**mediodía** *m.* midday (9)
**mejor** better (9)
**melocotón** *m.* peach (1)
**menor** younger (18)
**menos... que** less . . . than (18)
**mercado** *m.* market (7)
  **mercado al aire libre** *m.* open-air market (17)
**merienda** *f.* snack (1)
**mermelada** *f.* jelly (1)
**mes** *m.* month (14)
**metro** *m.* subway (11)
  **estación de metro** *f.* subway station (11)
**mexicano(a)** *m. (f.)* Mexican (3)
**México** Mexico (3)
**mi(s)** my (plural) (4)
**mí** me (1)
**mientras** in the meantime
**miércoles** *m.* Wednesday (10)
**mil** thousand (12)
**milla** *f.* mile (12)
**millón** *m.* million (12)
**minuto** *m.* minute (14)
**mirar** to look at, to watch (2)
  **¡Mira!** Look! (3)
**mismo(a)** same
**mitad** *f.* half
**mochila** *f.* knapsack (4)
**moda** *f.* style (18)
**moderno(a)** modern (18)
**montar en bicicleta** to ride a bicycle (13)
**moreno(a)** *m. (f.)* dark-haired, brunet(te) (6)
**morir** to die
**motocicleta** *f.* motorcycle (4)
**muchísimo** very much (1)
**mucho(a)** a lot (1)
  **Muchas gracias.** Thank you very much. (1)
  **Mucho gusto.** Nice to meet you. (1)
**muerte** *f.* death
**mujer** *f.* woman (3)
**mundo** *m.* world
**museo** *m.* museum (7)
**música** *f.* music (5)
  **música clásica** *f.* classical music (5)
  **música rock** *f.* rock music (5)
**muy** very (1)
  **Muy bien, gracias.** Very well, thank you. (1)

**nacer** to be born
**nacionalidad** *f.* nationality (3)
**nada** nothing (13)
**nadar** to swim (13)
**nadie** nobody
**naranja** *f.* orange (17)
**natación** *f.* swimming (14)
**naturaleza** *f.* nature (5)
**necesitar** to need (2)
**negocio** *m. (f.)* business (3)
  **hombre (mujer) de negocios** *m. (f.)* businessman (businesswoman) (3)
**Nicaragua** Nicaragua (3)
**nicaragüense** *m. or f.* Nicaraguan (3)
**niña** *f.* girl, baby
**niño** *m.* boy, baby
**nivel** *m.* level
**no** no (1)
**noche** *f.* night (9)
**nombre** *m.* name (6)
**norte** *m.* north
**norteamericano(a)** *m. (f.)* North American (3)
**nosotros(as)** *m. (f.)* we (1)
**novecientos(as)** nine hundred (12)
**noventa** ninety (7)
**nuestro(a)** our (4)
**nuevo(a)** new (12)
**número** *m.* number (7)
**nunca** never (7)

**o** or (12)
**ochenta** eighty (7)
**ochocientos(as)** eight hundred (12)
**oferta** *f.* sale (16)
  **¿No está(n) en oferta?** It's not on sale? (16)
**oficina de correos** *f.* post office (7)
**ofrecer** to offer (17)

**ojo** *m.* eye
**orden** *m.* order (12)
  **a sus órdenes** at your service (12)
**oreja** *f.* ear
**oro** *m.* gold
**otro(a)** other (11)
  **otra cosa** *f.* another thing (11)

## P

**padre** *m.* father (6)
  **padres** *m.* parents (6)
**pagar** to pay (12)
**país** *m.* country (8)
**paisaje** *m.* landscape
**pájaro** *m.* bird (5)
**palabra** *f.* word
**pan** *m.* bread (2)
  **pan dulce** *m.* any kind of sweet roll (1)
  **pan tostado** *m.* toast (1)
**panadería** *f.* bakery (7)
**Panamá** Panama (3)
**panameño(a)** *m. (f.)* Panamanian (3)
**pantalones** *m.* trousers (18)
**papa** *f.* potato (17)
**papel** *m.* paper (16)
  **papel de avión** *m.* air mail stationery (16)
  **papel para escribir a máquina** *m.* typing paper (16)
**papelería** *f.* stationery store (16)
**paquete** *m.* package (17)
**para** for, in order to (9)
  **para que** in order that
**Paraguay** Paraguay (3)
**paraguayo(a)** *m. (f.)* Paraguayan (3)
**parque** *m.* park (7)
  **parque zoológico** *m.* zoo (13)
**pasar** to pass (17)
  **pasar tiempo** to pass time (13)
**paseo** *m.* walk (10)
  **dar un paseo** to take a walk (10)
**pasta** *f.* pasta (17)
**pastel** *m.* pastry, pie (1)
**patata** *f.* potato (2)
  **patatas bravas** *f.* cooked potatoes diced and served in spicy sauce (2)
**patinar** to skate (14)
  **patinar en ruedas** to roller skate (14)
**pedazo** *m.* piece (17)
**pedir** to ask for (something), to request (8)
**peine** *m.* comb
**película** *f.* film, movie (5)
  **película cómica** *f.* comedy movie (5)
  **película de aventura** *f.* adventure movie (5)
  **película de ciencia ficción** *f.* science fiction movie (5)
  **película de horror** *f.* horror movie (5)
**peligro** *m.* danger
**peligroso(a)** dangerous
**pelirrojo(a)** redheaded (6)
**pelota** *f.* ball (16)
  **pelota de tenis** *f.* tennis ball (16)
**pendiente** *m.* earring
**pensar** to think (11)
**peor** worse, worst (18)
**pequeño(a)** small (6)
**pera** *f.* pear (17)
**perder** to lose (13)
**perdón** excuse me (8)
**periodista** *m. or f.* journalist (3)
**pero** but (1)
**perro** *m.* dog (5)
**perseguir** to persecute, to pursue
**persona** *f.* person (6)
**Perú** Peru (3)
**peruano(a)** *m. (f.)* Peruvian (3)
**a pesar de** in spite of
**pescado** *m.* fish (17)
**picante** spicy (3)
**piedra** *f.* stone
**pimienta** *f.* pepper (17)
**pintura** *f.* painting (5)
**piscina** *f.* swimming pool (7)
**planear** to plan (12)
**plano del metro** *m.* subway map (11)
**planta** *f.* plant, floor (4)
**plata** *f.* silver
**plato** *m.* dish
**playa** *f.* beach (12)
**playa de estacionamiento** *f.* parking lot (8)
**plaza** *f.* plaza, square (7)
**pluma** *f.* fountain pen (4), feather
**poco** a little (1)
**poder** to be able to (10)
**policía** *f.* police, *m.* or *f.* police officer (7)
  **estación de policía** *f.* police station (7)
**política** *f.* politics (5)
**pollo** *m.* chicken (3)
**por** for (11)
  **por eso** that is why (16)
  **por fin** finally (14)
  **por la mañana** in the morning (11)
  **por la noche** at night (11)
  **por la tarde** in the afternoon (11)
  **por supuesto** of course (9)
**¿por qué?** why? (6)
**porque** because (6)
**portafolio** *m.* briefcase (4)
**posesión** *f.* possession (4)
**póster** *m.* poster (4)
**practicar** to practice (1)
  **practicar el surfing** to surf (14)
  **practicar la vela** to sail (14)
**precio** *m.* price (16)
**preferencia** *f.* preference (17)
**preferir** to prefer (7)
**preguntar** to ask a question (9)
**premio** *m.* prize (9)
**preocupar** to preoccupy, to worry
**presentación** *f.* presentation, introduction (2)
**presentar** to present, introduce (1)
**primero** first (7)
**primo(a)** *m. (f.)* cousin (6)
**producto** *m.* product (17)
**profesión** *f.* profession (3)
**profesor(a)** *m. (f.)* professor, teacher (3)
**pronto** soon
**propina** *f.* tip (12)
**proteger** to protect
**próximo(a)** next (10)
**prueba** *f.* test
**pueblo** *m.* town
**Puerto Rico** Puerto Rico (3)
**puertorriqueño(a)** *m. (f.)* Puerto Rican (3)
**pues** then (1)

## Q

**que** that (1)
**¿qué?** what? (6)
  **¿Qué día es hoy?** What day is today? (10)
  **¿Qué hay?** What's new? (1)
  **¿Qué hora es?** What time is it? (9)
  **¿Qué pasó?** What's going on? (1)
  **¿Qué tal?** How are you? (1)
**¡Qué... !** How . . . ! (3)
  **¡Qué bueno(a)!** Great! (3)
  **¡Qué comida más rica!** What delicious food! (3)

    **¡Qué horrible!** How terrible! (3)
    **¡Qué pena!** What a pity! (16)
**quemado(a)** burned
**quemar** to burn
**quedar** to stay (8)
**querer** to want (7)
    **Yo quisiera...** I would like . . . (1)
**queso** *m.* cheese (1)
**¿quién?** who? (3)
**química** *f.* chemistry (5)
**quinientos(as)** five hundred (12)
**quiosco de periódicos** *m.* newspaper kiosk (8)

## R

**radio despertador** *m.* clock radio (4)
**raqueta** *f.* racket (16)
**rara vez** rarely (7)
**razón** *f.* reason
**rebanada de pan** *f.* slice of bread (1)
**receta** *f.* recipe
**recibir** to receive (5)
**recordar** to remember
**recuerdo** *m.* memory (3)
**refresco** *m.* soft drink (1)
**regalo** *m.* gift
**regatear** to bargain (17)
**regresar** to return
**reina** *f.* queen
**repaso** *m.* review (3)
**República Dominicana** Dominican Republic (3)
**restaurante** *m.* restaurant (1)
**revista** *f.* magazine
**rey** *m.* king
**riquísimo(a)** delicious (3)
**rojo(a)** red (17)
**ropa** *f.* clothes
    **ropa de marca** *f.* designer clothes
**rubio(a)** blond(e) (6)
**ruido** *m.* noise
**Rusia** Russia (3)
**ruso(a)** *m. (f.)* Russian (3)

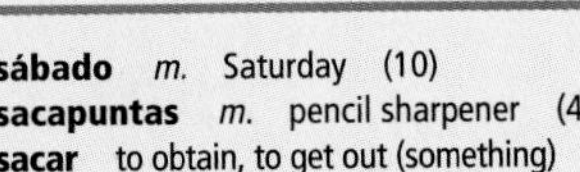

## S

**sábado** *m.* Saturday (10)
**sacapuntas** *m.* pencil sharpener (4)
**sacar** to obtain, to get out (something) (14)
**sal** *f.* salt (17)
**salir (de)** to go out, leave (13)

**salir con** to go out with (13)
**salsa** *f.* sauce, type of music (3)
**salud** *f.* health
**saludar** to greet (2)
**saludo** *m.* greeting (2)
**salvadoreño(a)** *m. (f.)* Salvadoran (3)
**sandalia** *f.* sandal (18)
**sándwich** *m.* sandwich (1)
**secretario(a)** *m. (f.)* secretary (3)
**seguir** to follow, to continue
**segundo(a)** second
**seguro(a)** sure (18)
**seiscientos(as)** six hundred (12)
**semana** *f.* week (14)
**sentido** *m.* sense
**sentir** to feel
    **Lo siento.** I'm sorry. (7)
**señor** *m.* Mr. (1)
**señora** *f.* Mrs. (1)
**señorita** *f.* Miss (1)
**ser** to be (3)
    **Es de...** Is from . . . , It belongs to . . . (4)
    **Es la una y media.** It is 1:30. (9)
    **Son de...** They are from . . . , They belong to . . . (4)
    **Son las tres.** It is 3 o'clock. (9)
**serie** *f.* series, sequence (14)
**serio(a)** serious (6)
**servir** to serve (12)
**sesenta** sixty (7)
**setecientos(as)** seven hundred (12)
**setenta** seventy (7)
**si** if (12)
**sí** yes (1)
**siempre** always (1)
**silla** *f.* chair (4)
**simpático(a)** nice (6)
**sin** without
**sin límite** unlimited (11)
**sino** but
**sobre** *m.* envelope (16)
**sobre** *prep., adv.* above
**soda** *f.* soda (1)
**sol** *m.* sun
**su(s)** his, her, your, their (4)
**subir** to raise
**suerte** *f.* fortune, luck
**suéter** *m.* sweater (18)
**suficiente** enough (16)
**¡Super!** Super! (16)
**sur** *m.* south
**suroeste** *m.* southwest

## T

**taco** *m.* taco, corn tortilla filled with meat and other things (3)
**también** also (2)
**tampoco** neither (2)
**tan** so (8)
    **tan / tanto... como** as / as much . . . as (18)
**tapa española** *f.* Spanish snack (2)
**taquilla** *f.* booth (11)
**tarde** *f.* afternoon, late (9)
**tarjeta** *f.* card (16)
    **tarjeta de abono transportes** *f.* commuter pass (11)
    **tarjeta de cumpleaños** *f.* birthday card (16)
    **tarjeta del Día de la Madre** *f.* Mother's Day card (16)
**taxi** *m.* taxi (7)
**té** *m.* tea (1)
**teatro** *m.* theatre (7)
**teléfono** *m.* telephone (7)
**televisor (a colores)** *m.* (color) television set (4)
**temer** to fear
**temporada** *f.* (sports) season
**tener** to have (6)
    **tener... años** to be . . . years old (7)
    **tener ganas de...** to feel like . . . (10)
    **tener hambre** to be hungry (7)
    **tener que** to have to (6)
    **tener sed** to be thirsty (7)
**tenis** *m.* tennis (5)
**tercero(a)** third
**terminar** to end
**terremoto** *m.* earthquake
**tía** *f.* aunt (6)
**tiempo** *m.* time (14)
    **tiempo libre** *m.* free time
**tienda** *f.* store (7)
    **tienda de deportes** *f.* sporting goods store (16)
    **tienda de música** *f.* music store (16)
    **tienda de ropa** *f.* clothing store (18)
**tierra** *f.* earth
**tío** *m.* uncle (6)
**tocar** to touch, to play an instrument (2)
    **te toca a ti** it's your turn
**todavía** still
**todo(a)** all (9)
    **todos los días** *m.* every day (1)

**tomar** to drink, to take (1)
**tomar el sol** to sunbathe (14)
**tomate** *m.* tomato (17)
**tonto(a)** silly, stupid, foolish (6)
**torre** *f.* tower
**tortilla** *f.* omelette (Spain) or cornmeal pancake (Mexico) (3)
**trabajador(a)** *m. (f.)* worker
**trabajar** to work (1)
**trabajo** *m.* work
**traer** to bring
**tratar de** to try, to endeavor
**tren** *m.* train (7)
**estación de trenes** train station (7)
**trescientos(as)** three hundred (12)
**triste** sad (9)
**tú** you (familiar) (1)
**tu(s)** your (plural) (4)
**turista** *m.* or *f.* tourist (11)

## U

**un(a)** a, an (1)
**universidad** *f.* university (7)
**uno** one (2)
**Uruguay** Uruguay (3)
**uruguayo(a)** *m. (f.)* Uruguayan (3)
**usted (Ud.)** you (formal) (1)
**ustedes (Uds.)** you (formal plural) (1)
**usualmente** usually (10)
**útil** useful
**uva** *f.* grape (17)

## V

**valiente** brave
**valor** *m.* value
**vaqueros** *m.* jeans
**varios(as)** various (17)
**vaso** *m.* glass (1)
**vegetal** *m.* vegetable (17)
**veinte** twenty (7)
**vendedor(a)** *m. (f.)* salesman (woman) (17)
**vender** to sell (5)
**venezolano(a)** *m. (f.)* Venezuelan (3)
**Venezuela** Venezuela (3)
**venir** to come (7)
**venta** *f.* sale
**ver** to see (9)
**Nos vemos.** See you. (farewell) (1)
**¿verdad?** right? (2)
**verdadero(a)** true, real
**verde** green (17)
**vestido** *m.* dress (18)
**vestir** to dress
**vez** *f.* time, instance (9)
**una vez** once (17)
**una vez al año** once a year (9)
**vía** *f.* (railway) track
**viajar** to travel (1)
**viaje** *m.* trip (12)
**agencia de viajes** *f.* travel agency (12)
**vida** *f.* life (13)
**vídeo** *m.* video (16)
**videocasetera** *f.* videocassette player (4)
**viejo(a)** old (6)
**viernes** *m.* Friday (10)
**visitar** to visit (7)
**vista** *f.* sight
**vivir** to live (5)
**vólibol** *m.* volleyball (5)
**volver** to go back (13)
**vosotros(as)** *m. (f.)* you (familiar plural) (1)
**voz** *f.* voice

## W

**waterpolo** *m.* waterpolo (14)
**windsurf** *m.* windsurfing (14)

## Y

**y** and (1)
**yo** I (1)
**yogur** *m.* yogurt (17)

## Z

**zanahoria** *f.* carrot (17)
**zapatería** *f.* shoe store (18)
**zapato** *m.* shoe (18)
**zapato de tacón** *m.* high-heeled shoe (18)
**zapato de tenis** *m.* tennis shoe (16)

## English-Spanish

*The numbers in parentheses refer to the chapters in which the words or phrases may be found.*

ability **habilildad** *f.*
(to be) able to **poder** (10)
above **sobre**
accountant **contador(a)** *m. (f.)* (3)
across from **frente a** (8)
action **acción** *f.* (15)
adventure movie **película de aventura** *f.* (5)
advertisement **anuncio** *m.*
after **después** (1)
afternoon **tarde** *f.*
afterwards **luego** (14)
against **contra**
age **edad** *f.* (7)
air mail stationery **papel de avión** *m.* (16)
airport **aeropuerto** *m.* (7)
all **todo(a)** (9)
almost **casi**
also **también** (2)
alteration **cambio** *m.* (12)
although **aunque**
always **siempre** (1)
ambassador **embajador** *m.*
American **americano(a)** *m. (f.)* (3), (from the United States) **estadounidense** *m.* or *f.* (3)
amusing **divertido(a)** (6)
and **y** (1)
angry **enojado(a)** (9)
animal **animal** *m.* (5)
(to) announce **anunciar** (9)
another **otro(a)** (11)
  another thing **otra cosa** *f.* (11)
(to) answer **contestar** (1)
any **cualquier** (13)
apartment **apartamento** *m.* (4)
(to) apologize **disculparse** (7)
apple **manzana** *f.* (17)
appointment **cita** *f.* (10)
architect **arquitecto(a)** *m. (f.)* (3)
Argentina **Argentina** (3)
Argentine **argentino(a)** *m. (f.)* (3)
(to) argue **discutir** (12)
around **alrededor**
(to) arrive **llegar** (8)
arrow **flecha** *f.*
art **arte** *m.* or *f.* (5)
as **como** (11)
  as / as much . . . as **tan / tanto... como** (18)
  as usual **como de costumbre** (11)
(to) ask a question **preguntar** (9)
(to) ask for (something) **pedir** (8)
at **a** (1)
  at night **por la noche** (11)
  at some other time **en otra oportunidad** (7)
  at this moment **en este momento** (15)
  At what time? **¿A qué hora?** (9)
  at your service **a sus órdenes** (12)
(to) attend **asistir a** (13)
aunt **tía** *f.* (6)

bad **malo(a)** (6)
bakery **panadería** *f.* (7)
ball **pelota** *f.* (16)
balloon **globo** *m.* (1)
banana **banana** *f.* (17)
bank **banco** *m.* (7)
(to) bargain **regatear** (17)
baseball **béisbol** *m.* (5)
basketball **básquetbol** *m.* (5); **baloncesto** *m. (14)*
battle **batalla** *f.*
(to) be **estar** (8), **ser** (3)
  to be in shape **estar en forma**
beach **playa** *f.* (12)
beans **frijoles** *m.* (3)
beautiful **hermoso(a)** (12)
beauty **belleza** *f.*
because **porque** (6)
bed **cama** *f.* (4)
before **antes**
(to) begin **empezar**
behind **detrás de** (8)
belt **cinturón** *m.* (18)
beside **al lado de** (8)
besides **además** (17)
better **mejor** (9)
between **entre** (8)
bicycle **bicicleta** *f.* (4)
bike path **carril-bici** *m.*
biology **biología** *f.* (5)
bird **pájaro** *m.* (5), **ave** *f.*
birthday card **tarjeta de cumpleaños** *f.* (16)
biscuit **galleta** *f.* (17)
blond(e) **rubio(a)** (6)
blouse **blusa** *f.* (18)
boat **barco** *m.*
body **cuerpo** *m.*
Bolivia **Bolivia** (3)
Bolivian **boliviano(a)** *m. (f.)* (3)
book **libro** *m.* (4)
bookshelf **estante** *m.* (4)
bookstore **librería** *f.* (7)
boot **bota** *f.* (18)
booth **taquilla** *f.* (11)
bored, boring **aburrido(a)** (6)
(to) be born **nacer**
bottle **botella** *f.* (17)
boutique **boutique** *f.* (18)
boy **chico** *m.*, **niño** *f.*
brave **valiente**
bread **pan** *m.* (2)
  bread, slice of **rebanada de pan** *f.* (1)
breakfast **desayuno** *m.* (1)
briefcase **portafolio** *m.* (4)
(to) bring **traer**
brother **hermano** *m.* (6)
brunet(te) **moreno(a)** (6)
(to) build **construir**
building **edificio** *m.* (7)
bunch **atado** *m.* (17)
(to) burn **quemar**
burned **quemado(a)**

bus **autobús** *m.* (4)
  bus terminal **estación de autobuses** *m.* (7)
business **negocio** *m.* (3)
businessman(woman) **hombre (mujer) de negocios** (3)
but **pero**
butcher shop **carnicería** *f.* (7)
butter **mantequilla** *f.* (1)
(to) buy **comprar** (13)

café **café** *m.* (1)
calculator **calculadora** *f.* (4)
(to be) called **llamarse** (4)
camera **cámara** *f.* (4)
can **lata** *f.* (17)
Canada **Canadá** (3)
Canadian **canadiense** *m.* or *f.* (3)
canned good **preserva** *f.* (17)
car **coche** *m.* (4)
card **tarjeta** *f.* (16)
career **carrera** *f.*
carpet **alfombra** *f.* (4)
carrot **zanahoria** *f.* (17)
(to) carry **llevar** (4)
cat **gato** *m.* (5)
cathedral **catedral** *f.* (7)
(to) celebrate **celebrar** (9)
center **centro** *m.* (16)
chair **silla** *f.* (4)
change **cambio** *m.* (12)
(to) change **cambiar** (11)
chart **esquema** *m.*
(to) chat **charlar** (1)
cheap **barato(a)** (16)
cheese **queso** *m.* (2)
chemistry **química** *f.* (5)
chicken **pollo** *m.* (3)
Chile **Chile** (3)
Chilean **chileno(a)** *m. (f.)* (3)
China **China** (3)
Chinese **chino(a)** *m. (f.)* (3)
chocolate **chocolate** *m.* (1)
church **iglesia** *f.* (7)
city **ciudad** *f.*
classical music **música clásica** *f.* (5)
clay **barro** *m.*
clock radio **radio despertador** *m.* (4)
close (to) **cerca (de)** (8)
(to) close **cerrar**
clothes **ropa** *f.*
  designer clothes **ropa de marca**
clothing store **tienda de ropa** *f.* (18)
club **club** *m.* (7)
coat **abrigo** *m.* (18)
coffee **café** *m.* (1)
cold **frío(a)**
Colombia **Colombia** (3)
Colombian **colombiano(a)** *m. (f.)* (3)
comb **peine** *m.*
(to) come **venir** (7)
(to) comment **comentar** (3)
commentary **comentario** *m.*
commuter pass **tarjeta de abono transportes** *f.* (11)
compact disc **disco compacto** *m.* (4)
company **compañía** *f.* (3)
comparison **comparación** *f.* (18)
computer **computadora** *f.* (4)
concert **concierto** *m.* (13)
(to) continue **continuar** (9), **seguir**
cookie **galleta** *f.* (17)
cool **fresco(a)** (17)
corn **maíz** *m.* (17)
corner **esquina** *f.* (8)
cornmeal pancake (Mexico) **tortilla** *f.* (3)
Costa Rica **Costa Rica** (3)
Costa Rican **costarricense** *m.* or *f.* (3)
country **país** *m.* (8), (vs. city) **campo** *m.*
cousin **primo(a)** *m. (f.)* (6)
cream **crema** *f.* (17)
croissant **croissant** *m.* (1)
(to) cross **cruzar** (8)
Cuba **Cuba** (3)
Cuban **cubano(a)** *m. (f.)* (3)
custard, caramel **flan** *m.* (3)
custom **costumbre** *f.*
cycling **ciclismo** *m.* (14)

## D

dairy **lácteo(a)** (17)
  dairy product **producto lácteo** *m.* (17)
dance **baile** *m.* (9)
(to) dance **bailar** (1)
danger **peligro** *m.*
dangerous **peligroso(a)**
date **cita** *f.* (10)
daughter **hija** *f.* (6)
day **día** *m.* (14)
death **muerte** *f.*
delicious **delicioso(a), riquísimo** (3)
delighted **encantado(a)** (2)
dentist **dentista** *m.* or *f.* (3)
desert **desierto** *m.*
desk **escritorio** *m.* (4)
(to) die **morir**
dining room **comedor** *m.*
disagreeable **antipático(a)** (6)
discotheque **discoteca** *f.* (7)
dish **plato** *m.*
divorced **divorciado(a)** (6)
(to) do **hacer** (9)
  (to) do an errand **hacer un mandado** (10)
doctor **médico** *m.*, **doctor(a)** *m. (f.)* (3)
dog **perro** *m.* (5)
Dominican **dominicano(a)** *m. (f.)* (3)
Dominican Republic **República Dominicana** (3)
dozen **docena** *f.* (17)
drawing **dibujo** *m.*
dress **vestido** *m.* (18)
(to) dress **vestir**
dresser **cómoda** *f.* (4)
drink **bebida** *f.* (1)
(to) drink **tomar** (1)
drugstore **farmacia** *f.* (7)

each **cada** (17)
ear **oreja** *f.*
(to) earn **ganar** (2)
earring **pendiente** *m.*
earth **tierra** *f.*
earthquake **terremoto** *m.*
(to) ease pain **desahogar**
easy **fácil**
(to) eat **comer** (1)
  (to) eat breakfast **desayunar**
Ecuador **Ecuador** (3)
Ecuadoran **ecuatoriano(a)** *m. (f.)* (3)
eight hundred **ochocientos(as)** (12)
eighty **ochenta** (7)
El Salvador **El Salvador** (3)
(to) end **terminar**
enemy **enemigo(a)** *m. (f.)*
engineer **ingeniero(a)** *m. (f.)* (3)
England **Inglaterra** (3)

English **inglés (inglesa)** *m. (f.)* (3)
(to) enjoy **disfrutar**
enough **suficiente** (16), **bastante**
entrance ticket **entrada** *f.* (11)
envelope **sobre** *m.* (16)
equal **igual**
equality **igualdad** *f.* (18)
eraser **borrador** *m.* (4)
(to) establish **establecer** (18)
event **acontecimiento** *m.*
every **cada** (17)
 every day **todos los días** *m.* (1)
example **ejemplo** *m.*
 for example **por ejemplo**
excuse me **perdón** (8)
to exercise **hacer ejercicio** (13)
expensive **caro(a)** (16)
(to) express **expresar** (1)
expression **expresión** *f.* (6)
eye **ojo** *m.*
eyeglasses **gafas** *f. pl.*

## F

facing **frente a** (8)
fair **feria** *f.* (9)
to fall **caer**
family **familia** *f.* (6)
famous **famoso(a)** (12)
fan (person) **aficionado(a)** *m. (f.)*
far (from) **lejos (de)** (8)
fat **gordo(a)** (6)
father **padre** *m.* (6)
favorite **favorito(a)** (16)
(to) fear **temer**
(to) feel **sentir**
 (to) feel like . . . **tener ganas de...** (10)
festival (religious) honoring a town's patron saint **Fiesta del pueblo** *f.* (9)
field hockey **hockey sobre hierba** *m.* (14)
fifty **cincuenta** (7)
(to) fight **luchar**
film **película** *f.* (5)
finally **finalmente, por fin** (14)
(to) find **encontrar** (9)
fine **bien** (1)
fireworks **fuegos artificiales** *m.* (9)
first **primero** (7)
fish **pescado** *m.* (17)
five hundred **quinientos(as)** (12)
floor **planta** *f.* (4)
flour **harina** *f.* (17)
flower shop **florería** *f.* (7)
folk dance **baile folklórico** *m.* (9)
food **alimento** *m.* (17), **comida** *f.* (3)
foolish **tonto(a)** (6)
football **fútbol americano** *m.* (5)
for **para** (9), **por** (11)
fortune **suerte** *f.*
fortune-teller **adivino(a)** *m. (f.)*
forty **cuarenta** (7)
four hundred **cuatrocientos(as)** (12)
France **Francia** (3)
free **gratis**
French **francés (francesa)** *m. (f.)* (3)
frequently **a menudo** (7), **frecuentemente** (10)
Friday **viernes** *m.* (10)
friend **amigo(a)** *m. (f.)* (2)
from **de, desde** (9)
 from time to time **de vez en cuando** (7)
frozen **congelado(a)** (17)
fruit **fruta** *f.* (17)
 fruit salad **ensalada de frutas** *f.* (17)
full **lleno(a)** (17)
fun **divertido(a)** (6)
future **futuro** *m.* (15)

## G

garage **garaje** *m.* (3)
German **alemán (alemana)** *m. (f.)* (3)
Germany **Alemania** (3)
(to) get out (something) **sacar** (14)
gift **regalo** *m.*
girl **chica** *f.*, **niña** *f.*
glass **vaso** *m.* (1)
globe **globo** *m.* (1)
(to) go **ir** (7)
 go ahead! **¡adelante!**
 (to) go along **andar** (13)
 (to) go back **volver** (13)
 (to) go camping **ir de camping** (14)
 (to) go down **bajar** (11)
 (to) go fishing **ir de pesca** (14)
 (to) go out **salir (de)** (13)
 (to) go shopping **ir de compras** (10)
 (to be) going to . . . **ir a...** (10)
gold **oro** *m.*
good **bueno(a)** (1)
 Good afternoon. **Buenas tardes.** (1)
 Good evening. **Buenas noches.** (1)
 Good morning. **Buenos días.** (1)
 Good night. **Buenas noches.** (1)
good-bye **adiós, chao** (1)
grace **gracia** *f.*
gram **gramo** *m.* (17)
grandfather **abuelo** *m.* (6)
grandmother **abuela** *f.* (6)
grape **uva** *f.* (17)
Great! **¡Qué bueno(a)!** (3)
green **verde** (17)
(to) greet **saludar** (2)
greeting **saludo** *m.* (2)
grenadine **granadina** *f.* (1)
group **grupo** *m.* (1)
Guatemala **Guatemala** (3)
Guatemalan **guatemalteco(a)** *m. (f.)* (3)
guitar **guitarra** *f.* (14)
gym **gimnasio** *m.* (13)

## H

half **medio(a)** (17), **mitad** *f.*
 half kilo **medio kilo** (17)
ham **jamón** *m.* (1)
hamburger **hamburguesa** *f.* (3)
handsome **guapo(a)** (6)
happy **contento(a)** (9)
(to) have **tener** (6)
 (to) have just . . . **acabar de...** (2)
 (to) have supper **cenar** (13)
 (to) have to **tener que** (6)
he **él** (2)
health **salud** *f.*
heart **corazón** *m.*
Hello! **¡Hola!** (1)
 Hello! (answering the phone) **¡Bueno!, ¡Diga! / ¡Dígame!** (7)
(to) help **ayudar**
her **su(s)** (4)
here **aquí** (4)
high-heeled shoe **zapato de tacón** *m.* (18)
high school **escuela secundaria** *f.* (7)
his **su(s)** (4)
Hispanic **hispano(a)** *m. (f.)* (9)
Honduran **hondureño(a)** *m. (f.)* (3)
Honduras **Honduras** (3)
(to) hope **esperar** (12)
horrible **horrible** (3)

horse **caballo** *m.*
hospital **hospital** *m.* (7)
hot **caliente** (3)
hot pepper **chile** *m.* (3)
hotel **hotel** *m.* (7)
hour **hora** *f.* (14)
house **casa** *f.* (4)
how **como** (11)
  how? **¿cómo?** (1)
  How are you? **¿Qué tal?** (1)
  How are you? (formal) **¿Cómo está Ud.?** (2), (informal) **¿Cómo estás?** (1)
  How can I help you (plural)? **¿En qué puedo servirle(s)?** (12)
  How is it / are they? **¿Cómo es / son?** (6)
  How is it going? **¿Cómo te va?** (1)
  how many? **¿cuántos(as)?** (6)
  How many are there? **¿Cuántos hay?** (4)
  How much is it (are they)? **¿Cuánto cuesta(n)?** (16)
  How old are you? **¿Cuántos años tienes?** (7)
  How . . . ! **¡Qué… !** (3)
  How terrible! **¡Qué horrible!** (3)
hundred **cien** (7), **ciento** (12)
(to be) hungry **tener hambre** (7)
(to) hunt **cazar**
husband **esposo** *m.* (6)

## I

I **yo** (1)
ice cream **helado** *m.* (17)
if **si** (12)
impossible **imposible** (10)
in **en** (1)
  in front of **delante de** (8)
  in order to **para** (9)
  in order that **para que**
  in the afternoon **por la tarde** (11)
  in the meantime **mientras**
  in the morning **por la mañana** (11)
  In which direction? **¿En qué dirección?** (11)
Independence Day **Día de la Independencia** *m.* (9)
inside **dentro**
instance **vez** (7)
intelligent **inteligente** (6)
interesting **interesante** (6)
(to) introduce **presentar** (1)
introduction **presentación** *f.* (2)
invitation **invitación** *f.* (12)
It belongs to . . . **Es de…** (4)
It is 3 o'clock. **Son las tres.** (9)
It is 1:30. **Es la una y media.** (9)
It's at the end of . . . **Está a(l) final de…** (8)
It's not on sale? **¿No está(n) en oferta?** (16)
Italian **italiano(a)** *m. (f.)* (3)
Italy **Italia** (3)

## J

jacket **chaqueta** *f.* (18)
Japan **Japón** (3)
Japanese **japonés (japonesa)** *m. (f.)* (3)
jazz **jazz** *m.* (5)
jeans **vaqueros** *m.*
jelly **mermelada** *f.* (1)
jewel **joya** *f.*
journalist **periodista** *m.* or *f.* (3)
juice **jugo** *m.* (1)

key **llave** f. (4)
kilogram **kilo** *m.* (17)
kilometer **kilómetro** *m.* (17)
king **rey** *m.*
kiss **beso** *m.* (5)
knapsack **mochila** *f.* (4)

landscape **paisaje** *m.*
language **lengua** *f.* (5)
late **tarde** (9)
lawyer **abogado(a)** *m. (f.)* (3)
leaf **hoja** *f.* (16)
(to) learn **aprender** (5)
leather **cuero** *m.* (18)
(to) leave **salir (de)** (13)
leave (something) **dejar**
left **izquierda** (8)
legend **leyenda** *f.*
lemon **limón** *m.* (17)
lemonade **limonada** *f.* (1)
less . . . than **menos… que** (18)
Let's go . . . **Vamos …** (1)
Let's see. **A ver.** (16)
letter **carta** *f.*
lettuce **lechuga** *f.* (17)
level **nivel** *m.*
library **biblioteca** *f.* (7)
life **vida** *f.* (13)
(to) lift weights **levantar pesas** (14)
like **como** (11)
(to) like **gustar** (5)
line **línea** *f.* (11)
(to) listen **escuchar** (1)
liter **litro** *m.* (17)
little, a **poco(a)** (1)
(to) live **vivir** (5)
location **lugar** *m.* (7)
long **largo**
Look! **¡Mira!** (3)
  (to) look at **mirar** (2)
  (to) look for **buscar** (14)
(to) lose **perder** (13)
lot, a **mucho(a)** (1)
(to) lower **bajar** (11)
luck **suerte)** *f.*

machine **máquina** *f.* (4)
mad **enojado(a)** (9)
magazine **revista** *f.*
(to) maintain **mantener**
majority **mayoría** *f.*
(to) make **hacer** (9)
  (to) make the bed **hacer la cama** (13)
man **hombre** *m.* (3)
market **mercado** *m.* (7)
married **casado(a)** (6)
mayonnaise **mayonesa** *f.* (17)
me **mí** (1)
meal **comida** *f.* (1)
means of transportation **medio de transporte** *m.* (4)
meat **carne** *f.* (3)
mechanic **mecánico(a)** *m. (f.)* (3)
memory **recuerdo** *m.*
Mexican **mexicano(a)** *m. (f.)* (3)
  Mexican food **comida mexicana** (3)
Mexico **México** (3)
midday **mediodía** *m.* (9)
middle **medio** *m.* (4)
midnight **medianoche** *f.* (9)
mile **milla** *f.* (12)
milk **leche** *f.* (1)
milkshake **licuado** *m.* (1)
million **millón** (12)

minute **minuto** *m.* (14)
Miss **señorita** *f.* (1)
modern **moderno(a)** (18)
Monday **lunes** *m.* (10)
money **dinero** *m.* (2)
month **mes** *m.* (14)
more **más** (1)
more . . . than **más... que** (18)
morning **mañana** *f.* (10)
mother **madre** *f.* (6)
  Mother's Day card **tarjeta del Día de la Madre** *f.* (16)
motorcycle **motocicleta** *f.* (4)
mountain **montaña** *f.*
  mountain climbing **alpinismo** *m.* *(14)*
movie **película** *f.* (5)
  movie, comedy **película cómica** *f.* (5)
  movie, horror **película de horror** *f.* (5)
  movie theater **cine** *m.* (7)
Mr. **señor** *m.* (1)
Mrs. **señora** *f.* (1)
much **mucho** (1)
  very much **muchísimo** (1)
museum **museo** *m.* (7)
music **música** *f.* (5)
music store **tienda de música** (16)
must **deber** (10)
my **mi(s)** (4)

name **nombre** *m.* (6)
  last name **apellido** *m.* (6)
(to be) named **llamarse** (4)
nationality **nacionalidad** *f.* (3)
native **indígena**
nature **naturaleza** *f.* (5)
near **cerca (de)** (8)
(to) need **necesitar** (2)
neighborhood **barrio** *m.* (7)
neither **tampoco** (2)
never **nunca** (7)
new **nuevo(a)** (12)
newspaper kiosk **quiosco de periódicos** *m.* (8)
next **próximo(a)** (10)
  next to **al lado de** (8)
Nicaragua **Nicaragua** (3)
Nicaraguan **nicaragüense** *m.* or *f.* (3)
nice **simpático(a)** (6)
  Nice to meet you. **Mucho gusto.** (1)
night **noche** *f.* (9)
  last night **anoche** (13)
nine hundred **novecientos(as)** (12)
ninety **noventa** (7)
no **no** (1)
nobody **nadie**
noise **ruido** *m.*
north **norte** *m.*
North American **norteamericano(a)** *m. (f.)* (3)
notebook **cuaderno** *m.* (4)
nothing **nada** (13)
now **ahora** (9)
number **número** *m.* (7)
nurse **enfermero(a)** *m. (f.)* (3)

(to) obtain **sacar** (14)
of **de** (3)
  of the **de la / del** (8)
of course **por supuesto** (9)
  Of course! **¡Claro!** (5)
  Of course!! (reaffirmed) **¡Claro que sí!** (10)
(to) offer **ofrecer** (17)
often **a menudo** (7)
oil **aceite** *m.* (17)
OK **de acuerdo** (9)
old **viejo(a)** (6)
older **mayor** (18)
olive **aceituna** *f.* (2)
  olive oil **aceite de oliva** *m.*
omelette (Spain) **tortilla** *f.* (3)
on **en** (1)
  on foot **a pie** (10)
  on the corner of **en la esquina de** (8)
once **una vez** (17)
  once a year **una vez al año** (9)
one **un(a)** (1), **uno** (2)
one hundred **ciento** (12)
onion **cebolla** *f.* (17)
open-air market **mercado al aire libre** *m.* (17)
or **o** (12)
orange **naranja** *f.* (17)
order **orden** *m.* (12)
other **otro(a)** (11)
our **nuestro(a)** (4)
over there **allá** (17)
(to) owe **deber** (10)
owner **dueño(a)** *m. (f.)*

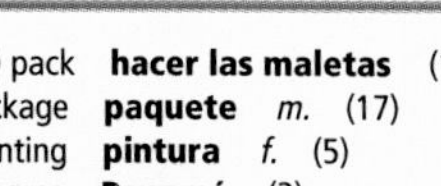

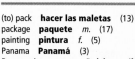

(to) pack **hacer las maletas** (13)
package **paquete** *m.* (17)
painting **pintura** *f.* (5)
Panama **Panamá** (3)
Panamanian **panameño(a)** *m. (f.)* (3)
pants **pantalones** *m.* (18)
paper **papel** *m.* (16)
  piece of paper **hoja** *f.* (16)
parade **desfile** *m.* (9)
Paraguay **Paraguay** (3)
Paraguayan **paraguayo(a)** *m. (f.)* (3)
(to) pardon **disculpar** (7)
parents **padres** *m.* (6)
park **parque** *m.* (7)
parking lot **playa de estacionamiento** *f.* (8)
party **fiesta** *f.* (9)
(to) pass **pasar** (17)
  (to) pass time **pasar tiempo** (13)
pasta **pasta** *f.* (17)
pastry **pastel** *m.* (1)
(to) pay **pagar** (12)
pea **guisante** *m.* (17)
peach **melocotón** *m.* (1)
peanut **cacahuete** *m.* (2)
pear **pera** *f.* (17)
pen, ball point **bolígrafo** *m.* (4)
pen, fountain **pluma** *f.* (4)
pencil **lápiz** *m.* (4)
  pencil sharpener **sacapuntas** *m.* (4)
people **gente** *f.*
pepper **pimienta** *f.* (17)
to persecute **perseguir**
person **persona** *f.* (6)
Peru **Perú** (3)
Peruvian **peruano(a)** *m. (f.)* (3)
pharmacy **farmacia** *f.* (7)
pie **pastel** *m.* (1)
piece **pedazo** *m.* (17)
place **lugar** *m.* (7)
plain **feo(a)** (6)
(to) plan **planear** (12)
plane **avión** *m.* (12)
plant **planta** *f.* (4)
(to) play (a sport or game) **jugar** (11)
  (to) play basketball **jugar al baloncesto** (14)
  (to) play field hockey **jugar al hockey sobre hierba** (14)
  (to) play golf **jugar al golf** (14)
  (to) play hockey **jugar al hockey** (14)

(to) play (an instrument) **tocar** (2)
player **jugador(a)** *m. (f.)*
plaza **plaza** *f.* (7)
poetry contest **concurso de poesía** *m.* (9)
police **policía** *f.* (7)
police officer **policía** *m.* or *f.* (7)
police station **estación de policía** *f.* (7)
politics **política** *f.* (5)
pool **piscina** *f.* (7)
poorly **mal** (1)
popular dance **baile popular** *m.* (9)
possession **posesión** *f.* (4)
post office **oficina de correos** *f.* (7)
poster **póster** *m.* (4)
potato **papa** *f.* (17), **patata** *f.* (2)
potatoes: cooked, diced, and served in spicy sauce **patatas bravas** *f.* (2)
pound **libra** *f.* (17)
(to) practice **practicar** (1)
(to) prefer **preferir** (7)
preference **preferencia** *f.* (17)
(to) present **presentar** (1)
presentation **presentación** *f.* (2)
preserve **conserva** *f.* (17)
pretty **bonito(a)** (6)
Pretty good. **Bastante bien.** (1)
price **precio** *m.* (16)
prize **premio** *m.* (9)
product **producto** *m.* (17)
profession **profesión** *f.* (3)
professor **profesor(a)** *m. (f.)* (3)
(to) protect **proteger**
Puerto Rican **puertorriqueño(a)** *m. (f.)* (3)
Puerto Rico **Puerto Rico** (3)
purse **bolsa** *f.* (4)

## Q

quality **calidad** *f.* (3)
quantity **cantidad** *f.* (17)
queen **reina** *f.*

## R

racket **raqueta** *f.* (16)
(to) rain **llover**
raincoat **impermeable** *m.* (18)
(to) raise **subir**
rarely **rara vez** (7)
(to) reach **alcanzar**
(to) read **leer** (5)
ready **listo(a)** (9)
reason **razón** *f.*
(to) receive **recibir** (5)
recipe **receta** *f.*
red **rojo(a)** (17)
redhead **pelirrojo(a)** (6)
remember **recordar**
(to) rent a video **alquilar un vídeo** (13)
(to) request **pedir** (8)
(to) rest **descansar** (9)
restaurant **restaurante** *m.* (1)
(to) return **regresar**
review **repaso** *m.*
rice **arroz** *m.* (3)
(to) ride a bicycle **montar en bicicleta** (13)
right **derecha** (8)
right? **¿verdad?** (2)
right now **ahora mismo** (15)
rock music **música rock** *f.* (5)
(to) roller-skate **patinar en ruedas** (14)
room **cuarto** *m.* (4)
round-trip ticket **billete de ida y vuelta** *m.* (12)
rug **alfombra** *f.* (4)
(to) run **correr** (5)
Russia **Rusia** (3)
Russian **ruso(a)** *m. (f.)* (3)

## S

sad **triste** (9)
(to) sail **practicar la vela** (14)
salad **ensalada** *f.* (17)
sale **oferta** *f.* (16), **venta** *f.*
salesman(woman) **vendedor(a)** *m. (f.)* (17)
salt **sal** *f.* (17)
Salvadoran **salvadoreño(a)** *m. (f.)* (3)
same **mismo(a)**
sandal **sandalia** *f.* (18)
sandwich **sándwich** *m.* (1), (French bread) **bocadillo** *m.* (1)
Saturday **sábado** *m.* (10)
sauce **salsa** *f.* (3)
sausage **chorizo** *m.* (2)
(to) say **decir** (10)
(to) say good-bye **despedirse** (1)
schedule **horario** *m.* (11)
school **colegio** *m.* (7), **escuela** *f.* (4)
science **ciencia** *f.* (5)
science fiction movie **película de ciencia ficción** *f.* (5)
sculpture **escultura** *f.* (5)
season (sports) **temporada** *f.*
secretary **secretario(a)** *m. (f.)* (3)
(to) see **ver** (9)
See you. **Nos vemos.** (1)
See you later. **Hasta luego.** (1)
(to) sell **vender** (5)
sense **sentido** *m.*
sequence, series **serie** *f.* (14)
serious **serio(a)** (6)
seven hundred **setecientos(as)** (12)
seventy **setenta** (7)
(to) share **compartir** (5)
she **ella** (2)
shirt **camisa** *f.* (18)
shoe **zapato** *m.* (18)
shoe store **zapatería** *f.* (18)
(to) shop **ir de compras** (10)
shopping cart **carrito** *m.* (17)
shopping center **centro comercial** (16)
short **bajo(a),** (in length) **corto(a)** (6)
should **deber** (10)
sick **enfermo(a)** (9)
sight **vista** *f.*
(to) sign **firmar**
silly **tonto(a)** (6)
silver **plata** *f.*
(to) sing **cantar** (1)
singer **cantante** *m.* or *f.*
sister **hermana** *f.* (6)
six hundred **seiscientos(as)** (12)
sixty **sesenta** (7)
(to) skate **patinar** (14)
ski **esquí** *m.* (16)
skirt **falda** *f.* (18)
slice of bread **rebanada de pan** *f.* (1)
slow **despacio** (8)
small **pequeño(a)** (6)
snack **merienda** *f.* (1)
snack, Spanish **tapa española** *f.* (2)
(to) snorkel **bucear** (14)
snorkeling **buceo** *m.*
so **tan** (8)
so-so **más o menos** (1)
soccer **fútbol** *m.* (5)
sock **calcetín** *m.* (18)
soda **soda** *f.* (1)
soft drink **refresco** *m.* (1)
some **alguno(a)**
someday **algún día** (12)

something **algo** (1)
sometimes **a veces** (1)
son **hijo** *m.* (6)
song **canción** *f.*
soon **pronto**
I'm sorry. **Lo siento.** (7)
south **sur** *m.*
southwest **suroeste** *m.*
space **espacio** *m.*
Spain **España** (3)
Spaniard **español(a)** *m. (f.)* (3)
special **especial** (11)
species **especie** *f.*
(to) spend **gastar**
sphere **globo** *m.* (1)
spice **especia** *f.*
spicy **picante** (3)
spirit **espíritu** *m.*
sport **deporte** *m.* (5)
sporting goods store **tienda de deportes** *f.* (16)
sportsman (sportswoman) **deportista** *m.* or *f.*
square **plaza** *f.* (7), (geometry) **cuadrado** *m.*
squid **calamares** *m.* (2)
stadium **estadio** *m.* (7)
stage (phase) **etapa**
star **estrella** *f.*
station **estación** *f.* (7)
stationery store **papelería** *f.* (16)
(to) stay **quedar** (8)
stereo **estéreo** *m.* (4)
still **todavía**
stocking **media** *f.* (18)
stone **piedra** *f.*
store **tienda** *f.* (7)
story **cuento** *m.*, **historia** *f.*
strawberry **fresa** *f.* (17)
street **calle** *f.* (8)
strength **fuerza** *f.*
student **alumno(a)** *m. (f.)* (4), **estudiante** *m.* or *f.* (3)
(to) study **estudiar** (1)
stupid **tonto(a)** (6)
style **moda** *f.* (18)
subway **metro** *m.* (11)
  subway map **plano del metro** *m.* (11)
  subway station **estación de metro** *f.* (11)
success **éxito** *m.*
sugar **azúcar** *m.* (17)
sun **sol** *m.*
(to) sunbathe **tomar el sol** (14)
Sunday **domingo** *m.* (10)
Super! **¡Super!** (16)
sure **seguro(a)** (18)
(to) surf **practicar el surfing** (14)
survey **encuesta** *f.* (12)
sweater **suéter** *m.* (18)
sweet roll, any kind **pan dulce** *m.* (1)
(to) swim **nadar** (13)
swimming **natación** *f.* (14)
swimming pool **piscina** *f.* (7)

T

T-shirt **camiseta** *f.* (18)
tail **cola** *f.*
(to) take **tomar** (1), **llevar** (4)
  (to) take a trip **hacer un viaje** (13)
  (to) take a walk **dar un paseo** (10)
(to) talk **hablar** (1)
tall **alto(a)** (6)
tape (cassette) **cinta** *f.* (4)
  tape recorder **grabadora** *f.* (4)
taste **gusto** *m.* (5)
taxi **taxi** *m.* (7)
tea **té** *m.* (1)
teacher **profesor(a)** *m. (f.)* (3)
team **equipo** *m.* (3)
telephone **teléfono** *m.* (7)
  telephone conversation **conversación telefónica** *f.* (7)
television set, (color) **televisor (a colores)** *m.* (4)
(to) tell (a story) **contar**
tennis **tenis** *m.* (5)
  tennis ball **pelota de tenis** *f.* (16)
  tennis shoe **zapato de tenis** *m.* (16)
thank you **gracias** (1)
  Thank you very much. **Muchas gracias.** (1)
Thanksgiving Day mass **la misa de Acción de Gracias** *f.* (9)
that **aquel(la), ese(a)** (17), **que** (1)
  that is why **por eso** (16)
  that one **ése(a)** *m. (f.)* (17)
  that one over there **aquél(la)** *m. (f.)* (17)
the **el** *m.*, **la** *f.*, (plural) **los** *m.*, **las** *f.* (4)
theatre **teatro** *m.* (7)
  movie theatre **cine** *m.* (7)
their **su(s)** (4)
then **entonces** (9), **luego** (14), **pues** (1)
there **allí** (4)
there is / are **hay** (4)
they **ellos(as)** *m. (f.)* (2)
thin **delgado(a)** (6)
thing **cosa** *f.* (11)
  another thing **otra cosa** *f.* (11)
(to) think **pensar** (11)
(to be) thirsty **tener sed** (7)
this **este(a)** (17)
this one **éste(a)** *m. (f.)* (17)
thousand **mil** (12)
three hundred **trescientos(as)** (12)
Thursday **jueves** *m.* (10)
ticket **billete** *m.* (11)
  ticket, ten-trip **billete de diez viajes** *m.* (11)
  ticket, one-way **billete sencillo** *m.* (11)
time **tiempo** *m.* (14), **vez** *f.* (9)
tin **lata** *f.* (17)
tip **propina** *f.* (12)
tired **cansado(a)** (9)
to **a** (1)
  to the **al** (7)
toast **pan tostado** *m.* (1)
today **hoy** (10)
together **junto(a)** (17)
tomato **tomate** *m.* (17)
tomorrow **mañana** (10)
tongue **lengua** *f.* (5)
(to) touch **tocar** (2)
tourist **turista** *m.* or *f.* (11)
tower **torre** *f.*
town **pueblo** *m.*
toy **juguete** *m.*
track (railw.) **vía** *f.*
train **tren** *m.* (7)
  train station **estación de trenes** (7)
(to) travel **viajar** (1)
travel agency **agencia de viajes** *f.* (12)
trip **viaje** *m.* (12)
trousers **pantalones** *m.* (18)
true **verdadero(a)**
(to) try (endeavor) **tratar de**
Tuesday **martes** *m.* (10)
tuna **atún** *m.* (17)
(to) turn **doblar** (8)
twenty **veinte** (7)
two hundred **doscientos(as)** (12)
typewriter **máquina de escribir** *f.* (4)
typing paper **papel para escribir a máquina** *m.* (16)

## U

ugly **feo(a)** (6)
uncle **tío** *m.* (6)
(to) understand **comprender** (5)
unemployment **desempleo** *m.*
United States **Estados Unidos** (3)
university **universidad** *f.* (7)
unknown **desconocido(a)**
unlimited **sin límite** (11)
until **hasta** (17)
Uruguay **Uruguay** (3)
Uruguayan **uruguayo(a)** *m. (f.)* (3)
useful **útil**
usually **usualmente** (10)

value **valor** *m.*
various **varios(as)** (17)
vegetable **vegetal** *m.* (17)
  vegetable salad **ensalada de vegetales (verduras)** *f.* (17)
Venezuela **Venezuela** (3)
Venezuelan **venezolano(a)** *m. (f.)* (3)
very **muy, bien** (1)
  very much **muchísimo** (1)
  Very well, thank you. **Muy bien, gracias.** (1)
video **vídeo** *m.* (16)
videocassette player **videocasetera** *f.* (4)
(to) visit **visitar** (7)
voice **voz** *f.*
volleyball **vólibol** *m.* (5)

(to) wait **esperar** (12)
waiter (waitress) **camarero(a)** *m. (f.)* (1)
(to) walk **caminar, andar** (13)
(to) walk on the beach **caminar en la playa** (14).
  a walk **paseo** *m.* (10)
walking **a pie** (10)
wallet **cartera** *f.* (4)
(to) want **desear** (1), **querer** (7)
  I would like . . . **Yo quisiera...** (1)
(to) watch **mirar** (2)
water **agua** *f.* (1)
water ski **esquí acuático** *m.* (14)
we **nosotros(as)** *m. (f.)* (1)
Wednesday **miércoles** *m.* (10)
week **semana** *f.* (14)
weekend **fin de semana** *m.* (10)
well **bien** (1)
what? **¿qué?, ¿cómo?** (1)
  What a pity! **¡Qué pena!** (16)
  What day is today? **¿Qué día es hoy?** (10)
  What delicious food! **¡Qué comida más rica!** (3)
  What's going on? **¿Qué pasó?** (1)
  What's new? **¿Qué hay (de nuevo)?** (1)
  What time is it? **¿Qué hora es?** (9)
  What's your name? **¿Cómo te llamas?** (4)
where? **¿adónde?** (7), **¿dónde?** (6)
  Where are you from? **¿De dónde es (eres)?** (3)
  Where is / are there . . . ? **¿Dónde hay... ?** (4)
  Where is . . . ? **¿Dónde está... ?** (8)
which? **¿cuál?** (17)
who? **¿quién?** (3)
whole **entero** (11)
Whose is it? **¿De quién es... ?** (4)
why? **¿por qué?** (6)
wife **esposa** *f.* (6)
store window **escaparate** *m.* (16)
winter **invierno** *m.*
(to) wish for **desear** (1)
with **con** (2)
  with me **conmigo** (10)
  with pleasure **con mucho gusto** (1)
without **sin** *m.* (16)
woman **mujer** *f.* (3)
word **palabra** *f.*
(to) work **trabajar** (1)
work **trabajo** *m.*
worker **trabajador(a)** *m. (f.)*
world **mundo** *m.*
(to) worry **preocupar**
worse, worst **peor** (18)
(to) write **escribir** (5)
written **escrito**

year **año** *m.* (14)
(to be) . . . years old **tener... años** (7)
yellow **amarillo(a)** (17)
yes **sí** (1)
yesterday **ayer** (13)
yogurt **yogur** *m.* (17)
you (familiar) **tú**, (familiar plural) **vosotros (as)** *m. (f.)*, (formal) **usted (Ud.)**, (formal plural) **ustedes (Uds.)** (1)
you're welcome **de nada** (3)
young **joven** (18)
younger **menor** (18)
your **su(s)** (18), **tu(s)** (4)
youth **juventud** *f.*

zoo **parque zoológico** *m.* (13)